CLYMER®

KAWASAKI JET SKI®

SHOP MANUAL
1992-1994

D1616337

The World's Finest Publisher of Mechanical How-To Manuals

PRIMEDIA
Intertec

P.O. Box 12901, Overland Park, Kansas 66282-2901

Copyright ©1995 PRIMEDIA Intertec

FIRST EDITION
First Printing July, 1995
Second Printing November, 1998

Printed in U.S.A.

CLYMER and colophon are registered trademarks of PRIMEDIA Intertec.

ISBN: 0-89287-644-1

Library of Congress: 95-79866

Technical illustrations by Steve Amos and Robert Caldwell.

COVER: Photograph courtesy of Kawasaki Motors Corporation, U.S.A.

PRIMEDIA *Intertec* Book Division

President and CEO Raymond E. Maloney
Vice President, Book Division Ted Marcus

EDITORIAL

Director
Randy Stephens

Senior Editor
Mark Jacobs

Editors
Mike Hall
Tom Fournier
Frank Craven
Paul Wyatt

Associate Editors
Robert Sokol
Eric Stone

Technical Writers
Ron Wright
Ed Scott
George Parise
Mark Rolling
Michael Morlan

Warehouse and Production Manager
Terry Distin

Editorial Production Supervisor
Shirley Renicker

Editorial Production Coordinator
Dylan Goodwin

Editorial Production Assistants
Carolyn Foster
Renee Colley

Advertising Coordinator
Jodi Donohoe

Advertising Production Specialist
Kim Sawalich

Technical Illustrators
Steve Amos
Robert Caldwell
Mitzi McCarthy
Michael St. Clair

MARKETING/SALES AND ADMINISTRATION

Product Development Manager
Michael Yim

Advertising & Promotions Coordinator
Liz Olivarez

Marketing Assistant
Melissa Abbott

Art Director
Al Terwelp

Associate Art Director
Jennifer Ray

Sales Manager/Marine
Dutch Sadler

Sales Manager/Manuals
Ted Metzger

Sales Manager/Motorcycles
Matt Tusken

Sales Coordinator
Paul Cormaci

Telephone Sales Supervisor
Terri Cannon

Telemarketing Sales Representatives
Susan Kay
Joelle Stephens

Customer Service/Fulfillment Manager
Caryn Bair

Fulfillment Coordinator
Susan Kohlmeyer

Lead Customer Service Representative
Janet Rogers

Customer Service Representatives
Angela Stephens
Erin Baker
Mildred Cofield
Jackie Hart

The following books and guides are published by **PRIMEDIA** *Intertec.*

CLYMER SHOP MANUALS
Boat Motors and Drives
Motorcycles and ATVs
Snowmobiles
Personal Watercraft

ABOS/INTERTEC/CLYMER BLUE BOOKS AND TRADE-IN GUIDES
Recreational Vehicles
Outdoor Power Equipment
Agricultural Tractors
Lawn and Garden Tractors
Motorcycles and ATVs
Snowmobiles and Personal Watercraft
Boats and Motors

AIRCRAFT BLUEBOOK-PRICE DIGEST
Airplanes
Helicopters

AC-U-KWIK DIRECTORIES
The Corporate Pilot's Airport/FBO Directory
International Manager's Edition
Jet Book

I&T SHOP SERVICE MANUALS
Tractors

INTERTEC SERVICE MANUALS
Snowmobiles
Outdoor Power Equipment
Personal Watercraft
Gasoline and Diesel Engines
Recreational Vehicles
Boat Motors and Drives
Motorcycles
Lawn and Garden Tractors

Contents

Quick Reference Data

GENERAL ENGINE SPECIFICATIONS—440 AND 550 CC MODELS

Engine type	2-stroke; vertical twin
Displacement	
440 cc	436 cc (26.6 cu. in.)
550 cc	530 cc (32.3 cu. in.)
Bore & stroke	
440 cc	68X60 mm (2.68 × 2.36 in.)
550 cc	75X60 mm (2.95 × 2.36 in.)
Compression ratio	
440 cc	6.1:1
550 cc	7.2:1

GENERAL ENGINE SPECIFICATIONS—650 & 750 CC MODELS

Engine type	2-stroke; vertical twin; reed valve
Displacement	
650 cc	635 cc
750 cc	743 cc
Bore and stroke	
650 cc	76 × 70 mm (2.99 × 2.76 in.)
750 cc	80 × 74 mm (3.15 × 2.92 in.)
Compression ratio	
650 cc	7.2:1
750 cc	7.0:1

RECOMMENDED SPARK PLUGS

Model	NGK part No.	Gap mm (in.)
JS440SX	BR7ES	0.7-0.8 (0.028-0.031)
All 650 and 750 cc models	BR8ES	0.7-0.8 (0.028.031)

CARBURETOR MODEL IDENTIFICATION*

Model	Carburetor	Venturi size
JS440SX	Mikuni BN38	34 mm
JS550SX	Keihin CDK38	32 mm
JF650X2		
1992-1993	Keihin CDK38	32 mm
1994	Keihin CDK40-34	38 mm
JF650TS	Keihin CDK38	32 mm
JL650SC	Keihin CDK38	32 mm
JS650SX	Keihin CDK38	32 mm

(continued)

CARBURETOR MODEL IDENTIFICATION* (continued)

Model	Carburetor	Venturi size
JB650 Jet Mate	Keihin CDK34	28 mm
JH750SS	Keihin 40-34	38 mm
JS750SX	Keihin CDK40-34	38 mm
JT750ST	Keihin CDK40-34	38 mm
JH750 Super Sport Xi	Keihin CDK40-34	38 mm
JH750 XiR	Keihin CDK40-34	38 mm

*All models are equipped with a diaphragm-type carburetor.

IDLE SPEED

Model	Rpm
JS440SX	1700-1900 (in water)
JS550SX	1400-1600 (in water)
	1800-2000 (out of water)
JF650X-2	1150-1350 (in water)
	1700-1900 (out of water)
JF650TS	1150-1350 (in water)
	1700-1900 (out of water)
JL650SC	1200-1300 (in water)
	1700-1900 (out of water)
JS650SX	1150-1350 (in water)
JH750SS	1150-1350 (in water)
	1600-1800 (out of water)
JS750SX	1150-1350 (in water)
	1600-1800 (out of water)
JT750ST	1150-1350 (in water)
	1600-1800 (out of water)
JH750 Super Sport Xi	1150-1350 (in water)
	1600-1800 (out of water)
JH750XiR	1150-1350 (in water)
	1600-1800 (out of water)

INITIAL CARBURETOR MIXTURE SETTING

Model	Low-speed screw (turns out)	High-speed screw (turns out)
JS440SX	7/8	5/8
JS550SX, JF650X-2	1-1/8	5/8
JL650TS	1	5/8
JL650SC, JS650SX	1-1/8	5/8
JB650 Jet Mate	1-1/8	3/8
JH750SS, JS750SX, JH750Xi, JH750XiR	7/8	7/8
JT750ST	1	1

ENGINE LUBRICATION SYSTEM*

440 cc, 550 cc	Premix 40:1
650 cc, 750 cc (except JH750XiR)	Oil injection

*On models equipped with oil injection, add premix fuel (40:1 [440 and 550 cc], 50:1 [all others]) to the fuel tank during the break-in period.

CLYMER®

KAWASAKI JET SKI®

SHOP MANUAL
1992-1994

Introduction

This Clymer shop manual covers Kawasaki Jet Skis produced from 1992-1994.

Troubleshooting, tune-up, maintenance and repair are not difficult, if you know what tools and equipment to use and how to perform the job. Step-by-step instructions guide you through jobs ranging from simple maintenance to complete engine, drive train and steering overhaul.

This manual can be used by anyone from a first time do-it-yourselfer to a professional mechanic. Detailed drawings and clear photographs give you all the information you need to do the job right.

Chapter One

General Information

Special tools are required to perform some of the procedures in this manual. A resourceful mechanic may be able, in some cases, to fabricate an acceptable substitute for a particular special tool. This can be as simple as using a few pieces of threaded rod, washers and nuts to remove or install a bushing or bearing. However, using a substitute for a special tool is generally not recommended as it can cause personal injury and may damage the part. But, if you find that a tool can be designed and safely made, you may want to search out a local community college or high school that has a machine shop curriculum. Shop teachers sometimes welcome outside work that can be used as practical shop applications for advance students.

Table 1 lists model coverage with hull serial numbers on Jet Ski models covered in this manual.

Metric and U.S. standards are used throughout this manual. U.S. to metric conversion is given in **Table 2**.

Tables 1-5 are found at the end of this chapter.

MANUAL ORGANIZATION

This chapter provides general information useful to Jet Ski owners and mechanics. In addition, information in this chapter discusses the tools and techniques used for preventive maintenance, troubleshooting and repair.

Chapter Two provides troubleshooting methods and suggestions for quick and accurate diagnosis and repair of problems. Troubleshooting procedures discuss typical symptoms and logical methods to pinpoint the trouble.

Chapter Three explains the periodic lubrication and routine maintenance necessary to keep your Jet Ski in top operating condition. Chapter Three also includes recommended tune-up procedures, eliminating the need to consult other chapters constantly on the various assemblies.

Subsequent chapters describe specific systems, providing disassembly, repair, reassembly and adjustment procedures in simple step-by-step form. If a specific repair procedure is impractical for a home mechanic, it is so indicated. In some cases, it could even be faster and less expensive to take such repairs to a dealer or qualified repair shop. Specifications concerning a specific system are located at the end of the appropriate chapter.

NOTES, CAUTIONS AND WARNINGS

The terms NOTE, CAUTION and WARNING have specific meanings in this manual. A NOTE provides additional information to make a step or procedure clearer or easier to understand. Disregarding a NOTE may cause inconvenience, but should not result in damage or personal injury.

A CAUTION emphasizes areas where equipment damage might occur. Disregarding a CAUTION could cause permanent mechanical damage; however, personal injury is unlikely.

A WARNING emphasizes areas where personal injury or even death could result from negligence. Mechanical damage may also occur. WARNINGS *are to be taken seriously.* Serious injury or death can result from disregarding warnings.

SAFETY FIRST

Professional mechanics can work for years and never sustain a serious injury. If you observe a few rules of common sense and safety, you too can enjoy many safe hours servicing your own machine. If you ignore these rules you can hurt yourself or damage the equipment.
1. Never use gasoline as a cleaning solvent.
2. Never smoke or use a torch in the vicinity of flammable liquids, such as cleaning solvent, and especially gasoline.
3. If welding or brazing is required on the machine, remove the fuel tank and move to a safe distance, at least 50 feet away.
4. Use the proper sized wrenches to avoid damage to fasteners and injury to yourself.
5. When loosening a tight or stuck fastener, be guided by what would happen if the wrench should slip. Be careful and protect yourself accordingly.

6. When replacing a fastener, make sure to use one with the same measurements and strength as the old one. Incorrect or mismatched fasteners can result in damage to the watercraft and possible personal injury. Beware of fastener kits that are filled with cheap and poorly made nuts, bolts, washers and cotter pins. Refer to *Fasteners* in this chapter for additional information.
7. Keep all hand and power tools in good condition. Always clean greasy and oily tools after using them. Greasy or oily tools are difficult to hold and can cause injury. Replace or repair worn or damaged tools.
8. Keep your work area clean and uncluttered.
9. Wear safety goggles during all operations involving drilling, grinding, the use of a cold chisel, punch or *anytime* you feel unsure about the safety of your eyes. Safety goggles should also be worn anytime solvent and compressed air is used to clean parts.
10. Keep an approved fire extinguisher nearby. Be sure it is rated for gasoline (Class B) and electrical (Class C) fires.
11. When drying bearings or other rotating parts with compressed air, never allow the air jet to rotate the bearing or part. The air jet is capable of rotating them at speeds far in excess of those for which they were designed. The bearing or rotating part is very likely to disintegrate causing serious personal injury. To prevent bearing damage when using compressed air, hold the inner bearing race by hand.

SERVICE HINTS

Most of the service procedures covered are straightforward and can be performed by anyone reasonably skillful with tools. It is suggested, however, that you consider your own capabilities carefully before attempting any operation involving major disassembly.
1. "FRONT" as used in this manual, refers to the front or bow of the Jet Ski; the front of any component is the end closest to the front of the

Jet Ski. The terms, "left-" and "right-hand" sides refer to the position of the watercraft or parts as viewed by a rider sitting or standing on the Jet Ski, facing forward. For example, the throttle control is on the right-hand side. These rules are simple, but confusion can cause a major inconvenience during service.

2. When disassembling any engine or drive component, mark the parts for original location and direction. Mark all parts which mate together, for location and direction. Small parts, such as bolts, can be identified by placing them in plastic sandwich bags (**Figure 1**). Seal the bags and label them with masking tape and a marking pen. When reassembly will take place immediately, an accepted practice is to place nuts, screws, bolts and other fasteners in a cupcake tin or egg carton in the order of disassembly.

3. Finished surfaces should be protected from physical damage or corrosion. Keep gasoline and solvent off painted surfaces.

4. Use a suitable penetrating oil on frozen or tight bolts, then tap the bolt head a few times with a hammer and punch (use a screwdriver on screws). Avoid the use of heat where possible, as it can warp, melt or affect the temper (hardness) of the component. Heat also ruins finishes, especially paint and plastics.

5. No component removed or installed (other than bushings and bearings) in the procedures given in this manual should require unusual force during disassembly or reassembly. If a part is difficult to remove or install, find out why before proceeding.

6. Cover all openings after removing components or assemblies to prevent small tools, parts, dirt or other contamination from entering.

7. Read each procedure *completely* while looking at the actual parts before starting a job. Make sure you thoroughly understand what is required, then carefully follow the procedure, step-by-step.

8. Recommendations are occasionally made to refer service or maintenance to a Jet Ski dealer or a specialist in a particular field. In some cases, the work may even be done more quickly and economically than if you performed the job yourself.

9. In procedural steps, the term "replace" means to discard a defective part and replace it with a new or exchange unit. "Overhaul" means to remove, disassemble, inspect, measure, repair or replace defective parts, then reassemble and install major systems or parts.

10. Some operations require the use of a hydraulic or an arbor press. If a suitable press is not available, it would be wise to have these operations performed by a shop equipped for such work, rather than to try to do the job yourself with makeshift equipment that may damage your machine.

11. Repairs go much faster and easier if your machine is clean before you begin work. There are many special cleaners on the market, like Bel-Ray Degreaser, for washing the engine and related parts. Follow the manufacturer's instruction on the container for the best results. Clean all oily or greasy parts with cleaning solvent as remove them.

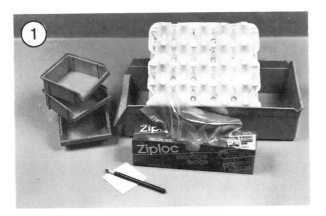

WARNING
Never use gasoline as a cleaning agent. It presents an extreme fire hazard. Be sure to work in a well-ventilated area when using cleaning solvent. Keep a fire extinguisher, rated for gasoline fires, handy in any case.

12. If special tools are necessary, make arrangements to obtain them before starting work. If is frustrating and time-consuming to get partially into a job, then be unable to complete it.

13. Make diagrams (or take a Polaroid picture) whenever similar parts are found. For example, crankcase bolts are often not the same length. You may think you can remember where everything came from; but mistakes can be costly. It is also possible that you may be sidetracked and not return to the work for days or even weeks, during such time, carefully arranged parts may become disturbed.

14. When reassembling parts, be sure all shims and washers are replaced exactly as they were removed.

15. Whenever a rotating part contacts a stationary part, look for a shim or washer.

16. Always install new gaskets, seals and O-rings during reassembly. Gaskets are usually installed dry (without sealant), unless otherwise specified.

17. Should it become necessary to make a gasket, and the old gasket is not available for use as a guide, use the outline of the cover or part. Apply engine oil to the gasket surface, then place the part on the new gasket material. Apply pressure to the part and the oil will leave a very accurate outline on the gasket material.

> *CAUTION*
> *If purchasing gasket material to fabricate a gasket, measure the thickness of the old gasket. The gasket material must have the same approximate thickness as the original gasket.*

18. Heavy grease can be used to hold small parts in place if they tend to fall from position during assembly. Keep grease and oil away from electrical components, however. In addition, any grease used inside the power head should be gasoline soluable.

19. A carburetor is best cleaned by disassembling it and soaking the parts in a commercial carburetor cleaner. Never soak gaskets and rubber parts in these cleaners. Never use wire to clean carburetor jets and air passages. Use compressed air to blow out the carburetor passages.

20. Most of all, take your time and do the job right. Do not forget that a newly rebuilt engine must be correctly broken-in, just like a new one.

ENGINE OPERATION

All Kawasaki Jet Ski models are equipped with a 2-stroke marine engine. During this discussion, assume that the crankshaft is rotating

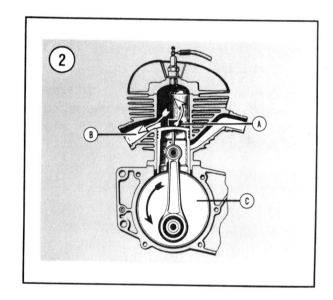

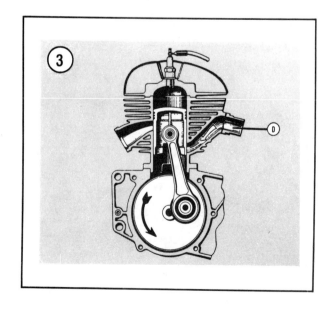

counterclockwise in **Figure 2**. As the piston travels downward, a transfer port (A, **Figure 2**) between the crankcase and cylinder is uncovered. The exhaust gases leave the cylinder through the exhaust port (B, **Figure 2**), which is also opened by the downward movement of the piston. A lightly compressed, fresh fuel-air charge travels from the crankcase (C, **Figure 2**) to the cylinder through the transfer port (A) as the port opens. Since the incoming charge is under pressure, it rushes into the cylinder

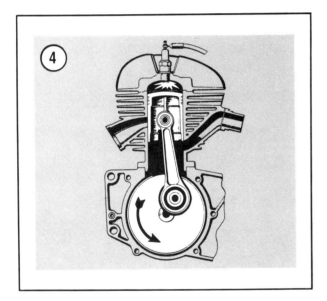

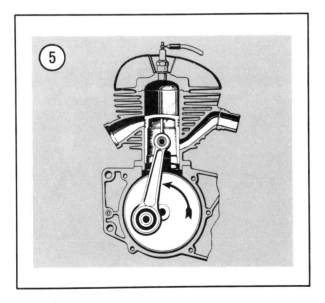

quickly and helps to scavenge (expel) the exhaust gases from the previous combustion.

Figure 3 illustrates the next phase of the cycle. As the crankshaft continues to rotate, the piston moves upward, closing the exhaust and transfer ports. As the piston continues upward, the air-fuel mixture in the cylinder is compressed. Notice also that a vacuum is being created in the crankcase at the same time. Further upward piston movement uncovers the intake port (D, **Figure 3**). A fresh fuel-air charge is then drawn into the crankcase through the intake port because of the vacuum created by the upward piston movement.

The third phase is shown in **Figure 4**. As the piston approaches top dead center (TDC), the spark plug fires, igniting the compressed fuel-air mixture. The piston is then driven downward by the expanding gases.

When the top of the piston uncovers the exhaust port, the fourth phase begins, as shown in **Figure 5**. The exhaust gases leave the cylinder through the exhaust port. As the piston continues downward, the intake port is closed and the mixture in the crankcase is compressed in preparation for the next cycle.

CLEARING A SUBMERGED JET SKI

If the Jet Ski is submerged while the engine cover is off, water may get into the engine and fuel tank. To prevent internal engine corrosion and serious damage to the engine, the following steps must be performed as soon as possible and before trying to restart the engine.

CAUTION
When a procedure calls for rolling the Jet Ski on its side, always roll the craft in the direction of its exhaust system. If rolled to the side opposite the exhaust, water from the exhaust system can enter the engine which can result in serious engine damage.

1. Remove the engine cover.

2A. *JS440SX and JS550SX*—Perform the following:

   a. Remove the spark plugs and ground their leads to the engine to prevent damage to the ignition system.

   b. Using a protective pad, roll the Jet Ski over onto its left side, then hold it upside down to allow the water to drain from the engine (**Figure 6**).

> *CAUTION*
> *If sand may have entered the engine, do not try to start the engine or severe internal damage can occur.*

   c. Wait several minutes until no more water comes out, then open the throttle and crank the engine a few revolutions with the start button.

> *WARNING*
> *Keep your hands away from the jet pump while cranking the engine.*

> *CAUTION*
> *Do not force the engine if it does not turn over. This may be an indication of a hydraulic lock (water in cylinders) or of internal engine damage.*

   d. Allow another minute for water to drain from the cylinders.

   e. Repeat until all the water has drained from the cylinders, then turn the Jet Ski right side up.

2B. *All models except JS440SX and JS550SX*—Perform the following:

   a. Pull up the engine drain knob (**Figure 7**) and operate the starter button for 5 seconds. Then allow the starter motor to cool for 15 seconds and repeat starter operation for another 5 seconds. Opening the engine drain knob while operating the starter will pump water from the crankcase.

> *CAUTION*
> *When a procedure calls for rolling the Jet Ski on its side, always roll the craft in the direction of its exhaust system. If rolled to the side opposite the exhaust, water from the exhaust system can enter the engine which can result in serious engine damage.*

   b. On JS750ST models, remove the drain screw from the stern and allow any water in the hull to drain. On all other models, roll the Jet Ski over on its side and tip it over slightly to allow the water to drain from the engine compartment. Use a protective pad to prevent damage to the hull.

   c. Remove the spark plugs and ground their leads to the engine to prevent damage to the ignition system.

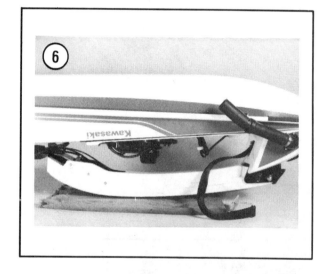

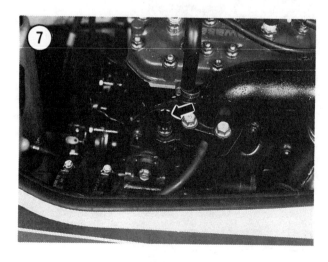

3. Spray WD-40, or an equivalent water displacing lubricant into the cylinders through the spark plug holes.

4. Install new dry spark plugs or thoroughly clean and dry the original plugs.

5. On models equipped with oil injection, check the oil tank (**Figure 8**) for water contamination. If necessary, drain the oil tank by disconnecting the intake hose (**Figure 9**) at the oil pump. Reconnect the oil line and bleed the oil pump as described in Chapter Nine.

CAUTION
If the oil tank is contaminated, remove the tank (Chapter 9) and flush it thoroughly.

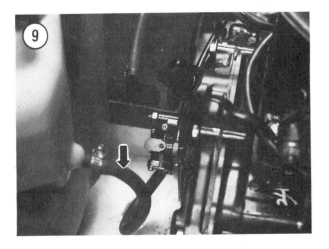

6. Start the engine and run it for less than 15 seconds to clear any remaining water from the engine.

CAUTION
Do not run the engine for more than 15 seconds without a supply of cooling water or the rubber parts used in the exhaust system will be damaged. Prolonged running without coolant will cause serious engine damage. Do not operate the engine at maximum speed out of the water.

7. If the engine does not start, remove the spark plugs and spray them again with water displacing lubricant (WD-40). Reinstall the plugs and attempt to start the engine. If water fouling continues there may be water in the fuel.

8. Clean the fuel sediment bowl and filter as described in Chapter Three. Water in the bowl may indicate that the fuel tank is contaminated.

9. If water is present in the fuel tank, use a pump or siphon to empty the contaminated fuel. Refill the tank with fresh fuel.

NOTE
It may be necessary to repeat this procedure several times before all water is removed from the engine. Continued trouble may require disassembly of the fuel pump to drain water. See Chapter Seven.

11. To dry out the electrical components and keep them from rusting, remove the magneto cover plug and spray water displacing lubricant or electrical contact cleaner into the cover.

12. Install the engine cover.

13. To completely clean all water out of the crankcase and cylinders, run the watercraft *in the water* for at least 5 minutes, at or close to wide-open throttle.

TORQUE SPECIFICATIONS

Torque specifications throughout this manual are given in Newton-meters (N.m) and foot-pounds (ft.-lb.).

Table 3 (steel bolts) and **Table 4** (stainless bolts) list general torque specifications for nuts and bolts that are not listed in the respective chapters. To use the table, first determine the size of the fastener by measuring it with a vernier caliper. See **Figure 10** and **Figure 11**.

FASTENERS

The design and material used to manufacture the various fasteners used on your Jet Ski are not selected by chance or accident. Fastener design determines the type of tool required to turn the fastener. Fastener material is carefully selected to decrease the possibility of physical failure from breakage, corrosion or other factors.

Nuts, bolts and screws are manufactured in a wide range of thread patterns. To join a nut and bolt, the diameter of the bolt and the diameter of the hole in the nut must be the same. It is just as important that the threads on both are properly matched.

The best way to determine if the threads on 2 fasteners are matched is to turn the nut on the bolt (or the bolt into a threaded hole) using the fingers only. Be sure the threads on both fasteners are clean and undamaged. If much force is required, check the thread condition on each fastener. If the thread condition is good but the fasteners jam, the threads are not compatible. A thread pitch gauge can also be used to determine thread pitch. Kawasaki Jet Skis are manufactured with ISO (International Organization for Standardization) metric fasteners. The threads on metric fasteners are cut differently from that of U.S. Standard fasteners. See **Figure 12**.

Most threads are cut so the fastener must be turned clockwise to tighten it. These are called right-hand threads. Some fasteners have left-

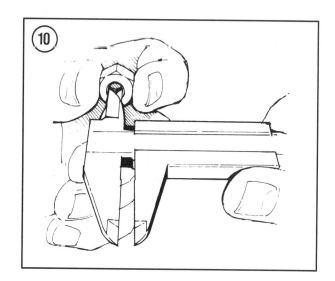

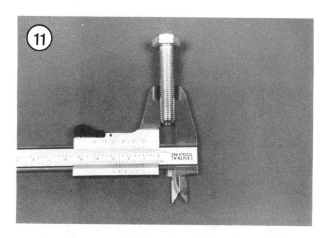

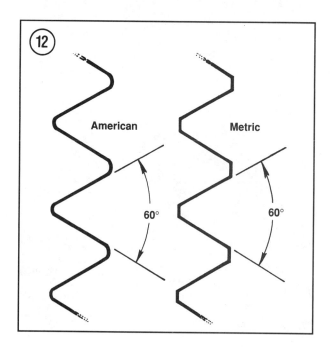

hand threads; they must be turned counterclockwise to tighten. Left-hand threads are used in locations where normal rotation of the equipment would tend to loosen a right-hand threaded fastener.

ISO Metric Screw Threads

ISO (International Organization for Standardization) metric threads are available in 3 standard thread sizes: coarse, fine and constant pitch. The ISO coarse pitch is used for most common fastener applications. The fine pitch thread is used on certain precision tools and instruments. The constant pitch thread is used mainly on machine parts and is not generally used on fasteners. The constant pitch thread is, however, used on all metric thread spark plugs.

ISO metric threads are specified by the capital letter M followed by the diameter in millimeters and the pitch (or distance between each thread) in millimeters separated by the sign "×." For example a M8 × 1.25 bolt is one that has a diameter of 8 millimeters with a distance of 1.25 millimeters between each thread. The measurement across 2 flats on the head of the bolt indicates the proper wrench size used to turn the fastener. **Figure 11** shows how to determine bolt diameter.

NOTE
When purchasing a bolt from a dealer or parts store, it is important to know how to specify bolt length. The correct way to measure bolt length is by measuring the length starting from under the bolt head to the end of the bolt. Always measure bolt length in this manner to avoid purchasing bolts that are too long.

Machine Screws

There are many different types of machine screws. **Figure 13** shows a number of screw heads which require different types of tools to turn them. The screw heads are also designed to either protrude above the metal (round) or to be slightly recessed (flat) in the metal. See **Figure 14**.

Bolts

Commonly called a bolt, the correct technical name for this type of fastener is cap screw. Metric bolts are described by the diameter and pitch (or the distance between each thread).

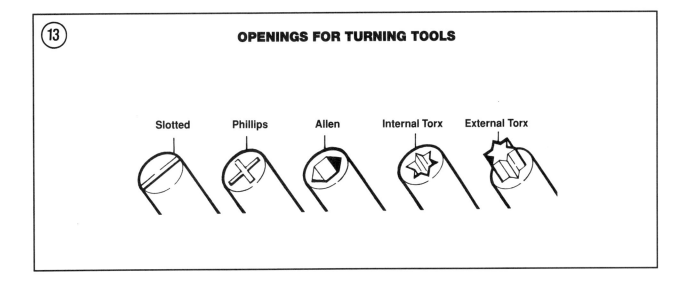

(13) OPENINGS FOR TURNING TOOLS

Slotted   Phillips   Allen   Internal Torx   External Torx

Nuts

Nuts are manufactured in a variety of types and sizes. Most are hexagonal (6 sides) and fit on bolts, screws and studs having the same diameter and pitch.

Figure 15 shows several types of nuts. The common nut is generally used with a lockwasher. Self-locking nuts have a nylon insert which prevents the nut from loosening. Self-locking fasteners do not normally require lockwashers. Wing nuts are designed for fast removal by hand and are used for convenience in noncritical locations.

To indicate the size of a metric nut, manufacturers specify the diameter of the opening and the thread pitch. This is similar to bolt specifications, but without the length dimension. The measurement across 2 flats on the nut indicates the proper wrench size used to turn the nut.

Prevailing Torque Fasteners

Several types of bolts, screws and nuts incorporate a system that develops an interference between the bolt, screw, nut or threaded hole. Interference is achieved in various ways: by slightly distorting the threads, coating the threads with dry adhesive or nylon, or distorting the top of an all-metal nut.

Prevailing torque fasteners offer greater holding strength and better vibration resistance than a plain nut and lockwasher. Some prevailing

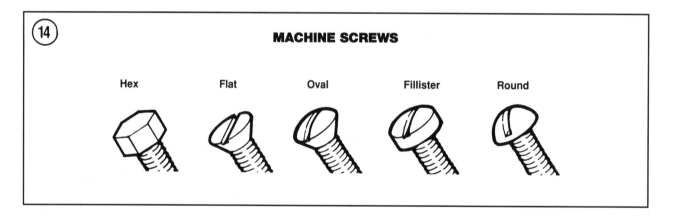

(14)　　**MACHINE SCREWS**

Hex　　　Flat　　　Oval　　　Fillister　　　Round

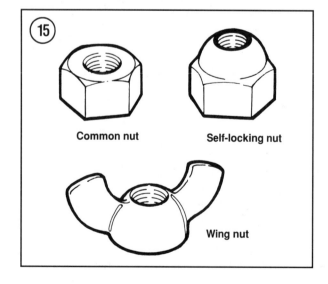

(15)

Common nut　　　Self-locking nut

Wing nut

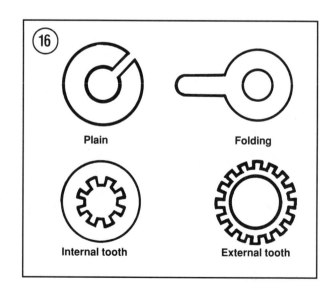

(16)

Plain　　　Folding

Internal tooth　　　External tooth

torque fasteners can be reused if still in good condition. Others, like the nylon insert nut, form an initial locking condition when the nut is first installed. Once installed, however, the nylon insert conforms closely to the bolt thread pattern. Therefore, once the fastener is removed, it should be replaced to offer the greatest security.

Washers

There are 2 basic types of washers: flat washers and lockwashers. Flat washers are simple discs with a hole to fit a screw, bolt or stud. Lockwashers are designed to prevent a fastener from working loose due to causes such as vibra-

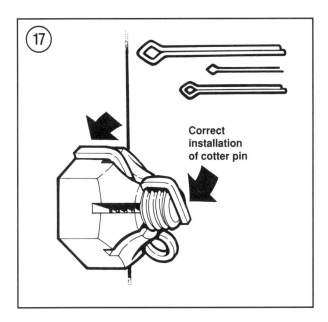

Correct installation of cotter pin

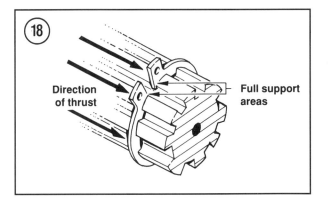

Direction of thrust — Full support areas

tion, expansion or contraction. **Figure 16** shows several types of lockwashers. Washers are also used in the following functions:

a. As spacers.
b. To prevent galling or damage of the equipment by the fastener.
c. To help distribute fastener load during tightening.
d. As seals.

Note that flat washers are often used between a lockwasher and a fastener to provide a smooth bearing surface.

Cotter pins

Cotter pins (**Figure 17**) are used to secure special kinds of fasteners. The stud or bolt must have a hole in it and the nut or nut lock piece must have 2 castellations through which the cotter pin is inserted. Cotter pins should not be reused after removal.

Snap Rings

Snap rings can be an internal or external design. They are used to retain items on shafts (external) or within housings (internal). In some applications, snap rings of varying thicknesses are used to control the thrust or end play of shafts or assemblies. This type of snap ring is called a "selective snap ring." Snap rings should normally be replaced during installation, as removal often weakens or deforms them.

Two basic types of snap rings are available: machined and stamped. Machined snap rings (**Figure 18**) can be installed in either direction (shaft or housing) because both faces are machined, thus creating two sharp edges. Stamped snap rings (**Figure 19**) are manufactured with one sharp edge and one rounded edge. When installing stamped snap rings in a thrust situation, the sharp edge must face away from the part producing the thrust. When installing snap rings, observe the following:

    a. Compress or expand the snap ring only enough to permit installation.

    b. After the snap ring is installed, make sure it is completely seated in its groove.

LUBRICANTS

Periodic lubrication ensures long life for any type of equipment. Regular lubrication is especially important to marine equipment because it is exposed to salt or brackish water or other harsh environments. The *type* of lubricant used is just as important as the lubrication service itself, although in an emergency the wrong type of lubricant is much better than none at all. The following paragraphs described the types of lubricants most often used on mechanical equipment. Be sure to follow the manufacturer's recommendations for lubricant use.

Generally, all liquid lubricants are called "oil." They may be mineral-based (petroleum base), natural-based (vegetable and animal base), synthetic-based or emulsions (mixtures). "Grease" is an oil to which a thickening base has been added so the end product is semi-solid. The resulting material is then usually enhanced with anticorrosion, antioxidant and extreme pressure (EP) additives. Grease is often classified by the type of thickener added. Lithium and calcium soap are commonly used thickeners.

4-Stroke Engine Oil

Oil designed for use in 4-stroke engines is graded by the American Petroleum Institute (API) and the Society of Automotive Engineers (SAE) in several categories. Oil containers display these ratings on the top or label.

API oil grade is indicated by letters. Oil for gasoline engines is identified by an "S" and oil for diesel engines is identified by a "C." Most modern gasoline engines require SF or SG graded oil. Automotive and marine diesel engines use CC or CD graded oil.

Viscosity is an indication of the oil's thickness, or resistance to flow. The SAE uses numbers to indicate viscosity; thin oil has a low number and thick oil has a high number. A "W" after the number indicates that the viscosity testing was done at low temperature to simulate cold weather operation. Engine oil falls into the 5W-20 to 20-50 range.

Multigrade oil (for example, 10W-40) is less viscous (thinner) at low temperature and more viscous (thicker) at high temperature. This allows the oil to perform efficiently across a wide range of engine operating temperatures.

> *CAUTION*
> *Four-stroke oil is only discussed to provide a comparison. Kawasaki Jet Ski engines are 2-stroke engines. Never use 4-stroke oil in a 2-stroke engine.*

2-Stroke Engine Oil

Lubrication for a 2-stroke engine is provided by oil mixed with the incoming fuel-air mixture. Some of the oil mixture settles out in the crankcase, lubricating the crankshaft and lower end of the connecting rods. The rest of the oil enters the combustion chamber to lubricate the piston, rings and cylinder wall. This oil is then burned

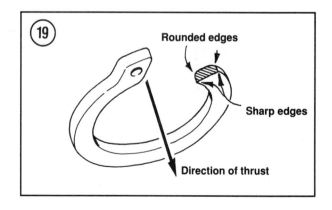

(19) Rounded edges

Sharp edges

Direction of thrust

along with the fuel-air mixture during the combustion process.

Engine oil must have several special qualities to work well in a 2-stroke engine. It must mix easily and stay in suspension in gasoline. When burned, it can't leave behind excessive deposits. It must also be able to withstand the high temperatures associated with 2-stroke engines.

The National Marine Manufacturer's Association (NMMA) has set standards for oil used in 2-stroke, water-cooled engines. This is the NMMA TC-W (two-cycle, water-cooled) grade. The oil's performance in the following areas is evaluated:

    a. Lubrication (prevention of wear and scuffing).

    b. Spark plug fouling.

    c. Preignition.

    d. Piston ring sticking.

    e. Piston carbon and varnish (piston coking).

    f. General engine condition (including deposits).

    g. Exhaust port blockage.

    h. Rust prevention.

    i. Mixing ability with gasoline.

In addition to oil grade, manufacturers specify the ratio of gasoline to oil required during break-in and normal operation.

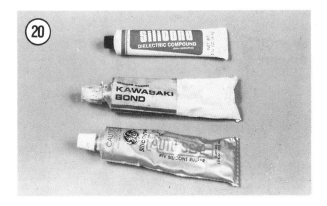

Grease

Grease is graded by the National Lubricating Grease Institute (NLGI). Greases are graded by number according to the consistency of the grease. These classifications range from No. 000 to No. 6, with No. 6 being the most solid. A typical multipurpose grease is NLGI No. 2. For specific applications, equipment manufacturers may require grease with a particular additive, such as molybdenum disulfide (MOS2).

GASKET SEALANT

Gasket sealant is used instead of pre-formed gaskets on some applications, or as a gasket dressing on others. Two types of gasket sealant are commonly used: room temperature vulcanizing (RTV) and anaerobic. Because these two materials have different sealing properties, they cannot be used interchangeably.

RTV Sealant

Room temperature vulcanizing (RTV) sealant is used on some pre-formed gaskets and to seal some components, such as the jet pump, during Jet Ski service. RTV is a silicone gel supplied in tubes (**Figure 20**).

Moisture in the air causes RTV to cure. Therefore, always place the cap on the tube as soon as possible when using RTV. RTV has a shelf life of approximately one year and will not cure properly when the shelf life has expired. Check the expiration date on RTV tubes before using and keep partially used tubes tightly sealed. RTV sealant can generally fill gaps up to 6.3 mm (1/4 in.) and works well on slightly flexible surfaces.

Apply RTV Sealant

Clean all gasket material from mating surfaces. If scraping is necessary, use a broad, flat scraper or a somewhat dull putty knife to avoid nicks, scratches or other damage to mating surfaces. Before applying RTV sealant, the mating surfaces must be absolutely free of gasket material, old sealant, dirt, oil, grease or other contamination. Lacquer thinner, acetone, isopropyl alcohol or similar solvents work well for cleaning mating surfaces. Avoid using solvents with an oil, wax or petroleum base as they may not be compatible with some sealants. Remove all RTV gasket material from blind attaching holes because it can create hydraulic pressure in the hole and affect fastener torque.

Apply RTV sealant in a continuous bead 2-3 mm (0.08-0.12 in.) thick. Avoid excess application as some of the sealant could be forced into bearings or seals. Circle all mounting holes unless otherwise specified. Tighten the fasteners within 10 minutes after application.

Anaerobic Sealant

Anaerobic sealant is a gel supplied in tubes and is used to seal rigid case assemblies instead of a gasket. It cures only in the absence of air, as when squeezed tightly between two machined mating surfaces. For this reason, it will not spoil if the cap is left off the tube. It should not be used if one mating surface is flexible. Anaerobic sealant is able to fill gaps up to 0.8 mm (0.030 in.) and generally works best on rigid, machined flanges or surfaces.

Applying Anaerobic Sealant

Clean all gasket material from mating surfaces. If scraping is necessary, use a broad, flat scraper or a somewhat dull putty knife to avoid nicks, scratches or other damage to mating surfaces. Before applying anaerobic sealant, the mating surfaces must be absolutely free of gasket material, old sealant, dirt, oil, grease or other contamination. Lacquer thinner, acetone, isopropyl alcohol or similar solvents work well for

cleaning mating surfaces. Avoid using solvents with an oil, wax or petroleum base as they may not be compatible with some sealants. Remove all anaerobic sealant from blind attaching holes because it can create hydraulic pressure in the hole and affect fastener torque.

Apply anaerobic sealant in a 1 mm (0.04 in.) or less bead to one sealing surface. Circle all mounting holes. Tighten mating parts with 15 minutes after application.

THREADLOCKING COMPOUND

Because of the Jet Ski's operating conditions, a threadlocking compound is required to help secure many of the fasteners used throughout the watercraft. A threadlocking compound will secure fasteners against vibration loosening and also seal against leaks. Loctite 242 (blue) and 271 (red) are recommended for many threadlocking requirements described in this manual.

Loctite 242 is a medium strength threadlocking compound and component disassembly can be performed with normal hand tools. Loctite 271 is a high strength threadlocking compound. Heat or special tools, such as a press or puller, are sometimes necessary for component disassembly.

Applying Threadlocking Compound

Fastener threads must be clean and dry before applying threadlocking compound. If necessary,

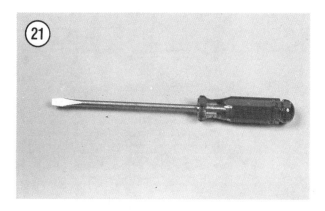

remove old threadlocking compound using a wire brush or similar tool. Remove oil, grease or other contamination using lacquer thinner, acetone or isopropyl alcohol. Apply the compound sparingly to the fastener, following the instructions on the container.

PARTS REPLACEMENT

Kawasaki makes frequent changes during a model year, some minor, some relatively major. Therefore, the hull and engine numbers must be provided when placing an order for replacement parts. The hull number is stamped in the outside of the vehicle. The engine number is stamped in the crankcase. Record the numbers for reference when ordering parts. Compare new parts to old before purchasing them. If they are not alike, have the parts manager explain the difference. **Table 1** lists hull serial numbers for all Jet Ski models covered in this manual.

BASIC HAND TOOLS

Many of the procedures in this manual can be performed with simple hand tools and test equipment familiar to the average home mechanic. Keep your tools clean and well organized in a tool box. After using a tool, wipe off any dirt, oil or grease then return the tool to its correct place.

Top quality tools are essential. They are also more economical in the long run. If you are just

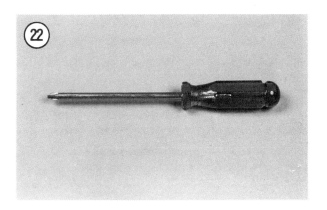

now starting to build your tool collection, avoid inexpensive tools that are thick, heavy and clumsy and are made of inferior material. Quality tools are made of alloy steel and are heat treated for greater strength. The initial cost of good quality tools may be more, but they are less expensive in the long term.

The following tools are required to perform virtually any repair job. Each tool is described and the recommended size given for starting a tool collection. Additional tools and some duplicates may be added as you become familiar with the vehicle. The Kawasaki Jet Ski is built with metric standard fasteners, so if you are starting your tool collection now, buy metric sizes.

Screwdrivers

The screwdriver is a very basic tool, but if used improperly, it can do more damage than good. The slot on a screw has a definite dimension and shape. A screwdriver must be selected to conform with this shape. Use a small screwdriver for small screws and a large one for large screws or the screw head will be damaged.

Two basic types of screwdrivers are required: common (flat-blade) screwdriver (**Figure 21**) and Phillips screwdriver (**Figure 22**).

Screwdrivers are available in sets which often include an assortment of common and Phillips blades. If you buy them individually, buy at least the following:

   a. Common screwdriver—5/16 × 6 in. blade.
   b. Common screwdriver—3/8 × 12 in. blade.
   c. Phillips screwdriver—size 2 tip, 6 in. blade.

Use screwdrivers only for removing and installing screws. Never use a screwdriver for prying or chiseling metal. Do not try to remove a Phillips or Allen head screw with a common screwdriver. The screw head can be damaged so that even the correct tool will be unable to remove it.

Keep screwdrivers in the proper condition and they will last long and perform well. Always keep the tip of a common screwdriver in good condition. **Figure 23** shows how to dress the tip to the proper shape if it becomes damaged. Note the symmetrical sides of the tip.

Pliers

Pliers come in a wide range of types and sizes. Pliers are useful for cutting, bending and crimping. They should never be used to cut hardened objects or to turn bolts or nuts. **Figure 24** shows several pliers useful in Jet Ski service.

Each type of pliers has a specialized function. Combination or slip-joint pliers are general purpose pliers and are used mainly for holding and bending. Needlenose pliers are used to grasp or bend small objects or objects in a difficult to reach area. Adjustable pliers can be adjusted to hold various sizes of objects while the jaws remain parallel to grip round objects such as pipe or tubing. There are many more types of specialized pliers.

Locking pliers

Locking pliers (**Figure 25**) are used as pliers or to hold objects very tightly while another task is performed on the object. Locking pliers can sometimes be used to remove a rounded-off fastener. Locking pliers are available in many types for more specific tasks.

Snap Ring Pliers

Snap ring pliers (**Figure 26**) are special in that they are only used to remove snap rings from shafts or from within a housing. When purchasing snap ring pliers, there are two basic types to consider. External pliers (spreading) are used to remove snap rings that fit on the outside of a shaft. Internal pliers (squeezing) are used to remove snap rings which fit inside a housing.

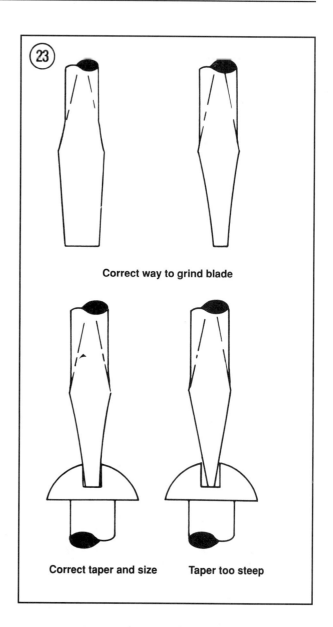

Correct way to grind blade

Correct taper and size   Taper too steep

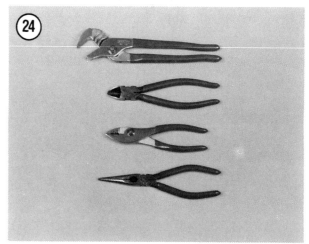

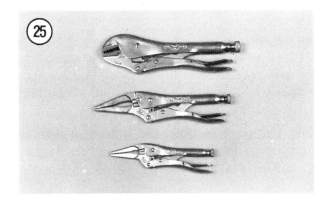

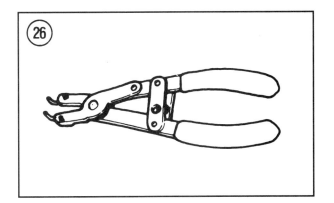

Box and Open-end Wrenches

Box and open-end wrenches (**Figure 27**) are available in sets or separately in a variety of sizes. The size number stamped near the end refers to the distance between 2 parallel flats on the hex-head bolt or nut.

Box wrenches usually have superior fastener turning ability compared to open-end wrenches. Open-end wrenches grip the fastener only on 2 flats. Unless a wrench fits well, it may slip and round of the points on the fastener. A box wrench contacts the fastener on 6 flats, providing a much more secure grip. Both 6-point and 12-point openings on box wrenches are available. The 6-point provides better holding power, but the 12-point allows a shorter swing.

Combination wrenches which are open on one end and boxed on the other are also available. Both ends are the same size on combination wrenches. See **Figure 28**.

Adjustable Wrenches

An adjustable wrench can be adjusted to fit a variety of fasteners. See **Figure 29**. However, it can loosen and slip, causing damage to the fastener and possible injury to your knuckles. Use an adjustable wrench only when other wrenches are not available.

Adjustable wrenches are available in various sizes.

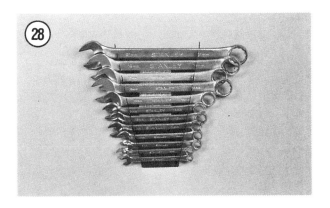

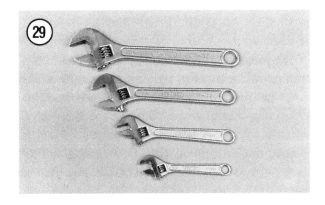

Socket Wrenches

Socket wrenches are undoubtedly the fastest, safest and most convenient to use. Sockets which attach to a ratchet handle (**Figure 30**) are available with 6- or 12-point openings and 1/4, 3/8, 1/2 and 3/4 in. drives (**Figure 31**). The drive size indicates the size of the square hole which mates with the ratchet handle.

Torque Wrench

A torque wrench (**Figure 32**) is used with a socket to measure how tightly a fastener is installed. Torque wrenches are available in a wide range of price ranges, with either a 3/8 in. (in.-lb.) or 1/2 in. (ft.-lb.) drive size. A beam-type torque wrench is shown in **Figure 32**. A beam torque wrench has a pointer which is read against a scale near the wrench handle. Other common types of torque wrench are dial type and click type. A click type torque wrench makes an audible "click" when the desired torque is obtained. A click type torque wrench is useful in hard to reach areas because the user does not have to closely watch the wrench for a reading.

Impact Driver

An impact driver makes removal of tight screws easy and eliminates damage to screw heads (especially screws secured with thread-locking compound). Impact drivers with inter-changeable bits (**Figure 33**) are available at most large hardware and automotive parts stores. Sockets can also be used with a hand impact driver. However, make sure the socket is designed for impact use. Do not use regular hand type sockets, as they may shatter during use.

Hammers

The correct hammer (**Figure 34**) is necessary for many procedures during repair and mainte-nance. Always use a hammer with a face (or head) of rubber or plastic or the soft-face type that is filled with lead shot, whenever a steel hammer could cause damage to a component. *Never* use a metal-face hammer on engine or drive train parts, as severe damage will likely

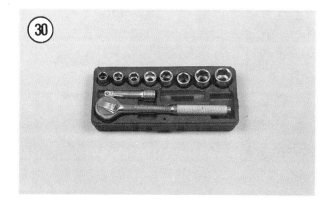

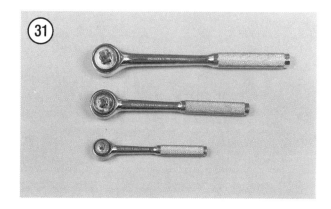

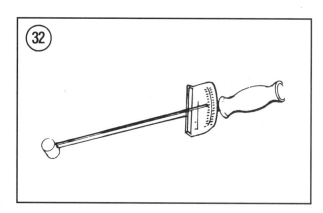

result. You can generally produce the same amount of force with a soft-face hammer as a metal-face hammer. A metal-face hammer may be necessary, however, when using a hand impact driver or using a punch or chisel.

PRECISION MEASURING TOOLS

Precision measurement is an important part of Jet Ski service. When performing many of the

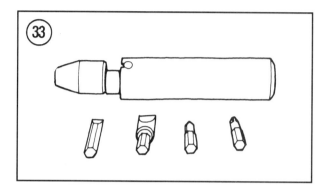

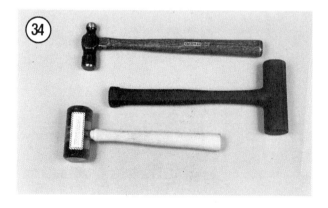

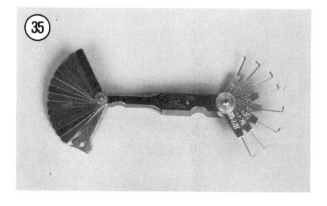

procedures in this manual, you will be required to make a number of measurements. These include such basic checks as engine compression and spark plug gap. During major engine disassembly and service, however, highly accurate, precision measurements are required to determine the condition of internal engine components such as the pistons, cylinders and crankshaft. When performing these measurements, the degree of accuracy will dictate which tool is required.

Precision measuring tools are relatively expensive. If this is your first experience at engine service, it may be worthwhile to have the measurements taken at a dealership or other qualified repair shop. However, as your skills increase, you may want to purchase some of these specialized measuring tools. The following is a description of the measuring tools required to perform engine service.

Because precision measuring instruments are somewhat fragile, they must be stored, handled and used carefully to ensure continued accuracy.

Feeler Gauge

The feeler gauge (**Figure 35**) is made of either a flat or round piece of hardened steel of a specified thickness. Feeler gauges are available in U.S. standard or metric, although some are marked with both measurements. The feeler gauge is used to accurately measure small gaps such as spark plug electrode gap, breaker point gap, valve clearance (4-stroke engines) and crankshaft end play. Wire gauges are mostly used to measure spark plug gap. Flat feeler gauges are used for all other measurements. Feeler gauges are also used with a straightedge or surface plate to measure warpage of mating surfaces. When using a feeler gauge, insert feelers of various thicknesses into the gap being measured until a slight drag is felt as the gauge is moved through the gap.

Vernier Caliper

A vernier caliper is used to take inside, outside and depth measurements. See **Figure 36** for a typical vernier caliper. Although a vernier caliper is not as precise as a micrometer, it allows reasonably accurate measurements, typically to within 0.02 mm (metric) or 0.001 in. (U.S.).

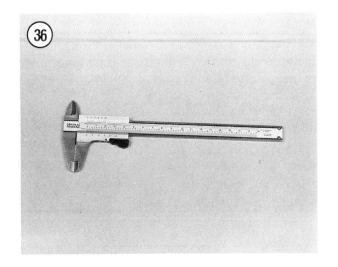

Outside Micrometer

An outside micrometer is one of the most accurate instruments for precision measurement. Outside micrometers are required to measure piston diameter, piston pin diameter, crankshaft journal and crankpin diameter precisely. Used with a telescopic gauge, an outside micrometer can be used to measure cylinder bore size and to determine cylinder taper and out-of-round. Outside micrometers are delicate instruments; if dropped on the floor, they most certainly will be knocked out of calibration. Always handle and use micrometers carefully to ensure accuracy. Store micrometers in their padded case when not in use to prevent damage.

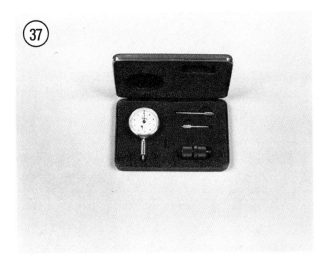

Dial Indicator

Dial indicators (**Figure 37**) are precision tools used to check ignition timing, gear lash and runout of shafts. Dial indicators take precision measurements to within 0.02 mm (metric) or 0.001 in. (U.S.). A dial indicator is typically mounted on a holder or bracket and the indicator plunger is positioned against the shaft or component being checked. The dial should then be rotated to align zero with the indicator needle. Always make sure the indicator plunger is set at a right angle to the shaft, gear or other component for accurate results.

For watercraft service, select a dial indicator with a continuous dial (**Figure 38**). A continuous dial is required to accurately measure piston position during timing adjustments.

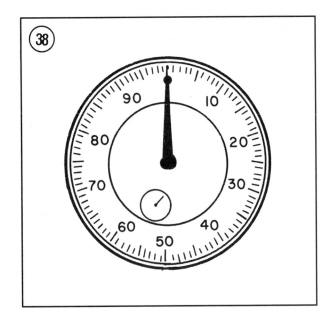

Cylinder Bore Gauge

The cylinder bore dial gauge set shown in **Figure 39** is comprised of a dial indicator, handle and a number of length adapters (anvils) and shims to adapt the gauge to different bore sizes. The bore gauge can be used to make cylinder

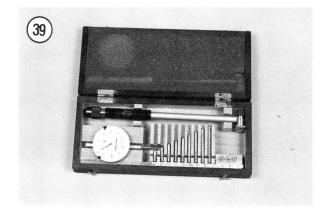

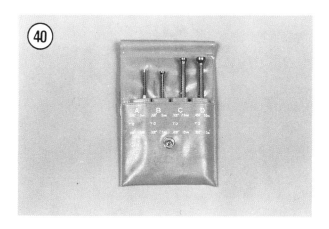

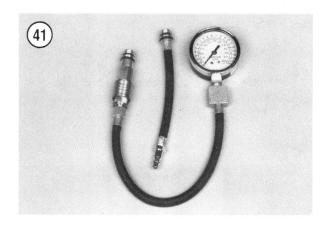

bore measurements such as bore size, taper and out-of-round. An outside micrometer of the correct size must be used to calibrate the bore gauge to the correct cylinder bore size. Refer to Chapters Four and Five (Engine) for correct setup, calibration and use of a cylinder bore gauge.

Small Hole Gauges

A set of small hole gauges (**Figure 40**) allows measurement of a hole, groove or slot ranging in size up to 13 mm (0.512 in.). An outside micrometer must be used together with the hole gauge to determine the size.

Compression Gauge

An engine with low compression cannot be properly tuned and will not develop full power. A compression gauge (**Figure 41**) measures the amount of pressure present in the engine's combustion chamber during the compression/power stroke. Compression readings can be interpreted to pinpoint specific engine mechanical problems. The gauge shown (**Figure 41**) has a flexible stem with an extension. Although compression gauges with press-in rubber tips are available, a gauge with screw-in adapters are generally more accurate and easier to use. See Chapter Three for instruction regarding the use of a compression gauge and interpretation of test results.

Strobe Timing Light

A timing light is used to accurately check ignition timing. By flashing light at the precise instant the spark plug fires, the position of the timing mark can be seen. The flashing light makes a moving mark appear to stand still opposite a stationary pointer or mark.

Suitable timing lights range from inexpensive neon bulb types to powerful xenon strobe lights.

See **Figure 42**. A light with an inductive pickup is recommended to eliminate any possible damage to ignition components or wiring.

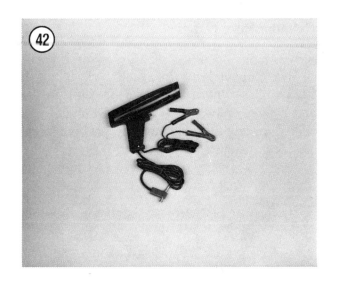

Multimeter

A multimeter (**Figure 43**) is invaluable for electrical system troubleshooting and service. It combines a voltmeter, an ohmmeter and an ammeter into one unit, so it is often called VOM.

Two types of multimeter are commonly available, analog and digital. Analog meters have a moving needle with marked bands indicating the volt, ohm and amperage scales. The digital meter (DVOM) is ideally suited for troubleshooting because it is easy to read, more accurate than analog, contains internal overload protection, is auto-ranging (analog meters must be calibrated each time the scale is changed) and has automatic polarity compensation.

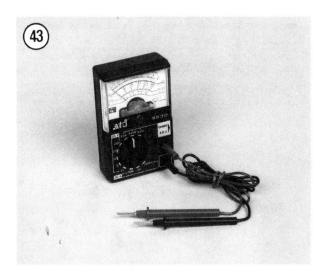

Tachometer

A portable tachometer is necessary for tuning and carburetor adjustments. Ignition timing and carburetor adjustments must be performed at specified engine speeds. The best instrument for this purpose is one with a low range of 0-1000 or 0-2000 rpm and a high range of 6000 rpm. Extended range instruments sometimes lack accuracy at lower speeds. The tachometer should be capable of detecting speed changes as low as 25 rpm.

Battery Hydrometer

A hydrometer (**Figure 44**) is used to determine a battery's state of charge. A hydrometer measures the specific gravity of the electrolyte in each battery cell. Specific gravity is the weight or density of the electrolyte as compared to pure water. As a battery is charged, the specific gravity goes up; when a battery is discharged, the spe-

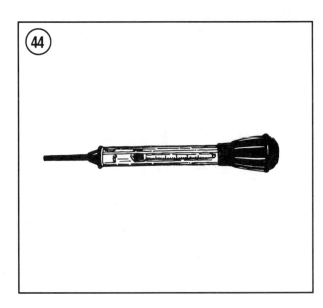

cific gravity goes down. See Chapter Eight for hydrometer testing instructions.

Screw Pitch Gauge

A screw pitch gauge (**Figure 45**) determines the thread pitch of bolts, screws, studs and other fasteners. The gauge is made up of a number of

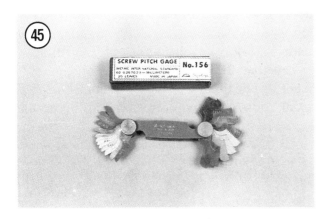

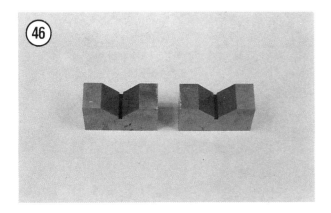

thin plates. Each plate has a thread shape cut on one edge to match one thread pitch. When using a screw pitch gauge to determine a thread pitch size, try to fit different thread pitch sizes onto the fastener until a perfect match is obtained.

Magnetic Stand

A magnetic stand is used to securely hold a dial indicator when checking the runout of a round object or when checking the end play of a shaft.

V-blocks

V-blocks (**Figure 46**) are precision ground blocks used to hold a round object (shaft) when checking its runout or condition. The shaft is placed into the V-blocks and rotated to check for excessive runout using a dial indicator.

SPECIAL TOOLS

This section described special tools unique to Jet Ski service and repair.

Flywheel Puller

A flywheel puller (**Figure 47**) is required to remove the flywheel from the engine. Flywheel removal is necessary to service the stator plate or adjust the ignition timing. In addition, the flywheel must be removed before the crankcase halves can be split during major engine disassembly.

There is not suitable substitute for a flywheel puller. Because the flywheel is a taper fit on the crankshaft, makeshift removal often results in crankshaft and flywheel damage. Do not attempt to remove the flywheel without the correct flywheel puller. Refer to Chapter Eight for the recommended flywheel puller part No. and flywheel removal procedures.

Flywheel Holder

The flywheel holder (**Figure 48**) is used to hold the flywheel during flywheel or coupling removal. Refer to Chapter Eight for flywheel holder part No. and flywheel removal procedures.

Coupling Holder

The coupling holder (**Figure 49**) is required when removing or installing the engine or drive shaft coupler half. Because the coupler half arms are brittle, the use of an improper tool will easily damage the coupler half. See Chapters Four and Five for coupling holder part No.

Pressure Cable Lube Tool

A cable lubricator is used to help force cable lubricant throughout a control cable.

This tool (**Figure 50**) is clamped to one end of a control cable and has a tube fitting to allow a cable lubricant to be forced throughout the length of the cable.

Expendable Supplies

Certain expendable supplies are also required for Jet Ski service and maintenance. These include the recommended grease, oil and gasket sealant. In addition, shop towels and a suitable cleaning solvent are necessary. Ask your Jet Ski dealer for the special threadlocking compounds, silicone sealants and lubrication products that are required for maintaining your watercraft. Cleaning solvent is generally available at automotive parts stores.

> *WARNING*
> *Having a stack of clean shop towels readily available is important when performing engine work. However, to prevent the possibility of a fire from spontaneous combustion, store oil or*

solvent soaked towels inside a sealed container until they can be washed.

MECHANIC'S TIPS

Removing Frozen Fasteners

When a fastener rusts and cannot be removed, several methods may be used to loosen it. First, apply penetrating oil such as Liquid Wrench or WD-40 (available at hardware or automotive parts stores). Apply the oil liberally and allow it to penetrate for 10-15 minutes. Tapping the fastener several times with a small hammer helps to break loose rust and corrosion and loosen the

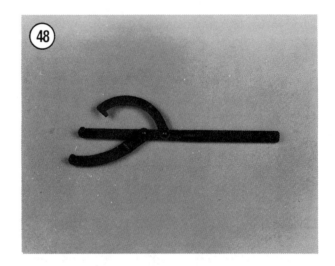

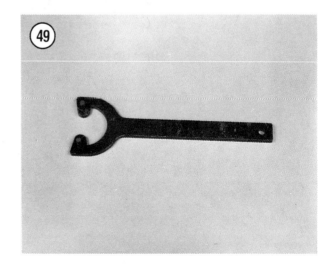

fastener. But, do not strike the fastener hard enough to cause damage. Reapply the penetrating oil as necessary.

For frozen screws, apply penetrating oil as previously described, then insert a screwdriver in the slot and tap the screwdriver with a hammer. If the screw head becomes damaged, apply a small amount of valve grinding compound to the screw head. The compound helps the screwdriver grip the damaged screw head. If the screw head is excessively damaged, it may be necessary to grip the head with locking pliers and attempt to remove it.

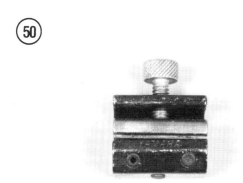

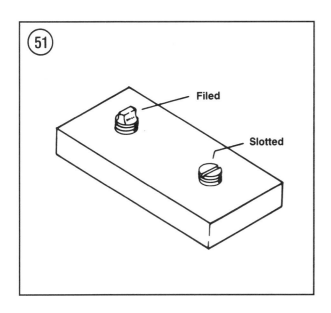

Filed

Slotted

Avoid applying heat unless specifically instructed, as it may melt, warp or remove the hardness from the components.

Removing Broken Fasteners

If the head breaks off a screw or bolt, several methods are available to remove the remaining portion.

If a large piece of the broken fastener projects above the part, try gripping it with locking pliers. If the projecting piece is too small, file it to fit a wrench or cut a slot in it to fit a screwdriver. See **Figure 51**.

If the head breaks off flush, use a screw extractor to remove the broken fastener. To do this, centerpunch the exact center of the remaining piece of the screw or bolt. Placing the centerpunch exactly in the center of the fastener is not an easy task; take your time and be precise. Drill an appropriately sized hole into the fastener at the centerpunch, then tap the screw extractor into the hole. Then, place a wrench on the screw extractor and back out the broken fastener. See **Figure 52**.

Repairing Damaged Threads

Occasionally, threads are damaged through carelessness or impact damage. Often, the threads can be cleaned up by running a tap (internal threads) or die (external threads) through the threads. See **Figure 53**. To clean or repair spark plug threads, a spark plug tap can be used.

NOTE
*Tap and dies can be purchased individually or in a set as shown in **Figure 54**.*

If an internal thread is damaged it may be necessary to install a Helicoil (**Figure 55**) or other type of thread insert. Follow the insert manufacturer's instructions when installing the insert.

REMOVING BROKEN SCREWS AND BOLTS

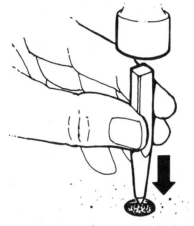

1. Center punch broken stud

2. Drill hole in stud

3. Tap in screw extractor

4. Remove broken stud

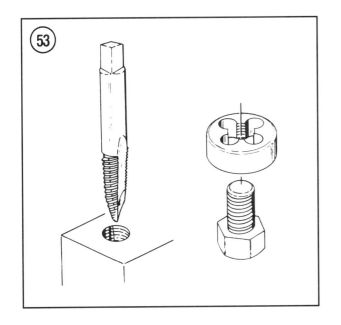

If it is necessary to drill and tap a hole, refer to **Table 5** for metric tap drill sizes.

Removing Broken or Damaged Studs

If a stud is broken (**Figure 56**) or the threads severely damaged, perform the following. A tube of Loctite 271, 2 nuts and 2 wrenches are required during this procedure (**Figure 57**).

1. Thread the 2 nuts onto the damaged stud as shown in **Figure 58**. Then tighten the 2 nuts against each other so that they are locked.

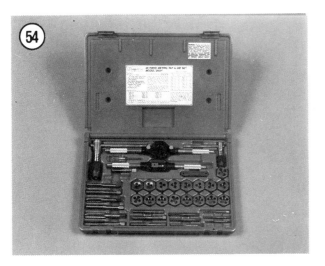

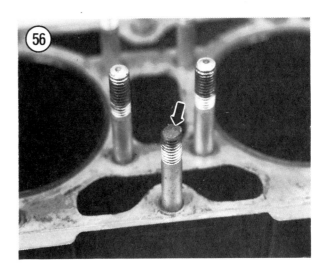

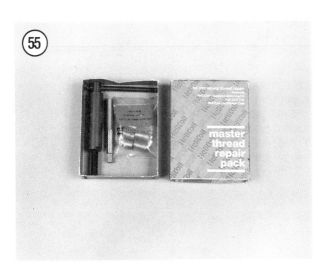

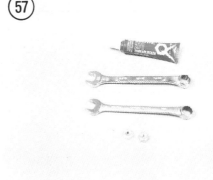

NOTE
If the threads on the damaged stud do not allow installation of the 2 nuts, remove the stud with a pair of locking pliers.

2. Turn the bottom nut counterclockwise (**Figure 59**) to unscrew and remove the broken stud.
3. Clean the threads with clean solvent and allow to dry thoroughly.
4. Install 2 nuts on the top half of the new stud as in Step 1. Make sure they are securely locked.
5. Coat the bottom threads of a new stud with Loctite 271.
6. Install the stud and tighten securely by turning the top nut (**Figure 60**).
7. Remove the nuts and repeat for each stud to be replaced.
8. Allow sufficient time for the Loctite to cure before returning the unit to service.

Table 1 HULL IDENTIFICATION (HIN) NUMBERS

Year and model	Starting HIN
1992	
JS440SX-A16	KAW
JS550SX-C2	KAW20001/192
JF650X-2-A7	KAW30001/192
JF650TS-B4	KAW40001/192
JL650SC-A2	KAW60001/192
JS650SX-B2	KAW10001/192
JH750SS-A1	KAW90001/292
JS750SX-A1	KAW80001/192
1993	
JS550SX-C3	KAW20001/293
JF650X-2-A8	KAW30001/293
JF650TS-B5	KAW40001/293
(continued)	

Table 1 HULL IDENTIFICATION (HIN) NUMBERS (continued)

Year and model	Starting HIN
1993 (cont.)	
JL650SC-A3	KAW50001/293
JS650SX-B3	KAW10001/293
JH750SS-A2	KAW80001/293
JS750SX-A2	KAW60001/293
JH750 Super Sport Xi-B1	KAW70001/393
1994	
JS550SX-C4	KAW20001/394
JF650X-2-A9	KAW30001/394
JF650TS-B6	KAW50001/394
JL650SC-A4	KAW50001/394
JH750SS-A3	KAW20001/394
JS750SX-A3	KAW70001/394
JH750 Super Sport Xi-B2	KAW40001/394
JT750ST-A1	KAW00001/394
JH750XiR-D1	KAW05001/494

TABLE 2 DECIMAL AND METRIC EQUIVALENTS

Fractions	Decimal in.	Metric mm	Fractions	Decimal in.	Metric mm
1/64	0.015625	0.39688	33/64	0.515625	13.09687
1/32	0.03125	0.79375	17/32	0.53125	13.49375
3/64	0.046875	1.19062	35/64	0.546875	13.89062
1/16	0.0625	1.58750	9/16	0.5625	14.28750
5/64	0.078125	1.98437	37/64	0.587125	14.68437
3/32	0.09372	2.38125	19/32	0.59375	15.08125
7/64	0.109375	2.77812	39/64	0.609375	15.47812
1/8	0.125	3.1750	5/8	0.625	15.87500
9/64	0.140625	3.57187	41/64	0.640625	16.27187
5/32	0.15625	3.96875	21/32	0.65625	16.66875
11/64	0.171875	4.36562	43/64	0.671875	17.06562
3/16	0.1875	4.76250	11/16	0.6875	17.46250
13/64	0.203125	5.15937	45/64	0.703125	17.85937
7/32	0.21875	5.55625	23/32	0.71875	18.25625
15/64	0.234375	5.95312	47/64	0.734375	18.65312
1/4	0.250	6.35000	3/4	0.750	19.05000
17/64	0.265625	6.74687	49/64	0.765625	19.44687
9/32	0.28125	7.14375	25/32	0.78125	19.84375
19/64	0.296875	7.54062	51/64	0.796875	20.24062
5/16	0.3125	7.93750	13/16	0.8125	20.63750
21/64	0.328125	8.33437	53/64	0.828125	21.03437
11/32	0.34375	8.73125	27/32	0.84375	21.43125
23/64	0.359375	9.12812	55/64	0.859375	21.82812
3/8	0.375	9.52500	7/8	0.875	22.22500
25/62	0.390625	9.92187	57/64	0.890625	22.62187
13/32	0.40625	10.31875	29/32	0.90625	23.01875
27/64	0.421875	10.71562	59/64	0.921875	23.41562
7/16	0.4375	11.11250	15/16	0.9375	23.81250
29/64	0.453125	11.50937	61/64	0.953125	24.20937
15/32	0.46875	11.90625	31/32	0.96875	24.60625
31/64	0.484375	12.30312	63/64	0.984375	25.00312
1/2	0.500	12.70000	1	1.00	25.40000

Table 3 GENERAL TORQUE SPECIFICATIONS (STEEL BOLTS)

Thread diameter	N·m	in.-lb.	ft.-lb.
5 mm	3.4-4.9	30-43	
6 mm	5.9-7.8	52-69	4.3-5.7
8 mm	14-19	—	10-14
10 mm	25-39	—	19-25
12 mm	44-61	—	33-45
14 mm	73-98	—	54-72
16 mm	115-155	—	83-115
18 mm	165-225	—	125-165
20 mm	225-325	—	165-240

Table 4 GENERAL TORQUE SPECIFICATIONS (STAINLESS BOLTS)

Thread diameter	N·m	in.-lb.	ft.-lb.
6 mm	5.9-8.8	52-78	—
8 mm	16-22	—	12-16
10 mm	30-41	—	22-30

TABLE 5 METRIC TAP DRILL SIZES

Metric tap (mm)	Drill size	Decimal equivalent	Nearest fraction
3 × 0.50	No. 39	0.0995	3/32
3 × 0.60	3/32	0.0937	3/32
4 × 0.70	No. 30	0.1285	1/8
4 × 0.75	1/8	0.125	1/8
5 × 0.80	No. 19	0.166	11/64
5 × 0.90	No. 20	0.161	5/32
6 × 1.00	No. 9	0.196	13/64
7 × 1.00	16/64	0.234	15/64
8 × 1.00	J	0.277	9/32
8 × 1.25	17/64	0.265	17/64
9 × 1.00	5/16	0.3125	5/16
9 × 1.25	5/16	0.3125	5/16
10 × 1.25	11/32	0.3437	11/32
10 × 1.50	R	0.339	11/32
11 × 1.50	3/8	0.375	3/8
12 × 1.50	13/32	0.406	13/32
12 × 1.75	13/32	0.406	13/32

Chapter Two

Troubleshooting

Diagnosing mechanical problems is relatively simple if you use orderly procedures and keep a few basic principles in mind. The first step in any troubleshooting procedure is to define the symptoms as closely as possible and then localize the problem. Subsequent steps involve testing and analyzing those areas which could cause the symptoms. A haphazard approach may eventually solve the problem, but it can be very costly in terms of wasted time and unnecessary parts replacement.

Proper lubrication, maintenance and periodic tune-up as described in Chapter Three reduces the necessity for troubleshooting. Even with the best of care, however, all watercraft are prone to problems which require troubleshooting.

When troubleshooting, never assume anything, but do not overlook the obvious either. If the engine won't start, is the stop button OFF? Is the engine cranking speed slow because the battery is discharged? Is the engine flooded with fuel from excessive use of the choke?

If the engine suddenly stops, check the easiest, most accessible area first. Is there sufficient gasoline in the tank? Have the spark plug wires fallen off? Is there water in the fuel filter sediment bowl? Is the fuel vent check valve allowing air to enter the tank as it should?

If nothing obvious is evident, look further. Learning to recognize and describe symptoms make repairs easier for you or a professional mechanic. Describe problems accurately and fully.

Gather as many symptoms as possible to aid in diagnosis. Note whether the engine lost power gradually or all at once, what color smoke (if any) came from the exhaust and so on. Remember that the more complicated a machine is, the easier it is to troubleshoot because symptoms point to specific problems.

After the symptoms are defined, areas which could cause problems are tested and analyzed. Guessing at the cause of a problem may provide the solution, but it can easily lead to frustration, wasted time and a series of expensive, unnecessary parts replacements.

You do not need expensive equipment or complicated test gear to determine if repairs can be attempted at home. A few simple checks could save a large repair bill and lost time while the watercraft sits in a service department. On the other hand, be realistic and do not attempt repairs beyond your abilities. Service departments tend to charge heavily for putting together a disassembled engine that may have been abused. Some will not even take on such a job. So, use common sense and do not get in over your head.

Tables 1-4 are located at the end of this chapter.

OPERATING REQUIREMENTS

An engine needs 3 basic requirements to run properly: correct fuel-air mixture, compression and a spark at the correct time (**Figure 1**). If one basic requirement is missing, the engine will not run. Two-stroke engine operating principles are described in Chapter One under *Engine Operation*. The ignition system is often the weakest link of the 3 systems. More problems result from ignition failures that from any other source. Keep that in mind before you begin tampering with the carburetor adjustments.

If the Jet Ski has been sitting for any length of time and refuses to start, check and clean the spark plugs. Then check the condition of the battery to make sure it has an adequate charge. If these items are good, then check the fuel delivery system. This includes the tank, fuel shutoff valve, inline fuel filter and fuel hose to the carburetor. Gasoline deposits may have gummed up carburetor jets and air passages. Gasoline tends to lose its potency after standing for long periods. Condensation may contaminate it with water. Drain the old fuel and try starting with a fresh tankful.

STARTING SYSTEM

An electric starter motor (**Figure 2**) is used on all Jet Ski models. The motor is mounted horizontally on the front of the engine. When battery

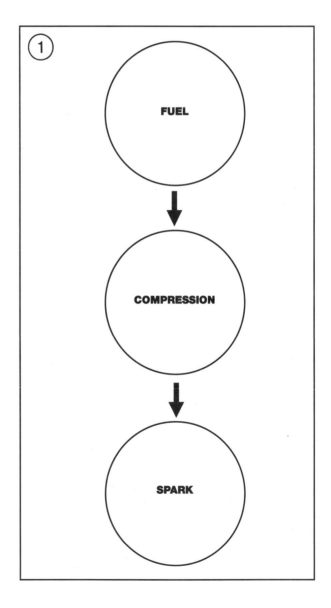

FUEL

COMPRESSION

SPARK

current is supplied to the starter motor, its pinion gear is thrust forward to engage the teeth on the engine flywheel. Once the starter switch is released, the pinion gear disengages from the flywheel.

The electric starting system requires a fully charged battery to provide the large amount of current required to operate the starter motor. Because there are no lights on the Jet Ski, the battery is only used to power the starting system. A charge coil (mounted on the stator plate) and a voltage regulator, connected to the battery, maintains battery charge while the engine is running. The battery can also be charged externally.

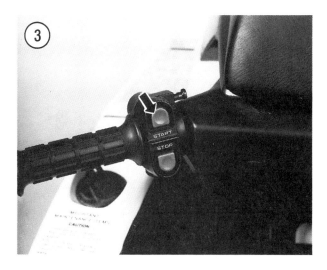

The starting circuit consists of the battery, stop switch, start switch, starter relay, starter motor and connecting wiring.

The starter relay carries the heavy electrical load to the starter motor (**Figure 2**). Depressing the starter switch (**Figure 3**, typical) allows current to flow through the relay coil. The relay contacts close and allow current to flow from the battery through the relay to the starter motor.

CAUTION
Do not operate the starter motor continuously for more than 5 seconds. Allow the motor to cool for at least 15 seconds between attempts to start the engine.

Troubleshooting

Before troubleshooting the starting system, make certain that:

  a. The battery is fully charged and in acceptable condition.
  b. The battery cables are the proper size and length. Replace the cables if undersize or damaged.
  c. All electrical connections are clean and tight.
  d. The wiring harness is in good condition with no worn or frayed insulation or loose harness sockets or connections.
  e. The fuel system is filled with an adequate supply of fresh gasoline. Make sure the gasoline is properly mixed with a recommended engine oil on models without oil injection. See Chapter Three.

Starter Circuit Voltage Drop Testing

Before performing the following troubleshooting procedures, remove the spark plugs (Chapter Three) and securely ground the spark plug leads to the engine.

NOTE
During the following voltage drop tests, set the voltmeter to its lowest DC volt scale (preferable 2.5 volt). Make sure the voltmeter test leads are correctly connected during testing.

Test 1

Test the condition of the positive battery cable (**Figure 4**) as follows:
1. Connect the voltmeter leads to the positive battery terminal and relay as shown in **Figure 5**.
2. Depress the starter button while noting the voltmeter. If the voltage drop exceeds 0.25 volt), clean the positive battery cable connections and repeat this step. If excessive voltage drop is still noted, replace the cable.
3. Disconnect the voltmeter leads.

Test 2

Test the condition of the negative battery cable as follows:
1. Connect the voltmeter leads to the battery negative terminal and a good engine ground as shown in **Figure 6**.
2. Depress the starter button while noting the voltmeter.
3. If the voltage drop exceeds 0.25 volt, clean the negative battery cable connections and repeat Step 2. If the voltage drop is still over 0.25 volt, replace the negative battery cable.

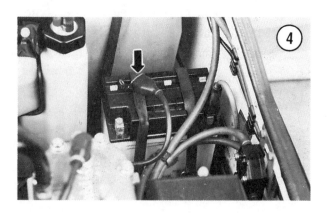

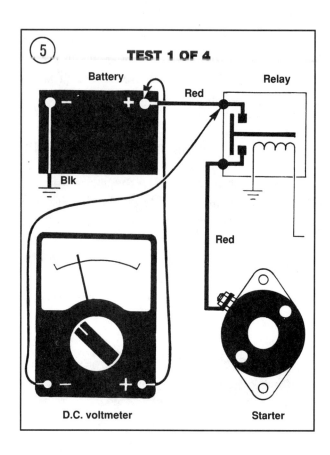

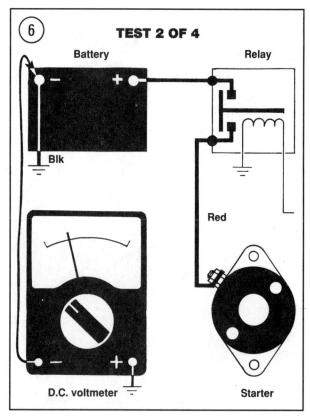

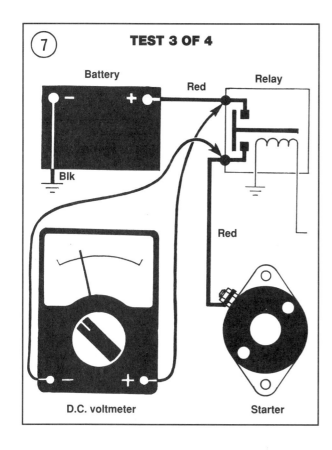

TEST 3 OF 4

Battery

Red

Relay

Blk

Red

D.C. voltmeter

Starter

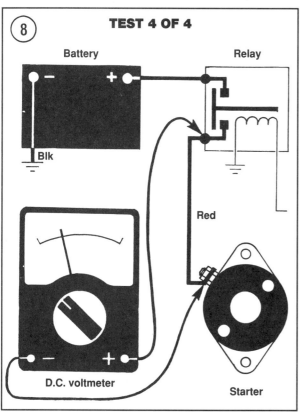

TEST 4 OF 4

Battery

Relay

Blk

Red

D.C. voltmeter

Starter

4. Disconnect the voltmeter.

Test 3

Test the condition of the starter relay as follows:

> *CAUTION*
> *Connect the voltmeter leads to the relay **only** while the starter button is depressed (engine cranking) and disconnect the leads **before** releasing the starter button. Failure to observe this precaution may cause voltmeter damage.*

1. Have an assistant depress the starter button and hold it down. Do not release the button.

2. Connect the voltmeter leads to the starter relay as shown in **Figure 7**. Be sure to observe the correct meter polarity. Quickly note the voltmeter reading, disconnect the test leads, *then* release the starter button.

3. The voltage reading should be 0.25 volt or less.

4. If the voltage drop reading in Step 2, exceeds 0.25 volt, remove the starter relay and test it according to the instructions in this chapter.

Test 4

Test the condition of the starter relay-to-starter motor cable as follows:

1. Connect the voltmeter leads to the battery and relay as shown in **Figure 8**.

2. Depress the starter button while observing the voltmeter. The reading should be 0.25 volt or less.

3. If the voltage drop reading in Step 2 exceeds 0.25 volt, remove the cable between the relay and starter motor. Thoroughly clean both connections, reinstall the cable and repeat this test.

4. If the voltage drop is still excessive (over 0.25 volt), replace the cable.

2

Starter Relay Continuity Test

1. Remove the starter relay as described in Chapter Eight.

2. Connect an ohmmeter between the 2 large relay terminals as shown in **Figure 9** or **Figure 10**. Place the ohmmeter on the R × 1 scale.

3. The ohmmeter should indicate infinity. If not, the relay is defective and must be replaced.

4. If the meter reads infinity, perform the *Starter Relay Activated Resistance Test* as described in this chapter.

Starter Relay Activated Resistance Test

An ohmmeter, a fully charged 12-volt battery and 2 jumper leads are required for this test.

1. Remove the starter relay as described in Chapter Eight.

2. Connect an ohmmeter between the 2 large relay terminals as shown in **Figure 11** or **Figure 12**. Place the ohmmeter on the R × 1 scale.

3. Using jumper leads, connect the 12-volt battery to the relay black and yellow/red wires as shown in **Figure 11** (late style relay) or the black and white wires as shown in **Figure 12** (early style relay). Note the ohmmeter reading as the battery is connected.

    a. If the relay clicks and the ohmmeter indicates zero ohms when the battery is connected, the relay is functioning properly.

    b. If no click is noted, and the ohmmeter indicates high resistance (or infinity), the relay is defective and must be replaced.

Starter Motor Testing

Refer to Chapter Eight for starter motor removal, disassembly and testing procedures.

Start/Stop Switch Testing

Refer to *Switches* in Chapter Nine.

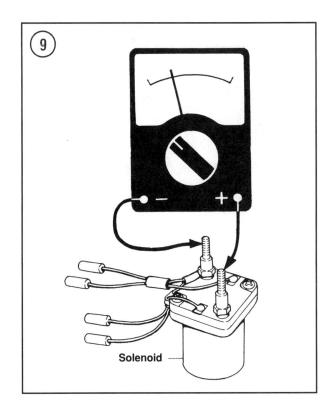

Solenoid

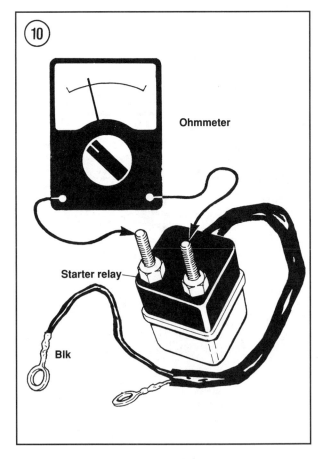

Ohmmeter

Starter relay

Blk

CHARGING SYSTEM

The battery charging system consists of a charge coil mounted on the stator plate (under the flywheel), permanent magnets located within the flywheel rim, a voltage regulator/rectifier assembly, a battery and related wiring.

A malfunction in the charging system generally results in an undercharged or dead battery. Should charging system problems occur, the problem is often in the battery, regulator/rectifier or wiring, since the battery charge coil is protected by its location behind the flywheel.

Troubleshooting

Before performing a battery charging coil or voltage regulator test, visually check the following items:

1. Make sure the battery cables are properly connected. If battery polarity is reversed, check for a damaged voltage regulator/rectifier.

2. Carefully inspect all wiring between the magneto base and the battery for worn or cracked insulation and corroded or loose connections. Repair or replace any faulty wiring and clean and tighten connections as necessary.

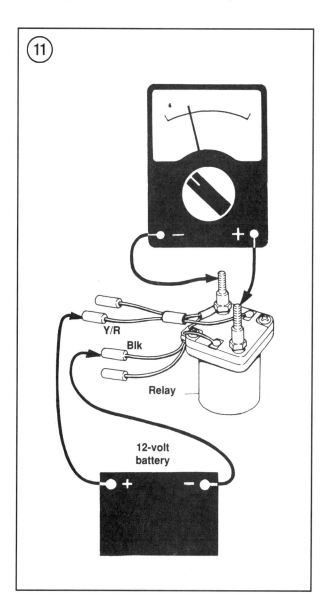

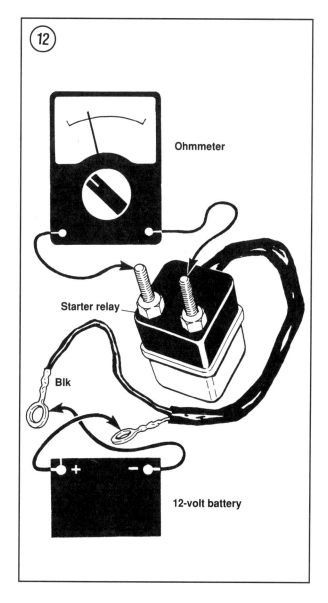

3. Check the battery condition. Clean and charge is necessary. See Chapter Eight.

Charge Coil Test

The charge coil (**Figure 13**) is mounted on the stator plate assembly behind the flywheel. A voltmeter capable of measuring alternating current (AC) is required to test charging coil output.

WARNING
To prevent an electrical shock, do not perform the output test with the Jet Ski in the water. Instead, use an auxiliary water supply during this test. Refer to Chapter Three. Never operate the engine at maximum speed with no load on the engine.

CAUTION
Never operate the engine for more than 15 seconds without a cooling water supply or engine damage from overheating will result.

440 and 550 cc models

Refer to **Figure 14** or **Figure 15** as necessary during this procedure.

1. Disconnect the negative battery cable from the battery.

2. Connect an auxiliary cooling water supply to the engine as described in Chapter Three.

3. Connect a tachometer to the engine according to its manufacturer's instructions.

4. Remove the wiring harness cover from the electrical box, exposing the 6-pin harness connector.

5. Disconnect the 6-pin harness connector. See **Figure 16**.

6. Locate the 2 light green wire pins in the charging coil side of the connector.

7. Using a pair of needlenose pliers, compress the spring retainer in each light green wire pin and pull the wire and pin out of the connector.

8. With the 2 light green wires isolated, reconnect the 6-pin connector.

9. Connect an AC voltmeter between the light green wire (charging coil side) and a good engine ground.

10. Reconnect the negative battery cable. Start the engine, then turn on the auxiliary water supply.

11. Gradually increase engine speed to 6000 rpm and note the voltmeter reading. Charging coil output should be 12-15 volts AC.

   a. If the output voltage is as specified, the charging coil is functioning properly. Check the voltage regulator/rectifier as described in this chapter.

   b. If the output voltage is less than 12 volts AC, check the charging coil resistance as described in Steps 12 and 13.

12. Connect an ohmmeter between the light green charging coil wire and a good engine ground.

13. Charging coil resistance should be 1.2-1.8 ohms. If resistance is not as specified, replace the charging coil as described in Chapter Eight.

NOTE
If charging coil voltage output is low, but resistance is within specification, the flywheel magnets may be weak. If so, the

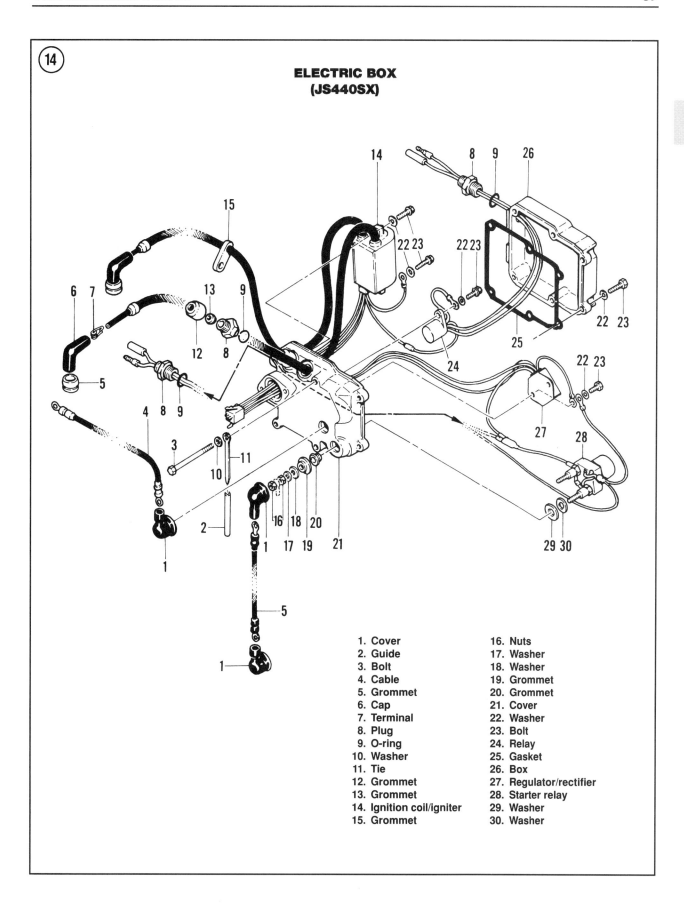

**ELECTRIC BOX
(JS440SX)**

1. Cover
2. Guide
3. Bolt
4. Cable
5. Grommet
6. Cap
7. Terminal
8. Plug
9. O-ring
10. Washer
11. Tie
12. Grommet
13. Grommet
14. Ignition coil/igniter
15. Grommet
16. Nuts
17. Washer
18. Washer
19. Grommet
20. Grommet
21. Cover
22. Washer
23. Bolt
24. Relay
25. Gasket
26. Box
27. Regulator/rectifier
28. Starter relay
29. Washer
30. Washer

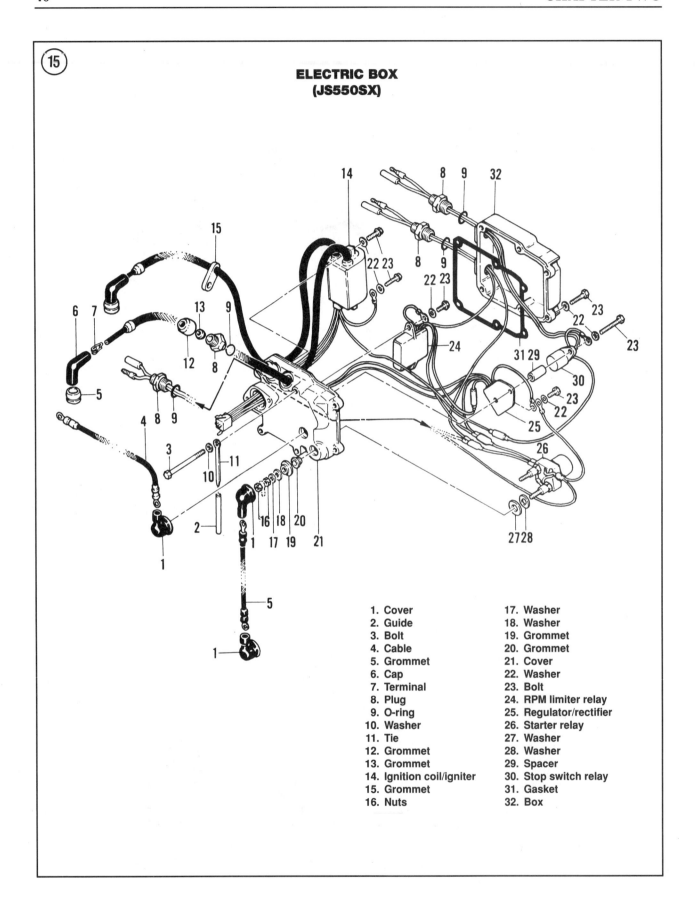

⑮ ELECTRIC BOX
(JS550SX)

1. Cover
2. Guide
3. Bolt
4. Cable
5. Grommet
6. Cap
7. Terminal
8. Plug
9. O-ring
10. Washer
11. Tie
12. Grommet
13. Grommet
14. Ignition coil/igniter
15. Grommet
16. Nuts
17. Washer
18. Washer
19. Grommet
20. Grommet
21. Cover
22. Washer
23. Bolt
24. RPM limiter relay
25. Regulator/rectifier
26. Starter relay
27. Washer
28. Washer
29. Spacer
30. Stop switch relay
31. Gasket
32. Box

flywheel must be replaced to restore proper charging system operation.

14. After performing the output test, throttle back to idle, turn off the auxiliary water supply then stop the engine.

15. Remove the test equipment. Reinstall all components and reconnect any disconnected circuits.

JS650SX

Refer to **Figure 17** for this procedure.

1. Remove the electric box as described in Chapter Eight.

2. Remove the box cover. Disconnect the 2 yellow stator wire bullet connectors at the voltage regulator/rectifier.

3. Connect an AC voltmeter across the 2 yellow wires (leading from stator).

4. Temporarily reconnect the spark plug leads, battery cables, starter motor cable and reinstall the flame arrestor so the engine can be started for the output test.

5. Connect a tachometer to the engine according to its manufacturer's instructions.

6. Connect an auxiliary water supply to the engine as described in Chapter Three.

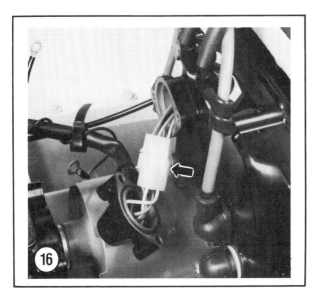

7. Start the engine then turn on the auxiliary water supply.

8. Gradually increase engine speed to 3000 rpm while observing the voltmeter. Charging coil output should be 38 volts AC at 3000 rpm. After checking output, throttle back to idle, turn off the auxiliary water supply, then stop the engine.

   a. If output is as specified, the charging coil is functioning properly. Check the voltage regulator as described in this chapter.

   b. If output is less than specified, check the charging coil resistance as described in Steps 9-11.

9. Connect an ohmmeter between the yellow charging coil wires. Resistance should be 1.5-1.8 ohms.

10. Next, connect the ohmmeter between the black charging coil wire and alternately to each yellow wire while noting the meter. Resistance should be 0.7-1.3 ohms at each connection.

11. If resistance is not as specified, replace the charging coil as described in Chapter Eight.

> *NOTE*
> *If charging coil voltage output is low, but resistance is within specification, the flywheel magnets may be weak. If so, the flywheel must be replaced to restore proper charging system operation.*

12. Remove the test equipment. Reinstall all components and reconnect any disconnected circuits.

JF650X-2

Refer to **Figure 18** during this procedure.

1. Disconnect the negative battery cable from the battery.

2. Remove the electric box as described in Chapter Eight. Open the box and disconnect the 2 yellow charging coil wires from the voltage regulator/rectifier, at their bullet connectors.

3. Connect an AC voltmeter between the 2 yellow wires leading from the stator plate.

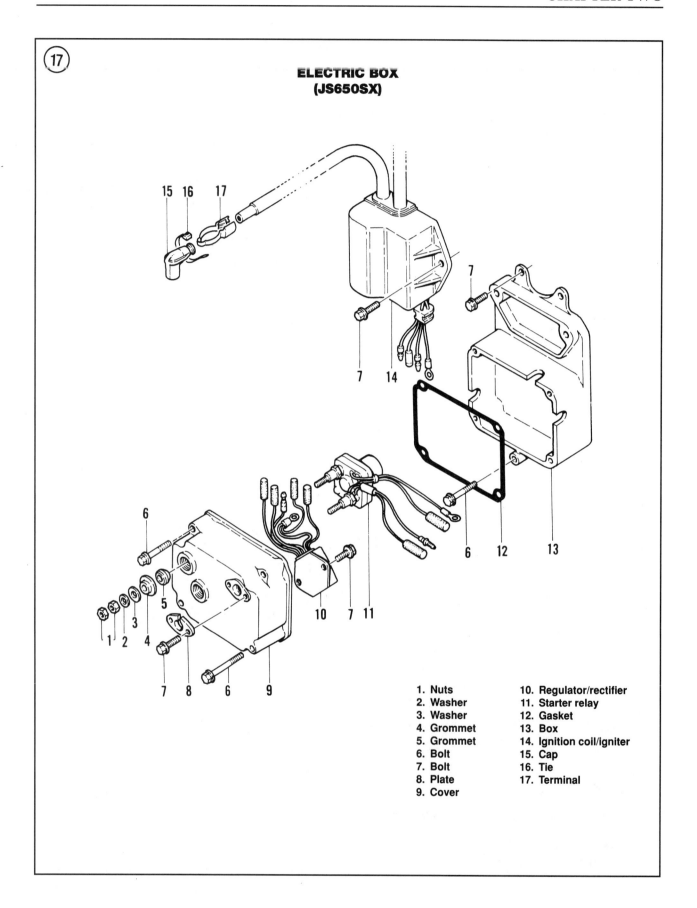

**ELECTRIC BOX
(JS650SX)**

1. Nuts
2. Washer
3. Washer
4. Grommet
5. Grommet
6. Bolt
7. Bolt
8. Plate
9. Cover
10. Regulator/rectifier
11. Starter relay
12. Gasket
13. Box
14. Ignition coil/igniter
15. Cap
16. Tie
17. Terminal

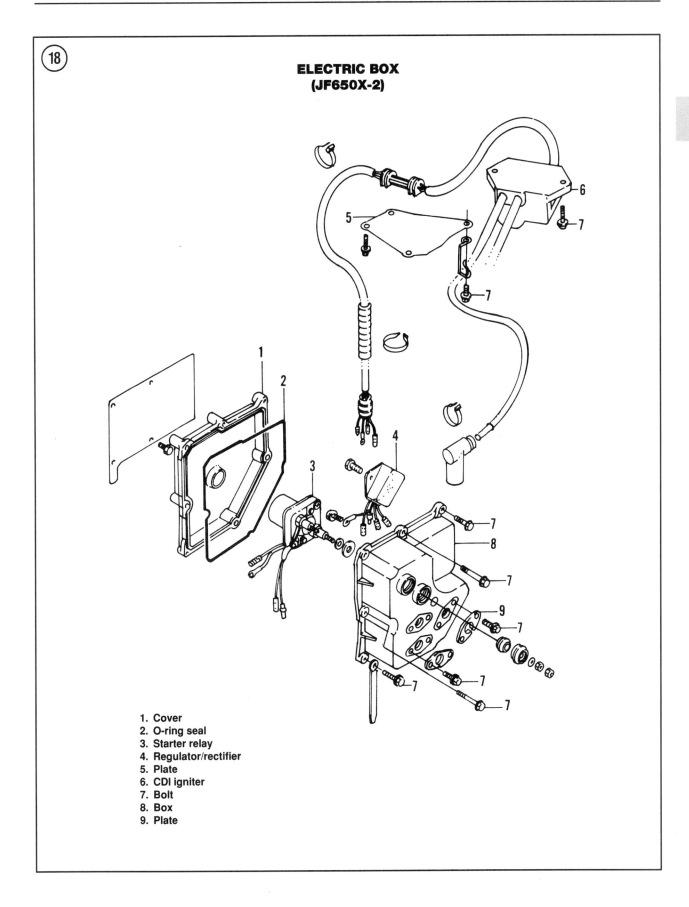

⑱

**ELECTRIC BOX
(JF650X-2)**

2

1. Cover
2. O-ring seal
3. Starter relay
4. Regulator/rectifier
5. Plate
6. CDI igniter
7. Bolt
8. Box
9. Plate

4. Connect a tachometer to the engine according to its manufacturer's instructions.

5. Attach an auxiliary water supply to the engine as described in Chapter Three.

6. Reconnect any wires/cables disconnected during electric box removal so the engine can be started. Start the engine, then turn on the auxiliary water supply.

7. Gradually increase engine speed to 3000 rpm and note the voltmeter. Then, throttle back to idle, turn off the auxiliary water supply and stop the engine.

8. Charging coil output should be 38 volts AC at 3000 rpm.

   a. If output is as specified, the charging coil is functioning properly. Check the voltage regulator/rectifier as described in this chapter.

   b. If output is less than specified, check charging coil resistance as described in Steps 9-11.

9. Connect an ohmmeter between the yellow charging coil wires. Resistance should be 1.5-1.8 ohms.

10. Next, connect the ohmmeter between the black charging coil wire and alternately to each yellow wire while noting the meter. Resistance should be 0.7-1.3 ohms at each connection.

11. If resistance is not as specified, replace the charging coil as described in Chapter Eight.

NOTE
If charging coil voltage output is low, but resistance is within specification, the flywheel magnets may be weak. If so, the flywheel must be replaced to restore proper charging system operation.

12. Remove the test equipment, reinstall all components and reconnect all circuits.

JF650SC, JL650TS and JB650 Jet Mate

Refer to **Figure 19** (JF650TS), **Figure 20** (JL650SC) or **Figure 21** (JB650 Jet Mate) as necessary for this procedure.

1. Disconnect the negative battery cable from the battery.

2. Open the electric box and disconnect the 2 brown charging coil wires from the voltage regulator/rectifier.

3. Connect an AC voltmeter between the 2 brown wires leading from the stator plate.

4. Connect a tachometer to the engine according to its manufacturer's instructions.

5. Attach an auxiliary water supply to the engine as described in Chapter Three.

6. Reconnect any wires/cables disconnected during electric box removal so the engine can be started. Start the engine, then turn on the auxiliary water supply.

7. Gradually increase engine speed to 3000 rpm and note the voltmeter. Next, throttle back to idle, turn off the auxiliary water supply then stop the engine.

8. Charging coil output should be 38 volts AC at 3000 rpm.

   a. If output is as specified, check the voltage regulator/rectifier as described in this chapter.

   b. If output is less than specified, check charging coil resistance as described in Steps 9-11.

9. Connect an ohmmeter between the 2 brown charging coil wires. Resistance should be 1.5-2.3 ohms.

10. Next, connect the ohmmeter between the black/yellow charging coil wire, and alternately to each brown wire while noting the meter. Resistance should be 0.7-1.3 ohms at each connection.

11. If charging coil resistance is not as specified, replace the charging coil as described in Chapter Eight.

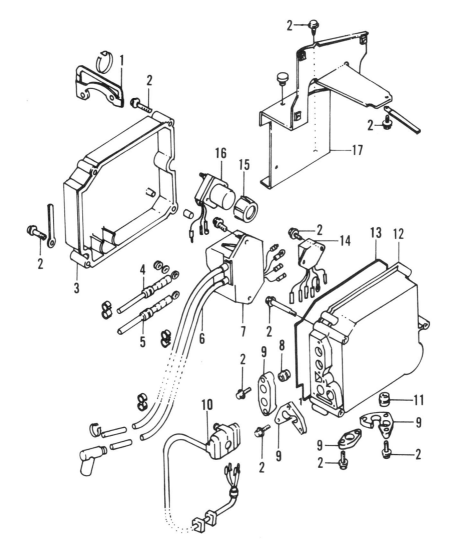

**ELECTRIC BOX
(JS650TS)**

1. Bracket
2. Bolt
3. Cover
4. Cable
5. Cable
6. Cable
7. CDI igniter
8. Grommet
9. Plate
10. Switch
11. Grommet
12. Box
13. O-ring seal
14. Regulator/rectifier
15. Rubber cushion
16. Starter relay
17. Bracket

(20)

**ELECTRIC BOX
(JL650SC)**

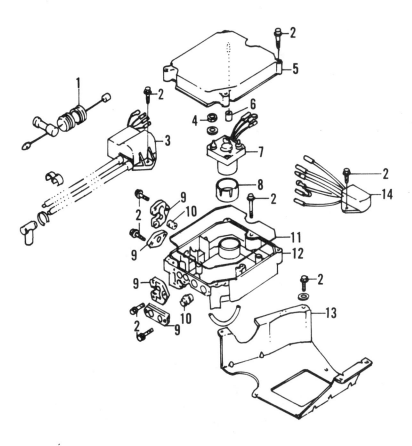

1. Fuse
2. Bolt
3. CDI igniter
4. Nut
5. Cover
6. Cap
7. Starter relay
8. Rubber cushion
9. Plate
10. Grommet
11. O-ring seal
12. Box
13. Bracket
14. Regulator/rectifier

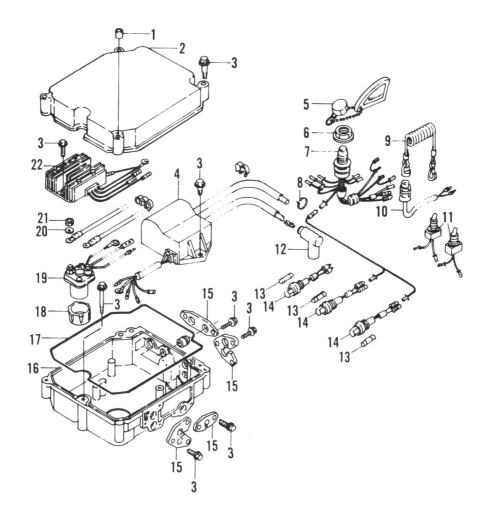

ELECTRIC BOX
(JB650 JET MATE)

2

1. Cap
2. Cover
3. Bolt
4. CDI igniter
5. Cap
6. Nut
7. Main switch
8. Clamp
9. Tether
10. Stop switch
11. Switches

12. Cap
13. Fuse
14. Fuse holder
15. Plate
16. Box
17. O-ring seal
18. Rubber cushion
19. Starter relay
20. Washer
21. Nut
22. Regulator/rectifier

NOTE
If charging coil voltage output is low, but resistance is within specification, the flywheel magnets may be weak. If so, the flywheel must be replaced to restore proper charging system operation.

12. Remove the test equipment, reinstall all components and reconnect all circuits.

All 750 cc models

1. Disconnect the negative battery cable from the battery.
2. Remove the electric box cover (**Figure 22**) to expose the 3- and 4-pin connectors.
3. Disconnect the 3-pin connector (**Figure 22**). Then, connect the black wire terminals in each connector half together, using a jumper wire.
4. Connect an AC voltmeter between the 2 brown wire terminals in the connector half leading from the stator plate.
5. Connect a tachometer according to its manufacturer's instructions.

6. Attach an auxiliary water supply to the engine as described in Chapter Three.

7. Reconnect the negative battery cable to the battery. Start the engine, then turn on the auxiliary water supply.

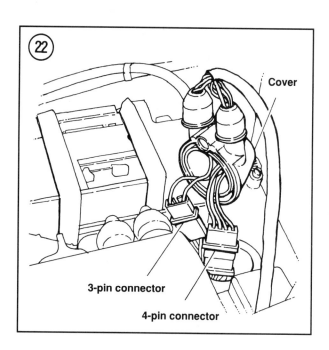

㉒

Cover

3-pin connector

4-pin connector

㉓ **VOLTAGE REGULATOR/RECTIFIER TEST (JS440SX)**

		Ohmeter posititive (+) lead connection				
	Wire color	Red/Purple	Red	Brown	Brown	Black
Ohmeter negative (−) lead connection	Red/Purple	[shaded]	Zero ohm	∞	∞	∞
	Red	Zero ohm	[shaded]	∞	∞	∞
	Brown	continuity	continuity	[shaded]	∞	continuity
	Brown	continuity	continuity	∞	[shaded]	continuity
	Black	∞	∞	∞	∞	[shaded]

∞ Indicates infinity

⌣ Indicates continuity

8.. Gradually increase engine speed to 3000 rpm and note the voltmeter. Next, throttle back to idle, turn off the auxiliary water supply then stop the engine.

9. Charging coil output should be 20 volts AC at 3000 rpm.

   a. If output is as specified, check the voltage regulator/rectifier as described in this chapter.

   b. If output is less than specified, check charging coil resistance as described in Steps 10 and 11.

10. Connect an ohmmeter between the 2 brown charging coil wires. Resistance should be 0.7-1.1 ohms.

11. If charging coil resistance is not as specified, replace the charging coil as described in Chapter Eight.

NOTE
If charging coil voltage output is low, but resistance is within specification, the flywheel magnets may be weak. If so, the flywheel must be replaced to restore proper charging system operation.

12. Remove the test equipment, reinstall all components and reconnect all circuits.

Voltage Regulator/Rectifier Test

Perform the following test if a charging system malfunction is evident, but charging coil output voltage is within specification. An ohmmeter is required to perform this test.

440 and 550 cc models

Refer to **Figure 14** and **Figure 15** for an exploded view of the electric box assembly.

1. Disconnect the negative battery cable from the battery.

2. Unbolt the electric box connector to expose the 6-pin connector (**Figure 16**).

3. Disconnect the 6-pin connector (**Figure 16**).

4. Calibrate the ohmmeter on the R × 100 scale.

5. Refer to **Figure 23** (JS440SX) or **Figure 24** (JS550SX) for the correct ohmmeter connections and the desired test results. Connect the ohmmeter to the regulator/rectifier wires in the 6-pin connector as indicated. Replace the regu-

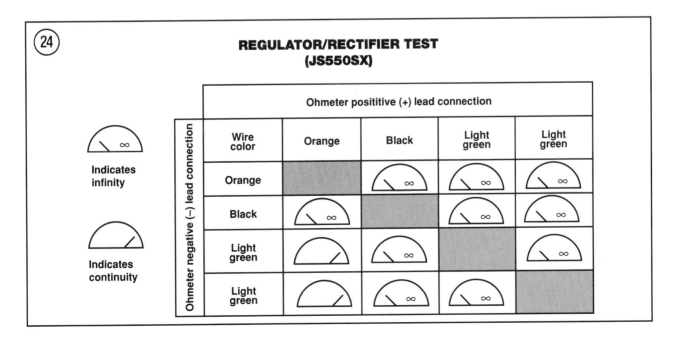

lator/rectifier assembly if any reading is different from that shown.

JS650SX and JF650X-2

Refer to **Figure 17** (JS650SX) or **Figure 18** (JF650X-2) for an exploded view of the electric box assembly.

1. Disconnect the negative battery cable from the battery.

2. Remove the electric box as described in Chapter Eight.

3. Remove the electric box cover and disconnect the voltage regulator/rectifier wires. See **Figure 25**.

4. Calibrate the ohmmeter on the R × 1000 scale.

5. Refer to **Figure 26** for the correct ohmmeter connections and the desired test results. Connect the ohmmeter to the regulator/rectifier wires as indicated. Replace the regulator/rectifier assembly if any reading is different from that shown.

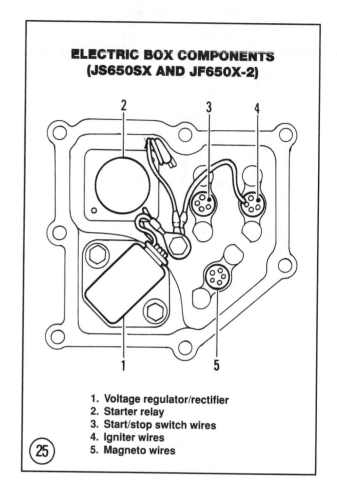

ELECTRIC BOX COMPONENTS (JS650SX AND JF650X-2)

1. Voltage regulator/rectifier
2. Starter relay
3. Start/stop switch wires
4. Igniter wires
5. Magneto wires

(25)

(26) **REGULATOR/RECTIFIER RESISTANCE TEST (JF650X-2 AND JS650SX)**

Ohmeter negative (−) connection	Wire color	Ohmeter positive (+) connection			
		Red	Red/purple	Brown	Brown
	Red		∞	∞	∞
	Red/purple	∞			∞
	Brown	1-5 KΩ	2-10 KΩ		∞
	Brown	1-5 KΩ	2-10 KΩ	∞	

JF650TS, JL650SC and
JB650 Jet Mate

Refer to **Figure 19** (JF650TS), **Figure 20** (JL650SC) or **Figure 21** (JB650 Jet Mate) for an exploded view of the electric box assembly.

1. Disconnect the negative battery cable from the battery.

2. Remove the electric box cover.

3. Disconnect the voltage regulator/rectifier wires.

4. Calibrate the ohmmeter on the R × 1000 scale.

5. Refer to **Figure 27** (JL650SC and JF650TS) or **Figure 28** (JB650 Jet Mate) for the correct ohmmeter connections and the desired test results. Connect the ohmmeter to the regulator/rectifier wires as indicated. Replace the

2

(27) REGULATOR/RECTIFIER RESISTANCE TEST (JF650TS AND JL650SC)

		Ohmeter positive (+) connection				
	Wire color	Red	Black (ground)	Brown	Brown	Red/purple
Ohmeter negative (−) connection	Red		∞	∞	∞	0 Ω
	Black (ground)	∞		∞	∞	∞
	Brown	1-6 KΩ	1.5-8 KΩ		∞	1-6 KΩ
	Brown	1-6 KΩ	1.5-8 KΩ	∞		1-6 KΩ
	Red/purple	0 Ω	∞	∞	∞	

(28) REGULATOR/RECTIFIER RESISTANCE TEST (JB650 JET MATE)

		Ohmeter positive (+) connection			
	Wire color	Red/purple	Brown	Brown	Black
Ohmeter negative (−) connection	Red/purple		20-100	20-100	15-80
	Brown	1-5		30-200	20-100
	Brown	1-5	30-200		20-100
	Black	2-10	1-5	1-5	

regulator/rectifier assembly if any reading is different from that shown.

All 750 cc models

1. Disconnect the negative battery cable from the battery.
2. Remove the voltage regulator as described in Chapter Eight.
3. Calibrate the ohmmeter on the R × 1000 scale.
4. Refer to **Figure 29** (JH750SS, JS750SX, JH750 Super Sport Xi, JT750ST) or **Figure 30** (JH750XiR) for the correct ohmmeter connections and desired results. Connect the ohmmeter to the regulator/rectifier wires as indicated. Replace the regulator/rectifier assembly if any reading is different from that shown.

IGNITION SYSTEM

All Jet Ski models are equipped with a capacitor discharge ignition (CDI) system. This solid state system uses no breaker points or other moving parts (other than the flywheel). Because of the solid state design, problems with the CDI system are relatively few. However, if an ignition system malfunction occurs, it results in one of the following symptoms:

   a. Weak spark.

   b. No spark.

It is relatively easy to troubleshoot and repair a CDI system with weak or no spark, or broken or damaged wires. It is more difficult to troubleshoot an intermittent ignition malfunction caused by excessive vibration or problems that only occur when the engine is hot and/or under load. As intermittent ignition malfunctions are often difficult to duplicate, they are sometimes best solved by parts replacement.

General troubleshooting procedures are provided in **Figure 31**.

Many tests described in this manual require the use of an ohmmeter. An ohmmeter, although useful, is not always a good indicator of ignition system condition. This is primarily because resistance tests do not simulate actual operating conditions. For example, the power source in most ohmmeters is only 6-9 volts. An ignition coil, however, commonly produces several thousand volts during normal operation. Such high voltage can cause coil insulation leakage that can not be detected with an ohmmeter.

Because resistance generally increases with temperature, perform resistance tests with the

REGULATOR/RECTIFIER RESISTANCE TEST
(JH750SS, JH750 SUPER SPORT Xi, JS750SX AND JT750ST)

		Ohmmeter positive (+) lead connection					
	Terminal	Red	Red/purple	Brown	Brown	Black	Black
Ohmeter negative (−) lead connection	Red		0	18 ~ 110 KΩ	18 ~ 110 KΩ	15 ~ 80 KΩ	15 ~ 80 KΩ
	Red/purple	0		18 ~ 110 KΩ	18 ~ 110 KΩ	15 ~ 80 KΩ	15 ~ 80 KΩ
	Brown	1.0 ~ 6.0 KΩ	1.0 ~ 6.0 KΩ		30 ~ 160 KΩ	18 ~ 110 KΩ	18 ~ 110 KΩ
	Brown	1.0 ~ 6.0 KΩ	1.0 ~ 6.0 KΩ	30 ~ 160 KΩ		18 ~ 110 KΩ	18 ~ 110 KΩ
	Black	2.0 ~ 12 KΩ	2.0 ~ 12 KΩ	1.0 ~ 6.0 KΩ	1.0 ~ 6.0 KΩ		0
	Black	2.0 ~ 12 KΩ	2.0 ~ 12 KΩ	1.0 ~ 6.0 KΩ	1.0 ~ 6.0 KΩ	0	

engine cold (room temperature). Resistance tests on hot components will indicate increased resistance and may result in unnecessary parts replacement without solving the basic problem.

Precautions

Certain precautions must be taken during troubleshooting to prevent damage to the capacitor discharge system. Instant ignition system damage can occur if the following steps are not observed.

1. Do not reverse the battery connections. Reverse battery polarity will immediately destroy the CDI ignition unit and the voltage regulator/rectifier.

2. Do not disconnect the battery while the engine is running. A voltage surge will occur that can damage the regulator/rectifier.

3. Do not "spark" the battery terminals with the battery cable connections to check polarity. A serious battery explosion can occur if sparks are created near the battery.

4. Do not crank the engine if the CDI unit is not securely grounded to the engine.

5. Do not disconnect any ignition component when the engine is running or while the battery cables are connected.

6. Keep all wiring connections between the various units clean and tight. Be sure that the wiring connectors are firmly pushed together.

Troubleshooting Preparation

NOTE
To test the wiring harness for poor connections in Step 1, bend and pull the molded rubber connector while checking each wire for continuity.

1. Check the wiring harness and all plug-in connections to make sure that all terminals are tight and free of corrosion or other damage. Make sure all wire insulation is in good condition.

2. Check all electrical components that are grounded to the engine for a good ground connection.

3. Make sure that all ground wires have clean, tight connections.

4. Check the remainder of the wiring for disconnected wires or short or open circuits.

5. Make sure there is an adequate supply of fresh and properly mixed fuel available to the engine. On oil injection models, make sure the oil tank is filled with a recommended oil.

6. Check the battery condition, Clean the battery terminals and charge the battery, if necessary. See Chapter Eight.

7. Check spark plug lead routing. Make sure the leads are properly connected to their respective spark plugs.

8. Remove all spark plugs, keeping them in the order removed. Check the condition of each plug. See Chapter Three.

9. Perform the following spark test:

<table>
<tr><td colspan="5">(30)   **REGULATOR/RECTIFIER RESISTANCE TEST**
(JH750XiR)</td></tr>
<tr><td rowspan="2">Ohmmeter negative (−) lead connection</td><td colspan="4">Ohmmeter positive (+) lead connection</td></tr>
<tr><td>Terminal</td><td>Red</td><td>Brown</td><td>Brown</td><td>Black</td></tr>
<tr><td>Red</td><td></td><td>20 ~ 100 KΩ</td><td>20 ~ 100 KΩ</td><td>15 ~ 60 KΩ</td></tr>
<tr><td>Brown</td><td>1 ~ 10 KΩ</td><td></td><td>30 ~ 150 KΩ</td><td>20 ~ 100 KΩ</td></tr>
<tr><td>Brown</td><td>1 ~ 10 KΩ</td><td>30 ~ 150 KΩ</td><td></td><td>20 ~ 100 KΩ</td></tr>
<tr><td>Black</td><td>2 ~ 20 KΩ</td><td>1 ~ 10 KΩ</td><td>1 ~ 10 KΩ</td><td></td></tr>
</table>

(31) **IGNITION TROUBLESHOOTING**

Engine won't start, but fuel and spark are good

Check:
- Defective or dirty spark plug
- Spark plug gap set too wide
- Incorrect ignition timing
- Shorted stop switch
- Broken piston ring(s)
- Cylinder, crankcase or cylinder sealing faulty
- Worn or damaged crankcase seal(s)
- Damaged CDI unit
- Damaged magneto coil(s)
- Damaged ignition coil

Engine misfires @ idle

Check:
- Incorrect spark plug gap
- Defective, dirty or loose spark plug
- Incorrect heat range spark plug
- Leaking or broken high tension wire
- Incorrect ignition timing
- Damaged CDI unit
- Damaged magneto coil
- Dirty wiring connection
- Damaged ignition coil

Engine misfires @ high speed

Check:
- See "Engine misfires @ idle"
- Coil breaks down
- Coil shorts through insulation
- Spark plug gap too wide
- Incorrect spark plug heat range
- Incorrect ignition timing

Engine backfires through exhaust

Check:
- Cracked spark plug insulator
- Incorrect ignition timing
- Damaged CDI unit

Engine preignition

Check:
- Incorrect ignition timing
- Incorrect spark plug heat range
- Burned spark plug electrodes

Spark plug burns and fouls

Check:
- Incorrect spark plug heat range
- Fuel mixture too rich
- Overheated engine
- Poor quality fuel
- Excessive carbon build-up in combustion chamber
- Incorrect ignition timing

WARNING
During this test, do not hold the spark plug, wire or connector with the fingers or a serious electrical shock may result. If necessary, use a pair of insulated pliers to hold the spark plug or wire.

a. Remove one of the spark plugs.

b. Connect the spark plug wire and connector to the spark plug. Then touch the spark plug base to a good engine ground. Position the spark plug so you can see the electrode.

c. Crank the engine while observing the spark plug. A crisp blue spark should be noted.

d. If weak or no spark is noted, check for loose connections at the ignition coil and battery. If all wiring connections are good, a problem with one or more ignition components is likely.

Ignition Coil Test
(All Models Except 750 cc)

The ignition coil and capacitor discharge unit (except 750 cc models) are integrated into a 1-piece assembly called an igniter. The igniter is

located inside the electric box. See **Figure 32**, typical. Although the coil primary windings can not be tested on these models, the secondary winding resistance can be checked without removing or opening the electric box. Also refer to *Igniter Test* in this chapter for additional igniter tests.

To test the ignition coil for shorted or open secondary windings, proceed as follows.

1. Disconnect the spark plug leads from the spark plugs. Remove the spark plug caps from the spark plug leads.

2. Calibrate the ohmmeter on the appropriate scale.

3. Connect the ohmmeter between the 2 disconnected spark plug leads and note the meter. The resistance reading should be:

a. *440 cc models—4480-6720 ohms.*

b. *550 cc models—4500-6700 ohms.*

c. *JF650TS and JL650SC—2500-3300 ohms.*

d. *JF650X-2 and JS650SX—2100-3100 ohms.*

NOTE
If the coil secondary winding resistance is within specification, but the coil is still suspected as being defective, the coil must be tested using a Kawasaki CD ignition tester (part No. T56019-201). Take the igniter assembly to a Kawasaki dealer or other qualified marine specialist.

4. Replace the igniter assembly (Chapter Eight) if the secondary winding resistance is not as specified.

Ignition Coil Test
(All 750 cc Models)

The ignition coil assembly is separate from the CD igniter on 750 cc models. The ignition coils for each cylinder are molded into a 1-piece unit assembly. The coil assembly is located inside the electric box.

NOTE
If primary and secondary resistance is within specification, but the coil is still suspected as being defective, the coil should be tested using Kawasaki Coil Tester part No. 57001-1242. If the tester is not available, remove the coil from the electric box (Chapter Eight) and have it tested by a Kawasaki dealer or other qualified marine specialist.

1. Disconnect the negative battery cable from the battery.

2. Open the electric box as described in Chapter Eight.

3. Disconnect the orange and black/white wires from the ignition coil primary terminals.

4. Calibrate the ohmmeter on the R × 1 scale.

5. Connect the ohmmeter between the coil primary terminals and note the meter. Coil primary winding resistance should be 0.08-0.10 ohm.

6. Next, calibrate the ohmmeter on the R × 1000 scale.

7. Cut the plastic tie strap clamp from the spark plug caps. Remove the spark plug caps from the spark plug leads by turning them counterclockwise.

8. Connect the meter between the spark plug leads and note the meter. Coil secondary resistance should be 3500-4700 ohms.

9. Replace the ignition coil assembly if resistance is not as specified.

10. Install the coil and reassemble the electric box as described in Chapter Eight. Securely clamp the spark plug caps to the plug leads using new tie straps.

Igniter Test

On all models (except 750 cc models), the capacitor discharge unit and the ignition coil are integrated into a 1-piece assembly called an igniter. On 750 cc models, the ignition coil and igniter are separate components. The igniter assembly is located inside the electric box on all models.

440 and 550 cc models

Kawasaki Ignition Tester part No. T56019-201 is necessary to thoroughly test the CD igniter on 440 and 550 cc models. If the tester is not available, remove the igniter as described in Chapter Eight and have it tested by a Kawasaki dealer.

---

(33)

IGNITER RESISTANCE TEST
(JF650X-2)

Range × 1 KΩ		Meter positive (+) lead connection		
		Black/red	Black/white	Black/yellow
Meter negative (−) lead connection	Black/red		1-5 KΩ	500 KΩ ∞
	Black/white	∞		∞
	Black/yellow	1-5 KΩ	5-17 KΩ	

The secondary windings in the ignition coil portion of the igniter can be tested with an ohmmeter. Refer to *Ignition Coil Test* in this chapter.

650 and 750 cc models

The resistance values provided in the following test is based on the use of a Kawasaki Hand Tester part No. 57001-983. If an ohmmeter other than the Kawasaki Hand Tester is used, the readings obtained may not agree with those specified, due to the different internal resistance of each specific ohmmeter. To prevent unnecessary parts replacement, use caution when using an ohmmeter other than what the manufacturer recommends.

Resistance tests on the CD igniter assembly are often not absolutely accurate. If in doubt about the validity of a resistance test, first check all other ignition components, then pass or fail the igniter using a process of elimination.

CAUTION
Only use a small portable ohmmeter, such as that used for radio or other electronic repair. An ohmmeter with a high-capacity battery (megger or insulation tester) can damage the CD igniter.

1. Disconnect the negative battery cable from the battery.
2. Remove the CD igniter assembly as described in Chapter Eight.
3. Calibrate the ohmmeter on the R × 1000 scale.
4. Refer to the following figures for the correct ohmmeter connections and desired results. Connect the ohmmeter to the igniter terminals as indicated. Replace the igniter assembly if any reading is different from that shown.
   a. **Figure 33**: JF650X-2
   b. **Figure 34**: JS650SX
   c. **Figure 35**: JF650TS
   d. **Figure 36**: JL650SC

(34) **IGNITER RESISTANCE TEST (JS650SX)**

Range × 1 KΩ		Meter positive (+) lead connection			
		Black/red	Black/yellow	Black	Blue
Meter negative (–) lead connection	Black/red		500* ↓ ∞	∞	500 ∞
	Black/yellow	3-6		∞	∞
	Black	15-25* ↓ 50-100	15-25* ↓ 50-100		15-25* ↓ 50-100
	Blue	3-6	0	∞	

*If measuring resistance twice, wait 30 minutes for capacitor charging

IGNITER RESISTANCE TEST
(JS650TS)

Range × 1 KΩ		Meter positive (+) lead connection			
		Purple	Black (ground)	White	Black (stop switch)
Meter negative (−) lead connection	Purple		500* ↓ ∞	∞	500* ↓ ∞
	Black (ground)	3-6		∞	0
	White	15-25* ↓ 50-100	15-25* ↓ 50-100		15-25* ↓ 50-100
	Black (stop switch)	3-6	0	∞	

*If measuring resistance twice, wait 30 minutes for capacitor charging

IGNITER RESISTANCE TEST
(JL650SC)

Range × 1 KΩ		Meter positive (+) lead connection			
		Black (1)	Purple	White	Black(2)
Meter negative (−) lead connection	Black (1)		2-6	∞	0
	Purple	∞		∞	∞
	White	50-240*	50-240*		50-240*
	Black (2)	0	2-6	∞	

*If measuring resistance twice, wait 30 minutes for capacitor charging

e. **Figure 37**: JB650 Jet Mate

f. **Figure 38**: JS750SX.

g. **Figure 39**: JT750ST and 1992-1993 JH750XiR.

h. **Figure 40**: 1994 JH750XiR.

i. **Figure 41**: JH750SS.

j. **Figure 42**: 1992-1993 JH750 Super Sport Xi.

k. **Figure 43**: 1994 JH750 Super Sport Xi.

Exciter and Pulser Coil Resistance Test (440 and 550 cc Models)

1. Disconnect the negative battery cable from the battery.

2. Remove the electric box connector to expose the 6-pin connector. See **Figure 44**, typical.

3. Disconnect the 6-pin connector.

4. Calibrate the ohmmeter on the R × 1 scale.

5. To check exciter coil resistance, connect the ohmmeter between the red and black wires in the

2

---

(37)

IGNITER RESISTANCE TEST
(JB650 JET MATE)

Range × 1 KΩ		Meter positive (+) lead connection				
		Purple	Green	Black (1)	White	Black (2)
Meter negative (–) lead connection	Purple		500* ↓ ∞	500* ↓ ∞	∞	500* ↓ ∞
	Green	500* ↓ ∞		500* ↓ ∞	∞	500* ↓ ∞
	Black (1)	3-4	20-30		∞	0
	White	40-150* ↓ 200-1000	14-22* ↓ 50-150	14-22* ↓ 50-150		14-22* ↓ 50-150
	Black (2)	3-4	20-30	0	∞	

*If measuring resistance twice, wait 30 minutes for capacitor charging

(38)

IGNITER RESISTANCE TEST
(JS750SX)

Unit: KΩ

Ohmeter negative (–) lead connection	Wire color	Orange	Black/white	Blue	Green	Red	Purple	Red/yellow	Black/yellow	White	Black	Black/blue
		Tester positive (+) lead connection										
	Orange		2~4	2~4	12~20	6~13	6~13	10~20	2~4	∞	2~4	2~4
	Black/white	∞		0	6~13	2~5	2~5	4~10	0	∞	0	0
	Blue	∞	0		6~13	2~5	2~5	4~10	0	∞	0	0
	Green	∞	6~12	6~12		11~22	11~22	12~23	6~12	∞	6~12	6~12
	Red	∞	20~60	20~60	20~60		40~110	14~28	20~60	∞	20~60	20~60
	Purple	∞	100~200	100~200	100~200	130~400		130~400	100~200	∞	100~200	100~200
	Red/yellow	∞	20~60	20~60	40~100	60~200	60~200		20~60	∞	20~60	20~60
	Black/yellow	∞	0	0	6~13	2~5	2~5	4~10		∞	0	0
	White	∞	10~30	10~30	25~60	30~300	30~300	30~300	10~30		10~30	10~30
	Black	∞	0	0	6~13	2~5	2~5	4~10	0	∞		0
	Black/blue	∞	0	0	6~13	2~5	2~5	4~10	0	∞	0	

(39)

IGNITER RESISTANCE TEST
(JT750ST AND 1992-1993 JH750XiR)

Unit: KΩ

Ohmeter negative (–) lead connection	Wire color	Orange	Black/white	Blue	Green	Red	Purple	Red/yellow	Black/yellow	White	Black	Black/blue
		Tester positive (+) lead connection										
	Orange		2~4	2~4	12~20	6~13	6~13	20~60	2~4	∞	2~4	2~4
	Black/white	∞		0	6~13	2~5	2~5	8~25	0	∞	0	0
	Blue	∞	0		6~13	2~5	2~5	8~25	0	∞	0	0
	Green	∞	6~12	6~12		11~22	11~22	15~45	6~12	∞	6~12	6~12
	Red	∞	20~60	20~60	20~60		40~110	30~150	20~60	∞	20~60	20~60
	Purple	∞	100~200	100~200	100~200	130~400		150~500	100~200	∞	100~200	100~200
	Red/yellow	∞	∞	∞	∞	∞	∞		∞	∞	∞	∞
	Black/yellow	∞	0	0	6~13	2~5	2~5	8~25		∞	0	0
	White	∞	10~30	10~30	25~60	30~300	30~300	80~500	10~30		10~30	10~30
	Black	∞	0	0	6~13	2~5	2~5	8~25	0	∞		0
	Black/blue	∞	0	0	6~13	2~5	2~5	8~25	0	∞	0	

40

IGNITER RESISTANCE TEST
(1994 JH750XiR)

Unit: KΩ

	Tester positive (+) lead connection										
Wire color	Orange	Black/white	Blue	Green	Red	Purple	Red/yellow	Black/yellow	White	Black	Black/blue
Orange		2~4	2~4	12~22	6~18	6~18	20~110	2~4	∞	2~4	2~4
Black/white	∞		0	6~13	2~5	2~5	1~28	0	∞	0	0
Blue	∞	0		6~13	2~5	2~5	1~28	0	∞	0	0
Green	∞	6~12	6~12		11~22	11~22	15~50	6~12	∞	6~12	6~12
Red	∞	20~60	20~60	20~60		50~150	30~200	20~60	∞	20~60	20~60
Purple	∞	120~240	120~240	120~240	150~500		150~600	100~200	∞	150~300	150~300
Red/yellow	∞	∞	∞	∞	∞	∞		∞	∞	∞	∞
Black/yellow	∞	0	0	6~13	2~5	2~5	8~25		∞	0	0
White	∞	10~30	10~30	25~70	30~300	30~300	80~600	10~30		10~30	10~30
Black	∞	0	0	6~13	2~5	2~5	8~25	0	∞		0
Black/blue	∞	0	0	6~13	2~5	2~5	8~25	0	∞	0	

Ohmeter negative (−) lead connection

41

IGNITER RESISTANCE TEST
(JH750SS)

Unit: KΩ

	Tester positive (+) lead connection										
Wire color	Orange	Black/white	Blue	Green	Red	Purple	Red/yellow	Black/yellow	White	Black	Black/blue
Orange		2~4	2~4	12~20	6~13	6~13	10~20	2~4	∞	2~4	2~4
Black/white	∞		0	6~13	2~5	2~5	4~10	0	∞	0	0
Blue	∞	0		6~13	2~5	2~5	4~10	0	∞	0	0
Green	∞	6~12	6~12		11~22	11~22	12~23	6~12	∞	6~12	6~12
Red	∞	20~60	20~60	20~60		42~110	14~28	20~60	∞	20~60	20~60
Purple	∞	100~200	100~200	100~200	130~400		130~400	100~200	∞	100~200	100~200
Red/yellow	∞	20~60	20~60	40~100	60~200	60~200		20~60	∞	20~60	20~60
Black/yellow	∞	0	0	6~13	2~5	2~5	4~10		∞	0	0
White	∞	10~30	10~30	25~60	30~300	30~300	30~300	10~30		10~30	10~30
Black	∞	0	0	6~13	2~5	2~5	4~10	0	∞		0
Black/blue	∞	0	0	6~13	2~5	2~5	4~10	0	∞	0	

Ohmeter negative (−) lead connection

2

(42) IGNITER RESISTANCE TEST (1992-1993 JH750 SUPER SPORT Xi) — Unit: KΩ

Tester positive (+) lead connection / Ohmeter negative (–) lead connection

Wire color	Orange	Black/white	Blue	Green	Red	Purple	Red/yellow	Black/yellow	White	Black	Black/blue
Orange		2~4	2~4	12~20	6~13	6~13	20~60	2~4	∞	2~4	2~4
Black/white	∞		0	6~13	2~5	2~5	8~25	0	∞	0	0
Blue	∞	0		6~13	2~5	2~5	8~25	0	∞	0	0
Green	∞	6~12	6~12		11~22	11~22	15~45	6~12	∞	6~12	6~12
Red	∞	20~60	20~60	20~60		40~110	30~150	20~60	∞	20~60	20~60
Purple	∞	100~200	100~200	100~200	130~400		150~500	100~200	∞	100~200	100~200
Red/yellow	∞	∞	∞	∞	∞	∞		∞	∞	∞	∞
Black/yellow	∞	0	0	6~13	2~5	2~5	8~25		∞	0	0
White	∞	10~30	10~30	25~60	30~300	30~300	80~500	10~30		10~30	10~30
Black	∞	0	0	6~13	2~5	2~5	8~25	0	∞		0
Black/blue	∞	0	0	6~13	2~5	2~5	8~25	0	∞	0	

(43) IGNITER RESISTANCE TEST (1994 JH750 SUPER SPORT Xi) — Unit: KΩ

Tester positive (+) lead connection / Ohmeter negative (–) lead connection

Wire color	Orange	Black/white	Blue	Green	Red	Purple	Red/yellow	Black/yellow	White	Black	Black/blue	Grey
Orange		2~4	2~4	12~20	6~13	6~13	20~60	2~4	∞	2~4	2~4	8~30
Black/white	∞		0	6~13	2~5	2~5	8~25	0	∞	0	0	3~20
Blue	∞	0		6~13	2~5	2~5	8~25	0	∞	0	0	3~20
Green	∞	6~12	6~12		11~22	11~22	15~45	6~12	∞	6~12	6~12	8~30
Red	∞	20~60	20~60	20~60		40~110	30~150	20~60	∞	20~60	20~60	10~60
Purple	∞	100~200	100~200	100~200	130~400		150~600	100~200	∞	100~200	100~200	100~250
Red/yellow	∞	∞	∞	∞	∞	∞		∞	∞	∞	∞	∞
Black/yellow	∞	0	0	6~13	2~5	2~5	8~25		∞	0	0	3~20
White	∞	10~30	10~30	25~60	30~300	30~300	80~500	10~30		10~30	10~30	3~150
Black	∞	0	0	6~13	2~5	2~5	8~25	0	∞		0	3~20
Black/blue	∞	0	0	6~13	2~5	2~5	8~25	0	∞	0		3~20
Grey	∞	8~25	8~25	20~60	20~60	20~60	10~30	8~25	∞	8~25	8~25	

connector half leading from the stator plate. Resistance should be 112-168 ohms.

6. To check pulser coil resistance, connect the ohmmeter between the red and gray wires in the connector half leading from the stator plate. Resistance should be 14.4-21.6 ohms.

7. Replace the exciter coil or pulser coil if resistance is not as specified. See Chapter Eight.

8. Reconnect the 6-pin connector and install the electric box connector. Reconnect the negative battery cable.

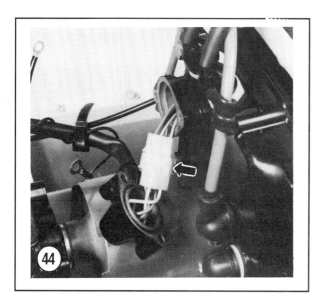

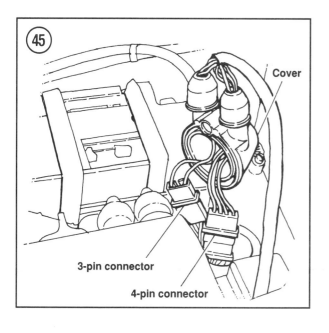

Exciter Coil Resistance Test (650 cc Models)

1. Disconnect the negative battery cable from the battery.

2. Open the electric box (Chapter Eight) and disconnect the purple and black/yellow wires from the igniter assembly.

3. Calibrate the ohmmeter on the R × 100 scale.

4. Connect the ohmmeter between the purple and black/yellow wires leading to the stator plate and note the meter.

5. Exciter coil resistance should be 255-380 ohms.

6. Replace the exciter coil (Chapter Eight) if resistance is not as specified.

7. Reconnect all circuits and reassemble the electric box.

Pickup Coil Resistance Test (750 cc Models)

1. Disconnect the negative battery cable from the battery.

2. Remove the electric box connector to expose the 3- and 4-pin connectors. See **Figure 45**.

3. Disconnect the 4-pin connector.

4. Calibrate the ohmmeter on the R × 100 scale. Connect the ohmmeter between the green and blue wires in the connector leading to the stator plate.

5. Pickup coil resistance should be 396-594 ohms.

6. Replace the pickup coil (Chapter Eight) if the resistance is not as specified.

7. Reconnect all circuits and reassemble the electric box.

STOP SWITCH RELAY

Some Jet Ski models are equipped with a relay connected to the stop switch so that the stop button need only be pressed once and released to ground the CD igniter and stop the engine.

1. Disconnect the negative battery cable from the battery.

2. Remove the electric box connector and disconnect the stop switch relay black/white, blue, black and brown wires at their bullet connectors.

3. Calibrate the ohmmeter on the R × 100 scale.

4. Refer to **Figure 46** for ohmmeter connections and test values. Make each connection and compare the reading to the specified value in **Figure 46**. If any of the meter readings differ from the specified values, replace the stop switch relay as described in Chapter Eight.

FUEL SYSTEM

When a watercraft begins to run poorly, owners often assume the carburetor(s) is at fault. The owner then attempts to make the repair by adjusting the carburetor(s). Although carburetor problems are not uncommon, adjustment is seldom the answer. Many times, such adjustments only complicates the situation by making the engine perform worse.

Fuel system troubleshooting should start at the fuel tank and proceed through the system, reserving the carburetor(s) for last. Most fuel system problems result from an empty fuel tank, plugged or restricted fuel filter, malfunctioning fuel pump or old, sour fuel. **Figure 47** provides a series of symptoms and causes that is useful for localizing fuel system malfunctions.

The carburetor choke valve (**Figure 48**) is a frequent source of fuel system problems. A choke valve that sticks in the open position

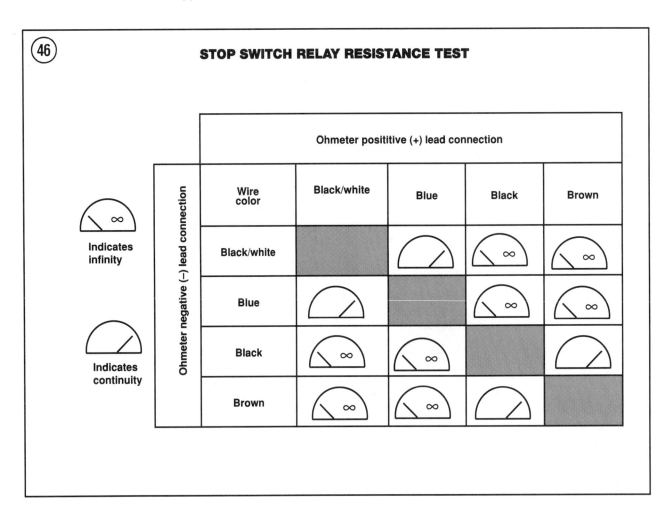

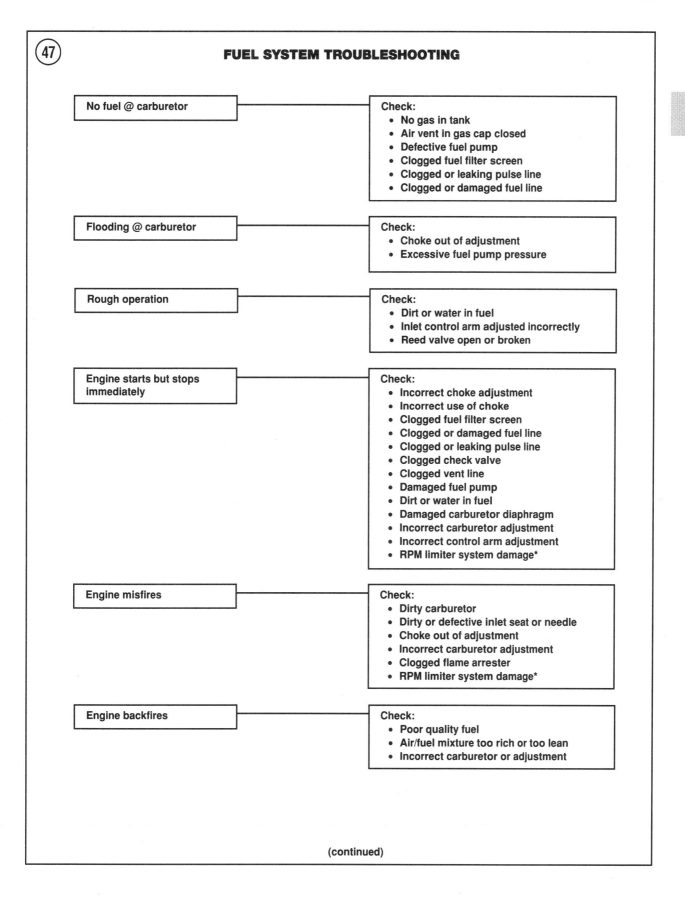

47

FUEL SYSTEM TROUBLESHOOTING

| No fuel @ carburetor | Check:
• No gas in tank
• Air vent in gas cap closed
• Defective fuel pump
• Clogged fuel filter screen
• Clogged or leaking pulse line
• Clogged or damaged fuel line |

| Flooding @ carburetor | Check:
• Choke out of adjustment
• Excessive fuel pump pressure |

| Rough operation | Check:
• Dirt or water in fuel
• Inlet control arm adjusted incorrectly
• Reed valve open or broken |

| Engine starts but stops immediately | Check:
• Incorrect choke adjustment
• Incorrect use of choke
• Clogged fuel filter screen
• Clogged or damaged fuel line
• Clogged or leaking pulse line
• Clogged check valve
• Clogged vent line
• Damaged fuel pump
• Dirt or water in fuel
• Damaged carburetor diaphragm
• Incorrect carburetor adjustment
• Incorrect control arm adjustment
• RPM limiter system damage* |

| Engine misfires | Check:
• Dirty carburetor
• Dirty or defective inlet seat or needle
• Choke out of adjustment
• Incorrect carburetor adjustment
• Clogged flame arrester
• RPM limiter system damage* |

| Engine backfires | Check:
• Poor quality fuel
• Air/fuel mixture too rich or too lean
• Incorrect carburetor or adjustment |

(continued)

2

causes the watercraft to start hard, stall and run poorly when cold; a choke that sticks closed (or nearly closed) results in hard or impossible starting when warm, stalling, poor performance and excessive exhaust smoke due to an overly rich air-fuel mixture.

Refer to the following figures for a diagram of the various fuel systems used on models covered in this manual:

a. **Figure 49**: JS440SX.

b. **Figure 50**: JS550SX.

c. **Figure 51**: JB650 Jet Mate.

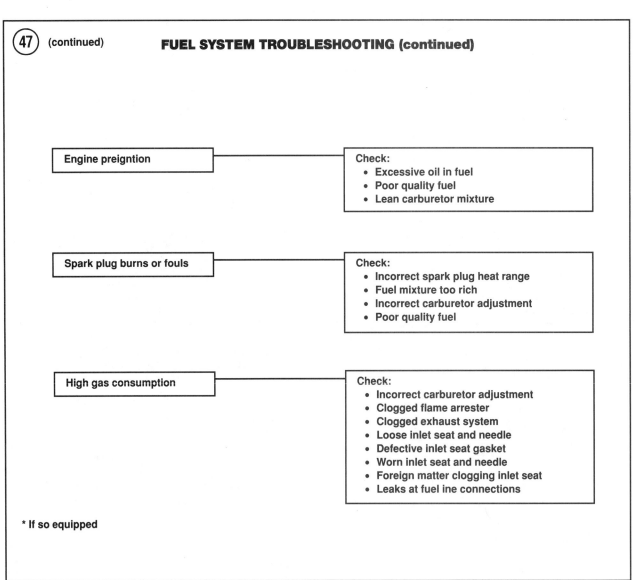

(47) (continued) **FUEL SYSTEM TROUBLESHOOTING (continued)**

| Engine preigntion | Check:
• Excessive oil in fuel
• Poor quality fuel
• Lean carburetor mixture |

| Spark plug burns or fouls | Check:
• Incorrect spark plug heat range
• Fuel mixture too rich
• Incorrect carburetor adjustment
• Poor quality fuel |

| High gas consumption | Check:
• Incorrect carburetor adjustment
• Clogged flame arrester
• Clogged exhaust system
• Loose inlet seat and needle
• Defective inlet seat gasket
• Worn inlet seat and needle
• Foreign matter clogging inlet seat
• Leaks at fuel ine connections |

* If so equipped

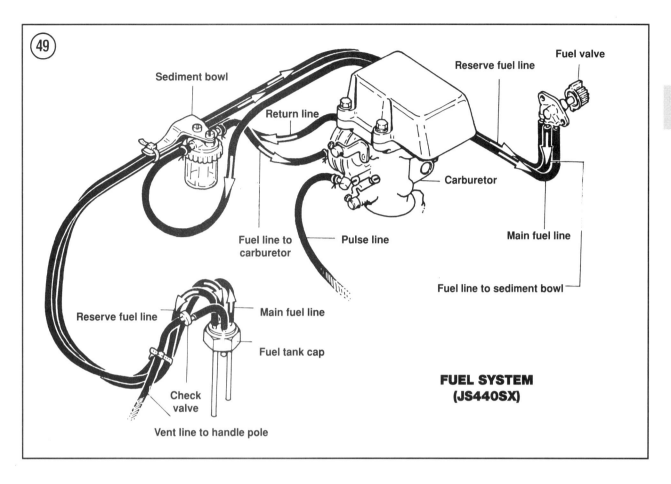

Sediment bowl

Return line

Reserve fuel line

Fuel valve

Carburetor

Fuel line to carburetor

Pulse line

Main fuel line

Fuel line to sediment bowl

Reserve fuel line

Main fuel line

Fuel tank cap

Check valve

Vent line to handle pole

**FUEL SYSTEM
(JS440SX)**

2

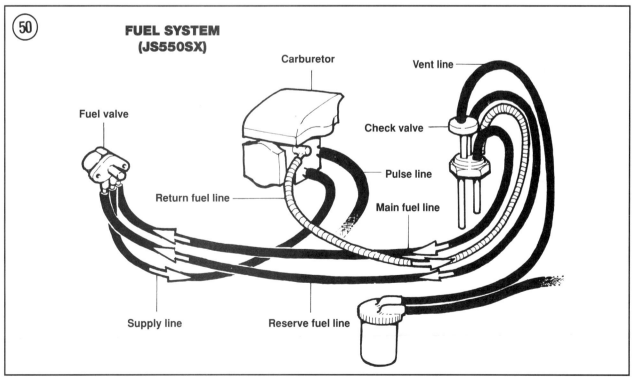

**FUEL SYSTEM
(JS550SX)**

Carburetor

Vent line

Check valve

Fuel valve

Pulse line

Return fuel line

Main fuel line

Supply line

Reserve fuel line

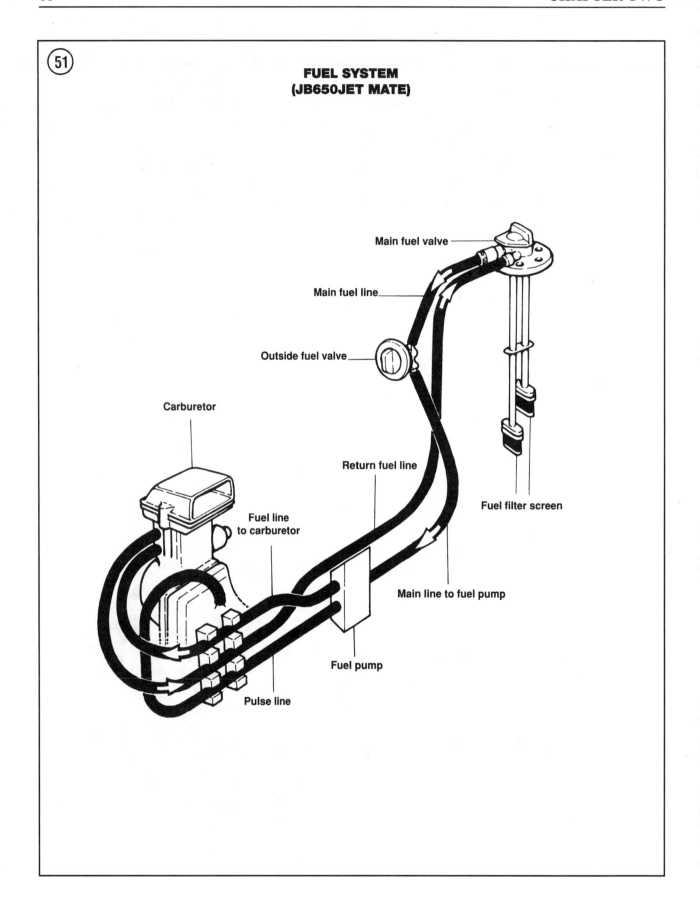

(51)

**FUEL SYSTEM
(JB650JET MATE)**

Main fuel valve

Main fuel line

Outside fuel valve

Carburetor

Fuel filter screen

Return fuel line

Fuel line
to carburetor

Main line to fuel pump

Fuel pump

Pulse line

d. **Figure 52**: JF650X-2 and JS650SX.

e. **Figure 53**: JF650TS.

f. **Figure 54**: JL650SC

g. **Figure 55**. JS750SX.

h. **Figure 56**: JH750SS and JT750ST.

i. **Figure 57**: JH750 Super Sport Xi and JH750XiR.

ENGINE

Engine problems are generally symptoms of something wrong in another system, such as ignition, fuel or starting system. If properly maintained and serviced, the engine should experience no problems other than those caused by age and wear.

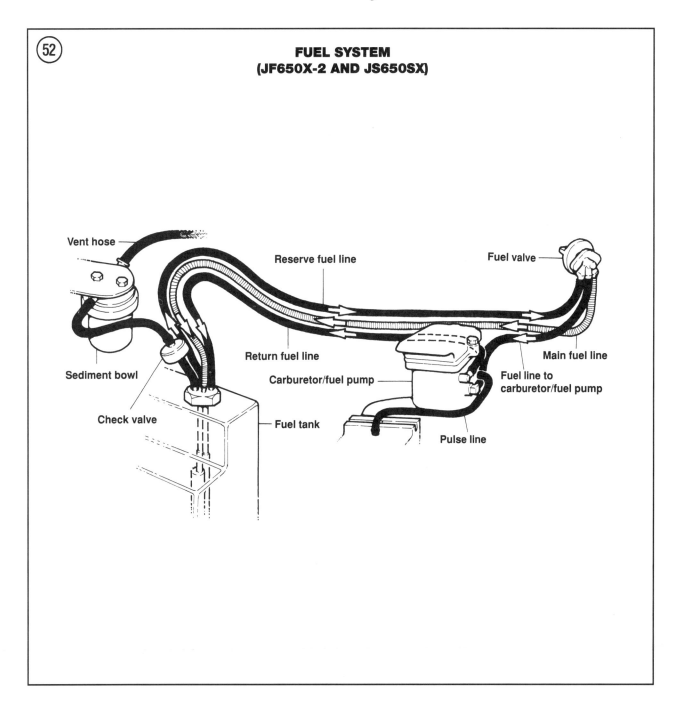

(52)

FUEL SYSTEM
(JF650X-2 AND JS650SX)

Vent hose

Reserve fuel line

Fuel valve

Return fuel line

Main fuel line

Sediment bowl

Carburetor/fuel pump

Fuel line to carburetor/fuel pump

Check valve

Fuel tank

Pulse line

Overheating and Lack of Lubrication

Overheating and lack of lubrication cause the majority of engine mechanical problems. Jet Ski engines create a great deal of heat and are not designed to operate at a standstill; the Jet Ski cooling system does not circulate water at idle speed. Make sure the cooling system is not plugged with sand or silt. See *Cooling System Cleaning* in Chapter Three. Using a spark plug

of the wrong heat range can burn a piston. Incorrect ignition timing, a faulty cooling system or an excessively lean fuel mixture can also cause the engine to overheat.

Preignition

Preignition is the premature burning of the fuel and air charge and is usually caused by

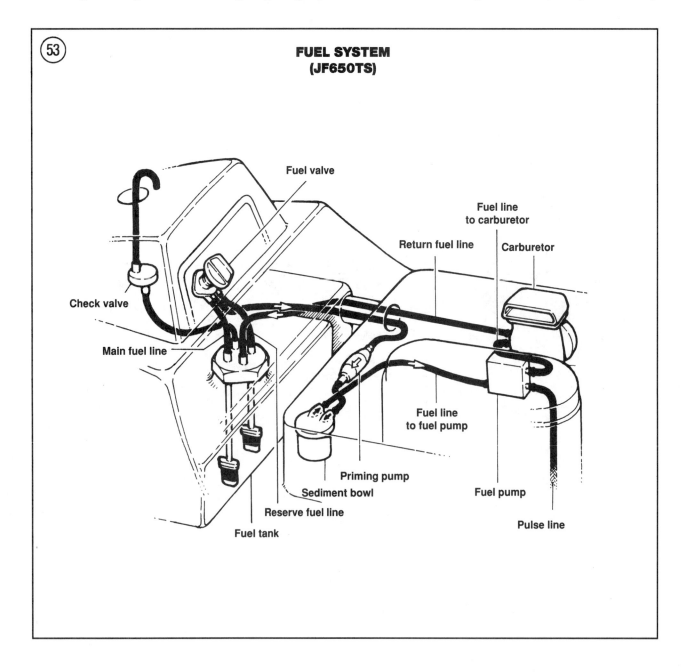

FUEL SYSTEM (JF650TS)

Fuel valve

Fuel line to carburetor

Return fuel line

Carburetor

Check valve

Main fuel line

Fuel line to fuel pump

Priming pump

Sediment bowl

Reserve fuel line

Fuel pump

Pulse line

Fuel tank

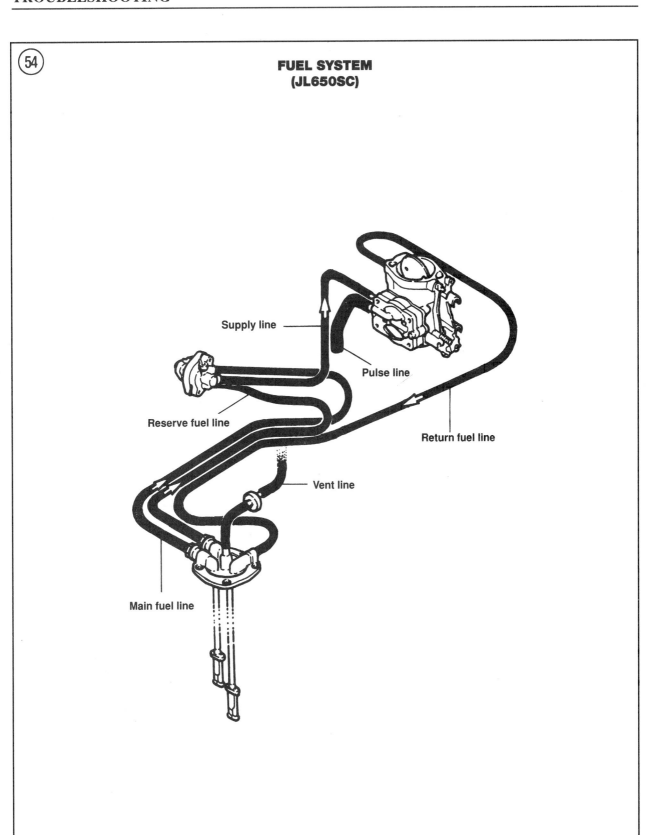

**FUEL SYSTEM
(JL650SC)**

Supply line

Pulse line

Reserve fuel line

Return fuel line

Vent line

Main fuel line

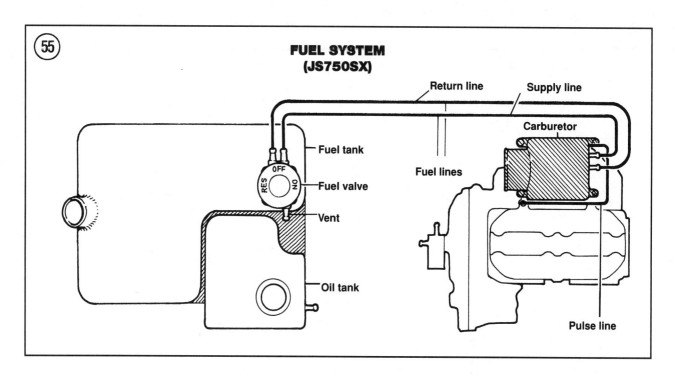

55

**FUEL SYSTEM
(JS750SX)**

Return line

Supply line

Carburetor

Fuel tank

Fuel lines

OFF

RES

ON

Fuel valve

Vent

Oil tank

Pulse line

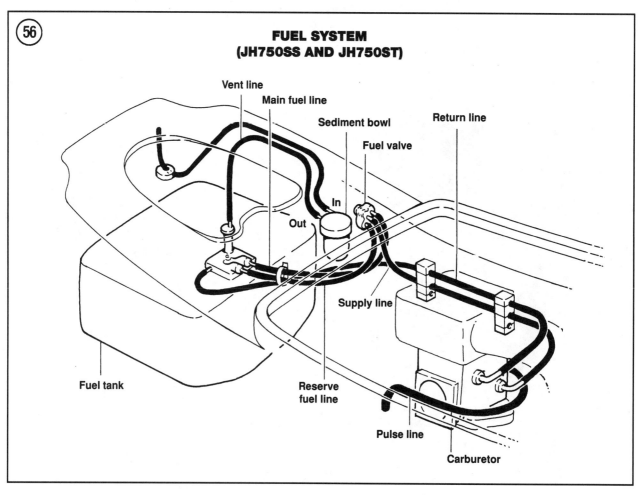

56

**FUEL SYSTEM
(JH750SS AND JH750ST)**

Vent line

Main fuel line

Sediment bowl

Return line

Fuel valve

In

Out

Supply line

Fuel tank

Reserve
fuel line

Pulse line

Carburetor

2

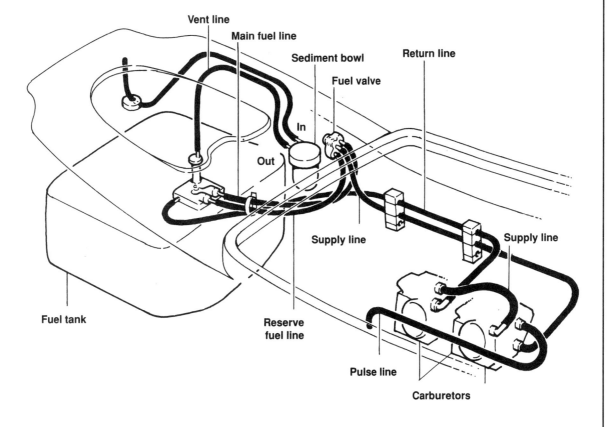

(57)

**FUEL SYSTEM
(JSH750 SUPER SPORT Xi AND JH750XiR)**

Vent line

Main fuel line

Sediment bowl

Return line

Fuel valve

In

Out

Supply line

Supply line

Fuel tank

Reserve
fuel line

Pulse line

Carburetors

hot spots in the combustion chamber (**Figure 58**). The fuel-air charge actually ignites before it is supposed to. Glowing deposits in the combustion chamber, inadequate cooling, overheated spark plugs can all cause preignition. Preignition is first noticed in the form of a power loss, but will eventually result in extensive damage to internal engine components because of excessive combustion chamber temperature and pressure.

Detonation

Commonly called "spark knock," detonation is the violent explosion of the fuel-air charge in the combustion chamber prior to the proper time of combustion (**Figure 59**). Severe damage can result from severe detonation. Use of low octane gasoline and over-advanced ignition timing are the most common causes of detonation.

Other frequent causes of detonation are excessive cylinder compression, excessively lean fuel-air mixture at or near full throttle, air (vacuum) leakage, engine overheating, cross firing spark plugs or excessive accumulation of deposits on the pistons or in the combustion chamber (causing excessive compression pressure).

Since the Jet Ski engine is covered, engine knock or detonation is likely to remain unnoticed, especially at high speeds. Such inaudible detonation, as it is called, is often the cause when piston and engine damage occurs for no apparent reason.

Poor Idling

A poor idle can be caused by improper carburetor adjustment, incorrect ignition timing or ignition system malfunctions. Check the carburetor pulse and vent lines for a restriction. Also check for loose carburetor mounting bolts or a faulty carburetor flange gasket.

Misfiring

Misfiring can result from a weak spark or a dirty spark plug. Check for fuel contamination. If misfiring occurs only under a heavy load, as when accelerating, is it is usually caused by a defective spark plug or spark plug wire.

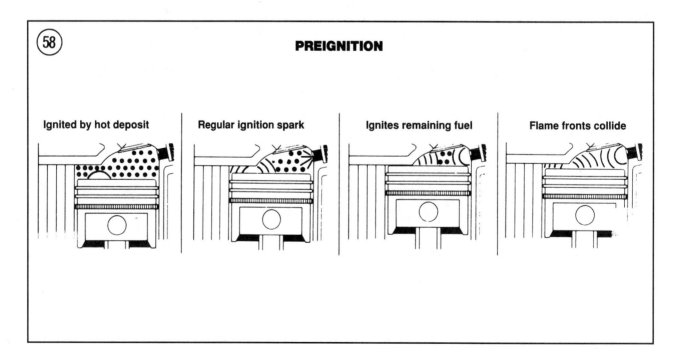

(58) **PREIGNITION**

Ignited by hot deposit | Regular ignition spark | Ignites remaining fuel | Flame fronts collide

Water Leakage into the Cylinders

The fastest and easiest method to check for water leakage into a cylinder is to check the spark plugs. Water in the combustion chamber tends to clean the spark plug. If one spark plug in a twin-cylinder engine is clean and the other has normal deposits, a water leak is likely in the cylinder with the clean plug.

To determine if a water leak is present, install used spark plugs with normal deposits into each cylinder. Run the engine in the water for 5-10 minutes. Stop the engine and remove the spark plugs. If one plug is clean and the other shows normal deposits (or both are clean), a water leak is present in that cylinder.

Flat Spots

If the engine seems to die momentarily when the throttle is opened and then recovers (hesitation), check for a dirty or contaminated carbure-tor, water in the fuel or an excessively lean or rich low speed mixture.

Power Loss

Several factors can cause a lack of power and speed. Look for air leaks in the fuel line or fuel pump, a plugged fuel filter or a choke/throttle valve that does not operate properly. Check the ignition timing at full advance with the engine running at wide-open throttle. See Chapter Three. This will allow you to make sure that the ignition system is operating properly. If the ignition timing is incorrect when checked dynamically, but was correctly set statically with a dial indicator, there may be a problem with an ignition component (igniter assembly).

A piston or cylinder that is galling, incorrect piston clearance or worn or sticky piston rings may be responsible for gradual power loss. Check for loose bolts, defective gaskets or leaking machined mating surfaces on the cylinder

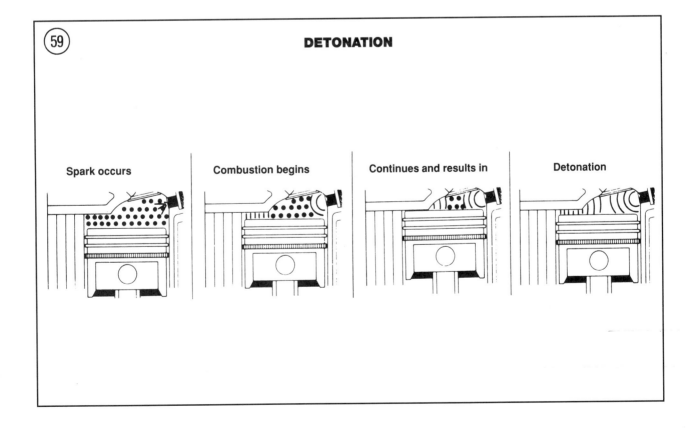

(59) DETONATION

Spark occurs   Combustion begins   Continues and results in   Detonation head, cylinder or crankcase. Also check the crankcase and crankshaft seals. Refer to *Two-stroke Engine Pressure Testing* in this chapter.

Exhaust fumes leaking within the engine compartment can slow and stop the engine.

If the engine runs correctly but you are experiencing performance related problems while in the water, check the jet pump assembly for case or impeller damage, weeds or other contamination or excessive impeller-to-pump case clearance.

Refer to **Figure 60** for a general listing of engine problems.

Piston Seizure

Piston seizure is commonly caused by incorrect bore clearance, improper piston ring end gap, compression leakage, incorrect engine oil, spark plugs with incorrect heat range (too hot), incorrect ignition timing or incorrect fuel-air mixture. Overheating from any cause can result in piston seizure.

Excessive Vibration

Excessive vibration may be cause by loose engine mount bolts, worn engine or drive shaft bearings, a generally poor running engine, incorrect drive shaft alignment, loose jet pump bolts, bent drive shaft or a damaged jet pump or impeller.

Engine Noises

Experience is needed to diagnose accurately in this area (**Figure 61**). Noises are difficult to differentiate and even harder to describe.

TWO-STROKE ENGINE PRESSURE TESTING

Sometimes an older or high-hour 2-stroke engine may be hard to start and generally runs poorly for no apparent reason. The fuel and ignition systems are functioning properly and a compression test indicates the engine's upper end is in acceptable condition.

What a compression test does not show, however, is the possible lack of *primary* compression. Primary compression is the ability of the crankcase assembly to be air and vacuum tight. In a 2-stroke engine, the crankcase must be alternately under pressure and vacuum. After the piston closes the intake port, further downward movement of the piston causes the entrapped mixture in the crankcase to be pressurized so that it can rush quickly into the cylinder when the scavenging ports are opened. Upward piston movement creates a vacuum in the crankcase, enabling the fuel-air mixture to pass into the crankcase from the carburetor.

NOTE
*The operational sequence of a 2-stroke engine is illustrated in **Chapter One** under **Engine Operation**.*

If the crankcase seals or cylinder gaskets leak, the crankcase cannot hold pressure or vacuum and proper engine operation becomes impossible. Any other source of leakage such as a defective cylinder base gasket or a porous or cracked crankcase casting results in the same condition.

It is possible to test for and isolate engine pressure leakage. The test is simple, but requires special equipment. A typical 2-stroke pressure test kit is shown in **Figure 62**. When pressure testing an engine, all engine openings are sealed, then air pressure is applied to the crankcase. If the crankcase does not hold the pressure, leakage is indicated.

The following procedure describes a typical pressure test.

1. Remove the carburetor(s). See Chapter Seven.
2. Insert a suitable rubber plug into the intake manifold. Make sure the manifold is securely sealed.

ⓍⓍ ENGINE TROUBLESHOOTING

Ignition system trouble

Check:
- Faulty ignition coil
- Incorrect ignition timing
- Incorrect spark plug heat range
- Loose wiring connectors

Fuel system trouble

Check:
- Contaminated fuel filter
- Contaminated fuel filter screen
- Throttle valve does not open fully
- Clogged high speed nozzle
- Clogged pulse line
- Leaking pulse line
- Insufficient fuel supply
- Faulty check valve diaphragm
- Faulty regulator diaphragm
- Faulty pulse diaphragm

Overheating

Check:
- See "Ignition system trouble"
- See "Fuel system trouble"
- Incorrect ignition timing
- Excessive carbon buildup in combustion chamber
- Incorrect fuel/oil mixture
- Incorrect oil type
- Incorrect fuel type
- Incorrect carburetor adjustment
- Clogged or leaking cooling system water line
- Clogged flame arrester
- Clogged exhaust system

Other

Check:
- Dirt or water in fuel
- Clogged flame arrester
- Clogged exhaust system

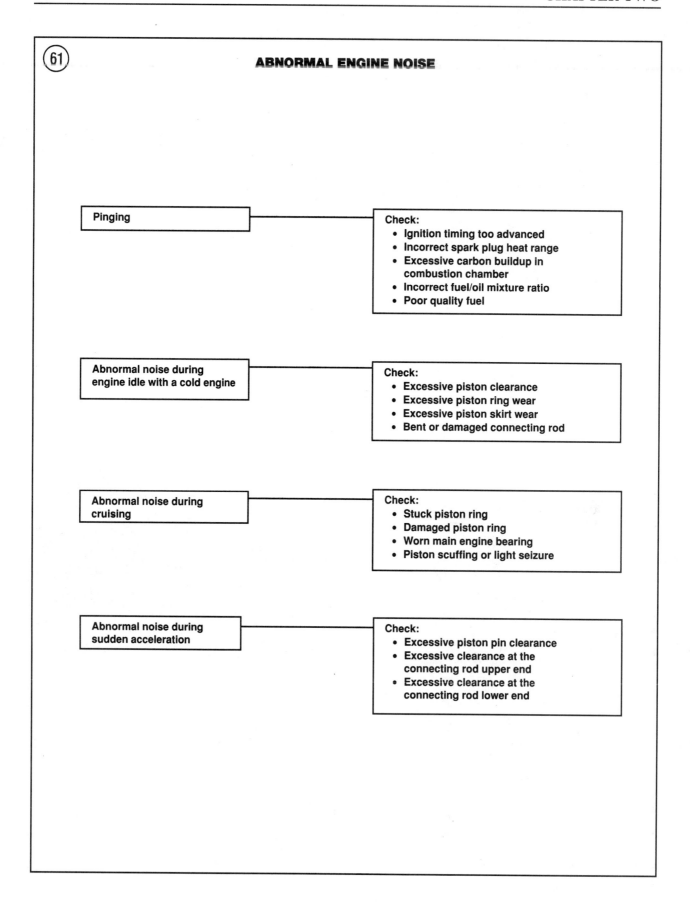

61

ABNORMAL ENGINE NOISE

Pinging

Check:
- Ignition timing too advanced
- Incorrect spark plug heat range
- Excessive carbon buildup in combustion chamber
- Incorrect fuel/oil mixture ratio
- Poor quality fuel

Abnormal noise during engine idle with a cold engine

Check:
- Excessive piston clearance
- Excessive piston ring wear
- Excessive piston skirt wear
- Bent or damaged connecting rod

Abnormal noise during cruising

Check:
- Stuck piston ring
- Damaged piston ring
- Worn main engine bearing
- Piston scuffing or light seizure

Abnormal noise during sudden acceleration

Check:
- Excessive piston pin clearance
- Excessive clearance at the connecting rod upper end
- Excessive clearance at the connecting rod lower end

3. Remove the exhaust pipe and block the exhaust port, using suitable adapters and fittings.

4. Remove a spark plug and install the pressure gauge adapter into the spark plug hole. Connect the pump and gauge to the pressure fitting adapter. Pressurize the crankcase until the gauge reads approximately 9 psi (62 kPa).

NOTE
The cylinders cannot be checked individually because of the seal installed on the crankshaft between the crankcase chambers. Pressurizing one cylinder also pressurizes the other.

5. Observe the pressure gauge. If the engine is in good condition, the pressure should not drop more than 1 psi (7 kPa) in several minutes. Any pressure loss of 1 psi (7 kPa) in one minute indicates considerable leakage.

6. If leakage is indicated, first make sure that no leaks are present in the test equipment. Then closely inspect the entire engine. Large leaks are easily found by listening. Small leaks can be located by checking every engine joint with a solution of liquid detergent and water. Common points of leakage are listed below:

    a. Crankshaft seals (**Figure 63**).

    b. Spark plugs.

    c. Cylinder head joint.

    d. Cylinder base joint.

    e. Carburetor base joint.

    f. Crankcase joint.

STEERING

The steering on the Jet Ski should operate smoothly. **Figure 64** provides a series of causes that can be useful in locating steering problems. Refer to Chapter Eleven for complete steering system service.

2

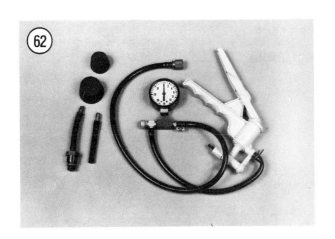

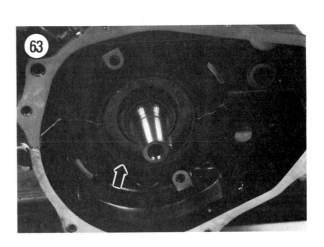

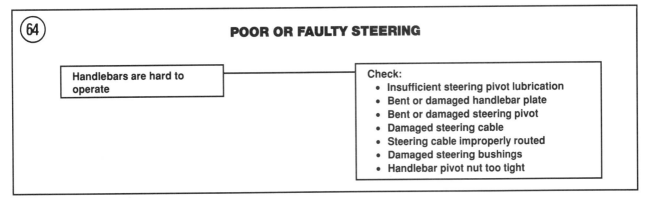

POOR OR FAULTY STEERING

Handlebars are hard to operate

Check:
- Insufficient steering pivot lubrication
- Bent or damaged handlebar plate
- Bent or damaged steering pivot
- Damaged steering cable
- Steering cable improperly routed
- Damaged steering bushings
- Handlebar pivot nut too tight

Table 1 ELECTRICAL SPECIFICATIONS (JS440SX)

Battery	12 volt, 19 amp hour
Maximum alternator output	42 watts AC @ 6000 rpm
Charging coil resistance	
Light green to ground	1.2-1.8 ohms
Light green to light green	2.4-3.6 ohms
Ignition coil secondary resistance	4480-6720 ohms
Exciter coil resistance	
Red to black	112-168 ohms
Pulser coil resistance	
Red to gray	1.4-1.8 ohms

Table 2 ELECTRICAL SPECIFICATIONS (JS550SX)

Battery	12 volt, 19 amp hour
Maximum alternator output	3.25 amps @ 6000 rpm
Regulated voltage	14-15 volts
Charging coil output	
Light green to black	12-15 volts AC
Charging coil resistance	
Light green to black	1.2-1.8 ohms
Light green to light green	2.4-3.6 ohms
Ignition coil secondary resistance	4500-6700 ohms
Exciter coil resistance	
Red to black	112-168 ohms
Pulser coil resistance	
Red to gray	14.4-21.6 ohms

Table 3 ELECTRICAL SPECIFICATIONS (650 CC MODELS)

Battery	12 volts, 19 amp hours
Maximum alternator output	
JS650SX	3.5 amps @ 6000 rpm
All others	4.0 amps @ 6000 rpm
Regulated voltage	12-15 volts
Charging coil output	38 volts AC
Charging coil resistance	
JF650X-2 & JS650SX	
Yellow to yellow	1.5-2.3 ohms
Yellow to black	0.7-1.3 ohms
All others	
Brown to brown	1.5-2.3 ohms
Brown to black/yellow	0.7-1.3 ohms
Ignition coil secondary resistance	
JL650SC	2500-3300 ohms
All others	2100-3100 ohms
Exciter coil resistance	255-380 ohms

Table 4 ELECTRICAL SPECIFICATIONS (750 CC MODELS)

Battery	12 volts, 19 amp hour
Maximum alternator output	6.6 amps @ 6000 rpm
Regulated voltage	14-15 volts
Charging coil output	
Brown to brown	20 volts AC
Charging coil resistance	
Brown to brown	0.7-1.1 ohms
Ignition coil	
Primary resistance	0.08-0.10 ohm
Secondary resistance	3500-4700 ohms
Pickup coil resistance	396-594 ohms

2

Chapter Three

Lubrication, Maintenance and Tune-up

This chapter covers all regular maintenance required to keep your Jet Ski in top shape. Because the Jet Ski is a high-performance marine watercraft, proper lubrication, maintenance and tune-up is absolutely necessary to provide long reliable service.

You can do your own lubrication, maintenance and tune-up if you follow the correct procedures and use common sense. Always remember that engine damage can result from improper tuning and adjustment. In addition, where special tools or testers are called for during a particular maintenance or adjustment procedure, the tool should be used or you should refer the service to a dealer or qualified marine repair shop.

The following information is based on the manufacturer's recommendations to keep your Jet Ski operating at its peak level.

Tables 1 and **2** list maintenance schedules for Jet Ski models covered in this manual. **Tables 1-9** are at the end of this chapter.

NOTE
Be sure to follow the correct procedure and specifications for your specific model and year. Also be certain to use the correct quantity and type of lubricant as indicated in the tables.

OPERATIONAL CHECK LIST

An important part of Jet Ski upkeep and operation is the preparation prior to riding and the maintenance after riding.

Pre-ride

Before launching your Jet Ski, remove the engine cover or seat and check the following items:

1. Release any vapor pressure from the fuel tank by loosening the fuel fill cap (**Figure 1**, typical). After releasing the pressure, securely tighten the fuel cap.

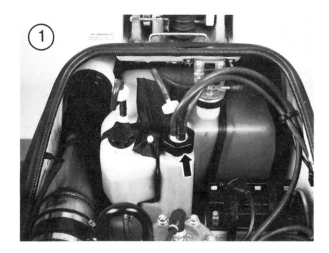

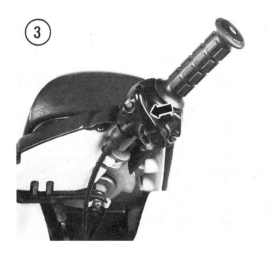

2. Check the throttle cable clamp pivot at the carburetor (**Figure 2**). If necessary, lubricate the pivot with a suitable water-resistant grease. Refer to *General Lubrication* in this chapter.

3. Lubricate the choke and steering control with WD-40, Bel-Ray 6 in 1 or a similar water-displacing lubricant. Refer to *General Lubrication* in this chapter.

4. Operate the throttle control to make sure the throttle lever returns to the idle position (**Figure 3**). Also check for proper throttle operation at the carburetor(s).

5. Operate the steering handlebar from side-to-side while checking operation of the jet pump steering nozzle. Make sure the nozzle moves from side-to-side corresponding to handlebar movement.

6. Check all fuel hoses for leakage, loose clamps or damage. Do not operate the craft until all leaks are repaired. Be *certain* that any fuel spilled inside the hull is thoroughly cleaned up.

CAUTION
When rolling the Jet Ski on its side in Step 7, protect the hull by supporting it with a heavy towel, a blanket or 2 discarded motorcycle tires as shown in Figure 4. On models not equipped with a handlepole, protect the handlebar or steering wheel assembly from damage during this step.

7. Roll the Jet Ski on its side to allow any water in the engine compartment to run out.

3

CAUTION
*Prior to rolling the watercraft on its side, note which side the exhaust system is on. Be sure the Jet Ski is rolled **toward** the exhaust side of the craft. If rolled in the opposite direction, water in the exhaust system can enter the engine, causing severe damage when the engine is started.*

8. Remove weeds or foreign objects from the water inlet, jet pump or around the drive shaft. Check the pump cover and intake grate mounting fasteners. If loose, tighten the fasteners securely.

9. Inspect the hull for damage.

10. Check the electrolyte level in the battery. Fill with distilled water as described in Chapter Eight.

11. Tighten any loose fasteners or hose clamps. Pay particular attention to the following items:

    a. Fuel hoses and tank outlet retainer nut.

    b. Fuel and oil tank mounting straps.

    c. Cooling system and bilge hoses.

    d. Exhaust system clamps.

    e. Oil injection hose clamps on models so equipped.

12. On models equipped with oil injection, make sure the oil tank is full of the recommended oil. See **Figure 5**, typical.

End of Day

The following procedures should be observed after riding:

1. Remove the Jet Ski from the water and lift the aft end 10 in. (25.4 cm) or more to allow water in the expansion chamber to drain away from the engine.

2. If the craft is operated in saltwater, the cooling system must be flushed as described under *Cooling System Cleaning* in this chapter. Also clean the jet pump assembly by spraying with clean freshwater.

3. Clear the excess water from the exhaust system by starting the engine and running for approximately 5 seconds.

CAUTION
Do not run the engine for more than 15 seconds without a cooling water supply or the rubber exhaust components will be damaged. Prolonged running without coolant can cause serious engine damage. Never operate the engine at wide-open throttle with the craft out of the water (no load).

4. Stop the engine and remove the engine cover or seat. If water is present in the bilge, roll the craft on is side (toward exhaust system) to drain the water. Be sure the protect the hull from damage when rolling the craft over.

5. Dry the engine compartment and reinstall the engine cover.

6. When storing the craft, loosen or remove the engine cover to allow air to circulate inside the hull and bilge.

LUBRICATION

WARNING
Gasoline is a serious fire hazard. Never smoke in areas where fuel is being mixed or while refueling the watercraft. A fire extinguisher, rated for gasoline and electrical fires must always be readily available.

Proper Fuel Selection

Two-stroke engines are lubricated by mixing oil with the fuel. The various components of the engine are lubricated as the fuel and oil mixture passes through the crankcase and cylinders. Since 2-stroke fuel serves the dual function of producing combustion and distributing the lubrication, the use of poor quality gasoline should be avoided due to its low octane rating and tendency to cause ring sticking and port plugging.

Kawasaki recommends using a good quality gasoline with a minimum pump octane rating of 87.

Break-in Procedure

Following cylinder servicing (honing, boring, new piston rings) and major lower end service, the engine should be broken in just as if it were new. The performance and service life of the engine depends greatly on a careful break-in procedure.

For the first 5 hours of operation (approximately 3 tanks of fuel), no more than 3/4 throttle should be used and the speed should be varied as much as possible. Prolonged steady running at one speed, no matter how moderate, is to be avoided, as is hard acceleration and heavy loads (lugging).

During the break-in period on models without oil injection, use a 25:1 fuel and oil mixture in the fuel tank to provide the additional lubrication required for break in. After the break-in period, switch to a 50:1 fuel-oil mixture.

During break in on models equipped with oil injection, use a 50:1 gasoline and oil mixture in the fuel tank in addition to the normal oil injection system. This double oil provides the additional lubrication required by the engine during break in. After the break-in period, switch to straight gasoline in the fuel tank.

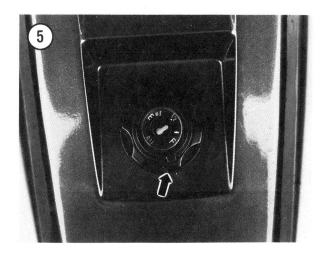

Sour Fuel

Fuel should not be stored for more than 2-3 weeks under ideal conditions. As gasoline ages, it forms gum and varnish deposits that can restrict carburetor passages and other fuel system components. A suitable fuel stabilizer can be used to prevent gum and varnish formation during periods of storage, but it is preferred to drain the fuel system in such cases. Always use fresh gasoline when mixing fuel for your watercraft.

Recommended Fuel Mixture (Models Equipped with Oil Injection)

All 650 and 750 cc models (except JH750XiR) are equipped with an oil injection system. A mechanical pump driven by the crankshaft is mounted on the generator cover located at the front of the engine. An oil line is attached to a nozzle on the oil pump and connects to a nozzle mounted in the intake manifold. A separate hose attaches the oil tank reservoir to the inlet side of the oil pump. During engine operation, oil is automatically injected into the engine at a variable ratio depending on engine speed.

On some models, the oil level in the tank can be monitored by the gauge attached to the oil fill cap (**Figure 5**, typical). Refer to Chapter Nine for a complete description of the oil injection system.

To refill the oil tank, remove the oil fill cap and pour in the required amount of the recommended engine oil. See **Table 4**.

Recommended Fuel Mixture (JS440SX and JS550SX)

These engines are lubricated by oil mixed with the gasoline. The recommended oil is a good quality engine oil with NMMA certification TCW-II or TCW-3. **Table 3** lists fuel and oil mixture ratios. Refer to **Table 4** for fuel tank capacities.

Correct Fuel-Oil Mixing

Mix the fuel and oil outdoors or in a well ventilated indoor location. Mix the fuel in a separate container and pour the mixture into the fuel tank after it is properly mixed.

Using less than the specified amount of oil can result in insufficient lubrication and serious engine damage. Using more oil than specified, causes spark plug fouling, excessive exhaust smoke, poor performance and rapid carbon accumulation which can cause preignition.

Cleanliness is of prime importance when mixing fuel. Even a very small particle of dirt can cause carburetor problems. Always use fresh gasoline with an octane rating of 87 or higher. Use of sour fuel can result in carburetor problems, spark plug fouling and poor performance.

Mix the oil and gasoline thoroughly in a clean sealable container. Allow room in the container for proper agitation of the mixture. Always measure the quantities exactly and consistently.

Use a suitable container with graduations in both cubic centimeters (cc) and fluid ounces (fl. oz.) to measure the oil. Pour the required amount of oil into the mixing container and add approximately 1/2 the required gasoline. Agitate the mixture thoroughly, then add the remaining fuel and agitate again until well mixed.

To avoid any contaminants entering into the fuel system, use a funnel with a filter, when pouring the fuel into the tank.

Consistent Fuel Mixtures

The carburetor idle adjustment is sensitive to fuel mixture variations which result from the use of different oil and gasoline or from inaccurate measuring and mixing. This may require readjustment of the carburetor fuel mixture. To prevent the necessity for constant carburetor readjustment, prepare each batch of fuel exactly the same as previous ones.

General Lubrication

The following components (if so equipped) should be lubricated at the intervals listed in

Tables **1** and **2**. Unless specified otherwise, use WD-40, Bel-Ray 6 in 1 or an equivalent water-displacement, rust inhibiting lubricant.

1. At the handlebar, lubricate the throttle lever pivot and the steering cable end pivot and sliding shaft.

2. Pull the choke knob out and lubricate its shaft.

3. Lubricate the choke fitting pivot at the carburetor and the carburetor throttle cable fitting pivot with waterproof grease.

4. Remove the engine cover or seat.

5. Locate the grease fittings (if so equipped) on the bearing box (**Figure 6**, typical) inside the hull. Wipe the grease fittings off with a clean shop towel. Then, pump a suitable water-resistant grease into the fitting using a grease gun. Keep pumping grease until resistance is noted on the grease gun handle.

3

CAUTION
Prior to rolling the watercraft on its side, remove the seat or engine cover and note on which side the exhaust system is located. Only roll the craft toward its exhaust side to prevent water in the exhaust system from entering the engine.

6. Roll the watercraft on its side. Be sure to adequately protect the side of the hull with a heavy towel or blanket.

7. Remove the intake grate (A, **Figure 7**) and jet pump cover (B, **Figure 7**).

CAUTION
When applying grease to the jet pump in Step 8, do not force grease in after the housing is full or the housing seals could rupture. A damaged seal will allow water to enter the housing and result in bearing damage.

8. Lubricate the grease fittings on the jet pump, if so equipped. See **Figure 8**, typical. Wipe off the grease fitting with a clean shop towel. Then, pump grease into the fitting until resistance if noted on the grease gun handle.

9. Lubricate the steering nozzle and reverse gate pivot points, joints and the steering cable (**Figure 9**, typical).

10. Reinstall the pump cover and grate. Tighten the fasteners securely.

11. Lubricate the shift and steering cable ball joints, using water-resistant grease.

Steering Pivot Lubrication

Complete steering pivot lubrication requires partial disassembly of the steering assembly. Refer to Chapter Eleven.

Throttle and Choke Cable Lubrication

Lubricate the throttle and choke cables at the intervals specified in **Tables 1** and **2**. In addition, the cables should be carefully inspected at this time. Check for fraying, chafing or other damage. Replace the cables as necessary.

Lubricate the cable using Bel-Ray 6 in 1 lubricant (or equivalent) and a suitable cable lubricator tool.

1. Lubricate the choke cable as follows:

   a. Disconnect the cable from the carburetor (A, **Figure 10**).

   b. Attach a cable lubricator (Kawasaki part No. K56019-021) to the end of the cable.

   c. Insert the nozzle of the lubricant can into the lubricator (**Figure 11**). Then inject lubricant into the cable until the lubricant flows from the other end of the cable.

   d. Reconnect the choke cable. Adjust the cable as described in this chapter.

2. Lubricate the throttle cable as follows:

   a. Loosen the set screw at the carburetor or disconnect the throttle cable from the carburetor lever (B, **Figure 10**).

   b. Remove the throttle case screws and separate the throttle case housing (**Figure 12**, typical).

   c. Attach a cable lubricator to the end of the throttle cable.

   d. Inject lubricant into the cable until it flows from the other end. See **Figure 11**.

   e. Reconnect the throttle cable. Adjust the cable as described in this Chapter.

Magneto Housing Lubrication (JS440SX and JS550SX)

At the intervals listed in **Table 1**, remove the magneto housing breather plug (**Figure 13**) and spray the inside of the magneto cavity with WD-40, Bel-Ray 6 in 1 or equivalent.

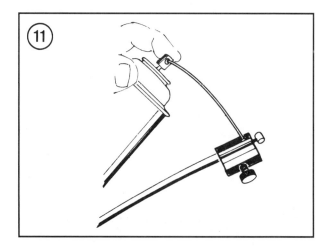

PERIODIC MAINTENANCE

The following periodic maintenance items should be inspected at the intervals specified in **Tables 1** and **2**.

Fuel Line Check Valve Inspection

The fuel tank must be vented to the atmosphere to allow fuel to be drawn from the tank without creating a vacuum in the tank. The fuel vent check valve (A, **Figure 14**) allows air to

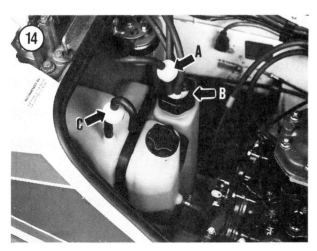

enter the fuel tank for venting, but prevents fuel from spilling from the tank during riding or if the watercraft should capsize. Note that the check valve has an arrow stamped in it. The arrow should always face toward the fuel tank.

> *WARNING*
> *Prior to disconnecting any fuel hoses, loosen the fuel tank fill cap (B, **Figure 14**) to relieve any pressure that may be present in the tank.*

1. Locate the fuel vent check valve (A, **Figure 14**) near the fuel tank fill cap. Disconnect the 2 fuel hoses from the valve, then remove the valve.
2. Thoroughly clean each end of the valve with a clean towel.
3. The check valve can be tested by blowing through it from both ends. Air should only pass through the valve in one direction. If air passes through the valve in both directions, or not at all, replace the check valve.
4. Install the valve so the arrow faces toward the fuel tank. Make sure the vent hoses are attached to the check valve securely.

Oil Tank Vent Check Valve
(Models Equipped with Oil Injection)

The oil tank must be vented to the atmosphere to allow oil to be drawn from the tank without creating a vacuum within the tank. The oil tank vent check valve (C, **Figure 14**) is connected to the oil tank vent hose. The valve allows air to enter the tank, but prevents oil from spilling during riding or if the watercraft capsizes.

The arrow on the check valve must always face toward the oil tank.

The check valve can be tested by blowing through it from both ends. Air should only pass through the valve in one direction. If air passes through in both directions, or not at all, replace the check valve.

3

Fuel Filter
(JS440SX)

A fuel filter (**Figure 15**) is mounted inside the engine compartment on 440 cc models to prevent dirt and water from entering the carburetor. Clean the filter at the specified service intervals (**Table 1**) or whenever water, or other contamination is present in the filter bowl.

1. Remove the engine cover.

WARNING
Some fuel may spill during this procedure. Work in a well-ventilated area at least 50 ft. (15 m) from any sparks or flame, including gas appliance pilot lights. Never smoke during this procedure.

2. Place a shop towel under the filter bowl to absorb any spilled fuel.

3. Unscrew the filter bowl ring and remove the bowl, spring and filter. See **Figure 16**.

4. Clean the filter and bowl in solvent. Replace the filter element if excessively contaminated, torn or damaged.

5. Make sure the small O-ring is in position in the filter neck (arrow, **Figure 16**). Then, insert the filter element into the outlet tube.

6. Install the bowl with its large O-ring. Tighten the mounting ring securely.

Sediment Bowl

Some models are equipped with a sediment bowl to prevent dirt, water or other contamination from entering the carburetor. See **Figure 17**. Clean the sediment bowl at the specified service interval (**Tables 1** and **2**) or whenever water or other contamination is present in the bowl.

NOTE
On some models, access to the sediment bowl and mounting ring is limited. If necessary, remove the fuel hoses from the sediment bowl base, then remove the mounting fasteners and remove the entire bowl assembly.

WARNING
Some fuel may spill during this procedure. Work in a well-ventilated area at least 50 ft. (15m) from any sparks or flame, including gas appliance pilot lights. Never smoke during this procedure.

1. Place a shop towel under the sediment bowl to absorb any spilled fuel.

2. Loosen and unscrew the bowl mounting ring (**Figure 17**).

3. Remove the bowl and ring. Empty the bowl into a suitable container.

4. Clean the bowl using a suitable solvent. Dry with compressed air or a clean towel.

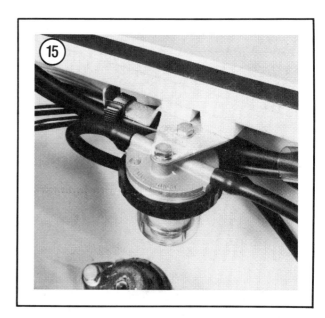

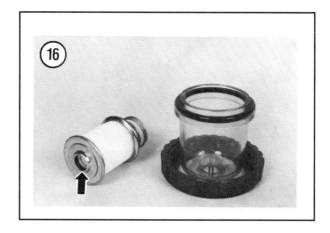

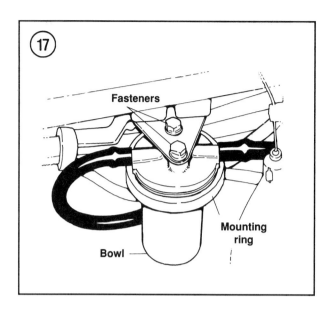

Fasteners

Mounting ring

Bowl

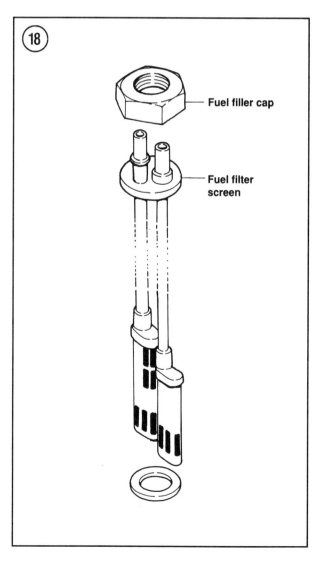

Fuel filler cap

Fuel filter screen

5. Closely inspect the bowl O-ring seal. Replace the seal if damaged or deteriorated.

6. Place the O-ring on the bowl. Lightly lubricate the O-ring with clean engine oil. Install the bowl and mounting ring. Tighten the mounting ring securely. If the entire sediment bowl is removed, install it by reversing the removal procedure. Make sure the fuel hoses are securely clamped to prevent fuel leakage into the bilge.

3

Fuel Filter Screen

Model not equipped with a fuel filter or sediment bowl are equipped with a filter screen attached to the fuel filler cap mounted on the tank. See **Figure 18**. Note that some models are equipped with both types of filters. To service the filter, observe the following steps.

> *WARNING*
> *Some fuel may spill during this procedure. Work in a well- ventilated area at least 50 ft. (15 m) from any sparks or flame, including gas appliance pilot lights. Never smoke during this procedure.*

1. Label the hoses connected to the fuel tank fill cap for identification during installation.

2. Disconnect each hose from its fitting on the cap.

3. Unscrew the retainer cap and remove the filter screen (**Figure 18**). Place a shop towel under the screen to prevent gasoline from spilling into the bilge.

4. Wash the filter screen in solvent and allow to air dry. Replace the screen if excessively contaminated or damaged.

5. Install the filter screen by reversing the removal procedure.

Flame Arrester

The flame arrestor should be removed and cleaned at the service intervals specified in **Ta-**

bles **1** and **2**. Refer to Chapter Seven for service procedures.

Impeller Inspection

Inspect the impeller assembly (**Figure 19**) for nicks, deep scratches or gouges at the specified service intervals (**Tables 1** and **2**). The impeller should also be inspected whenever the watercraft's performance deteriorates, although the engine is performing properly. Refer to Chapter Six for drive train service procedures.

Rubber coupler

Inspect the rubber coupler (**Figure 20**) at the specified service intervals listed in **Tables 1** and **2**. Refer to Chapter Four or Chapter Five.

Magneto Nut or Bolt

Torque the magneto nut or bolt at the specified service intervals (**Tables 1** and **2**). Refer to Chapter Eight.

> *NOTE*
> *On models equipped with oil injection, the magneto bolt also engages with and drives the oil pump (**Figure 21**). When the tightening the bolt, check the bolt slot for cracks, excessive wear, breakage or other damage. Replace the bolt if necessary. After reinstalling the oil pump, be sure to bleed the oil injection pump as described in Chapter Nine.*

Throttle Valve (Mikuni Carburetor)

Inspect the throttle valve nylon bushing for excessive wear and make sure the throttle return spring is firmly closing the throttle. Replace worn or damaged parts. Refer to Chapter Seven.

Throttle Valve (Keihin Carburetor)

Make sure the throttle return spring is firmly closing the throttle valve. If the spring is weak or damaged, replace the carburetor. Refer to Chapter Seven.

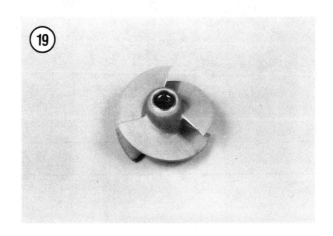

Cylinder Head Nuts

Retighten the cylinder head fasteners at the intervals specified in **Tables 1** and **2**. Refer to *Engine Tune-up* in this chapter.

Cooling System Cleaning

The cooling system can become restricted or blocked by sand, silt or salt deposits if it is not

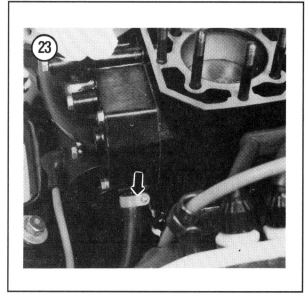

flushed occasionally. Flush the cooling system at the intervals specified in **Tables 1** and **2**. Flush the cooling system after *each* use when operated in saltwater. Refer to *On-shore Cooling* in this chapter.

Bilge Pump System Cleaning

The bilge pump system can become restricted or blocked and should be flushed at the intervals indicated in **Tables 1** and **2**. Refer to Chapter Ten.

3

ON-SHORE COOLING

NOTE
*Follow the **On-Shore Cooling** procedure when flushing the cooling system. Make sure clean freshwater is used to flush the system.*

If it is necessary to run the engine during maintenance, the watercraft should be in the water. However, a temporary cooling water supply system can be used if this is not possible.

CAUTION
Do not run the engine for more than 15 seconds without cooling water or the rubber components of the exhaust system will be damaged. Furthermore, prolonged running without cooling water will cause serious engine damage. Also, never run the engine at wide-open throttle with the craft out of the water (no load).

1A. *JS440SX and JS550SX*—Perform the following:
    a. Obtain a garden hose and a 3/8 in. adapter (**Figure 22**). Screw the adapter onto the garden hose.
    b. Locate the cooling hose that runs from the bulkhead to the exhaust manifold (**Figure 23**). Disconnect the hose from the bulkhead.

c. Attach the garden hose adapter to the cooling hose from the exhaust pipe.

1B. *650 and 750 cc models*—Perform the following:

a. Loosen the clamp and remove the cap (**Figure 24**) from the hose fitting on the cylinder head.

b. Attach the garden hose to the hose fitting and tighten securely.

2. Attach the garden hose to a faucet.

3. Start the engine and allow it to idle, *then* turn on the water. Should the engine stop running, immediately turn off the water to prevent flooding the cylinders. Adjust the water flow so a trickle flows from the bypass outlet on the left side of the hull.

> *CAUTION*
> *If the water flow is insufficient, exhaust system and engine damage can occur from overheating. Excessive water flow can stop the engine and flood the cylinders with water. Water in the cylinders will result in a hydraulic lock and severe engine damage. If the engine stops during the flushing procedure, **immediately** turn off the water supply.*

4. Allow the engine to idle for several minutes to ensure the cooling system is flushed.

5. After flushing is completed, first turn off the water, then stop the engine. Accelerate the engine 2-3 times to clear the remaining water from the exhaust system. Remove the garden hose, reinstall the cap (**Figure 24**) and clamp securely.

STEERING CABLE ADJUSTMENT

JB650 Jet Mate

1. Position the control stick in the upright position.

2. With the control stick in this position, the steering nozzle should be the same distance from each side of the hull cavity. If the steering nozzle is not centered, perform the following steps.

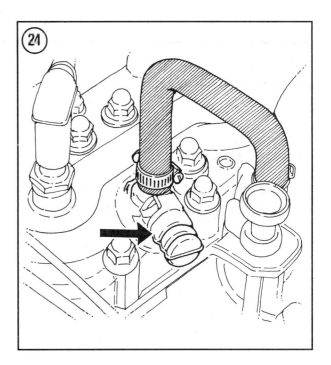

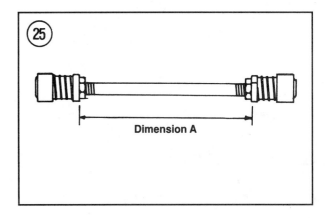

Dimension A

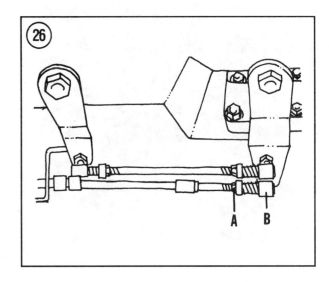

3. Remove the engine cover.

4. The steering rod should have a Dimension A length of 118-120 mm (4.65-4.72 in.). See **Figure 25**.

5. Loosen the locknut (A, **Figure 26**) and disconnect the steering cable connector (B, **Figure 26**) from the ball.

6. Center the steering nozzle in the hull cavity.

7. Again, position the control stick in the upright position.

8. Turn the steering cable connector until its hole aligns with the ball.

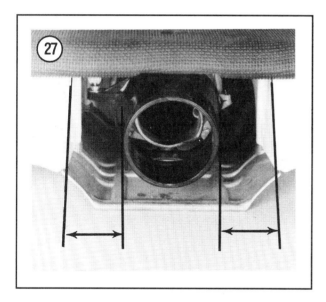

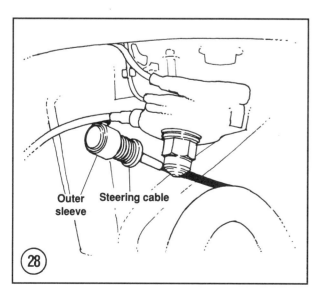

Outer sleeve   Steering cable

9. Connect the steering cable to the ball and recheck adjustment. If steering adjustment is acceptable, tighten the locknut securely.

JS440SX, JS550SX, JS650SX, JF650X-2, JF650TS and JS750SX,

1. Lower the handlepole on models so equipped. Center the handlebar in the straight-ahead position.

2. With the handlebar centered, the steering nozzle should be centered in the jet pump cavity. See **Figure 27**.

3. If adjustment is necessary, raise the handlepole (if so equipped) or remove the engine cover, and loosen the steering cable locknut. See **Figure 28**. On JF650TS models, remove the storage case to access the steering cable connector.

4. Disconnect the steering cable from the ball by sliding the outer sleeve away from the ball, the lifting the cable off the ball.

5. Turn the steering cable connector as necessary to adjust. Temporarily reinstall the steering cable on the ball and repeat Steps 1 and 2. Repeat adjustment as necessary, then retighten the steering cable locknut securely.

JL650SC, JH750 Super Sport Xi, JH750SS, JT750ST and JH750XiR

1. Center the steering wheel (JL650SC) or handlebar (all others) in the straight-ahead position.

2. With the steering wheel or handlebar centered, the steering nozzle should be centered in the jet pump cavity. See **Figure 27**. If the nozzle is not centered, the steering cable should be adjusted.

3. *JL650SC*—Place the shift lever into the REVERSE position, then disconnect the reverse cable from the reverse gate.

4. Loosen the locknut on the steering cable. Then, disconnect the steering cable connector from the ball by sliding the cable outer sleeve

away from the ball and lifting off the cable. See **Figure 29**.

5. Turn the steering cable connector as necessary to adjust the cable. Reinstall the steering cable and repeat Steps 1 and 2 to check the adjustment.

6. Readjust the cable as necessary. When the correct adjustment is obtained, securely tighten the steering cable locknut. Reinstall the reverse cable to the reverse gate on JL650SC models.

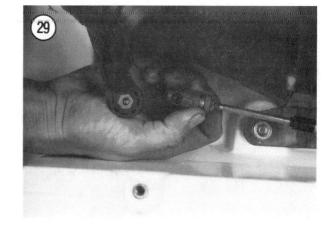

TRIM CABLE ADJUSTMENT

JF650X-2

1. Turn the trim adjusting knob all the way clockwise and check the steering nozzle position. The nozzle should nearly contact the jet pump cover (**Figure 30**). If not, adjust the trim cable.

2. Raise the handlebar to its highest position. Loosen the trim cable adjusting locknut located behind the trim adjusting knob. Slide the cable outer sleeve away from the ball and remove the cable from the ball.

3. Turn the connector clockwise to lower the steering nozzle or counterclockwise to raise it. Then reconnect the linkage and recheck nozzle position. After the correct adjustment is obtained, securely tighten the cable adjuster locknut.

4. Next, turn the trim adjusting knob fully counterclockwise. Turn the handlebar from side-to-side to be sure the steering nozzle does not drag or rub against the rubber pad.

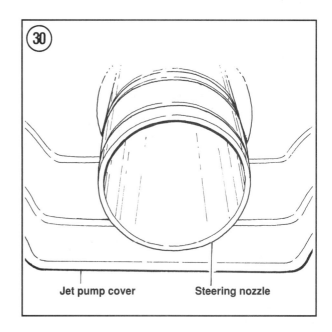

Jet pump cover   Steering nozzle

JH750 Super Sport Xi and JH750XiR

1. Place the watercraft on a level surface.

2. Disconnect the handle return spring (**Figure 31**).

3. Place the trim adjusting knob in the "N" position (neutral trim). On models equipped with electric trim, start the engine and push the trim

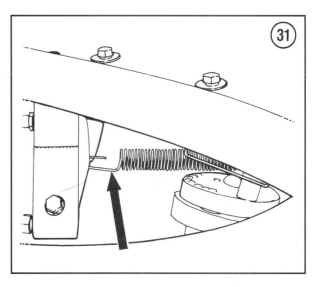

button until the trim meter needle points at the level position.

4. Place a suitable rule or straight edge on the level area near the steering nozzle pivot bolt (**Figure 32**).

5. Lightly lift upward on the steering nozzle to remove any play (**Figure 32**) and note the position of the straightedge. It should be approxi-

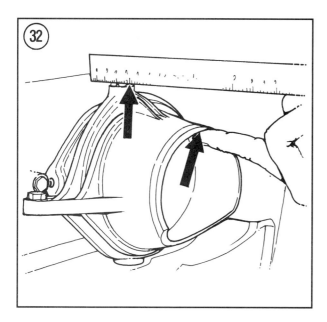

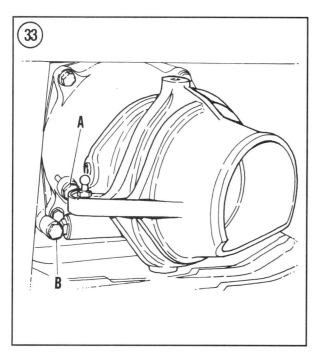

mately level with the surface the watercraft is setting on.

6. If not, disconnect the steering cable (A, **Figure 33**) from the nozzle to gain access to the trim cable (B, **Figure 33**). Slide the cable outer sleeve away from the ball and lift the cable off the ball. Then disconnect the trim cable and turn the cable connector as necessary to obtain the correct adjustment (Step 5).

7. Reconnect the trim cable and recheck adjustment as described in Steps 2-5. Readjust the cable as necessary. Reconnect the steering cable.

THROTTLE CABLE ADJUSTMENT

JS440SX

Refer to **Figure 34** for this procedure. Model JS440SX is equipped with a Mikuni BN38 carburetor.

1. With the throttle lever released, the idle adjusting screw should contact the throttle stop and light slack should be present in the throttle cable.

2. Open the throttle to the wide-open throttle position. With the throttle wide open, the pivot pulley should be touching its stop.

3. To adjust, loosen the throttle cable locknut (B, **Figure 35**) and adjust the cable so the idle adjusting screw rests against the throttle stop with light cable slack. Tighten the locknut.

4. Swing the handlebar fully in each direction. Make sure that the throttle cable does not catch or bend sharply at the steering pivot nut.

All 550, 650 and 750 cc Models

Refer to **Figure 36** for this procedure. These models are equipped with a Keihin CDK34, CDK38-32 or CDK40-34 carburetors. JH750XiR models are equipped with twin carburetors.

1. With the throttle lever released, the idle adjusting screw should contact the stop on the

throttle shaft lever and slight slack should be present in the throttle cable.

2. With the throttle at the wide-open position, the stop on the throttle shaft lever should contact the stop on the carburetor.

3. If adjustment is necessary, loosen the throttle cable locknuts and adjust the cable so the idle adjusting screw rests against the throttle shaft lever stop and light slack is present in the cable. Then, securely tighten the locknuts.

4. Swing the handlebar or steering wheel fully in each direction to make sure the throttle cable does not bind, catch or bend sharply at the steering pivot.

CHOKE CABLE ADJUSTMENT

JS440SX

Refer to **Figure 37** for this procedure.

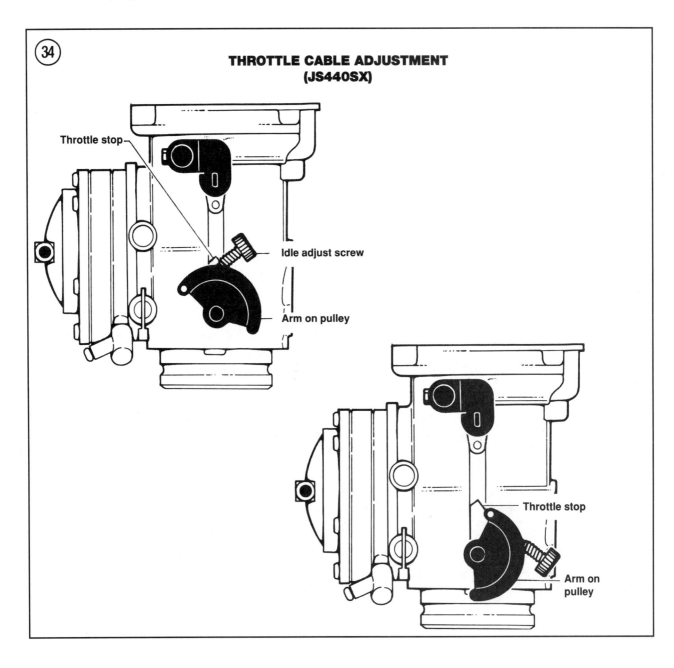

(34) THROTTLE CABLE ADJUSTMENT (JS440SX)

Throttle stop

Idle adjust screw

Arm on pulley

Throttle stop

Arm on pulley

1. The choke valve (**Figure 38**) should fully open with the choke knob pushed in. There should also be a slight amount of slack in the choke cable.

2. With the choke knob pulled out, the choke valve (**Figure 38**) should be fully closed.

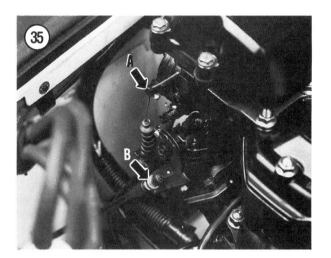

3. If adjustment is necessary, loosen the choke cable adjusting nuts (**Figure 39**). Turn the adjusting nuts as necessary to move the cable up or down to obtain the correct adjustment, then securely tighten the nuts. This adjustment can also be achieved by loosening the set screw on the choke pivot arm and sliding the inner cable up or down in the pivot arm connector.

All 550, 650 and 750 cc Models

Refer to **Figure 36** for this procedure. Three different methods are used to activate the choke on these models. On 550 cc models, the choke is closed by pulling the choke knob out. Pushing the knob in, opens the choke valve. On JF650X-2 models, a choke lever located on the right handlebar is used. Pushing the lever to the left closes the choke and to the right opens the choke. On all other models, turning the choke knob

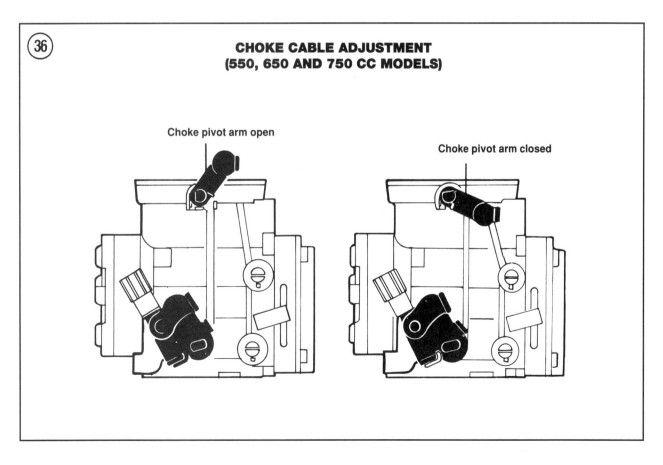

CHOKE CABLE ADJUSTMENT
(550, 650 AND 750 CC MODELS)

Choke pivot arm open

Choke pivot arm closed

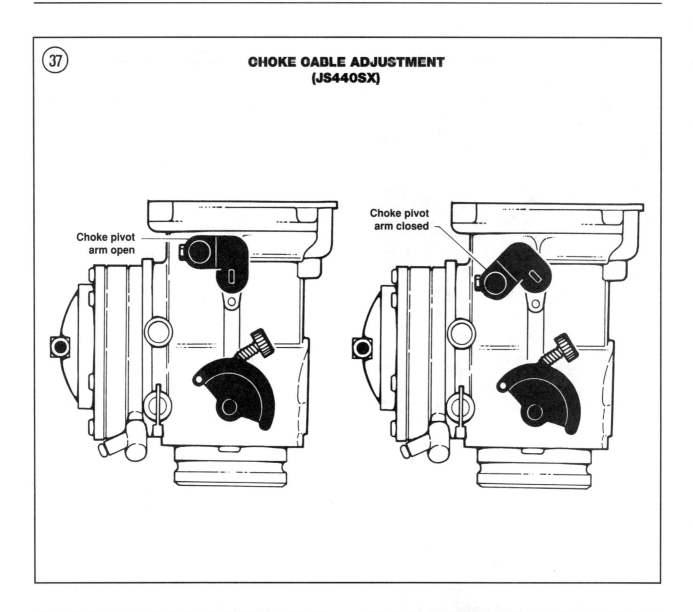

(37)

**CHOKE CABLE ADJUSTMENT
(JS440SX)**

Choke pivot
arm open

Choke pivot
arm closed

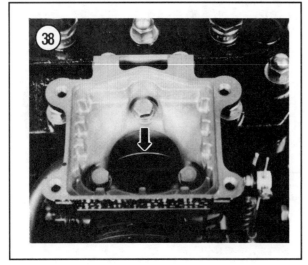

(38)

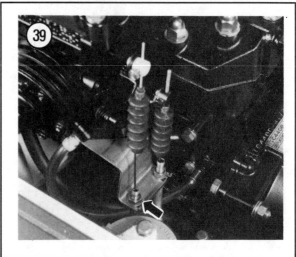

(39)

clockwise closes the choke valve and counter-clockwise opens the choke.

1. The choke valve (A, **Figure 40**) should be fully open with the choke lever or knob in the OFF position.

2. With the choke activated, the choke valve (A, **Figure 40**) should be fully closed.

NOTE
On JL650SC models, it is necessary to remove the electric box and bracket to access the choke cable locknuts. Refer to Chapter Eight.

3. If adjustment is necessary, loosen the choke cable locknuts (B, **Figure 40**). Turn the nuts to

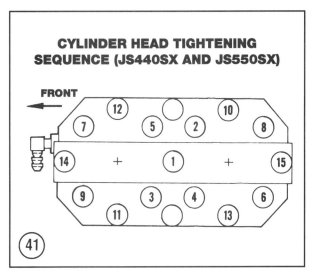

move the cable as necessary for correct adjustment. Securely tighten the locknuts.

ENGINE TUNE-UP

For the purposes of this manual, a tune-up is considered the general adjustment, parts replacement and maintenance necessary to ensure optimum engine performance.

The following paragraphs discuss each part of a tune-up. The instructions are presented in the order the tune-up procedure should be performed.

The following tools and equipment is necessary to properly tune the Jet Skis covered in this manual:

    a. 14 mm spark plug wrench.

    b. Socket wrench and assorted sockets.

    c. Phillips screwdriver.

    d. Spark plug wire feeler gauge and gap adjusting tool.

    e. Dial indicator.

    f. Flywheel puller.

    g. Compression gauge.

    h. Timing light.

    i. Torque wrench.

Retorquing Cylinder Head Fasteners

The cylinder head fasteners should be retorqued after the first 10 hours of operation and after every 25 hours of operation thereafter.

The engine must be cool (room temperature) before retorquing the cylinder head.

Retighten the cylinder head fasteners in 3 incremental steps to the specified torque (**Table 5**). Tighten the fasteners in the sequence shown.

    a. **Figure 41**: 440 and 550 cc.

    b. **Figure 42**: 650 and 750 cc.

Compression Test

A compression test is a good indicator of the condition of the cylinders, pistons, piston rings and head gasket. It is good practice to check compression at each tune-up, recording the results of each test for comparison with the results of the next test. Doing so can help identify developing engine problems.

1. Start the engine and warm it to normal operating temperature. If the watercraft is not in the water, an auxiliary water supply must be connected to the engine as described in this chapter.

> *CAUTION*
> *Do not run the engine for more than 15 seconds without cooling water or the rubber components of the exhaust system will be damaged. Furthermore, prolonged running without cooling water will cause serious engine damage. Also, never run the engine at wide-open throttle with the craft out of the water (no load).*

2. Remove both spark plugs. Securely ground the spark plug leads to the engine. Pull the engine shut-off lanyard from the stop switch.

> *CAUTION*
> *The CD igniter can be damaged if the spark plug leads are not properly grounded to the engine while cranking.*

3. Thread a compression gauge into one spark plug hole. If a press-in type of gauge is used, hold it firmly in the spark plug hole.

4. Hold the throttle in the wide-open position and crank the engine until the compression gauge reaches its highest reading. Record the figure.

5. Repeat Steps 3 and 4 for the remaining cylinder.

6. Refer to **Table 6** for the recommended compression readings. If more than a 10% difference in compression pressure between cylinders is noted, a problem is indicated.

7. If excessive compression pressure is noted, check for excessive carbon deposits in the combustion chamber. If compression is low, check for compression leaking around the cylinder head gasket, or damaged or excessively worn piston(s), piston rings or cylinder(s).

Spark Plug Heat Range

The proper spark plug is very important for maximum performance and reliability. The condition of a used spark plug can tell an experienced mechanic a lot about the condition of the carburetion system and engine.

Select spark plugs of the heat ranged designed for the loads and conditions under which the watercraft will be operated. Use of incorrect spark plugs may result in a seized piston, scored cylinder wall and damaged piston crown.

In general, use a hotter plug for low speeds and low temperatures. Use a colder plug for high speed, high load and/or high temperature operation. The spark plug should operate hot enough to burn off unwanted deposits, but not so hot that they burn themselves or cause preignition. A spark plug running at the correct temperature has a light tan color on the plug insulator. See **Figure 43** for various spark plug conditions.

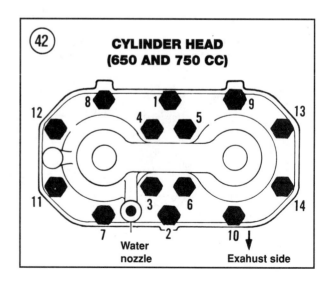

(43)   **SPARK PLUG CONDITIONS**

3

NORMAL USE

OIL FOULED

CARBON FOULED

OVERHEATED

GAP BRIDGED

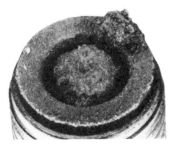

SUSTAINED PREIGNITION

WORN OUT

The reach (length) of a spark plug is also an important consideration. A longer than specified spark plug could interfere with the piston, causing permanent and severe engine damage. See **Figure 44** for an explanation of spark plug reach.

The spark plugs recommended for use in the watercraft covered in this manual are listed in **Table 7**.

Spark Plug Removal/Cleaning

1. Grasp the spark plug lead (**Figure 45**) as near the plug as possible and pull it off the spark plug. If the lead is stuck, twist is slightly to break it loose from the plug.

2. Blow away any dirt or other contamination from around the base of the spark plugs.

> *CAUTION*
> *Dirt or other contamination can fall into the cylinder when the plug is removed, causing major engine damage.*

3. Remove the spark plug using a 14 mm spark plug wrench.

> *NOTE*
> *If the spark plug is difficult to remove, apply penetrating oil (WD-40, Liquid Wrench) around the base of the plug. Allow the oil to soak for 10-20 minutes, then attempt to remove the plug.*

4. Inspect the spark plug carefully and compare it to **Figure 43**. Check for broken porcelain, excessive wear, excessive carbon or fouling.

> *NOTE*
> *A common spark plug problem on watercraft is water fouling. Water or a water/oil emulsion on the spark plug usually indicates water in the fuel.*

Gapping and Installing Spark Plugs

The gap on a new spark plug should be carefully adjusted to ensure a reliable, consistent

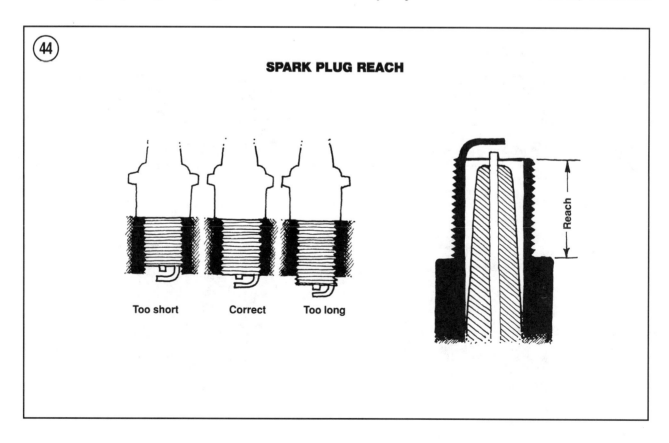

SPARK PLUG REACH

Too short   Correct   Too long

Reach

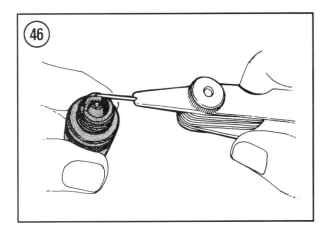

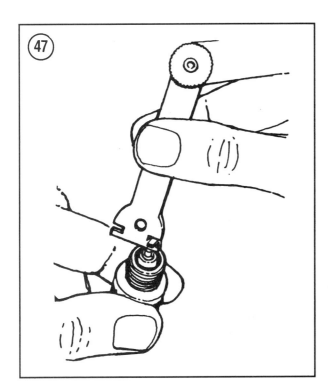

spark. A spark plug gapping tool and a wire feeler gauge must be used to gap the plugs.

1. Insert the wire feeler gauge between the center and side electrode (**Figure 46**). The correct gap is listed in **Table 7**. If the gap is correct, a slight drag on the feeler gauge is noted. If adjustment is required, bend the side electrode with the gapping tool (**Figure 47**) to set the proper gap.

2. Apply a light coat of a suitable antiseize lubricant to the spark plug threads.

3. Thread the spark plug in by hand until it bottoms. Very little effort is required to screw the plug into the cylinder head. If force is necessary, the plug may be cross threaded. Remove the plug and reinstall it.

4. After the plug bottoms, tighten it an additional 1/4 (used plug) to 1/2 (new plug) turn.

NOTE
Do not overtighten the spark plugs. Excessive tightness will damage the plug gasket and destroy its sealing ability.

5. Reconnect the spark plug leads.

Reading Spark Plugs

Much information about engine and spark plug performance can be determined by careful examination of the spark plugs. However, this information is only valid after performing the following steps.

1. Ride the watercraft a short distance at full throttle.

2. With the craft running at full throttle, push the engine stop switch before closing the throttle. Coast back to the dock.

3. Remove the spark plugs and examine them. Compare them to **Figure 43**.

4. If the insulator is white or burned, the plug is too hot and should be replaced with a colder plug.

5. A too-cold plug will have sooty or oily deposits.

6. If the plug has a light tan or gray deposit and no abnormal electrode wear, the plug and the engine are functioning properly.

7. If the spark plug has a black insulator tip, damp oil film over the firing end and a carbon layer over the entire tip, it is oil fouled. An oil fouled plug can be cleaned, but it is always better to replace it.

Ignition Timing

NOTE
Ignition timing is fixed (not adjustable)
on 750 cc models.

All models are equipped with an electronic capacitor discharge ignition (CDI) system. This system uses no breaker points and greatly simplifies ignition timing adjustment. The CDI system is also much less susceptible to failure caused by dirt, moisture and wear than conventional breaker-point ignition.

Since there are no components to wear, adjusting the ignition timing is only necessary after the engine has been disassembled or if the stator plate mounting screws have loosened from vibration.

JS440SX and JS550SX

During the ignition timing procedure, the front piston must be positioned at top dead center (TDC). A suitable dial indicator is required to accurately position the piston at TDC. The manufacturer recommends using Kawasaki Top Dead Center Finder part No. 57001-402.

1. Remove the fuel tank from the watercraft as described in Chapter Seven. Lay the tank next to the craft and connect the fuel hoses to the carburetor.

2. Remove the flywheel cover as described in Chapter Eight.

3. Reinstall the 2 front starter mounting bolts to hold the starter motor in position.

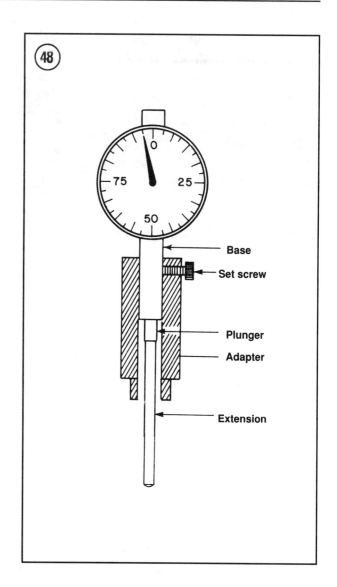

4. Remove the front spark plug.

5. Install and position the dial indicator as follows:

   a. Screw the extension onto the dial indicator and insert the dial indicator into the adapter. See **Figure 48**.

   b. Screw the dial indicator adapter into the front spark plug hole (**Figure 49**). Do not lock the dial indicator in the adapter at this time.

   c. Rotate the flywheel until the dial indicator rises all the way up in its holder, indicating the piston is approaching top dead center.

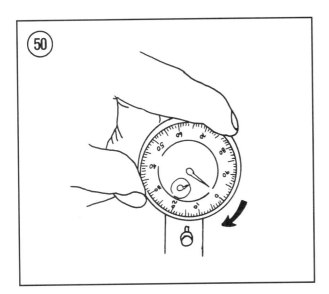

   d. Lightly tighten the set screw on the dial indicator adapter to secure the dial gauge.

   e. Rotate the flywheel until the dial needle stops moving and reverses direction. Top dead center (TDC) is the exact point the dial needle reverses direction. With the piston at TDC, zero the dial indicator (**Figure 50**).

   f. Firmly tighten the set screw on the dial indicator adapter securely.

6. Attach a rigid pointer to one of the flywheel cover bolts. See **Figure 51**. Align the pointer with the "T" mark on the flywheel (piston at TDC).

7. Remove the dial indicator, install the spark plug and connect the spark plug lead.

8. Connect a timing light according to its manufacturer's instructions.

9. Connect a tachometer to the engine according to its manufacturer's instructions.

10. Connect an auxiliary cooling water supply to the engine. Refer to *On-shore Cooling* in this chapter.

> *CAUTION*
> *Do not run the engine for more than 15 seconds without cooling water or the rubber components of the exhaust system will be damaged. Furthermore, prolonged running without cooling water will cause serious engine damage. Also, never run the engine at wide-open throttle with the craft out of the water (no load).*

11. Start the engine and warm it to normal operating temperature. Point the timing light at the pointer and timing marks. Then, increase engine speed to 6000 rpm and note the timing marks and pointer. If the timing is correctly adjusted, the "F" mark on the flywheel aligns with the pointer.

12. If the timing is not correct, loosen the stator plate set screw through the holes in the flywheel (**Figure 52**). Then, turn the stator plate as required to obtain the correct timing. Securely retighten the stator screws and recheck the timing as described in Step 11.

13. Remove the timing light and tachometer. Remove the 2 front starter mounting bolts and reinstall the flywheel cover as described in Chapter Eight. Reinstall the fuel tank as described in Chapter Seven.

650 cc models

1. Connect a timing light according to its manufacturer's instructions.
2. Connect a tachometer according to its manufacturer's instructions.
3. Connect an auxiliary water supply as described in this chapter. Refer to *On-shore Cooling*.

> *CAUTION*
> *Do not run the engine for more than 15 seconds without cooling water or the rubber components of the exhaust system will be damaged. Furthermore, prolonged running without cooling water will cause serious engine damage. Also, never run the engine at wide-open throttle with the craft out of the water (no load).*

4. Remove the breather plug (**Figure 53**) from the flywheel cover.
5. Start the engine and warm to normal operating temperature. Point the flywheel at the flywheel cover pointer (**Figure 54**). Increase engine speed to 6000 rpm and note the timing marks. Ignition timing should be 15° BTDC at 6000 rpm on JL650SC and JF650TS models and 17° BTDC at 6000 rpm on JF650X-2, JS650SX and JB650 Jet Mate models.

> *NOTE*
> ***Figure 54*** *shows the flywheel cover pointer with the cover removed for clarity.*

6. If the timing is not correct, remove the flywheel as described in Chapter Eight. Loosen the stator plate set screws (**Figure 55**) and turn the stator plate as required to obtain the specified timing.

7. Then, tighten the stator set screws, reinstall the flywheel and recheck the timing (Step 5).

Carburetor Identification

A Mikuni Model BN38 carburetor is used on JS440SX models. A Keihin Model CDK34 carburetor is used on JB650 Jet Mate models. All other models are equipped with Keihin Model CDK38-32 or CDK40-34 carburetors. On JH750 Super Sport Xi and JH750XiR models, a twin carburetor arrangement is used.

Carburetor Adjustment

The carburetor settings described in the following procedures are for operation at sea level to approximately 3300 ft. (1000 m) above sea level. When operating the watercraft at elevations over 3300 ft. (1000 m), additional high-

speed mixture adjustment is necessary. Spark plug readings are the best determining factor when adjusting the carburetor(s) for operation at higher elevation.

When adjusting the carburetor(s), bear in mind:

a. Turning the mixture adjusting screws counterclockwise, enrichens the fuel-air mixture.

b. Turning the mixture adjusting screws clockwise, leans the fuel-air mixture.

Initial Mixture Screw Setting

The carburetors are adjusted at the factory using a flow meter, then a limiter cap is installed on the mixture screws. Unless the mixture screws must be removed for cleaning during an overhaul, do not remove the limiter caps or disturb the initial setting. If, however, the mixture screws must be removed from the carburetor, use the following procedure to adjust the mixture screw initial setting.

Refer to the following figures for the location of the low- and high-speed mixture screws.

a. **Figure 56** (low speed) and **Figure 57** (high speed): JS440SX (Mikuni carburetor).

b. **Figure 58**: All other models (Keihin carburetor).

1. Remove the limiter cap from the mixture screw.

2. Turn the screw inward (clockwise) until *lightly* seated in the carburetor body. Do not force the screw or the screw and carburetor body will be damaged.

3. Back out (counterclockwise) the mixture screw the specified number of turns. Refer to **Table 9**.

4. Adjust the carburetor under load as described in this chapter.

Mixture Screw Adjustment Under Load

The mixture screws are adjusted at the factory using a flow meter. After the adjustment is correctly set, a limiter cap is installed over the mixture screws to prevent tampering with the adjustment. Further mixture adjustment is not necessary unless the position of the screws has been disturbed.

Prior to adjusting the mixture under load, perform the *Initial Mixture Screw Setting* as described in this chapter.

The low- and high-speed mixture adjustment must be performed with the Jet Ski in the water to apply the correct load on the engine.

Low-speed mixture

> *WARNING*
> *The Jet Ski produces enormous thrust at high engine speeds. Make sure at least 100 ft. (30.5 m) are open in front of the watercraft in case the anchor rope fails. Keep clothing, hands and feet away from the jet pump intake and outlet.*

Refer to **Figure 56** (low speed) and **Figure 57** (high speed) for JS440SX (Mikuni carburetor). Refer to **Figure 58** for all other models (Keihin carburetor).

1. Place the Jet Ski in at least 2 ft. (0.6 m) of water.

2. Secure the craft to a stationary object (**Figure 59**) using a strong rope (minimum 500 lb. test) secured to the rear of the craft. Be sure to choose an object that is strong enough to withstand the full thrust of the watercraft.

3. Remove the engine cover or seat and set both mixture screws at their initial settings as described in this chapter. Refer to **Table 9** for initial setting specifications.

4. Start the engine and warm it to normal operating temperature.

5. Check to be sure the anchor rope has no slack and is secure at both ends. Then, quickly accel-erate 2 or 3 times. The engine should accelerate cleanly without hesitation. If the engine stalls, hesitates or backfires, the slow-speed mixture should be adjusted. Turn the mixture screw as necessary until the engine accelerates smoothly without hesitation or stalling.

High-speed mixture

> *WARNING*
> *The Jet Ski pumps a large volume of water and produces enormous thrust at high engine speeds. Make sure at least 100 ft. (30.5 m) are open in front of the watercraft in case the anchor rope fails. Also, provide for at least a 50 ft. (15 m) clear area behind the craft. Keep cloth-*

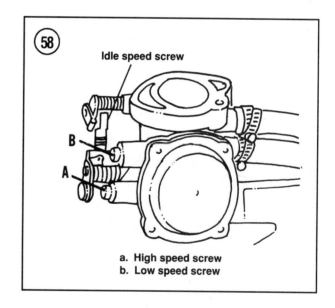

58

Idle speed screw

B

A

a. High speed screw
b. Low speed screw

59

ing, hands and feet away from the jet pump intake and outlet.

1. Make sure the pump intake stays submerged at full throttle by placing a 50 lb. (25 kg) weight on the riding platform.

2. Check to make sure the anchor rope has no slack and is secure at both ends. Then, gradually accelerate to full throttle.

3. Turn the high-speed screw inward (clockwise) until the engine begins to misfire and lose speed.

4. Then, slowly turn the high-speed screw counterclockwise until the highest smooth engine speed is obtained.

CAUTION
To prevent engine damage, do adjust the high-speed mixture leaner than necessary to provide acceptable running characteristics. It is better to set the mixture slightly rich rather than too lean.

5. After adjusting the mixture under load, install new spark plugs and check the mixture by reading the plugs. Ride the watercraft a short distance at full throttle. Then, without decelerating, stop the engine and drift back to the dock. Remove the spark plugs and examine the insulator tip.

   a. If the insulator is white or burned, the fuel mixture is too lean.

   b. Black, smoothe deposits indicate the mixture is too rich.

   c. The mixture is correct if the insulator is light tan or gray.

NOTE
Spark plug readings are only accurate if the correct heat range plugs are used.

Idle Speed

The best idle speed for the Jet Ski is the lowest at which it will run reliably and have just enough thrust to circle back to the rider after a spill. See **Table 8** for the standard idle speed specifications. Experimentation with different idle speeds is the best way to set the idle speed. Turn the idle adjusting screw as required. The idle speed location is identified as follow:

   a. **Figure 60**: JS440SX (Mikuni carburetor).

   b. **Figure 58**: All others (Keihin carburetor).

**Carburetor Synchronization
(JH750 Super Sport Xi and JH750XiR)**

On twin-carburetor equipped models, the throttle valves must open and close at exactly the same time or the engine will idle and accelerate poorly. Use the following procedure to synchronize the carburetors.

1. Remove the carburetors as described in Chapter Seven.

2. Back out the idle speed screw until a small clearance is present between the screw and the throttle shaft lever. See **Figure 61**.

3. Next, turn the idle speed screw inward until the screw just contacts the throttle shaft lever. Then, turn the idle speed screw inward an additional 3/4 turn.

4. Measure the distance from the bottom of the carburetor body casting to the bottom tip of the throttle valve on the front carburetor. See D, **Figure 61**.

5. Now, adjust the synchronizing screw (**Figure 62**) so the throttle valve on the rear carburetor is at the same distance (D, **Figure 61**) as the front carburetor.

6. Reinstall the carburetors (Chapter Seven). Adjust the throttle and choke cables as described in this chapter.

STORAGE

Several months of inactivity can cause many problems and a general deterioration of the watercraft unless the proper care is taken. This is especially true in areas of weather extremes. To prevent these problems, always prepare your Jet Ski carefully for storage (30 days or more).

Storage Preparation

Careful preparation will minimize deterioration and make it easier to restore the watercraft to service after storage. Use the following procedure to properly prepare the watercraft for storage.

> *WARNING*
> *Exhaust gases are poisonous. Do not run the engine in an enclosed areas. Make sure adequate ventilation is provided before starting the engine.*

> *CAUTION*
> *Do not run the engine for more than 15 seconds without cooling water or the rubber components of the exhaust system will be damaged. Furthermore, prolonged running without cooling water will cause serious engine damage. Also, never run the engine at wide-open throttle with the craft out of the water (no load).*

1. Flush the cooling system. See *Cooling System Cleaning* in this chapter.
2. After flushing the cooling system, all water should be cleared from the cooling and exhaust systems. Lift the rear of the watercraft and run the engine for 15 seconds, accelerating the engine several times. Wait 5 minutes to allow the engine to cool, then repeat this Step.
3. Clean the bilge system as described in Chapter Ten.

4. Perform the lubrication as described in this chapter.

> *WARNING*
> *Some fuel may spill during the following steps. Work in a well-ventilated area at least 50 ft. (15 m) from sparks or flames, including gas appliance pilot lights. Do not smoke in the area. Make sure a fire extinguisher rated for gasoline fires is at hand.*

5. Drain all gasoline from the fuel tank, fuel hoses, fuel filter and carburetor(s). Run the engine in 15 second intervals until the fuel in the carburetor(s) is consumed.

6. Remove the carburetor cover and clean the flame arrestor element. See Chapter Seven. Open the choke and throttle and spray WD-40, Bel-Ray 6 in 1 or an equivalent rust inhibiting lubricant into the carburetor bore(s). Reinstall the flame arrestor and cover.

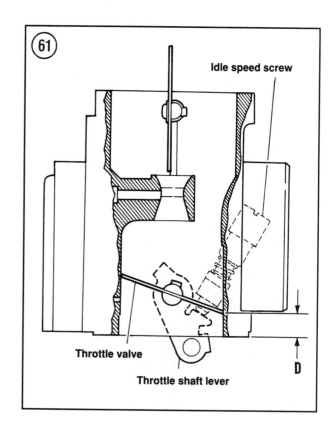

(61)

Idle speed screw

Throttle valve

Throttle shaft lever

D

7. Remove the spark plugs and add an ounce of engine oil to each cylinder. Briefly crank the engine to distribute the oil.

CAUTION
Do not add more than a small amount of oil to the cylinders to prevent a hydraulic lock.

8. Remove the battery and coat the cable terminals with petroleum jelly. See Chapter Eight. Check the battery electrolyte level and fill as necessary with distilled water. Store the battery in an area that will remain above freezing. Recharge the battery once per month.

9. Lightly spray the entire engine with WD-40, Bel-Ray 6 in 1 or an equivalent rust inhibiting lubricant. Wipe off the excess.

10. Wash the watercraft completely using clean, freshwater. Dry the watercraft and drain the water from the bilge. Apply a suitable wax to all painted and polished surfaces.

11. Place the engine cover or seat on the watercraft, but prop it up off the gasket so air can circulate freely inside the engine compartment.

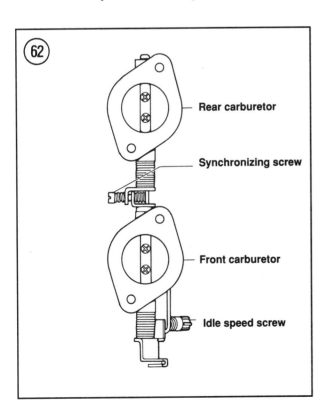

12. Cover the watercraft with a cover that will allow air circulation. Don't use plastic.

Removal From Storage

1. Perform the lubrication procedures as described in this chapter.

2. Install the battery as described in Chapter Eight.

3. Fill the fuel tank with fresh gasoline. Check carefully for fuel leaks.

4. Inspect or replace the fuel filter element, if so equipped.

5. *Oil injection models*: Fill the oil injection tank with a recommended engine oil. If the tank was completely empty or an oil hose is disconnected, bleed the injection system as described in Chapter Nine.

6. Start the engine and run for 15 seconds. Allow the engine to cool for 5 minutes. Repeat this step a few times to check for fuel or exhaust leakage.

WARNING
Exhaust gases are poisonous. Do not run the engine in an enclosed areas. Make sure adequate ventilation is provided before starting the engine.

CAUTION
Do not run the engine for more than 15 seconds without cooling water or the rubber components of the exhaust system will be damaged. Furthermore, prolonged running without cooling water will cause serious engine damage. Also, never run the engine at wide-open throttle with the craft out of the water (no load).

7. Perform an engine tune-up as described in this chapter.

8. Check all rubber bilge and cooling hoses for cracking, deterioration and weathering. Replace any faulty components.

9. Check the steering for proper operation.

10. Check all controls for proper operation.

11. Make sure the on-board fire extinguisher is fully charged.

Table 1 MAINTENANCE SCHEDULE JS440SX AND JS550SX*

Initial 10 hours	• Check all nuts, bolts and fasteners for tightness • Check all hose clamps for tightness
Every 25 hours of operation	• Check all nuts, bolts and fasteners for tightness • Lubricate throttle pulley fitting • Lubricate choke cable fitting at the carburetor • Clean and check spark plug gap; replace plug if necessary • Check battery electrolyte level; check more frequently in hot weather • Lubricate throttle and choke cables • Lubricate drive shaft bearing holder • Lubricate the jet pump bearing • Lubricate the handlebar pivot assembly • Inspect fuel filter (if so equipped); replace if necessary • Clean the fuel sediment bowl and fuel filter screens; replace worn or damaged parts as required • Check the fuel vent and engine oil vent; check valves • Check carburetor cable play, idle speed and mixture; adjust if necessary • Lubricate magneto housing • Flush the bilge line and filter system • Flush cooling system (flush after riding vehicle in salt water) • Inspect and clean flame arrester
Every 100 hours of operation	• Remove impeller blade and inspect for damage; replace if necessary • Decarbonize piston, cylinder head and exhaust system • Check ignition timing; adjust if necessary • Check flywheel nut torque; tighten if necessary • Remove coupling rubber for inspection; replace if necessary • Check carburetor throttle shaft spring and bushing for wear; replace carburetor if necessary

* This Kawasaki factory maintenance schedule should be considered a guide to general maintenance and lubrication intervals. Harder than normal use will naturally dictate more frequent attention to most maintenance items.

Table 2 MAINTENANCE SCHEDULE ALL 650 AND 750 CC MODELS*

Initial 10 hours	• Check all nuts, bolts and fasteners for tightness • Check all hose clamps for tightness
Every 25 hours of operation	• Check all nuts, bolts and fasteners for tightness • Lubricate throttle pulley fitting • Lubricate choke cable fitting at the carburetor • Clean and check spark plug gap; replace if necessary • Check battery electrolyte level; check more frequently in hot weather • Lubricate throttle and choke cables • Lubricate the handlebar pivot assembly • Lubricate steering nozzle and reverse bucket pivots (models so equipped) • Clean the filter screens; replace worn or damaged parts as required

(continued)

Table 2 MAINTENANCE SCHEDULE ALL 650 AND 750 CC MODELS* (continued)

Every 25 hours **of operation (continued)**	• Check the fuel vent and engine oil vent check valves • Check carburetor cable play, idle speed and mixture; adjust if necessary • Flush the bilge line and filter system • Flush cooling system (flush after riding vehicle in saltwater) • Inspect and clean flame arrester

Every 100 hours	• Remove impeller blade and inspect for damage;
	  replace if necessary
	• Decarbonize piston, cylinder head and exhaust system
	• Check ignition timing; adjust if necessary
	• Check flywheel nut torque; tighten if necessary
	• Remove coupling rubber for inspection; replace if necessary
	• Check carburetor throttle shaft spring for wear;
	  replace carburetor if necessary
	• Check steering and trim cables (models so equipped)
	• Inspect and clean anti-siphon valve (JB650 Jet Mate)

* This Kawasaki factory maintenance schedule should be considered a guide to general maintenance and lubrication intervals. Harder than normal use will naturally dictate more frequent attention to most maintenance items.

Table 3 FUEL/OIL PREMIX RATIO

Gasoline	Oil	
U.S. gal.	Oz.	cc
RATIO 24:1		
1	5.3	157
2	10.7	316
3	16	473
4	21.3	630
5	26.7	790
RATIO 50:1		
1	2.6	77
2	5.1	151
3	7.7	228
4	10.2	302
5	12.8	378

Table 4 APPROXIMATE REFILL CAPACITES

Fuel tank	
JS440SX, JS550SX	
Full	13 L (3.4 gal.)
Reserve	3.4 L (0.9 gal.)
JB650 Jet Mate	
Full	30 L (7.9 gal.)
Reserve	4 L (1.0 gal.)

(continued)

Table 4 APPROXIMATE REFILL CAPACITES (continued)

JF650X-2	
Full	16 L (4.23 gal.)
Reserve	3 L (0.8 gal.)
JF650TS	
Full	24 L (6.3 gal.)
Reserve	4 L (1.0 gal.)
JL650SC	
Full	25 L (6.6 gal.)
Reserve	3.2 L (0.8 gal.)
JS650SX	
Full	17.5 L (4.6 gal.)
Reserve	4 L (1.0 gal.)
JH750SS, JH750 Super Sport Xi	
Full	33 L (8.7 gal.)
Reserve	6 L (1.6 gal.)
JS750SX	
Full	16 L (4.2 gal.)
Reserve	2.3 L (0.6 gal.)
JT750ST	
Full	46 L (12.1 gal.)
Reserve	7.5 L (2.0 gal.)
JH750XiR	
Full	33 L (8.7 gal.)
Reserve	6 L (1.6 gal.)
Oil injection tank	
JB650 Jet Mate	5.5 L (5.8 qt.)
JF650X-2	2.7 L (2.8 qt.)
JF650TS	2.3 L (2.4 qt.)
JL650SC	3.0 L (3.2 qt.)
JS650SX	2.8 L (3.0 qt.)
JH750SS, JH750 Super Sport Xi,	
JT750ST, JH750XiR	2.3 L (2.4 qt.)
JS750SX	2.6 L (2.7 qt.)

Table 5 CYLINDER HEAD TIGHTENING TORQUE

	N•m	ft.-lb.
440 and 550 cc	25	18
650 and 750 cc	29	21

Table 6 ENGINE COMPRESSION

Model	kPa	psi
440cc	580-920	84-133
550 cc	930-1420	135-206
650 cc	865-1325	125-192
JS750SX, JH750SS	835-1294	121-188
JT750ST	892-1373	129-199
JH750 Super Sport Xi,		
JH750XiR	890-1370	142-198

Table 7 RECOMMENDED SPARK PLUGS

Model	NGK part No.	Gap mm (in.)
JS440SX	BR7ES	0.7-0.8 (0.028-0.031)
All 650 and 750 cc models	BR8ES	0.7-0.8 (0.028.031)

3

Table 8 IDLE SPEED

Model	In water	Out of water
JS440SX	1700-1900	–
JS550SX	1400-1600	1800-2000
All 650 cc models	1150-1350	1700-1900
All 750 cc models	1150-1350	1600-1800

Table 9 INITIAL MIXTURE SCREW SETTING (TURNS OUT FROM LIGHTLY SEATED)

Model	Low-speed	High-speed
JS440SX	7/8	3/4
JS550SX	1-1/8	5/8
JB650 Jet Mate	1-1/8	3/8
JF650X-2	1	5/8
JF650TS	1-1/8	3/4
JL650SC	5/8	1
JS650SX	1-1/4	5/8
JH750SS	5/8	1
JS750SX	7/8	7/8
JH750 Super Sport Xi	1	3/4
JT750ST	1	1
JH750XiR	1	3/4

Chapter Four

Engine (440 and 550 cc)

The 440 and 550 cc engines are 2-stroke, twin-cylinder marine engines. The engine is mounted inside the hull and is secured to 2 sets of engine mounts with stainless steel fasteners. An aluminum coupler half is mounted onto the end of the crankshaft and to the front of the stainless steel drive shaft. A rubber coupler is used to engage the crankshaft and drive shaft coupler halves. The coupler cushions crankshaft and drive shaft engagement and absorbs small amounts of drive train misalignment resulting from engine vibration and drive shaft runout.

This chapter covers information to provide routine top-end service as well as crankcase disassembly and crankshaft service.

Work on the Jet Ski engine requires considerable mechanical ability. Carefully consider your own capabilities before attempting any operation involving major disassembly of the engine.

Much of the labor charge for dealer repairs involves the removal and disassembly of other parts to reach the defective component. Even if you decide not to attempt the entire engine overhaul after studying the text and illustrations in this chapter, it can be less expensive to perform the preliminary operations yourself, then deliver the engine to your dealership service department or other qualified marine specialist. Since dealership service departments often have lengthy waiting lists for service (especially during the boating season), this practice can reduce the time your unit is down for repair. If much of the preliminary work is already done, your repairs can be scheduled and performed much quicker.

General engine specifications are listed in **Table 1**. **Tables 1-3** are located at the end of this chapter.

ENGINE LUBRICATION

Engine lubrication is provided by the fuel-oil mixture used to power the engine. Refer to Chapter Three for oil and ratio recommendations.

SERVICE PRECAUTIONS

The following precautions should always be closely observed during engine disassembly, inspection and reassembly.

1. Included in the text, is frequent mention of the left- and right-hand side of the engine. This refers to the engine as it is mounted in the hull, with the operator in the normal riding position.

2. Always replace a worn or damaged fastener with one of the same size, type and torque requirement. Stainless steel fasteners are used throughout the watercraft. Be sure to identify each fastener before replacing it. Fastener threads should be lubricated with engine oil, unless otherwise specified. If a tightening specification is not listed in **Table 3**, refer to the torque and fastener information in Chapter One.

3. Use special tools where noted, In some cases, it may be possible to perform the procedure with makeshift tools, but this procedure is not recommended. The use of makeshift tools can damage the components and may cause serious personal injury. Special tools may be purchased through

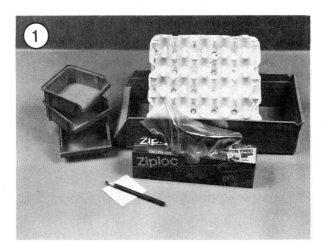

any Jet Ski or Kawasaki dealer. Other tools can be purchased through a tool supplier, or from a motorcycle or automotive accessory store. When purchasing tools from an automotive accessory dealer, remember that all Kawasaki Jet Skis are manufactured with ISO metric fasteners.

4. Before removing the first fastener, obtain a number of boxes, plastic bags and containers to store the parts as they are removed (**Figure 1**). Use masking tape and a permanent, waterproof marking pen to label each part or assembly as required. If your watercraft was purchased second hand and it appears that some of the wiring may have been changed, it may be necessary to label each electrical connection for reference during reassembly.

5. Use a vise with protective jaws to hold parts. If protective jaws are not available, insert wooden blocks on each side of the part(s) before clamping in the vise.

6. Remove and install press-fit parts with an appropriate mandrel, support and hydraulic or arbor press. *Do not* pry, hammer or otherwise force a part on or off.

7. Refer to the tables at the end of the chapter for torque specifications. Proper torque is essential to ensure long life and satisfactory service from marine components.

8. Discard all O-rings, seals and gaskets during disassembly. Apply a small amount of a suitable grease to the inner lips of each oil seal to prevent damage during initial start up.

9. Record the size and location of all shims and thrust washers.

10. If reused, all wearing components must be reinstalled in the same location, facing the same direction from which removed. Always mark wearing components for reference during reassembly.

11. Work in an area with sufficient lighting and room for storage.

12. When it is necessary to work on the bottom of the watercraft, roll it toward the exhaust side of the engine only. To protect the hull finish,

4

support the craft with 2 discarded motorcycle tires, a heavy blanket or towel. See **Figure 2**.

> *CAUTION*
> *Always roll the watercraft toward the exhaust side of the engine. Do not roll the watercraft in a direction that will allow water in the exhaust system to drain into the engine. Water from the exhaust system can enter the cylinders through the exhaust ports and create a hydraulic lock, which can result in serious damage should the engine be started.*

SERIAL NUMBERS

The Jet Ski is identified by hull and engine identification numbers. The hull number is stamped on a plate mounted on the starboard side or at the stern of the craft (**Figure 3**); the exact location varies between models. The engine number is stamped in the crankcase at the front of the engine (**Figure 4**).

Because the manufacturer may make a number of design changes during the production run, hull and engine numbers should always be used when ordering replacement parts. Record the hull and engine identification numbers in the front of this book for reference.

SERVICING ENGINE IN HULL

The following components can be serviced without removing the engine from the hull:

a. Cylinder head.
b. Cylinder.
c. Piston.
d. Carburetor.
e. Magneto.

ENGINE

Engine removal and crankcase separation is required for repair of the "bottom end" (crank-

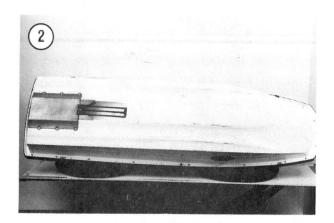

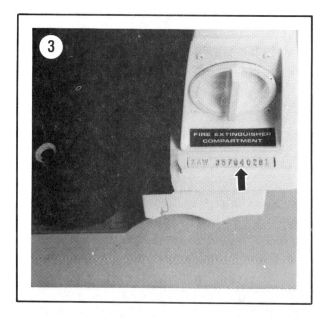

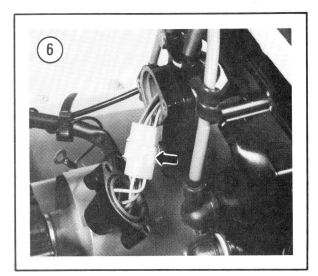

shaft, connecting rods and bearings) and for removal of the drive shaft and bearing box.

Removal

1. Support the Jet Ski on a stand or on wooden boxes so that it is secure.

2. Remove the engine cover.

3. Remove the battery as described in Chapter Eight.

4. Remove the carburetor and exhaust pipe/expansion chamber assembly as described in Chapter Seven. On 550 cc models, remove the sediment bowl assembly as described in Chapter Three.

5. Disconnect the spark plug wires at the plugs. Then, loosen but do not remove the spark plugs.

6. If necessary, the engine top end (cylinder head, pistons, and cylinder) can be removed before removing the engine from the hull. Refer to *Cylinder* in this chapter.

7. Remove the bolts holding the coupler guard to the mounting lugs in the bottom of the hull. Remove the guard.

8. Disconnect the electric box ground wire at the engine.

9. Remove the 2 bolts securing the magneto wiring cap to the electric box (**Figure 5**). Don't loose the O-ring between the cap and the box.

10. Remove the electric box cap and disconnect the 5- or 6-pin connector at the electric box (**Figure 6**).

11. Disconnect the starter cable at the starter motor (**Figure 7**).

12. Loosen the 4 engine bed bolts (**Figure 8**). Note any shims under each of the 4 engine bed corners for installation in their original location. Remove the bolts and shims.

13. Slide the engine to the front to disengage it from the coupler and lift it up out of the hull. Place the engine on a suitable workbench for further disassembly.

4

Installation

1. Examine the engine mounts (**Figure 9**) for cracks or other damage. Check each of the mount threads for damage. Repair, if necessary, with a thread tap. Replace engine mounts as required. Check the engine mounting bolts for looseness and tighten to specification (**Table 3**).

2. Check each of the engine mounting bolts for damage. Replace the bolts as necessary.

3. Remove and clean the bilge filter as described in Chapter Ten.

4. Check inside the hull for tools or other objects that may interfere with engine installation. Make sure all wiring harnesses are properly routed and secured.

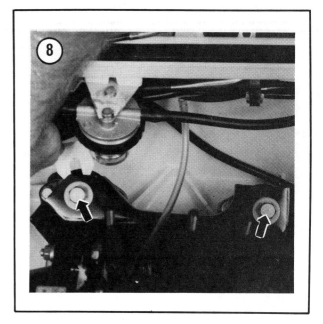

5. Check the rubber coupler (**Figure 10**) for excessive wear or damage. Wear grooves or deterioration of the rubber are signs of wear. Especially check for wear on the round outer knobs. Replace the coupler if any rotational play is present between the engine and the drive shaft coupler halves.

6. Install the rubber coupler. Slide the coupler onto the drive shaft coupler half so that the hollow side of the coupler faces forward.

7. Place the engine inside the hull and slide it backward, meshing the engine and drive shaft coupler halves into the rubber coupler.

8. Loosely install the 4 engine bed bolts and insert the original engine bed shims under the engine bed.

9. Check the coupler alignment as follows:

   a. Tighten the engine bed mounting bolts temporarily.

   b. Hold a straightedge against one side of the coupling halves (**Figure 11**). Push the straightedge against the flat sides of the couplings. If a gap is present between one coupling flat and the straightedge, or if the straightedge rocks as you push it against one coupling flat and then the other, there is *offset* (**Figure 12**) or angular (**Figure 13**) misalignment. Repeat this check with the

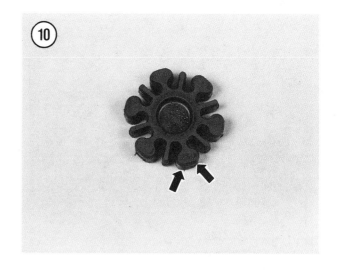

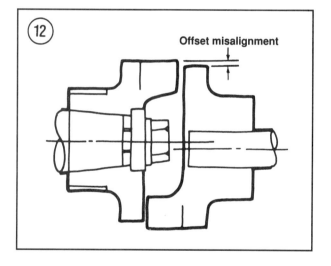

Offset misalignment

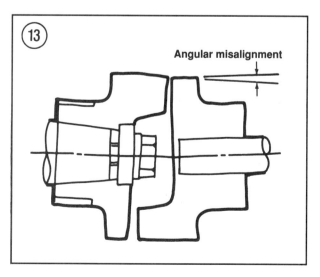

Angular misalignment

straightedge against the other side, and then on top of the coupler halves.

c. To correct *offset* misalignment, loosen the bed bolts and slide the engine left or right. Shim the engine up or down at both the back and front as required to align the coupler halves. Tighten the bed bolts temporarily and recheck alignment with the straightedge.

d. To correct *angular* misalignment, loosen the bed bolts and twist the engine left or right. Shim the engine up or down at the front or rear as required to align the coupler halves. Temporarily tighten the bed bolts and recheck alignment with the straightedge.

NOTE
Shims can be purchased through Jet Ski dealers in thicknesses of 0.2, 0.5, 1.0 and 1.5 mm.

CAUTION
The coupler must be aligned as closely as possible. Any significant degree of misalignment will cause vibration which will result in damage to the rubber coupler and possible damage to the watercraft.

10. With a feeler gauge, measure the gap between the rubber coupler and the front and rear coupler halves. See **Figure 14** and **Figure 15**. The total front and rear gap clearance should not exceed 0.5 mm (0.020 in.). If the clearance is excessive, loosen all engine bed bolts and push the engine toward the front or rear as necessary. Recheck the clearance.

11. After the drive shaft and engine are properly aligned, tighten the engine bed bolts to the specification listed in **Table 3**. Apply Loctite 242 to the bolt threads before tightening them the final time. Each engine bed bolt should be equipped with a lockwasher and a flat washer.

NOTE
To prevent altering the coupler alignment, remove one engine bed bolt at a

time to apply Loctite. Then install the bolt before removing the next one. Repeat until all the bolts are installed. Then, tighten the bolts to specification (Table 3).

12. After tightening the engine bed bolts, re-check the coupler alignment.

13. Apply Loctite 242 to each of the coupler guard housing bolts (**Figure 16**). Then install the coupler guard with the bolts, flat washers and lockwasher. Turn the drive shaft and check that the coupler assembly does not contact the coupler guard.

14. If removed, reinstall the engine top end components as described in this chapter.

15. Install the starter cable on the starter and slide the boot down over the nut.

16. Attach the magneto wiring plug to the electric box connector (**Figure 6**). Lubricate the O-ring and install the cap. Make sure the electric box ground wire is attached to one of the cap bolts.

17. Tie the ground wire, switch loom and magneto loom together with a plastic tie strap.

ENGINE TOP END

The engine "top end" consists of the cylinder head, cylinder housing, pistons, piston rings, piston pins and the connecting rod small-end bearings. See **Figure 17** (440 cc) and **Figure 18** (550 cc) and **Figure 19**.

The engine top end can be serviced without engine removal.

Cylinder Head Removal/Installation

Refer to **Figure 17** and **Figure 19** for this procedure.

CAUTION
To prevent warpage or damage to any component, remove the cylinder head only when the engine is at room temperature.

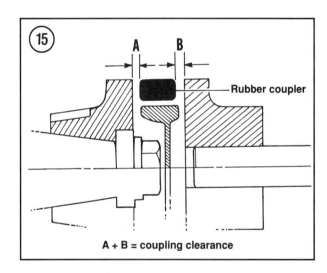

A + B = coupling clearance

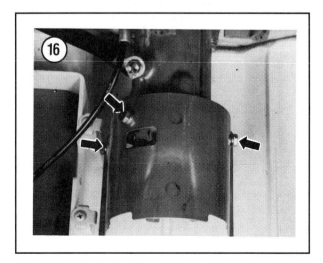

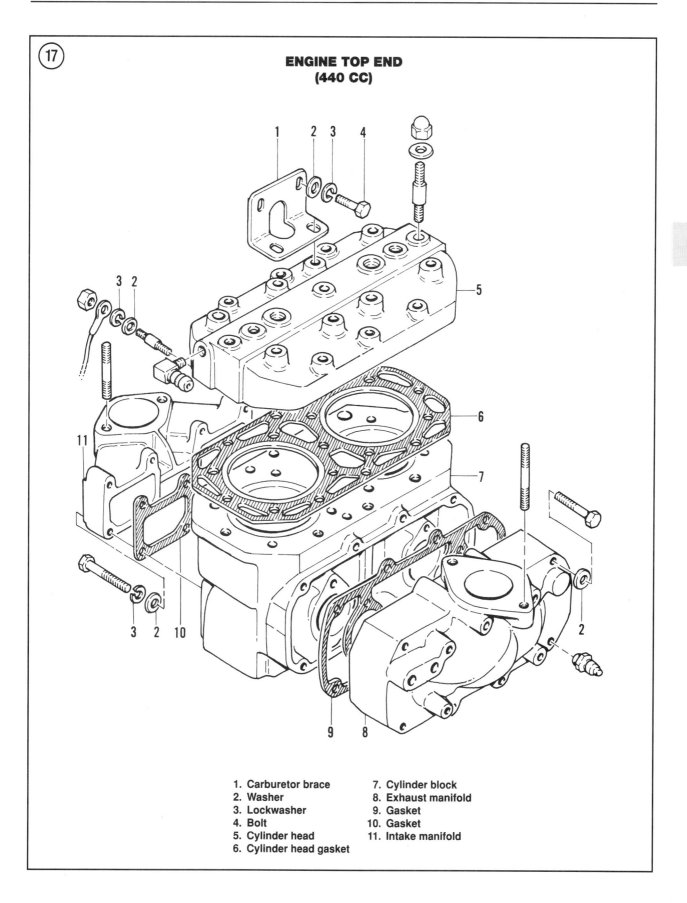

**ENGINE TOP END
(440 CC)**

4

1. Carburetor brace
2. Washer
3. Lockwasher
4. Bolt
5. Cylinder head
6. Cylinder head gasket
7. Cylinder block
8. Exhaust manifold
9. Gasket
10. Gasket
11. Intake manifold

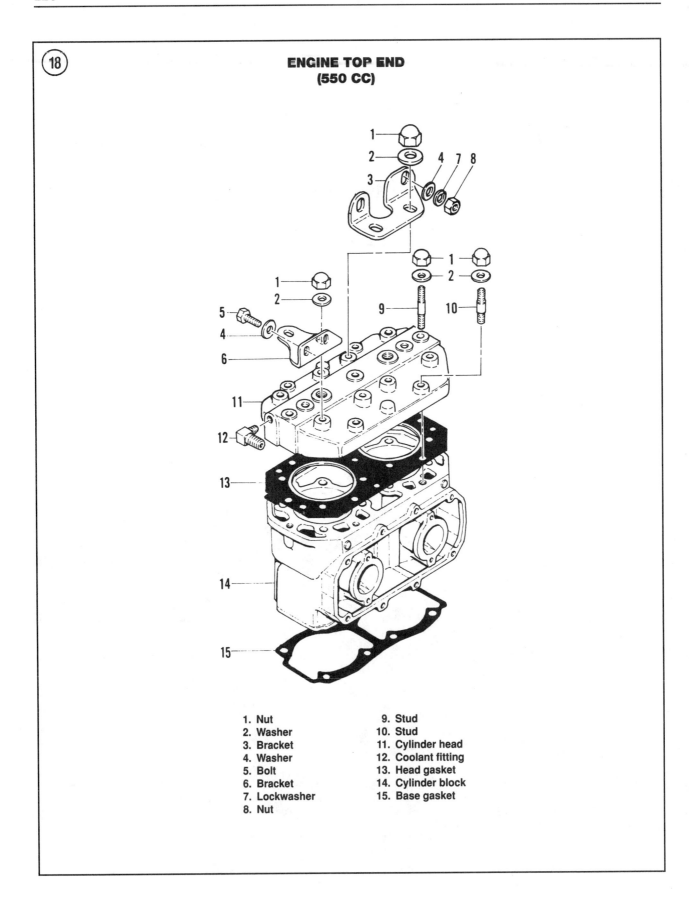

(18) **ENGINE TOP END
(550 CC)**

1. Nut
2. Washer
3. Bracket
4. Washer
5. Bolt
6. Bracket
7. Lockwasher
8. Nut
9. Stud
10. Stud
11. Cylinder head
12. Coolant fitting
13. Head gasket
14. Cylinder block
15. Base gasket

1. Remove the engine cover.

2. Disconnect the negative battery cable at the engine. See **Figure 20**.

3. Remove the bolts holding the exhaust manifold to the cylinder block. Remove the manifold and gasket. If necessary, lightly tap the manifold with a soft-face mallet to loosen it.

4. Disconnect the water hose from the fitting at the front of the cylinder head.

5. Remove the flame arrestor as described in Chapter Seven.

6. Remove the cylinder head nuts and washers in reverse of the sequence shown in **Figure 21**.

7. Dislodge the cylinder head by lightly tapping around its perimeter with a rubber or plastic mallet. Remove the cylinder head (**Figure 22**).

8. Remove and discard the cylinder head gasket.

9. Lay a shop towel over the cylinder block to prevent dirt or other contamination from falling into the cylinders.

10. Inspect the cylinder head as described in this chapter.

4

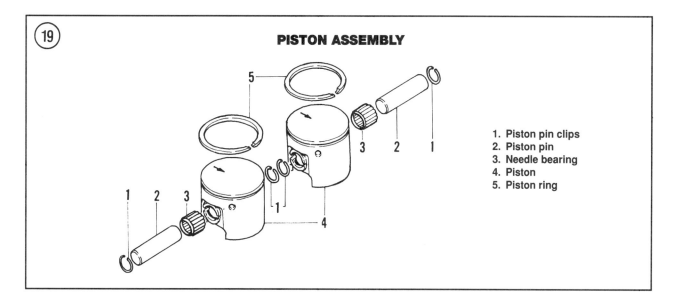

PISTON ASSEMBLY

1. Piston pin clips
2. Piston pin
3. Needle bearing
4. Piston
5. Piston ring

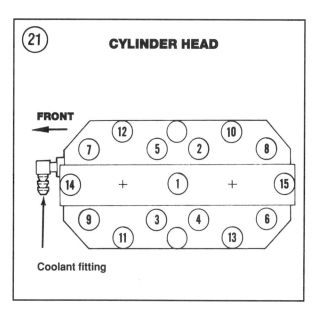

CYLINDER HEAD

FRONT

Coolant fitting

11. Install a new head gasket so the tab on the gasket aligns with the tab on the front side of the cylinder. See **Figure 23**.

12. Install the cylinder head so the coolant fitting faces forward. See **Figure 21**.

13. Install the cylinder head nuts and washers finger-tight.

14. Install the carburetor and flame arrestor mounting brackets.

15. Tighten the cylinder head nuts in 2-3 steps following the sequence shown in **Figure 21**. Tighten the nuts to the specification listed in **Table 3**.

16. Complete flame arrestor installation after tightening the cylinder head nuts.

17. Install the exhaust manifold using a new gasket. Tighten the manifold bolts to the specification listed in **Table 3**.

18. Install the exhaust pipe assembly as described in Chapter Seven.

19. Connect the water hose from the exhaust pipe to the fitting at the front of the cylinder head. Securely clamp the hose.

20. Connect the negative battery at the engine (**Figure 20**).

21. Install the spark plugs and wires.

Inspection

1. Thoroughly clean the cylinder head. Hard deposits can be removed with a wire brush mounted in a drill or with a soft metal scraper. Be careful not to scratch, nick or gouge the aluminum surfaces. Burrs created from improper cleaning can cause preignition and heat erosion.

2. Inspect the spark plug threads in the cylinder head (**Figure 24**) for carbon deposits, cracking or other damage. Any carbon deposits can be removed using a 14 mm spark plug thread chaser (**Figure 25**).

> *NOTE*
> *Lubricate the thread chaser and spark plug threads with kerosene or light oil during Step 2.*

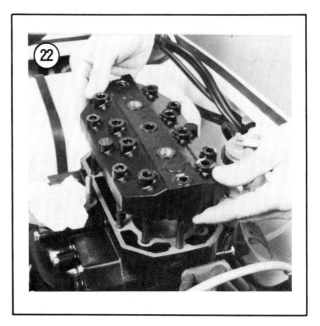

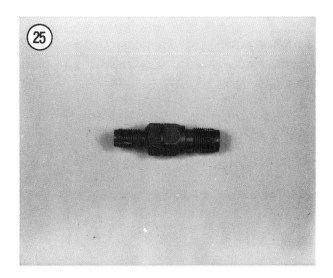

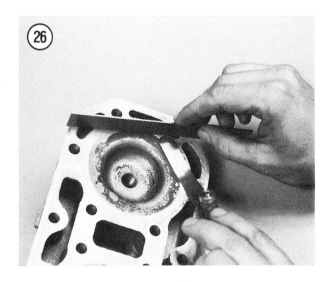

3. Check the water hose fitting on the cylinder head for plugging from silt, sand or sludge.

4. Using a straightedge and feeler gauge, measure the flatness of the cylinder head (**Figure 26**). If the cylinder head is warped in excess of the service limit in **Table 2**, resurface the head as follows:

    a. Tape a piece of 400-600 grit wet emery sandpaper on a piece of thick plate glass or a surface plate.

    b. Slowly resurface the head by moving it in figure-eight patterns on the sandpaper.

    c. Rotate the head several times to avoid removing too much material from one side. Check progress often with the straightedge and feeler gauge.

    d. If the cylinder head cannot be trued using this method, have the head resurfaced by a qualified machine shop. Note that removing material from the cylinder head mating surface will change the compression ratio. Consult with the machinist regarding the amount of material removed from the head.

5. Wash the cylinder head using hot soapy water and rinse thoroughly with clean water.

CYLINDER

All models are equipped with a cast iron cylinder block. Pistons and rings are available in 0.5 mm and 1.00 mm oversize should piston-to-cylinder bore clearance become excessive.

Removal

1. Remove the cylinder head as described in this chapter.

2. Remove the carburetor as described in Chapter Seven.

3. Disconnect the cooling system water supply hose at the bottom rear of the exhaust manifold (**Figure 27**).

4. Disconnect the electric box ground wire at the upper rear intake manifold bolt (**Figure 20**).

5. Loosen the cylinder block by tapping around its perimeter with a rubber or plastic mallet.

6. Remove the cylinder block by lifting it straight up (**Figure 28**).

7. Remove and discard the cylinder block base gasket.

8. Place clean shop towels around the connecting rods to prevent dirt and loose parts from entering the crankcase.

9. Do not remove the manifolds from the cylinder block unless the gaskets are leaking or manifold inspection is necessary.

   a. Remove the intake (**Figure 29**) or exhaust (**Figure 30**) manifold bolts and washers.

   b. Remove the manifold and gaskets from the cylinder block. If necessary, lightly tap the manifold with a soft-face mallet to dislodge it.

Inspection

Cylinder bore measurement requires a precision inside micrometer or bore gauge. If the correct instruments are not available, have the measurements performed by a qualified machine shop.

1. Wash the cylinder block in solvent and then with soap and water to remove any oil and carbon. The cylinder bore must be cleaned thoroughly before attempting the bore measurements.

2. Remove all gasket material from the top and bottom gasket surfaces.

3. Measure the cylinder bore diameter as described under *Piston-To-Cylinder Clearance* in this chapter.

4. If the cylinder is not excessively worn, carefully inspect the cylinder wall for scratches or gouges. If scratches or gouges are present, the cylinder may still require reconditioning.

5. If the cylinder has been rebored or honed, wash the bore in hot soapy water. This is the only way to properly clean the cylinder wall of the fine grit material left from the bore or honing job. After washing the cylinder wall, run a clean white cloth through it. The cylinder wall should show no traces of grit or other debris. If the cloth is dirty, the cylinder wall is not clean enough and must be washed again. After cleaning, lubricate the cylinder bore with clean engine oil to prevent rusting.

CAUTION
A combination of soap and hot water is the only solution recommended to com-

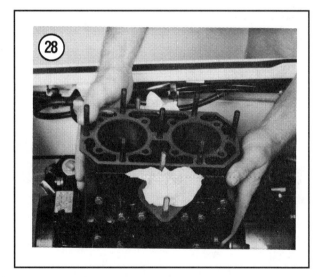

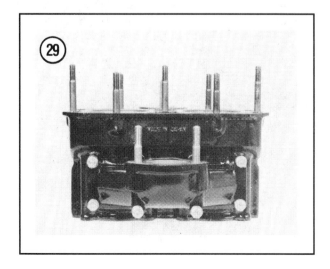

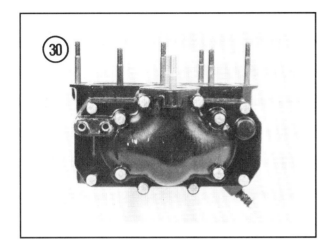

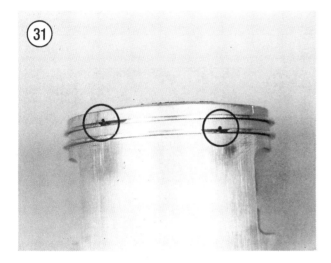

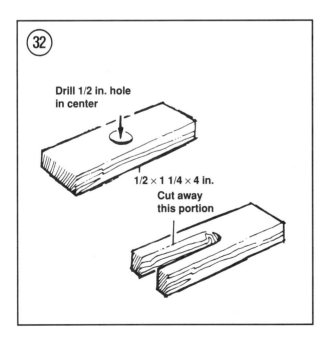

**Drill 1/2 in. hole
in center**

1/2 × 1 1/4 × 4 in.

**Cut away
this portion**

pletely clean the cylinder bore. Solvent or kerosene cannot wash the fine grit out of the cylinder. Grit left in the cylinder will act as a grinding compound and cause premature wear to the new rings.

6. Check the intake and exhaust manifold thread holes for thread damage. If the damage is minor, clean up the threads using the correct size metric tap.

Installation

1. Clean the cylinder bore as described under *Inspection* in this chapter.

2. If removed, install the manifolds as follows:

    a. Install new manifold gaskets.

    b. Install the manifold and secure with the bolts and washers. Apply Loctite 242 to the threads on the manifold bolts before installation.

    c. Tighten the manifold bolts to the specification listed in **Table 3**.

3. Make sure the top surface of the crankcase and the bottom cylinder block surface are clean prior to installation.

4. Install new cylinder base gaskets.

5. Make sure the piston ring end gaps are aligned with the locating pins in the ring grooves (**Figure 31**). Lightly oil the piston rings and the inside of the cylinder bore.

6. Place a piston holding tool under one piston and turn the crankshaft until the piston is firmly against the tool. This will make cylinder block installation easier. You can make such a tool from wood as shown in **Figure 32**.

> *NOTE*
> *If the magneto cover was removed, slip the 2 upper magneto cover bolts into their holes from the rear (cylinder) side of the crankcase flange (**Figure 33**).*

7. Install the cylinder block on the crankcase studs, compressing each piston ring with your

fingers as the cylinder starts to slide over it (**Figure 34**). After one piston is installed in its cylinder, lower the cylinder block and install the opposite piston. If the rings are difficult to compress, use a large hose clamp as an effective ring compressor as shown in **Figure 35**. Make sure the cylinder block is fully seated on the crankcase. Remove the piston holding tool and hose clamps, if used.

8. Connect the cooling system water supply hose at the rear of the exhaust manifold. Tighten the clamp securely.

9. Connect the electric box ground wire to the upper rear intake manifold bolt (**Figure 20**).

10. Install the cylinder head as described in this chapter.

11. Install the exhaust pipe and carburetor as described in Chapter Seven.

12. Follow the *Break-in Procedure* in Chapter Three if the cylinder block was reconditioned or replaced.

PISTON, PISTON PIN AND PISTON RINGS

The piston is made of an aluminum alloy. The piston pin is a precision fit and is held in place by a clip at each end. A caged needle bearing is used on the small end of the connecting rod.

Piston and Piston Ring Removal

1. Remove the cylinder head and cylinder block as described in this chapter.

2. Mark the cylinder number and directional reference on the piston. In addition, keep each piston together with its pin, bearing and rings to avoid intermixing parts.

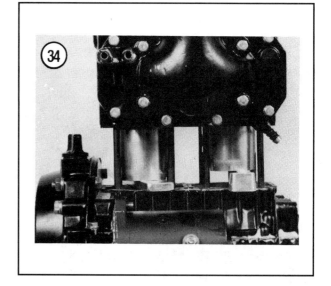

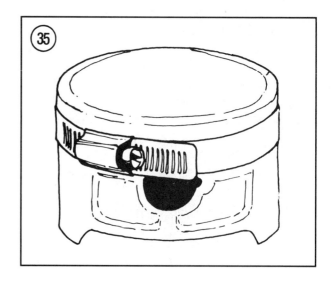

NOTE
Do not confuse rocking motion in Step 3
with the normal sliding motion of the
piston on the piston pin.

3. Before removing the piston, hold the rod tightly and rock the piston as shown in **Figure 36**. Any rocking motion indicates wear on the

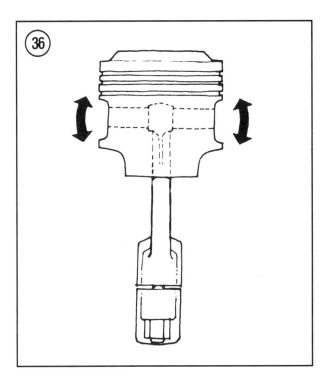

piston pin, needle bearing, piston, or a combination of all three.

NOTE
Wrap a clean shop towel under the piston
to prevent the clips from falling into the
crankcase in Step 4.

CAUTION
Safety glasses must be worn when removing the clips in Step 4.

4. Remove the clips from each side of the piston pin (**Figure 37**) using a small screwdriver or awl. Hold your thumb over one edge of the clip when removing it to prevent it from springing out. Discard the clips.

5. Push the piston pin from the piston using an appropriately size tool.

CAUTION
If the engine has overheated or seized, the piston pin may be very difficult to remove. However, do not drive the piston pin from the piston. Driving the pin will result in piston, needle bearing and connecting rod damage. Instead, remove the piston pin as described in Step 6.

6. If the piston pin will not slide out of the piston, fabricate the tool shown in **Figure 38**. Assemble the tool onto the piston and pull the piston pin out of the piston. Be sure to install a pad between the piston and piece of pipe to prevent scoring the side of the piston.

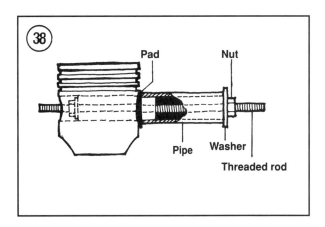

7. Lift the piston off the connecting rod.

8. Remove the needle bearing from the connecting rod (**Figure 39**).

9. Repeat Steps 4-8 for the remaining piston.

10. A single Keystone type piston ring is used on 440 cc models. See **Figure 40**. On 550 cc models a keystone (top) ring and a square (bottom) ring are used. Remove the ring(s) by spreading the ends with your thumbs just enough to slide it up over the piston. See **Figure 41**.

Piston Pin and Needle Bearing Inspection

1. Clean the needle bearing (A, **Figure 42**) in solvent and dry with compressed air. Using a magnifying glass, closely inspect the bearing cage for cracks at the corners of the needle slots (**Figure 43**). Inspect the needle bearing rollers for cracks, pitting, corrosion or other damage. Replace the bearing if any defects are noted.

2. Check the piston pin (B, **Figure 42**) for excessive wear, scoring or chrome flaking. Also check the pin for cracks along the top and side. Replace the piston pin if any defects are noted.

3. Oil the needle bearing and pin, then reinstall them into the piston. Slowly rotate the pin and check for radial and axial play (**Figure 44**). If

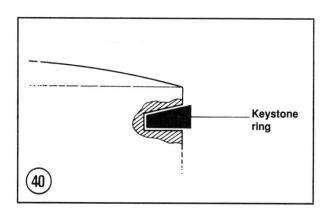

Keystone ring

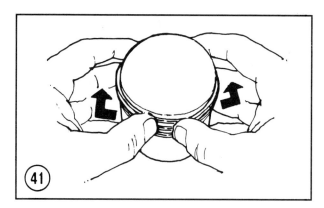

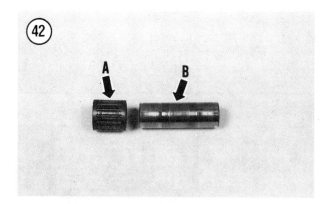

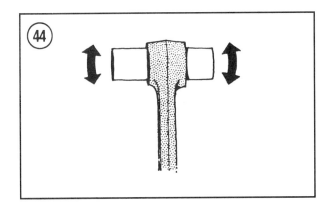

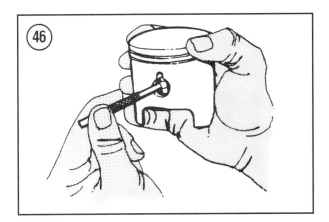

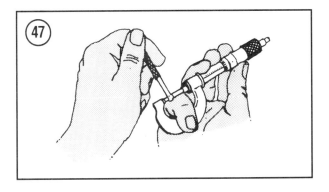

any play is present, the pin and bearing should be replaced, providing the rod bore is in acceptable condition. If the condition of the rod bore is questionable, the old pin and bearing can be checked in a new connecting rod.

4. Measure the piston pin outside diameter with a micrometer (**Figure 45**). Replace the pin if the diameter is less than the service limit in **Table 2**.

5. Measure the piston pin bore in the piston with a small hole gauge (**Figure 46**). Then, measure the gauge with an outside micrometer to determine the bore inside diameter (**Figure 47**). Replace the piston if the bore diameter exceeds the wear limit listed in **Table 2**.

> *CAUTION*
> *If signs of piston seizure and/or overheating is noted, replace the piston pins and bearings.*

4

Connecting Rod Inspection

1. Clean the piston pin bore in the connecting rod, then check it for galling, scratches, excessive wear or other damage. Replace the connecting rod if any of these conditions are noted. Also refer to *Crankshaft Inspection* in this chapter.

2. Check the connecting rod big end bearing play. Rock the connecting rod side-to-side as shown in **Figure 48**. A slight amount of side-to-side play is normal. But, if more than just a slight

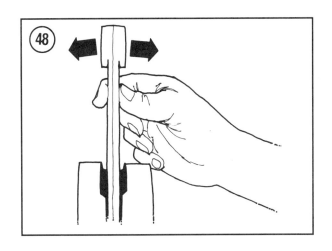

rocking motion is noted, measure the connecting rod side clearance with a feeler gauge (**Figure 49**). If the play exceeds the wear limit listed in **Table 2**, the connecting rod and bearing must be replaced. Refer to *Crankcase Disassembly* in this chapter. Remove the crankshaft and refer it to a Jet Ski Dealer or a qualified machine shop experienced in rebuilding twin-cylinder crankshafts.

3. Measure the inside diameter of the piston pin bore with a small hole gauge (**Figure 50**). Then measure the gauge with an outside micrometer to determine the bore diameter. See **Figure 47**. If the diameter exceeds the wear limit listed in **Table 2**, have the connecting rods and bearings replaced by a Jet Ski dealer or qualified machine shop experienced in twin-cylinder crankshaft rebuilding.

Piston and Ring Inspection

1. Carefully check the piston for cracks at the top edge of the transfer cutaways (**Figure 51**). Replace the piston(s) if any cracks or other damage is noted. Also, check the piston skirt (**Figure 52**) for excessive varnish deposits and clean as required.

2. Check the piston skirt for galling, scoring and abrasion which may indicate piston seizure. If light galling is present, smooth the area with No. 400 emery paper and oil or a fine oilstone. However, if the damage is severe, the pistons must be replaced.

3. Check the piston ring locating pins in the piston ring grooves (**Figure 53**). The locating pins should be tight. If a locating pin is loose, or if cracks are present in the ring groove, the piston must be replaced. A loose locating pin will eventually fall out and cause severe piston and cylinder damage.

4. Check the piston pin retaining clip grooves (**Figure 54**) for cracks or other damage. Replace the pistons if the grooves are not in acceptable condition.

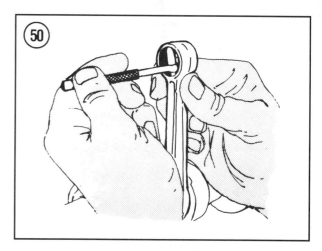

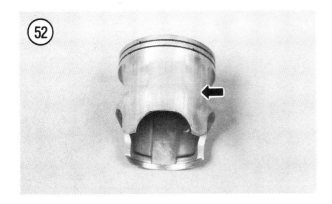

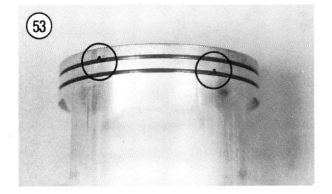

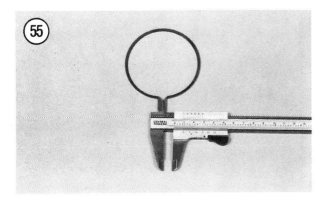

NOTE
Always replace both pistons at the same time. Always install new piston rings when installing new pistons.

NOTE
The correct piston ring end gap must be maintained to ensure peak engine performance. Always check ring end gap at the intervals specified in Chapter Three. Excessive gap reduces engine performance and can cause overheating. Insufficient gap will cause the ring ends to butt together and cause the ring to break.

5. *440 cc models*—Check piston ring tension by measuring the free end gap with a vernier caliper as shown in **Figure 55**. If the free end gap is less than the service limit in **Table 2**, replace the piston ring.

6. Measure piston ring end gap. Place the ring into the bottom of the cylinder approximately 20 mm (3/4 in.) from the cylinder mating surface. Push the ring in with the crown of the piston (**Figure 56**) so the ring is square in the bore. Measure the gap with a flat feeler gauge (**Figure 57**). Compare the gap with the specification in **Table 2**. If the gap exceeds the specified wear limit, the ring should be replaced (providing the cylinder bore is within specification).

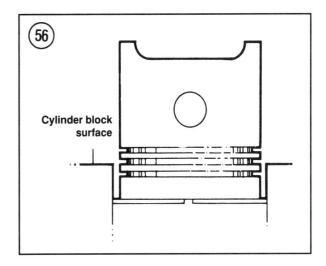

Cylinder block surface

4

NOTE
*Always measure the ring end gap on new piston rings. If the gap is less than specified, first make sure you have the correct piston rings. If the replacement rings are correct, but the end gap is too small, carefully file the ends with a fine-cut file (**Figure 58**).*

7. Carefully remove all carbon deposits from the ring grooves with a broken ring (**Figure 59**). Carefully inspect the ring grooves for burrs, nicks or broken or cracked ring lands.

8. To check piston ring side clearance, first install the ring on its piston. Then, install the piston into its correct cylinder. Position the piston so the ring is visible through the intake or exhaust port. Insert the feeler gauge through the port and measure the clearance between the bottom side of the piston ring (untapered side) and the ring groove. See **Figure 60**. If the side clearance exceeds the wear limit in **Table 2**, measure the ring thickness with a micrometer. Compare the ring thickness with the specification in **Table 2**. If the piston ring thickness is too thin, replace the ring and recheck the side clearance. If the ring thickness is within specification, but the side clearance is still excessive, the piston ring groove in the piston is worn. Replace the pistons.

NOTE
Always replace both pistons at the same time. Always install new piston rings when installing new pistons.

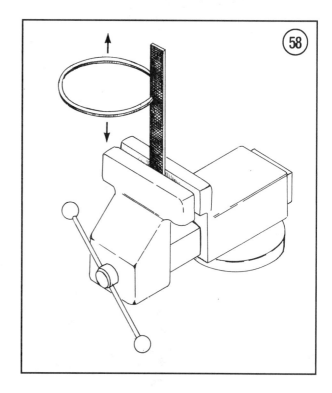

9. Inspect the condition of the piston crown (**Figure 61**). If the piston shows signs of overheating, pitting, erosion or other abnormal conditions, the engine my be experiencing preignition or detonation.

10. Measure the piston outside diameter as described under *Piston-To-Cylinder Clearance* in this chapter.

11. If new piston rings are installed, the cylinders should be honed before engine reassembly. See *Cylinder Honing* in this chapter.

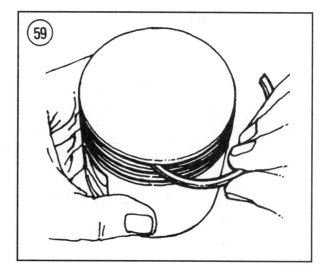

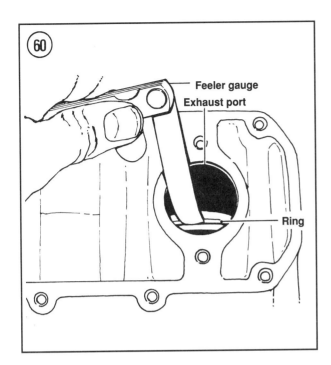

60

Feeler gauge

Exhaust port

Ring

61

Piston-To-Cylinder Clearance

The following procedure requires the use of specialized measuring instruments, such as a cylinder bore gauge, inside micrometer or telescopic gauge. If this equipment is not available, have the measurements performed by a qualified machine shop.

A cylinder bore gauge is generally considered the easiest to use and most accurate instrument for measuring cylinder bore diameter. Therefore, the following procedure is based on the use of a cylinder bore gauge. An inside micrometer or telescopic gauge can be substituted for the bore gauge, however, by skipping the steps which apply to bore gauge set up and calibration.

The cylinder bore gauge consists of a dial indicator (A, **Figure 62**), handle assembly (B), anvils (C) and shims (D). The dial indicator is marked in 0.01 mm increments, from 0.01-10 mm. Anvils are included in 40-80 mm sizes in 5 mm increments. The shims are included in 1 mm, 2 mm and 3 mm sizes.

1A. *440 cc*—Using an outside micrometer, measure the piston diameter at a point approximately 5 mm (3/16 in.) above the bottom of the piston skirt, at a 90° angle to the piston pin (**Figure 63**). If the diameter is not within the specification listed in **Table 2**, replace the pistons.

1B. *550 cc*—Using an outside micrometer, measure the piston diameter at a point approxi-

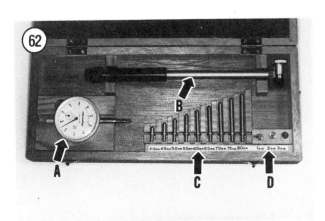

62

A   B   C   D

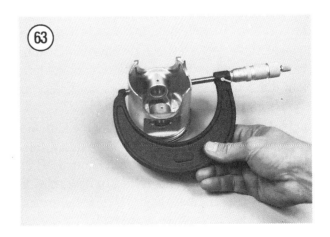

63

mately 9 mm (11/32 in.) from the bottom of the piston skirt, at a 90° angle to the piston pin (**Figure 63**). If the diameter is not within the specification listed in **Table 2**, replace the pistons.

NOTE
Always replace both pistons and piston rings at the same time.

2. Thoroughly clean the cylinder block with solvent, then with detergent and hot water. Make sure all oil, grease and carbon is removed. To prevent incorrect measurements, the cylinder bore must be absolutely clean.

3. Attach the dial indicator to the bore gauge handle assembly.

4. Next, refer to **Table 2** and note the standard bore size for the models being serviced. Then, select an anvil, and shim if necessary, which will add up to the standard bore diameter (or as close as possible). For example, if the standard bore size is 68 mm, assemble the gauge using the 65 mm anvil and the 3 mm shim (68 mm total). Place the shim (**Figure 64**) on the anvil, insert the anvil and shim into the gauge, then install the nut over the anvil and tighten it securely. See **Figure 65** for a fully assembled bore gauge.

NOTE
Although not absolutely necessary, a suitable micrometer stand is very helpful in Steps 5 and 6.

5. Again, note the standard cylinder bore diameter for your model in **Table 2**. Then set the outside micrometer at exactly this dimension, then lock the micrometer thimble. If the standard bore diameter is 68 mm, set the micrometer at *exactly* 68 mm.

6. Next, place the bore gauge in the outside micrometer as shown in **Figure 66**. While firmly holding the gauge in the micrometer, turn the dial indicator face to align the indicator needle with the zero mark. The bore gauge is now calibrated for use.

7. Place the bore gauge into the cylinder bore (**Figure 67**) and slowly rock it back and forth to obtain the highest reading on the indicator. Because zero on the indicator is calibrated to the standard bore diameter, any reading over zero

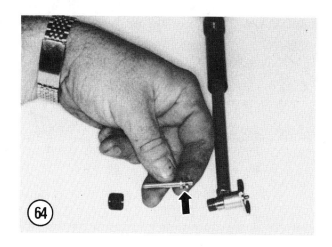

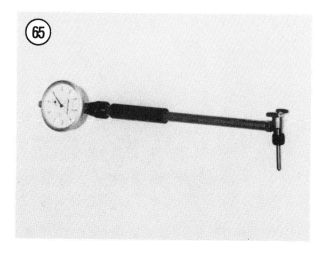

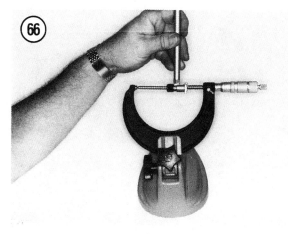

indicates cylinder wear. A perfect cylinder would read zero on the bore gauge indicator.

8. Measure the cylinder bore at the top, center and bottom of the piston ring travel area. Record each measurement. Then, repeat each measurement at 90° to the first measurement. See **Figure 68** for the measurement points. Using these dimensions, calculate cylinder bore out-of-round, taper and wear.

9. If the taper, out-of-round or wear exceeds the specifications listed in **Table 2**, the cylinders must be bored oversize and oversize pistons and rings fitted to the cylinders.

NOTE
Obtain the oversize pistons before the cylinders are bored. The pistons must be measured and the cylinders bored to fit the pistons.

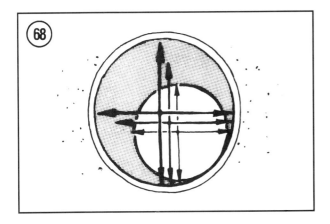

10. Piston-to-cylinder clearance is the difference between the maximum piston diameter and the maximum cylinder diameter. For a used piston and cylinder, subtract the dimension of the piston from the cylinder dimension. If the clearance exceeds the specification in **Table 2**, the cylinders must be bored and oversize pistons and rings installed.

Cylinder Honing

The surface of a well-worn cylinder wall is normally glazed and almost mirror smooth. Cylinder honing, often referred to as deglazing, is required whenever new piston rings are installed in a used cylinder. For new piston rings to seal correctly, the ring face and cylinder wall must establish a smooth compatible surface between them. This is known as "seating in." New piston rings will not properly seat to a cylinder that has not been honed or deglazed. When a cylinder bore is honed, a cross-hatch pattern of small scratches is formed on the cylinder wall. This surface allows the piston rings to break through the oil film on the cylinder wall and create the friction necessary for the rings to seat to the cylinder. Once the seating-in process is complete, very little metal-to-metal contact will occur thereafter.

Honing service can be performed by a dealership service department or a qualified machine shop. If, however, you choose to hone the cylinders yourself, purchase a quality hone and follow the hone manufacturer's instructions closely. Ball or bead-type hones commonly used in automotive service do not work well on 2-stroke engines because the abrasive beads catch in the ports in the cylinders.

CAUTION
*After a cylinder has been reconditioned by boring or honing, the bore must be thoroughly cleaned to remove all material left from the machining operation. Refer to **Inspection** under **Cylinder** in*

this chapter. Improper cleaning will not remove all of the machining residue resulting in rapid piston and piston ring wear.

Piston Installation

1. Apply clean engine oil to the needle bearing and install it in the connecting rod (**Figure 69**).

2. Lubricate the piston pin and slide it into the piston until the end of it extends slightly beyond the inside of the boss (**Figure 70**).

3. Place the piston over the connecting rod. Make sure the arrow on the piston crown is pointing toward the left (exhaust) side of the engine. Align the piston pin with the bearing and push the pin into the piston until it is centered in the piston.

4. Install new piston pin clips (**Figure 71**). Make sure the clips are securely seated in their grooves.

5. Check the installation by rocking the piston back and forth around the pin axis and from side-to-side along the axis. It should rotate freely back and forth but not from side-to-side.

6A. *440 cc*—Install the piston ring by carefully spreading the ends of the ring with your thumbs and slipping the ring over the top of the piston. Make sure the manufacturer's mark on the piston ring faces toward the top of the piston (**Figure 72**).

6B. *550 cc*—Install the piston rings, first the bottom, then the top. Carefully spread the ring with your thumbs and slip it over the top of the piston. Make sure the manufacturer's mark on the rings are facing toward the top of the piston (**Figure 72**).

7. Make sure the rings are seated completely in the grooves, around the entire circumference of the piston. Make sure the ring end gaps are aligned with the ring locating pins. See **Figure 73** (440cc) or **Figure 74** (550 cc).

8. Follow the *Break-in Procedure* in Chapter Three.

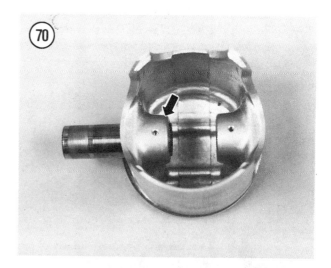

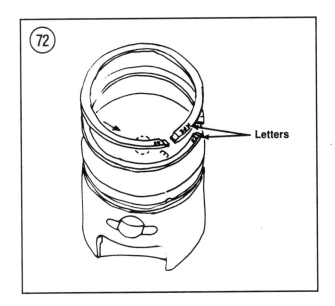

Letters

CRANKCASE AND CRANKSHAFT

Disassembly of the crankcase and removal of the crankshaft requires that the engine be removed from hull. Remove the engine along with the cylinder head, cylinder block and all other attached assemblies as described under *Removal* in this chapter.

The crankcase is made in 2 halves of precision diecast aluminum alloy and is of the "thin-walled" type (**Figure 75**, typical). To avoid damage to the crankcase halves, never hammer or pry on any of the interior or exterior walls. These areas are easily damaged if stressed beyond what they are designed for. They are assembled without a gasket: only gasket sealer is used while dowel pins align the crankcase halves when they are bolted together. The crankcase halves are sold as a matched set only . If one half becomes damaged, both must be replaced.

The procedure which follows is presented as a complete, step-by-step major lower end overhaul.

Special Tools

A few special tools are necessary to split the crankcase assembly. These tools allow easy disassembly and reassembly of the engine without prying or hammering. Remember, the crankcase is easily destroyed using improper disassembly or reassembly techniques. The following tools are required:

   a. Kawasaki coupling holder (part No. T57001-276) or equivalent. See **Figure 76**. The coupling holder is used to remove and install the coupler half installed on the end of the crankshaft or drive shaft. Because the coupler halves are made of cast aluminum, they can be easily damaged by the use of incorrect tools or procedures.

   b. Universal gear puller (**Figure 77**). This tool is used to pull the coupler off of the crankshaft.

4

(75)

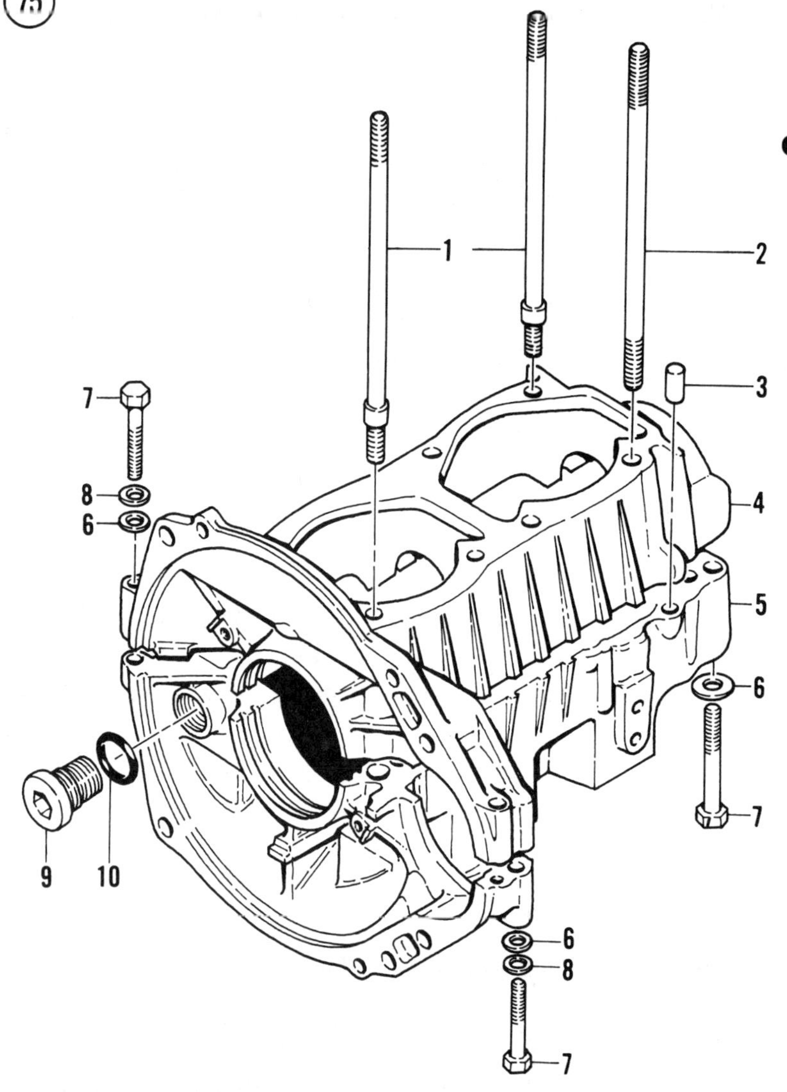

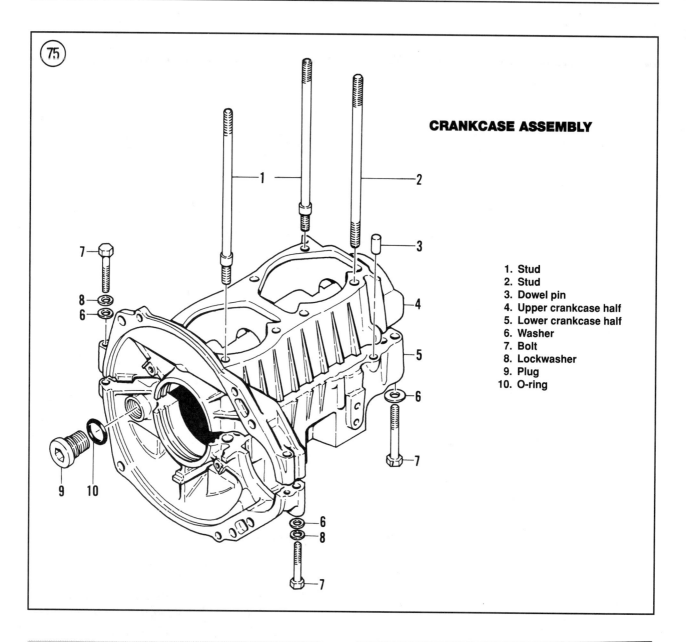

CRANKCASE ASSEMBLY

1. Stud
2. Stud
3. Dowel pin
4. Upper crankcase half
5. Lower crankcase half
6. Washer
7. Bolt
8. Lockwasher
9. Plug
10. O-ring

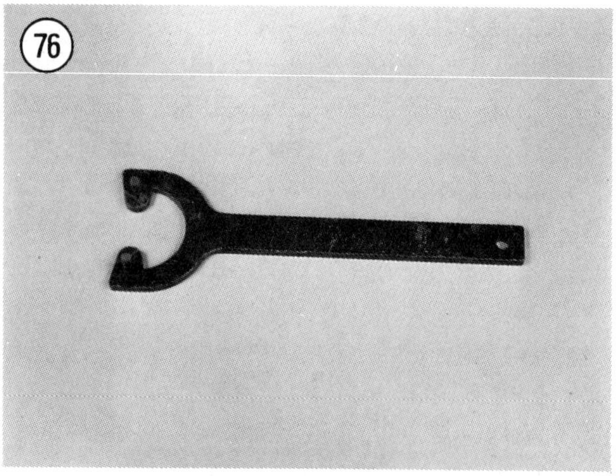

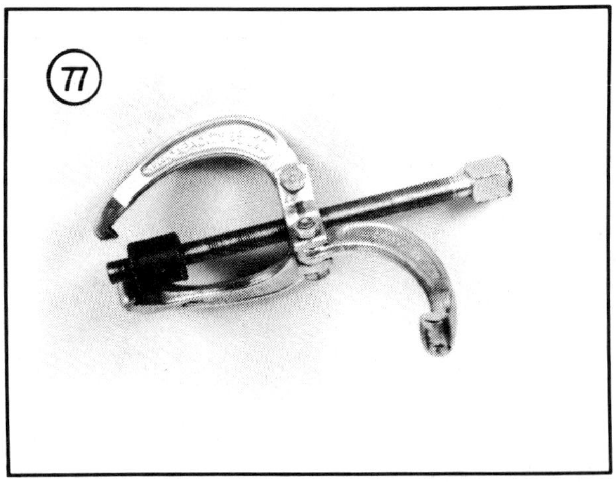

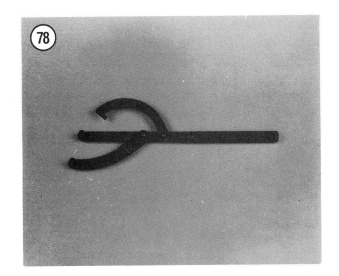

c. Flywheel holder (part No. 57001-306) or equivalent (**Figure 78**). A flywheel holder is required to hold the flywheel from turning while the crankshaft coupler half is removed.

d. A hydraulic or arbor press. A press is necessary to remove and install the crankshaft outside main bearings.

Crankcase Disassembly

This procedure describes the disassembly of the crankcase halves and removal of the crankshaft.

1. Remove the engine from the hull as described in this chapter.

2. Remove the starter motor as described in Chapter Eight.

3. Remove the 4 magneto cover bolts (**Figure 79**). Remove the magneto cover.

4. Hold the flywheel firmly with the flywheel holding tool and unscrew the coupler half from the rear of the crankshaft (**Figure 80**).

5. Remove the flywheel as described in Chapter Eight. Remove the stator plate mounting bolts.

> *NOTE*
> *The bolts removed in Step 6 are secured with thread locking compound and are very tight. If the bolts are difficult to remove, heat the bolts with a torch.*

6. Turn the engine over and remove the bolts holding the engine bed to the engine. Remove the engine bed (**Figure 81**).

> *NOTE*
> *The engine bed mounting bolts have special threads. Do not intermix these bolts with other fasteners.*

7. Loosen the 3 bolts securing the side of the flywheel housing (**Figure 82**). Remove the bolts and washers.

8. Remove the 10 bolts or cap nuts that hold the crankcase halves together. See **Figure 83**.

4

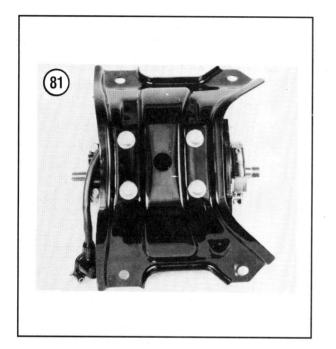

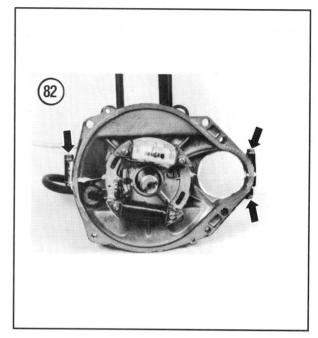

CAUTION
Make sure all fasteners are removed in Step 8. If the case halves are difficult to separate, double-check to be certain all fasteners are removed.

9. Thread an end case bolt 10 mm into the case and lightly tap on it (**Figure 84**) to separate the crankcase halves.

10. After separating the crankcase halves, remove the crankshaft assembly from the lower case half (**Figure 85**). Remove the center oil seal locating pin from the crankcase (**Figure 86**).

11. Remove the 2 dowel pins (**Figure 87**).

CAUTION
*The stator grommet cap (**Figure 88**) is made of brittle plastic. Be very careful to*

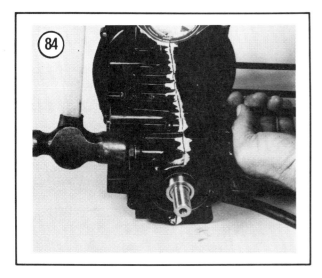

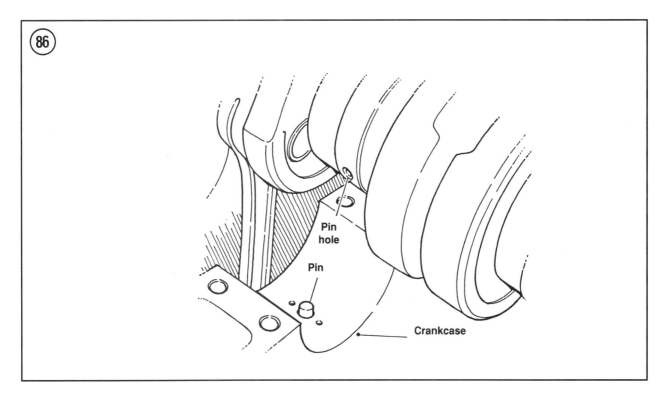

Pin hole

Pin

Crankcase

avoid cracking or damaging this cap, as replacement requires removal of the individual stator wires.

NOTE
The stator leads pass through the lower crankcase half. Do not detach the leads or connectors unless stator replacement is required.

Crankcase Inspection

1. Clean both crankcase halves with cleaning solvent. Thoroughly dry with compressed air. Be sure to remove all traces of old gasket sealant from the mating surfaces.

2. Carefully inspect the case halves for cracks and fractures. Also check the areas around the stiffening ribs, around bearing bosses and threaded holes. If any cracks are found, have them repaired by a shop specializing in the repair of precision aluminum castings. If repair is not possible, replace the crankcase assembly.

3. Check the threaded holes in both crankcase halves for thread damage, dirt or oil accumulation. If necessary, clean or repair the threads with a metric tap. Coat the threads with kerosene or an aluminum tap fluid before use.

4. Check the cylinder studs on both crankcase halves for thread damage. If necessary, replace the studs as described under *Stud Replacement* in Chapter One.

Crankshaft Inspection

Refer to **Figure 89**. The crankshaft and connecting rod assembly is pressed together. The bearings on the ends of the crankshaft can be replaced with little trouble, but the 2 center main bearings require crankshaft disassembly for their replacement. This is a job which should be entrusted to a shop equipped and experienced in this type of service.

1. Check connecting rod big-end radial clearance with a dial indicator. Position the indicator

so its plunger rests against the connecting rod small end (**Figure 90**). Then support the crankshaft and push the connecting rod up and then down. Note the dial indicator gauge movement each time the connecting rod is moved. The difference in the 2 gauge readings is the radial clearance. Repeat this procedure on the remaining rod. If the clearance exceeds the service limit listed in **Table 2**, the crankshaft must be rebuilt using new connecting rods and bearings.

NOTE
The connecting rod radial clearance can also be checked roughly by hand. Support the crankshaft with the crank pin at

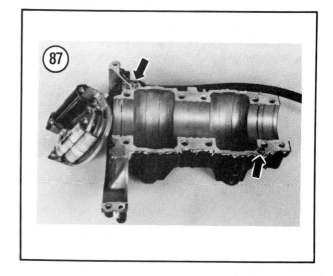

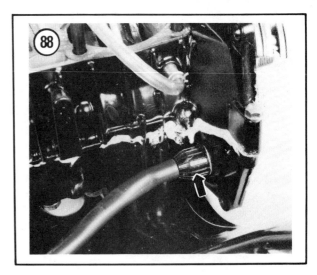

CRANKSHAFT ASSEMBLY

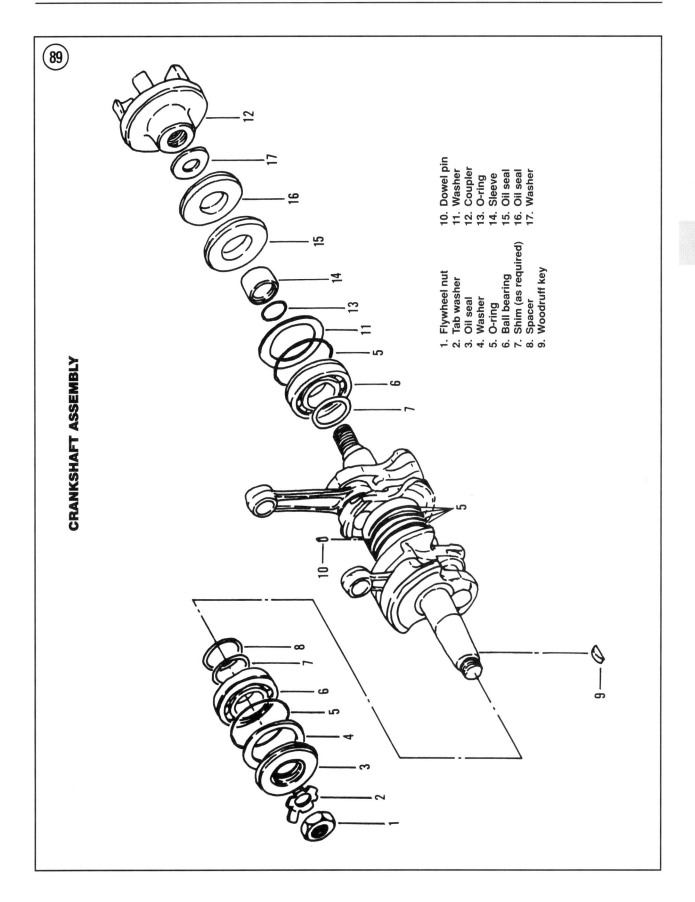

1. Flywheel nut
2. Tab washer
3. Oil seal
4. Washer
5. O-ring
6. Ball bearing
7. Shim (as required)
8. Spacer
9. Woodruff key
10. Dowel pin
11. Washer
12. Coupler
13. O-ring
14. Sleeve
15. Oil seal
16. Oil seal
17. Washer

4

the top. Grasp the connecting rod firmly and pull upward on it. Tap sharply on the top of the rod with your free hand. If the bearing and crank pin are in good condition, there should be no movement felt in the rod. If movement if noted, or if there is a sharp metallic click, the bearing may be unserviceable and the crankshaft should be replaced or rebuilt.

2. Check connecting rod big-end side clearance with a feeler gauge. Insert the gauge between the crankshaft and the connecting rod as shown in **Figure 91**. If the clearance exceeds the service limit (**Table 2**), the crankshaft assembly must be rebuilt or replaced.

3. Carefully examine the condition of the crankshaft ball bearings. Clean the bearings in solvent and roll each bearing around by hand. Check that it turns quietly and smoothly with no rough spots. There also should be no apparent radial play. Defective end bearings can be replaced individually. The 2 center bearings must be replaced together. Lightly oil the bearings after inspection to prevent rust formation.

4. Support the crankshaft by placing it on 2 V-blocks at the points shown in **Figure 92**. Then check crankshaft runout with a dial indicator at the 4 points shown (**Figure 92**). Turn the crankshaft slowly and note the indicator reading. The maximum difference recorded is the crankshaft runout at that position. If the runout at any position exceeds the service limit in **Table 2**, the crankshaft must be trued or rebuilt.

Main Bearing Replacement and Shim Selection

All models are equipped with cutaway crank wheels (**Figure 89**). When new outer crankshaft bearings are installed, they must be shimmed to achieve the proper crankshaft end play at the front and rear of the crankshaft to avoid rapid crankshaft and bearing wear. Shims of different thicknesses are available from your Jet Ski dealer. A press is required to remove and install the bearings.

1. Measure the outside width across the forward cylinder's crank wheels (A, **Figure 93**). If distance A is 49.66-49.87 mm (1.955-1.963 in.), no shim is necessary. If distance A is less than 49.66 mm (1.955 in.), add shims as required to total

4

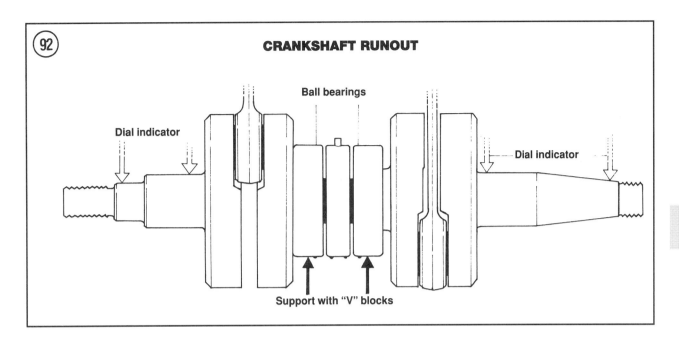

CRANKSHAFT RUNOUT

Dial indicator

Ball bearings

Dial indicator

Support with "V" blocks

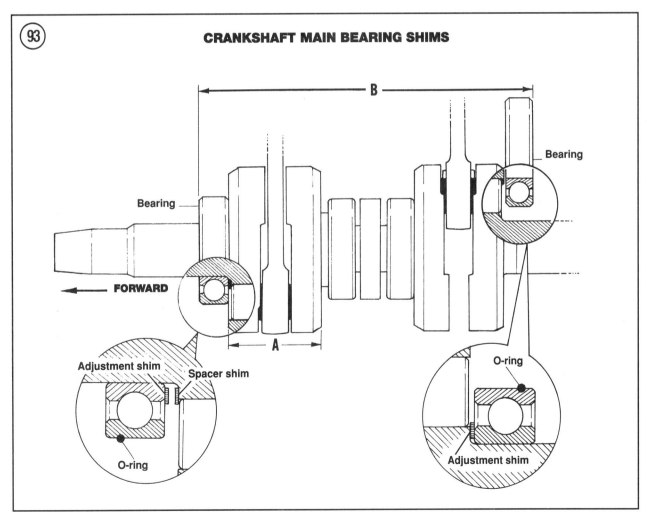

CRANKSHAFT MAIN BEARING SHIMS

B

Bearing

Bearing

FORWARD

A

Adjustment shim

Spacer shim

O-ring

O-ring

Adjustment shim

49.75 ±0.1 mm (1.959 ±0.004 in.) when the bearing is installed. Slide the wide 1 mm thick spacer on the crankshaft against the forward crank wheel, then add the selected shim and install the front bearing with its O-ring groove toward the front.

2. Temporarily hold the rear bearing against the back cylinder's rear crank wheel and measure the distance between the forward face of the front bearing and the rear face of the rear bearing (B, **Figure 93**). If distance B is 188.77-188.98 mm (7.432-7.440 in.), no shim is necessary. If distance is less than 188.77 mm (7.432 in.), add shims as required to total 188.82 ±0.05 mm (7.434 ±0.002 in.) when the bearing is installed. Place the selected shim against the rear crank wheel and install the rear bearing with its O-ring groove toward the rear.

Crankshaft Installation

Refer to **Figure 89** for this procedure.

1. Lubricate the crankshaft bearings with engine oil and check that each bearing's O-ring is in position (**Figure 94**).

2. Install the washer in front of the front main bearing. Lubricate the front oil seal thoroughly with high-temperature grease. Install the seal on the front of the crankshaft with its open side facing toward the connecting rod (**Figure 95**).

3. Install the washer to the rear of the rear main bearing.

4. Install the O-ring and sleeve on the rear of the crankshaft (**Figure 96**). The recessed end of the sleeve faces the O-ring.

5. Lubricate the 2 rear oil seals with high-temperature grease. Slide the oil seals on the crankshaft as shown in **Figure 97**.

6. Fit the locating pin into the pin hole in the upper crankcase (**Figure 86**).

7. Align the crankshaft with the upper crankcase half and install the crankshaft (**Figure 98**). Be certain to align the center seal pin hole with the locating pin in the case (**Figure 86**).

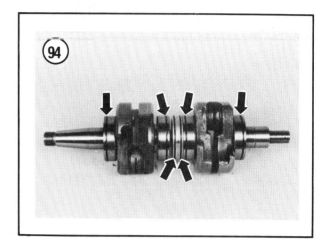

8. Check that the bearing stop rings, the bearing O-rings and the oil seal ridges are located in their respective crankcase grooves (**Figure 99**).

Crankcase Assembly

NOTE
The magneto stator leads pass through the lower crankcase half. If the stator or its leads are removed, refer to Chapter Eight for reassembly.

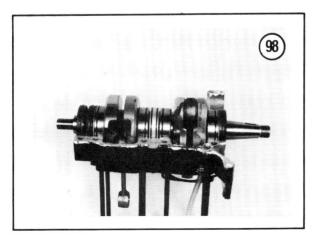

1. Install the crankshaft in the upper crankcase half as described in this chapter.

2. Install the 2 dowel pins into the lower crankcase half (**Figure 100**).

3. Make sure the crankcase mating surfaces are completely clean and free of oil, grease or other contamination. Apply a light coat of Kawasaki Bond part No. 92104-1003 (or equivalent) on the mating surfaces of one case half.

4. Place the lower case half onto the upper case half, fitting the magneto stator over the end of the crankshaft. Check the mating surfaces all the

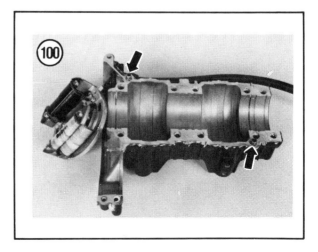

way around the case halves to make sure they are even and that the locating pins are properly positioned.

5. Apply a light coat of engine oil on the crankcase stud or bolt threads before installation.

6. Loosely install the 10 bolts or cap nuts and washers. Tighten the fasteners gradually, in the sequence shown in **Figure 101**, to the specification in **Table 3**.

CAUTION
While tightening the crankcase fasteners, make frequent checks to ensure the crankshaft turns freely and the crankshaft locat-

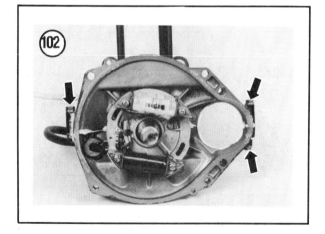

ing rings and crankcase dowel pins fit into place in the case halves.

7. Be certain the crankshaft turns freely, without unusual noise or binding. If binding or noise is noted, separate the crankcase halves and determine the cause before proceeding with assembly.

8. Install the 3 magneto housing bolts and washers (**Figure 102**). Tighten the bolts securely.

9. Position the magneto stator so the mark on the stator plate aligns with the parting line of the crankcase halves (**Figure 103**). Apply a small amount of silicone sealant on the threads of the 2 mounting screws (**Figure 104**), slip on their lockwashers and flat washers, then install and tighten them securely.

10. Set the engine bed in position with the right-angle mounting tabs at the front and the 45° sloping tabs at the rear (**Figure 105**). Apply Loctite 242 (or equivalent thread locking compound) to the threads of the 4 engine bed bolts. Then install the bolts with their lockwashers and flat washers and tighten to the specification in **Table 3**.

NOTE
The engine bed bolts have a special thread pitch. Be certain the correct bolts are used to mount the engine bed.

11. Place the engine right side up.

12. Install the flywheel as described in Chapter Eight.

13. Install the engine coupler half by first coating the rear crankshaft threads with grease. Install the coupler washer and hold the flywheel firmly using a flywheel holding tool (part No. 57001-306) as the coupler is screwed onto the crankshaft. See **Figure 106**. Tighten the coupler to the specification in **Table 3**.

14. Install the starter as described in Chapter Eight.

15. Reassemble the engine top end as described in this chapter.

16. Install the engine into the hull as described in this chapter.

Table 1 GENERAL ENGINE SPECIFICATIONS (440 AND 550 CC MODELS)

Engine type	2-stroke vertical twin
Displacement	
440 cc	436 cc (24.3 cu. in.)
550 cc	530 cc (32.3 cu. in.)
Bore	
440 cc	68 mm (2.68 in.)
550 cc	75 mm (2.95 in.)
Stroke	60 mm (2.36 in.)
Compression ratio	
440 cc	6:1
550 cc	7.2:1
Ignition	Magneto CDI
Lubrication	Gasoline/oil premix 50:1 ratio

Table 2 ENGINE SERVICE SPECIFICATIONS (440 AND 550 CC MODELS)

Item	Specification mm (in.)	Wear limit mm (in.)
Cylinder head warpage limit		0.25 (0.010)
Cylinder bore diameter		
440 cc	68.075-68.094 (2.68-2.681)	68.17 (2.684)
550 cc	75.075-75.090 (2.955-2.956)	75.18 (2.96)
Maximum cylinder bore taper & out-of-round	–	0.05 (0.0020)
Piston diameter		
440 cc	67.96-67.98 (2.675-2.676)	67.79 (2.669)
550 cc	74.985-75.000 (2.952-2.953)	74.835 (2.946)
Piston-to-cylinder clearance		
440 cc	0.095-0.133 (0.0037-0.0052)	–
550 cc	0.075-0.105 (0.0029-0.0041)	–
Piston pin bore diameter (in piston)	15.999-16.005 (0.6298-0.6301)	16.08 (0.6331)
Piston pin outside diameter	15.994-16.000 (0.6297-0.6299)	–
Piston pin clearance	0.001-0.011 (0.00004-0.0004)	–
Piston ring free end gap		
440 cc	8.0 (0.31)	5.0 (0.20)
Piston ring end gap		
440 cc	0.2-0.4 (0.008-0.016)	0.7 (0.027)

(continued)

Table 2 ENGINE SERVICE SPECIFICATIONS (440 AND 550 CC MODELS) (continued)

Item	Specification mm (in.)	Wear limit mm (in.)
Piston ring end gap (continued)		
550 cc		
Top & bottom rings	0.20-0.35 (0.008-0.014)	0.65 (0.026)
Piston ring side clearance		
440 cc	0.12-0.17 (0.005-0.007)	0.22 (0.009)
550 cc		
Bottom ring	1.23-1.25 (0.048-0.049)	1.33 (0.052)
Piston ring thickness		
440 cc	1.97-1.99 (0.077-0.078)	1.92 (0.076)
550 cc		
Bottom ring	1.17-1.19 (0.046-0.047)	1.10 (0.043)
Connecting rod		
Small end inside diameter	20.003-20.014 (0.7875-0.7879)	20.05 (0.7894)
Connecting rod side		
clearance	0.4-0.5 (0.016-0.020)	0.7 (0.027)
Connecting rod radial		
clearance	0.02-0.03 (0.0008-0.0012)	0.08 (0.0031)
Maximum connecting rod		
twist or bend	0-0.05 (0.0020)	0.2 (0.008)
Crankshaft runout	0-0.05 (0-0.0020)	0.08 (0.0031)
Crankshaft end play	0-0.75 (0.029)	—

Table 3 ENGINE TIGHTENING TORQUES (440 AND 550 CC MODELS)

Fastener	N·m	in.-lb.	ft.-lb.
Coupler half (engine side)	54	—	40
Crankcase			
Large bolts	29	—	21
Small bolts	7.8	69	5.7
Cylinder head bolts	25	—	18
Engine bed bolts	37	—	27
Engine mounting bolts	16	—	12
Engine mount damper bolts	22	—	16
Exhaust manifold bolts	7.8	69	5.7
Exhaust pipe flange bolts	16	—	12
Exhaust pipe/expansion chamber junction bolts (550 cc)	16	—	12

(continued)

Table 3 ENGINE TIGHTENING TORQUES (440 AND 550 CC MODELS) (continued)

Fastener	N·m	in.-lb.	ft.-lb.
Expansion chamber bracket bolts	16	–	12
Flywheel cover bolts	16	–	12
Flywheel nut	165	–	122
Spark plugs	27	–	20
Starter mounting bolts			
440 cc			
Front	16	–	12
Rear	6	53	4.4
550 cc			
Front & rear	16	–	12

Chapter Five

Engine (650 and 750 CC)

The 650 and 750 engines are 2-stroke, twin-cylinder, marine engines. The engine is mounted inside the hull and is secured to 2 sets of engine mounts with stainless steel bolts. An aluminum coupler half is mounted on the end of the crankshaft and to the front of the stainless steel drive shaft. A rubber coupler is used to engage the crankshaft and drive shaft couplings. The coupler cushions crankshaft and drive shaft engagement and absorbs small amounts of drive train misalignment resulting from engine vibration and drive shaft runout.

This chapter covers information to provide routine top-end service as well as crankcase disassembly and crankshaft service.

Work on the Jet Ski engine requires considerable mechanical ability. You should carefully consider your own capabilities before attempting any operation involving major disassembly of the engine.

Much of the labor charge for dealer repairs involves the removal and disassembly of other parts to reach the defective component. Even if you decide not to attempt the entire engine overhaul after studying the text and illustrations in this chapter, it can be less expensive to perform the preliminary operations yourself, then deliver the engine to your dealership service department or other qualified marine specialist. Since dealership service departments often have lengthy waiting lists for service (especially during the boating season), this practice can reduce the time your unit is down for repair. If much of the preliminary work is already done, your repairs can be scheduled and performed much quicker.

General engine specifications are listed in **Table 1**. **Tables 1-3** are located at the end of this chapter.

ENGINE LUBRICATION

All models (except JH750XiR) are equipped with an oil injection system. Refer to Chapter Nine for a complete description of the injection system.

SERVICE PRECAUTIONS

The following precautions should always be closely observed during engine disassembly, inspection and reassembly.

1. Included in the text, there is frequent mention of the left- and right-hand side of the engine. This refers to the engine as it is mounted in the hull, with the operator in the normal riding position.

2. Always replace a worn or damaged fastener with one of the same size, type and torque requirement. Stainless steel fasteners are used throughout the watercraft. Be sure to identify each fastener before replacing it. Fastener threads should be lubricated with engine oil, unless otherwise specified. If a tightening specification is not listed in **Table 3**, refer to the torque and fastener information in Chapter One.

3. Use special tools where noted, In some cases, it may be possible to perform the procedure with makeshift tools, but this procedure is not recommended. The use of makeshift tools can damage the components and may cause serious personal injury. Special tools may be purchased through any Jet Ski or Kawasaki dealer. Other tools can be purchased through a tool supplier, or from a motorcycle or automotive accessory store. When purchasing tools from an automotive accessory dealer, remember that all Kawasaki Jet Skis are manufactured with ISO metric fasteners.

4. Before removing the first fastener, obtain a number of boxes, plastic bags and containers to store the parts as they are removed (**Figure 1**). Use masking tape and a permanent, waterproof marking pen to label each part or assembly as required. If your watercraft was purchased second hand and it appears that some of the wiring may have been changed, it may be necessary to label each electrical connection for reference during reassembly.

5. Use a vise with protective jaws to hold parts. If protective jaws are not available, insert wooden blocks on each side of the part(s) before clamping in the vise.

6. Remove and install press-fit parts with an appropriate mandrel, support and hydraulic or arbor press. *Do not* pry, hammer or otherwise force a part on or off.

7. Refer to the tables at the end of the chapter for torque specifications. Proper torque is essential to ensure long life and satisfactory service from marine components.

8. Discard all O-rings, seals and gaskets during disassembly. Apply a small amount of a suitable grease to the inner lips of each oil seal to prevent damage during initial start up.

9. Record the size and location of all shims and thrust washers.

10. If reused, all wearing components must be reinstalled in the same location, facing the same

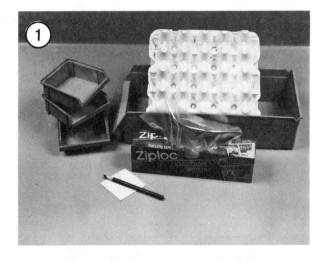

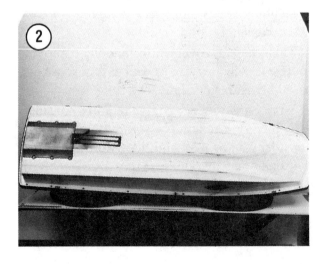

direction from which removed. Always mark wearing components for reference during reassembly.

11. Work in an area with sufficient lighting and room for storage.

12. When it is necessary to work on the bottom of the watercraft, roll it toward the exhaust side of the engine only. To protect the hull finish, support the craft with 2 discarded motorcycle tires, a heavy blanket or towel. See **Figure 2**.

CAUTION
Always roll the watercraft toward the exhaust side of the engine. Do not roll the watercraft in a direction that will allow water in the exhaust system to drain into

the engine. Water from the exhaust system can enter the cylinders through the exhaust ports and create a hydraulic lock, which can result in serious damage should the engine be started.

SERIAL NUMBERS

The Jet Ski is identified by hull and engine identification numbers. The hull number is stamped on a plate mounted on the starboard side or at the stern of the craft (**Figure 3**); the exact location varies between models. The engine number is stamped in the crankcase at the front of the engine (**Figure 4**).

Because the manufacturer may make a number of design changes during the production run, hull and engine numbers should always be used when ordering replacement parts. Record the hull and engine identification numbers in the front of this book for reference.

SERVICING THE ENGINE IN THE HULL

Some of the components can be serviced while the engine is mounted in the hull:

   a. Cylinder head.

   b. Cylinder.

   c. Pistons.

   d. Carburetor(s).

   f. Oil pump.

   g. Starter motor.

ENGINE

Engine removal and crankcase separation is required for repair of the "bottom end" (crankshaft, connecting rods and bearings) and for removal of the drive shaft.

5

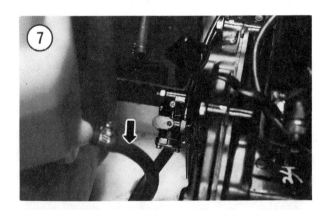

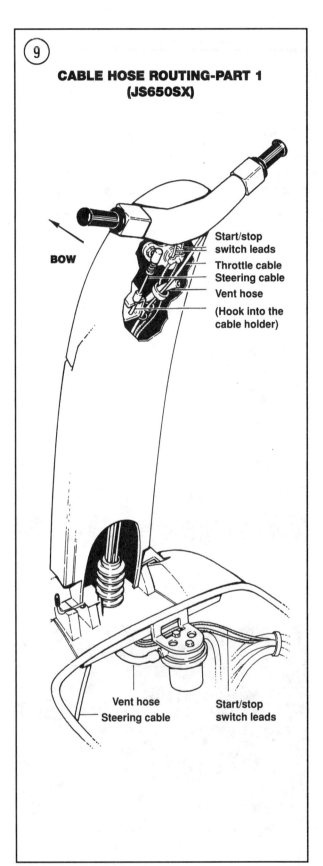

**CABLE HOSE ROUTING-PART 1
(JS650SX)**

BOW

Start/stop
switch leads
Throttle cable
Steering cable
Vent hose
(Hook into the
cable holder)

Vent hose   Start/stop
Steering cable   switch leads

Removal
(650 cc Models)

NOTE
This sequence of steps represents a typical engine removal procedure. Where differences between models occur, they are specifically noted.

1. Securely support the watercraft on a stand or on wooden boxes.
2. Remove the engine cover.
3. Remove the battery as described in Chapter Eight.
4. Disconnect the spark plug wires from the spark plugs (**Figure 5**). Loosen, but do not remove the spark plugs.
5. Remove the carburetor and exhaust pipe/expansion chamber assembly as described in Chapter Seven.

6. Drain or pump all the fuel from the fuel tank (A, **Figure 6**) into a suitable container. If necessary, siphon the fuel using a length of hose.
7. Disconnect the oil delivery hose (**Figure 7**) from the engine. Plug the hose to prevent oil leakage or contamination. On all models except JF650TS, JL650SC and JB650 Jet Mate, remove the oil tank (B, **Figure 6**) as described in Chapter Nine and the fuel tank (**Figure 8**) as described in Chapter Seven.
8A. *JF650X-2*—Perform the following:
   a. Remove the electric box as described in Chapter Eight.
   b. Open the box and disconnect the 2 yellow stator wires at their bullet connectors.
8B. *JS650SX*—Refer to **Figures 9-11** and perform the following:
   a. Remove the bolts securing the igniter and remove it (**Figure 12**).

5

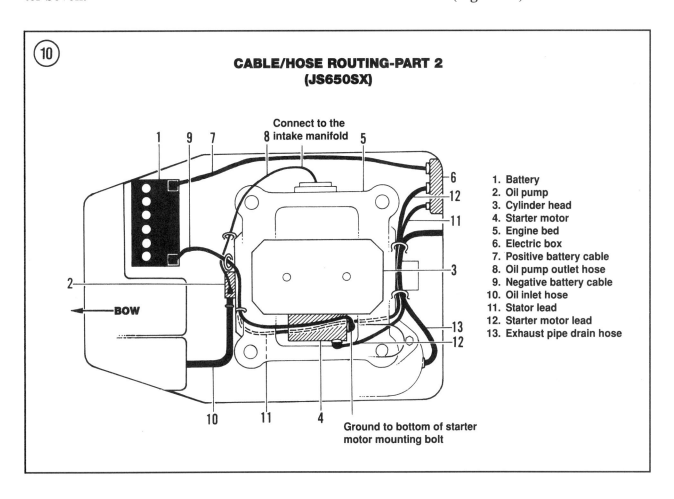

CABLE/HOSE ROUTING-PART 2
(JS650SX)

Connect to the intake manifold

BOW

Ground to bottom of starter motor mounting bolt

1. Battery
2. Oil pump
3. Cylinder head
4. Starter motor
5. Engine bed
6. Electric box
7. Positive battery cable
8. Oil pump outlet hose
9. Negative battery cable
10. Oil inlet hose
11. Stator lead
12. Starter motor lead
13. Exhaust pipe drain hose

⑪

CABLE/HOSE ROUTING-PART 3
(JS650SX)

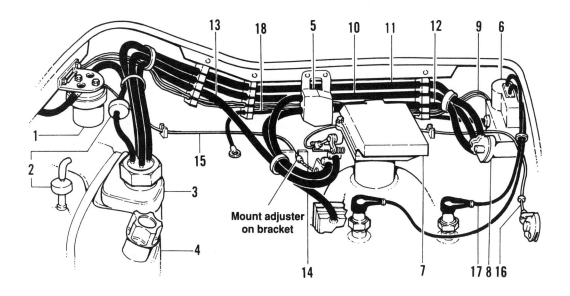

Mount adjuster
on bracket

1. Sediment bowl
2. Check valve
3. Fuel tank
4. Oil tank
5. Fuel pump
6. CDI igniter
7. Flame arrester
8. Fuel valve
9. Start/stop leads
10. Fuel hose (ON)
11. Fuel hose (RES)
12. Fuel hose (MAIN)
13. Fuel hose (RETURN)
14. Pulse hose
15. Throttle cable
16. Choke cable
17. Spark plug leads
18. Positive battery cable

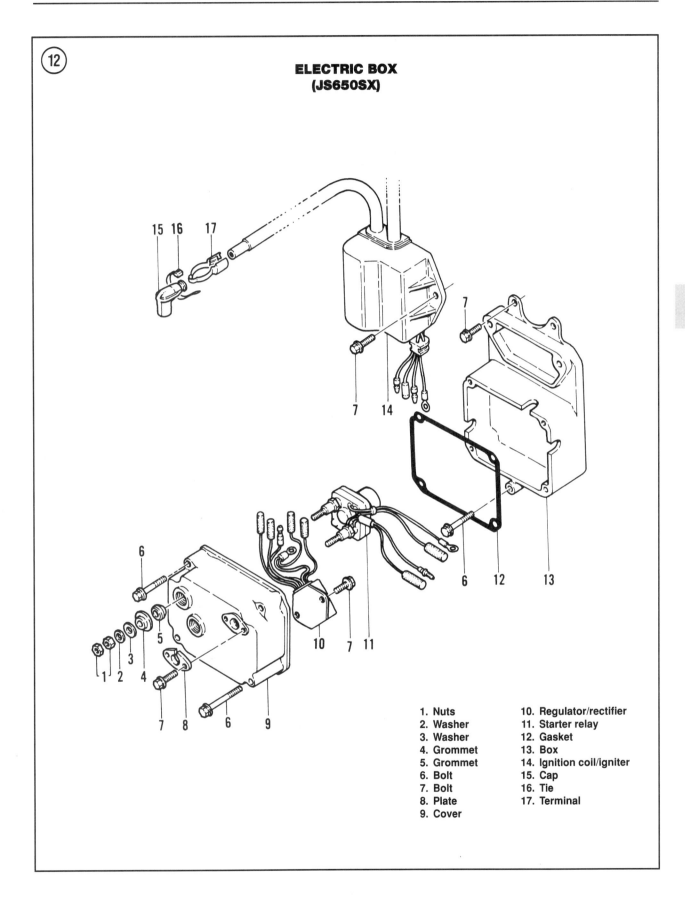

ELECTRIC BOX
(JS650SX)

5

1. Nuts
2. Washer
3. Washer
4. Grommet
5. Grommet
6. Bolt
7. Bolt
8. Plate
9. Cover
10. Regulator/rectifier
11. Starter relay
12. Gasket
13. Box
14. Ignition coil/igniter
15. Cap
16. Tie
17. Terminal

b. Remove the bolts (**Figure 13**) securing the electric box to the back of the engine compartment. See **Figure 14**.

c. Remove the grommet cap bolts (**Figure 14**) and pull the stator wires out of the electric box. Disconnect the wires.

d. Disconnect the battery cable at the electric box.

e. Disconnect the starter cable at the electric box.

8C. *JF650TS and JB650 Jet Mate*—Perform the following:

a. Remove the bolts securing the top to the electric case and remove the top.

b. Disconnect the stator wires.

c. Remove the bolts securing the stator wire holder to the side of the electric box and withdraw the stator wires from the box.

8D. *JL650SC*—Perform the following:

a. Remove the bolts securing the top to the electric box and remove the top.

b. Remove the bolts securing the electric box and mounting bracket. Remove the electric box and bracket.

9. Disconnect the pulse hose from the engine (**Figure 15**).

10. Disconnect the inlet cooling hose at the exhaust manifold.

11. If necessary, the engine top end (cylinder head, pistons and cylinder block) can be removed before removing the engine from the hull. Refer to *Cylinder* in this chapter.

12. Remove the magneto breather plug, if necessary, for additional room to maneuver the engine.

13. Remove the bolts holding the coupling guard to the mounting lugs in the bottom of the hull. Remove the guard.

14. Loosen the 4 engine bed bolts (**Figure 16**). Note any shims under each of the 4 engine bed corners so that the shims can be reinstalled in their original location. Remove the bolts and shims.

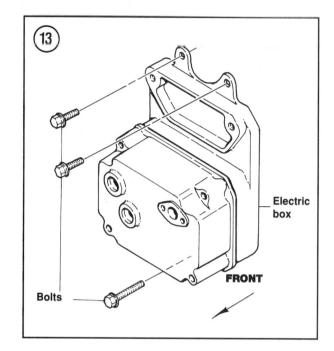

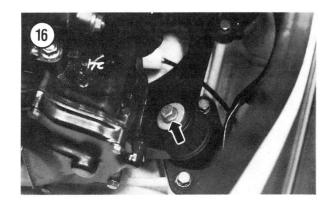

15. Make sure all wiring and hoses have been disconnected from the engine.

16. Slide the engine to the front of the hull to disengage it from the coupler. Lift the engine out of the hull and place it on a suitable workbench.

Installation
(650 cc Models)

1. Inspect the engine mounts for cracks or other damage. Check the threads on each of the mounts for damage and repair if necessary. Check the engine mount fasteners for looseness and tighten to specification (**Table 3**) as required.

2. Check the engine mounting bolts for cracks, damaged threads or other defects. Replace the bolts as required.

3. Remove and clean the bilge filter as described in Chapter Ten.

4. Check inside the hull for tools or other objects that could interfere with engine installation. Make sure all wiring harnesses are properly routed and secured.

5. Check the rubber coupler (**Figure 17**) for excessive wear or damage. Wear grooves or deterioration of the rubber are signs of wear. Especially check for wear on the round outer knobs. Replace the coupler if any rotational play is present between the engine and drive shaft coupler halves.

6. Install the rubber coupler. Slide the coupler on the drive shaft coupling so the hollow side of the coupler faces forward.

7. JS650SX: Make sure the 3 rubber dampers are installed in the bottom of the hull.

8. Place the engine into the hull and slide it backward, meshing the engine and drive shaft coupler halves into the rubber coupler (**Figure 18**).

9. Loosely install the 4 engine bed bolts and insert the original engine bed shims under the engine bed. On JS650SX models, install the cable bracket on the right front engine mount as shown in **Figure 19**.

5

10A. *JF650X-2, JL650SC and JS650SX*—The magneto cover has a vertical alignment mark cast in the cover (A, **Figure 20**) and an arrow is present on a raised boss cast in the bottom of the hull (B). After the engine is installed in the hull, make sure the mark on the magneto cover aligns with the arrow on the bottom of the hull. If not, reposition the engine.

10B. *JF650TS*—Place a suitable straightedge on the cylinder head, against the inside of the 2 projections on the head. See **Figure 21**. If the engine is properly positioned, the straightedge will align with the projection on the deck plate (**Figure 21**). If not, reposition the engine as necessary.

11. Rock the engine back and forth and side-to-side. If the engine rocks at all, a gap is present between the engine bed and mounting dampers. Install an appropriate size shim where necessary to eliminate the gap. Shims are available in 0.3, 0.5, 1.0 and 1.5 mm thicknesses.

12. After the engine is properly shimmed, apply Loctite 242 to the engine bed bolt threads. Install and tighten the bolts to specification (**Table 3**).

13. Apply Loctite 242 to the threads of the coupler guard housing bolts. Then, install the coupler guard with the bolts, flat washers and lockwashers. Turn the drive shaft and check that the coupler assembly does not contact the coupler guard.

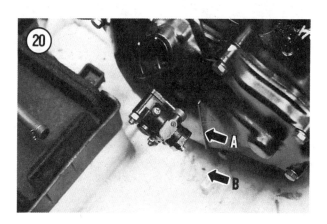

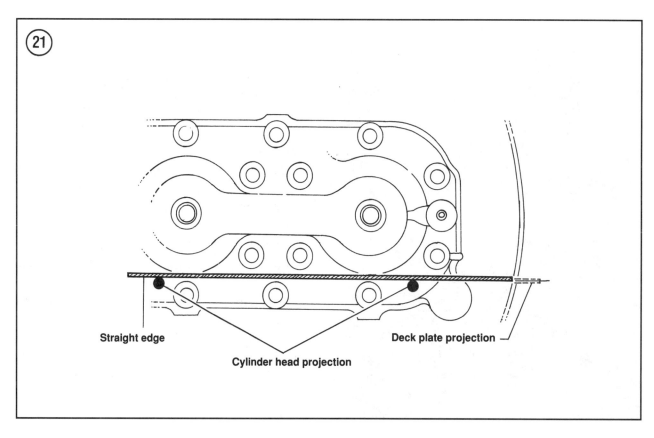

Straight edge

Cylinder head projection

Deck plate projection

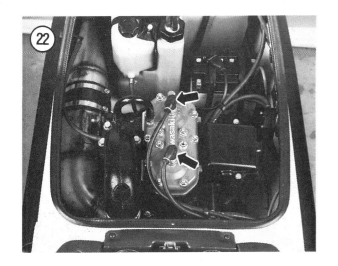

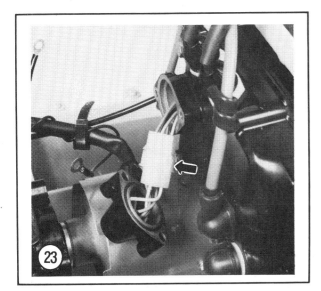

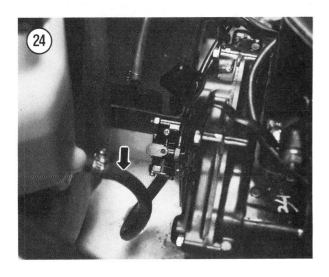

14. Reverse Steps 1-12 under *Removal (650 cc Models)* to complete installation. Note the following points:

    a. JS650SX: Apply a thin coat of silicone sealant to both sides of a *new* electric box gasket. Also, apply Loctite 242 to the threads of the electric box fasteners.

    b. Bleed the oil injection system as described in Chapter Nine.

Removal
(750 cc Models)

NOTE
This sequence of steps represents a typical engine removal procedure. Where differences between models occur, they are specifically noted.

1. Securely support the watercraft on a stand or wooden boxes.

2. Remove the engine cover or seat.

3. Remove the battery as described in Chapter Eight.

4. Disconnect the spark plug leads (**Figure 22**) from the spark plugs. Loosen, but do not remove the spark plugs.

5A. *JS750SX*—Remove the electric box connector and disconnect the magneto wire connectors (**Figure 23**, typical).

5B. *Except JS750SX*—Remove the electric box as described in Chapter Eight.

6. Remove the carburetor(s) and exhaust pipe/expansion chamber assembly as described in Chapter Seven.

7. Remove the air intake cover and flame arrestor. See Chapter Seven.

8. Disconnect the oil delivery hose from the oil pump. See **Figure 24**). Plug the hose to prevent leakage and contamination.

9. On JH750 Super Sport Xi and JH750XiR models, remove the throttle and choke cable mounting bracket from the front of the cylinder head.

5

10. Disconnect the inlet cooling hose from its fitting on the cylinder head (**Figure 25**, typical).

11. On JT750ST models, remove the oil pump from the engine as described in Chapter Nine.

12. Remove the fasteners holding the coupling cover to the mounting bracket in the bottom of the hull. Remove the cover.

13. Remove the red starter motor cable from the starter motor terminal. If necessary, remove the black ground wire from the engine.

14. Make sure all wiring and hoses are disconnected from the engine.

15. Loosen the 4 engine bed bolts (**Figure 26**, typical). Note any shims under each of the engine bed bolts for reference during installation. Remove the bolts and shims.

16. Slide the engine forward to disengage the couplings. Then, lift the engine out of the hull. Place the engine on a suitable workbench.

Installation
(750 cc Models)

1. Inspect the engine mounts for cracks or other damage. Check each mount for thread damage. Repair thread damage or replace mount(s) as necessary. Inspect each engine mounting fastener for looseness. Tighten the bolts to specification (**Table 3**).

2. Check each engine mounting bolt for thread damage or other damage. Replace the bolts as necessary.

3. Remove and clean the bilge filter as described in Chapter Ten.

4. Check inside the hull for tools or other objects that could interfere with engine installation. Make sure all wiring harnesses are properly routed and secured.

5. Inspect the rubber coupler (**Figure 27**) for excessive wear, deterioration or damage. Especially check the round outer knobs for excessive wear. Replace the coupler if any rotational play is present between the engine and drive shaft coupler halves.

6. Install the rubber coupler. Slide the coupler on the drive shaft coupling so the hollow side of the coupler is facing forward.

7. Install the engine into the hull. Slide the engine backward, engaging the engine and drive shaft coupling halves into the rubber coupler (**Figure 28**).

8. Loosely install the 4 engine bed bolts and insert the original engine bed shim(s) under the engine bed.

NOTE
On models without engine alignment marks, engine alignment is achieved by visually aligning the engine and drive shaft couplers.

9. On some models, the magneto cover has a vertical alignment mark cast into the cover. See A, **Figure 29**. In addition, an arrow is present on a raised boss cast into the bottom of the hull (B, **Figure 29**). The engine is correctly aligned when the mark on the magneto cover is aligned with the arrow on the bottom of the hull. If necessary,

reposition the engine to obtain the specified alignment.

10. Rock the engine back and forth and side-to-side. If the engine rocks at all, a gap is present between the engine bed and mounting dampers. Install an appropriate size shim where necessary to eliminate the gap. Shims are available in 0.3, 0.5, 1.0 and 1.5 mm thicknesses.

11. After the engine is properly shimmed, apply Loctite 242 to the engine bed bolt threads. Install and tighten the bolts to specification (**Table 3**).

12. Apply Loctite 242 to the threads of the coupling guard housing bolts. Then, install the coupler guard with the bolts, flat washers and lockwashers. Turn the drive shaft and check that the coupler assembly does not contact the coupler guard.

13. Next, reverse Steps 1-13 under *Removal (750 cc Models)* to complete installation. Bleed the oil injection system as described in Chapter Nine.

ENGINE TOP END

The engine "top end" consists of the cylinder head, cylinder housing, pistons, piston rings, piston pins and the connecting rod small-end bearings. See **Figure 30**. The engine top end can generally be serviced without removing the engine from the hull.

Cylinder Head Removal/Installation

Refer to **Figure 30** for this procedure.

CAUTION
To prevent warpage and damage to any component, remove the cylinder head only when the engine is cool (room temperature).

1. Remove the engine cover or seat.

2. If the engine is mounted in the hull, perform the following:

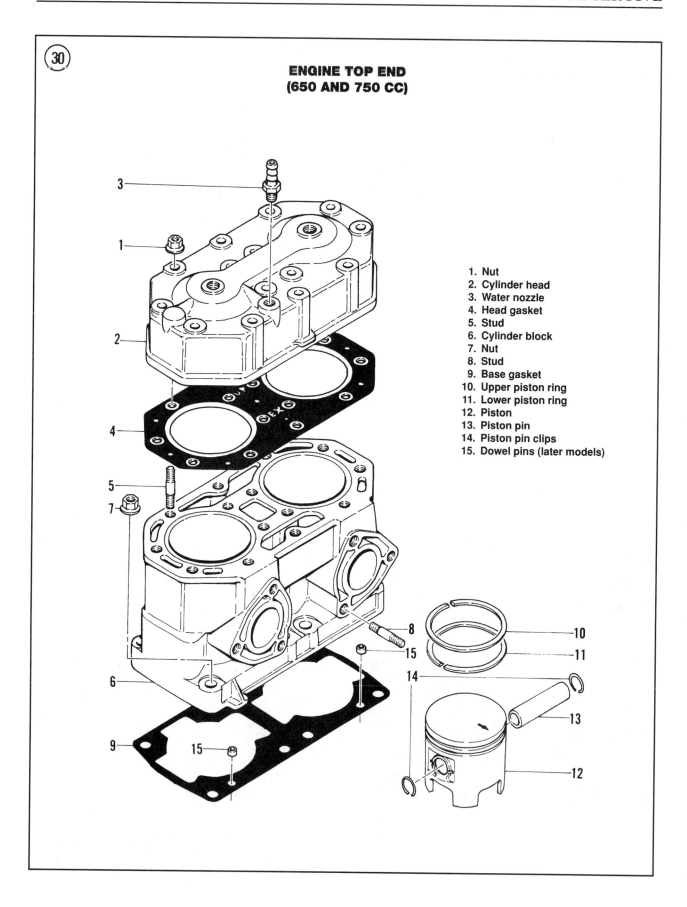

**ENGINE TOP END
(650 AND 750 CC)**

1. Nut
2. Cylinder head
3. Water nozzle
4. Head gasket
5. Stud
6. Cylinder block
7. Nut
8. Stud
9. Base gasket
10. Upper piston ring
11. Lower piston ring
12. Piston
13. Piston pin
14. Piston pin clips
15. Dowel pins (later models)

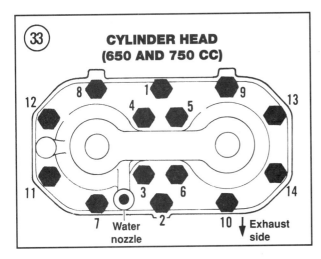

**CYLINDER HEAD
(650 AND 750 CC)**

7   Water
     nozzle

10 ↓ Exhaust
       side

a. Disconnect the negative battery cable from the battery (**Figure 31**).

b. Remove the air intake cover and spark arrestor.

c. Disconnect the coolant hose at the cylinder head fitting (A, **Figure 32**).

d. Disconnect the spark plug leads from the spark plugs (B, **Figure 32**).

e. Remove the carburetor(s) and exhaust pipe/expansion chamber. See Chapter Seven. On JH750 Super Sport Xi, JH750SS and JH750XiR, remove the throttle/choke cable mounting bracket from the cylinder head.

3. Loosen, but do not remove the spark plugs.

4. Loosen the cylinder head nuts in reverse of the sequence shown in **Figure 33**. After all nuts are loose, remove the nuts and washers.

5. Loosen the cylinder head by tapping around its perimeter with a rubber or plastic mallet. Remove the cylinder head (**Figure 34**) and gasket (**Figure 35**). Discard the gasket. Place a shop towel over the cylinder block to prevent anything from falling into the cylinders.

6. Inspect the cylinder head as described in this chapter.

7. The new cylinder head gasket is marked "UP" and "EX" (**Figure 35**). Install the gasket so the "UP" mark is facing upward and the "EX"

mark is facing toward the exhaust port as shown in **Figure 36**).

8. Install the cylinder head so the coolant fitting is facing the exhaust pipe.

9. Install the cylinder head nuts and washers. Tighten the nuts finger tight.

10. Tighten the cylinder head nuts in 2-3 steps to the specification in **Table 3**. Tighten the nuts in the sequence shown in **Figure 33**.

11. Install the spark plugs. Tighten the plugs to specification (**Table 3**). Reconnect the spark plug leads to the plugs.

12. Connect the water inlet hose to its fitting on the cylinder head. See A, **Figure 32**. Tighten the hose clamp securely.

13. Reverse Steps 1 and 2 to complete installation.

Inspection

1. Thoroughly clean any soft deposits off the cylinder head mating surface (**Figure 37**). Remove carbon and hard deposits using a wire brush and soft metal scraper. *Do not* scratch, nick or gouge the cylinder head mating surface.

2. Closely inspect the spark plug holes (**Figure 38**) for cracking or damaged threads. Excessive carbon deposits or mildly damaged threads can be cleaned up using a 14 mm spark plug thread chaser (**Figure 39**).

> *NOTE*
> *When repairing spark plug threads, lubricate the spark plug thread chaser with kerosene or aluminum thread fluid to prevent aluminum galling.*

3. Check the water inlet fitting (**Figure 40**) for silt, sand or sludge accumulation, looseness or damage. If necessary, remove the fitting and thoroughly clean it. Clean the fitting threads and apply a suitable sealant to the threads. Reinstall it and tighten to 9.8 N•m (87 in.-lb.).

4. Measure the flatness of the cylinder head mating surface using a straightedge and feeler

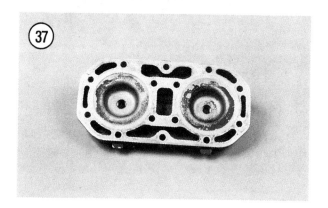

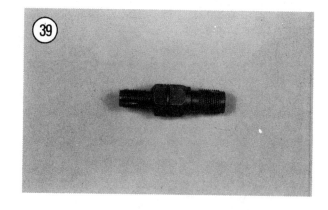

gauge (**Figure 41**). If the cylinder head is warped in excess of the specification in **Table 2**, resurface the head as follows:

a. Tape a piece of 400-600 grit wet emery sandpaper on a thick plate glass or surface plate.

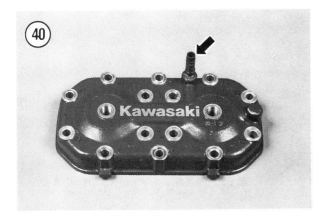

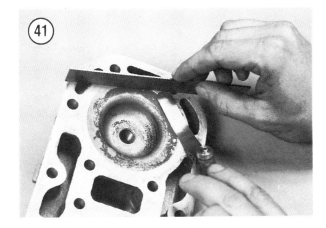

b. Slowly resurface the cylinder head mating surface by moving it in a figure eight pattern on the sandpaper.

c. Rotate the head several times to avoid removing too much material from one side. Check progress often with the straightedge and feeler gauge.

d. If the cylinder head warpage still exceeds the service limit (**Table 2**), have the head resurfaced by a qualified machine shop. Note that removing material from the cylinder head mating surface will change the compression ratio. Consult with the machinist to determine how much material was removed.

5. Wash the cylinder head in hot soapy water and rinse thoroughly before installation.

CYLINDER

An aluminum cylinder block with cast iron cylinder liners is used on all models. The cylinders can be bored oversize should wear be excessive. Pistons and piston rings are available in 0.5 mm and 1.0 mm oversize.

Removal

1. Remove the cylinder head as described in this chapter.

2. If the engine is installed in the hull, perform the following:

a. Remove the carburetor(s) as described in Chapter Seven.

b. Remove the exhaust pipe/expansion chamber as described in Chapter Seven.

c. On JF650TS models, remove the fuel pump as described in Chapter Seven.

3. Loosen and remove the cylinder block base nuts (**Figure 42**) on both sides of the cylinder block. Mark the location of any cable ties mounted on the cylinder studs (**Figure 43**) for reference during reinstallation.

5

4. Dislodge the cylinder block by tapping around its perimeter with a rubber or plastic mallet.

5. Lift the cylinder block (**Figure 44**) up and off the crankcase.

6. Remove the 2 dowel pins (**Figure 45**), if so equipped.

7. Remove and discard the cylinder base gasket.

8. Stuff clean shop towels around the connecting rods to prevent dirt or loose parts from entering the crankcase.

9. It is not necessary to remove the manifolds from the cylinder block unless the gaskets are leaking or manifold inspection is required.

    a. *Exhaust manifold*—Remove the bolts holding the exhaust manifold to the cylinder block. If necessary, tap the manifold with a soft-face mallet to dislodge it from the cylinder block. Remove the manifold. Remove and discard the manifold gasket.

    b. *Intake manifold*—Remove the intake manifold as described under Reed Valve Assembly in this chapter.

Inspection

Cylinder measurement requires a precision inside micrometer or a cylinder bore gauge. If the correct instruments are not available, have the cylinder bores measured by a dealer or qualified machine shop.

1. Thoroughly wash the cylinder block in solvent, then with detergent and hot water. All oil, carbon or other contamination must be removed from the cylinder bores before attempting cylinder measurements, to prevent incorrect readings.

2. Remove all gasket material from the top (**Figure 46**) and bottom (**Figure 47**) mating surfaces.

3. Measure the cylinder bore diameters as described under *Piston/Cylinder Clearance* in this chapter.

4. If the cylinders are within the service limit, check the bore carefully for scratches, nicks,

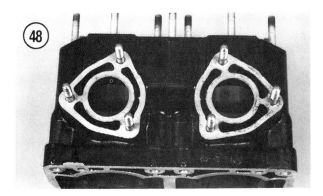

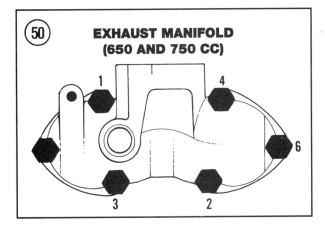

EXHAUST MANIFOLD (650 AND 750 CC)

gouges or other damage. Recondition the cylinder bores as required.

5. Check the cylinder studs (**Figure 46**) and manifold studs (**Figure 48**) for thread damage or looseness. Repair minor thread damage using the correct size metric die. Tighten loose studs. If the studs are damaged, they must be replaced. See Chapter One.

6. After the cylinder block is serviced, wash the bores with detergent and hot water to remove the fine grit left from the honing or boring process. After washing the cylinders, wipe the bores with a clean white cloth. If the cloth is dirty, the cylinders must be washed again. Once the bores are thoroughly clean, apply a thin coat of clean engine oil to the bores to prevent rusting.

> *CAUTION*
> *A combination of detergent and hot water is the only solution that will completely clean the cylinder walls. Solvent will not clean the fine grit left over from the cylinder machining process. Any grit remaining in the cylinders acts as a grinding compound resulting in premature internal engine wear.*

Installation

1. Clean the cylinder bores as described under *Inspection* in this chapter.

2. If the manifolds are removed, reinstall them as follows:

   a. *Intake manifold*—Install the intake manifold as described under *Reed Valve Assembly* in this chapter.

   b. *Exhaust manifold*—Install a new exhaust manifold gasket. If a 1-piece exhaust manifold gasket is used, install the gasket so the hole (**Figure 49**) in the center of the gasket is facing up. If 2 separate gaskets are used, install the gaskets so the arrows on the gaskets are facing up. Then install the manifold, nuts and washers. Tighten the nuts in the sequence shown in **Figure 50** to the specification in **Table 3**.

3. Make sure the cylinder block and crankcase mating surfaces are completely clean.

4. Install a new cylinder block base gasket on the crankcase mating surface.

5. Install the 2 dowel pins (**Figure 45**), if so equipped, into the crankcase.

6. Make sure the piston ring end gaps are aligned with the locating pins in the piston ring grooves. See **Figure 51**. Lightly lubricate the piston skirt, piston rings and cylinder walls.

7. Place a piston holding tool under one piston and turn the crankshaft until the piston is drawn down firmly against the tool. This makes cylinder block installation easier. A suitable piston holding tool can easily be made of wood. See **Figure 52**.

8. Install the cylinder block on the crankcase studs, compressing each piston ring with your fingers as the cylinder starts to slide over it. After one piston is installed in its cylinder, lower the cylinder block and install the opposite piston. If the rings are hard to compress, use a large hose clamp as a ring compressor as shown in **Figure 53**. Make sure the cylinder block is fully seated on the crankcase. Remove the piston holding tool and hose clamps (if used).

9. Install the cylinder head as described in this chapter.

10. Install the exhaust pipe/expansion chamber and carburetor(s) as described in Chapter Seven.

PISTON, PISTON PIN AND PISTON RINGS

The piston is made of aluminum alloy. The piston pin is a precision fit in the piston and is held in place by a retainer clip at each end. The piston pin rides in a caged needle bearing installed in the connecting rod small end.

Piston and Piston Ring Removal

1. Remove the cylinder head and cylinder block as described in this chapter.

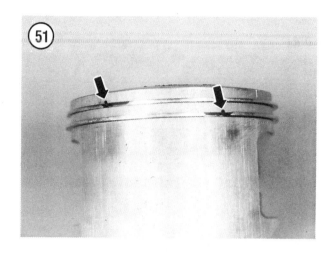

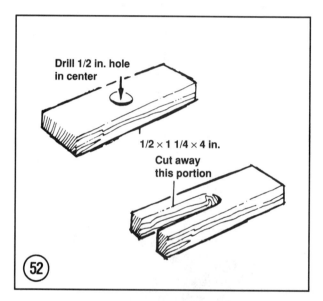

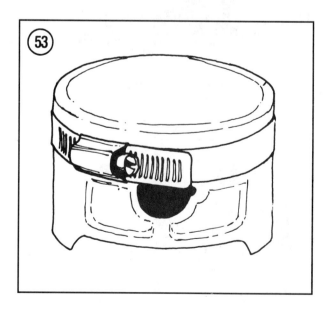

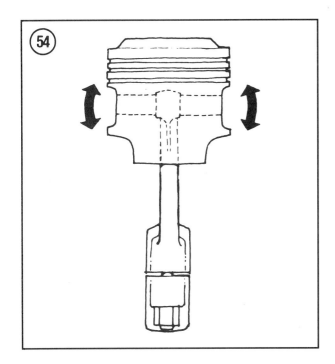

2. Mark the cylinder number on the top of each piston. Also mark each piston for directional reference during reassembly. Always keep each piston together with its piston pin, bearing and rings to avoid intermixing components.

3. Before removing the piston from the connecting rod, hold the rod tightly and rock the piston as shown in **Figure 54**. Any rocking motion indicates excessive wear on the piston pin, bearing, piston, or a combination of all three.

> *NOTE*
> *Place a clean shop towel under the piston to prevent the piston pin retaining clip from falling into the crankcase.*

> *WARNING*
> *Wear safety glasses when performing Step 4.*

4. Remove the piston pin retaining clips from each side of the piston pin bore (**Figure 55**) with a small screwdriver or similar tool. Hold your thumb over one edge of the clip to prevent it from springing out. Discard the retaining clips.

> *CAUTION*
> *If the piston pin is difficult to remove from the piston, remove it as described in Step 6. Do not drive the pin out of the piston. This will damage the piston, needle bearing and connecting rod.*

5. Push the piston pin out of the piston (**Figure 56**) using a wooden dowel or similar tool.

6. If the piston pin is tight, fabricate the tool shown in **Figure 57**. Assemble the tool onto the

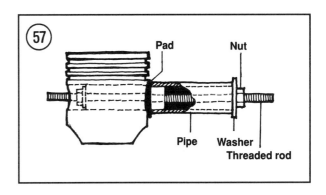

piston and pull the piston pin out of the piston by tightening the nut on the threaded rod. Make sure to install a pad between the piston and piece of pipe to avoid scoring the side of the piston.

7. Lift the piston off the connecting rod.

8. Remove the needle bearing assembly **Figure 58**) from the connecting rod.

9. Repeat Steps 3-8 for the remaining piston.

10. Remove the upper piston ring by spreading the ends with your thumbs just enough to slide it up and off the crown of the piston. See **Figure 59**. Then repeat for the bottom ring.

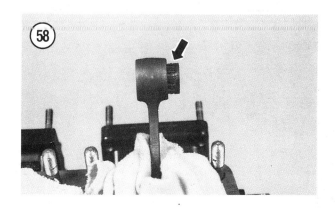

Piston Pin and Needle Bearing Inspection

1. Clean the needle bearing (A, **Figure 60**) in solvent and dry thoroughly. Using a magnifying glass, closely inspect the bearing cage for cracks at the corners of the needle slots (**Figure 61**). Closely inspect the needle rollers for pitting, cracks, corrosion, excessive wear or other damage. Replace the bearing if *any* defects are noted.

2. Check the piston pin (B, **Figure 60**) for excessive wear, scoring, flaking, pitting, corrosion or other damage. Also check the pin for cracks along the top and side. Replace the pin if *any* defects are noted.

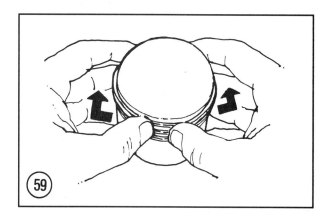

3. Lightly lubricate the piston pin and needle bearing with clean engine oil. Install the bearing and pin into its respective connecting rod. Slowly rotate the pin while checking for radial and axial play (**Figure 62**). If any play is noted, the pin and bearing (and possibly the connecting rod) should be replaced. If the pin and bearing are excessively worn, the connecting rod small end bore may also be worn. See *Connecting Rod Inspection* in this chapter.

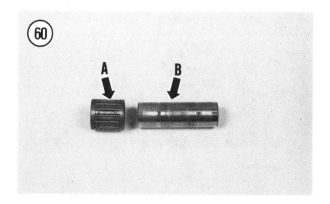

> *CAUTION*
> *If piston seizure or obvious signs of engine overheating are noted, replace the piston pins and bearings. Excessive heat can weaken these components which can result in premature failure.*

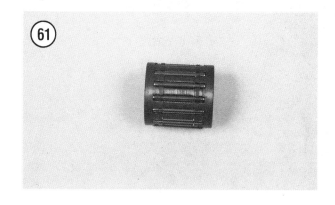

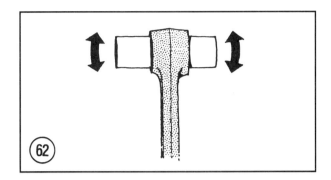

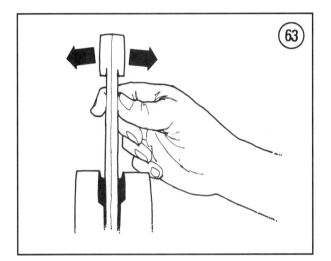

Connecting Rod Inspection

1. Wipe the connecting rod small end bore with a clean shop towel. Inspect the bore for galling, scratches, excessive wear, corrosion or other damage. Note that the connecting rods are not available separately from the crankshaft.

NOTE
*In Step 2, do not confuse the normal side-to-side sliding motion of the connecting rod with a rocking motion (**Figure 63**) which indicates excessive wear.*

2. Check the connecting rod big end bearing play. Rock the connecting rod side-to-side as shown in **Figure 63**. If more that a very slight rocking motion is noted, measure the connecting rod side clearance with a feeler gauge. Measure the clearance between the side of the crankshaft and connecting rod as shown in **Figure 64**. If the clearance exceeds the wear limit specified in **Table 2**, the crankshaft assembly must be repaired or replaced.

Piston and Piston Ring Inspection

1. Carefully inspect the piston for cracks at the top edge of the transfer cutaways (**Figure 65**). Replace the piston if any cracks are noted.

2. Check the piston skirt (**Figure 66**) for scoring, excessive wear, cracks, galling or other dam-

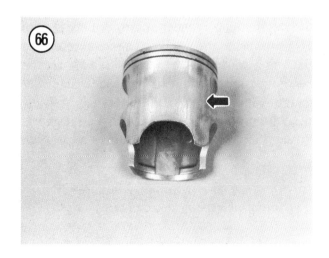

5

age. Light galling and abrasion (resulting from piston seizure) can be cleaned with No. 400 emery paper, or oil and a fine-cut oilstone. Replace the piston, however, if the damage is severe.

3. Check the piston ring locating pins in the ring grooves. See **Figure 67**. The pins must be tight with no cracks in the area around the pins. If a loose pin is noted, the piston must be replaced. A loose pin will eventually fall out resulting in severe engine damage.

4. Check the piston pin retaining clip grooves (**Figure 68**) for cracks or other damage that could allow a retaining clip to fall out. Replace the piston if damage to either groove is noted.

NOTE
*Always replace both pistons as a set. In addition, always install new piston rings when using new pistons. Refer to **Cylinder Honing** in this chapter.*

NOTE
Maintaining the correct piston ring end gap helps to ensure peak engine performance. Always check piston ring end gap at the intervals specified in Chapter Three. Excessive ring end gap reduces engine performance and can cause overheating. Insufficient end gap will cause the ring ends to butt together resulting in ring breakage.

5. Measure the piston ring end gap. Place the ring into the bottom of the cylinder. Then, push the ring into the cylinder approximately 20 mm (3/4 in.), using the crown of a piston to ensure the ring is square in the cylinder. See **Figure 69**. Next, measure the ring end gap with a flat feeler gauge (**Figure 70**). Compare the gap with the wear limit specified in **Table 2**. If the gap is greater than specified, replace the rings as a set.

NOTE
Measure the end gap on new piston rings using the same method as for used rings. If the gap is less than specified, first make sure the rings are the correct part

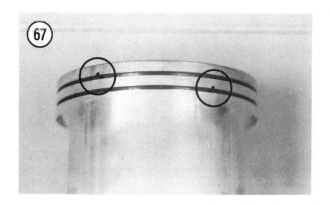

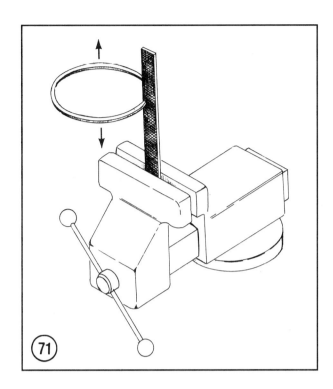

*number. If the rings are correct, carefully file the ends with a fine-cut file to obtain the correct end gap. See **Figure 71**.*

6. Carefully remove all carbon deposits from the ring grooves with a broken ring (**Figure 72**). Inspect the ring grooves for burrs, nicks, cracks or broken lands. Replace the pistons as necessary.

7. Inspect the condition of the piston crown (**Figure 73**). Normal deposits can be removed by carefully scraping the crown. Do not scratch or gouge the piston. If the piston crown shows pitting, erosion or other abnormal wear, preignition or detonation may have occurred during operation. See Chapter Two for a description of preignition and detonation.

8. Measure the piston diameter as described under *Piston-to-Cylinder Clearance* in this chapter.

9. Hone the cylinders as described under *Cylinder Honing* in this chapter.

Piston-to-Cylinder Clearance

The following procedure requires the use of specialized measuring instruments, such as a cylinder bore gauge, inside micrometer or telescopic gauge. If the proper instruments are not available, have the measurements performed by dealership personnel or a qualified machine shop.

A cylinder bore gauge is generally considered the easiest to use and most accurate instrument for measuring cylinder bore diameter. Therefore, the following procedure is based on the use of a cylinder bore gauge. An inside micrometer or telescopic gauge can be substituted for the bore gauge, however, by skipping the steps which apply to bore gauge set up and calibration.

The cylinder bore gauge consists of a dial indicator (A, **Figure 74**), handle assembly (B), anvils (C) and shims (D). The dial indicator is marked in 0.01 mm increments, from 0.01-10 mm. Anvils are included in 40-80 mm sizes in 5

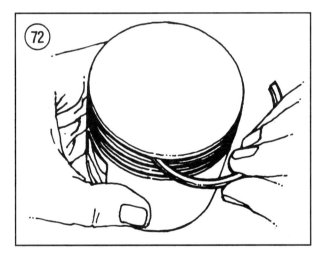

5

mm increments. The shims are included in 1 mm, 2 mm and 3 mm sizes.

1. Using an outside micrometer, measure the piston diameter at a point approximately 18 mm (0.71 in.) up from the bottom of the piston skirt, at a 90° angle to the piston pin (**Figure 75**). If the diameter is not within the specification listed in **Table 2**, replace the pistons.

NOTE
Always replace both pistons and piston rings at the same time.

2. Thoroughly clean the cylinder block with solvent, then with detergent and hot water. Make sure all oil, grease and carbon is removed. To prevent incorrect measurements, the cylinder bore must be absolutely clean.

3. Attach the dial indicator to the bore gauge handle assembly.

4. Next, refer to **Table 2** and note the standard bore size for the models being serviced. Then, select an anvil, and shim if necessary, which will add up to the standard bore diameter (or as close as possible). For example, if the standard bore size is 76.0 mm, assemble the gauge using the 75 mm anvil and the 1 mm shim (76 mm total). Place the shim (**Figure 76**) on the anvil, insert the anvil and shim into the gauge, then install the nut over the anvil and tighten it securely. See **Figure 77** for a fully assembled bore gauge.

NOTE
Although not absolutely necessary, a suitable micrometer stand is very helpful in Steps 5 and 6.

5. Again, note the standard cylinder bore diameter for your model in **Table 2**. Then set the outside micrometer at exactly this dimension, then lock the micrometer thimble. If the standard bore diameter is 76.0 mm, set the micrometer at *exactly* 76 mm.

6. Next, place the bore gauge in the outside micrometer as shown in **Figure 78**. While firmly holding the gauge in the micrometer, turn the dial

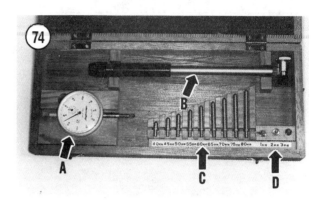

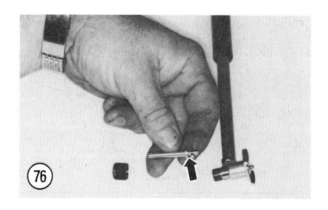

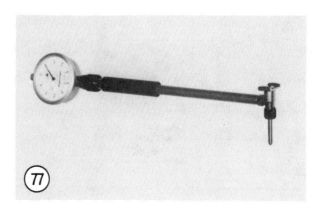

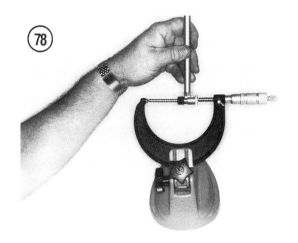

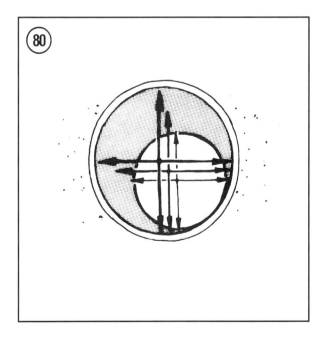

indicator face to align the indicator needle with the zero mark. The bore gauge is now calibrated for use.

7. Place the bore gauge into the cylinder bore (**Figure 79**) and slowly rock it back and forth to obtain the highest reading on the indicator. Because zero on the indicator is calibrated to the standard bore diameter, any reading over zero indicates cylinder wear. A perfect cylinder would read zero on the bore gauge indicator.

8. Measure the cylinder bore at the top, center and bottom of the piston ring travel area. Record each measurement. Then, repeat each measurement at 90° to the first measurement. See **Figure 80** for the measurement points. Using these dimensions, calculate cylinder bore out-of-round, taper and wear.

9. If the taper, out-of-round or wear exceeds the specifications listed in **Table 2**, the cylinders must be bored oversize and oversize pistons and rings fitted to the cylinders.

NOTE
Obtain the oversize pistons before the cylinders are bored. The pistons must be measured and the cylinders bored to fit the pistons.

10. Piston-to-cylinder clearance is the difference between the maximum piston diameter and the maximum cylinder diameter. For a used piston and cylinder, subtract the piston outside diameter from the cylinder bore diameter. If the clearance exceeds the specification in **Table 2**, the cylinders must be bored and oversize pistons and rings installed.

Cylinder Honing

The surface of a well-worn cylinder wall is normally glazed and almost mirror smooth. Cylinder honing, often referred to as deglazing, is required whenever new piston rings are installed in a used cylinder. For new piston rings to seal correctly, the ring face and cylinder wall must

5

establish a smooth compatible surface between them. This is known as "seating in." New piston rings will not properly seat to a cylinder that has not been honed or deglazed. When a cylinder bore is honed, a cross-hatch pattern of small scratches is formed on the cylinder wall. This surface allows the piston rings to break through the oil film on the cylinder wall and create the friction necessary for the rings to seat to the cylinder. Once the seating-in process is complete, very little metal-to-metal contact will occur thereafter.

Honing service can be performed by a dealership service department or a qualified machine shop. If, however, you choose to hone the cylinders yourself, purchase a quality hone and follow the hone manufacturer's instructions closely. Ball or bead-type hones commonly used in automotive service do not work well on 2-stroke engines because of the ports in the cylinders.

> *CAUTION*
> *After a cylinder has been reconditioned by boring or honing, the bore must be thoroughly cleaned to remove all material left from the machining operation. Refer to* **Inspection** *under* **Cylinder** *in this chapter. Improper cleaning will not remove all of the machining residue resulting in rapid piston and piston ring wear.*

Piston Installation

1. Lubricate the connecting rod small end needle bearing with engine oil. Install the bearing into the connecting rod small end bore (**Figure 81**).

2. Lubricate the piston pin and slide it into the piston until the end extends slightly beyond the inside of the boss (**Figure 82**).

3. Position the piston over the connecting rod. Make sure the arrow on the piston crown is facing toward the exhaust (left) side of the engine. Align the piston pin with the needle bearing

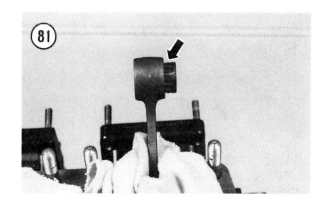

and push the pin (**Figure 83**) into the piston until it is even with the pin retaining clip grooves.

4. Install *new* piston pin retaining clips (**Figure 84**). Position the clips so their end gap is facing either up or down and make sure the clips are securely seated in their grooves.

5. Check piston installation by rocking the piston back and forth around the pin axis and from side-to-side along the axis. The piston should rotate freely back and forth but not from side-to-side.

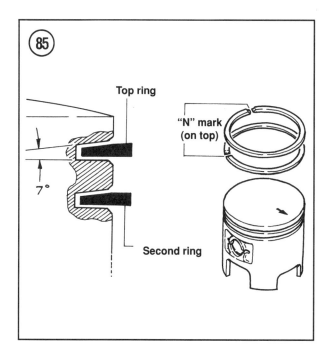

Top ring

"N" mark (on top)

7°

Second ring

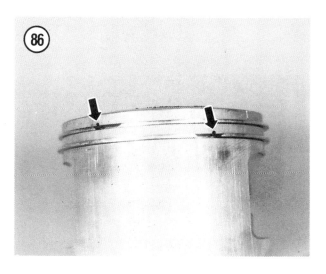

6. Next, install the piston rings. Install the bottom ring first, by carefully spreading the end gap and slipping the ring over the top of the piston and into its groove. Install the top ring using the same method. Make sure the "N" (650 cc) or "R" (750 cc) mark on the ring is facing the piston crown (**Figure 85**).

7. Make sure the rings are completely seated in their grooves, around the entire piston circumference, and that the ring end gaps are aligned with the locating pins. See **Figure 86**.

8. Follow the *Break-in Procedure* in Chapter Three to properly break in the engine.

REED VALVE ASSEMBLY

All models are equipped with a reed valve assembly located between the intake manifold and crankcase. The reed valves are thin flexible diaphragms make of stainless steel or a fiber material. The reed valves are designed to control the passage of air-fuel mixture into the crankcase by opening and closing as crankcase pressure changes. When crankcase pressure is high, the reeds maintain contact with the reed plate to which they are attached. As crankcase pressure drops on the compression stroke, the reeds move away from the plate and allow the air-fuel mixture to enter the crankcase. Reed travel is limited by the reed stop.

Removal/Installation

The reed valves can be removed with the engine installed in the hull.

1. Remove the carburetor(s) as described in Chapter Seven.

2. Disconnect the oil hoses at the fitting on the intake manifold. See **Figure 87**. On models with twin carburetors, disconnect 2 oil hoses from the intake manifold.

3. Mark all wire cable guides mounted on the intake manifold for reference during reassembly.

4. Remove the fasteners holding the intake manifold (**Figure 88**, typical) to the engine.

5. Remove and discard the gasket(s) located between the manifold and reed cage (**Figure 89**).

6. Pull the reed cage assemblies (**Figure 90**) out of the intake tract.

7. Remove and discard the gaskets installed between the reed cages and cylinder (**Figure 91**).

8. Carefully remove all gasket material from all mating surfaces.

9. Inspect the studs in the cylinder block for damaged threads. If necessary, replace damaged studs as described in Chapter One.

10. Place a clean shop towel into each intake opening in the cylinder to prevent foreign objects from entering the cylinders.

11. Inspect the reed valve assembly as described in this chapter.

12. Install a new gasket(s) on the cylinder block (**Figure 91**).

13A. *650 cc models*—Insert the reed cage assemblies into the intake passage (**Figure 90**) so the small hole in the reed cage is at the bottom. See **Figure 92**.

13B. *750 cc models*—Install the reed cage assemblies into the intake passage so the "UP" mark on the reed cage is facing up.

14. Install a new gasket on each reed cage (**Figure 89**).

15. Install the intake manifold so the studs on the manifold face up (**Figure 88**). Apply Loctite 242 to the threads of the manifold nuts. Install and tighten the nuts securely.

16. Reconnect the oil hose(s) at the intake manifold fitting(s).

17. Bleed the oil injection system as described in Chapter Ten.

Reed Valve Inspection

1. Carefully inspect the reed valve assembly (**Figure 93**) for visible wear, distortion or other damage. Check the rubber coating on the reed cage for separation or other damage.

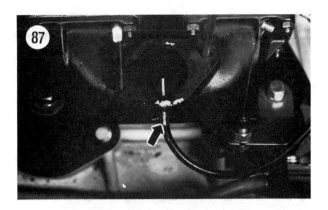

2. Using a flat feeler gauge, check the clearance between the reed and the valve holder (**Figure 94**). Repeat for each reed tip. Replace the reeds if the clearance exceeds 0.2 mm (0.008 in.).

3. Remove the screws (A, **Figure 95**) securing the reed stop (B) to the reed cage. Be careful not to damage the reed plate with the screwdriver. Remove the reed stop (B, **Figure 95**) and reed plate (C).

4. Carefully inspect the reed plate and reed stop. Check for cracks, metal fatigue, distortion or other damage. Closely inspect the rubber seal. The reed stops and plates are available for replacement, but if the rubber seal is damaged the reed cage assembly must be replaced.

5. Check the threaded holes in the reed cage. If the threads are stripped, do not repair the threads. If a screw loosens and falls into the engine, severe damage will result. If any threads are damaged, replace the reed cage.

6. Reassemble the unit. Apply Loctite 242 to the threads prior to installation and tighten securely.

5

NOTE
Make sure all parts are clean and free of any small particles or lint from shop towels.

7. Reinstall the reed valve assembly as previously described.

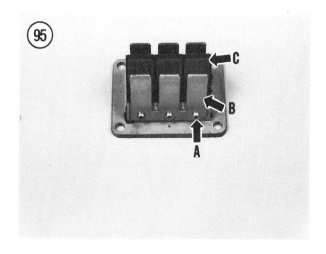

CRANKCASE AND CRANKSHAFT

Disassembly of the crankcase and removal of the crankshaft assembly requires engine removal from the bull. However, the cylinder head, cylinder block and all other attached assemblies can be removed with the engine in the hull.

The crankcase is made in 2 halves of precision diecast aluminum alloy and is of the "thin-walled" type. See **Figure 96**. To avoid damage to the crankcase halves, never hammer or pry on any of the interior or exterior projected walls. These areas are easily damaged if stressed beyond what they are designed for.

The crankcase halves are assembled without a gasket; only gasket sealer is used while dowel pins align the halves.

The crankcase halves are a machined and matched set (**Figure 97**). If one half is damaged, both must be replaced.

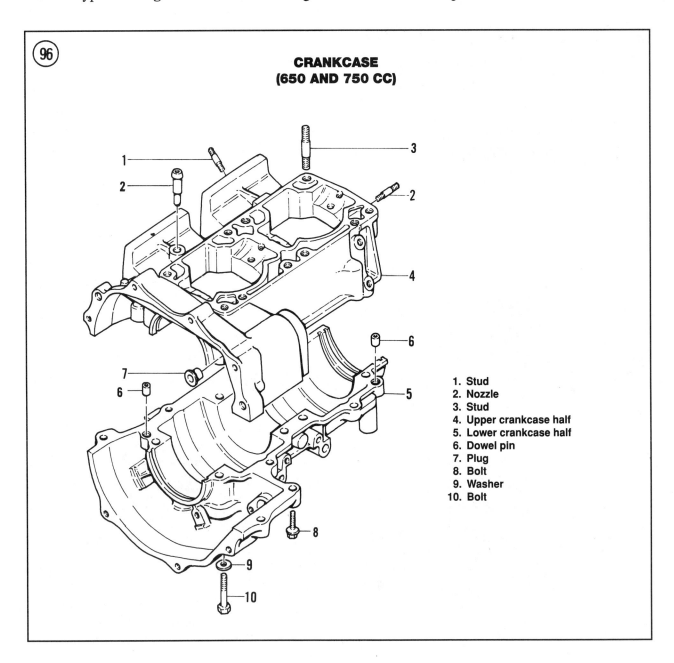

96

**CRANKCASE
(650 AND 750 CC)**

1. Stud
2. Nozzle
3. Stud
4. Upper crankcase half
5. Lower crankcase half
6. Dowel pin
7. Plug
8. Bolt
9. Washer
10. Bolt

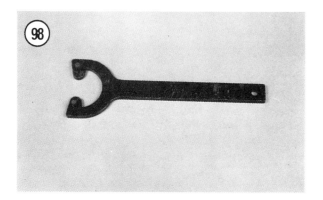

The procedure which follows is presented as a complete, step-by-step lower end overhaul that should be closely followed if the engine is to be completely reconditioned.

Special Tools

A few special tools are necessary to split the crankcase assembly. These tools allow easy disassembly and reassembly of the engine without prying or hammering. Remember, the crankcase is easily destroyed using improper disassembly or reassembly techniques. The following tools are required:

a. Kawasaki coupling holder (part No. T57001-276) or equivalent. See **Figure 98**. The coupling holder is used to remove and install the coupler half installed on the end of the crankshaft or drive shaft. Because the coupler halves are made of cast aluminum, they can be easily damaged by the use of incorrect tools or procedures.

b. Flywheel holder (part No. 57001-306) or equivalent (**Figure 99**). A flywheel holder is required to hold the flywheel from turning while the crankshaft coupler half is removed.

c. A hydraulic or arbor press. A press is necessary to remove and install the crankshaft outside main bearings.

Crankcase Disassembly

This procedure describes the disassembly of the crankcase halves and removal of the crankshaft.

1. Remove the engine from the hull as described in this chapter.

2. Remove the starter motor as described in Chapter Eight.

3. Remove the oil pump (if so equipped) as described in Chapter Nine.

4. Remove the magneto cover bolts and the cover (**Figure 100**).

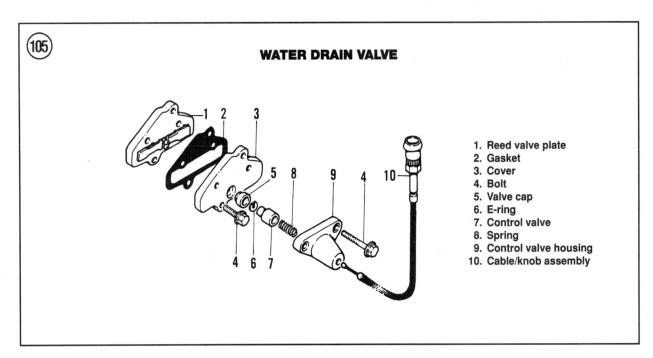

WATER DRAIN VALVE

1. Reed valve plate
2. Gasket
3. Cover
4. Bolt
5. Valve cap
6. E-ring
7. Control valve
8. Spring
9. Control valve housing
10. Cable/knob assembly

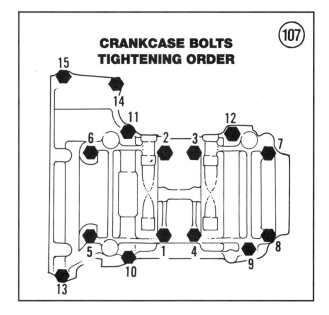

CRANKCASE BOLTS TIGHTENING ORDER

5. Hold the flywheel steady with a flywheel holding tool (**Figure 101**) and unscrew the coupler half from the rear end of the crankshaft (**Figure 102**). Remove the coupler (**Figure 103**).

6. Remove the flywheel, stator and starter clutch as described in Chapter Eight.

> *NOTE*
> *The bolts removed in Step 7 are secured with thread locking compound and are very tight.*

7. Invert the engine and remove the bolts holding the engine bed to the engine. Remove the engine bed (**Figure 104**).

> *NOTE*
> *The engine bed mounting bolts are a special design. Do not mix these fasteners with others.*

8. Remove the water drain valve assembly from the crankcase. See **Figure 105**.

9. Place the engine up-side-down on wooden blocks as shown in **Figure 106**.

10. Loosen the 6 mm bolts from the bottom of the crankcase half (**Figure 107**).

11. Loosen the 8 mm bolts from the bottom of the crankcase half (**Figure 107**).

12. Remove the 6 and 8 mm bolts.

> *CAUTION*
> *Make sure all fasteners are removed. If the cases are hard to separate, check for fasteners that might have been missed.*

13. Locate the pry points (**Figure 108**) on both sides of the crankcase. Then, using a large screwdriver, carefully pry the crankcase halves apart (**Figure 109**). Do not pry between the crankcase mating surfaces.

14. Lift the lower crankcase half up and remove it (**Figure 110**).

15. Remove the crankshaft assembly (**Figure 111**) from the upper crankcase half.

16. Remove the center block locating pin (**Figure 112**), if so equipped. Remove the center

bearing locating ring (**Figure 113**), if so equipped.

17. Remove the 2 dowel pins (**Figure 114**).

Crankcase Inspection

Refer to **Figure 96** for this procedure.

1. Clean both crankcase halves (**Figure 115**) with solvent. Thoroughly dry with compressed air, then wipe them off with a clean shop towel.

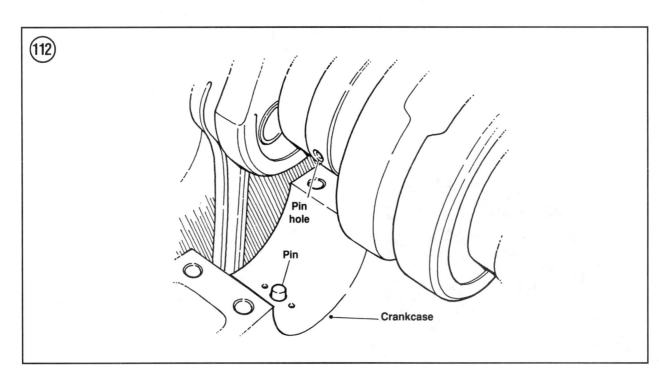

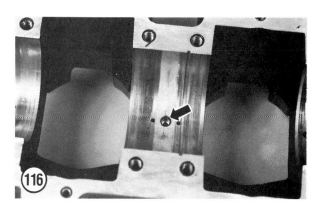

Be sure to remove all traces of old sealant from the mating surfaces.

2. Carefully inspect the case halves for cracks and fractures. Also check the areas around the stiffening ribs, around bearing bosses and threaded holes. Defects can sometimes be repaired by shops specializing in precision aluminum casting repair. If not, replace the crankcase assembly.

3. Check the center block locating pin hole (**Figure 116**) in the upper crankcase for cracks or other damage.

4. Check the threaded holes (**Figure 117**) in both crankcase halves for thread damage, dirt or oil buildup. If necessary, clean or repair the threads with a suitable size metric tap. Coat the tap threads with kerosene or an aluminum tap fluid before using.

5. Check the cylinder studs (**Figure 118**) on both crankcase halves for thread damage. If necessary, replace the studs as described in Chapter One.

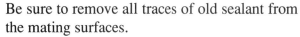

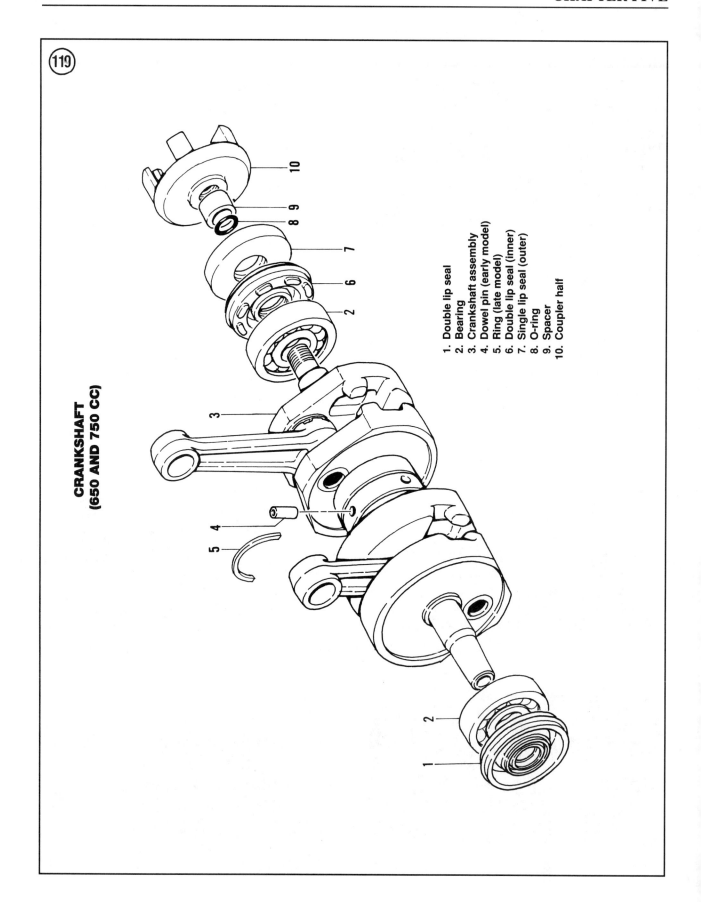

CRANKSHAFT (650 AND 750 CC)

1. Double lip seal
2. Bearing
3. Crankshaft assembly
4. Dowel pin (early model)
5. Ring (late model)
6. Double lip seal (inner)
7. Single lip seal (outer)
8. O-ring
9. Spacer
10. Coupler half

Crankshaft Inspection

Refer to **Figure 119** for this procedure. The crankshaft and connecting rod assembly is pressed together. However, because Kawasaki does not offer replacement connecting rods and bearings for replacement, the crankshaft must be replaced as a unit assembly if excessively worn or damaged.

1. The crankshaft is equipped with 2 double-lip seals (A, **Figure 120**) and 1 single-lip seal (B). Remove the seals by pulling them off the end of the crankshaft.

2. Remove the spacer (**Figure 121**) and O-ring (**Figure 122**) from the of the crankshaft.

3. Check the connecting rod big-end radial clearance with a dial indicator. Place the end of a dial indicator so its plunger rests against the connecting rod big end (**Figure 123**). Then support the crankshaft and push the connecting rod up and down. Note the dial indicator gauge movement each time the connecting rod is moved. The difference between the 2 readings is the radial clearance. Repeat this procedure for the remaining connecting rod. Replace the crankshaft assembly if the clearance exceeds the service limit specified in **Table 2**.

4. Check connecting rod big-end side clearance with a feeler gauge. Insert the gauge between the crankshaft and connecting rod as shown in **Figure 124**. If the clearance exceeds the service limit in **Table 2**, the crankshaft assembly must be replaced.

5

5. Carefully inspect the condition of the crankshaft ball bearings (**Figure 125**). Clean the bearings in solvent and allow to dry. Then, lubricate each bearing with engine oil. Roll each bearing around by hand, making sure it turns quietly and smoothly, and that no rough spots are present. No apparent radial play should be noted. Defective end bearings (A, **Figure 125**) can be replaced using a press and bearing plate. The center bearings (B, **Figure 125**) can only be replaced as an assembly with the crankshaft.

6. Support the crankshaft by placing it on 2 V-blocks at the points shown in **Figure 126**. Then check runout with a dial indicator at the 2 points shown (**Figure 126**). Turn the crankshaft slowly while noting the dial indicator. The maximum difference noted is the crankshaft runout at that position. Replace the crankshaft assembly if runout exceeds the service limit specified in **Table 2**.

Crankshaft Oil Seal Installation

The crankshaft is equipped with 2 double-lip oil seals (A, **Figure 120**) and 1 single-lip seal (B). Refer to **Figures 119** and **120** and install the seals as follows.

1. Install a new O-ring in the groove on the rear of the crankshaft (**Figure 122**).

2. Lubricate the inside of the spacer and slide in on the rear of the crankshaft (**Figure 121**) until it bottoms out.

3. Install the front crankshaft double-lip seal (A, **Figure 120** as follows:

    a. Pack the area between the seal lips with a suitable heat-resistant grease. See **Figure 127**.

(125)

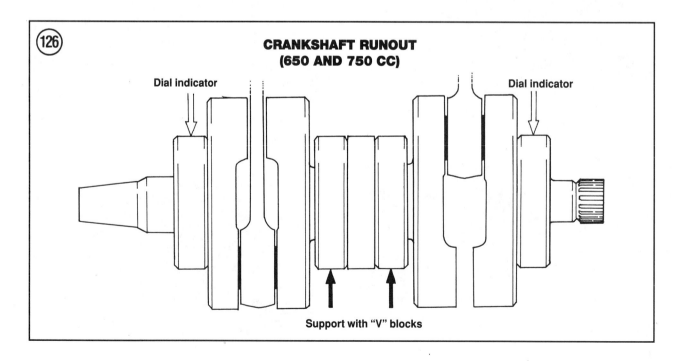

(126) **CRANKSHAFT RUNOUT (650 AND 750 CC)**

Dial indicator

Dial indicator

Support with "V" blocks

b. Slide the seal on the crankshaft so that projection side faces toward the front crankshaft bearing (**Figure 128**). Push the seal all the way on the crankshaft.

4. Install the rear crankshaft double-lip seal (A, **Figure 120**) and single-lip seal (B) as follows:

a. Lubricate the seals with a suitable heat-resistant grease, as shown in **Figure 129**.

b. Mate the 2 seals together (**Figure 130**).

c. Slide the oil seals on the end of the crankshaft so the projection on the double-lip seal faces toward the rear crankshaft bearing (**Figure 131**). Push the seals fully onto the crankshaft.

5. Make sure the front and rear seals are seated against the crankshaft bearings. See **Figure 132**.

5

Crankshaft Installation

Refer to **Figure 119** for this procedure.

1. Install the oil seals on the crankshaft as described in this chapter.

2. Place the upper crankcase half on wooden blocks as shown in **Figure 133**.

3A. *If equipped with center block locating pin*—Perform the following:

    a. Fit the pin into the pin hole in the upper crankcase half (**Figure 134**).

    b. Align the crankshaft with the upper crankcase half and install the crankshaft (**Figure 135**). Align the center block pin hole with the pin in the case (**Figure 134**).

3B. *If equipped with center bearing locating ring*—Perform the following:

    a. Install the locating ring into its groove in the upper crankcase half. See **Figure 136**.

    b. Align the ring groove in the center bearing with the locating ring installed in the upper crankcase half (**Figure 137**) and install the crankshaft. See **Figure 135**. Make sure the locating ring fits in the center bearing ring groove (**Figure 138**).

NOTE
On late models, align the ring in the bearing with the crankcase groove.

4. Make sure the oil seal ridges are located in their crankcase grooves. See **Figure 139** (front) and **Figure 140** (rear).

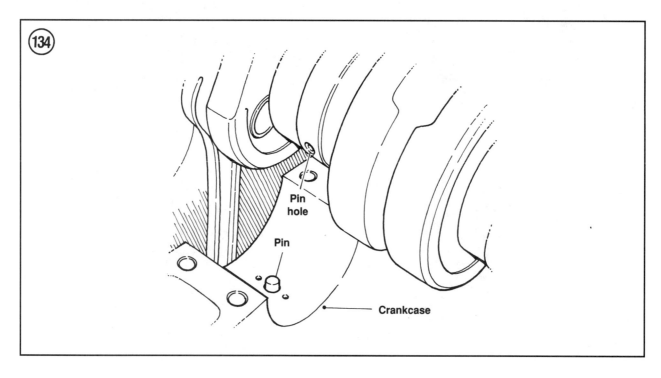

Crankcase Assembly

1. Install the crankshaft in the upper crankcase half as described in this chapter.

2. Install the 2 dowel pins in the lower crankcase half (**Figure 114**).

3. Make sure the crankcase mating surfaces are completely clean. Apply a light coat of Kawasaki Bond (part No. 92104-1003) or equivalent on the mating surface of one case half.

4. Place the lower case half on the upper case half (**Figure 141**). Make sure the mating surfaces around the entire crankcase are even and that a dowel pin or locating ring has not worked loose. See **Figure 142**.

5. Install washers on each of the 6 and 8 mm crankcase fasteners.

5

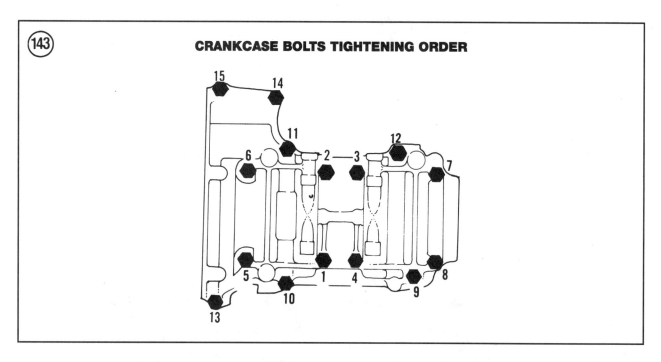

CRANKCASE BOLTS TIGHTENING ORDER

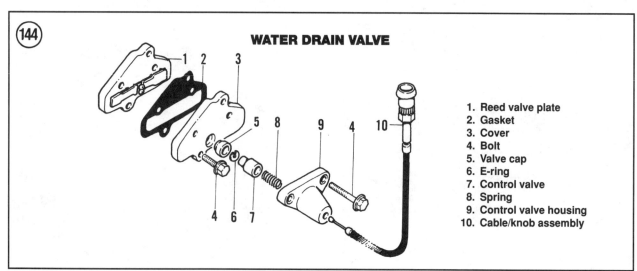

WATER DRAIN VALVE

1. Reed valve plate
2. Gasket
3. Cover
4. Bolt
5. Valve cap
6. E-ring
7. Control valve
8. Spring
9. Control valve housing
10. Cable/knob assembly

6. Apply Loctite 242 to the threads of the crankcase fasteners. Install the fasteners.

7. Tighten the crankcase fasteners in the sequence shown in **Figure 143** to the torque specification in **Table 3**.

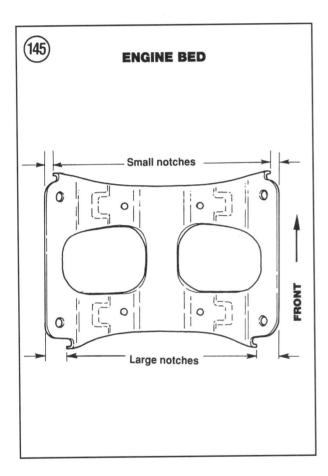

ENGINE BED

Small notches

FRONT

Large notches

CAUTION
Frequently rotate the crankshaft while tightening the crankcase fasteners. Make sure the crankshaft turns freely without unusual noise. Also make sure the crankshaft locating rings and crankcase dowel pins are properly located.

8. After tightening all crankcase fasteners to the proper torque, make sure the crankshaft turns freely without unusual noise. If binding or unusual noise is noted, the crankcase must be separated to determine the problem before proceeding with reassembly.

9. Install the water drain valve (**Figure 144**) on the lower crankcase half as described in this chapter.

10. The engine bed has a notch machined into each corner (**Figure 145**). Install the engine bed so the side with the small notches is facing toward the magneto side of the engine. Apply Loctite 242 to the threads of the engine bed mounting bolts. Install the bolts with their flat washers and lockwasher and tighten to the specification in **Table 3**.

NOTE
The engine bed bolts have special threads. Be certain the correct bolts are installed.

11. Place the engine right-side up.

12. Install the stator plate, flywheel and starter clutch as described in Chapter Eight.

13. Install the engine coupler half as follows:

  a. Make sure the spacer is installed and pushed all the way in **Figure 146**).

  b. Coat the rear crankshaft threads with grease.

  c. Screw the coupler half on the end of the crankshaft.

  d. Hold the flywheel steady with a holding tool, then tighten the coupler half with the special tool (**Figure 147**). Tighten the coupler half to the specification in **Table 3**.

5

14. Install the starter motor as described in Chapter Eight.

15. Install the engine into the hull as described in this chapter.

16. Reinstall the engine top end as described in this chapter.

WATER DRAIN VALVE

Removal/Installation/Installation

A water drain valve is mounted on the lower crankcase half. A pull handle (**Figure 148**) is connected to the valve by a cable. When pulled, any water in the crankcase is released.

Refer to **Figure 144** for this procedure.

1. If the engine is installed in the hull, remove the following components:

    a. Exhaust pipe, expansion chamber and exhaust manifold (Chapter Seven).

    b. Starter motor (Chapter Eight).

2. Remove the bolts securing the water drain valve to the lower crankcase half. Remove the valve and cable assembly (**Figure 149**).

3. Remove the 2 housing bolts (**Figure 150**) and separate the housings (**Figure 151**).

4. Check the reed valve (**Figure 152**) for cracks, tears or other damage. Replace the reed valve as necessary.

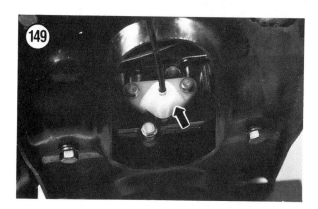

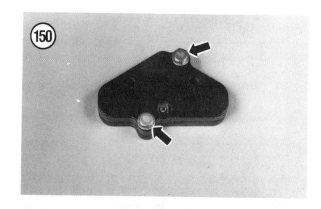

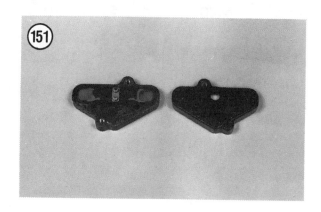

5. To disassemble the control valve assembly, remove the valve cap and remove the E-ring (**Figure 144**). Remove the parts in the order shown in **Figure 144**.

6. Inspect all control valve components for excessive wear or damage and replace as necessary.

7. Reassemble the control valve by reversing the disassembly sequence in **Figure 144**.

8. Install a new gasket when reassembling the reed valve housing. Apply Loctite 242 to the threads of the housing bolts and tighten them securely

9. Install the water drain by reversing Steps 1 and 2. When installing the control valve housing, push the control valve into the housing. Apply Loctite 242 to the threads of the mounting bolts. Then align the housings with the crankcase and install the mounting bolts.

10. After the assembly is installed, operate the control knob to make sure the control valve fits tightly in the drain hole when closed.

STARTER REDUCTION GEAR

Removal/Installation

1. Remove the flywheel as described in Chapter Eight.

2. Remove the washer (**Figure 153**).

3. Remove the starter reduction gear assembly (**Figure 154**).

4. Installation is the reverse of these steps. Apply molybdenum disulfide grease to both shaft ends.

Inspection

1. Check the reduction gear teeth (**Figure 155**) for excessive wear or damage. Replace the reduction gear as necessary.

2. Check the reduction gear operation as follows:

a. Turn the pinion gear (**Figure 156**) counter-clockwise by hand. It should turn freely.

b. Turn the pinion gear (**Figure 156**) clockwise until it stops against the stopper (**Figure 157**).

Then release the pinion gear. It should return to its original starting position.

c. If the pinion gear failed to operate correctly, replace the starter reduction gear assembly.

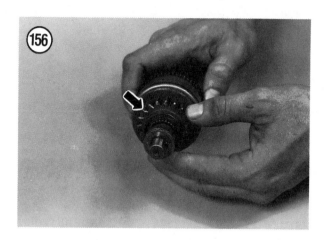

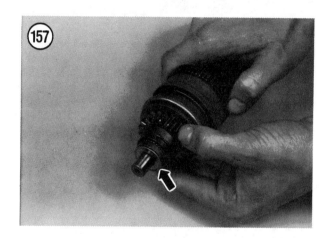

Table 1 GENERAL ENGINE SPECIFICATIONS (650 AND 750 CC MODELS)

Engine type	2-stroke, vertical twin, reed valve
Displacement	
650 cc	635 cc (38.73 cu. in.)
750 cc	743 cc (45.34 cu. in.)
Bore	
650 cc	76.0 mm (2.99 in.)
750 cc	80.0 mm (3.15 in.)
Stroke	
650 cc	70.0 mm (2.75 in.)
750 cc	74.0 mm (2.91 in.)
Compression ratio	
650 cc	7.2:1
750 cc	7:1

Table 2 ENGINE SERVICE SPECIFICATIONS (650 AND 750 CC MODELS)

Item	Specification mm (in.)	Wear limit mm (in.)
Cylinder head warpage	–	0.05 (0.002)
Cylinder bore diameter		
650 cc	76.050-76.065 (2.994-2.995)	76.100 (2.996)
750 cc	80.00-80.015 (3.149-3.150)	80.100 (3.153)
Maximum taper	–	0.05 (0.002)
Maximum out-of-round	–	0.01
	–	(0.0004)

(continued)

Table 2 ENGINE SERVICE SPECIFICATIONS (650 AND 750 CC MODELS) (continued)

Item	Specification mm (in.)	Wear limit mm (in.)
Piston diameter		
650 cc	75.961-75.976 (2.991-2.992)	75.81 (2.985)
750 cc	79.900-79.915 (3.145-3.146)	79.75 (3.140)
Piston-to-cylinder clearance		
650 cc	0.084-0.094 (0.0033-0.0041)	−
750 cc	0.095-0.115 (0.0037-0.0045)	−
Piston ring end gap		
650 cc	0.2-0.4 (0.008-0.016)	0.7 (0.027)
750 cc	0.25-0.40 (0.010-0.016)	0.7 (0.027)
Crankshaft runout	0.0-0.04 (0.0-0.0016)	0.10 (0.004)
Connecting rod		
Side clearance	0.45-0.55 (0.018-0.022)	0.8 (0.031)
Radial clearance		
650 cc	0.045-0.055 (0.0018-0.0022)	0.11 (0.004)

Table 3 ENGINE TIGHTENING TORQUES (650 AND 750 MODELS)

Fastener	N·m	in.-lb.	ft.-lb.
Crankcase bolts			
6 mm	7.8	69	5.7
8 mm	29	−	21
Coupler half	98	−	72
Cylinder base nuts	34	−	25
Cylinder head nuts	29	−	21
Engine bed mounting bolts	32	−	24
Engine mount bolts	16	−	12
Engine mounting bolts	36	−	26
Exhaust manifold nuts	20	−	15
Exhaust pipe bolts			
650 cc			
8 mm	25	−	18
10 mm	49	−	36
750 cc	49	−	36
Flywheel cover bolts	7.8	69	5.7
Flywheel bolt			
650 cc	98	−	72
750 cc	125	−	92
Magneto cover bolts	7.8	69	5.7
Magneto cover stud	7.8	69	5.7
Spark plugs	27	−	20
Water pipe fitting	9.8	87	7.2

5

Chapter Six

Drive Train

The Jet Ski drive train consists of the engine/drive shaft coupling, drive shaft bearing housing and jet pump.

Tables 1-3 list drive train specifications. Tables 1-6 are located at the end of this chapter.

DRIVE SHAFT (JS440SX)

The front end of the stainless steel drive shaft is supported by 2 ball bearings in the bearing housing at the hull bulkhead. The rear of the drive shaft is supported by the pump case bushing. See **Figure 1**.

Grease fittings are provided at the bearing housing, pump housing and steering nozzle for periodic lubrication.

Drive Shaft Removal

Refer to **Figure 1** for this procedure.

1. Remove the engine as described in Chapter Four or Chapter Five.
2. Remove the jet pump and impeller as described in this chapter.
3. Remove the bolts securing the coupling cover to the hull (**Figure 2**), then remove the cover.
4. Remove the bearing housing mounting bolts (**Figure 3**). Then, label and remove the shims located under the bearing housing mounting lugs.

CAUTION
Always keep any original factory-installed shims between the bearing housing and the hull bulkhead (A, Figure 3). These shims effect alignment of the drive

(1)

DRIVE SHAFT AND BEARING HOUSING
(JS440SX)

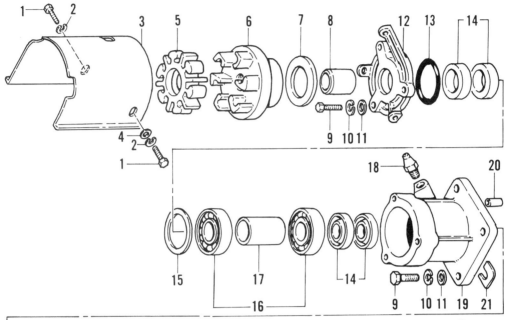

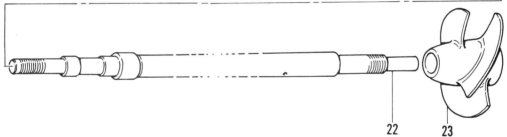

1. Bolt	13. O-ring
2. Washer	14. Oil seals
3. Coupling cover	15. Shim (as required)
4. Washer	16. Bearing
5. Rubber coupler	17. Spacer
6. Coupler half	18. Grease fitting
7. Washer	19. Bearing housing
8. Sleeve	20. Dowel pin
9. Bolt	21. Shim
10. Lockwasher	22. Drive shaft
11. Washer	23. Impeller
12. Bearing housing cover	

shaft with the jet pump as well as alignment with the engine.

5. Loosen the bearing housing by wiggling the rear of the drive shaft back and forth to break the seal at the bulkhead.

> *NOTE*
> *If the seal between the bearing housing and hull bulkhead is tight, it may be necessary to cut the seal edge at the bearing housing to help loosen it.*

6. Pull the bearing housing and drive shaft out of the hull (**Figure 4**).

Bearing Housing Disassembly

Refer to **Figure 1** for this procedure.

1. Unscrew the coupling half from the front of the drive shaft as follows:

   a. Open the drive shaft holder, part No. W56019-003 (**Figure 5**). Engage the holder pin with the hole in the end of the drive shaft (**Figure 6**). Pivot the end of the holder over the drive shaft and lock it with the Allen bolt.

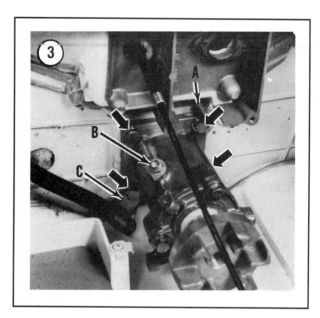

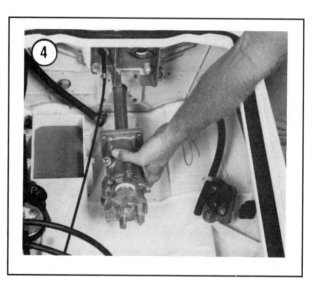

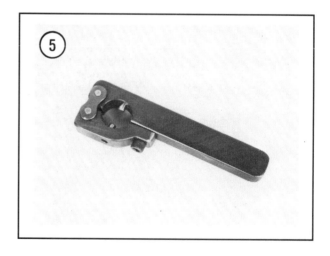

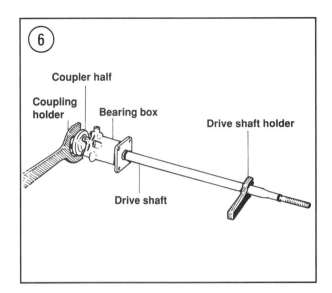

b. Unscrew the coupling half with the coupling holder part No. T57001-276 (**Figure 7**). See **Figure 6**.

2. Remove the bearing housing cover bolts (**Figure 8**). Then, tap the cover free with a soft-face mallet.

CAUTION
To prevent breakage, do not tap or hit on the cover mounting brackets.

3. Remove any bearing shim(s) located between the cover and the bearing (**Figure 9**).

4. Mount the drive shaft in a vise with protective (soft) jaws. Then, gently tap the bearing housing toward the rear and off the bearings (**Figure 10**).

6

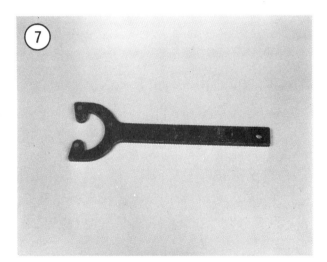

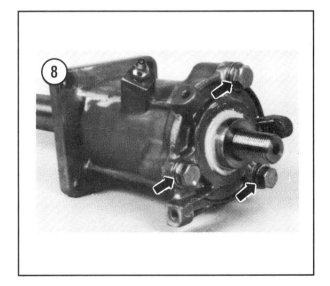

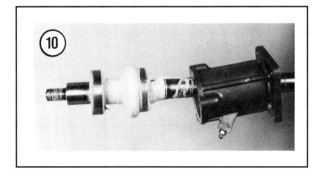

CAUTION
If protective jaws for the vise are not available, clamp the drive shaft between 2 blocks of wood. Do not damage the drive shaft.

Inspection

1. Check the cover O-ring (**Figure 11**) for flat spots, nicks, cuts or other damage. Replace the O-ring as necessary.

2. Check the cover oil seals (**Figure 11**) for wear or damage. If necessary, replace the seals as described in this chapter.

3. Check the bearing housing seals for wear or damage. If necessary, replace the oil seals as described in this chapter.

4. If the seals can be reused, do not remove them. Wash the seals thoroughly with solvent and allow to dry. Then, pack the seal lips with a suitable water-resistant grease.

NOTE
The seals and bearings are damaged during removal. If removed, always replace oil seals and bearings.

5. Clean the bearings on the drive shaft using solvent. Turn each bearing by hand to be sure it turns smoothly and quietly with no rough spots or other apparent damage. If any defects are noted, replace the bearing(s) as described in this chapter.

6. Mount the drive shaft on V-blocks at the points shown in **Figure 12**. Turn the drive shaft slowly while checking for runout using a dial indicator at the 4 test points shown in **Figure 12**. runout is the difference between the highest and lowest dial indicator reading. Replace the drive shaft if runout exceeds the following service limits:

a. Test position A: 0.1 mm (0.004 in.).

b. Test position B: 0.5 mm (0.020 in.).

Oil Seal and Bearing Replacement

Use a marine-grade, water-resistant grease when lubrication is required during this procedure. See **Figure 1** for seal and bearing alignment.

1. Replace the oil seals as follows:

a. Pry the 2 seals from the bearing housing cover using a large flat screwdriver or similar tool. Place a shop towel between the tool and cover to prevent damage to the cover.

b. Pry the 2 seals from the bearing housing using a large flat screwdriver or similar tool. Work the screwdriver around the outer seal until it pops out. Repeat for the second seal. Place a shop towel between the tool and housing to prevent damage to the housing.

2. Install the new oil seals as follows:

a. Lubricate the seal lips before installation.

b. Install the 2 seals into the bearing housing cover so their open sides face the front (**Figure 13**).

c. Install the 2 seals into the bearing box so their open sides face to the rear (**Figure 14**).

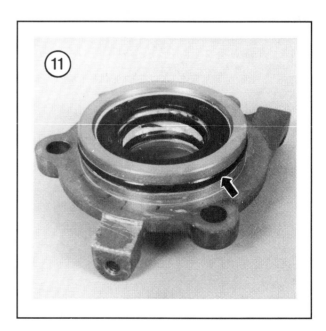

d. Install the seals by driving them into the cover or bearing housing using a socket placed on the outer portion of the seal. Do not drive on the inside of the seal or it will be damaged.

e. Thoroughly coat the seal lips with grease.

3. To remove the bearings mounted on the drive shaft, a press or bearing remover is required. The following steps describe bearing removal using a press. If a bearing remover is used, follow the tool manufacturer's instructions during bearing removal. Perform the following to remove the drive shaft bearings:

a. Mount the drive shaft into a press bed so the front bearing is supported by an adapter (**Figure 14**). Press the sleeve and bearing off the drive shaft. Catch the drive shaft as the bearing is pressed.

b. Remove the spacer (**Figure 14**).

c. Support the lower bearing in a press and press it off the drive shaft. Catch the drive shaft as the bearing is removed.

4. Install the drive shaft bearings as follows:

a. Lightly lubricate the drive shaft bearing mounting areas to ease installation.

b. Drive the rear bearing onto the drive shaft using a piece of pipe with the same diameter as the bearing inner race. Drive the bearing onto the drive shaft until fully bottomed.

c. Lubricate the inside of the spacer and slide in on the drive shaft so it bottoms against the rear bearing (installed in sub-step b).

d. Drive the front bearing onto the drive shaft with a piece of pipe with the same diameter as the bearing inner race. Drive the bearing on the shaft until fully bottomed against the spacer.

e. Install the front sleeve on the drives shaft so it is bottomed against the front bearing.

5. Lubricate the bearings with marine, water-resistant grease.

Bearing Housing Assembly

Refer to **Figure 1** for this procedure.

1. Make sure the bearings and seals are thoroughly lubricated using water-resistant grease.

2. Slide the bearing housing over the rear of the drive shaft (**Figure 10**).

3. Mount the drive shaft in a vise with protective jaws.

CAUTION
If protective jaws for the vise are not available, clamp the drive shaft between 2 blocks of wood. Do not damage the drive shaft.

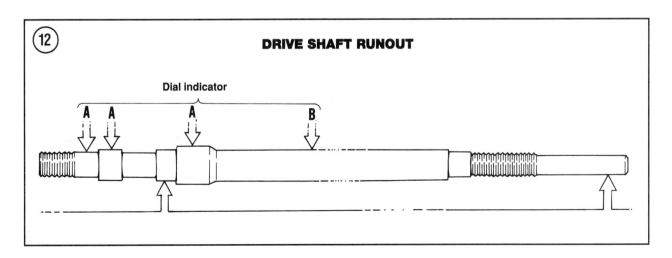

(12) **DRIVE SHAFT RUNOUT**

Dial indicator

A   A   A   B

4. Align the bearing housing with the bearings and gently tap the bearing housing toward the bearings. Tap the housing on all the way.

5. If the original drive shaft bearings are used, install the original shims outside the outer bearing (**Figure 9**).

6. If new bearings are used, it is necessary to determine bearing housing clearance.

With the bearings fully seated in the bearing housing, measure the distance from the end face of the housing to the outer face of the bearing using a vernier caliper as shown in **Figure 15**. Interpret the measurement as follows:

a. If the distance is 12.9-13.05 mm (0.508-0.514 in.), no shim is required.

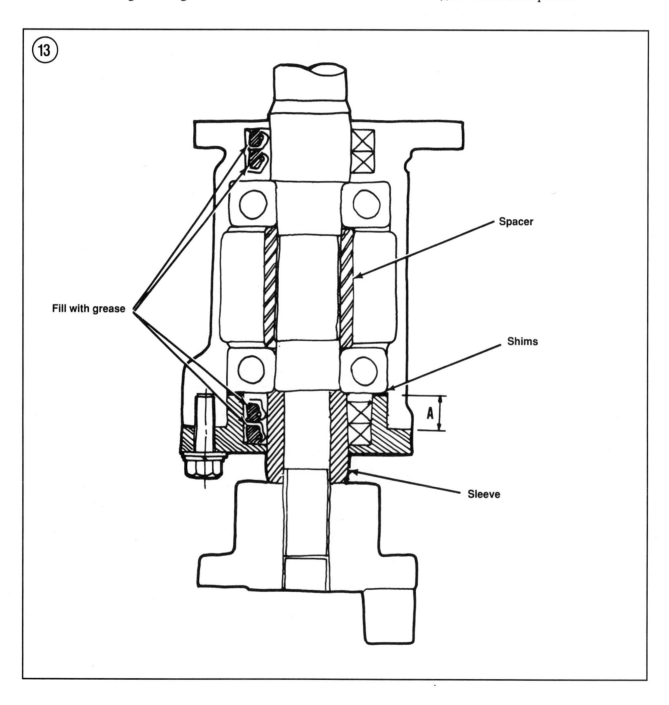

(13)

Fill with grease

Spacer

Shims

A

Sleeve

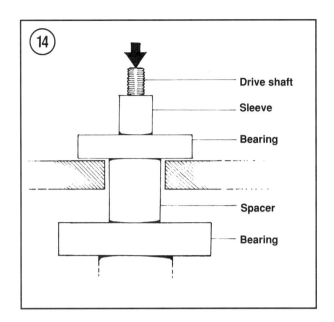

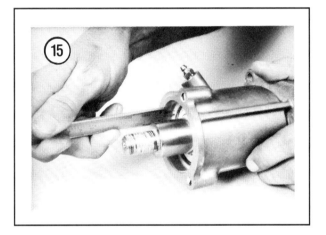

b. If the distance is 13.05-13.20 mm (0.514-0.520 in.), install a 0.15 mm (0.006 in.) shim (part No. 92025-502).

c. If the distance is 13.20-13.32 mm (0.520-0.524 in.), install a 0.30 mm (0.012 in.) shim (part No. 92-25-503).

d. If the distance exceeds 13.32 mm (0.524 in.), check for a damaged drive shaft, bearing housing or spacer.

7. Install a new O-ring on the bearing housing end cover (**Figure 11**). Coat the O-ring with water-resistant grease.

8. Install the end cover as follows:

a. While the end cover bolts are symmetrical, the cover must be installed only one way for correct alignment. If the cover is installed incorrectly, the coupling cover cannot be installed in the hull.

b. Slip the end cover over the drive shaft.

c. The end cover is equipped with 3 mounting tabs. Align the mounting tab that is adjacent to the word "made" on the cover with the grease fitting on the bearing housing. See **Figure 16**.

d. Push the cover into the bearing housing while making sure the cover O-ring remains in position.

6

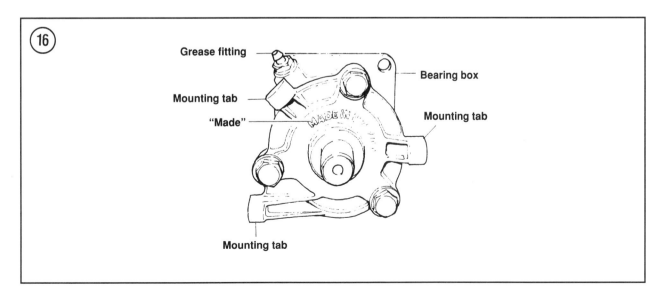

e. Install the cover bolts (**Figure 8**) and tighten securely.

9. Connect a grease gun to the grease fitting on the bearing housing. Pump grease into the housing until resistance is felt on the grease gun handle.

10. Install the coupling half as follows:

a. Apply water-resistant grease on the coupling threads.

b. Thread the coupling half on the end of the drive shaft.

c. Using drive shaft holder (part No. W56019-003) and coupling holder (part No. T57001-276), tighten the coupling half to the specification in **Table 4**. See **Figure 6**.

Drive Shaft Installation

1. Coat the mounting surfaces of the bearing housing with silicone sealant, then slide the bearing housing and drive shaft into position in the hull (**Figure 4**). The dowel pins in the back of the bearing housing (**Figure 17**) fit into the holes in the bulkhead. The grease fitting must be on the upper right side of the housing (B, **Figure 3**).

2. Loosely install the 4 bearing housing mounting bolts and washer (**Figure 3**).

3. Reinstall any shims in the same location from which removed during disassembly. If the shims were lost or the hull replaced, proceed to Step 4. Tighten the bolts to the torque specification in **Table 4**.

> *CAUTION*
> *Always keep the original factory-installed shims between the bearing housing and the hull bulkhead. These shims effect alignment of the drive shaft with the jet pump as well as alignment with the engine.*

4. If the factory-installed shims were lost or misplaced or the hull replaced, align the drive shaft/bearing housing as follows:

a. Measure the distance from the side of the hull to the end of the drive shaft (**Figure 18**). Take measurements on the left and right sides. Then, measure the distance from the top of the hull to the end of the drive shaft.

b. The distance from the shaft to the top of the hull should be 77 mm (3.03 in.). The distance from the shaft to the left and right sides should be equal.

c. If necessary, install shims between the hull and the bearing housing flanges until the distances are correct.

d. Tighten the bearing housing mounting bolts to the specification listed in **Table 4**.

5. Install the impeller and jet pump as described in this chapter.

DRIVE SHAFT
(550, 650 AND 750 CC MODELS)

The stainless steel drive shaft is supported by a ball bearing in the drive shaft holder mounted at the front of the bulkhead and by the bearing mounted in the jet pump at the rear. See **Figure 19**.

Drive Shaft Removal/Installation

Refer to **Figure 19** for this procedure.

1. Remove the engine as described in Chapter Four or Chapter Five.

2. *JS550SX, JS650SX and JS750SX*—Remove the fuel tank as described in Chapter Seven.

3. Grasp the drive shaft coupling half and slide the drive shaft out of the hull. See **Figure 20**. **Figure 21** shows the drive shaft and coupling removed.

4. To install the drive shaft, first apply a suitable water-resistant grease to the drive shaft splines (**Figure 22**).

5. Apply water-resistant grease to the lips drive shaft holder seals. See **Figure 19**.

6. Slide the drive shaft into the holder. Rotate the shaft to engage the impeller and drive shaft splines.

Coupling Half Removal/Installation

1. Remove the drive shaft as described in this chapter.

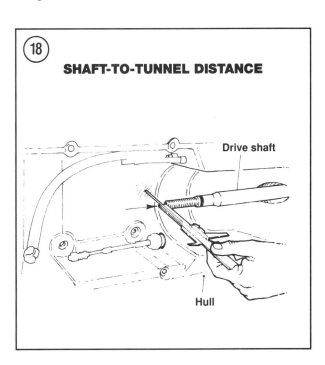

(18)

SHAFT-TO-TUNNEL DISTANCE

Drive shaft

Hull

2. Open the drive shaft holder tool (**Figure 5**) part No. W56019-003 (JS550SX, JB650 Jet Mate, JF650X-2 and JS650SX) or part No. 57001-1327 (all other models). Install holder adapter, part No. 57001-1348 (JL650SC and JH650TS) or part No. 57001-1231 (all other models) on the drive shaft.

3. Engage the holder pin with the adapter (**Figure 23**). Pivot the end of the holder over the drive shaft and lock it in place with the Allen bolt.

4. Unscrew the coupling half (**Figure 24**) using coupling holder part No. 57001-1230. See **Figure 23**.

5. Reverse Steps 1-3 to install the coupling. Tighten the coupling to the specification listed in **Table 5** or **Table 6**. Install the drive shaft as described in this chapter.

Drive Shaft and Coupling Half Inspection

1. Mount the drive shaft on V-blocks at the points indicated in **Figure 25**. Turn the drive shaft slowly while checking runout with a dial indicator situated at the 2 test points shown in **Figure 25**. Runout is the difference between the highest and lowest indicator readings. On JS550SX, JF650SX, JS650SX and JB650 Jet Mate models, drive shaft runout must not exceed 0.6 mm (0.024 in.) measured as shown (top, **Figure 25**). On all other models, drive shaft runout must not exceed 0.2 mm (0.008 in.) measured at point A (bottom, **Figure 25**) or 0.6 mm (0.024 in.) measured at point B. Replace the drive shaft if the runout exceeds the specified limit.

2. Inspect the coupling half for excessive wear, cracks or other damage. Replace the coupling half as required. If the drive shaft coupling half is damaged, be sure to carefully check the crankshaft coupling half and rubber coupling half for damage.

6

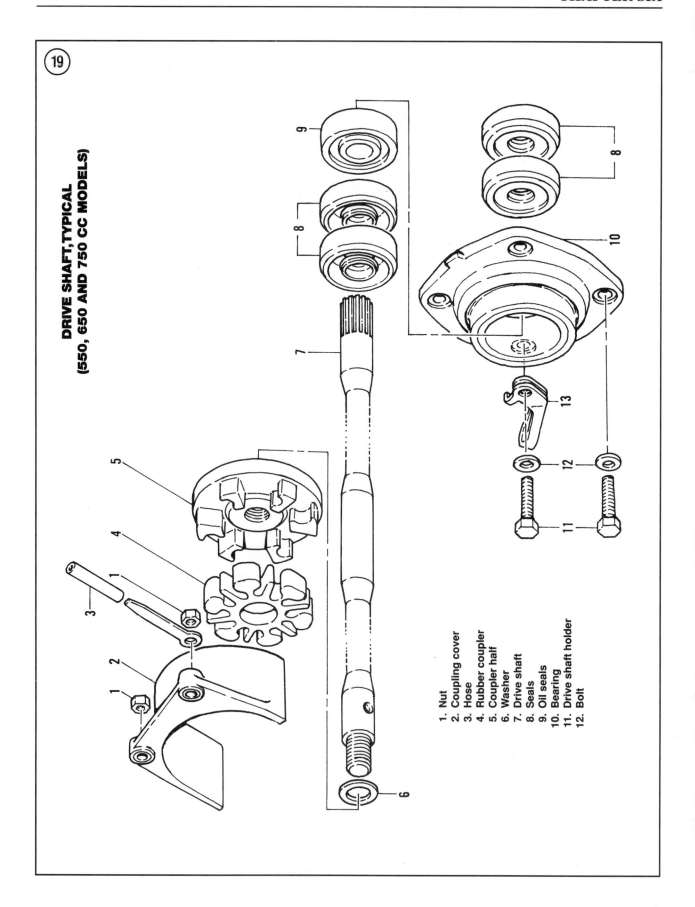

⑲

**DRIVE SHAFT, TYPICAL
(550, 650 AND 750 CC MODELS)**

1. Nut
2. Coupling cover
3. Hose
4. Rubber coupler
5. Coupler half
6. Washer
7. Drive shaft
8. Seals
9. Oil seals
10. Bearing
11. Drive shaft holder
12. Bolt

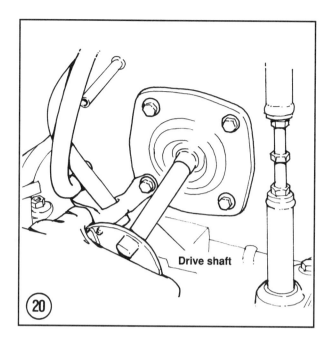

Drive shaft

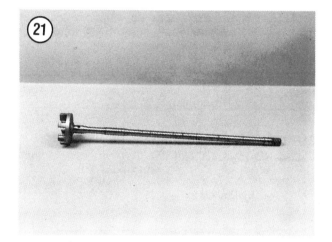

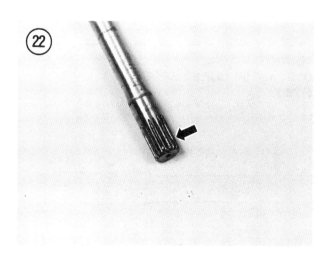

Drive Shaft Holder Removal/Installation

1. Remove the drive shaft as described in this chapter.

2. Remove the bolts holding the drive shaft holder to the bulkhead (**Figure 26**). Remove the drive shaft holder from the bulkhead.

3. Spin the bearing mounted in the drive shaft holder. Replace the bearing if it turns roughly, grabs or is noisy.

4. Closely inspect the front and rear seals for leakage. Replace the seals if any leakage is noted.

6

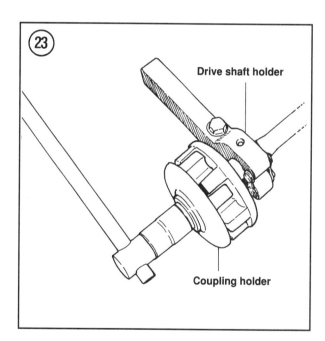

Drive shaft holder

Coupling holder

CAUTION
The following drive shaft installation procedure must be followed to ensure proper coupling alignment. Improper alignment will result in excessive vibration and premature bearing failure.

5. Coat the mounting surfaces of the drive shaft holder with Kawasaki Bond (part No. 56019-120) or equivalent silicone sealant.

6. Install the drive shaft holder so the side with the snap ring faces to the front (**Figure 27**). Install the holder bolts finger tight. Be sure to reinstall any clamps or brackets attached to the bolts.

7. Install the drive shaft as described in this chapter.

8. After the engine bed is securely bolted in the hull, remove the holder bolts one at a time and apply Loctite 242 to the threads. Reinstall the bolts finger tight. Then, tighten the bolts in a crossing pattern to the specification listed in **Table 5** or **Table 6**.

Drive shaft Holder Oil Seal and Bearing Replacement

The drive shaft holder houses a single ball bearing and 4 grease seals. See **Figure 28**. Do not remove the seals or bearing unless replacement is necessary.

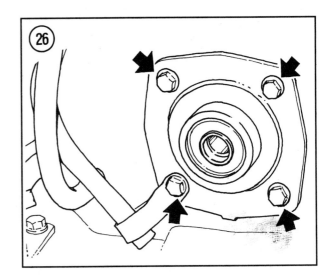

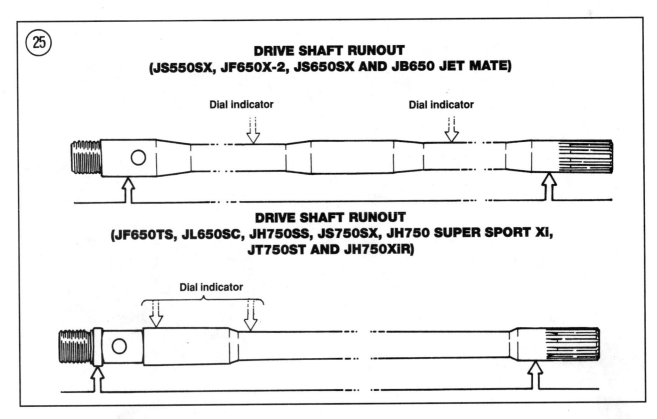

DRIVE SHAFT RUNOUT
(JS550SX, JF650X-2, JS650SX AND JB650 JET MATE)

Dial indicator   Dial indicator

DRIVE SHAFT RUNOUT
(JF650TS, JL650SC, JH750SS, JS750SX, JH750 SUPER SPORT Xi, JT750ST AND JH750XiR)

Dial indicator

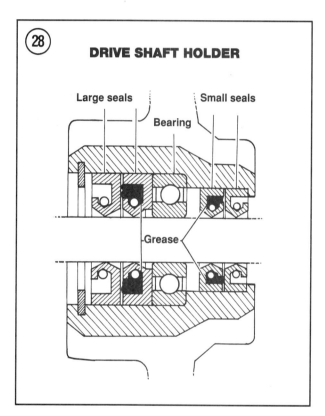

DRIVE SHAFT HOLDER

Large seals   Small seals

Bearing

Grease

1. Remove the snap ring from the end of the holder (**Figure 29**).

2. Place the drive shaft holder on wooden blocks as shown in **Figure 30**.

3. Using a suitable bearing driver positioned against the small seals, press the small seals, bearing and large seals from the holder (**Figure 30**). Discard the bearing and seals.

4. Thoroughly clean the holder with solvent and allow to dry.

5. Install the 2 small seals as follows:

   a. Pack the grease seal lips with water-resistant grease.

   b. Install the small seals so their open side faces toward the rear of the holder.

   c. Using a suitable seal installer or driver, install the lower seal so it seats against the

6

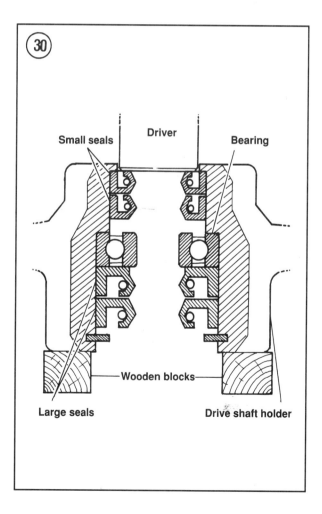

Small seals   Driver   Bearing

Wooden blocks

Large seals   Drive shaft holder

bottom shoulder in the holder. See **Figure 31**.

d. Drive the upper seal into the holder until it bottoms against the lower seal.

6. Install the bearing as follows:

a. Lubricate the bearing with water-resistant grease.

b. Using a suitable bearing driver, drive the bearing into the holder until it contacts the shoulder inside the holder (**Figure 28**). Make sure the driver contacts the bearing outer race only.

7. Install the 2 large seals as follows:

a. Pack the seal lips with water-resistant grease.

b. Install the large seals so their open sides face toward the front of the holder.

c. Drive the lower seal into the holder until it bottoms on the bearing.

d. Drive the upper seal into the holder until it bottoms against the lower seal.

11. Install the snap ring into its groove in the holder (**Figure 29**). Make sure the snap ring is completely seated in its groove.

JET PUMP (JS440SX)

The jet pump case contains the impeller mounted on the drive shaft. The end of the drive shaft rides in a bushing at the rear of the pump case. A grease fitting is provided at the pump outlet for regular lubrication.

The pump is carefully manufactured so very little clearance between the impeller and case is present. As the pump wears from the normal use, the clearance will increase causing pump thrust to decrease. The impeller and case should be inspected according to the maintenance schedule in Chapter Three. Replace the pump and case if excessively worn.

With extended use, the drive shaft bushing in the rear of the pump case can wear and may cause inaccurate impeller-to-case clearance.

Positioning of the impeller inside the case is controlled by the pump case bushing and shims placed under the pump case. See *Impeller and Jet Pump Installation* in this chapter.

> *NOTE*
> *Do not change the original factory installed shims between the jet pump and hull, unless it is necessary reposition the impeller within the pump case. This may be required after installing new bearings in the bearing housing or after replacing the bushing in the rear of the pump case.*

Jet Pump/Impeller Removal

Refer to **Figure 32** for this procedure.

1. Remove the battery. See Chapter Eight.

2. Disconnect the spark plug leads from the spark plugs to prevent accidental starting.

3. Roll the watercraft onto its left side (**Figure 33**). Support the watercraft with a heavy blanket to protect the hull finish.

> *NOTE*
> *Do not turn the watercraft on its right side or water in the exhaust system may drain into the cylinders.*

4. Remove the bolts holding the water intake grate (**Figure 34**) to the bottom of the hull. Remove the grate.

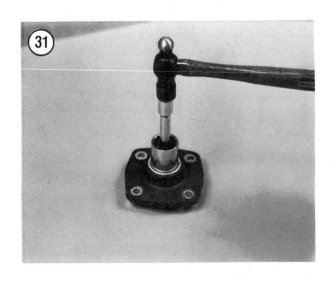

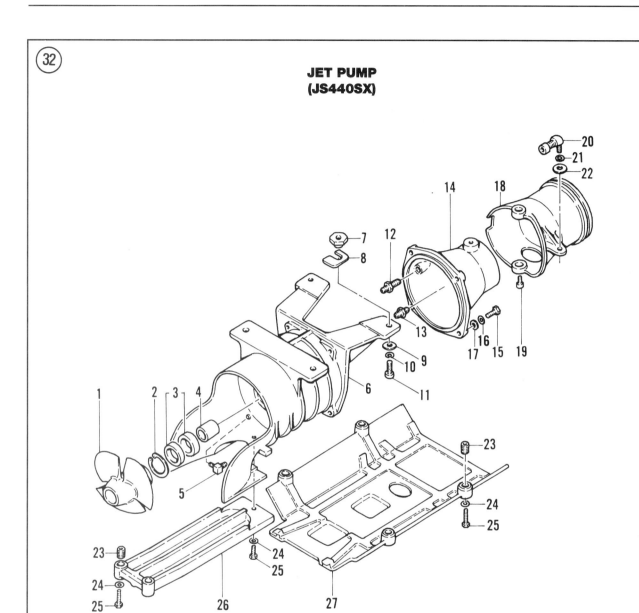

**JET PUMP
(JS440SX)**

1. Impeller
2. Snap ring
3. Oil seals
4. Bushing
5. Hose fitting
6. Pump housing
7. Nut (in hull)
8. Shim
9. Washer
10. Lockwasher
11. Allen bolt
12. Hose fitting
13. Grease fitting
14. Pump outlet
15. Bolt
16. Lockwasher
17. Washer
18. Steering nozzle
19. Bolt
20. Ball-joint
21. Lockwasher
22. Washer
23. Insert nut (in hull)
24. Washer
25. Bolt
26. Intake grate
27. Pump cover

6

5. Remove the bolts holding the pump cover (**Figure 35**) to the bottom of the hull. Remove the cover.

6. Detach the steering cable ball joint from the pump steering nozzle. Slide its spring-loaded sleeve forward and pull the connector off the ball (A, **Figure 36**).

7. Loosen the hose clamps and disconnect the cooling water supply hose (B, **Figure 36**) and the bilge discharge hose (C) from the pump case.

8. Remove the 4 Allen bolts that hold the jet pump to the hull (**Figure 37**).

CAUTION
Be sure to note the location and thickness (number) of any shims under the pump mounting lugs (A, Figure 37). These shims must be reinstalled in exactly the same position from which removed to ensure the correct pump alignment.

9. Cut the sealant at the pump intake area.

10. Remove the jet pump by pulling it to the rear. If necessary, lightly tap the pump case with a soft-face mallet. (See **Figure 38**).

CAUTION
The pump assembly may be difficult to remove because of the silicone sealant applied to the pump intake area (Figure 39). If you find it impossible to break the seal loose, do not hammer excessively on the pump case. The case is constructed of cast aluminum and is easily

broken. Instead, remove the engine as described in Chapter Four. Then remove the drive shaft bearing housing mounting bolts and pull the drive shaft forward slightly as described in this chapter. This will provide the clearance necessary to

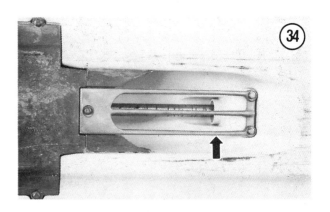

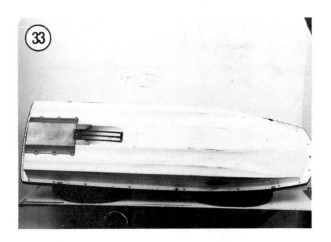

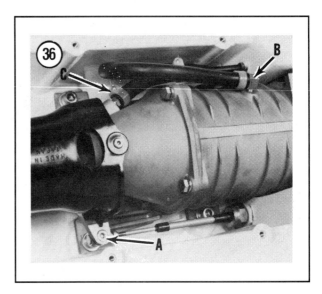

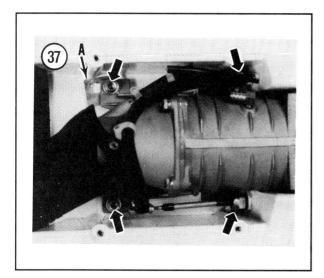

pull the pump case sideways and break the seal.

11. Remove the shims (**Figure 40**).

12. Hold the drive shaft steady with the Kawasaki drive shaft holding tool (part No. W56019-003). See **Figure 41**. Then, loosen the impeller with a 32 mm wrench or a large adjustable wrench placed on the hex section of the impeller (**Figure 42**).

13. Slide the impeller off the drive shaft.

Pump Case Disassembly

See **Figure 32** for this procedure.

6

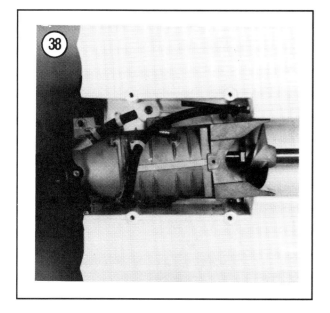

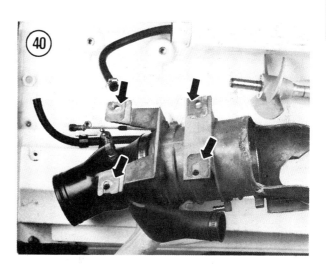

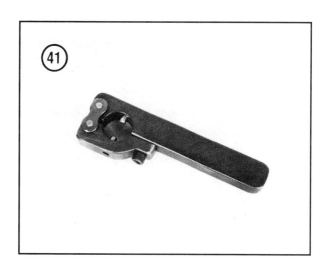

NOTE
Do not remove the bushing and seals in the jet pump unless replacement is required. The bushing and seals are damaged during the removal process.

1. Remove the 2 Allen bolts (**Figure 43**) securing the steering nozzle to the pump assembly. Remove the steering nozzle.

2. Remove the bolts holding the pump outlet to the pump case. See **Figure 44**. Tap the outlet with a soft-face mallet to dislodge the outlet.

Jet Pump/Impeller Inspection

Normal wear of the pump case and impeller can reduce pump thrust and top speed, even if the

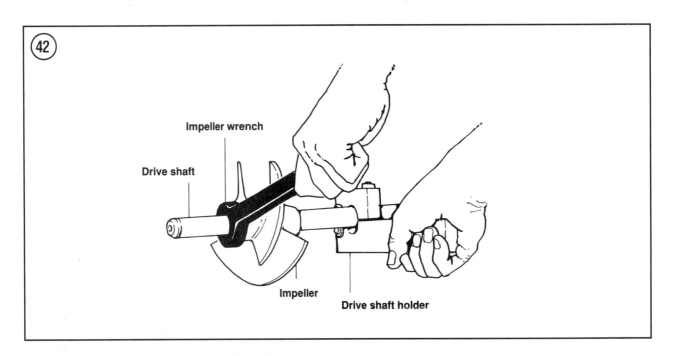

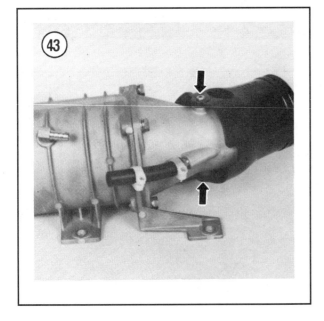

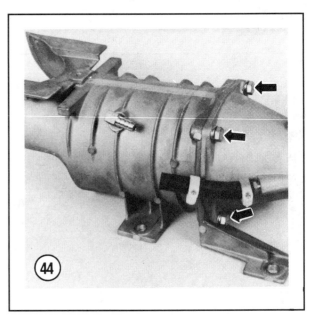

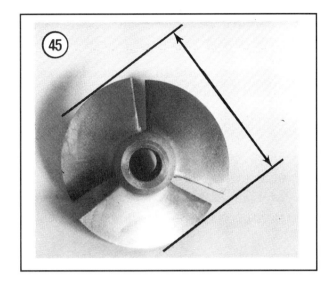

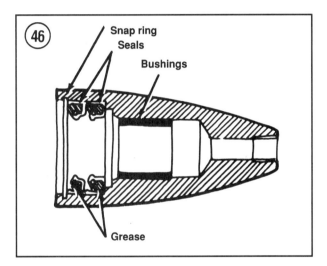

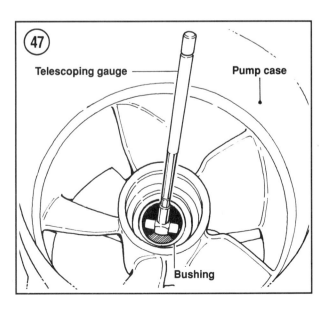

engine is operating properly. Thrust reduction can also be caused by obstructions in the pump or a damaged pump case or impeller. If the wide-open throttle engine speed has increased, but watercraft top speed and performance has declined, expect pump case/impeller damage or wear.

1. Inspect the impeller blades and pump case blades for nicks, gouges cracks or other damage. Minor damage can be smoothed with a file or sand paper. To prevent cavitation, it is especially important for the leading edges of the impeller blades to be smooth.

2. Measure the outside diameter of the impeller (**Figure 45**). If is smaller than the service limit specified in **Table 1**, replace the impeller.

3. Check the inside of the jet pump case for deep scratches. Measure the inside diameter of the section that houses the impeller. If it is damaged or the diameter is larger than the service limit specified in **Table 1**, replace the pump case or have the pump remachined. See *Remachined Pumps* in this chapter.

4. Clean the bushing (**Figure 46**) with solvent and check it for scratches or uneven wear. Measure the bushing's inside diameter with a telescopic gauge as shown in **Figure 47**. Then, measure the gauge with a micrometer to determine the bushing inside diameter. Replace the bushing if the inside diameter is larger than the service limit specified in **Table 1**.

6

Remachined Pumps

The jet pump's forward thrust declines as the impeller and wall of the pump wears. The inner wall of the pump and the outer edges of the impeller blades are gradually worn by sand, gravel and silt drawn into the pump during operation. Aftermarket accessory dealers can bore the inner diameter of the pump case, then install a precision, stainless steel wear ring insert, which generally has a tighter impeller-to-pump clearance than the factory pump. This tighter clearance increases pump efficiency which results in greater thrust. In addition, the modified pump generally has a longer service life than the original pump.

Bushing and Seal Removal/Installation

CAUTION
The bushing and seal are damaged during removal. Do not remove them unless replacement is required.

1. Remove the snap ring from the rear of the drive shaft bore (**Figure 48**).

2. Two seals are located in the rear of the pump case. Remove the outer seal using a suitable hooked tool. Work the tool around the seal and slowly pull the outer seal squarely out of the case. Remove the inner seal using the same procedure.

3. Heat the pump case to approximately 200°F (93°C) using a heat lamp or heat gun.

4. Next, pull the bushing from the case using Kawasaki seal and bearing remover (part No. 57001-1058) or an equivalent puller with internal jaws.

NOTE
*If a suitable bushing puller is not available, insert a brass or aluminum punch into the rear of the case. Locate the edge of the bushing (**Figure 46**) with the punch and **carefully** tap the bushing out. Move the punch around the edge of the bushing while tapping to ensure the bushing is driven out evenly.*

5. Place the new bushing in a freezer for about 1 hour. Once the bushing is thoroughly cooled, heat the pump case to approximately 200°F (93°C) using a heat lamp or heat gun.

6. Remove the bushing from the freezer and lubricate its outer diameter with grease. Quickly insert the bushing into its bore. Using a suitable driver, tap the bushing into the pump case until fully seated.

7. Install the drive shaft seals (**Figure 46**) into the pump case as follows:

a. Thoroughly lubricate the seal lips with water-resistant grease.

b. Install both seals so their open side is facing the front of the pump case.

c. Install the inner seal using a driver that contacts the outer diameter of the seal. Drive the seal squarely, until fully bottomed. Then, drive the outer seal into the case until it bottoms against the inner seal. When properly installed, the outer seal is

just below the snap ring groove in the case (**Figure 49**).

8. Install the snap ring (**Figure 48**) making sure it is fully seated in its groove.

Pump Case Assembly

Refer to **Figure 32** for this procedure.

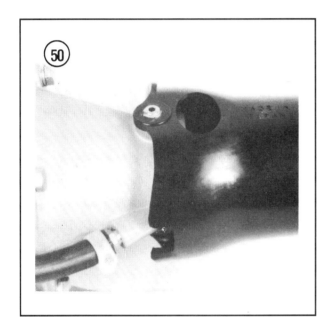

1. Apply a light coat of silicone sealant to the mating surface of the pump outlet. Mount the pump outlet on the pump case with the 4 bolts with flat washers and lockwashers. Apply Loctite 242 to the threads of the bolts. Make sure the hose fitting on the outlet is on the same side as the fitting on the pump case. See **Figure 44**. Tighten the bolts in a crossing pattern to the specification in **Table 4**.

2. Fit the steering nozzle on the pump case with its ball joint on the side opposite the pump case water hose fittings (**Figure 50**). Apply Loctite 242 to the threads of the nozzle pivot bolts, then install the bolts (**Figure 43**) and tighten securely. Make sure the nozzle moves smoothly.

Impeller/Jet Pump Installation

6

1. Lubricate the threaded end of the drive shaft with water-resistant grease.

2. Screw the impeller onto the drive shaft. Hold the drive shaft steady with the Kawasaki drive shaft holding tool (part No. W56019-003). See **Figure 41**. Then, tighten the impeller with a 32 mm wrench or a large adjustable wrench placed on the hex section of the impeller (**Figure 42**).

3. To prevent a hydraulic lock when installing the pump onto the drive shaft, remove the grease fitting from the rear of the pump case (**Figure 51**).

4. Make sure the water intake and bilge discharge hoses are in position in the pump cavity. See **Figure 52**.

5. Lightly lubricate the end of the drive shaft with water-resistant grease. Carefully slide the pump case over the drive shaft and impeller. Use caution not to damage the drive shaft seals.

6. Install the alignment shims on the pump mounting bolts exactly as originally installed (**Figure 53**).

7. Temporarily tighten the pump mounting bolts. Then, using a feeler gauge, make sure an even gap of at least 0.1 mm (0.004 in.) is present all around the impeller circumference. If the

clearancc is incorrect, change shims on the pump mounting bolts as necessary.

8. After the correct impeller-to-pump case clearance is obtained, tighten the pump mounting bolts to the specification listed in **Table 4**. Then, recheck impeller clearance and readjust if necessary.

9. Seal the gap between the hull and the edge of the pump intake area (**Figure 54**) with Loctite SuperFlex (Kawasaki part No. K61079-007) or equivalent silicone sealant. Remove all excess sealant from inside the pump intake to prevent impeller cavitation.

10. Reinstall the grease fitting on the pump outlet (**Figure 51**). Lubricate the bearing with water-resistant grease.

11. Connect the steering cable at the nozzle. See A, **Figure 55**.

12. Connect the engine cooling and bilge drain hoses. The cooling system supply hose connects to the fitting toward the front of the pump case (A, **Figure 56**). The bilge hose connects to the fitting at the rear of the pump (B, **Figure 56**). Tighten the hose clamps securely.

CAUTION
If the hoses are connected incorrectly, the engine will overheat and the engine compartment will fill with water.

13. Pivot the steering nozzle to make sure no binding or pinching of the hoses is noted.

14. Install the pump cover plate (**Figure 57**) and tighten the bolts securely.

15. Install the intake grate (**Figure 58**) and tighten its 2 bolts to the specification in **Table 4**.

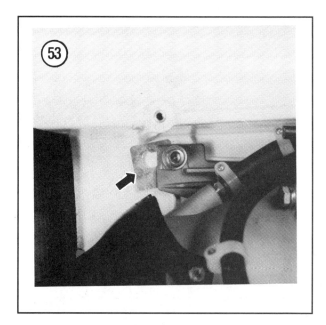

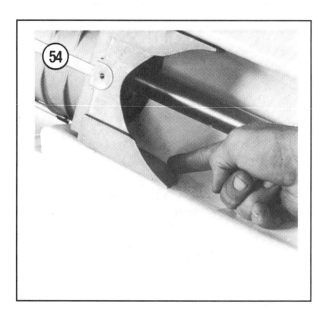

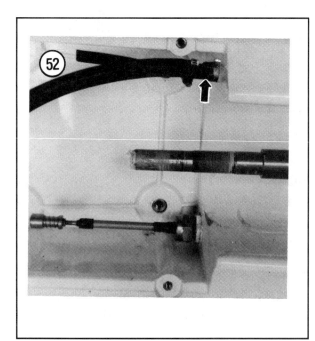

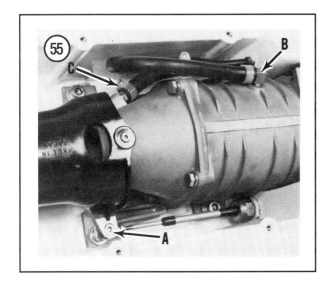

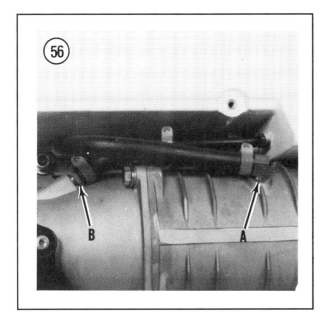

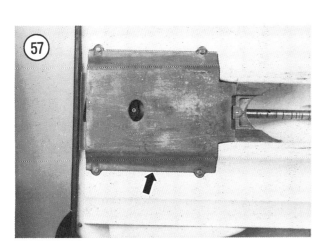

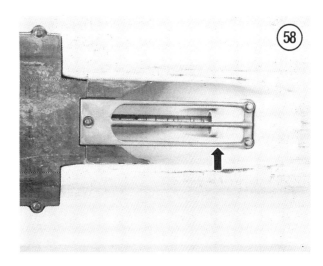

16. Place the watercraft upright. Reinstall the battery and reconnect the spark plug leads.

JET PUMP (JS550SX)

The jet pump case contains the impeller mounted on the pump shaft. The pump shaft is engaged with the rear of the drive shaft with splines. A grease fitting for regular lubrication is provided at the pump outlet.

The pump is carefully manufactured so very little clearance between the impeller and case is present. As the pump wears from the normal use, the clearance will increase causing pump thrust to decrease. The impeller and case should be inspected according to the maintenance schedule in Chapter Three. Replace the pump and case if excessively worn.

Positioning of the impeller inside the case is controlled by shims located behind the impeller. Refer to *Pump Case Assembly* in this chapter.

Jet Pump Removal

NOTE
*The impeller is mounted on the guide vane (**Figure 59**). To remove the impeller, the pump must be removed and partially disassembled.*

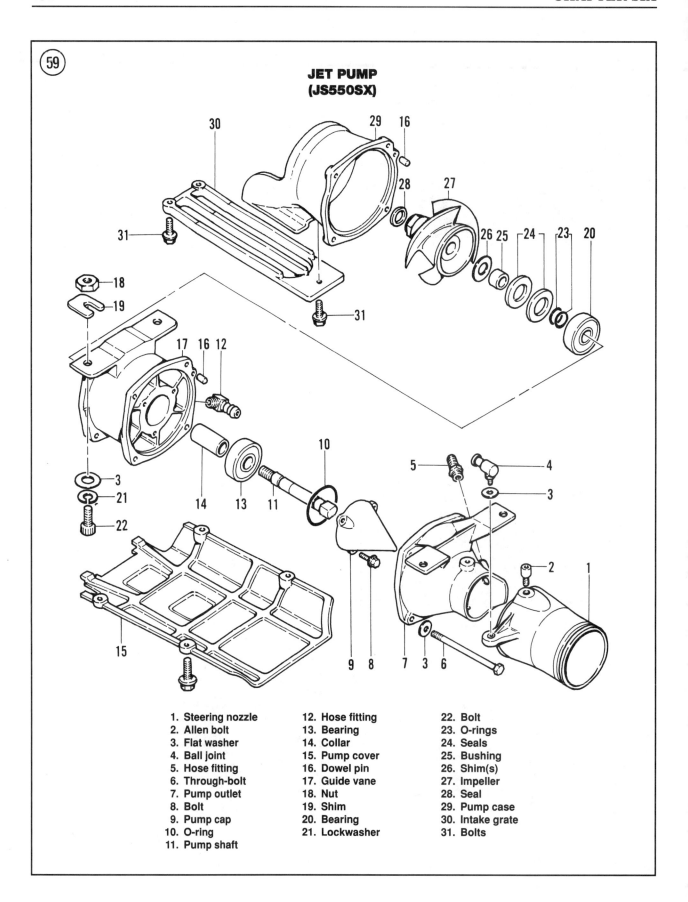

**JET PUMP
(JS550SX)**

1. Steering nozzle	12. Hose fitting	22. Bolt
2. Allen bolt	13. Bearing	23. O-rings
3. Flat washer	14. Collar	24. Seals
4. Ball joint	15. Pump cover	25. Bushing
5. Hose fitting	16. Dowel pin	26. Shim(s)
6. Through-bolt	17. Guide vane	27. Impeller
7. Pump outlet	18. Nut	28. Seal
8. Bolt	19. Shim	29. Pump case
9. Pump cap	20. Bearing	30. Intake grate
10. O-ring	21. Lockwasher	31. Bolts
11. Pump shaft		

Refer to **Figure 59** for this procedure.

1. Remove the battery.

2. Disconnect the spark plug leads from the spark plugs to prevent accidental starting.

3. Roll the watercraft on its left side (**Figure 60**). Place a heavy blanket under the watercraft to protect the hull finish.

CAUTION
Do not roll the watercraft on its right side or water in the exhaust system can drain into the cylinders.

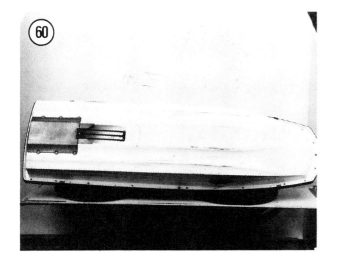

4. Remove the bolts holding the water intake grate (**Figure 58**) to the bottom of the hull. Remove the grate.

5. Remove the bolts holding the jet pump cover (**Figure 57**) to the hull. Remove the cover.

6. Detach the steering cable ball joint from the pump nozzle. Slide its spring-loaded sleeve forward and pull the connector off the ball (**Figure 61**).

7. Loosen the hose clamps and disconnect the cooling water supply hose and the bilge discharge hose from the pump case. See **Figure 61**.

8. Remove the 4 Allen bolts that hold the jet pump to the hull (**Figure 62**).

CAUTION
*Be sure to note the location and thickness (number) of any shims under the pump mounting lugs (**Figure 62**). These shims must be reinstalled in exactly the same position from which removed to ensure the correct pump alignment.*

9. Cut the sealant at the pump intake area.

10. Remove the pump assembly by pulling it to the rear and disengaging the drive shaft from the pump shaft. Lightly tap the pump to break the silicone seal.

6

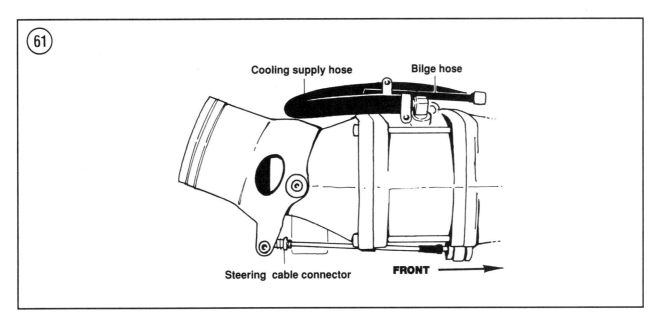

Cooling supply hose   Bilge hose

Steering cable connector   FRONT ➝

CAUTION
*The pump assembly may be difficult to remove because of the silicone sealant applied to the pump intake area (**Figure 63**). With the drive shaft and pump shaft engaged, it is necessary to pull the pump backward to remove it. If you find it impossible to break the seal loose, do not hammer excessively on the pump case. The case is constructed of cast aluminum and is easily broken. Instead, remove the engine as described in Chapter Four. The remove the drive shaft bearing housing mounting bolts and pull the drive shaft forward slightly as described in this chapter. This will provide the clear-*

ance necessary to pull the pump case sideways and break the seal.

11. Remove any shims located between the bottom of the hull and pump case mounting flanges.

Pump Case Disassembly

Refer to **Figure 59** for this procedure.

NOTE
Do not remove the seals from the pump housing unless replacement is necessary. The seals are damaged during removal.

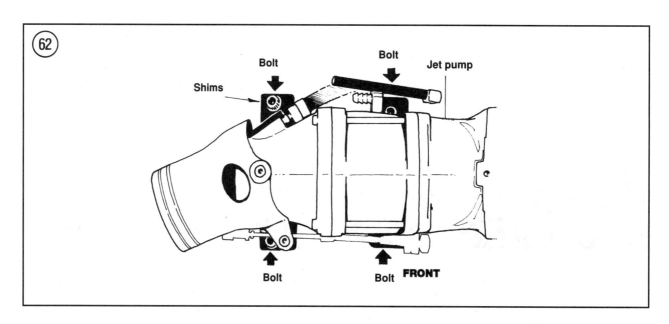

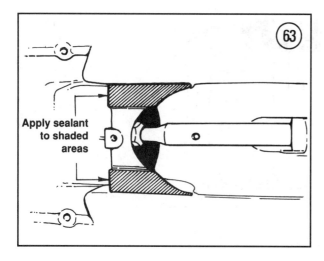

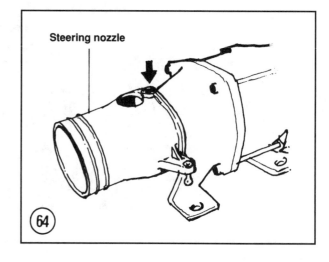

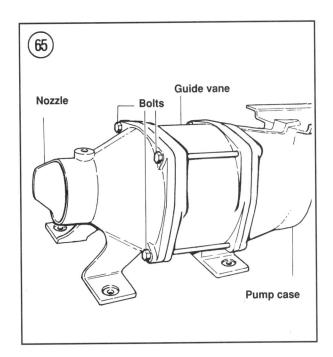

Figure 65

Nozzle
Bolts
Guide vane
Pump case

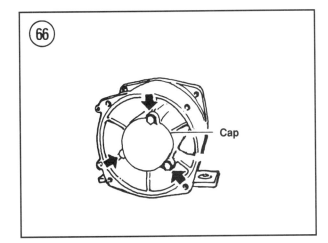

Figure 66

Cap

Figure 67

1. Remove the 2 Allen bolts securing the steering nozzle (**Figure 64**) to the pump assembly. Remove the steering nozzle.

2. Remove the long bolts holding the pump outlet, guide vane and pump case together. See **Figure 65**. Using a soft-face mallet, tap the pump outlet to break the seal, then separate it from the guide vane casting. Then, tap the pump case to break it loose from the guide vane. Remove the dowel pins from the mating surfaces.

3. Remove the 3 bolts securing the pump cap to the guide vane casting. See **Figure 66**. Remove the cap.

3. The impeller is threaded (right-hand threads) on the pump shaft. To remove it, proceed as follows:

a. Securely clamp the pump shaft (**Figure 67**) in a vise with protective jaws. Use caution not to damage the shaft.

b. Using an appropriately sized box-end wrench, turn the impeller counterclockwise (right-hand threads) to loosen it from the pump shaft. See **Figure 68**. Unscrew and remove the impeller (**Figure 69**).

6

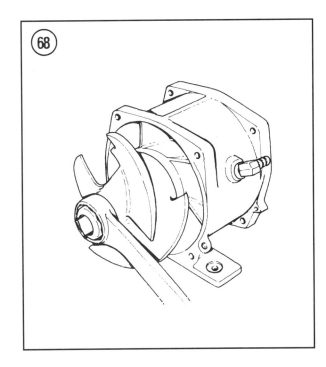

Figure 68

c. Remove any shims (**Figure 69**) located behind the impeller.

4. Slide the pump shaft (**Figure 70**) from the pump case.

5. Remove the bushing (**Figure 71**) from the pump case.

Jet Pump/Impeller Inspection

Normal wear of the pump case and impeller can diminish pump thrust and top speed, even if the engine is operating properly. Reduced thrust can also be caused by obstructions in the pump or a damaged pump case or impeller. If the wide-open throttle engine speed has increased, but watercraft top speed and performance has declined, expect pump case/impeller damage or wear.

1. Clean all components with solvent and allow to dry.

2. Clean all sealant from all mating surfaces.

3. Inspect the impeller and pump case for nicks, gouges, pitting or other damage. Minor damage can be smoothed with a file or sand paper. To prevent cavitation, it is especially important for the leading edges (A, **Figure 72**) of the impeller blades to be smooth.

4. Closely inspect the inside of the pump case for damage. If deep scratches are noted (deeper than 1 mm [0.039 in.]), replace the pump case or have the case remachined. See *Remachined Pumps* in this chapter.

5. Check the threads in the impeller (B, **Figure 72**) for damage. Repair damaged threads if possible or replace the impeller.

6. Check the impeller grease seal (**Figure 73**). Replace the seal by prying it out of the impeller with a screwdriver. Install the seal with a bearing driver or a socket with the same outer diameter as the seal.

7. Check the pump shaft (A, **Figure 74**) surface for cracks, scoring or excessive wear. Replace the O-ring (B, **Figure 74**) during reassembly.

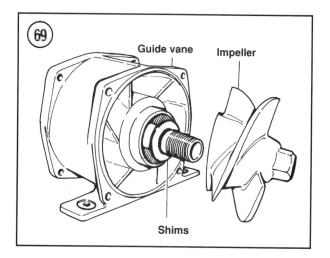
(69) Guide vane   Impeller   Shims

(70)

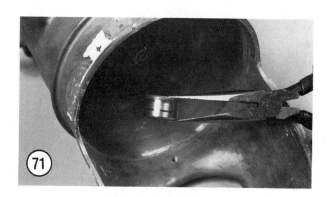
(71)

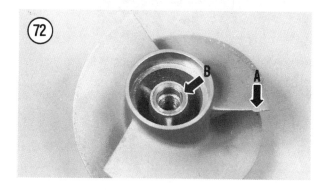
(72)   B   A

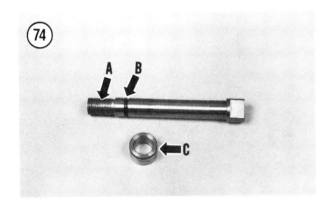

8. Check pump shaft bushing (C, **Figure 74**) for cracks, scoring, excessive wear or other damage. Replace the bushing if worn or damaged.

9. Check the 2 grease seals mounted in the guide vane (**Figure 75**, typical). Check the seal lips for tears, softness or signs of leakage. It is always good practice to replace all O-rings and seals during reassembly.

10. Check the 2 pump shaft bearings (**Figure 76**, typical) in the vane guide. Slowly turn each bearing and check for roughness, corrosion or excessive noise. The bearings must rotate smoothly. If necessary, replace the bearings as described in this chapter.

Remachined Pumps

The jet pump's forward thrust declines as the impeller and wall of the pump wears. The inner wall of the pump and the outer edges of the impeller blades are gradually worn by sand, gravel and silt drawn into the pump during operation. Aftermarket accessory dealers can bore the inner diameter of the pump case, then install a precision, stainless steel wear ring insert, which generally has a tighter impeller-to-pump clearance than the original arrangement. This tighter clearance increases pump efficiency which results in greater thrust. In addition, the modified pump generally has a longer service life than the original pump.

Bearing and Seal Removal/Installation

CAUTION
The seals and bearings are damaged during removal from the guide vane casting. Do not remove unless replacement is necessary.

1. Remove the 2 seals from the guide vane using Kawasaki bearing and seal remover (part No. 57001-1058) or an equivalent puller. Discard the seals.

6

2. Support the guide vane on wooden blocks. Remove the lower bearing by tapping around its inner bearing race with a punch as shown in **Figure 77**. When the bearing falls free, the collar can be removed. Then, invert the guide vane and remove the remaining bearing using the same procedure (**Figure 77**).

3. Thoroughly clean the guide vane casting with solvent and dry with compressed air.

4. Using a suitable bearing driver, tap the rear bearing into the guide vane until fully seated. See **Figure 78**. Make sure the driver contacts the bearing outer race only.

5. Invert the guide vane and place the collar into the guide vane. Then, tap the front bearing into the guide vane using the bearing driver (**Figure 78**.

NOTE
*Install the seals (Steps 6 and 7) so their open side faces the front of the guide vane. See **Figure 79**.*

6. Coat the guide vane seals with water-resistant grease. Drive the inner seal into the guide vane with a driver with the same outer diameter as the seal. Drive the seal until fully bottomed in the guide vane.

7. Next, drive the outer seal into the guide vane until fully bottomed against the inner seal.

8. Pack the area between the seals with water-resistant grease.

9. Lightly lubricate the outer diameter of the bushing (**Figure 71**) and install it into the guide vane.

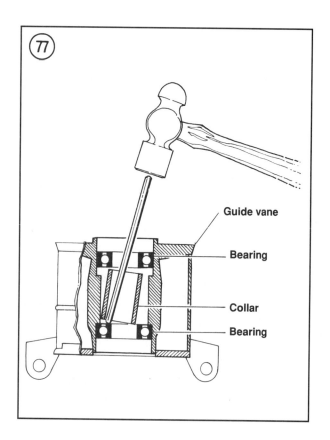

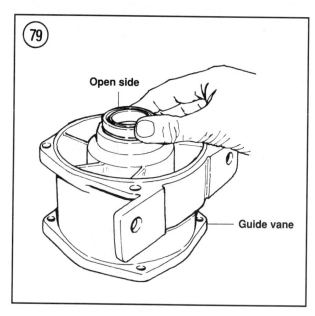

Pump Case Assembly

Refer to **Figure 59** for this procedure.

1. Lubricate the pump shaft with water-resistant grease. Install the shaft into the guide vane, from the rear side.

2. Install new O-rings on the pump shaft. Lubricate the O-rings with water-resistant grease.

3. Place the impeller shims on the pump shaft. See **Figure 69**.

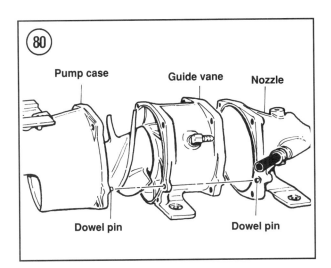

Pump case   Guide vane   Nozzle

Dowel pin   Dowel pin

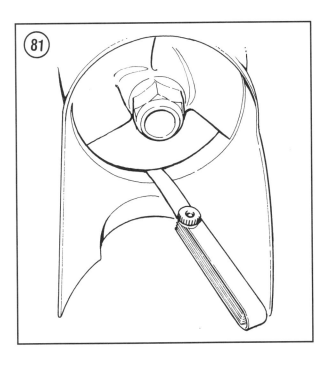

4. Lubricate the pump shaft threads with water-resistant grease. Install a new seal into the impeller (**Figure 73**), if removed. Pack the area around the seal with water-resistant grease. Then, install the impeller on the pump shaft (right-hand threads).

5. Clamp the rear end of the pump shaft (**Figure 70**) in a vise with protective jaws. Do not damage the pump shaft.

6. Using a box-end wrench, tighten the impeller to the specification listed in **Table 5**. See **Figure 68**.

7. Place a new O-ring on the pump cap. Install the cap and tighten the 3 mounting bolts (**Figure 66**) to the specification in **Table 5**.

8. Make sure the dowel pins are properly installed in the pump outlet and pump case. Temporarily assemble the pump case, guide vane and outlet (**Figure 80**). Tighten the through-bolts securely.

9. Measure the impeller-to-pump case clearance with a feeler gauge as shown in **Figure 81**. Compare the clearance with the specification in **Table 2**. If the clearance is not within the specification in **Table 2**, remove the impeller and change the thickness of the shim pack behind the impeller (**Figure 69**). Changing shim thickness by 1 mm changes impeller clearance by approximately 0.144 mm (0.006 in.). Shims are available in thicknesses of 1.0 mm, 1.5 mm and 2.0 mm.

10. Reinstall the impeller as described in this chapter and repeat Step 9.

11. When the correct impeller clearance is obtained, disassemble the pump case, guide vane and outlet housing.

12. Apply a thin coat of silicone sealant to the mating surfaces of the pump case, guide vane and outlet housing. Reassemble the housings, making sure the dowel pins (**Figure 80**) are properly installed.

13. Apply Loctite 242 to the threads of the pump through-bolts. Install the bolts and tighten in a crossing pattern to the specification in **Table 5**.

6

14. Install the steering nozzle (**Figure 64**) making sure the notch in the nozzle is aligned with the bilge discharge hose fitting in the pump outlet housing. Apply Loctite 242 to the threads of the nozzle mounting bolts, install the bolts and tighten securely. Move the nozzle from side-to-side to ensure the nozzle pivots freely.

Jet Pump Installation

1. Make sure the cooling system intake and the bilge discharge hoses are in position in the pump cavity.

2. Make sure all old sealant is removed from the pump intake area.

3. Lubricate the drive splines with water-resistant grease and make sure the O-ring is properly installed inside the pump shaft.

4. Place the pump assembly in position and carefully engage the drive shaft splines with the pump shaft. Loosely install the 4 pump mounting bolts with flat washers and lockwashers (**Figure 82**).

> *NOTE*
> *If the jet pump or hull has been replaced, the drive shaft-to-impeller alignment may have changed. Check alignment by observing the position of the 4 pump*

*mounting lugs (**Figure 83**) before tightening the mounting bolts. If gaps are present between the pump mounting lugs and the hull, insert shims as required to take up the clearance. Shims are available in 0.3, 0.5, 1.0 and 1.5 mm thicknesses. If no gaps are present, install the original shims (if used) in their original locations.*

5. Temporarily tighten the pump mounting bolts (**Figure 82**). Turn the drive shaft and check for binding. If binding is noted, realign the drive shaft and pump shafts by changing the alignment shims (**Figure 82**) as required. If no binding is noted, continue at Step 6.

6. Next, draw a line on the inside of the pump tunnel in the hull, along the front of the pump case.

7. Remove the pump mounting bolts and pump assembly.

8. Place a wide bead of silicone sealant just behind the line drawn in Step 6.

9. Reinstall the pump assembly. Hold the pump away from the sealant bead as much as possible. Once the pump assembly is installed, allow it to settle into the sealant bead. Install the pump mounting bolts and tighten securely.

10. Remove one pump mounting bolt. Apply Loctite 242 to the threads of the bolt. Reinstall the bolt and tighten to specification (**Table 5**).

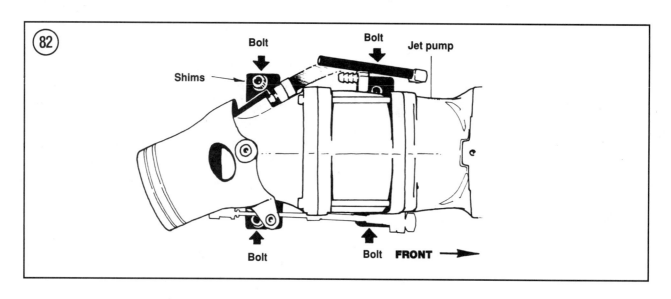

Repeat this procedure for the remaining pump mounting bolts.

11. Seal the gap between the hull and the edge of the pump intake area (**Figure 84**) with silicone sealant. Be sure all excess sealant is removed from the area around the pump intake. Excess sealant can disturb the water flow into the pump and cause impeller cavitation.

12. Connect the steering cable connector at the nozzle (**Figure 85**).

13. Connect the cooling water inlet and the bilge discharge hoses. The cooling water hose con-nects to the fitting at the front of the pump case. the bilge discharge hose connects to the fitting at the rear of the pump. See **Figure 85**.

CAUTION
If the hoses are incorrectly connected, the engine quickly overheat and the en-gine will fill with water.

14. Move the steering nozzle side-to-side to make sure there is no binding or pinching of the hoses.

6

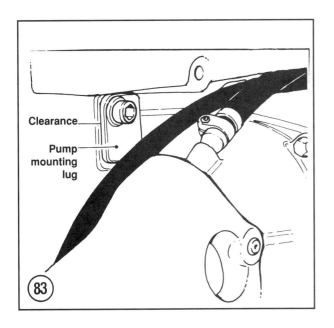

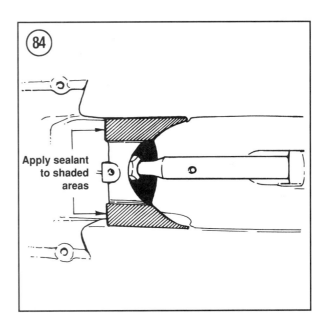

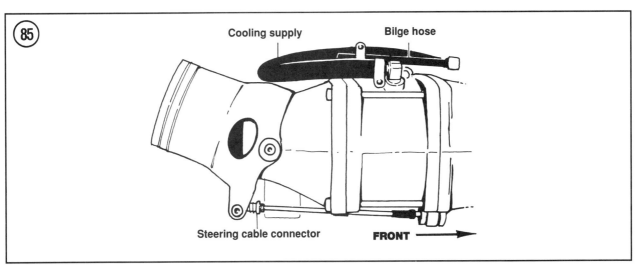

15. Install the pump cover plate (**Figure 57**). Tighten the fasteners to specification (**Table 5**).

16. Install the intake grate (**Figure 58**). Tighten the mounting fasteners to specification (**Table 5**).

17. Place the watercraft upright. Install the battery and reconnect the spark plug leads.

JET PUMP
(650 AND 750 CC MODELS)

The jet pump case contains the impeller which is mounted on the pump shaft. The pump shaft is engaged with and driven by the drive shaft.

The pump is carefully manufactured so very little clearance between the impeller and case is present. As the pump wears from the normal use, the clearance will increase causing pump thrust to decrease. The impeller and case should be inspected according to the maintenance schedule in Chapter Three. Replace the pump and case if excessively worn.

With extended used, the pump shaft bearings in the pump case can wear, resulting in inaccurate impeller-to-pump case clearance.

JL650SC, JB650 Jet Mate and JT750ST models are equipped with a reverse system. The reverse systems consists of a reverse gate, control lever and cable. The gate is attached to the brackets on the pump cover. When activated, the reverse gate moves down into the jet pump discharge stream and deflects the water toward the front of the watercraft, effectively reversing pump thrust.

Jet Pump Removal

NOTE
On these models, the impeller is mounted on the pump shaft located inside the pump case. To remove the impeller, the jet pump must be removed and then partially disassembled.

Refer to the following illustrations for this procedure:

    a. **Figure 86**: JL650SC, JF650TS and JT750ST.

    b. **Figure 87**: JF650X-2, JH750 Super Sport Xi and JH750XiR.

    c. **Figure 88**: JS650SX, JS750SX and JH750SS.

    d. **Figure 89**: JB650 Jet Mate.

1. Remove the battery to prevent electrolyte spillage. See Chapter Eight.

2. Disconnect the spark plug leads (**Figure 90**) to prevent accidental starting.

CAUTION
When rolling the watercraft onto its side in Step 3, protect the hull with a heavy blanket. Also, on models so equipped, protect the steering wheel assembly from damage.

3. Roll the watercraft on its side. See **Figure 91**. Be sure to roll the craft toward the exhaust side to prevent water in the exhaust system from entering the cylinders.

CAUTION
Do not turn the watercraft to the opposite side of the exhaust system or water in the exhaust system can drain into the cylinders through the exhaust ports. Should the engine be cranked or started with water in the cylinders, serious engine damage will result.

4. On JL650SC, JB650 Jet Mate and JT750ST models, disconnect the reverse cable connector from the reverse gate.

5. Remove the bolts holding the water intake grate (**Figure 92**) and pump cover (**Figure 93**) to the bottom of the hull. Remove the grate and cover.

6. Remove the steering cable ball joint connector from the pump nozzle (**Figure 94**). Slide its spring loaded sleeve forward and pull the connector off the ball (**Figure 95**).

JET PUMP
(JL650SC, JF650TS AND JT750ST)

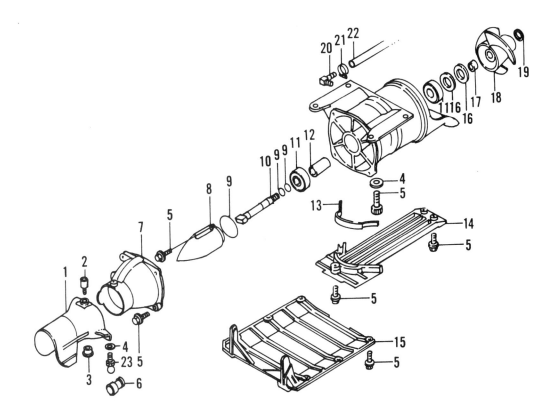

6

1. Steering nozzle
2. Allen bolt
3. Bushing
4. Washer
5. Bolt
6. Shaft joint
7. Pump nozzle
8. Pump cap
9. O-ring
10. Pump shaft
11. Bearing
12. Collar
13. Gasket
14. Intake grate
15. Pump cover
16. Washer
17. Bushing
18. Impeller
19. Seal
20. Hose elbow fitting
21. Clamp
22. Hose
23. Ball joint

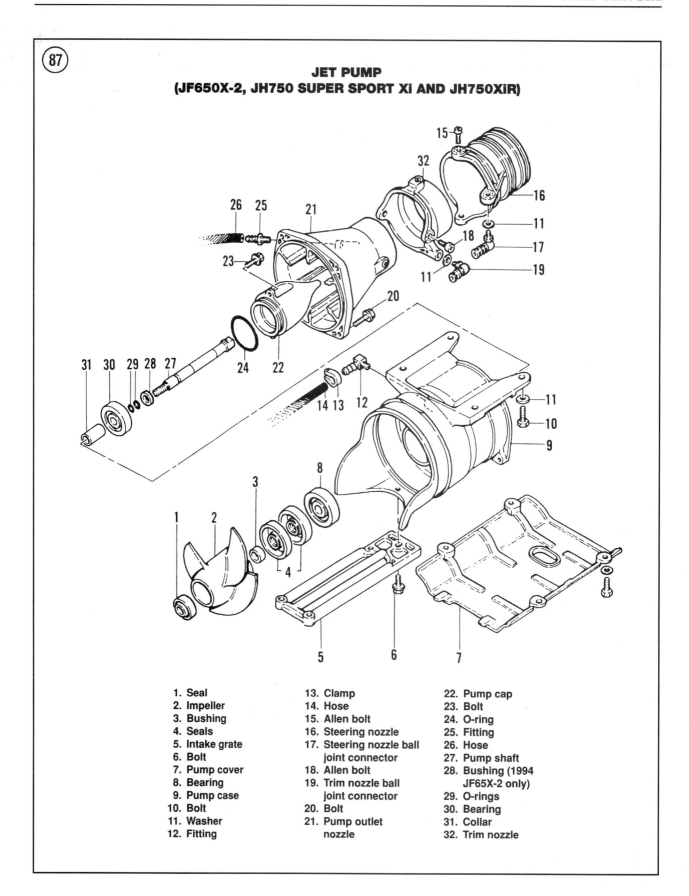

JET PUMP
(JF650X-2, JH750 SUPER SPORT Xi AND JH750XiR)

1. Seal	13. Clamp	22. Pump cap
2. Impeller	14. Hose	23. Bolt
3. Bushing	15. Allen bolt	24. O-ring
4. Seals	16. Steering nozzle	25. Fitting
5. Intake grate	17. Steering nozzle ball	26. Hose
6. Bolt	joint connector	27. Pump shaft
7. Pump cover	18. Allen bolt	28. Bushing (1994
8. Bearing	19. Trim nozzle ball	JF65X-2 only)
9. Pump case	joint connector	29. O-rings
10. Bolt	20. Bolt	30. Bearing
11. Washer	21. Pump outlet	31. Collar
12. Fitting	nozzle	32. Trim nozzle

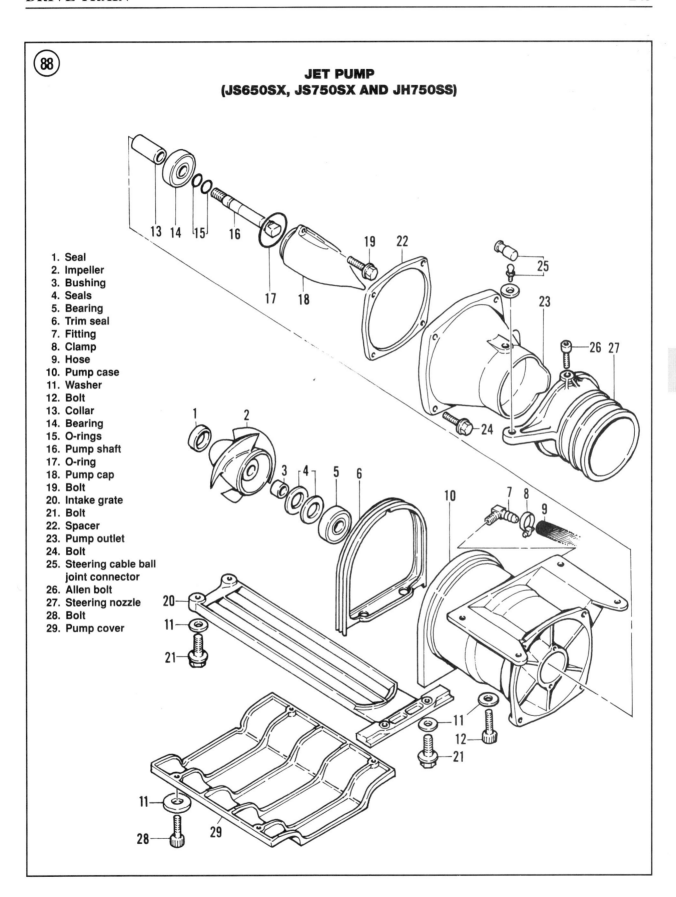

JET PUMP
(JS650SX, JS750SX AND JH750SS)

1. Seal
2. Impeller
3. Bushing
4. Seals
5. Bearing
6. Trim seal
7. Fitting
8. Clamp
9. Hose
10. Pump case
11. Washer
12. Bolt
13. Collar
14. Bearing
15. O-rings
16. Pump shaft
17. O-ring
18. Pump cap
19. Bolt
20. Intake grate
21. Bolt
22. Spacer
23. Pump outlet
24. Bolt
25. Steering cable ball joint connector
26. Allen bolt
27. Steering nozzle
28. Bolt
29. Pump cover

6

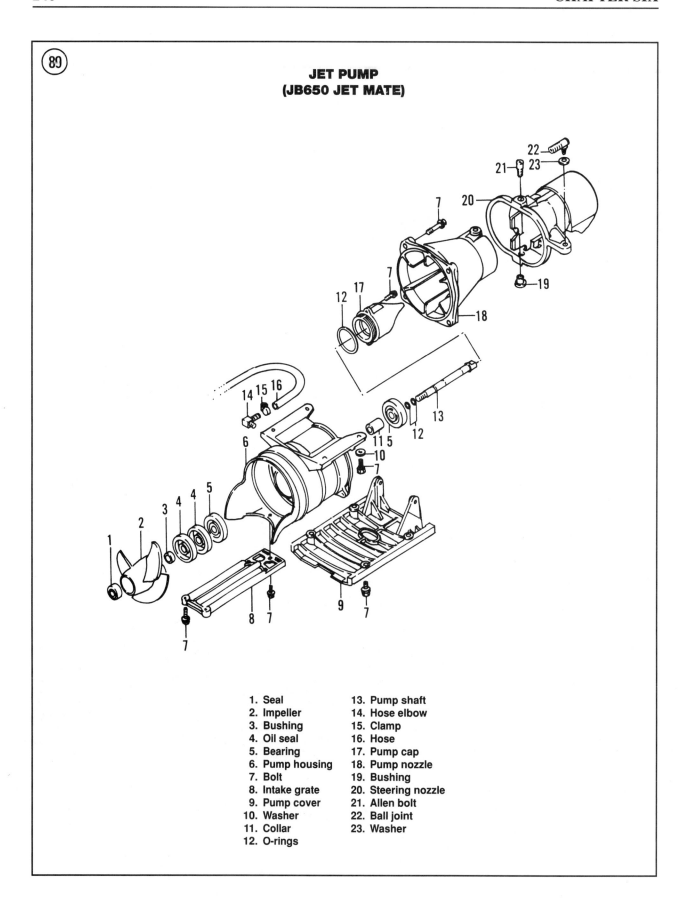

**JET PUMP
(JB650 JET MATE)**

1. Seal
2. Impeller
3. Bushing
4. Oil seal
5. Bearing
6. Pump housing
7. Bolt
8. Intake grate
9. Pump cover
10. Washer
11. Collar
12. O-rings
13. Pump shaft
14. Hose elbow
15. Clamp
16. Hose
17. Pump cap
18. Pump nozzle
19. Bushing
20. Steering nozzle
21. Allen bolt
22. Ball joint
23. Washer

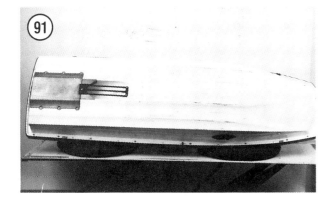

7. *JF650X-2, JH750 Super Sport Xi and JH750XiR*—Remove the trim cable ball joint connector from the rod (**Figure 96**). Slide its spring loaded sleeve forward and pull the connector off the ball.

8. Loosen the hose clamps and disconnect the cooling water supply hose (A, **Figure 97**) and the bilge discharge hose (B) from the fittings on the pump case.

9. Remove the 4 Allen bolts that hold the jet pump to the hull (**Figure 98**).

> *CAUTION*
> *During jet pump removal, note the number and position of any alignment shims under each pump mounting lug. The*

6

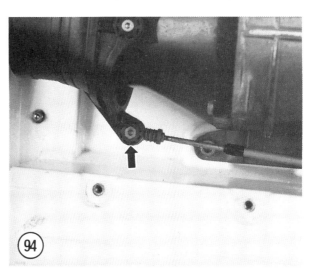

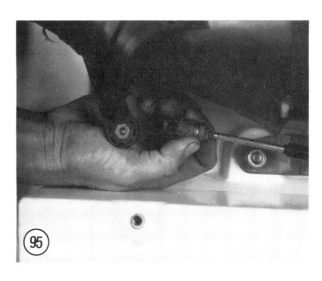

shims (if used) must be reinstalled in their original location for proper drive shaft-to-pump shaft alignment.

10. *650 cc models*—Using a thin, sharp knife cut the sealant at the pump intake area.

11. Remove the jet pump by pulling it to the rear and disengaging the drive shaft from the impeller. On 650 cc models, lightly tap the pump with a soft-face mallet to break the silicone seal.

CAUTION
On 650 cc models, the pump assembly may be difficult to remove due to the silicone sealant applied to the pump intake area (Figure 99). The pump must be moved backward to disengage it from the drive shaft. If it is impossible to break the seal loose, never hammer on the pump

casting to break the seal. Instead, remove the engine as described in Chapter Five. Then, slide the drive shaft forward to disengage it from the pump shaft. This will provide the necessary clearance to move the pump housing to the side and break the silicone seal.

12. On models so equipped, remove any shims from the mounting bolts holes.

Pump Case Disassembly

Refer to the following illustrations for this procedure:

   a. **Figure 86**: JL650SC, JF650TS and JT750ST.

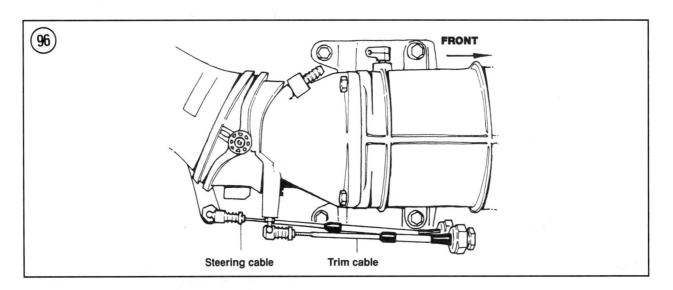

Steering cable   Trim cable

b. **Figure 87**: JF650X-2, JH750 Super Sport Xi and JH750XiR.

c. **Figure 88**: JS650SX, JS750SX and JH750SS.

d. **Figure 89**: JB650 Jet Mate.

NOTE
The seals and bearings in the pump case are damaged during removal. Do not remove the seals and bearings unless replacement is necessary.

1A. *Except adjustable trim*—Remove the 2 Allen bolts securing the steering nozzle to the pump outlet (**Figure 100**). Remove the steering nozzle.

1B. *Adjustable trim*—Remove the 2 Allen bolts (one each side) securing the steering nozzle and trim nozzle to the pump outlet. Remove the steering nozzle and trim nozzle as an assembly.

2. Remove the bolts holding the pump outlet (**Figure 101**) to the pump case. Remove the outlet.

3. Remove the bolts holding the pump cap (**Figure 102**) to the pump housing. Remove the pump cap.

4. Next, remove the impeller (**Figure 103**). Clamp the end of the pump shaft (**Figure 104**) in a vise with protective jaws. Use caution not to damage the shaft.

5. Insert Kawasaki impeller wrench (part No. 57001-1228) into the end of the impeller. Turn

6

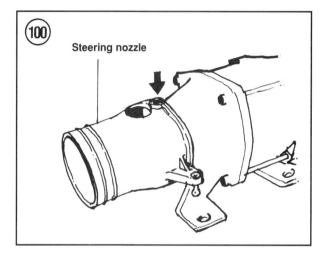

Steering nozzle

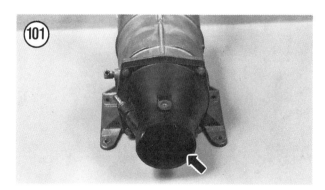

the impeller wrench (counterclockwise) using a box-end wrench and remove the impeller.

NOTE
*If Kawasaki impeller wrench (part No. 57001-1228) is not available, remove the drive shaft and insert it into the end of the impeller. Then, clamp the drive shaft in a vise with protective jaws and turn the end of the pump shaft (**Figure 104**) with a wrench.*

6. Slide the pump shaft (**Figure 105**) out of the pump case.

7. Remove the bushing (**Figure 106**).

Jet Pump/Impeller Inspection

Normal wear of the pump case and impeller can diminish pump thrust and top speed, even if the engine is operating properly. Reduced thrust can also be caused by obstructions in the pump or a damaged pump case or impeller. If the wide-open throttle engine speed has increased, but watercraft top speed and performance has declined, expect pump case/impeller damage or wear.

1. Clean all components in solvent and dry with compressed air.

2. Clean all sealant from all mating surfaces.

3. Inspect the impeller blades (A, **Figure 107**) for nicks, gouges, cracks, excessive wear or other damage. Also check the pump case blades (**Figure 108**) for nicks, gouges or damage. Minor damage to the pump case blades or impeller blades can be smoothed up using abrasive paper or a fine-cut file. The leading edges of the pump case and impeller blades must be smooth and not damaged to prevent impeller cavitation.

4. Inspect the impeller threads (B, **Figure 107**) for damage. Repair damaged threads if possible. If not, replace the impeller.

5. Measure the outside diameter of the impeller (**Figure 109**) using a vernier caliper. Compare the measurement to the specification in **Table 3**.

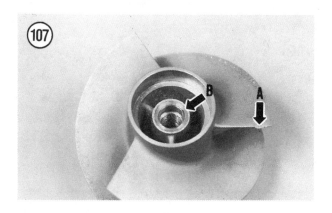

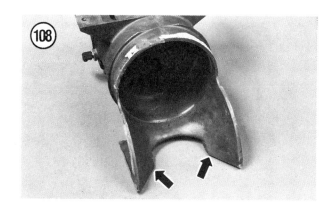

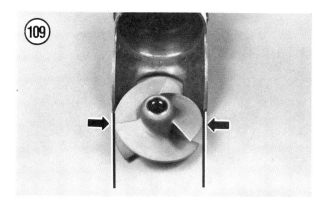

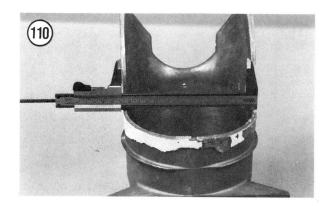

Replace the impeller if its diameter is less than the service limit specified in **Table 3**.

6. Measure the pump case machined surface inside diameter using a vernier caliper (**Figure 110**). If the pump case inside diameter exceeds the service limit specified in **Table 3**, replace the case or have it remachined as described in this chapter.

7. Inspect the impeller grease seal (**Figure 111**). Replace the seal by prying it out of the impeller using a screwdriver. Install the seal using a bearing driver or other tool with the same outer diameter as the seal.

8. Rotate the impeller needle bearing to check for roughness or other damage. The impeller and bearing are not available separately. If the bearing is rough, excessively worn or damaged, replace the impeller.

9. Inspect the pump shaft (A, **Figure 112**) for cracks, scoring, excessive wear or other damage. Replace the O-ring (B, **Figure 112**) during reassembly.

10. Check the pump shaft bushing (C, **Figure 112**) for cracks, scoring, excessive wear or other damage. Replace the bushing as necessary.

11. Inspect the 2 grease seals mounted in the front of the pump case (**Figure 113**). Check the seal lips for tears, softness, leakage or other

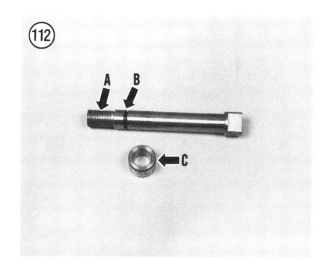

damage. Replace the seals as described in this chapter.

12. Check the 2 bearings (**Figure 114**) in the pump case. Slowly turn each bearing and check for roughness, excessive wear or noise. The bearings must rotate smoothly. If not, replace the bearings as described in this chapter.

13. Inspect the entire pump case (**Figure 115**) for cracks or other damage.

14. Replace the pump cap O-ring (**Figure 116**) upon reassembly.

Remachined Pumps

The jet pump's forward thrust declines as the impeller and wall of the pump wears. The inner wall of the pump and the outer edges of the impeller blades are gradually worn by sand, gravel and silt drawn into the pump during operation. Aftermarket accessory dealers can bore the inner diameter of the pump case, then install a precision, stainless steel wear ring insert. This type of repair usually results in a tighter impeller-to-pump clearance than the original arrangement. Tighter clearance increases pump efficiency which results in greater thrust. In addition, the modified pump generally has a longer service life than the original pump.

Bearing and Seal Removal/Installation

CAUTION
The seals and bearings are damaged during removal from the pump case. Do not remove unless replacement is necessary.

1. Remove the 2 seals from the pump case using Kawasaki bearing and seal remover (part No. 57001-1058) or an equivalent puller. Discard the seals.

2. Support the pump case on wooden blocks. Remove the lower bearing by tapping around its inner bearing race with a punch as shown in **Figure 117**. When the bearing falls free, the

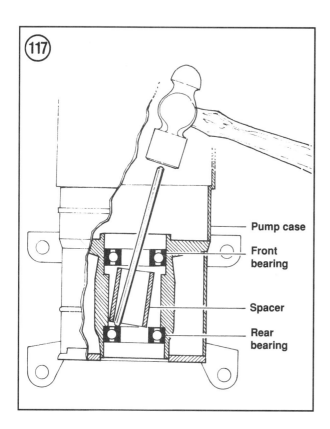

Pump case

Front bearing

Spacer

Rear bearing

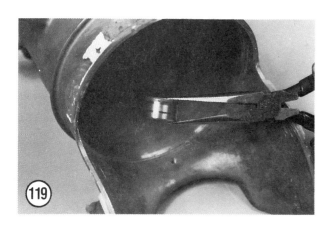

collar can be removed. Then, invert the pump case and remove the remaining bearing using the same procedure (**Figure 117**).

3. Thoroughly clean the pump case casting with solvent and dry with compressed air.

4. Using a suitable bearing driver, tap the rear bearing into the pump case until fully seated. See **Figure 118**. Make sure the driver contacts the bearing outer race only.

5. Invert the pump case and place the collar into the pump case. Then, tap the front bearing into the pump case using the bearing driver **Figure 118**.

NOTE
*Install the seals (Steps 6 and 7) so their open side faces the front of the pump case. See **Figure 113**.*

6. Coat the pump case seals with water-resistant grease. Drive the lower seal into the pump case with a driver with the same outer diameter as the seal. Drive the seal until fully bottomed in the pump case.

7. Next, drive the outer seal into the pump case until fully bottomed against the lower seal.

8. Pack the area between the seals with water-resistant grease.

9. Lightly lubricate the outer diameter of the bushing (**Figure 119**) and install it into the pump case.

Jet Pump/Impeller Reassembly

Refer to the following illustrations for this procedure:

a. **Figure 86**: JL650SC, JF650TS and JT750ST.

b. **Figure 87**: JF650X-2, JH750 Super Sport Xi and JH750XiR.

c. **Figure 88**: JS650SX, JS750SX and JH750SS.

d. **Figure 89**: JB650 Jet Mate.

1. Install a new O-ring into its groove in the pump shaft (B, **Figure 112**).

6

2. Lubricate the pump shaft with water-resistant grease. Insert the pump shaft (**Figure 120**) into the pump housing.

3. Lubricate the pump shaft bushing (**Figure 106**) with water-resistant grease. Install the bushing on the pump shaft until it bottoms against the front bearing. See **Figure 120**.

4. Install the impeller. Lubricate the threads on the pump shaft with water-resistant grease. Place the impeller on the shaft and turn it clockwise to install it (**Figure 103**).

5. Clamp the pump shaft (**Figure 104**) in a vise with protective jaws. Then, insert Kawasaki impeller wrench (part No. 57001-1228) into the end of the impeller. Then, tighten the impeller wrench using a box-end wrench, to the specification in **Table 6**. After properly tightening the impeller, check impeller-to-pump case clearance as described in this chapter.

NOTE
*If Kawasaki impeller wrench (part No. 57001-1228) is not available, remove the drive shaft and insert it into the end of the impeller. Then, clamp the drive shaft in a vise with protective jaws and turn the end of the pump shaft (**Figure 104**) with a wrench.*

6. Install a new O-ring into its groove in the pump cap (**Figure 116**). Install the pump cap on the pump case (**Figure 102**). Apply Loctite 242 to the threads of the pump cap mounting bolts, then install a tighten the bolts securely.

7. On models so equipped, place the spacer (22, **Figure 88**) on the pump case. On XiR models, the spacer is wedge shaped—mount the spacer so its thick side is facing down (to tilt outlet upward).

8. Install the pump outlet on the pump case as shown in **Figure 101**. Apply Loctite 242 to the threads of the outlet mounting bolts. Install and tighten the bolts to the specification in **Table 6**.

9A. *Except adjustable trim*—Install the steering nozzle to the pump outlet (**Figure 100**). Apply

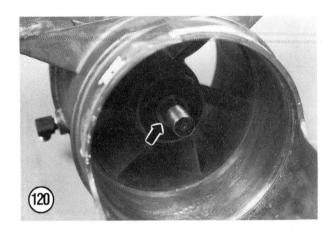

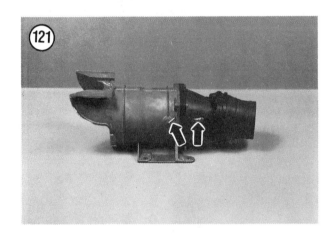

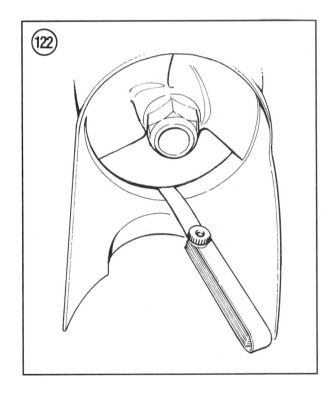

Loctite to the threads of the 2 Allen bolts. Install the bolts and tighten to specification (**Table 6**).

9B. *Adjustable trim*—Install the trim nozzle and steering nozzle as a unit on the pump outlet. Apply Loctite 242 to the threads of the 2 Allen bolts. Install the bolts and tighten to specification (**Table 6**).

10. Move the steering nozzle from side-to-side to check for freedom of movement.

11. If removed, install the cooling water inlet and bilge discharge hose fittings. Make sure the fittings are facing as shown in **Figure 121**.

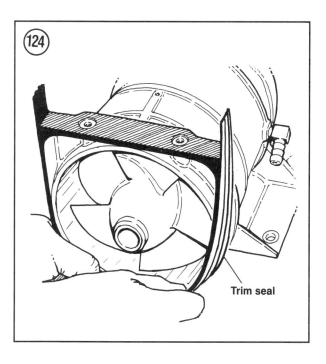

Trim seal

Impeller-to-Pump Case Clearance

Impeller-to-pump case clearance should be checked to determine if excessive impeller and/or pump case wear is present.

1. Make sure the impeller is properly installed and tightened as described under *Jet Pump/Impeller Reassembly* in this chapter.
2. Using a feeler gauge, measure the clearance between the tips of the impeller blades and the pump case inner wall (**Figure 122**).
3. Compare the clearance to the specification in **Table 3**. Excessive clearance indicates excessive impeller and/or pump case wear. Measure the impeller outside diameter and the pump case inside diameter as described under *Jet Pump/Impeller Inspection* to determine which components should be replaced.

Jet Pump Installation

1. Make sure the cooling system intake and the bilge discharge hoses are in the proper position in the pump cavity.
2. Remove all old sealant from the pump intake area.
3. Make certain the O-ring is properly installed on the pump shaft groove (**Figure 123**). Lubricate the drive shaft splines with water-resistant grease.
4A. *750 cc models*—Install the trim seal (**Figure 124**) on the pump case. Lubricate the outer edge of the trim seal with soapy water or light oil to ensure the seal slides into place during pump installation.
4B. *650 cc models*—Apply silicone sealant around the entire pump intake area (**Figure 125**). Do not allow the sealant into the inside of the pump intake. Sealant in this area will disturb the water flow causing impeller cavitation.
5. Install the pump assembly by engaging the drive shaft splines with the impeller. On 650 cc models, hold the pump away from the hull during installation to prevent scraping away the

6

sealant. After the pump is fully in place, allow it to settle into the sealant. On 750 cc models, make sure the trim seal is still in the proper position.

6. Install any alignment shims in their original locations.

7. Apply Loctite 242 to each pump mounting bolt. Install the bolts (**Figure 126**) and tighten to specification (**Table 6**).

8. Connect the steering cable at the nozzle (**Figure 127**). On models equipped with adjustable

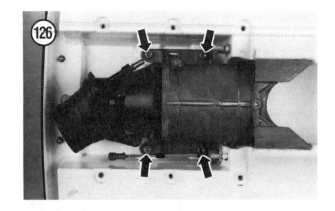

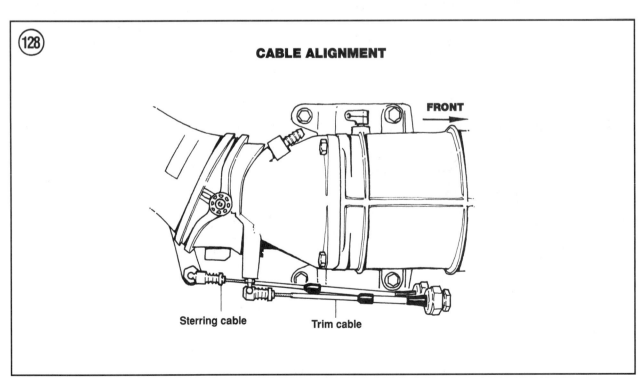

CABLE ALIGNMENT

FRONT

Sterring cable   Trim cable

trim, connect the trim cable at the nozzle (**Figure 128**).

9. Connect the cooling water inlet hose and the bilge discharge hose. See **Figure 129**. The cooling water hose connects to the fitting toward the front of the pump case (A, **Figure 129**). The bilge discharge hose connects to the fitting at the rear of the pump (B, **Figure 129**). Securely tighten the hose clamps.

> *CAUTION*
> *If the hoses are incorrectly connected, the engine will overheat from lack of cooling water and the engine compartment will flood with water.*

10. Pivot the steering nozzle from side-to-side to ensure no binding or pinching of the hoses will occur.

11A. *Models equipped with reverse gate*— Move the pump cover toward the front carefully moving the reverse gate over the end of the steering nozzle. Tighten the bolts securely. Then, connect the reverse cable connector on the reverse gate.

11B. *Except models equipped with reverse gate*—Install the pump cover (**Figure 130**). Apply Loctite 242 to the threads of the cover mounting bolts. Install the bolts and tighten securely.

12. Install the intake grate (**Figure 131**). Apply Loctite 242 to the threads of the grate bolts. Install the bolts and securely tighten.

13. Turn the watercraft upright. Install the battery and connect the spark plug leads.

REVERSE SYSTEM (JL650SC, JB650 JET MATE AND JT750ST)

Reverse Gate Removal/Installation

Refer to **Figure 132** (JL650SC and JT750ST) and **Figure 133** (JB650 Jet Mate) for this procedure.

1. Remove the battery to prevent electrolyte spillage. See Chapter Eight.

2. Disconnect the spark plug leads from the spark plugs to prevent accidental starting.

> *CAUTION*
> *When rolling the watercraft onto its side in Step 3, protect the hull with a heavy blanket. Also, protect the steering wheel or handle bar assembly from damage.*

3. Roll the watercraft on its side. Be sure to roll the craft toward the exhaust side to prevent water

6

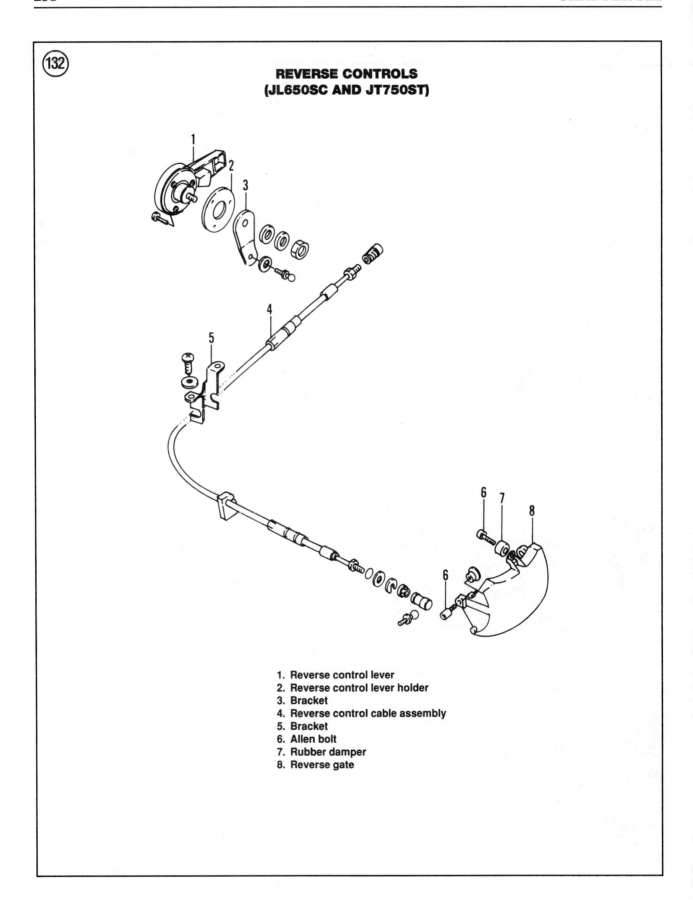

**REVERSE CONTROLS
(JL650SC AND JT750ST)**

1. Reverse control lever
2. Reverse control lever holder
3. Bracket
4. Reverse control cable assembly
5. Bracket
6. Allen bolt
7. Rubber damper
8. Reverse gate

in the exhaust system from entering the cylinders.

CAUTION
Do not turn the watercraft to the opposite side of the exhaust system or water in the exhaust system can drain into the cylinders through the exhaust ports. Should the engine be cranked or started with water in the cylinders, serious engine damage will result.

4. Disconnect the reverse cable connector from the reverse gate.

5. Remove the bolts holding the water intake grate to the bottom of the hull. Remove the grate.

6. Remove the bolts holding the pump cover to the hull. Move the cover toward the rear of the watercraft, carefully moving the reverse gate over the end of the steering nozzle.

7. To remove the reverse gate from the pump cover, perform the following:

    a. Remove the Allen bolt on each side securing the reverse gate to the pump cover.

    b. Pull the reverse gate off the pump cover and remove the collars from the gate pivot points.

8. Install the reverse gate by reversing these steps. Be sure to reinstall the collars into the reverse gate pivot points. Apply Loctite 242 to the threads of the Allen bolts and tighten the bolts to specification (**Table 6**).

9. Check the operation of the reverse shift cable. If necessary, adjust the cable as described in Chapter Three.

6

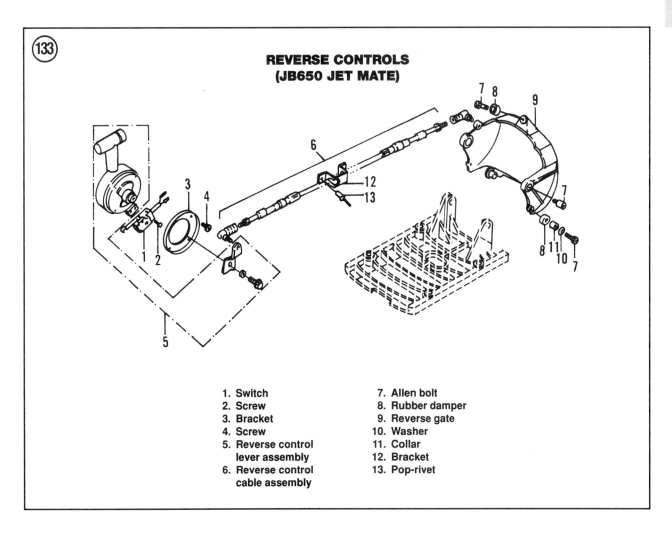

(133)

**REVERSE CONTROLS
(JB650 JET MATE)**

1. Switch
2. Screw
3. Bracket
4. Screw
5. Reverse control lever assembly
6. Reverse control cable assembly
7. Allen bolt
8. Rubber damper
9. Reverse gate
10. Washer
11. Collar
12. Bracket
13. Pop-rivet

Table 1 DRIVE TRAIN SERVICE SPECIFICATIONS (440 CC MODELS)

Item	Specification mm (in.)	Wear limit mm (in.)
Drive shaft runout	See text	See text
Impeller clearance	0.35-0.45	0.87
	(0.014-0.018)	(0.034)
Impeller outside diameter	121.0	120.0
	(4.764)	(4.724)
Pump bushing inside diameter	20.0	20.2
	(0.7874)	(0.7952)
Pump case inside diameter	121.7	122.7
	(4.79)	(4.83)

Table 2 DRIVE TRAIN SERVICE SPECIFICATIONS (550 CC MODELS)

Item	Specification mm (in.)	Wear limit mm (in.)
Drive shaft runout	0.2	0.6
	(0.008)	(0.024)
Impeller clearance	0.2-0.3	0.6
	(0.008-0.012)	(0.024)

Table 3 DRIVE TRAIN SERVICE SPECIFICATIONS (650 AND 750 CC MODELS)

Item	Specification mm (in.)	Wear limit mm (in.)
Drive shaft runout	See text	
Impeller clearance	0.2-0.3	0.6
	(0.008-0.012)	(0.024)
Impeller outside diameter	139.5-139.6	138.5
	(5.42-5.46)	(5.45)
Pump case inside diameter	140.0-140.1	141.1
	(5.51-5.52)	(5.55)

Table 4 DRIVE TRAIN TIGHTENING TORQUES (440 CC MODELS)

Fastener	N·m	in.-lb.	ft.-lb.
Bearing housing cover bolts	16	–	12
Bearing housing mounting bolts	16	–	12
Coupler half	27	–	20
Impeller	See text	–	–
Intake grate bolts	10	88	7.4
Pump cover bolts	10	88	7.4
Pump mounting bolts	22	–	16
Pump outlet bolts	16	–	12

Table 5 DRIVE TRAIN TIGHTENING TORQUES (550 CC MODELS)

Fastener	N·m	in.-lb.	ft.-lb.
Bearing housing mounting bolts	16	–	12
Coupling half	27	–	20
Coupling cover	6	53	–
Drive shaft holder bolts	20	–	14.5
Guide vane cap bolts	6	53	–
Impeller	20	–	14
Intake grate bolts	10	88	7.4
Pump case bolts	5.5	48.7	–
Pump cover bolts	10	88	7.4
Pump mounting bolts	22	–	16

Table 6 DRIVE TRAIN TIGHTENING TORQUES (650 AND 750 CC MODELS)

Fastener	N·m	in.-lb.	ft.-lb.
Ball joint connectors	7.8	69	
Coupling	39	–	29
Drive shaft holder bolts	20-22	–	15-16
Hose fittings	10	88	7.4
Impeller	98	–	72
Intake grate bolts	10	88	7.4
Pump cover bolts	10	88	7.4
Pump mounting bolts	22	–	16
Steering nozzle Allen bolts	10	88	7.4
Tilt nozzle Allen bolts	10	88	7.4

6

Chapter Seven

Fuel and Exhaust Systems

This chapter includes removal and repair procedures for the carburetor, fuel pump, fuel tank and exhaust system. See Chapter Three for idle speed and mixture adjustment procedures. **Table 1** (end of this chapter) identifies and lists the various carburetors used on models covered in this manual.

FLAME ARRESTOR

Removal/Cleaning/Installation (JS440SX)

Slight variations exist between the flame arrestor used on these models. It is important to note that some models use a flat washer and a lockwasher on the intake cover and the flame arrestor holder mounting bolts. Make sure to reinstall these bolts with washers. On all models, Loctite thread locking compound should be applied to the threads of the flame arrestor mounting bolts during reassembly.

Refer to **Figure 1** for this procedure.

1. Remove the engine hood.
2. Disconnect the negative battery cable from the engine (**Figure 2**) or battery.
3. Remove the bolts holding the intake cover to the flame arrestor holder. Remove the intake cover. See **Figure 3**.
4. Lift the flame arrestor element out of the holder. Handle the element carefully to prevent damage. See **Figure 4**.

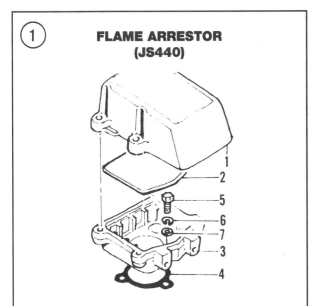

**FLAME ARRESTOR
(JS440)**

1. Intake cover
2. Flame arrestor
3. Flame arrestor holder
4. Gasket
5. Bolt
6. Lockwasher
7. Washer

5. If necessary, remove the flame arrestor holder. First, close the choke to prevent foreign objects from falling into the carburetor.

6. Remove the bolts securing the holder (**Figure 5**) to the carburetor. Remove the bolts holding the cylinder head bracket to the holder, if so equipped, and remove the holder.

7. Remove and discard the holder-to-carburetor gasket.

8. Place a shop towel over the carburetor opening to prevent contamination or small parts from falling into the carburetor.

9. Clean the flame arrestor with compressed air. Check the flame arrestor screen, expander plates and intake cover gasket for tearing or other damage. Replace as necessary.

7

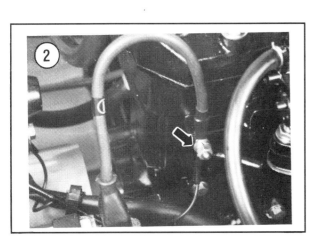

10. If removed, reinstall the flame arrestor holder as follows:

    a. Install a new holder gasket on the carburetor. See **Figure 6**.

    b. Install the holder (**Figure 5**).

    c. Install the bolts holding the cylinder head bracket (if so equipped) to the holder. Apply Loctite 242 to the threads of the bracket bolts, then install the bolts and tighten them securely.

    d. Apply Loctite 242 to the threads of the holder mounting bolts. Install the bolts and washers (if used) and tighten them evenly and securely.

11. Install the flame arrestor element (**Figure 4**) into the cover so the flat side is facing up. See **Figure 8**.

12. Install the intake cover. Apply Loctite 242 to the threads of the cover mounting bolts. Install the bolts and washers and tighten evenly and securely.

Removal/Cleaning/Installation (All 550 and 650 cc Models)

Refer to **Figure 8** for this procedure.

1. Remove the engine hood.

2. Disconnect the negative battery cable from the battery.

3. Loosen the locknuts and remove the throttle cable (JF650X-2 and JS650SX) or throttle and choke cables (JB650 Jet Mate and JF650TS) from the flame arrestor holder.

4. On JL650SC models, loosen the clamp securing the air silencer duct to the intake cover. Remove the duct from the cover.

5. Remove the bolts holding the intake cover to the flame arrestor holder. Remove the flame arrestor cover (**Figure 9**).

6. Lift the flame arrestor element from the holder.

7. To remove the flame arrestor holder, first bend the lock tabs on the lockwasher away from the holder fasteners.

8. Remove the holder fasteners and lift the holder off the carburetor. Remove and discard the holder-to-carburetor gasket.

9. Disassemble the flame arrestor and clean the screen and expander plates with compressed air. Check the screen, plates and intake cover gasket for tearing or other damage. Replace if necessary.

10. Assemble the flame arrestor by placing the screen between both expander plates.

11. If removed, reinstall the holder as follows:

    a. Install a new holder gasket on the carburetor. Install the holder on the carburetor.

    b. Install a *new* locking tab washer on the holder bolts or studs.

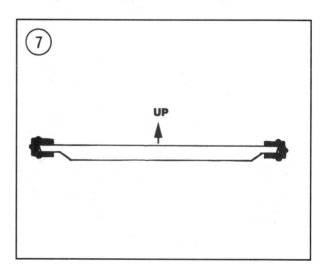

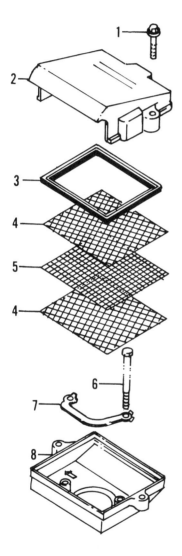

**FLAME ARRESTOR
(JS550SX, JF650X-2, JS650SX, JF650TS,
JL650SC AND JB650 JET MATE)**

1. Bolt
2. Cover
3. Gasket
4. Expander plate
5. Screen
6. Bolt
7. Lockwasher
8. Holder

c. Apply Loctite 242 to the threads of the holder mounting fasteners. Install the fasteners and tighten securely.

d. Bend the tabs of the lockwasher firmly against the bolt heads to lock the bolts in place.

12. Install the flame arrestor element into the holder. The element is symmetrical and can be installed either side up.

13. Install the intake cover. Apply Loctite 242 to the cover fasteners.

14. On JL650SC models, reconnect the air silencer duct to the flame arrestor assembly and clamp securely.

15. Reconnect the throttle and choke cables. Adjust the cables as described in Chapter Three.

16. Connect the negative battery cable and install the engine cover.

**Removal/Cleaning/Installation
(JH750SS, JS750SX and JT750ST)**

Refer to **Figure 10** for this procedure.

1. Disconnect the negative battery cable.

2. Remove the clamp (A, **Figure 11**) and disconnect the air silencer tube from the intake cover (C).

3. Remove the intake cover mounting bolts (B, **Figure 11**). Remove the cover.

7

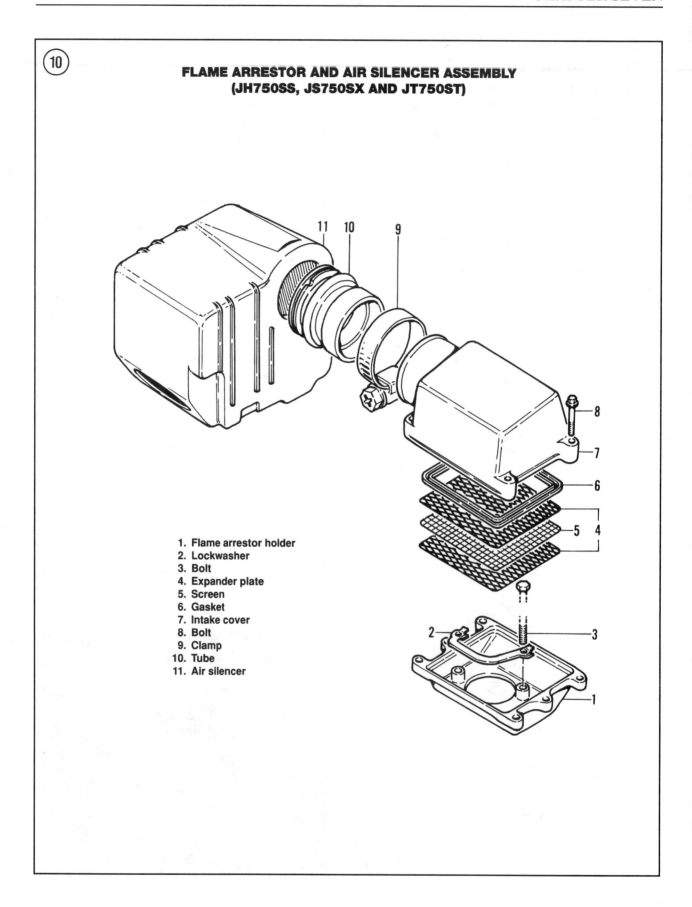

10

FLAME ARRESTOR AND AIR SILENCER ASSEMBLY
(JH750SS, JS750SX AND JT750ST)

1. Flame arrestor holder
2. Lockwasher
3. Bolt
4. Expander plate
5. Screen
6. Gasket
7. Intake cover
8. Bolt
9. Clamp
10. Tube
11. Air silencer

4. Lift the flame arrestor and expander plates from the holder.

5. If necessary, remove the flame arrestor holder as follows:

    a. Close the choke to prevent foreign objects from entering the carburetor. Bend the locking tabs away from the carburetor mounting bolts (3, **Figure 10**), then remove the bolts.

    b. Lift the flame arrestor holder off the carburetor.

    c. Cover the carburetor opening with a shop towel.

6. Disassemble the flame arrestor and clean the screen and expander plates with compressed air. Inspect the screen and plates for tearing or other damage. Replace as necessary. Inspect the intake cover gasket for tearing or damage and replace as required.

7. Reinstall the flame arrestor cover as follows:

    a. Place the holder on the carburetor.

    b. Apply Loctite 242 to the threads of the carburetor mounting bolts. Install the bolts and tighten evenly, to 7.8 N•m (69 in.-lb.).

    c. Bend the lock tabs on the lockwasher firmly against the bolt heads to lock the bolts in place.

8. Place the flame arrestor screen between the expander plates. Install all 3 parts into the holder.

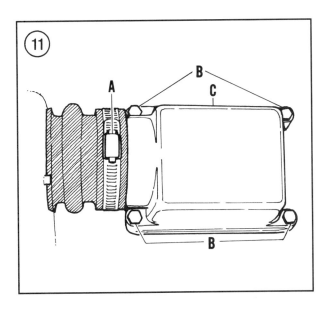

9. Install the intake cover. Apply Loctite 242 to the threads of the cover bolts. Install the bolts and tighten evenly and securely.

10. Connect the air silencer tube to the intake cover. Tighten the clamp securely.

Removal/Cleaning/Installation (JH750 Super Sport Xi and JH750XiR)

Refer to **Figure 12** for this procedure.

1. Disconnect the negative battery cable.

2. Remove the intake cover mounting bolts and remove the cover.

3. Lift the flame arrestor elements out of the arrestor base.

4. Disassemble the arrestor elements and clean with compressed air. Inspect the screens and expander plates for tears or other damage. Replace as required. Inspect the intake cover gasket for tearing or other damage and replace as required.

5. If necessary, remove the flame arrestor base as follows:

    a. Close the choke valves to prevent foreign objects from entering the carburetors. Bend the tabs on the lockwasher away from the carburetor mounting bolt heads.

    b. Remove the carburetor mounting bolts and lift the base off the carburetors.

    c. Cover the carburetor openings with a shop towel.

6. Install the flame arrestor base so its short side (from edge of base to carburetor inlets) is facing the engine.

7. Install new lockwashers on the carburetor mounting bolts then apply Loctite 242 to the threads. Install the carburetor mounting bolts, tighten them securely, then bend the lock tabs firmly against the bolt heads.

8. Place the flame arrestor screens between the expander plates. Then install the arrestor elements into the base.

7

9. If removed, apply a suitable contact cement to the outer surface of the ducts. Install the ducts into the intake cover.

10. Install the intake cover. Apply Loctite 242 to the threads of the cover mounting bolts. Install the bolts and tighten evenly and securely.

MIKUNI CARBURETOR (JS440SX)

NOTE
*Refer to **Table 1** for carburetor identification for each model covered in this manual.*

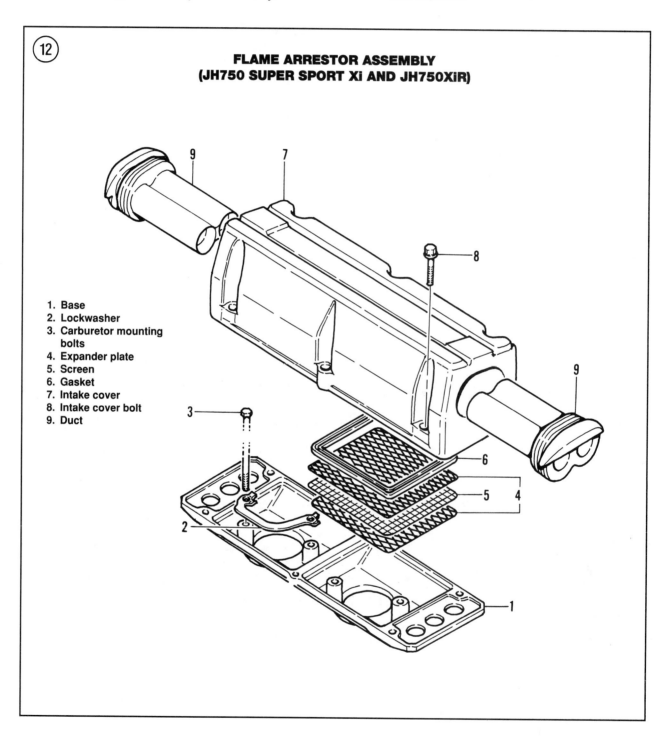

(12)

**FLAME ARRESTOR ASSEMBLY
(JH750 SUPER SPORT Xi AND JH750XiR)**

1. Base
2. Lockwasher
3. Carburetor mounting bolts
4. Expander plate
5. Screen
6. Gasket
7. Intake cover
8. Intake cover bolt
9. Duct

JS440SX models are equipped with a Mikuni Model BN38 carburetor. Refer to **Figure 13** for an exploded view of the carburetor. The BN38 carburetor is a down-draft diaphragm-type carburetor with an integral fuel pump.

Carburetor Removal

WARNING
Some fuel spillage can be expected during carburetor removal. Work in a well ventilated area at least 50 ft. (15 m) from any sparks or flames, including gas appliances pilot lights. Never smoke around gasoline. Always have a fire extinguisher rated for gasoline fires available.

1. Remove the engine cover.
2. Remove the flame arrestor and flame arrestor holder as described in this chapter.

WARNING
*Before disconnecting any fuel hoses, loosen the fuel tank cap (**Figure 14**) to relieve pressure in the fuel delivery system.*

7

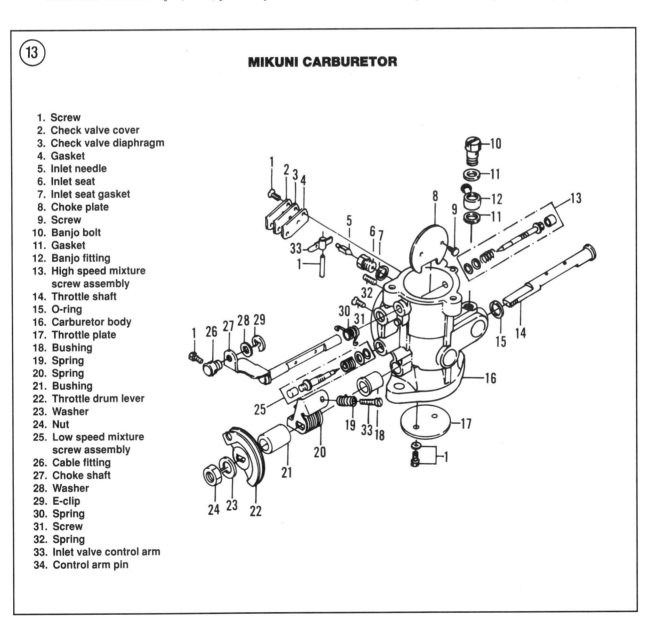

MIKUNI CARBURETOR

1. Screw
2. Check valve cover
3. Check valve diaphragm
4. Gasket
5. Inlet needle
6. Inlet seat
7. Inlet seat gasket
8. Choke plate
9. Screw
10. Banjo bolt
11. Gasket
12. Banjo fitting
13. High speed mixture screw assembly
14. Throttle shaft
15. O-ring
16. Carburetor body
17. Throttle plate
18. Bushing
19. Spring
20. Spring
21. Bushing
22. Throttle drum lever
23. Washer
24. Nut
25. Low speed mixture screw assembly
26. Cable fitting
27. Choke shaft
28. Washer
29. E-clip
30. Spring
31. Screw
32. Spring
33. Inlet valve control arm
34. Control arm pin

3. Label the fuel, pulse and vent hoses for reference during installation. Disconnect the fuel hoses from the carburetor. See **Figure 15**, typical.

4. Disconnect the vent and pulse hoses from the carburetor. See A, **Figure 16**, typical.

5. Loosen the choke cable set screw and pull the choke inner cable out of the choke fitting on the carburetor. See A, **Figure 17**. Unwind the throttle drum (B, **Figure 17**) at the carburetor and disconnect the throttle cable.

6. Remove the nuts holding the carburetor bracket to the cylinder head. See **Figure 18**, if so equipped.

7. Unscrew the nuts securing the carburetor to the intake manifold. Remove the carburetor from the manifold.

8. Remove the carburetor gaskets, insulator (**Figure 19**) and cable bracket (**Figure 20**). Discard the gaskets.

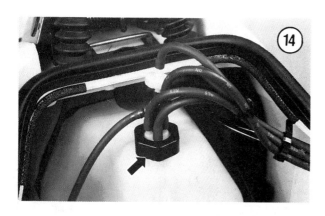

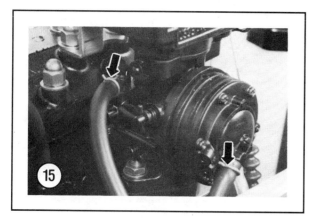

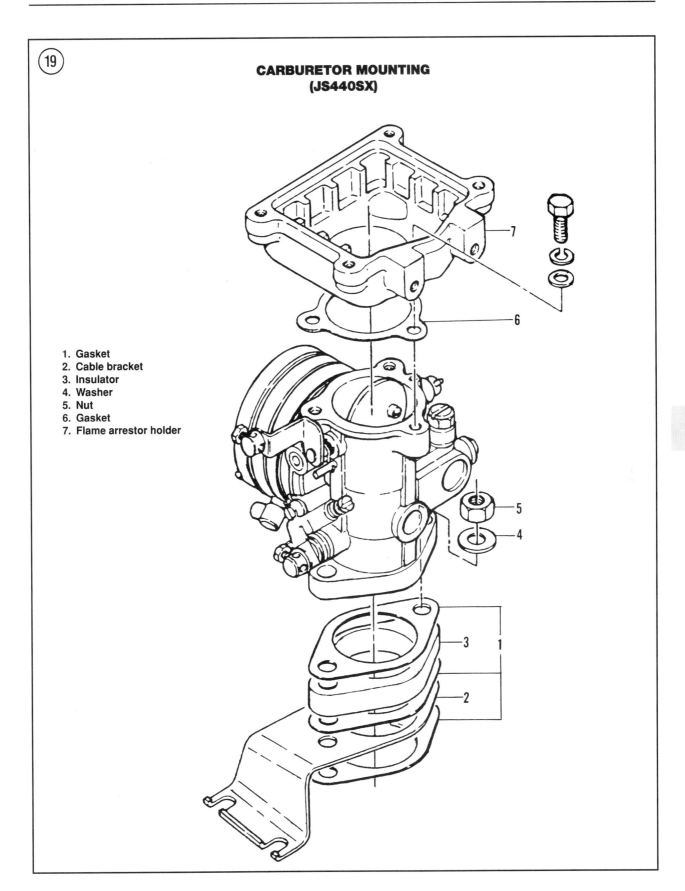

19

CARBURETOR MOUNTING
(JS440SX)

1. Gasket
2. Cable bracket
3. Insulator
4. Washer
5. Nut
6. Gasket
7. Flame arrestor holder

7

9. Installation is the reverse of these steps. Adjust the throttle and choke cables as described in Chapter Three.

> *CAUTION*
> *Make sure all hoses are properly connected and routed. Avoid sharp bends or kinks in the hoses. Make sure all hoses are routed away from engine components that can cut, chafe or damage the hose.*

Fuel Pump Disassembly

The carburetor is equipped with an integral fuel pump (**Figure 21**). The diaphragm-type fuel pump is operated by crankcase pulsations.

> *NOTE*
> *All fuel pump gaskets and diaphragms should be replaced if the pump is disassembled. Therefore, do not disassemble the pump unless leakage or internal damage is suspected.*

1. Remove the carburetor as described in this chapter.
2. Remove the screw (A, **Figure 22**) securing the fuel fitting to the fuel pump. remove the fuel fitting and gasket.
3. Remove the screws (B, **Figure 22**) holding the fuel pump to the carburetor. Then, carefully pry the pump assembly off the carburetor. See **Figure 23**.

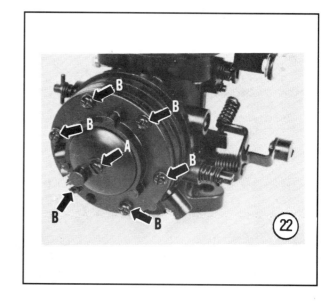

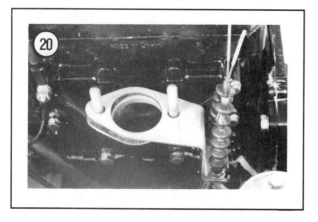

4. Separate the pump components (**Figure 24**). Arrange each part in the order of removal. See **Figure 25**.

Carburetor Disassembly

Refer to **Figure 13** when performing this procedure.

1. Remove the carburetor and fuel pump as described in this chapter.

2. Remove the control arm pivot pin screw (**Figure 26**). then remove the control arm, pivot pin (**Figure 27**) and spring (**Figure 28**).

3. Invert the carburetor and allow the fuel valve to fall out or lift it out using needlenose pliers (**Figure 29**). Remove the fuel valve seat and

7

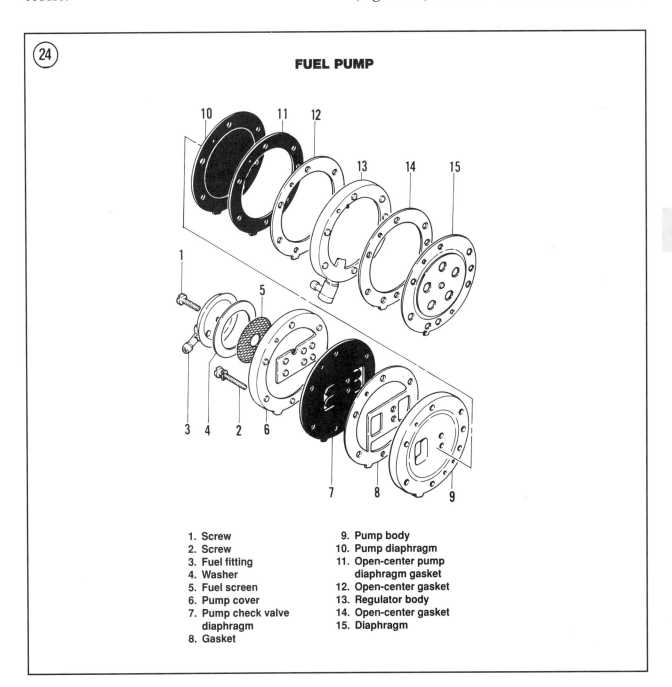

(24)

FUEL PUMP

1. Screw
2. Screw
3. Fuel fitting
4. Washer
5. Fuel screen
6. Pump cover
7. Pump check valve diaphragm
8. Gasket
9. Pump body
10. Pump diaphragm
11. Open-center pump diaphragm gasket
12. Open-center gasket
13. Regulator body
14. Open-center gasket
15. Diaphragm

gasket (A, **Figure 30**). A very thin walled socket is required to loosen the fuel valve.

4. Remove the high-speed check valve diaphragm assembly as follows:

    a. Remove the 2 screws (B, **Figure 30**) securing the high-speed check valve plate to the carburetor housing. Remove the plate (**Figure 31**).

    b. Remove the diaphragm (**Figure 32**).

    c. Remove the gasket (**Figure 33**).

5. Turn the low- and high-speed mixture screws clockwise, counting the number of turns required to lightly seat the screws. Record the number of turns for each screw, then remove the screws, springs, washers and O-rings (**Figure 34**).

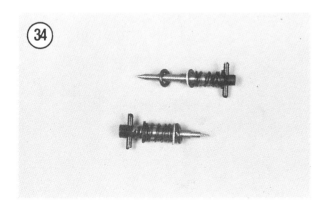

Carburetor Cleaning and Inspection

1. Thoroughly clean and dry all parts. If submerging the carburetor components in carburetor cleaning solvent, all nonmetal parts (O-rings) must be removed or they will be damaged.

2. Remove all gasket material from mating surfaces. Make sure all fuel and air passages are clean. Blow all passages out with compressed air. Never use wire or drill bits to clean passages or orifices. If the passages or orifices are altered, carburetor calibration will be changed resulting in poor performance.

3. Inspect the rubber gasket that fits between the fuel pump filter screen and the end cover (**Figure 35**).

4. Replace all 4 fuel pump gaskets.

5. Check the fuel pump diaphragm and regulator diaphragm for tears or small holes (**Figure 36**). Replace damaged diaphragms.

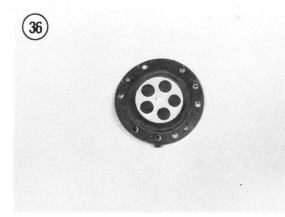

7

6. Inspect the carburetor control arm. Replace the arm if excessively worn. Replace the control arm spring if damaged or weakened.

7. Closely inspect the fuel valve (**Figure 37**) and fuel valve seat for wear, scratches or other damage. Replace the fuel valve and seat as a set if either part is defective.

8. Inspect the high-speed check valve diaphragm and gasket. Replace the diaphragm and gasket as necessary.

9. Inspect the tapered ends of the high- and low-speed mixture screws (**Figure 34**) for grooves, roughness or other damage. Replace the mixture screw(s) if any defects are noted. Inspect the O-rings and replace as required.

10. Operate the choke and throttle shafts (A, **Figure 38**) to check for shaft movement and proper operation. The shafts should move smoothly. Check each shaft for side play; excessive play indicates worn O-rings. If necessary, remove the choke or throttle valve screws (B, **Figure 39**) and remove the valve. Then remove the retaining ring or screw securing the end of the shaft, then withdraw the shaft (A, **Figure 39**) from the carburetor body. Replace worn or damage parts. Apply Loctite 242 to the threads of the choke or throttle valve screws during reassembly.

> *CAUTION*
> *A loose choke or throttle valve attaching screw will back out and fall into the engine, resulting in serious engine damage. Because of this, the screws are secured with thread locking compound at the factory. The screws are also made of relatively soft metal. Therefore, when removing the screws, use a screwdriver which fits the screws perfectly, to prevent rounding out the screw heads.*

Carburetor Reassembly

Refer to **Figure 13** while performing this procedure.

1. Install the high- and low-speed mixture screws with their springs, washers and new O-rings. The short (low-speed) screw must be installed on the side with the control linkage. Turn each screw clockwise until *lightly* seated, then back it out the number of turns recorded during removal.

> *CAUTION*
> *The mixture screws and carburetor body will be damaged if the screws are forced into their seats.*

2. Install the high-speed check valve diaphragm assembly as follows:

  a. Install the gasket, aligning it with the channel in the carburetor (**Figure 33**).

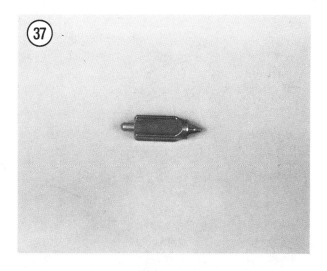

b. Install the diaphragm (**Figure 32**) on top of the gasket.

c. Install the plate (**Figure 31**) and secure it with the mounting screws (B, **Figure 30**).

3. Install the fuel valve seat (A, **Figure 30**) with a new gasket. Tighten the valve seat securely.

4. Place the fuel valve (**Figure 29**) into the valve seat (tapered end down).

5. Install the control arm spring (A, **Figure 40**) into its mounting hole in the carburetor housing.

6. Install the control arm assembly as follows:

a. Place the control arm (B, **Figure 40**) into position. Make sure the rounded projection is facing the top of the control arm spring (A, **Figure 40**). Insert the control arm pivot through the arm and install its retaining screw.

b. Make sure the long side of the arm is level with the base of the regulator chamber as shown in **Figure 41**. If it is not level, remove the arm and carefully bend it as necessary. Check this adjustment carefully; if not performed correctly, the fuel mixture will be excessively rich or lean throughout the entire rpm range.

7. Install the fuel pump as described in this chapter.

Fuel Pump Assembly

Refer to **Figure 42** while performing this procedure.

> *NOTE*
> *Assemble the fuel pump by stacking each component on the carburetor body. To ensure proper assembly, the fuel pump body pieces have locating pegs that align with the holes in the diaphragms and gaskets. In addition, each piece has a round projection (**Figure 43**) on its outer edge that aligns with a notch (**Figure 44**) on the carburetor body. If all components are not correctly aligned, the fuel pump will not function properly.*

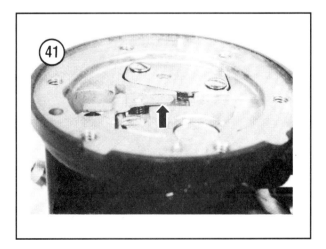

7

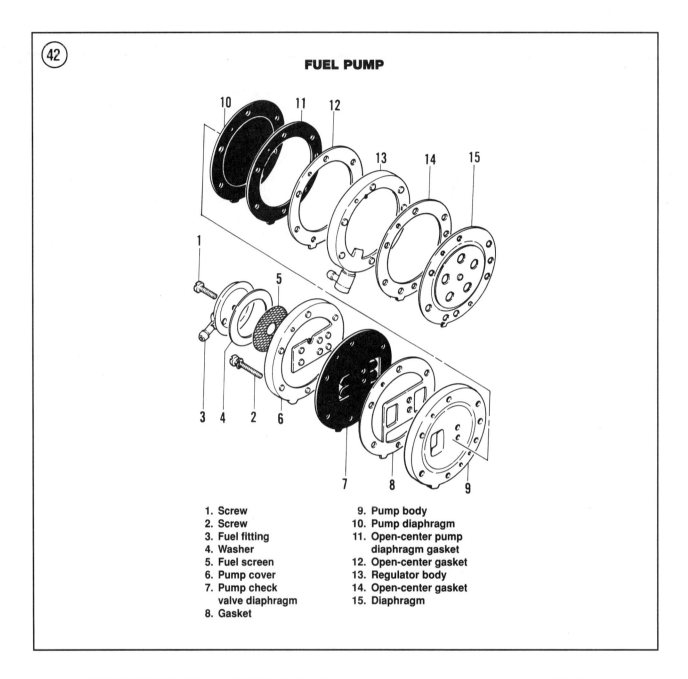

FUEL PUMP

1. Screw
2. Screw
3. Fuel fitting
4. Washer
5. Fuel screen
6. Pump cover
7. Pump check
   valve diaphragm
8. Gasket
9. Pump body
10. Pump diaphragm
11. Open-center pump
    diaphragm gasket
12. Open-center gasket
13. Regulator body
14. Open-center gasket
15. Diaphragm

1. Place the black regulator diaphragm and gasket on the carburetor (**Figure 45**). Make sure the perforated metal plate faces toward the carburetor.

2. Install an open-center gasket (14, **Figure 42**) over the regulator diaphragm.

3. Install the cast regulator body so the pulse line fitting (**Figure 46**) aligns with the carburetor alignment projection.

4. Align an open-center gasket (12, **Figure 42**) with the regulator body and install it.

5. Install the open-center pump diaphragm gasket (**Figure 47**).

6. Install the solid pump diaphragm (**Figure 48**).

7. Fit the center pump casting over the assembly (**Figure 49**). Then, install the open-center gasket (**Figure 50**) so it aligns with the pump casting.

7

8. Install the pump check valve diaphragm (**Figure 51**) over the gasket.

9. Install the pump cover (**Figure 52**) and its 6 screws. Tighten the screws evenly and securely.

> *CAUTION*
> *Be careful not to cross thread or strip the fuel pump screws. The aluminum threads in the carburetor casting are easily damaged, resulting in air or fuel leakage.*

10. Install the fuel fitting cover gasket (**Figure 53**).

11. Install the fuel fitting (A, **Figure 54**). Secure the fitting with the center screw (B, **Figure 54**).

12. Install the carburetor on the engine as described in this chapter.

KEIHIN CARBURETOR
(JS550SX AND ALL 650 AND
750 CC MODELS)

All models except JS440SX are equipped with Keihin carburetors. Twin carburetors are used on JH750 Super Sport Xi and JH750XiR models. Refer to **Table 1** for carburetor identification on all models.

The Keihin carburetors used on Jet Skis are down-draft diaphragm-type carburetors. A remote fuel pump is used with Keihin Model CDK34 carburetors (Jet Mate). Models CDK38 and CDK40 carburetors use an integral fuel pump. Refer to *Fuel Pump* in this chapter.

The following Keihin carburetors are used:

a. Model CDK34: JB650 Jet Mate. See **Figure 55**.

b. Model CDK38: JS550SX, JL650SC, JF650TS, JF650X-2 (1992-1993) and JS650SX. See **Figure 56**.

c. Model CDK40: JF650X-2 (1994) and all 750 cc models. See **Figure 56**. Note that JH750 Super Sport Xi and JF750XiR are equipped with twin carburetor arrangements.

**KEIHIN MODEL CDK34 CARBURETOR
(JB650 JET MATE)**

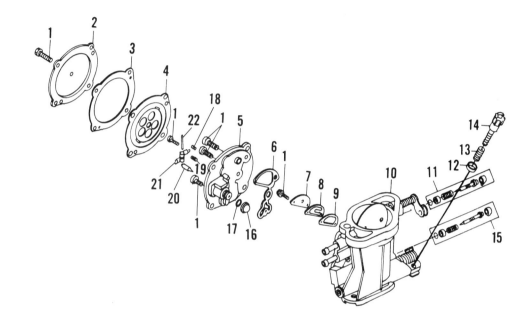

1. Screw
2. Cover
3. Gasket
4. Diaphragm
5. Case
6. Gasket
7. Check valve plate
8. Check valve
9. Gasket
10. Carburetor body
11. High-speed mixture screw

12. Washer
13. Spring
14. Idle screw
15. Low-speed mixture screw
16. Filter
17. O-ring
18. Pin
19. Spring
20. Inlet valve
21. Control arm
22. Control arm pin

7

Carburetor Removal/Installation (All Models Except JS440SX, JH750 Super Sport Xi and JH750XiR)

WARNING
Some fuel may spill during carburetor removal. Work in a well-ventilated area at least 50 ft. (15 m) from any sparks or flames, including gas appliance pilot lights. Never smoke in the area. Always have a fire extinguisher rated for gasoline fires nearby.

1. Remove the engine cover or seat.
2. On JL650SC models, unbolt the electric box bracket. Without disconnecting the wiring, place the electric box and bracket aside.
3. Remove the flame arrestor and flame arrestor holder or base as described in this chapter.

NOTE
The long bolts that are installed through the top of the flame arrestor holder or base are also the carburetor mounting bolts. After removing the flame arrestor

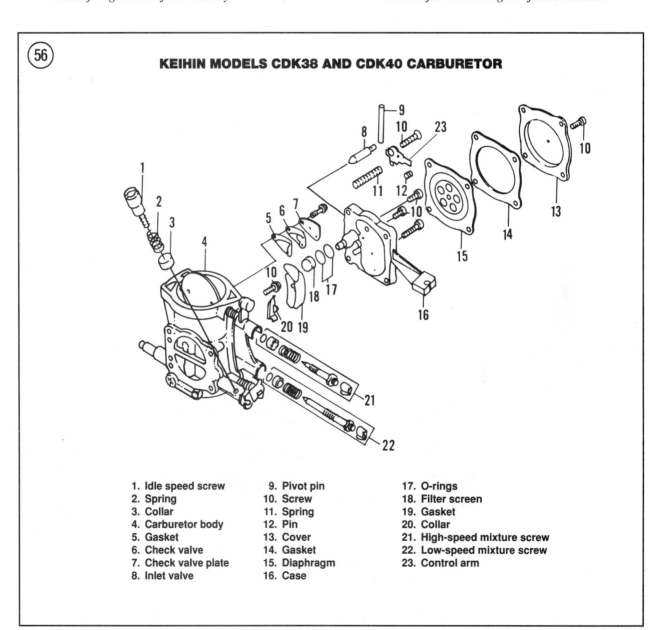

KEIHIN MODELS CDK38 AND CDK40 CARBURETOR

1. Idle speed screw	9. Pivot pin	17. O-rings
2. Spring	10. Screw	18. Filter screen
3. Collar	11. Spring	19. Gasket
4. Carburetor body	12. Pin	20. Collar
5. Gasket	13. Cover	21. High-speed mixture screw
6. Check valve	14. Gasket	22. Low-speed mixture screw
7. Check valve plate	15. Diaphragm	23. Control arm
8. Inlet valve	16. Case	

assembly, temporarily install the bolts to hold the carburetor in place while removing the fuel lines and control cables.

WARNING
*Before disconnecting any fuel hoses, loosen the fuel tank fill cap (**Figure 57**) to relieve any pressure in the fuel delivery system.*

4. Label the fuel and vent hoses for reference during installation. Label the pulse hose on all models except Jet Mate (remote fuel pump). See **Figure 58**, typical. Disconnect the hoses from the carburetor.

5. Loosen the choke (A, **Figure 59**) and throttle (B) cable locknuts. Then, disconnect the cables from the carburetor.

6. Remove the carburetor mounting bolts and lift the carburetor off the intake manifold. Remove and discard the carburetor-to-manifold gasket.

7. Installation is the reverse of these steps while noting the following points:

   a. Install a new gasket between the carburetor and intake manifold.

   b. Apply Loctite 242 to the threads of the carburetor mounting bolts. Install a new lockwasher when installing the flame arrestor holder or base. Tighten the carburetor/flame arrestor holder mounting bolts evenly and securely.

   c. Adjust the choke and throttle cables as described in Chapter Three.

CAUTION
Check the routing of all hoses. The hoses must be correctly routed without sharp bends or kinks. Make sure all fuel hoses are positioned away from engine components that could damage them.

Carburetor Removal/Installation
(JH750 Super Sport Xi and JH750XiR)

1. Remove the engine cover/seat.

2. Remove the flame arrestor and flame arrestor base as described in this chapter. Note that the long bolts that hold the flame arrestor base are also the carburetor mounting bolts.

3. Disconnect the choke and throttle cables.

4. Label the fuel and pulse hoses for reference during installation. Disconnect the hoses from the carburetors.

7

5. Lift both carburetors off the intake manifold as a unit. See **Figure 60**. Remove and discard the carburetor-to-intake manifold gaskets.

6. Installation is the reverse of these steps while noting the following points:

a. Install new gaskets between the carburetors and intake manifold.

b. Apply Loctite 242 to the threads of the carburetor mounting bolts. Install new lockwashers when installing the flame arrestor holder or base. Tighten the carburetor/flame arrestor base mounting bolts to 7.8 N•m (69 in.-lb.).

c. Adjust the choke and throttle cables as described in Chapter Three.

CAUTION
Check the routing of all hoses. The hoses must be correctly routed without sharp bends or kinks. Make sure all fuel hoses are positioned away from engine components that could damage them.

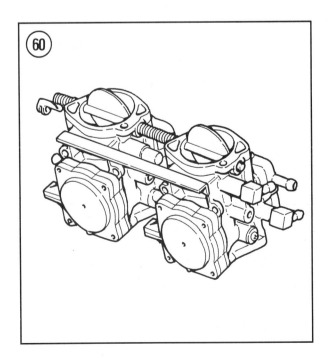

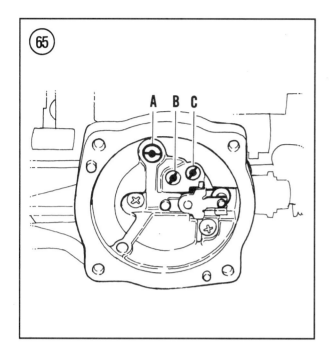

Carburetor Disassembly
(Keihin CDK34, CDK38 and CDK40)

Refer to **Figure 55** (CDK34) or **Figure 56** (CDK38 and CDK40) while performing this procedure.

1. Separate the carburetors on twin-carburetor arrangements.

2. Turn the high-speed mixture screw (A, **Figure 61**) clockwise until lightly seated, counting the turns required. Record the number of turns for reference during reassembly. Repeat this procedure on the low-speed mixture screw (B, **Figure 61**).

3. Remove the mixture screws, springs, washers, O-rings and limiter caps. See **Figure 61**.

4. Remove the screws securing the cover to the carburetor. Remove the cover (**Figure 62**) and diaphragm.

5A. *Model CDK34*—Remove the pilot jet (**Figure 63**) and main jet (**Figure 64**).

5B. *Models CDK38 and CDK40*—Remove the main jet (A, **Figure 65**), pilot jet (B) and intermediate jet (C).

6. Remove the screw (A, **Figure 66**) securing the carburetor case to the carburetor body. Separate the case (B, **Figure 66**) from the body. See **Figure 67**.

7. Remove the control arm pivot pin screw (A, **Figure 68**). Remove the control arm pivot pin

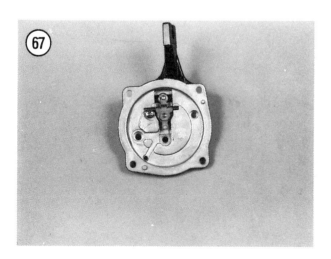

7

(B, **Figure 68**) and control arm. Remove the control arm spring (**Figure 69**).

8A. *Except JH750 Super Sport Xi and JH750XiR*—Remove the 2 screws (**Figure 70**) securing the check valve plate to the carburetor body.

8B. *JH750 Super Sport Xi and JH750XiR*—Remove the screws (A and B, **Figure 71**) securing the check valve plate and to the carburetor body.

9. Remove the plate(s) (**Figure 72**), check valve(s) (**Figure 73**) and gasket(s) (**Figure 74**).

10. Remove the fuel filter screen and O-ring(s) (**Figure 75**) from the fuel inlet fitting. Remove the O-ring seal (**Figure 76**) from the carburetor body.

NOTE
Do not disassemble the integral fuel pump used on Keihin CDK38 and CDK40 carburetors. There are no serviceable components contained within the pump. If leakage or a pump malfunction is evident, the pump must be replaced as an assembly. Do not remove the pump unless replacement is necessary.

11. *CDK38 and CDK40*—If necessary, remove the fuel pump assembly from the carburetor body. See *FUEL PUMP* in this chapter.

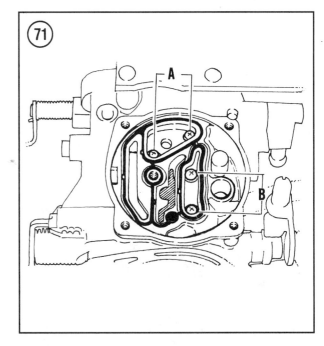

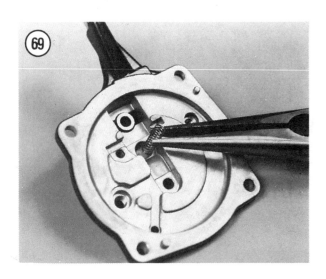

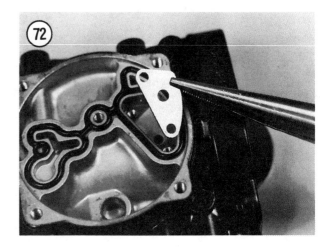

Cleaning and Inspection

1. Thoroughly clean all components and dry with compressed air. If submersing the carburetor components in a carburetor cleaning solution, all nonmetal parts (O-rings, plastic parts) must be removed first.

2. Thoroughly remove all old gasket material. Make sure all fuel and vent passages are clean. Blow out the passages with compressed air. Do not use wire or drill bits to clean any orifices or passages.

3. Inspect the carburetor control arm (A, **Figure 77**) for excessive wear or damage and replace the arm as required. Replace the control arm spring (B, **Figure 77**) if weakened or damaged.

4. Closely inspect the tapered area on the fuel inlet valve (**Figure 78**) and valve seat for scratches, excessive wear or damage. Leakage at

7

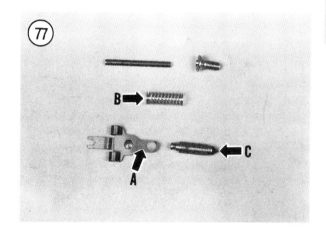

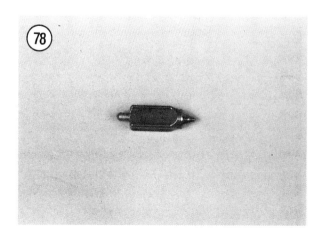

the inlet valve assembly will result in severe a flooding condition.

NOTE
The fuel valve and inlet seat should be replaced as a set. However, the inlet valve seat is an integral part of the carburetor body. So, if the seat is worn or damaged, replace the carburetor body and inlet valve.

5. Inspect the check valve(s) and gasket(s). Replace as required.

6. Inspect the tapered ends of the high- and low-speed mixture screws (**Figure 79**) for grooves, roughness or other damage. Replace the mixture screws if any defects are noted. Inspect the O-rings on the mixture screws for cuts, nicks, cracks, deterioration or other damage. Replace the O-rings if any defects are noted.

7. Inspect the diaphragm (**Figure 80**) for cuts, cracks, tears or other damage and replace as required.

8. Operate the choke and throttle shafts (A, **Figure 81**, typical) to check for shaft movement and proper operation. The shafts should move smoothly. Check each shaft for side play; excessive play indicates worn O-rings. If necessary, remove the choke or throttle valve screws (B, **Figure 81**) and remove the valve. Then remove the retaining ring or screw securing the end of the shaft, then withdraw the shaft from the carburetor body. Replace worn or damage parts. Apply Loctite 242 to the threads of the choke or throttle valve screws during reassembly.

CAUTION
A loose choke or throttle valve attaching screw will back out and fall into the engine, resulting in serious engine damage. Because of this, the screws are secured with thread locking compound at the factory. The screws are also made of relatively soft metal. Therefore, when removing the screws, use a screwdriver which fits the screws perfectly, to prevent rounding out the screw heads.

Carburetor Reassembly

Refer to **Figure 55** (CDK34) or **Figure 56** (CDK38 and CDK40) while performing this procedure.

1. Install new O-ring(s) in the fuel valve inlet (**Figure 75**). Install a new filter screen on the fuel inlet, if necessary.

2. Install a new O-ring seal into its groove in the carburetor body casting (**Figure 76**).

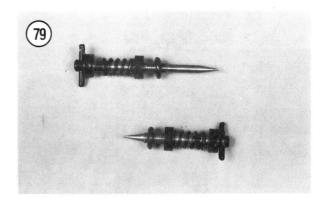

3. Install the check valve gasket(s) (**Figure 74**), diaphragm(s) (**Figure 73**) and plate(s) (**Figure 72**). Install the screws and tighten evenly and securely. See **Figure 70** and **Figure 71** as required.

4. Install the control arm spring (**Figure 69**) into its hole in the carburetor body.

5. Install the control arm assembly as follows:

   a. Engage the end of the fuel inlet valve in the control arm as shown in **Figure 82**. Slide the control arm pivot pin through the arm (**Figure 82**).

   b. Place the control arm (B, **Figure 68**) and pivot pin into position. The rounded projection on the control arm must face downward into the top of the control arm spring. Install

the pivot pin retaining screw (A, **Figure 68**) and tighten securely.

NOTE
The control arm adjustment must be performed correctly or the fuel mixture will be incorrect at all engine speeds.

   c. Measure the distance from the base of the carburetor body to the plastic tip on the end of the control arm (**Figure 83**). The distance should be 1.0-2.0 mm (0.039-0.079 in.). To adjust the control arm distance, remove the arm and carefully bend it as required.

6. Assemble the carburetor case and body assemblies. Secure the case to the body with the screw (A, **Figure 66**). Tighten the screw securely.

7A. *CDK34*—Install the main jet (**Figure 64**) and pilot jet (**Figure 63**).

7B. *CDK38 and CDK40*—Install the main jet (A, **Figure 65**), pilot jet (B) and intermediate jet (C).

8. Align the holes in the diaphragm with the pegs in the carburetor case. Install the diaphragm.

9. Install the diaphragm cover (**Figure 62**). Install the cover screws and tighten evenly and securely.

10. Install the high-speed mixture screw (A, **Figure 61**) along with its spring, washer and O-ring. Turn the screw clockwise until *lightly* seated, then back it out the number of turns recorded during removal. Repeat this procedure for the low-speed mixture screw (B, **Figure 61**). Install the limiter caps so their points are facing downward.

11. *JH750 Super Sport Xi and JH750XiR. Reassemble* the carburetors (**Figure 60**).

12. Install the carburetors as described in this chapter. Synchronize the carburetors (JH750 Super Sport Xi and JH750XiR) as described in Chapter Three. PAGE 111

82

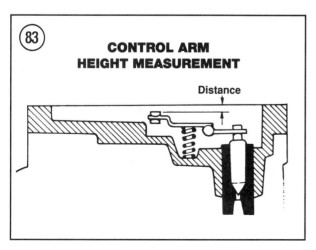

83

CONTROL ARM HEIGHT MEASUREMENT

Distance

7

FUEL PUMP

A remote fuel pump is used on JB650 Jet Mate models. All other models are equipped with an integral fuel pump assembly.

Remote Fuel Pump Removal/Installation (JB650 Jet Mate)

Jet Mate models are equipped with a remote fuel pump assembly. The fuel pump contains fragile diaphragms and gaskets that are easily damaged. Therefore, do not disassemble the pump unless leakage or internal defects are sus-

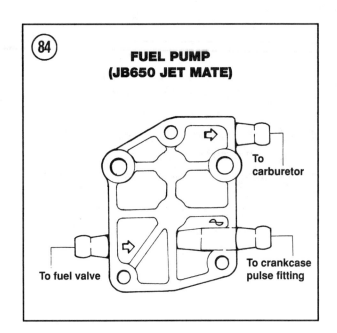

84

**FUEL PUMP
(JB650 JET MATE)**

To carburetor

To fuel valve

To crankcase
pulse fitting

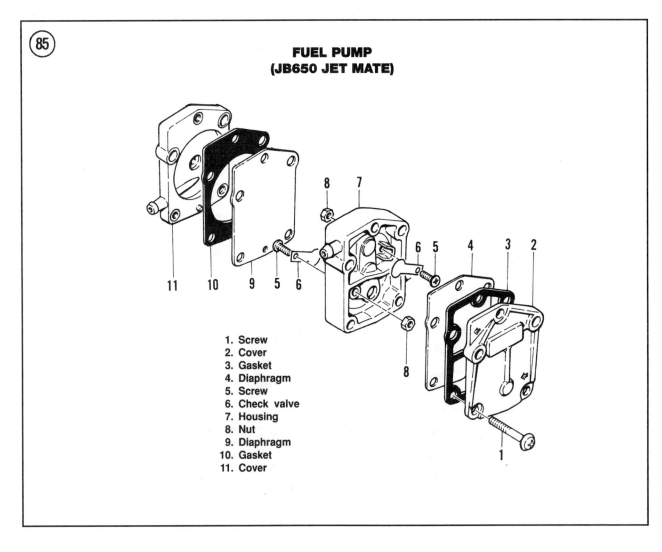

85

**FUEL PUMP
(JB650 JET MATE)**

1. Screw
2. Cover
3. Gasket
4. Diaphragm
5. Screw
6. Check valve
7. Housing
8. Nut
9. Diaphragm
10. Gasket
11. Cover

pected. Check the availability of replacement parts for the pump prior to disassembly.

1. Disconnect the cooling and bilge hoses from the bulkhead. Remove the bracket bolts and pull the bracket and fuel pump away from the bulkhead to gain access to the fuel hoses.

2. Disconnect the hoses from the pump.

3. Remove the screws securing the pump to the bracket and remove the pump.

4. Install the fuel pump by reversing Steps 1-3. Connect the fuel hoses as shown in **Figure 84**. Make sure fuel hoses are securely clamped to the pump fittings. Tighten the pump mounting screws securely, but do not overtighten to prevent damage to the pump assembly.

Disassembly/Inspection/Reassembly

NOTE
The fuel pump contains fragile diaphragms and gaskets that are easily damaged during disassembly. Therefore, do not disassemble the pump unless leakage or internal defects are suspected. Check the availability of pump replacement parts prior to disassembly.

Refer to **Figure 85** for this procedure.

1. Remove the fuel pump body screws.

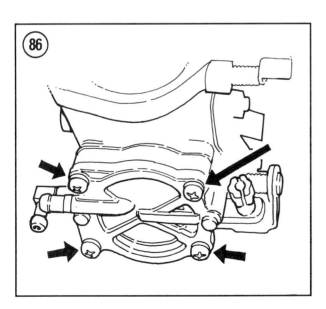

86

2. Carefully separate the 3 fuel pump body castings.

3. Remove the 2 gaskets and 2 diaphragms.

4. Inspect the diaphragms for holes, tears or other damage. The diaphragms should always be replaced once the pump is disassembled.

5. Inspect the check valves for cracks, chips or other damage and replace as required. The check valve should seat lightly against pump housing.

6. To reassemble the pump, carefully stack each component together in the order or disassembly. Make sure the gaskets and diaphragms are properly aligned with the pegs on each pump cover.

7. Install the pump body screws and tighten securely.

Integral Fuel Pump Removal/Installation (JS550SX, JF650X-2, JF650TS, JL650SC, JS650SX, JH750SS, JS750SX, JT750ST, JH750 Super Sport Xi and JH750XiR)

No replacement parts are available for the integral fuel pump used on Keihin Model CDK38 and CDK40 carburetors. If leakage or internal defects are suspected, the pump must be replaced as an assembly. The pump contains fragile diaphragms and gaskets that are easily damaged. Therefore, do not disassemble the pump for inspection purposes.

1. Remove the carburetor(s) as described in this chapter.

2. Remove the screws securing the fuel pump to the side of the carburetor. See **Figure 86**.

3. Separate the fuel pump assembly from the carburetor.

4. Install the fuel pump by reverse Steps 1-3. Tighten the pump mounting screws evenly and securely.

7

FUEL TANK

Removal/Installation
(JS440SX and JS550SX)

> *WARNING*
> *Some fuel may spill during these pro-*
> *cedures. Work in a well-ventilated area*
> *at least 50 ft. (15 m) from any sparks*
> *or flames, including gas appliance pi-*
> *lot lights. Never smoke around gaso-*
> *line. Keep a fire extinguisher rated for*
> *gasoline fires nearby.*

1. Remove the engine cover.

2. Pump or siphon the contents of the fuel tank into a container approved for gasoline storage.

3. Unhook the fuel tank rubber straps from the clips on the hull (**Figure 87**).

4. Unscrew the outlet retainer nut (A, **Figure 88**) and remove the fuel outlet assembly and fuel tubes.

5. Loosen the hose clamp at the front of the tank (**Figure 89**) and pull the tank free from the filler hose. Lift the tank out of the hull.

6. Discard any fuel remaining in the tank. If necessary, flush out the tank using clean, high-flash point solvent, then pour out the solvent and allow the tank to dry.

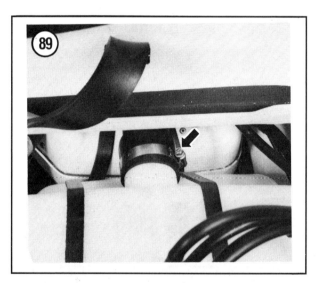

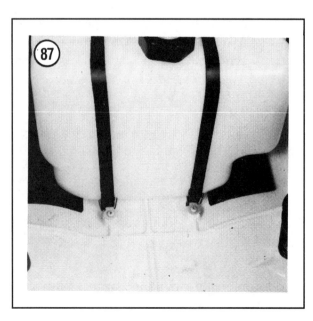

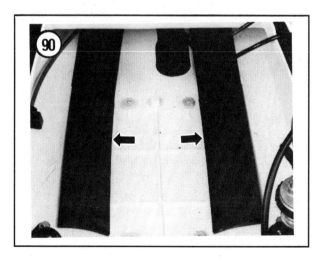

7. To install the fuel tank, reverse the removal steps, while noting the following:

    a. Make sure the fuel tank damper pads (**Figure 90**) are in good condition. Install new pads, if necessary, using water-resistant contact cement.

    b. When installing the tank retainer straps, position the strap ends with their tabs toward the tank (**Figure 87**) to keep the hooks from chafing the tank.

    c. Make sure the filler hose clamp and tank outlet connections are tight.

Removal/Installation (JS650SX and JF650X-2)

> *WARNING*
> *Some fuel may spill during these procedures. Work in a well-ventilated area at least 50 ft. (15 m) from any sparks or flames, including gas appliance pilot lights. Never smoke around gasoline. Keep a fire extinguisher rated for gasoline fires nearby.*

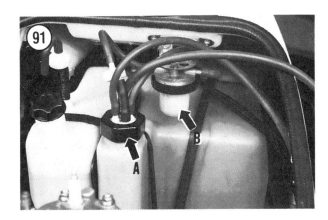

1. Remove the engine cover.

2. Remove the battery as described in Chapter Eight.

3. Pump or siphon the contents of the fuel tank into a container approved for gasoline storage.

4. Remove the oil tank. See Chapter Nine.

5. Unscrew the fuel outlet retainer nut (A, **Figure 91**) and remove the outlet assembly and fuel tubes.

6. Unhook the fuel tank rubber retainer straps from the clips on the hull.

7. *JS650SX*—Remove the bolts securing the sediment bowl (B, **Figure 91**) to the hull. Remove the sediment bowl and gasket.

8. Loosen the hose clamp at the fuel inlet hose. Pull the tank free of the filler hose. Lift the tank (**Figure 92**) out of the hull.

9. Properly discard any fuel remaining in the tank. If necessary, rinse out the tank using clean, high-flash point solvent, then allow the tank to dry.

10. To install the fuel tank, reverse the removal steps, while noting the following:

    a. Make sure the tank damper pads are in good condition. Install new pads, if necessary. Secure the pads using water-resistant contact cement.

    b. When installing the tank retainer straps, position the strap ends so their tabs face the tank, to keep the hooks from chafing the tank.

    c. Make sure the filler hose clamp and tank outlet connections are tight.

    d. Bleed the oil injection system as described in Chapter Nine.

7

**Removal/Installation
(JF650TS)**

> *WARNING*
> *Some fuel may spill during these pro-
> cedures. Work in a well-ventilated area
> at least 50 ft. (15 m) from any sparks
> or flames, including gas appliance pi-
> lot lights. Never smoke around gaso-
> line. Keep a fire extinguisher rated for
> gasoline fires nearby.*

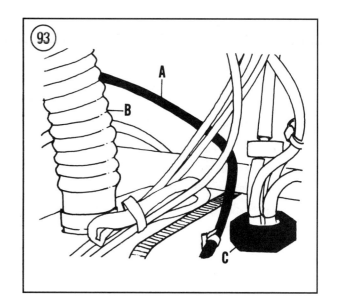

1. Open the storage compartment door.
2. Remove the screws securing the storage compartment case to the hull.
3. Remove the storage compartment case and
door as an assembly.
4. Pump or siphon the contents of the fuel tank
into a container approved for gasoline storage.
5. Loosen the clamp and disconnect the fuel
tank breather hose (A, **Figure 93**). Place the hose
out of the way.
6. Loosen the clamp and disconnect the fuel
tank filler tube (B, **Figure 93**). Place the tube out
of the way.
7. Unscrew the fuel outlet retainer nut (C, **Figure 93**) and remove the outlet assembly and fuel
tubes.

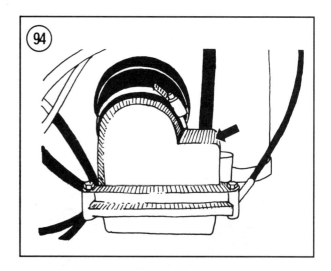

8. Unhook the fuel tank rubber retaining straps
from the clips on the hull. Lift the fuel tank out
of the hull.
9. Properly discard any fuel remaining in the
tank. If necessary, flush the tank with clean,
high-flash point solvent, then allow the tank to
dry.
10. To install the tank, reverse the removal
steps, while noting the following:

   a. When installing the tank retaining straps,
   position the strap ends so their tabs face the
   tank, to prevent the hooks from chafing the
   tank.

   b. Make sure the filler hose clamp, breather
   hose and tank outlet connections are tight.

   c. Inspect the seal on the storage compartment
   case. Replace the seal if necessary.

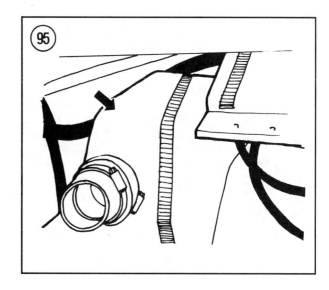

Removal/Installation
(JL650SC)

WARNING
Some fuel may spill during these procedures. Work in a well-ventilated area at least 50 ft. (15 m) from any sparks or flames, including gas appliance pilot lights. Never smoke around gasoline. Keep a fire extinguisher rated for gasoline fires nearby.

1. Remove the engine as described in Chapter Five.
2. Remove the intake silencer as follows:

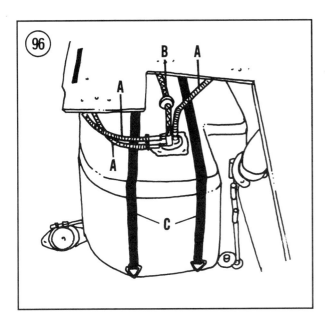

  a. Remove the electric box along with its mounting bracket. Place the electric box and bracket aside.

  b. Remove the air intake cover (**Figure 94**).

  c. Unhook the rubber strap and remove the intake silencer (**Figure 95**) from the hull.

3. Pump or siphon the contents of the fuel tank into a container approved for gasoline storage.

4. Label all fuel hoses for reference during installation.

5. Loosen the clamps and disconnect the fuel hoses (A, **Figure 96**) from the fuel valve. Plug the hoses to prevent leakage and contamination.

6. Loosen the clamp and disconnect the fuel tank vent hose (B, **Figure 96**) from the fuel valve.

7. Unhook the fuel tank rubber retaining straps (C, **Figure 96**) from the clips on the hull.

8. Loosen the clamps and disconnect the fuel tank filler tube (**Figure 97**).

9. Remove the fuel tank from the hull.

10. Properly discard any fuel remaining in the tank. If necessary, flush out the tank using high-flash point solvent, then allow the tank to dry.

11. To install the fuel tank, reverse the removal steps, while noting the following:

  a. Make sure the fuel tank damper pads are in good condition. Replace the pads if necessary. Secure the pads using water-resistant contact cement.

  b. When installing the tank retaining straps, position the strap ends so their tabs face the tank, to prevent the hooks from chafing the tank.

  c. Make sure the filler hose clamp, breather hose and tank outlet connections are tight.

12. Install the engine as described in Chapter Five.

7

Removal/Installation (JB650 Jet Mate)

> *WARNING*
> *Some fuel may spill during these procedures. Work in a well-ventilated area at least 50 ft. (15 m) from any sparks or flames, including gas appliance pilot lights. Never smoke around gasoline. Keep a fire extinguisher rated for gasoline fires nearby.*

1. Remove the rear seat assembly.

2. Pump or siphon the contents of the fuel tank into a container approved for gasoline storage.

3. Label all fuel hoses for reference during tank installation.

4. Loosen the clamps and disconnect the fuel hoses (**Figure 98**) from the main fuel valve. Plug the hoses to prevent leakage and contamination.

5. Unhook the fuel tank rubber retaining strap from the clip on the hull.

6. Loosen the clamps and disconnect the fuel tank filler tube (**Figure 99**).

7. Remove the fuel tank from the hull.

8. Properly discard any fuel remaining in the tank. If necessary, flush the tank using clean, high-flash point solvent, then allow the tank to dry.

9. To install the fuel tank, reverse the removal steps, while noting the following:

    a. Make sure the fuel tank damper pads are in good condition. Replace the pads if necessary. Secure the pads using water-resistant contact cement.

    b. When installing the tank retaining straps, position the strap ends so their tabs face the tank, to prevent the hooks from chafing the tank.

    c. Make sure the filler hose clamp, breather hose and tank outlet connections are tight.

Removal/Installation (JS750SX)

> *WARNING*
> *Some fuel may spill during these procedures. Work in a well-ventilated area at least 50 ft. (15 m) from any sparks or flames, including gas appliance pilot lights. Never smoke around gasoline. Keep a fire extinguisher rated for gasoline fires nearby.*

1. Place the main fuel valve in the OFF position.

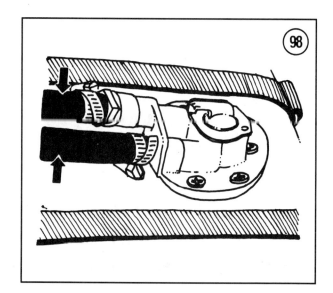

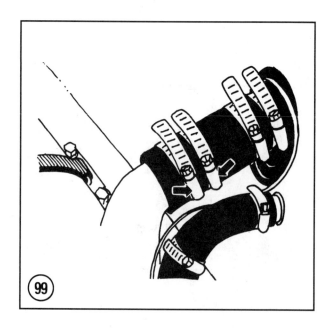

2. Pump or siphon the contents of the fuel tank into a container approved for gasoline storage.

3. Remove the air intake silencer as described in this chapter. Remove the intake silencer mounting bracket.

4. Remove the exhaust pipe and expansion chamber as described in this chapter.

5. Loosen the main fuel valve control cable locknuts (A, **Figure 100**) and disconnect the cables (B) from the valve.

6. Disconnect the fuel hoses (C, **Figure 100**) and vent hose from the main fuel valve.

7. Remove the 4 screws (D, **Figure 100**) securing the main fuel valve to the fuel tank.

8. Remove the main fuel valve assembly from the fuel tank.

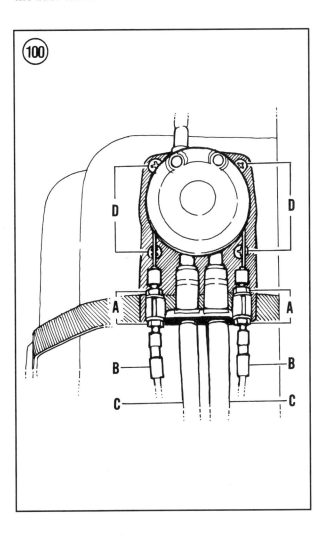

9. Disconnect the fuel tank rubber retaining straps from the clip in the hull.

10. Remove the oil tank as described in Chapter Nine.

11. Loosen the clamp and disconnect the fuel inlet hose from the tank.

12. Lift the fuel tank from the hull.

13. Properly discard any fuel remaining in the tank. If necessary, flush the tank using clean, high-flash point solvent.

14. To install the fuel tank, reverse the removal steps, while noting the following:

   a. Make sure the O-ring seal under the main fuel valve is in position and in good condition.

   b. Make sure the fuel tank damper pads are in good condition. Replace the pads if necessary. Secure the pads using water-resistant contact cement.

   c. When installing the tank retaining straps, position the strap ends so their tabs face the tank, to prevent the hooks from chafing the tank.

   d. Make sure all hose clamps are tight.

   e. Apply Loctite 242 to the threads of the air intake silencer mounting screws.

Removal/Installation
(JH750SS, JH750 Super Sport Xi and JH750XiR)

> *WARNING*
> *Some fuel may spill during these procedures. Work in a well-ventilated area at least 50 ft. (15 m) from any sparks or flames, including gas appliance pilot lights. Never smoke around gasoline. Keep a fire extinguisher rated for gasoline fires nearby.*

1. Pump or siphon the contents of the fuel tank into a container approved for gasoline storage.

2. Push the starter interlock switch. Place the main fuel valve in the OFF position.

7

3. Remove the engine as described in Chapter Five.

4. Disconnect the handlebar return spring (A, **Figure 101**).

5. Disconnect the steering cable (B, **Figure 101**). Slide the cable outer sleeve away from the ball joint. Pull the cable away from the ball joint.

6. Remove the steering cable mounting bracket.

7. Disconnect the fuel level sensor 2-pin connector (pink wires).

8. Disconnect the fuel hoses from the sediment bowl. Remove the sediment bowl and mounting bracket as a unit.

9. Unhook the fuel tank rubber retaining straps from the clips on the hull.

10. Loosen the clamps on the fuel filler tube (**Figure 102**).

11. Label all fuel hoses for reference during tank installation. Cut the tie strap clamps and disconnect the fuel hoses from the tank.

12. Remove the fuel tank from the hull.

13. Properly discard any fuel remaining in the tank. If necessary, flush out the tank using clean, high-flash point solvent. Allow the tank to dry.

14. To install the fuel tank, reverse the removal steps, while noting the following:

  a. Make sure the fuel tank damper pads are in good condition, if used. Replace the pads if necessary. Secure the pads using water-resistant contact cement.

  b. When installing the tank retaining straps, position the strap ends so their tabs face the tank, to prevent the hooks from chafing the tank.

  c. Make sure all hose clamps are tight.

Removal/Installation (JT750ST)

WARNING
Some fuel may spill during these procedures. Work in a well-ventilated area at least 50 ft. (15 m) from any sparks or flames, including gas appliance pilot lights. Never smoke around gasoline. Keep a fire extinguisher rated for gasoline fires nearby.

1. Place the main fuel valve in the OFF position.

2. Pump or siphon the contents of the fuel tank into a container approved for gasoline storage.

3. Remove the air intake cover fasteners (B, **Figure 103**). Remove the intake cover along with the intake duct.

4. Open the storage compartment hatch. Remove the storage compartment.

5. Label all fuel hoses for reference during tank installation.

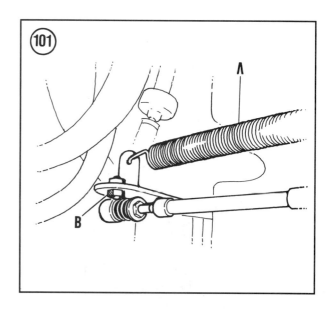

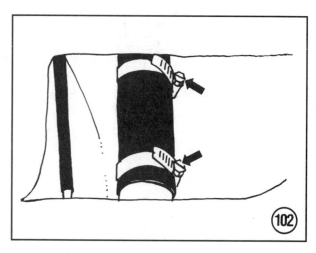

6. Cut the tie strap clamps and disconnect the fuel hoses from the tank. Disconnect the fuel level sensor 2-pin connector (pink wires).

7. Remove the main fuel valve (along with the fuel hoses) as described in this chapter.

8. Remove the steering cover as described in Chapter Eleven.

9. Remove the sediment bowl mounting bracket fasteners.

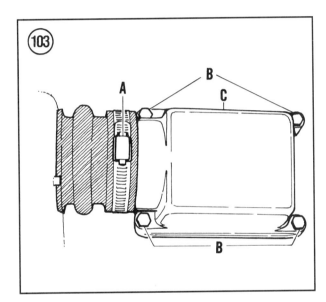

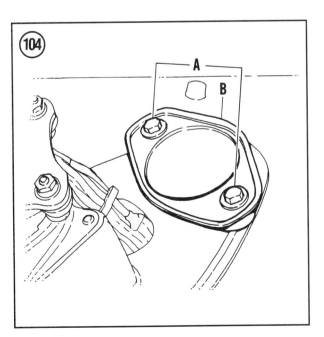

10. Remove the 2 intake duct mounting screws (A, **Figure 104**), then lift the duct (B) out of the hull.

11. Unhook the fuel tank rubber retaining straps from the clips on the hull.

12. Loosen the clamps on the fuel filler tube. Disconnect the filler tube from the fuel tank and lift the tank out of the hull.

13. Properly discard any fuel remaining in the tank. If necessary, flush out the tank using clean, high-flash point solvent, then allow the tank to dry.

14. To install the fuel tank, reverse the removal steps, while noting the following:

    a. When installing the tank retaining straps, position the strap ends so their tabs face the tank, to prevent the hooks from chafing the tank.

    b. Make sure all hose clamps are tight.

    c. Install the main fuel valve as described in this chapter.

    d. Apply Loctite 242 to the threads of the air intake cover fasteners.

MAIN FUEL VALVE

Fuel Valve Removal/Installation (JS440SX and JS550SX)

    Refer to **Figure 105** (JS440SX) or **Figure 106** (JS550SX) while performing this procedure.

> *WARNING*
> *Before disconnecting any fuel hoses, loosen the fuel filler cap (A, **Figure 88**) to relieve any pressure that may be present in the fuel system.*

1. Remove the engine hood.

2. Disconnect the negative battery cable.

3. Remove the electric box as described in Chapter Eight.

4. Remove the set screw from the fuel valve knob on the outside of the hull. Pull the knob from the valve shaft.

7

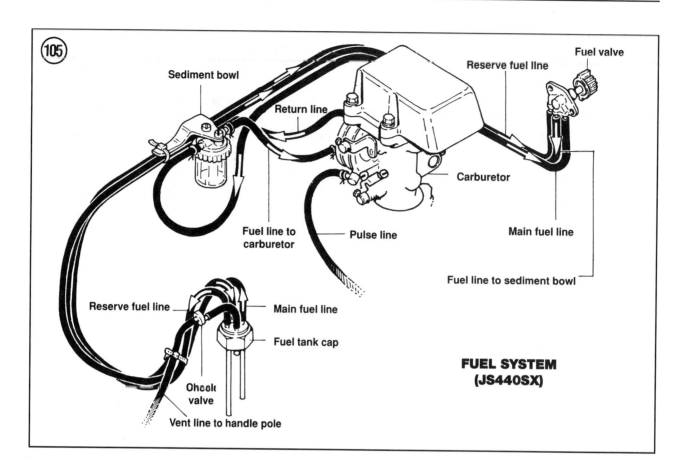

(105) Sediment bowl — Return line — Reserve fuel line — Fuel valve — Carburetor — Fuel line to carburetor — Pulse line — Main fuel line — Fuel line to sediment bowl — Reserve fuel line — Main fuel line — Fuel tank cap — Check valve — Vent line to handle pole

FUEL SYSTEM (JS440SX)

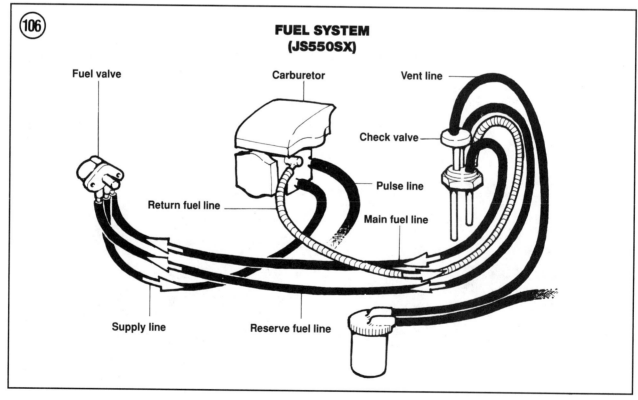

(106) **FUEL SYSTEM (JS550SX)**

Fuel valve — Carburetor — Vent line — Check valve — Pulse line — Return fuel line — Main fuel line — Supply line — Reserve fuel line

5. From inside the hull, label the fuel hoses at the fuel valve. Then, disconnect the hoses. Plug the hoses to prevent leakage and contamination.

6. Remove the screws securing the fuel valve (**Figure 107**) to the hull. Remove the valve.

7. Install the fuel valve by reversing the removal steps. Apply Loctite 242 to the threads of the fuel valve mounting screws and the fuel knob set screw. Tighten all fasteners securely.

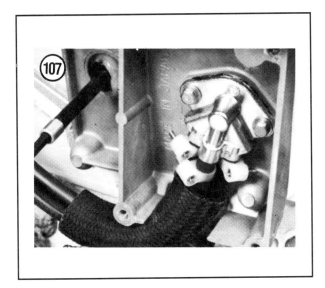

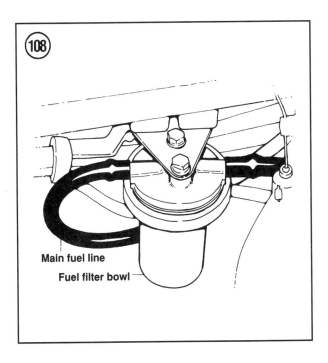

Main fuel line
Fuel filter bowl

Fuel valve cleaning
(JS440SX and JS550SX)

If the fuel valve is plugged or restricted, clean it as follows:

1. Remove the engine hood.

> *WARNING*
> *Before disconnecting any fuel hoses, loosen the fuel filler cap (A, **Figure 88**) to relieve any pressure that may be present in the fuel system.*

2. Disconnect the hose from the inlet side of the fuel filter (**Figure 108**). Then disconnect the hose from the fuel tank outlet.

> *NOTE*
> *To prevent damage to fuel hoses or other components, the air pressure should not exceed 25 psi (172 kPa) during Step 3.*

> *WARNING*
> *To prevent personal injury, wear eye protection anytime compressed air is used to clean or dry components.*

3. Using compressed air, blow through the main fuel hose while switching the fuel valve back and forth between the ON and RESERVE positions. Continue using compressed air and switching the valve until all debris is forced out of the valve.

4. Reconnect the main fuel hose to the fuel filter (**Figure 108**). Make sure the hoses is securely clamped.

Fuel Valve Removal/Installation
(JB650 Jet Mate)

Jet Mate models are equipped with 2 fuel valves. The main fuel valve is located on top of the fuel tank and the outside valve is located on the inner surface of the hull under the rear seat panel.

The main fuel valve has a built-in anti-siphon valve to prevent fuel flow from the fuel tank if

7

the fuel hose from the tank to the carburetor should break.

Refer to **Figure 109** while performing this procedure.

1. Remove the rear seat assembly.
2. Disconnect the negative battery cable.

> *WARNING*
> *Before disconnecting any fuel hoses, loosen the fuel filler cap to relieve any pressure that may be present in the fuel system.*

3. To remove the main fuel valve, perform the following steps in the storage area under the seat:

    a. Label the main fuel valve hoses for reference during valve installation. Then disconnect the hoses. Plug the hoses to prevent leakage and contamination.

    b. Remove the mounting screws (**Figure 110**) and withdraw the main fuel valve from the fuel tank.

4. To remove the outside fuel valve, perform the following steps in the storage area under the seat:

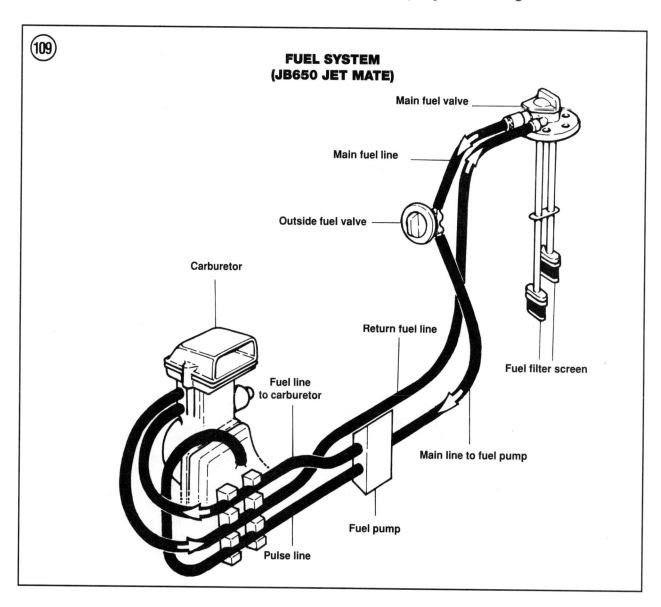

(109)

**FUEL SYSTEM
(JB650 JET MATE)**

Main fuel valve

Main fuel line

Outside fuel valve

Carburetor

Return fuel line

Fuel filter screen

Fuel line
to carburetor

Main line to fuel pump

Fuel pump

Pulse line

a. Label the fuel valve hoses for reference during installation. Disconnect the hoses from the outside fuel valve. Plug the hoses to prevent leakage and contamination.

b. Remove the set screw on the outside fuel valve knob (A, **Figure 111**). Then, pull the knob off the valve shaft.

c. Remove the cap (B, **Figure 111**) from the hull receptacle.

d. Within the receptacle, unscrew the nut (**Figure 112**) securing the fuel valve.

e. Prior to removing the fuel valve, note the orientation of the valve. The inlet hose fitting is located at the top. Mark this fitting so it will be reinstalled in the same position.

f. Remove the outside fuel valve.

5. Install the valves by reversing the removal steps, while noting the following points:

a. To prevent damage to the fuel tank threads, do not overtighten the main fuel valve mounting screws.

b. Install the outside fuel valve so the inlet hose fitting is positioned toward the top, as noted during removal.

c. On the outside fuel valve, inspect the large O-ring seal on the hull receptacle cap and the small O-ring on the inner surface of the fuel valve. Replace the O-ring(s) if any defects are noted.

d. Apply Loctite 242 to the threads of the outside fuel valve nut and on the knob set screw.

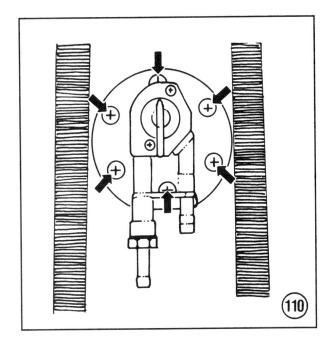

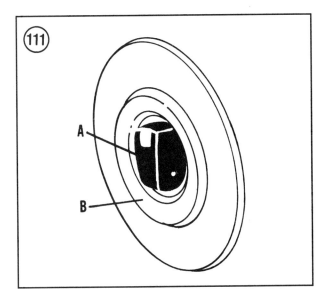

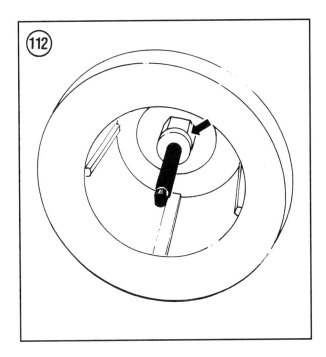

7

Main Fuel Valve Cleaning (JB650 Jet Mate)

If the main fuel valve is plugged or restricted, perform the following steps to clean it.

1. Remove the fuel valve as described in this chapter.

2. Remove the anti-siphon valve from the fuel valve.

WARNING
Before disconnecting any fuel hoses, loosen the fuel filler cap to relieve any pressure that may be present in the fuel system.

3. Using compressed air, blow through one of the valve fittings while rotating the valve knob back and forth. Continue until all debris is forced from the valve.

4. Reinstall the valve as described in this chapter.

Outside Fuel Valve Cleaning (JB650 Jet Mate)

If the outside fuel valve is plugged or restricted, perform the following steps to clean it.

1. Label the hoses at the outside fuel valve. Then, disconnect the hoses from the valve. Plug the hoses to prevent leakage and contamination.

WARNING
Before disconnecting any fuel hoses, loosen the fuel filler cap to relieve any pressure that may be present in the fuel system.

2. Using compressed air, blow through one of the valve fittings while rotating the valve knob back and forth. Continue until all debris is forced from the valve.

3. Reconnect the fuel hoses to the valve. Make sure all clamps are tight.

Anti-siphon Valve Inspection (JB650 Jet Mate)

WARNING
Some fuel may spill during these procedures. Work in a well-ventilated area at least 50 ft. (15 m) from any sparks or flames, including gas appliance pilot lights. Never smoke around gasoline. Keep a fire extinguisher rated for gasoline fires nearby.

1. Remove the front seat and engine hood.

2. The fuel tank must be full of fuel.

3. Place shop towels under the fuel hose at the fuel pump to absorb any spilled fuel.

4. Start the engine and run for several seconds to ensure all fuel hoses are full of fuel.

5. Disconnect the fuel hose (**Figure 113**) from the fuel pump inlet fitting. Place a suitable con-

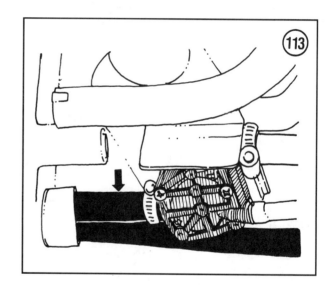

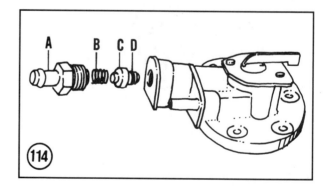

tainer under the end of the hose. Fuel should *not* flow from the hose. If no fuel flow is noted from the hose, the anti-siphon valve is functioning properly.

6. If fuel flows from the hose, the anti-siphon valve is not functioning properly and must be repaired. Continue at Step 7.

7. Remove the main fuel valve as described in this chapter.

8. Unscrew the fuel hose fitting (A, **Figure 114**) from the end of the main fuel valve.

9. Remove the spring (B, **Figure 114**) and plunger (C). from the main fuel valve housing.

10. Clean the main fuel and anti-siphon valve components in clean solvent and dry with compressed air. Make sure all foreign material is removed from the interior of the main fuel valve.

11. Inspect all components for excessive wear or damage. The only replacement parts available are the O-ring seals. Therefore, if any other part

is worn or damaged, the main fuel valve assembly must be replaced.

12. If all valve components are serviceable, install new O-rings on the plunger and fuel line fitting (D, **Figure 114**).

13. Install the plunger (O-ring end first) into the valve housing, then install the spring.

14. Make sure the O-ring is in place on the fuel hose fitting, then install the fitting into the main fuel valve. Tighten the fitting securely.

15. Install the main fuel valve as described in this chapter.

16. Complete reassembly by installing the engine hood and front seat.

Fuel Valve Removal/Installation (JF650X-2 and JS650SX)

Refer to **Figure 115** while performing this procedure.

7

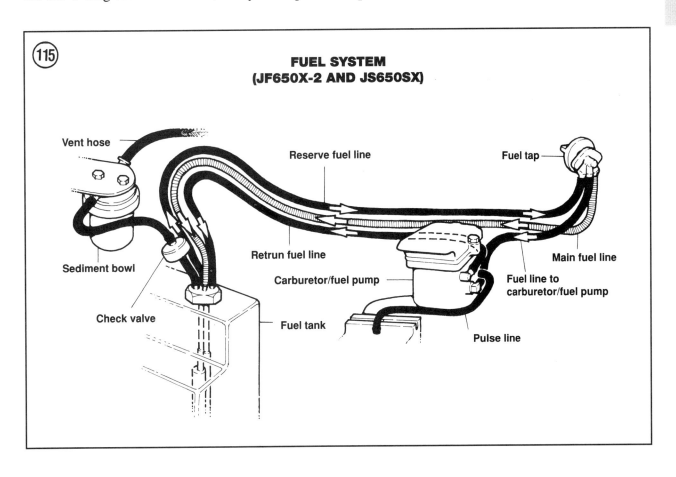

(115)

**FUEL SYSTEM
(JF650X-2 AND JS650SX)**

Vent hose

Reserve fuel line

Fuel tap

Retrun fuel line

Main fuel line

Sediment bowl

Carburetor/fuel pump

Fuel line to
carburetor/fuel pump

Check valve

Fuel tank

Pulse line

WARNING
Before disconnecting any fuel hoses, loosen the fuel filler cap to relieve any pressure that may be present in the fuel system.

1. Remove the engine hood.
2. Disconnect the negative battery cable.
3. Remove the set screw from the fuel valve knob (outside of hull), then pull the knob (2, **Figure 116**) off the valve shaft.
4. From inside the hull, label the fuel valve hoses for reference during installation. Next, disconnect the hoses from the valve. Plug the hoses to prevent leakage and contamination.
5. Remove the fuel valve bracket fasteners. Remove the valve along with its mounting bracket.

NOTE
Prior to removing the fuel valve from its mounting bracket, scribe match marks on both parts so they can be reassembled in their original positions.

6. Remove the fuel valve-to-mounting bracket fasteners. Separate the valve and mounting bracket.
7. Install the fuel valve by reversing the removal steps, while noting the following points:
    a. Align the match marks (made prior to valve and bracket disassembly) on the mounting bracket and fuel valve. Install the valve-to-bracket fasteners and tighten securely.
    b. Apply a silicone sealant on both sides of the fuel valve bracket.
    c. Apply Loctite 242 to the threads of the fuel valve bracket mounting bolts and to the valve knob set screw. Tighten the fasteners securely.

Fuel Valve Cleaning (JF650X-2 and JS650SX)

If the fuel valve is plugged or restricted, clean it as follows:
1. Remove the engine hood.

WARNING
Before disconnecting any fuel hoses, loosen the fuel filler cap to relieve any pressure that may be present in the fuel system.

2. Disconnect the main fuel hose from the fuel pump inlet fitting. See **Figure 115**. Label and disconnect the 2 remaining fuel hoses from the fuel valve.

NOTE
To prevent damage to fuel hoses or other components, the air pressure should not exceed 25 psi (172 kPa) during Step 3.

WARNING
To prevent personal injury, wear eye protection anytime compressed air is used to clean or dry components.

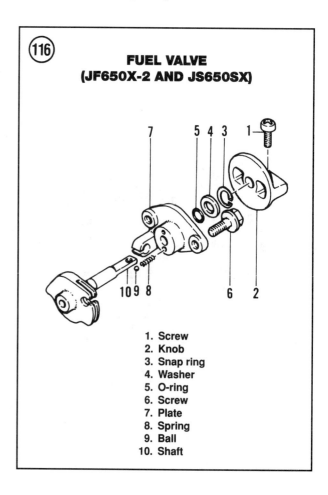

FUEL VALVE (JF650X-2 AND JS650SX)

1. Screw
2. Knob
3. Snap ring
4. Washer
5. O-ring
6. Screw
7. Plate
8. Spring
9. Ball
10. Shaft

3. Using compressed air, blow through the main fuel hose while switching the fuel valve back and forth between the ON and RESERVE positions. Continue using compressed air and switching the valve until all debris is forced out of the valve.

4. Reassemble by reversing Steps 1 and 2.

Fuel Valve Removal/Installation (JF650TS)

Refer to **Figure 117** while performing this procedure.

WARNING
Before disconnecting any fuel hoses, loosen the fuel filler cap to relieve any pressure that may be present in the fuel system.

1. Disconnect the negative battery cable.

2. Remove the set screws from the fuel valve knob and the choke knob. Pull the fuel valve and choke knobs off their shafts.

3. Remove the screws securing the panel cover and remove the panel cover.

4. Open the storage compartment door.

5. Remove the screws securing the storage compartment case.

6. Remove the storage compartment case and door as an assembly.

7. Remove the bolts securing the fuel valve to the inner metal panel.

8. Reach in through the storage compartment case opening and carefully pull the fuel valve and hoses down into the opening.

9. From inside the opening, label the fuel valve hoses for reference during valve installation. Then, disconnect the hoses from the valve. Plug the hoses to prevent leakage and contamination.

10. Remove the fuel valve.

7

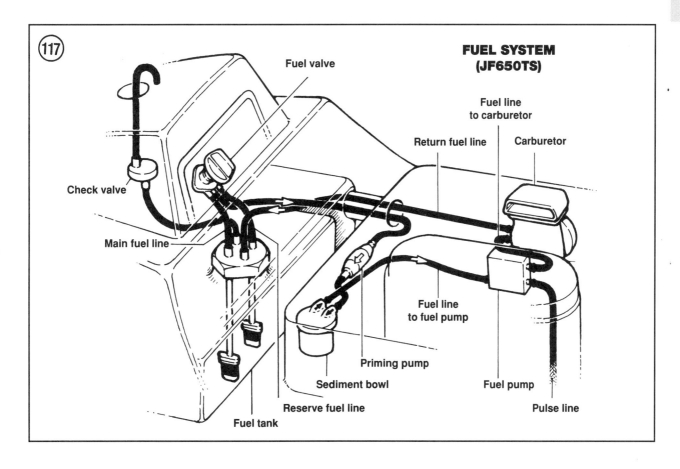

(117)

FUEL SYSTEM (JF650TS)

Fuel valve

Fuel line to carburetor

Return fuel line

Carburetor

Check valve

Main fuel line

Fuel line to fuel pump

Priming pump

Sediment bowl

Fuel pump

Pulse line

Reserve fuel line

Fuel tank

11. Install the fuel valve by reversing the removal steps. Make sure the fuel hoses are attached to the valve correctly. See **Figure 117**.

Fuel Valve Cleaning (JF650TS)

If the fuel valve is plugged or restricted, clean it as follows:

WARNING
Before disconnecting any fuel hoses, loosen the fuel filler cap to relieve any pressure that may be present in the fuel system.

1. Open the storage compartment door.

2. Remove the screws securing the storage compartment case.

3. Remove the storage compartment and door from the hull as an assembly.

4. Loosen the fuel hose outlet retainer nut at the fuel tank.

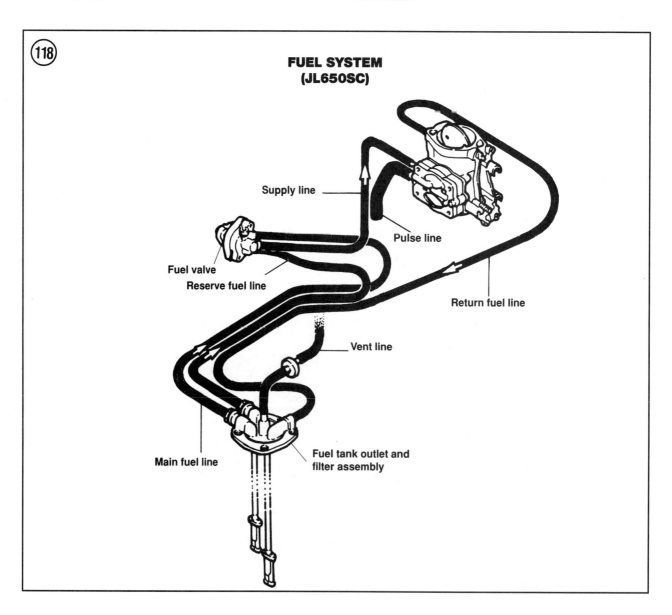

(118)

FUEL SYSTEM (JL650SC)

Supply line

Pulse line

Fuel valve

Reserve fuel line

Return fuel line

Vent line

Main fuel line

Fuel tank outlet and filter assembly

5. Disconnect the main fuel hose from the fuel tank. Label and disconnect the remaining 2 fuel hoses from the fuel valve. See **Figure 117**.

NOTE
To prevent damage to fuel hoses or other components, the air pressure should not exceed 25 psi (172 kPa) during Step 6.

WARNING
To prevent personal injury, wear eye protection anytime compressed air is used to clean or dry components.

6. Using compressed air, blow through the main fuel hose while switching the fuel valve back and forth between the ON and RESERVE positions. Continue using compressed air and switching the valve until all debris is forced out of the valve.

7. Reconnect the fuel hoses and clamp securely. Complete the remaining reassembly by reversing Steps 1-3.

Fuel Valve Removal/Installation (JL650SC)

Refer to **Figure 118** while performing this procedure.
1. Unlock the seat.
2. Remove the screws securing both seat base brackets and remove the seat.
3. Remove the rubber plugs covering the engine hood retaining screws. Remove the hood screws and washers and remove the engine hood.
4. Disconnect the negative battery cable.

WARNING
Before disconnecting any fuel hoses, loosen the fuel filler cap to relieve any pressure that may be present in the fuel system.

5. Remove the set screw from the fuel valve knob, then pull the knob off the valve shaft.
6. Remove the screws securing the knob trim plate and valve and remove the plate.

7. Reach in through the engine hood opening and carefully pull the fuel valve and hoses into the opening.
8. From inside the opening, label the fuel valve hoses for reference during installation. Then, disconnect the hoses from the valve. Plug the hoses to prevent leakage and contamination.
9. Remove the fuel valve from the hull.
10. Install the fuel valve by reversing the removal steps. Apply Loctite 242 to the threads of the fuel valve mounting screws and the valve knob set screw.

Fuel Valve Cleaning (JL650SC)

If the fuel valve is plugged or restricted, clean it as follows:

WARNING
Before disconnecting any fuel hoses, loosen the fuel filler cap to relieve any pressure that may be present in the fuel system.

1. Unlock the seat.
2. Remove the screws securing both seat base brackets and remove the seat.
3. Remove the rubber plugs covering the engine hood retaining screws. Remove the hood screws and washers and remove the engine hood.
4. Remove the screws securing the fuel tank outlet and filter assembly. See **Figure 118**. Remove the outlet assembly from the tank.
5. Disconnect the main fuel delivery hose from the carburetor.

NOTE
To prevent damage to fuel hoses or other components, the air pressure should not exceed 25 psi (172 kPa) during Step 6.

WARNING
To prevent personal injury, wear eye protection anytime compressed air is used to clean or dry components.

7

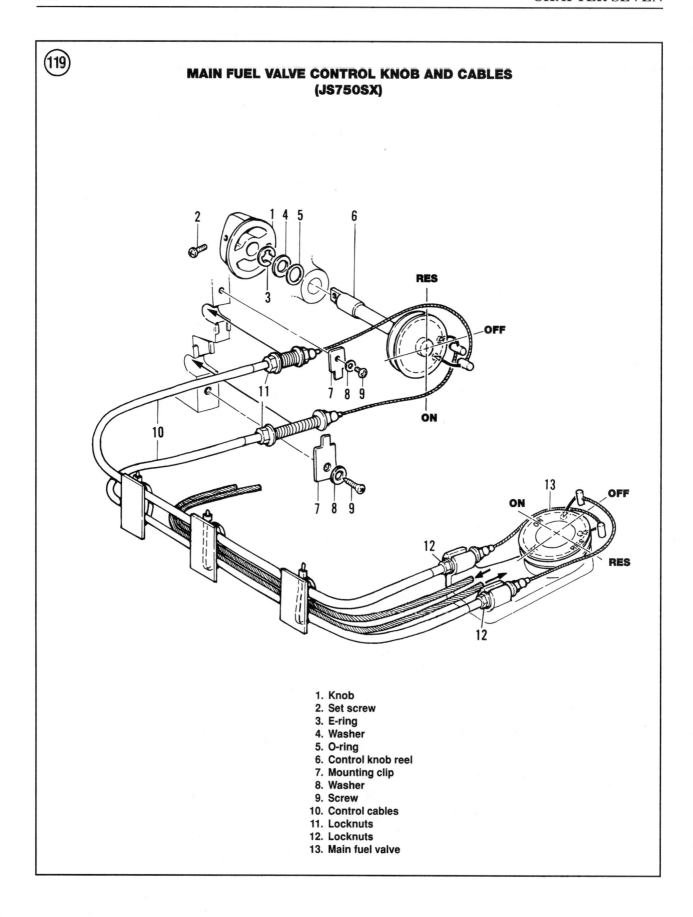

**MAIN FUEL VALVE CONTROL KNOB AND CABLES
(JS750SX)**

1. Knob
2. Set screw
3. E-ring
4. Washer
5. O-ring
6. Control knob reel
7. Mounting clip
8. Washer
9. Screw
10. Control cables
11. Locknuts
12. Locknuts
13. Main fuel valve

6. Using compressed air, blow through the main fuel hose while switching the fuel valve back and forth between the ON and RESERVE positions. Continue using compressed air and switching the valve until all debris is forced out of the valve.

7. Reconnect the fuel hoses and clamp securely. Complete the remaining reassembly by reversing Steps 1-4.

Fuel Valve Removal/Installation (JS750SX)

The main fuel valve control knob is mounted outside the hull. The fuel valve, however, is mounted on top of the fuel tank and is connected to the control knob with 2 cables. See **Figure 119**.

WARNING
Before disconnecting any fuel hoses, loosen the fuel filler cap to relieve any pressure that may be present in the fuel system.

1. Remove the engine hood.
2. Place the main fuel valve in the OFF position.
3. Remove the air intake silencer as described in this chapter.
3. Loosen the locknuts securing the control cables to the main fuel valve. See **Figure 120**. Disconnect the cables from the valve.
4. Disconnect the fuel hoses and vent hose from the fuel valve.
5. Remove the 4 screws (**Figure 120**) securing the fuel valve assembly to the fuel tank. Lift the fuel valve up and out of the fuel tank.
6. To remove the control cables, first remove the screws securing the cable mounting clips to the hull. See **Figure 119**.
7. Remove the electric box (Chapter Eight) to gain access to the tie strap clamps securing the control cables at the rear of the engine compartment.
9. Cut the tie strap clamps.
10. Loosen the locknuts at the cable mounting bracket and disconnect the cables from the control knob reel. Remove the cables from the hull.
11. To install the control cables, place the main fuel valve in the OFF position. The OFF mark on the valve must be aligned with the projection on the bracket as shown in **Figure 121**.
12. Install the cables in position. Connect the cables to the control knob reel, tighten the locknuts, install the mounting clips and screws, then secure the cables at the rear of the hull using new tie strap clamps.
13. Reinstall the electric box (Chapter Eight).
14. Make sure the fuel valve-to-fuel tank O-ring seal is properly positioned and in good condition.

7

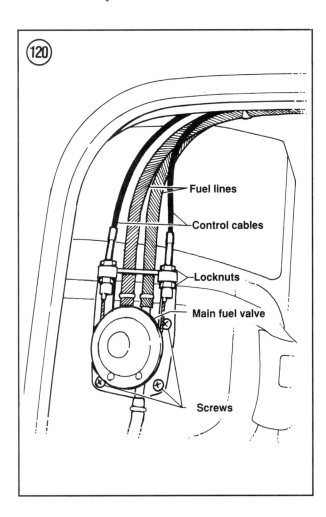

(120)

Fuel lines

Control cables

Locknuts

Main fuel valve

Screws

15. Install the fuel valve into the fuel tank. Secure the valve with its 4 screws. Do not overtighten the screws or the threads in the fuel tank could be damaged.

16. Attach the fuel hoses and control cables to the fuel valve. Turn the fuel valve control knob between the OFF, ON and RES positions. Make sure the fuel valve moves to the correct positions, corresponding to control knob position. If not, adjust the cables as necessary using the locknuts at the control knob reel. After adjusting, tighten the locknuts securely.

17. Complete the remaining installation by reversing the removal steps. Install the air intake silencer as described in this chapter.

Fuel Valve Cleaning
(JS750SX)

If the fuel valve is plugged or restricted, clean it as follows:

> *WARNING*
> *Before disconnecting any fuel hoses, loosen the fuel filler cap to relieve any pressure that may be present in the fuel system.*

1. Remove the engine hood.

2. Disconnect the fuel hoses from the carburetor. See **Figure 122**.

3. Remove the main fuel valve as described in this chapter.

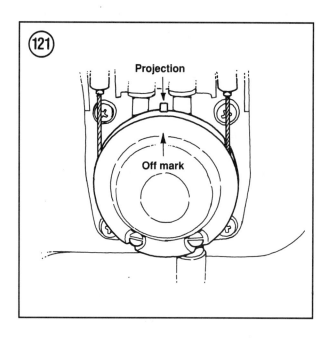

(121) Projection / Off mark

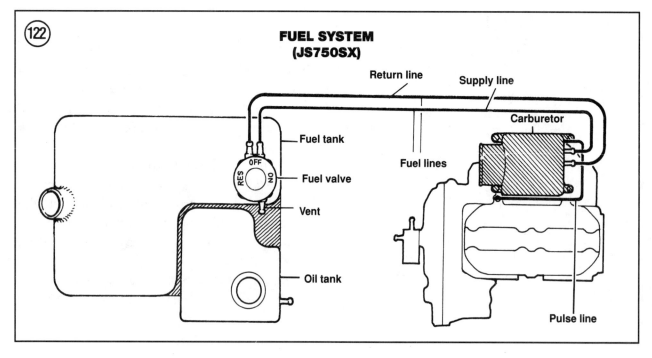

(122) **FUEL SYSTEM (JS750SX)** — Return line, Supply line, Carburetor, Fuel tank, Fuel valve, Vent, Oil tank, Fuel lines, Pulse line

NOTE
To prevent damage to fuel hoses or other components, the air pressure should not exceed 25 psi (172 kPa) during Step 4.

WARNING
To prevent personal injury, wear eye protection anytime compressed air is used to clean or dry components.

4. Using compressed air, blow through the main fuel hose while switching the fuel valve back and forth between the ON and RESERVE positions. Continue using compressed air and switching the valve until all debris is forced out of the valve.

7. Reconnect the fuel hoses and clamp securely. Complete the remaining reassembly by reversing Steps 1-3.

Fuel Valve Removal/Installation (JH750SS, JT750ST, JH750 Super Sport Xi and JH750XiR)

Refer to **Figure 123** or **Figure 124** while performing this procedure.

WARNING
Before disconnecting any fuel hoses, loosen the fuel filler cap to relieve any pressure that may be present in the fuel system.

1. Remove the seat.

2. *Except JT750ST*—Remove the 2 screws securing the sediment bowl mounting bracket to the hull. Place the sediment bowl assembly out of the way.

7

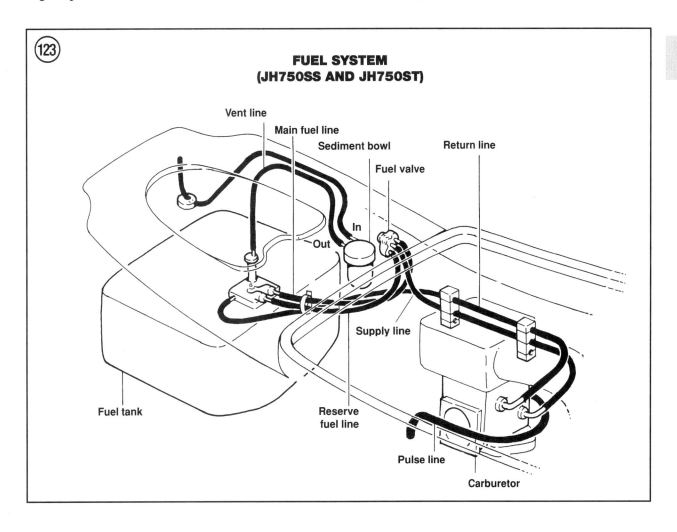

**FUEL SYSTEM
(JH750SS AND JH750ST)**

Vent line

Main fuel line

Sediment bowl

Return line

Fuel valve

In

Out

Supply line

Fuel tank

Reserve fuel line

Pulse line

Carburetor

3. Remove the set screw securing the fuel valve knob to the valve shaft. Pull the knob off the shaft.

4. Remove the 2 screws securing the fuel valve to the side of the hull.

5. Label the fuel hoses for reference during valve installation. Disconnect the hoses from the valve and remove the valve.

6. Install the fuel valve by reversing the removal steps, while noting the following:

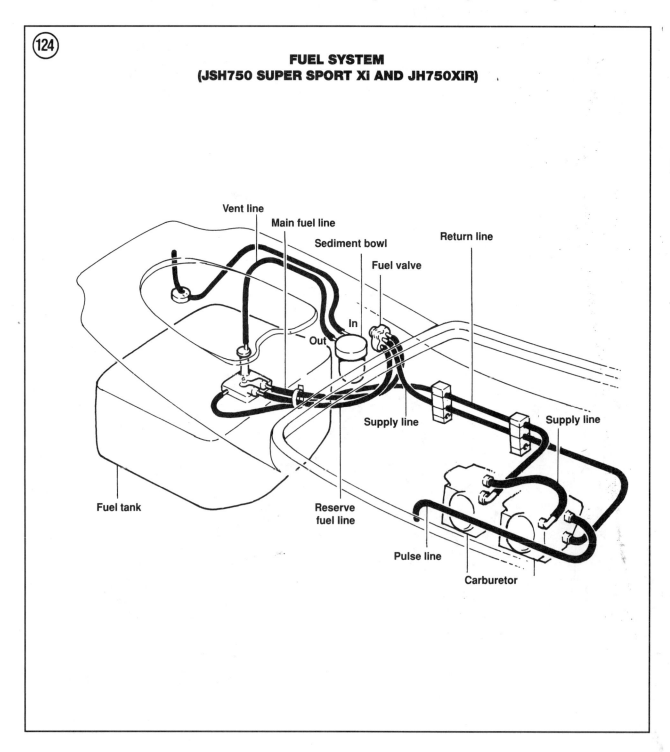

(124)

**FUEL SYSTEM
(JSH750 SUPER SPORT Xi AND JH750XiR)**

Vent line

Main fuel line

Sediment bowl

Return line

Fuel valve

In

Out

Supply line

Supply line

Fuel tank

Reserve
fuel line

Pulse line

Carburetor

a. Apply silicone sealant to the fuel valve and hull mating surfaces.

b. Make sure the fuel hoses are correctly connected to the valve and clamped securely.

c. Apply Loctite 242 to the threads of the fuel valve mounting fasteners. Tighten the fasteners securely.

Fuel Valve Cleaning (JH750SS, JT750ST, JH750 Super Sport Xi and JH750XiR)

If the fuel valve is plugged or restricted, clean it as follows:

WARNING
Before disconnecting any fuel hoses, loosen the fuel filler cap to relieve any pressure that may be present in the fuel system.

1. Remove the fuel valve as described in this chapter.

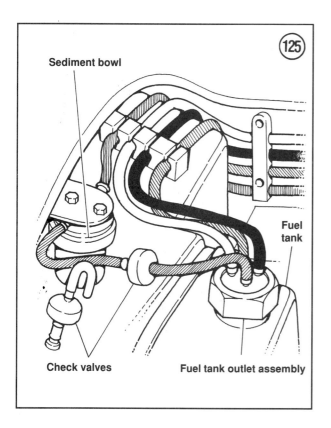

(125)

Sediment bowl

Fuel tank

Check valves

Fuel tank outlet assembly

NOTE
To prevent damage to fuel hoses or other components, the air pressure should not exceed 25 psi (172 kPa) during Step 4.

WARNING
To prevent personal injury, wear eye protection anytime compressed air is used to clean or dry components.

2. Using compressed air, blow through the inlet fitting of the fuel valve while switching the valve back and forth between the ON and RESERVE positions. Continue using compressed air and switching the valve until all debris is forced out of the valve.

3. Reinstall the fuel valve as described in this chapter.

Fuel Vent Check Valve

A check valve is installed in the fuel tank vent line to prevent fuel from spilling during hard riding. Because air must enter the fuel tank as the fuel is drawn from the tank, an atmospheric vent must be provided. The fuel vent check valve allows air to enter the tank as the fuel level drops, but prevents fuel from the tank from flowing out the vent line.

The check valve must be installed in the vent line so the arrow on the valve is facing the fuel tank. See **Figure 125** for a typical vent check valve installation.

To test the valve, disconnect it from the vent line. Then attempt to blow through the valve from each end. Air should pass through the valve from one direction only. If air flows through the valve in both directions, or not at all, the valve is defective and must be replaced.

EXHAUST SYSTEM (JS440SX)

Refer to **Figure 126** while performing the procedures in this section.

7

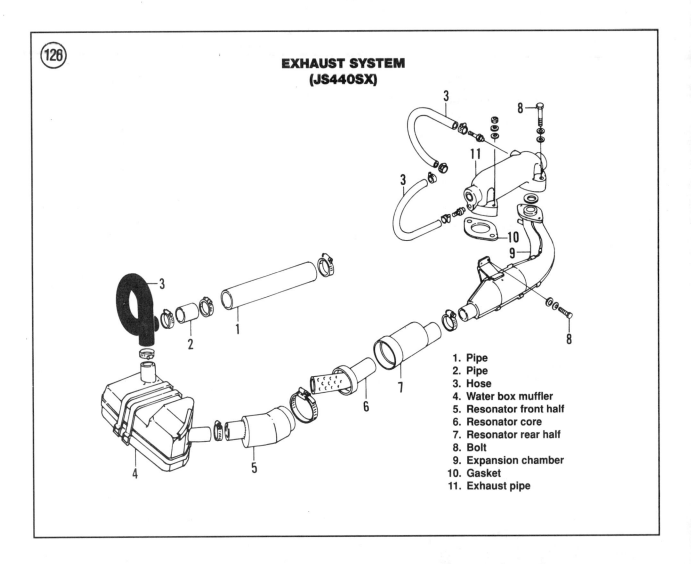

**EXHAUST SYSTEM
(JS440SX)**

1. Pipe
2. Pipe
3. Hose
4. Water box muffler
5. Resonator front half
6. Resonator core
7. Resonator rear half
8. Bolt
9. Expansion chamber
10. Gasket
11. Exhaust pipe

Exhaust Pipe/Expansion Chamber Removal/Installation

1. Loosen the clamp at the front of the cylinder head and disconnect the water hose (A, **Figure 127**).

2. Loosen the clamp (B, **Figure 127**) holding the exhaust resonator to the expansion chamber.

3. Remove the 2 expansion chamber brace bolts (A, **Figure 128**) and the 2 flange nuts (B).

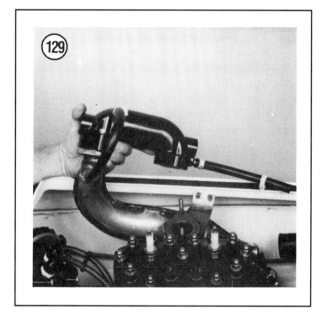

4. Remove the exhaust pipe and expansion chamber as one unit (**Figure 129**).

5. To separate the exhaust pipe from the expansion chamber, perform the following:

    a. Remove the 2 bolts and washers holding the exhaust pipe to the expansion chamber.

    b. Remove the exhaust pipe (**Figure 130**).

6. Loosen the front resonator clamp (**Figure 131**) and pull the resonator free from the water box muffler.

7. Clean the exhaust system components as described in this chapter.

8. Installation is the reverse of Steps 1-6, while noting the following steps:

9. Install new gaskets.

10. Clean all mating surfaces thoroughly before reassembly.

11. If the exhaust pipe was separated from the expansion chamber, use a new gasket at the junction and loosely install the 2 bolts with lockwashers and flat washers.

NOTE
Do not tighten the junction bolts until after the pipe and expansion chamber are securely mounted on the engine.

7

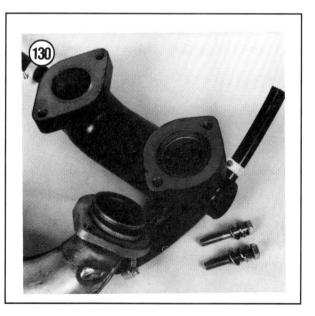

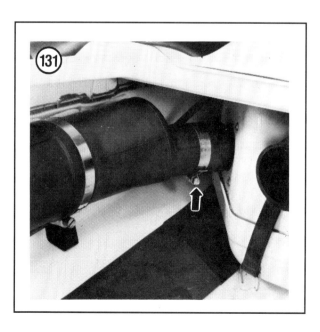

12. Install a new gasket on the exhaust manifold and fit the expansion chamber/exhaust pipe into place. Install the flat washers, lockwashers and exhaust pipe flange nuts on the he manifold studs (B, **Figure 128**). Do not tighten them yet.

13. Loosely install the 2 expansion chamber brace bolts (A, **Figure 128**). Tighten the exhaust pipe flange nuts and then the expansion chamber brace bolts.

14. If the exhaust pipe was separated from the expansion chamber, tighten the 2 junction bolts securely. Then, retighten the bolts after the engine has been operated at normal operating temperature and allowed to cool.

15. If the resonator was disassembled, assemble it with the core cutout at the bottom and align the arrows on the rubber halves at the top. The front half fits inside the rear half. Position the middle clamp so it will not chafe at the fuel tank.

16. Tighten all fasteners securely.

Water Box Muffler Removal/Installation

Refer to **Figure 126** while performing this procedure.

1. Remove the fuel tank as described in this chapter.

2. Remove the resonator as described under *Exhaust Pipe Removal/Installation* in this chapter.

3. Unhook the retainer straps (A, **Figure 132**) securing the water box to the hull.

4. Loosen the outlet tube hose clamp (B, **Figure 132**) at the top of the water box. Slide the hose clamp up the outlet tube.

5. Rotate the water box from the bottom up to disconnect the outlet tube at the top of the box. Remove the water box.

6. Install the water box by reversing Steps 1-5, plus the following steps.

7. If the outlet tube was removed, install it on the tail pipe fitting inside the hull before installing the water box.

8. Check that the water box damper pads are in good condition. Install new pads if necessary,

Secure the pads using water-resistant contact cement.

9. When installing the water box retainer straps, position the strap end with their tabs toward the water box to keep the hooks from chafing the box. Attach one end of the retainer strap to the front hook before installing the water box into the hull.

10. Reconnect and tighten all hose connections.

Water Box Muffler Inspection

A leaking or damage water box (**Figure 133**) will allow the engine compartment to fill with exhaust gases that will cause poor engine performance.

1. Discard any water in the water box.

2. Check the intake fitting for heat damage. If heat damage is noted, check the cooling system for proper operation.

3. Check the water box center seam for leakage. If a minor leak is noted, repair it with a suitable epoxy. If the leak is severe, replace the water box muffler.

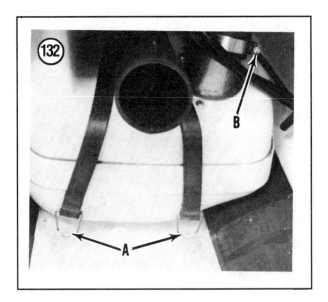

Tail Pipe and Cover Replacement

Refer to **Figure 126** while performing this procedure.

1. Remove the water box muffler as described in this chapter.

2. Remove the tail pipe tube from outside the hull.

3. From inside the hull, remove the inlet pipe at the tail pipe fitting.

4. The tail pipe and cover is secured to the hull with rivets. To remove the pipe and cover, first drill out the rivets with a 1/4 in. drill bit. Then remove all sealant between the tail pipe and the hull and from between the hull and cover. Pull the tail pipe and cover away from the hull.

5. Clean all mating surfaces thoroughly.

6. Coat all mating surfaces with silicone sealant.

7. Align the cover with the outside of the hull and press it into place. Then align the tail pipe with the inside of the hull and press it into place. Secure the assembly with new rivets.

8. Install the inlet pipe at the tail pipe and secure it with the hose clamp.

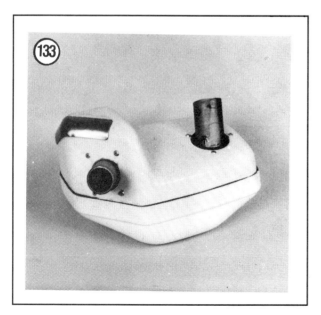

EXHAUST SYSTEM (JS550SX)

Exhaust Pipe Removal/Installation (JS550SX)

Refer to **Figure 134** while performing this procedure.

1. Remove the engine hood.

2. Disconnect the negative battery cable.

3. Loosen the hose clamp at the bottom of the muffler housing and disconnect the hose at the muffler.

4. Remove the exhaust pipe bracket at the manifold.

5. Remove the upper nuts that hold the exhaust pipe to the exhaust manifold. Remove the muffler assembly.

6. Disconnect the cooling system hose at the cylinder head.

7. Disconnect the bypass hose at the exhaust pipe.

8. Remove the bottom nuts that hold the exhaust pipe to the exhaust manifold. Remove the exhaust pipe.

9. Clean the exhaust system components as described in this chapter.

10. Install the exhaust pipe by reversing Steps 1-8, plus the following:

11. Install new gaskets.

12. Clean all gasket surfaces thoroughly before reassembly.

13. Tighten all fasteners securely.

Water Box Muffler Removal/Installation

Refer to **Figure 134** while performing this procedure.

1. Remove the fuel tank as described in this chapter.

2. Unhook the retainer straps (A, **Figure 132**) securing the water box to the hull.

3. Loosen the outlet tube hose clamp (B, **Figure 132**) at the top of the water box. Slide the hose clamp up the outlet tube.

7

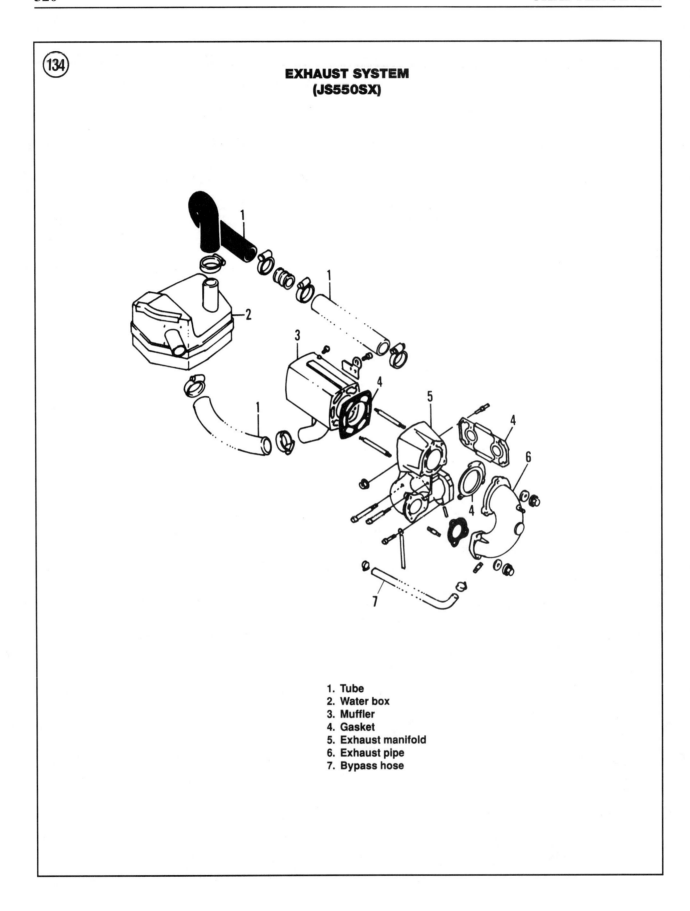

134

EXHAUST SYSTEM
(JS550SX)

1. Tube
2. Water box
3. Muffler
4. Gasket
5. Exhaust manifold
6. Exhaust pipe
7. Bypass hose

4. Rotate the water box from the bottom up to disconnect the outlet tube at the top of the box. Remove the water box.

5. Install the water box muffler by reversing Steps 1-4, plus the following:

6. If the outlet tube was removed, install it on the he tail pipe fitting inside the hull before installing the water box.

7. Make sure the water box damper pads are in good condition. Install new pads if necessary. Secure the pads using water-resistant contact cement.

8. When installing the water box retainer straps, position the strap ends with their tabs toward the water box to keep the hooks from chafing the box. Attach one end of the retainer strap to the front hook before installing the water box into the hull.

9. Reconnect and tighten all hose connections.

Water Box Muffler Inspection

A leaking or damage water box (**Figure 133**) will allow the engine compartment to fill with exhaust gases that will cause poor engine performance.

1. Discard any water in the water box.

2. Check the intake fitting for heat damage. If heat damage is noted, check the cooling system for proper operation.

3. Check the water box center seam for leakage. If a minor leak is noted, repair it with a suitable epoxy. If the leak is severe, replace the water box muffler.

Tail Pipe and Cover Replacement

Refer to **Figure 134** while performing this procedure.

1. Remove the water box muffler as described in this chapter.

2. Remove the tail pipe tube from the outside of the hull.

3. From inside the hull, remove the inlet pipe at the tail pipe fitting.

4. The tail pipe and cover is secured to the hull with rivets. To remove the pipe and cover, first drill out the rivets with a 3/16 in. drill bit. Then remove all sealant between the tail pipe and the hull and from between the hull and cover. Pull the tail pipe and cover away from the hull.

5. Clean all mating surfaces thoroughly.

6. Coat all mating surfaces with silicone sealant.

7. Align the cover with the outside of the hull and press it into place. Then align the tail pipe with the inside of the hull and press in into place. Secure the assembly with new rivets.

8. Install the inlet pipe at the tail pipe and secure it with the hose clamp.

EXHAUST SYSTEM
(JF650X-2 AND JS650SX)

Refer to **Figure 135** while performing the procedures in this section.

Exhaust Pipe Removal/Installation

1. Remove the engine hood.

2. *JS650SX*—Remove the oil tank as described in Chapter Nine.

3. Disconnect the negative battery cable.

4. Disconnect the cooling system hose (A, **Figure 136**) from the exhaust pipe.

5. Disconnect the bypass hose (B, **Figure 136**) from the exhaust pipe.

6. Disconnect the drain hose from the curved pipe.

7. Loosen the locknut at the water drain knob (**Figure 137**) and slide the knob off the exhaust pipe.

8. Loosen the hose clamp at the end of the straight pipe.

9. Remove the bolts holding the exhaust pipe at the manifold. Pull the exhaust pipe toward the rear and remove it. See **Figure 138**.

7

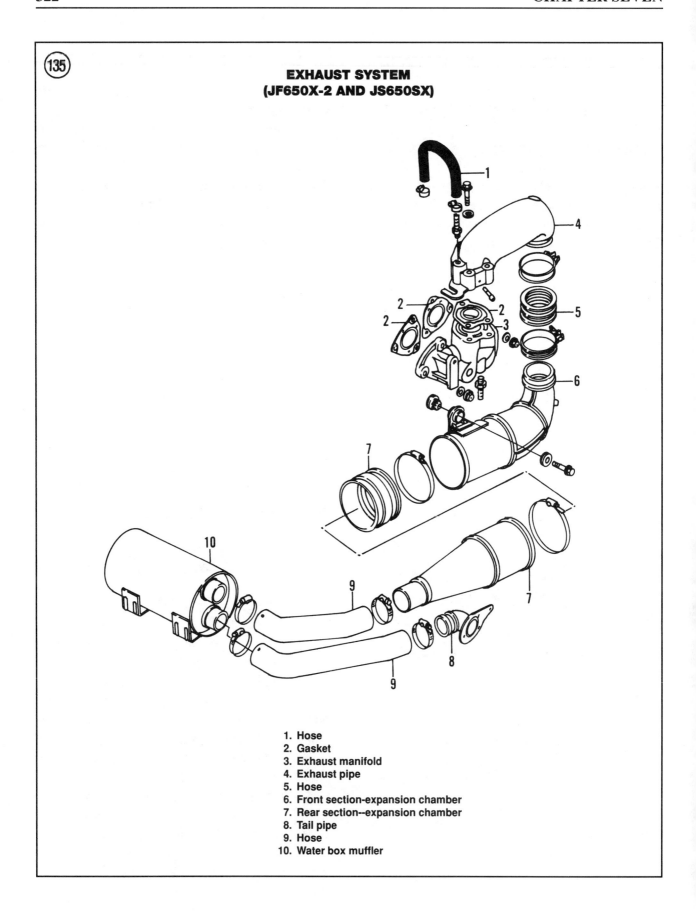

**EXHAUST SYSTEM
(JF650X-2 AND JS650SX)**

1. Hose
2. Gasket
3. Exhaust manifold
4. Exhaust pipe
5. Hose
6. Front section-expansion chamber
7. Rear section--expansion chamber
8. Tail pipe
9. Hose
10. Water box muffler

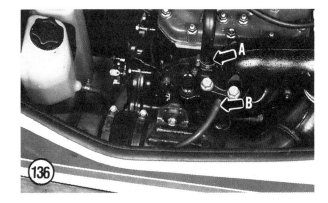

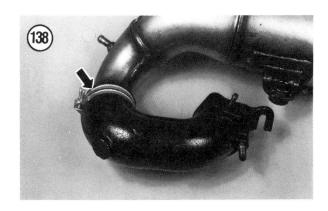

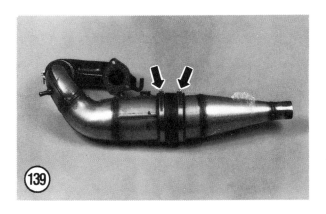

10. If necessary, loosen the hose clamps and separate the exhaust pipe assembly. See **Figure 138** and **Figure 139**.

11. Clean the exhaust system components as described in this chapter.

12. Install the exhaust pipe by reversing Steps 1-10, plus the following:

13. If the exhaust pipe assembly was disassembled, reconnect the center rubber holder so it is pushed all the way against the mounting bracket on the curved pipe. See **Figure 139**.

14. Install new gaskets.

15. Thoroughly clean all gasket mating surfaces before reassembly.

16. Apply Loctite 242 to the threads of the 10 mm bolts. Tighten all fasteners securely.

17. *JS650SX*—Bleed the oil injection system as described in Chapter Nine.

Water Box Muffler Removal/Installation

Refer to **Figure 135** while performing this procedure.

1. Remove the battery as described in Chapter Eight.

2. Remove the oil tank as described in Chapter Nine.

3. Remove the fuel tank as described in this chapter.

4. Remove the exhaust pipe assembly as described in this chapter.

5. Loosen the hose clamps at the water box. Then, slide the tubes off the water box.

6. Unhook the retainer straps securing the water box to the hull.

7. Install the water box by reversing Steps 1-6, plus the following.

8. If the inlet and outlet hose assembly was disassembled, refer to **Figure 135** during reassembly. Some models have alignment marks on the hoses and connectors. Reconnect the hoses so the arrows and marks are aligned.

9. Make sure the water box damper pads are in good condition. Install new pads if necessary.

7

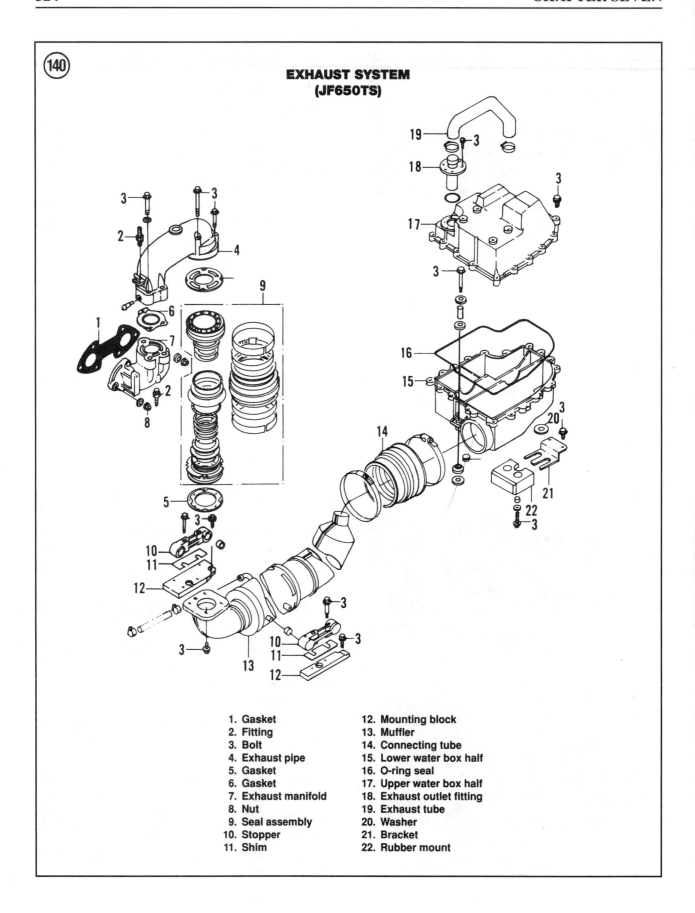

**EXHAUST SYSTEM
(JF650TS)**

1. Gasket
2. Fitting
3. Bolt
4. Exhaust pipe
5. Gasket
6. Gasket
7. Exhaust manifold
8. Nut
9. Seal assembly
10. Stopper
11. Shim
12. Mounting block
13. Muffler
14. Connecting tube
15. Lower water box half
16. O-ring seal
17. Upper water box half
18. Exhaust outlet fitting
19. Exhaust tube
20. Washer
21. Bracket
22. Rubber mount

Secure the pads with water-resistant contact cement.

10. When installing the water box retainer straps, position the strap ends with their tabs toward the water box to keep the hooks from chafing the box. Attach one end of the retainer straps to the front hook before installing the water box into the hull.

11. Reconnect and securely clamp all hose connections.

Water Box Inspection

A leaking or damage water box (**Figure 133**) will allow the engine compartment to fill with exhaust gases that will cause poor engine performance.

1. Discard any water in the water box.

2. Check the intake fitting for heat damage. If heat damage is noted, check the cooling system for proper operation.

3. Check the water box center seam for leakage. If a minor leak is noted, repair it with a suitable epoxy. If the leak is severe, replace the water box muffler.

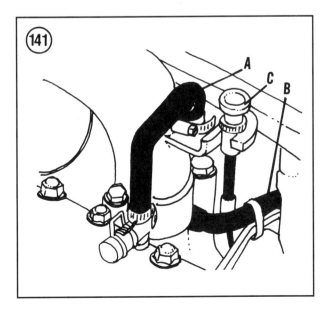

Tail Pipe and Cover Replacement

Refer to **Figure 135** while performing this procedure.

1. Remove the battery as described in Chapter Eight.

2. Remove the oil tank as described in Chapter Nine.

3. Remove the fuel tank as described in this chapter.

4. Remove the exhaust pipe assembly as described in this chapter.

5. Loosen the outlet tube hose clamp at the water box. Then, slide the outlet tube off the water box.

6. The tail pipe and cover is secured to the hull with rivets. To remove the tail pipe and cover, first drill out the rivets with a 3/16 in. drill bit. Then, remove all sealant between the tail pipe and the hull and from between the hull and cover. Pull the tail pipe and cover away from the hull.

7. Thoroughly clean all mating surfaces.

8. Coat all mating surfaces with silicone sealant.

9. Align the cover with the outside of the hull and press it into place. Then align the tail pipe with the inside of the hull and press it into place. Secure the assembly with new rivets.

10. Install the outlet pipe at the tail pipe and secure it with the hose clamp.

EXHAUST SYSTEM (JF650TS)

Refer to **Figure 140** while performing this procedure.

Exhaust Pipe and Muffler Removal/Installation

1. Remove the engine hood.

2. Disconnect the negative battery cable.

3. Disconnect the cooling system hose (A, **Figure 141**) from the exhaust pipe.

4. Disconnect the bypass hose (B, **Figure 141**) from the exhaust pipe.

7

5. Disconnect the drain hose from the curved pipe.

6. Loosen the locknut at the water drain knob (C, **Figure 141**) and slide the knob off the exhaust pipe.

7. Remove the electric box and bracket (**Figure 142**) as described in Chapter Eight.

8. Remove the bolts (A, **Figure 143**) holding the exhaust pipe to the exhaust manifold.

9. Remove the muffler mounting bolts (B, **Figure 143**).

10. Loosen the clamp (C, **Figure 143**) and remove the muffler from the water box. Remove the muffler/exhaust manifold assembly.

11. Remove the muffler stopper and shim(s), if used, from the mounting blocks. Note the number and location of the shims(s) under the mounting brackets. They must be reinstalled in the same location.

12. Thoroughly clean the exhaust system components as described in this chapter.

13. Install the exhaust pipe and muffler by reversing Steps 1-11, plus the following.

14. Install new gaskets and position the exhaust manifold-to-exhaust pipe gasket as shown in **Figure 144**.

15. Thoroughly clean all gasket surfaces before reassembly.

16. If the muffler-to-water box connecting tube was replaced, install the new one with the stepped edge ring on the end of the tube facing toward the front of the water craft.

17. Apply Loctite 242 to the muffler-to-exhaust pipe bolts. Tighten all fasteners securely.

Water Box Muffler Removal/Installation

Refer to **Figure 140** while performing this procedure.

1. Remove the battery as described in Chapter Eight.

2. Remove the electric box and bracket (**Figure 142**) as described in Chapter Eight.

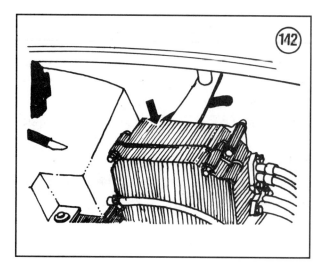

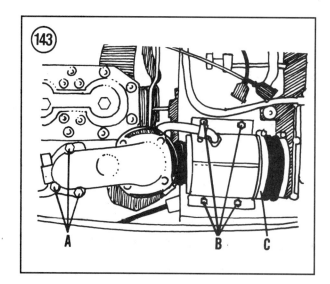

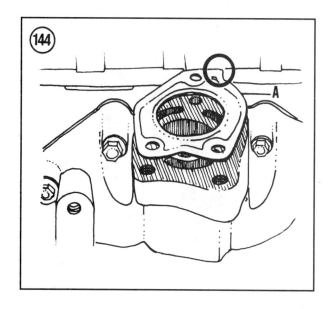

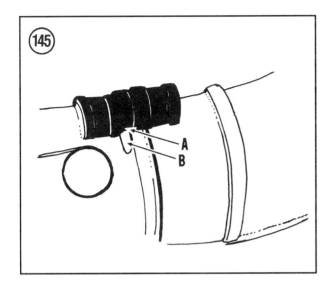

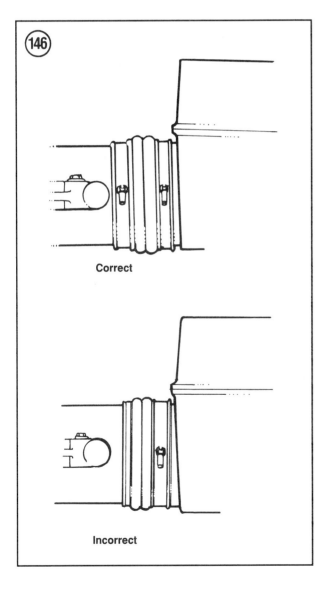

Correct

Incorrect

3. Remove the exhaust pipe assembly as described in this chapter.

4. Remove the oil tank as described in Chapter Nine.

5. Loosen the exhaust tube hose clamp at the water box. Then, slide the tube off the water box.

6. Remove the bolts, washer and rubber isolators securing the water box.

7. Slide the water box forward, out of the rear mounting plate and remove it.

8. Install the water box by reversing Steps 1-7, plus the following.

9. On models so equipped, make sure the water box damper pads are in good condition. Replace the damper pads if necessary, securing them with water-resistant contact cement.

10. Place the water box into position and make sure it properly engages the rear mounting plate.

11. If the muffler-to-water box connecting tube was replaced, perform the following steps:

    a. Install a new connecting tube with the stepped edge ring on the end of the tube facing toward the front of the water craft.

    b. Make sure the groove inside the tube (A, **Figure 145**) fits over the raised bead (B) on the muffler, then tighten the clamp on the engine side of the tube.

12. When installing the muffler into the water box, push it on completely over the fitting and make sure it is not cocked (**Figure 146**).

13. Apply Loctite 242 to the threads of the water box fasteners. Tighten all fasteners securely.

Water Box Inspection

Refer to **Figure 140** for this procedure.

A leaking or damage water box (**Figure 133**) will allow the engine compartment to fill with exhaust gases that will cause poor engine performance.

1. Discard any water in the water box.

2. Check the exhaust outlet fitting for heat damage. If heat damage is noted, check the cooling system for proper operation.

7

(147)

**EXHAUST SYSTEM
(JL650SC)**

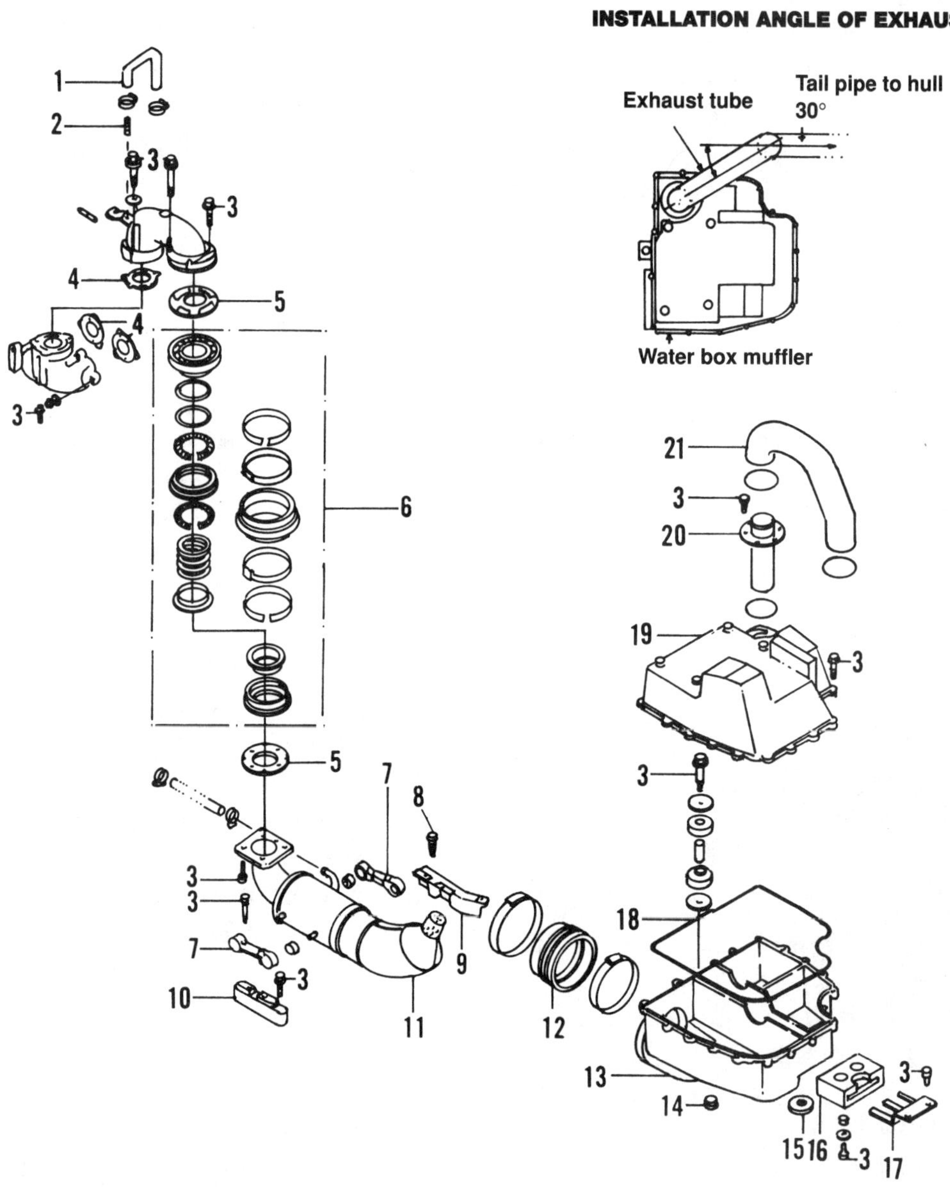

INSTALLATION ANGLE OF EXHAUST TUBE

Exhaust tube

Tail pipe to hull
30°

Water box muffler

1. Hose	8. Bolt	15. Washer
2. Fitting	9. Bracket	16. Rubber mount
3. Bolt	10. Stopper	17. Bracket
4. Gasket	11. Muffler	18. O-ring seal
5. Gasket	12. Connecting tube	19. Upper water box half
6. Seal assembly	13. Lower water box half	20. Exhaust outlet fitting
7. Stopper	14. Plug	21. Exhaust tube

3. To remove the exhaust outlet fitting, perform the following steps:
   a. Remove the bolts and remove the fitting and O-ring.
   b. Install the fitting with a new O-ring.
   c. Apply Loctite 242 to the threads of the bolts and tighten them securely.
4. Check the perimeter of the water box for leakage. If a minor leak is noted, perform the following:
   a. Remove the bolts securing the case halves together.
   b. Separate the case halves and remove the perimeter O-ring seal.
   c. Install a new O-ring seal and assemble the case halves.
   d. Apply Loctite 242 to the threads of the fasteners. Tighten the fasteners evenly and securely, but do not overtighten.
5. If severe leakage is noted, replace the water box assembly.

EXHAUST SYSTEM (JL650SC)

Refer to **Figure 147** while performing the procedures in this section.

Exhaust Pipe and Muffler Removal/Installation

1. Unlock the seat.
2. Remove the screws securing both seat base brackets and remove the seat.
3. Remove the rubber plugs covering the engine hood mounting screws. Remove the engine hood screws and engine hood.
4. Disconnect the negative battery cable.
5. Disconnect the cooling system hose from the exhaust pipe.
6. Disconnect the bypass hose from the exhaust pipe.
7. Remove the bolt, washer and rubber isolator securing the front of the water box.

8. Loosen the rear clamp where the muffler enters the water box.
9. Remove the bolts holding the exhaust pipe to the manifold.
10. Remove the muffler mounting bolts.
11. Remove the muffler from the water box and remove exhaust pipe and muffler assembly.
12. Remove the muffler stopper from the mounting blocks.
13. Clean the exhaust components as described in this chapter.
14. Install the exhaust pipe and muffler by reversing Steps 1-12, plus the following:
15. Install new gaskets and position the exhaust manifold-to-exhaust pipe gasket as shown in **Figure 144**.
16. Thoroughly clean all gasket mating surfaces prior to reassembly.
17. If the muffler-to-water box connecting tube was replaced, perform the following:
   a. Install the new connecting tube with the stepped edge ring on the end of the tube facing the front of the watercraft.
   b. Make sure the groove inside the tube (A, **Figure 145**) fits over the raised bead (B) on the muffler, then tighten the clamp on the engine side of the tube.
18. When installing the muffler into the water box, push it on completely over the fitting and make sure it is not cocked (**Figure 146**).
19. Apply Loctite 242 to the exhaust pipe-to-manifold and water box mounting fasteners. Tighten all fasteners securely.

Water Box Muffler Removal/Installation

Refer to **Figure 147** while performing this procedure.

1. Remove the exhaust pipe assembly as described in this chapter.
2. Loosen the exhaust tube hose clamp at the water box. Then, slide the tube off the water box.
3. Remove the front bolt, washer and rubber isolator securing the water box.

7

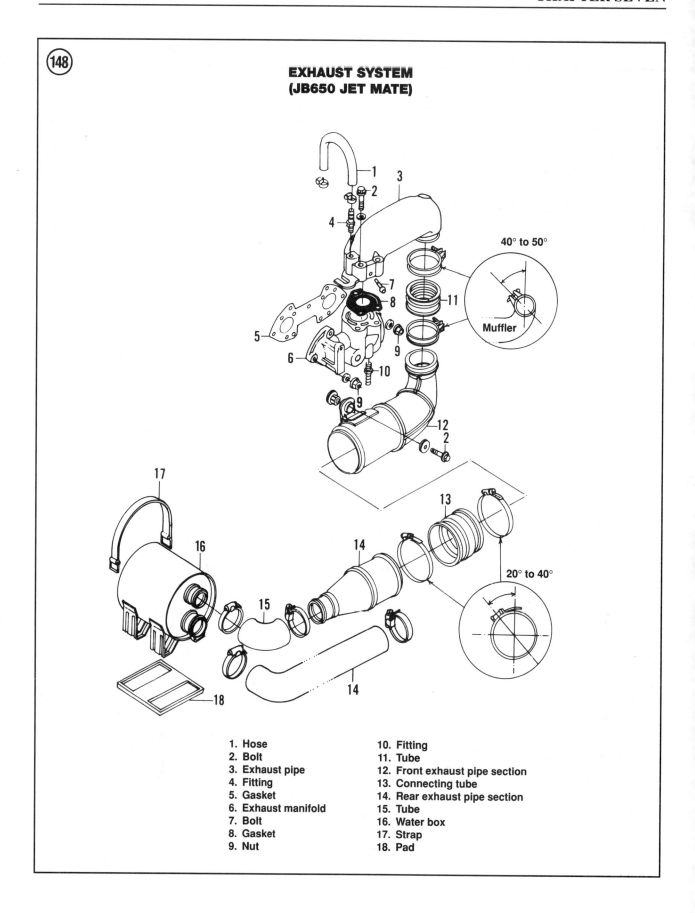

(148)

**EXHAUST SYSTEM
(JB650 JET MATE)**

40° to 50°

Muffler

20° to 40°

1. Hose
2. Bolt
3. Exhaust pipe
4. Fitting
5. Gasket
6. Exhaust manifold
7. Bolt
8. Gasket
9. Nut
10. Fitting
11. Tube
12. Front exhaust pipe section
13. Connecting tube
14. Rear exhaust pipe section
15. Tube
16. Water box
17. Strap
18. Pad

NOTE
There is very little space to remove the water box without first removing the fuel tank. If you cannot easily remove the water box, remove the fuel tank as described in this chapter.

4. Slide the water box forward, out of the rear mounting plate and remove it.

5. Install the water box by reversing Steps 1-4, plus the following.

6. On models so equipped, make sure the water box damper pads are in good condition. Install new pads if necessary, securing them using water-resistant contact cement.

7. If the muffler-to-water box connecting tube was replaced, perform the following:

    a. Install the new connecting tube with the stepped edge ring on the end of the tube facing toward the front of the watercraft.

    b. Make sure the groove inside the tube (A, **Figure 145**) fits over the raised bead (B) on the muffler, then tighten the clamp on the engine side of the tube.

8. Move the water box into position and make sure it properly engages the rear mounting plate.

9. Apply Loctite 242 to the threads of the water box mounting bolts. Tighten all fasteners securely.

Water Box Inspection

Refer to **Figure 147** for this procedure.

A leaking or damage water box (**Figure 133**) will allow the engine compartment to fill with exhaust gases that will cause poor engine performance.

1. Discard any water in the water box.

2. Check the exhaust outlet fitting for heat damage. If heat damage is noted, check the cooling system for proper operation.

3. To remove the exhaust outlet fitting, perform the following steps:

    a. Remove the bolts and remove the fitting and O-ring.

    b. Install the fitting with a new O-ring.

    c. Apply Loctite 242 to the threads of the bolts and tighten them securely.

4. Check the perimeter of the water box for leakage. If a minor leak is noted, perform the following:

    a. Remove the bolts securing the case halves together.

    b. Separate the case halves and remove the perimeter O-ring seal.

    c. Install a new O-ring seal and assemble the case halves.

    d. Apply Loctite 242 to the threads of the fasteners. Tighten the fasteners evenly and securely, but do not overtighten.

5. If severe leakage is noted, replace the water box assembly.

EXHAUST SYSTEM (JB650 JET MATE)

Refer to **Figure 148** while performing the procedures in this section.

Exhaust Pipe and Muffler Removal/Installation

1. Remove the rear seat assembly.

2. Disconnect the negative battery cable.

3. Disconnect the cooling system hose (A, **Figure 149**) from the exhaust pipe.

4. Disconnect the bypass hose (B, **Figure 149**) from the exhaust pipe.

5. Loosen the locknut at the water drain knob (C, **Figure 149**) and slide the knob off the exhaust pipe.

6. Loosen the hose clamp where the end of the pipe enters the water box (D, **Figure 149**).

7. Remove the bolt (E, **Figure 149**) securing the muffler to the engine block.

8. Remove the bolts (F, **Figure 149**) holding the exhaust pipe to the manifold. Pull the exhaust pipe toward the rear and remove it.

7

9. If necessary, loosen the hose clamps and separate the exhaust pipe assembly. See **Figure 138** and **Figure 139**.

10. Clean the exhaust system components as described in this chapter.

11. Install the exhaust pipe and muffler by reversing Steps 1-9, plus the following.

12. If the exhaust pipe assembly was removed, reconnect the center rubber holder so it is pushed all the way against the mounting bracket on the muffler (**Figure 139**).

13. Install new gaskets and position the exhaust manifold-to-exhaust pipe gasket as shown in **Figure 144**.

14. Thoroughly clean all gasket mating surfaces prior to reassembly.

Water Box Muffler Removal/Installation

Refer to **Figure 148** during this procedure.

1. Remove the engine hood.

2. Disconnect the negative battery cable.

3. Loosen the hose clamps (A, **Figure 150**) at the water box. Then, slide the tubes off the water box.

4. Unhook the retainer straps (B, **Figure 150**) securing the water box to the hull.

5. Remove the water box (C, **Figure 150**).

6. Install the water box by reversing Steps 1-5, plus the following.

7. Make sure the water box damper pads are in good condition. Replace the damper pads if necessary, securing them with water-resistant contact cement.

8. If the hose clamps were removed from the tubes, install them onto the tubes with their clamp screws facing up so you can get a screwdriver on them.

9. When installing the water box retainer straps, position the trap ends with their tabs toward the water box to keep the hooks from chafing the box.

10. Reconnect and tighten all hose connections securely.

Water Box Inspection

A leaking or damage water box (**Figure 133**) will allow the engine compartment to fill with exhaust gases that will cause poor engine performance.

1. Discard any water in the water box.

2. Check the intake fitting for heat damage. If heat damage is noted, check the cooling system for proper operation.

3. Check the water box center seam for leakage. If a minor leak is noted, repair it with a suitable epoxy. If the leak is severe, replace the water box muffler.

EXHAUST SYSTEM (JS750SX)

Refer to **Figure 151** while performing the procedures in this section.

Exhaust Pipe, Front Muffler and Expansion Chamber Removal/Installation

Refer to **Figure 151**.

1. Remove the engine cover.

2. Disconnect the negative battery cable.

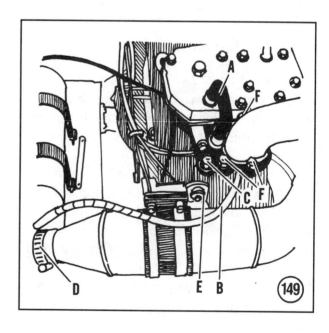

3. Remove the air intake silencer as described in this chapter.

4. Loosen the clamp and disconnect the cooling hose (A, **Figure 152**) from the exhaust pipe.

5. Loosen the clamp and disconnect the bypass hose (B, **Figure 152**) from the exhaust pipe.

6. Loosen the clamp securing the hose (15, **Figure 151**) to the expansion chamber. Slide the hose off the expansion chamber.

7. Loosen the locknut at the water drain knob (C, **Figure 152**) and slide the knob off the exhaust pipe bracket.

8. Remove the 2 bolts (A, **Figure 153**) securing the front muffler bracket to the cylinder block.

9. Remove the 5 bolts (B, **Figure 153**) securing the exhaust pipe to the exhaust manifold. Remove the exhaust pipe, front muffler and expansion chamber as an assembly.

10. If necessary, remove the fasteners and separate the exhaust pipe, front muffler and expansion chamber. See **Figure 154**.

11. Clean all exhaust components as described in this chapter.

12. Install the exhaust pipe, front muffler and expansion chamber by reversing Steps 1-10, plus the following.

13. Thoroughly clean all gasket mating surface prior to reassembly.

14. Reassemble the exhaust pipe, front muffler and expansion chamber (if disassembled) using new gaskets. Install the fasteners finger tight.

15. Install a new manifold-to-exhaust pipe gasket. Install the exhaust pipe, front muffler and expansion chamber assembly onto the exhaust manifold. Install and tighten the exhaust pipe mounting bolts (B, **Figure 153**) finger tight. Install the front muffler bracket and bolts (A, **Figure 153**) finger tight.

16. One-by-one, remove all fasteners and apply Loctite 242 to their threads. After all fasteners are treated and installed finger tight, tighten them to 20 N·m (14.7 ft.-lb.) in the following order:

    a. Exhaust pipe-to-exhaust manifold bolts.

    b. Exhaust pipe-to-front muffler bolts.

    c. Front muffler-to-expansion chamber bolts.

    d. Front muffler-to-cylinder block bracket mounting bolts.

Water Box Removal/Installation

Refer to **Figure 151** while performing this procedure.

1. Remove the exhaust pipe, front muffler and expansion chamber as an assembly as described in this chapter.

2. Remove the electric box as described in Chapter Eight.

3. Loosen the clamps and disconnect the outlet hose (A, **Figure 155**) and inlet hose (B) from the water box.

4. Next, remove the water box mounting bracket (C, **Figure 155**). Then, rotate the top of the water box outward until the water box can be removed from the hull.

5. Inspect the water box assembly as described in this chapter.

6. Install the water box by reversing Steps 1-4, plus the following.

7. Make sure the water box damper pads are in good condition. Replace the damper pads if nec-

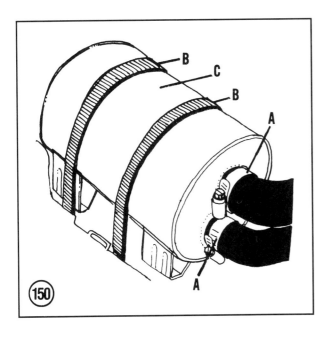

7

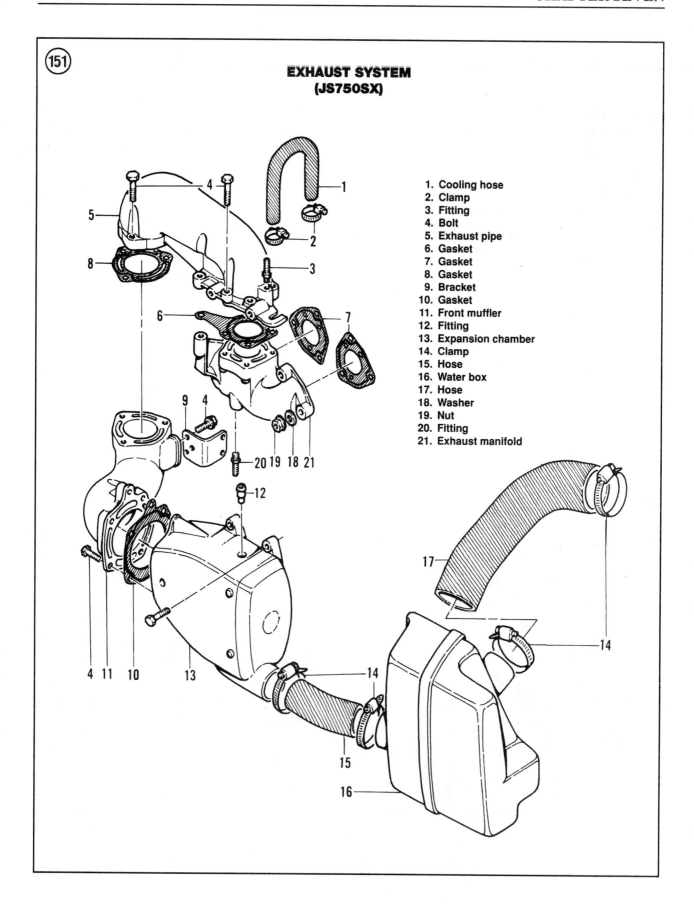

(151)

**EXHAUST SYSTEM
(JS750SX)**

1. Cooling hose
2. Clamp
3. Fitting
4. Bolt
5. Exhaust pipe
6. Gasket
7. Gasket
8. Gasket
9. Bracket
10. Gasket
11. Front muffler
12. Fitting
13. Expansion chamber
14. Clamp
15. Hose
16. Water box
17. Hose
18. Washer
19. Nut
20. Fitting
21. Exhaust manifold

essary, using water-resistant contact cement to secure them.

8. Make sure all hose connections are securely clamped.

Water Box Inspection

A leaking or damage water box (**Figure 133**) will allow the engine compartment to fill with exhaust gases that will cause poor engine performance.

1. Discard any water in the water box.

2. Check the intake fitting for heat damage. If heat damage is noted, check the cooling system for proper operation.

3. Check the water box center seam for leakage. If a minor leak is noted, repair it with a suitable epoxy. If the leak is severe, replace the water box muffler.

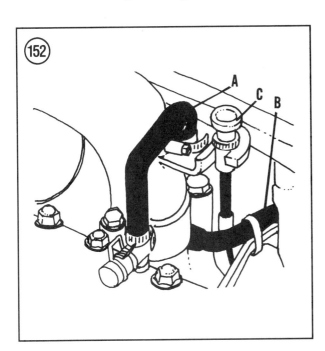

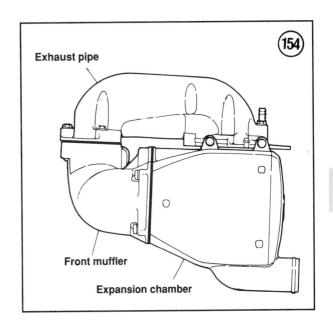

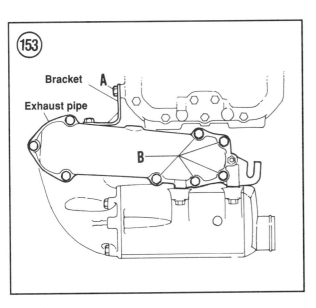

EXHAUST SYSTEM
(JT750ST, JH750SS AND
JH750 SUPER SPORT Xi)

Refer to **Figure 156** while performing the procedures in this section.

Exhaust Pipe and Expansion Chamber Removal/Installation

1. Remove the seat.
2. Disconnect the negative battery cable.
3. Disconnect the spark plug leads from the spark plugs.
4. Disconnect the starter motor cable from the starter.
5. Remove the electric box as described in Chapter Eight.
6. Loosen the clamp and disconnect the cooling hose from the expansion chamber or top of the water box.
7. Loosen the clamp and disconnect the cooling system hose (A, **Figure 152**) from the exhaust pipe.
8. Loosen the clamp and disconnect the bypass hose (B, **Figure 152**) from the exhaust pipe.
9. Loosen the locknut at the water drain knob (C, **Figure 152**) and slide the knob assembly off the exhaust pipe.
10. Remove the bolts securing the electric box mounting bracket. Remove the bracket.
11. Loosen the rear clamp where the expansion chamber enters the water box.
12. Remove the expansion chamber mounting bolts.
13. Remove the bolts holding the exhaust pipe to the exhaust manifold.
14. Remove the exhaust pipe and expansion chamber as a unit.
15. If any shims are present under the expansion chamber stoppers. Mark the shims so they can be reinstalled in their original locations.
16. Clean all exhaust components as described in this chapter.

**EXHAUST SYSTEM
(JT750ST, JH750SS AND
JH750 SUPER SPORT Xi)**

1. Cooling hose
2. Fitting
3. Bolt
4. Gasket
5. Gasket
6. Seal assembly
7. Stopper
8. Bolt
9. Bracket
10. Stopper
11. Expansion chamber
12. Connecting hose
13. Lower water box half
14. Plug
15. Washer
16. Rubber mount
17. Bracket
18. O-ring seal
19. Upper water box half
20. Exhaust outlet fitting
21. Exhaust hose
22. Hose fitting

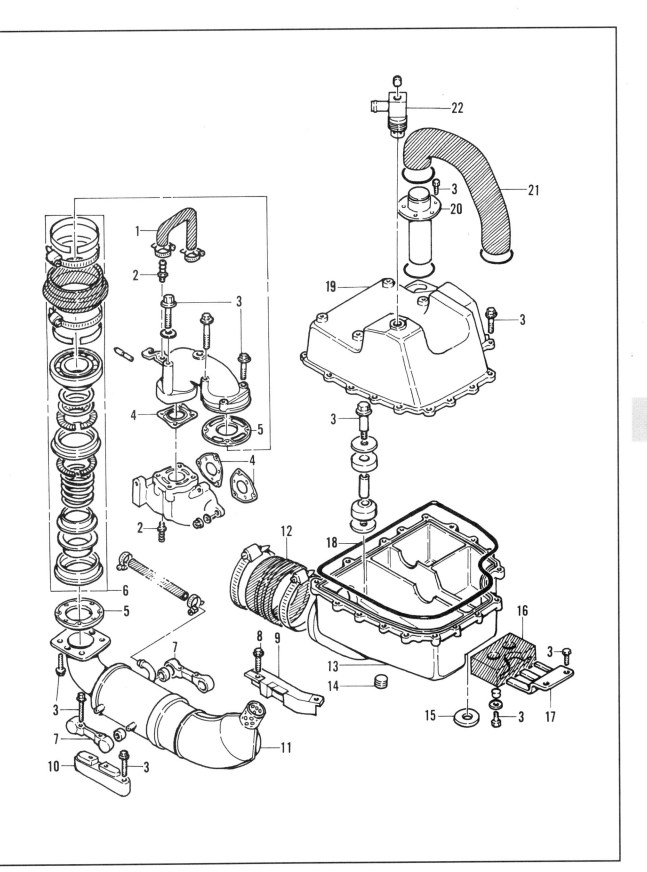

7

17. Install the exhaust pipe and expansion chamber assembly by reversing Steps 1-14, plus the following.

18. Install new gaskets and make sure all mating surfaces are clean.

19. If used, make sure the shims under the expansion chamber mounting stoppers are reinstalled in their original location.

20. If the expansion chamber-to-water box connecting tube was replaced, perform the following:

   a. Install the new connecting tube with the stepped edge ring on the end of the tube facing toward the front of the watercraft.

   b. Make sure the groove (A, **Figure 157**) fits over the raised bead (B), then tighten the clamp on the engine side of the tube.

21. When installing the expansion chamber into the water box, push it on completely over the fitting and make sure it is not cocked (**Figure 158**).

22. Apply Loctite 242 to the threads of the exhaust pipe-to-exhaust manifold bolts. Tighten the bolts to 49 N·m (36 ft.-lb.).

Exhaust Pipe-to-Expansion Chamber Joint Disassembly/Reassembly

Refer to **Figure 159** while performing this procedure.

1. Remove the exhaust pipe/expansion chamber assembly as described in this chapter.

2. Remove the exhaust pipe-to-expansion chamber joint mounting bolts (**Figure 160**). Lift off the exhaust pipe and remove the joint.

3. Remove the 2 clamps, bands and remove the outer boot.

4. Next, remove the inner clamps and remove the race, spring seat, spring and inner boot.

4. Closely inspect all components for wear, deterioration or other damage. Replace as required.

5. To reassemble the joint assembly, invert the upper joint half (A, **Figure 161**) and install the

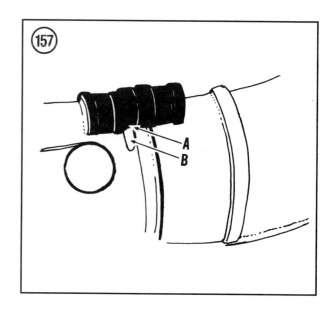

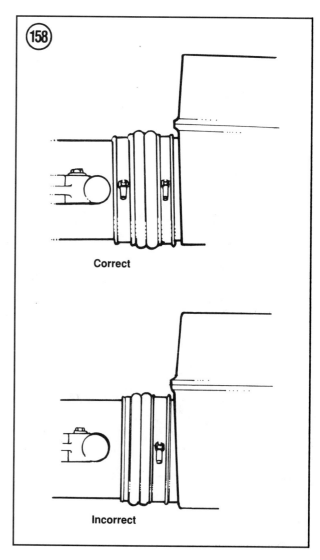

Correct

Incorrect

EXHAUST PIPE-TO-EXPANSION CHAMBER JOINT ASSEMBLY (JT750ST, JH750SS AND JH750 SUPER SPORT Xi)

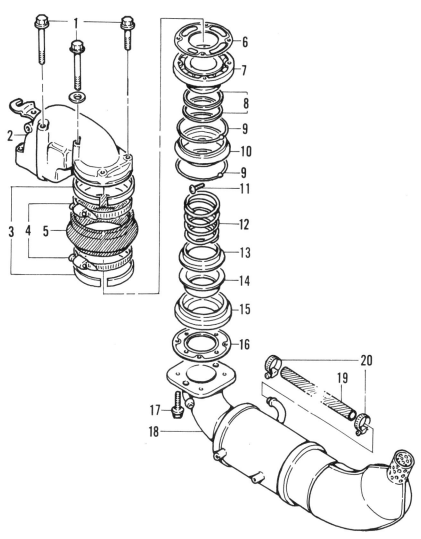

1. Bolts	11. Screw
2. Exhaust pipe	12. Spring
3. Band	13. Race
4. Clamp	14. Spring seat
5. Outer boot	15. Lower joint half
6. Gasket	16. Gasket
7. Upper joint half	17. Bolt
8. O-rings	18. Expansion chamber
9. Inner clamps	19. Hose
10. Inner boot	20. Clamp

7

inner boot (B), spring (C), spring seat (D) and race (E).

6. Then, with the upper joint still inverted, install the lower joint half onto the upper joint. Engage the groove in the lower joint with the lip on the inner boot. Align the left side of the notch in each joint with the alignment mark on the inner boot (**Figure 162**).

7. Install the inner clamps into the grooves of the inner boot. Apply Loctite 242 to the threads of the clamp screws. Arrange the clamp screws in opposite directions and align them as shown in **Figure 163** and tighten securely, but do not overtighten.

8. Place the joint assembly right-side up. Install the outer boot, making sure the arrow on the boot is facing the upper joint half.

9. Install the bands and outer clamps. Align the clamp worm gears with the end gaps in the bands. Tighten the clamps securely.

10. Coat the mating surfaces of the upper and lower joint halves with silicone sealant. Install the upper and lower gaskets. Make sure the UP mark in the upper gasket is facing upward.

11. Apply Loctite 242 to the threads of the joint assembly mounting bolts. Assemble the expansion chamber, joint assembly and exhaust pipe. Tighten the joint mounting bolts to 9.8 N·m (87 in.-lb.).

Water Box Removal/Installation

Refer to **Figure 156** while performing this procedure.

1. Remove the battery as described in Chapter Eight.

2. Remove the oil tank as described in Chapter Nine.

3. Remove the exhaust pipe/expansion chamber assembly as described in this chapter.

4. Loosen the exhaust tube hose clamp at the water box. Slide the tube off the water box.

5. Remove the bolts, washers and rubber isolators securing the water box in the hull.

6. Slide the water box forward, out of the rear mounting plate and remove it from the hull.

7. Install the water box by reversing Steps 1-6, plus the following.

8. Make sure the water box properly engages with the rear mounting plate.

9. If the expansion chamber-to-water box tube was replaced, perform the following:

    a. Install the new connecting tube with its stepped edge ring on the end of the tube facing toward the front of the watercraft.

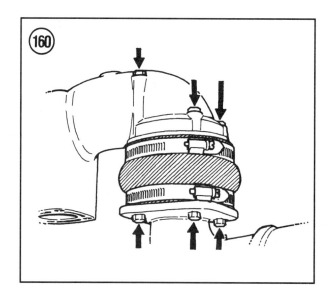

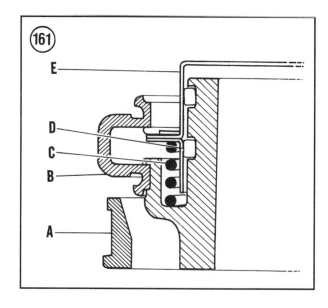

b. Make sure the groove inside the tube (A, **Figure 157**) fits over the raised bead (B) on the expansion chamber.

c. Apply Loctite 242 to the threads of the water box mounting fasteners. Tighten the fasteners to 7.8 N•m (69 in.-lb.).

10. When installing the expansion chamber into the water box, push it on completely over the fitting and make sure it is not cocked (**Figure 158**).

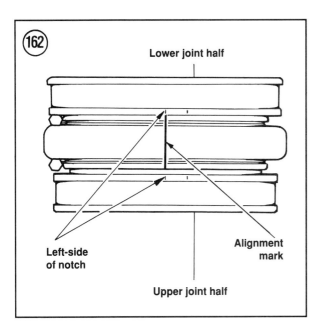

Lower joint half

Left-side of notch

Alignment mark

Upper joint half

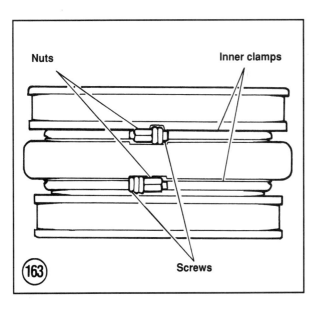

Nuts

Inner clamps

Screws

11. Bleed the oil injection system as described in Chapter Nine.

Water Box
Disassembly/Inspection/Reassembly

A leaking or damaged water box can allow the engine compartment to fill with exhaust gases resulting in poor engine operation

1. Remove the water box as described in this chapter.

2. Discard any water in the water box.

3. Remove the exhaust outlet fitting mounting bolts. Remove the outlet fitting and O-ring.

4. Remove the bolts securing the water box halves together.

5. Separate the water box halves and remove the perimeter O-ring seal.

6. To reassemble the water box, first apply a light coat of silicone sealant into the O-ring groove in the lower water box half. Then, place a new O-ring seal into the groove in the lower half.

7. Lower the upper water box half straight down onto the lower half, making sure the O-ring seal remains in position.

8. Apply Loctite 242 to the water box half retaining bolts. Tighten the bolts in a crossing pattern to 7.8 N•m (69 in.-lb.).

9. Install the outlet fitting using a new O-ring. Apply Loctite 242 to the threads of the outlet fitting bolts. Install the bolts and tighten to 7.8 N•m (69 in.-lb.).

EXHAUST SYSTEM (JH750XiR)

Exhaust Pipe and Expansion Chamber Removal/Installation

Refer to **Figure 164** when performing this procedure.

1. Loosen the clamp and disconnect the cooling hose from the fitting located at the small end of the expansion chamber.

7

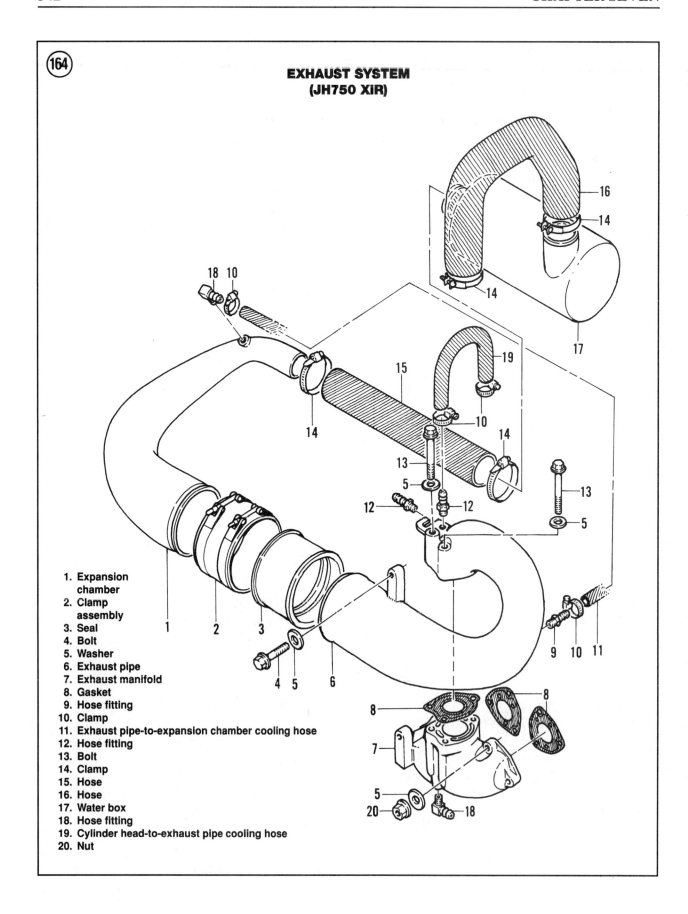

**EXHAUST SYSTEM
(JH750 XiR)**

1. Expansion
   chamber
2. Clamp
   assembly
3. Seal
4. Bolt
5. Washer
6. Exhaust pipe
7. Exhaust manifold
8. Gasket
9. Hose fitting
10. Clamp
11. Exhaust pipe-to-expansion chamber cooling hose
12. Hose fitting
13. Bolt
14. Clamp
15. Hose
16. Hose
17. Water box
18. Hose fitting
19. Cylinder head-to-exhaust pipe cooling hose
20. Nut

2. Loosen the clamps and disconnect the cooling hose between the exhaust pipe and cylinder head. See A, **Figure 165**.

3. Loosen the clamp and disconnect the bypass hose (B, **Figure 165**).

4. Loosen the locknut and slide the water drain knob out of the bracket on the exhaust pipe.

5. Loosen the clamps at each end of the expansion chamber. Remove the expansion chamber.

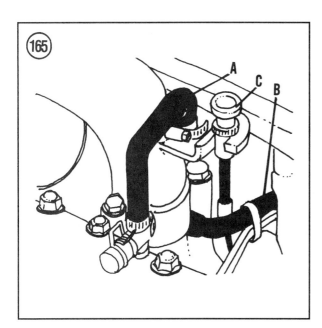

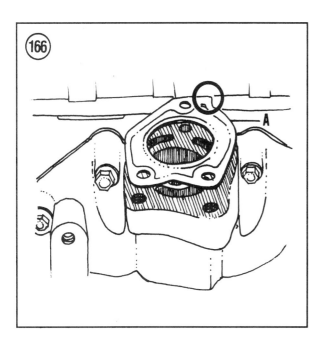

6. Remove the 3 exhaust pipe manifold bolts. Remove 1 exhaust p. ing bolt.

7. Remove the engine bed mounting ɔɹts as described in Chapter Five. Slide the engine toward the front just enough to remove the exhaust pipe toward the rear of the watercraft.

8. To install the exhaust pipe, place the pipe in position on the engine. Slide the engine back into position, following the alignment procedure described in Chapter Five. Install the engine bed bolts as described in Chapter Five.

9. Install the exhaust pipe onto the manifold using a new gasket. Make sure the tab on the gasket is facing the engine as shown in **Figure 166**. Apply Loctite 242 to the threads of the 3 exhaust pipe-to-manifold bolts and the exhaust pipe mounting bolt and tighten them to 49 N•m (36 ft.-lb.).

Water Box Removal/Installation

The water box is molded into the hull on JH750XiR models and is not removable.

EXHAUST SYSTEM CLEANING AND INSPECTION (ALL MODELS)

Read this entire procedure before starting.

1. Clean all accessible exhaust passages with a blunt, roundnose tool. To clean areas farther down the pipe, chuck a piece of stranded cable in an electric drill (**Figure 167**). Fray the loose end of the cable and run the drill while moving the cable back and forth inside the pipe.

> *WARNING*
> *Do not start the drill until the cable is inserted into the pipe. At no time should the drill be started with the cable free of the pipe. The whipping action of the cable could cause serious personal injury. Wear heavy gloves and a full-face shield when using this equipment.*

7

2. Flush the water passages with clean water. Make sure all debris is flushed from the passages.

3. Check the stainless steel pipe for cracks, especially along the seams. If necessary, have the pipe repaired by a qualified welder experienced with stainless steel.

4. Check all rubber holders for hardening. Also check for cracks or tears that would allow leakage.

5. Inspect the hose clamps for excessive wear, fatigue or damage.

6. If there is any doubt as to the condition of any component, replace it.

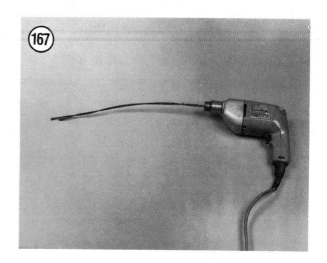

Table 1 CARBURETOR MODEL IDENTIFICATION*

Model	Carburetor	Venturi size
JS440SX	Mikuni BN38	34 mm
JS550SX	Keihin CDK38	32 mm
JF650X-2		
1992-1993	Keihin CDK38	32 mm
1994	Keihin CDK40-34	38 mm
JF650TS	Keihin CDK38	32 mm
JL650SC	Keihin CDK38	32 mm
JS650SX	Keihin CDK38	32 mm
JB650 Jet Mate	Keihin CDK34	28 mm
JH750SS	Keihin 40-34	38 mm
JS750SX	Keihin CDK40-34	38 mm
JT750ST	Keihin CDK40-34	38 mm
JH750 Super Sport Xi	Keihin CDK40-34	38 mm
JH750 XiR	Keihin CDK40-34	38 mm
*All models are equipped with a diaphragm-type carburetor.		

Chapter Eight

Electrical Systems

This chapter provides service procedures for the battery, charging system, starting system and the ignition system. Electrical troubleshooting procedures are described in Chapter Two. Wiring diagrams are located at the end of the manual.

BATTERY

The electric starting system requires a fully charged battery, in good condition, to operate the starter motor. Because there are no lights on the Jet Ski, the battery is only used to provide power to the starter motor. A charge coil mounted on the stator plate, and a voltage regulator, maintains the proper battery charge while the engine is running. The battery can also be charged externally, if necessary.

Care and Inspection

The battery is the heart of the electrical system. Electrical system troubles can often be attributed to neglect of this vital component.

The battery must be removed from the hull to correctly service the electrolyte level in the battery. The electrolyte level should be maintained between the two marks on the battery case. If the electrolyte level is low, remove the battery so it can be thoroughly cleaned, inspected and serviced.

All Jet Ski models are equipped with a negative ground electrical system. When removing the battery, disconnect the negative (–) ground cable first, then the positive (+) cable. This minimizes the chance of a tool shorting to ground when disconnecting the positive "hot" cable.

1. Remove the engine hood or seat.

2. Disconnect the negative battery cable from the engine (**Figure 1**) or battery (**Figure 2**).

3. Disconnect the positive battery cable from the battery.

4. Unlatch the battery hold down straps and lift the battery out of the hull.

> *WARNING*
> *Protect your eyes, skin and clothing when servicing the battery. If electrolyte gets into your eyes, flush your eyes thoroughly with clean water and obtain prompt medical attention.*

> *CAUTION*
> *Do not spill battery electrolyte on painted or polished surfaces. The liquid is highly corrosive and will damage the finish. If it is spilled, wash it off immediately with soapy water, then thoroughly flush with clean water.*

5. Check the entire battery case for cracks. Replace the battery if the case is damaged.

6. Inspect the battery tray (**Figure 3**) or container for corrosion. If necessary, clean the area with a solution of baking soda and water. Make sure the tray mounting screws are tight. Make sure the tray is equipped with a rubber damper and support plate (**Figure 4**).

> *CAUTION*
> *Do not allow the baking soda and water solution to enter the battery cells in Step 7. The solution severely weakens the battery electrolyte.*

7. Clean the top of the battery with a stiff bristle brush using the baking soda and water solution. Rinse the battery case with clean water and dry with a clean cloth or paper towel.

8. Check the battery cable terminal ends for corrosion. Clean the terminals with a wire brush and the baking soda and water mixture. Replace the battery cables if severely corroded.

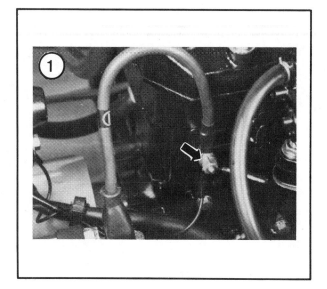

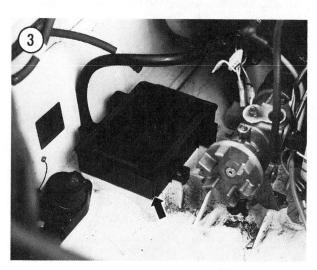

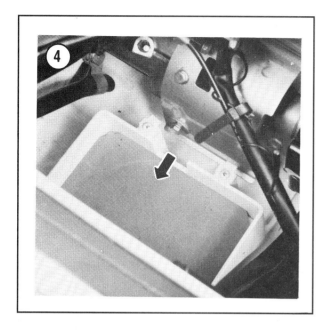

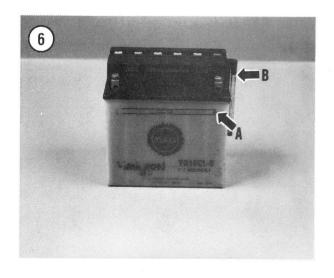

NOTE
Do not overfill the battery cells in Step 9. The electrolyte expands when heated by the charging process, and could overflow if the battery is overfilled.

9. Remove the battery caps (**Figure 5**) and check the electrolyte level. Add distilled water, if necessary, to bring the level within the upper and lower level lines (A, **Figure 6**) on the battery case.

10. Position the battery in the battery tray.

11. Reconnect the positive cable, then the negative cable.

WARNING
Be sure the battery cables are connected to their proper terminals. Connecting the battery backward will reverse system polarity, destroy the voltage regulator/rectifier and could result in a serious battery explosion.

WARNING
*After installing the battery, make sure the vent tube (B, **Figure 6**) is not pinched. A pinched or kinked tube would allow high pressure to accumulate in the battery and cause the battery electrolyte to overflow the cells.*

12. Tighten the battery connections. Coat the terminals with petroleum jelly or a light mineral grease.

13. Reconnect the battery hold down straps.

Battery Testing

Hydrometer testing is the best method to check the battery's state of charge (specific gravity). Use a hydrometer with numbered graduations from 1.100-1.300 points rather then one with color-coded bands. To use the hydrometer, squeeze the rubber bulb, insert the tip into a cell, then release the bulb to fill the hydrometer. See **Figure 7**.

NOTE
Do not test specific gravity immediately after adding water to the battery cells, as the water will dilute the electrolyte and lower the specific gravity. To obtain accurate hydrometer readings, the battery must be charged after adding water.

Draw sufficient electrolyte to raise the float inside the hydrometer. When using a temperature-compensated hydrometer, discharge the electrolyte back into the battery cell and repeat the process several times to adjust the temperature of the hydrometer to that of the electrolyte.

Hold the hydrometer upright and note the number on the float that is even with the surface of the electrolyte (**Figure 7**). This number is the specific gravity for that cell. Discharge the electrolyte into the cell from which it came.

The specific gravity of a cell is the indicator of the cell's state of charge. A fully charged cell will read 1.260 or more at 80° F (26.7° C). A cell that is 75% charged will read from 1.220-1.230 points specific gravity while a cell with a 50% charge will read from 1.170-1.180. Any cell reading 1.120 or less should be considered discharged. See **Figure 8**.

All cells should be within 30 points specific gravity of each other. If over 30 points variation is noted, the battery condition is questionable. Charge the battery and recheck the specific gravity. If 30 points or more variation remains between cells after charging, the battery has failed and should be replaced.

NOTE
If a temperature-compensated hydrometer is not used, add 4 points specific gravity to the actual reading for every 10° above 80° F (26.7° C). Subtract 4 points for every 10° below 80° F (26.7° C).

Battery Storage

Wet-cell batteries slowly discharge when stored. They discharge faster when warm than when cold. Before storing a battery, clean the case with a solution of baking soda and water. Rinse with clean water and wipe dry. The battery

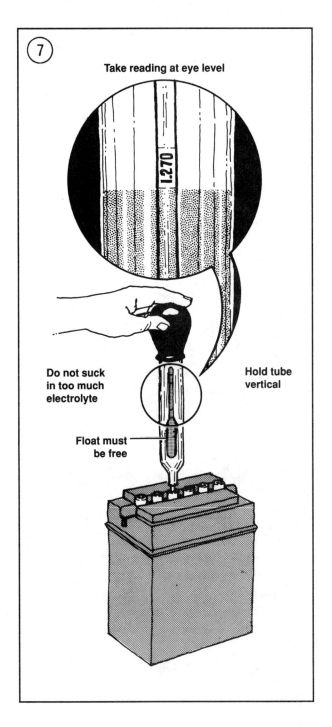

Take reading at eye level

1.270

Do not suck in too much electrolyte

Hold tube vertical

Float must be free

should be fully charged and then stored in a cool, dry location. Check electrolyte level and state of charge frequently (every 6-8 weeks) during storage. If the battery state of charge falls below 75%, charge the battery as described in this chapter.

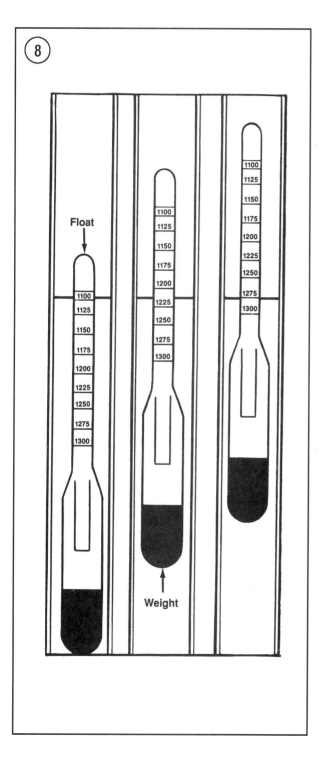

Charging

A good state of charge must be maintained in batteries used for starting. The battery does not have to be removed from the watercraft for charging, but it is a recommended safety procedure, since a charging battery releases highly explosive hydrogen gas. The area around the battery is not well ventilated and the gas may remain in the area for hours after the charging process has been completed. Sparks or flames occurring near the battery can cause it to explode, spraying battery electrolyte over a wide area. For this reason, it is critical to observe the following precautions:

a. Never smoke around batteries that are charging, or that have been recently charged.

b. Do not disconnect a live circuit at the battery creating a spark that can ignite any hydrogen gas that may be present.

When charging a battery, note the following:

a. During charging, the cells will show signs of gas bubbling. If one cell has no gas bubbles, or if its specific gravity is low, the cell is probably defective.

b. If a battery not in use loses its charge within a week after charging or if the specific gravity drops quickly, the battery is defective. A good battery should only self-discharge approximately 1% each day.

8

WARNING
*Always remove the battery from the watercraft before connecting charging equipment. During charging, highly explosive hydrogen gas is released from the cells. The battery should be charged only in a well-ventilated area, and open flames and sparks must be kept away. **Never** check the charge of the battery by arcing across the terminals. The resulting spark can create a dangerous explosion.*

1. Remove the battery from the watercraft as described in this chapter.

2. Connect the positive (+) charge lead to the positive battery terminal, then the negative (−) charger lead to the negative battery terminal.

3. Remove the battery vent caps from the battery, set the charger at 12 volts, and switch it on. Normally, a battery should be charged at a slow charge rate of 1/10 its given capacity. See **Table 1** for battery capacity.

> *CAUTION*
> *The electrolyte level must be maintained at the upper level during the charging cycle. Check and refill the cells with distilled water as necessary.*

4. The charging time necessary to fully charge the battery largely depends on the condition of the battery. The graph in **Figure 9** can be used to determine the approximate charging times at different specific gravity conditions. For example, if the specific gravity of the battery is 1.180, the approximate charging time would be 6 hours.

5. After the battery has charged for a sufficient time, switch the charger off, disconnect the charger leads and check the specific gravity. If the specific gravity is within the limits specified in **Table 2**, and remains stable for 1 hour, the battery is fully charged.

New Battery Installation

When replacing the battery, be sure to charge it completely (specific gravity 1.260-1.280) before installing it in the hull. Failure to do so, or using the battery with a low electrolyte level will result in premature battery failure.

Jump Starting

If the battery becomes severely discharged, it is possible to start and run an engine by jump starting it from another (fully charged) battery. If the proper procedure is not followed, however, jump starting can be extremely dangerous. Check the electrolyte level before jump starting any battery. If is not visible or if it appears to be frozen, do not attempt the jump start.

The booster battery must be the same voltage as the discharged battery.

> *WARNING*
> *Do avoid personal injury or damage to the system, use extreme caution when connecting a booster battery to a discharged battery. Never lean over the battery when making the connections. Wear eye protection whenever working around batteries.*

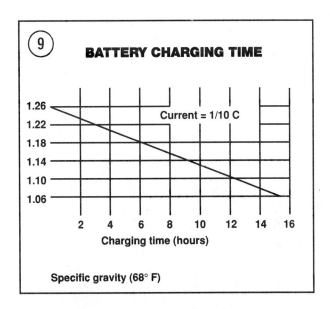

1. Secure the watercraft with a strong rope (minimum 500 lb. test) connected at one end to the rear of the watercraft and the other end to a stationary object (**Figure 10**). Be sure to choose an object that is strong enough to withstand the full thrust of the watercraft.

2. Remove the engine hood or seat.

3. Connect the jumper cables in the following order (**Figure 11**):

   a. Connect the positive jumper cable to the positive terminal of the booster battery, then to the positive terminal of the discharged battery.

   b. Connect the negative jumper cable to the negative terminal of the booster battery.

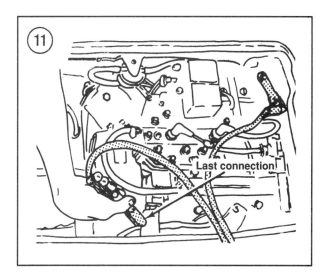

Then, connect the opposite end to a bolt on the exhaust pipe or other good engine ground. Do not connected the jumper cable to the negative terminal of the discharged battery.

> *WARNING*
> *An electrical arc may occur when the final connection is make. This could cause an explosion if it occurs near the battery. Therefore, the final connection should be made to a good ground away from the battery and not to the battery itself.*

5. Make sure that all jumper cables are out of the way of moving engine parts.

> *NOTE*
> *When attempting to start the watercraft in Step 6, do not operate the starter longer than 5 seconds. Excessive starter operation will overheat and damage the starter motor. Allow 15 seconds cooling time between starting attempts.*

6. Start the watercraft engine. Once it starts, run it at a moderate speed.

> *CAUTION*
> *Running the engine at wide-open throttle can damage the charging system.*

7. Remove the jumper cables in the exact reverse order of connection.

8. Install the engine hood/seat and remove the rope.

CHARGING SYSTEM

A battery charging system is standard on all Jet Ski models. The charging system consists of the battery, charge coil (**Figure 12**, typical) flywheel with attached permanent magnets and voltage regulator. The voltage regulator is a solid-state device that maintains the correct battery charge. The voltage regulator also contains the rectifier.

8

As the flywheel turns, the magnets located in the outer rim of the flywheel (**Figure 13**) rotate past the charging coil, inducing alternating current (AC) in the charge coil. From the charge coil, the AC current flows to the voltage regulator/rectifier assembly, where the AC current is rectified (converted) to direct current (DC) to charge the battery.

A charging system malfunction generally causes to the battery to be undercharged. Since the battery charge coil is protected by its location under the flywheel, it is more likely that the battery, voltage regulator or connecting wiring will cause problems. Perform the following visual inspection to help determine the cause of the problem. If the visual inspection does not locate the problem, test the charging system as described in Chapter Two.

1. Make sure the battery cables are properly connected. The red cable must be connected to the positive battery terminal. If the battery polarity is reversed, the voltage regulator/rectifier assembly will be damaged.

2. Inspect the battery terminals for loose or corroded connections. Tighten or clean the connections as required.

3. Inspect the physical condition of the battery. Look for bulges or cracks in the case, leaking electrolyte or corrosion.

4. Carefully check the wiring between the charge coil and battery for chafing, deterioration or other damage.

5. Check the circuit wiring for corroded or loose connections and open circuits (broken wires). Clean and tighten loose connections. Reconnect or repair open circuits as required.

ELECTRIC STARTING SYSTEM

The starting system consists of the stop switch, start switch, starter solenoid, battery and starter motor. Starting system operation and troubleshooting procedures are described in Chapter Two.

Starter Motor

The starter motor is capable of producing very high torque output, but only for a short time, because of the excessive heat generated by the motor. Never operate the starter motor continuously for more than 5 seconds. Allow the motor to cool for at least 15 seconds before operating it again.

If the starter motor does not function, check the battery and all connecting wiring for loose or corroded connections. If a visual inspection does not locate a problem, troubleshoot the starting system as describe in Chapter Two.

Starter Motor Removal/Installation (JS440SX and JS550SX)

1. Remove the engine cover.
2. Disconnect the ground cable from the engine (**Figure 1**).
3. Remove the exhaust pipe and expansion chamber as described in Chapter Seven.
4. Disconnect the cooling system water inlet hose from the exhaust manifold.
5. Pull back the rubber cap at the starter and disconnect the battery cable (**Figure 14**).
6. Remove the 2 bolts from the rear of the starter motor (**Figure 15**). Note any shims between the starter and the crankcase.
7. Remove the 2 bolts from the front of the starter (**Figure 16**) and remove the starter.
8. Install the starter motor by reversing Steps 1-7, plus the following:

   a. Apply a light coat of grease on the starter drive gear mechanism.

   b. Check the condition of the starter O-ring (**Figure 17**). Replace the O-ring as required. Lightly lubricate the O-ring prior to installation.

   c. Apply Loctite 242 to the threads of the starter motor fasteners.

   d. Apply a thin coat of silicone sealant to the crankcase-to-starter motor mating surface.

   e. Loosely install the starter, using the 2 bolts and washers at the front and the 2 bolts and washers at the rear bracket. Tighten the front mounting bolts securely.

   f. Measure the space between the crankcase and the rear starter bracket (**Figure 18**). Install shims or washers to take up any clearance, then tighten the mounting bolts securely.

8

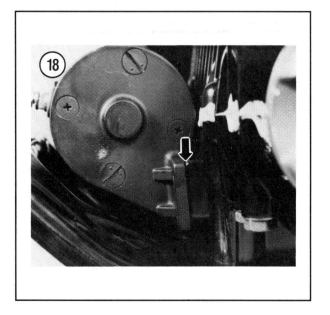

NOTE
Shims are available from Kawasaki in 0.4, 0.6 and 0.8 mm thicknesses.

Starter Motor Removal/Installation (JF650X-2 and JS650SX)

1. Remove the engine cover.

2. Disconnect the negative battery cable from the bottom starter motor mounting bolt.

3. Remove the exhaust pipe (Chapter Seven).

4. Remove the exhaust manifold. See Chapter Five.

5. Pull back the rubber cap at the starter and disconnect the starter cable (**Figure 16**).

6. Remove the 2 mounting bolts holding the starter motor to the engine. Remove the starter motor (**Figure 19**).

7. Install the starter motor by reversing Steps 1-7, plus the following:

   a. Clean the mounting lugs on the starter motor (**Figure 20**) and the engine (**Figure 21**) where the starter is grounded.

   b. Check the condition of the O-ring (**Figure 22**). Replace the O-ring if necessary. Lightly lubricate the O-ring with engine oil prior to installation.

   c. Apply a thin coat of silicone sealant to the crankcase-to-starter motor mating surface.

   d. Apply Loctite 242 to the threads of the starter mounting fasteners.

   e. Connect the ground cable to the bottom starter motor mounting bolt.

Starter Motor Removal/Installation (JL650SC and JF650TS)

1A. *JL650SC*—Unlock the seat. Remove the screws securing both seat base brackets and remove the seat. Remove the rubber plugs covering the engine hood retaining screws, then remove the screws and remove the engine hood panel.

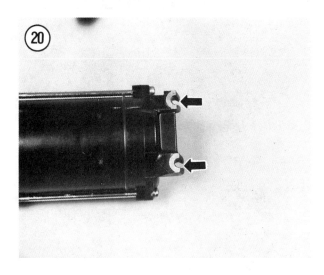

1B. *JF650TS*—Remove the engine hood/seat assembly.

2. Disconnect the negative battery cable.

3. Remove the inlet coolant hose from the engine.

4. Pull back the rubber cap at the starter and disconnect the starter cable (**Figure 16**).

5. Remove the 2 bolts securing the starter motor to the engine.

6. Install the starter motor by reversing Steps 1-5, plus the following:

   a. Clean the mounting lug on the starter motor and the crankcase where the starter is grounded.

b. Apply a light coat of grease on the starter motor drive gear mechanism.

c. Check the starter O-ring. Replace the O-ring as required. Lightly lubricate the O-ring with engine oil prior to starter motor installation.

d. Apply a thin coat of silicone sealant to the crankcase-to-starter motor mating surface.

e. Apply Loctite 242 to the threads of the starter motor mounting fasteners.

Starter Motor Removal/Installation (JB650 Jet Mate)

1. Remove the rear seat assembly.

2. Remove the exhaust pipe and expansion chamber as described in Chapter Seven.

3. Disconnect the negative battery cable from the battery.

4. Pull back the rubber boot at the starter motor and disconnect the starter cable (**Figure 16**) from the starter.

5. Remove the 2 bolts securing the starter motor to the engine. Remove the starter from the engine.

6. Install the starter motor by reversing Steps 1-5, plus the following:

   a. Clean the mounting lug on the starter motor and the crankcase where the starter is grounded.

   b. Apply a light coat of grease to the starter drive gear mechanism.

   c. Check the condition of the starter O-ring. Replace the O-ring if necessary. Lubricate the O-ring with engine oil prior to starter installation.

   d. Apply a thin coat of silicone sealant to the crankcase-to-starter motor mating surface.

   e. Apply Loctite 242 to the threads of the starter motor mounting fasteners.

   f. Connect the starter motor ground cable to the bottom starter mounting bolt.

8

Starter Motor Removal/Installation
(All 750 cc Models)

1. Remove the engine hood/seat assembly.

2. Disconnect the negative battery cable from the engine or battery.

3A. *JS750SX*—Remove the exhaust pipe, front muffler and expansion chamber as a unit assemble. See Chapter Seven.

3B. *Except JS750SX*—Remove the exhaust pipe and expansion chamber as a unit assembly. See Chapter Seven.

4. Disconnect the inlet cooling hose from the engine.

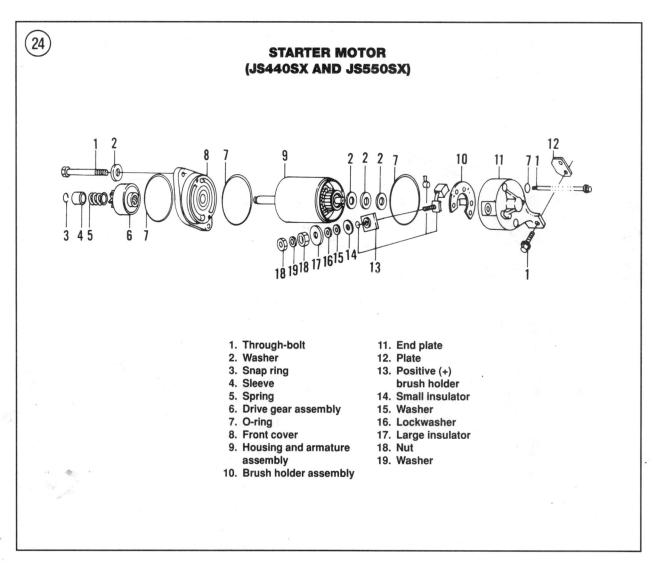

**STARTER MOTOR
(JS440SX AND JS550SX)**

1. Through-bolt
2. Washer
3. Snap ring
4. Sleeve
5. Spring
6. Drive gear assembly
7. O-ring
8. Front cover
9. Housing and armature assembly
10. Brush holder assembly
11. End plate
12. Plate
13. Positive (+) brush holder
14. Small insulator
15. Washer
16. Lockwasher
17. Large insulator
18. Nut
19. Washer

5. Pull back the rubber boot and disconnect the starter motor cable from the starter. See **Figure 23**, typical.

6. Remove the starter motor mounting bolts and remove the starter.

7. Install the starter motor by reversing Steps 1-6, plus the following:

   a. Clean the starter motor mounting lugs and the crankcase in the area where the starter motor grounds.

   b. Inspect the starter motor O-ring (**Figure 22**) and replace as required. Lightly lubricate the O-ring with engine oil prior to starter motor installation.

   c. Apply a thin coat of silicone sealant to the crankcase-to-starter motor mating surface.

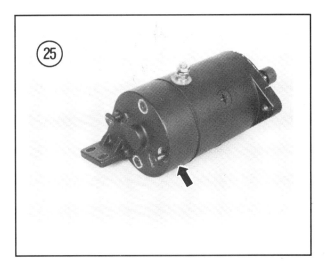

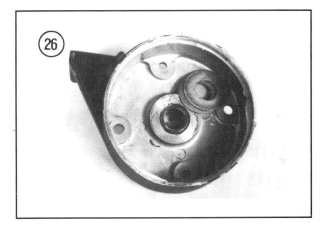

   d. Apply Loctite 242 to the threads of the starter motor mounting fasteners. Tighten the mounting fasteners securely.

Starter Motor Disassembly/Reassembly (JS440SX and JS550SX)

Refer to **Figure 24** while performing this procedure.

1. Place match marks on the front cover, housing and end plate for alignment reference during reassembly.

NOTE
An impact driver with a Phillips or straight-tip bit is required to loosen the starter housing screws. Attempting to loosen the screws with screwdriver may destroy the screw heads.

2. Loosen and remove the 2 through-bolts and O-rings (**Figure 25**).

3. Remove the end plate, then the housing from the armature assembly.

4. Remove any washers installed on the armature shaft next to the commutator (**Figure 26**).

5. If it is necessary to remove the drive gear assembly, mount the armature in a vise with soft jaws. Clamp the armature gently to prevent damage.

6. Pry the snap ring from its groove in the armature shaft (**Figure 27**). Then, remove the sleeve, spring, drive assembly and front cover.

7. Remove the nut, large insulator, spring washer, washer, small insulator and O-ring from the positive terminal.

8. To remove the brush holder assembly, remove the 2 mounting screws (**Figure 28**).

9. Carefully pry off the positive brush spring (A, **Figure 29**) and remove the positive brush and terminal (B).

10. Inspect the starter motor assembly and perform the electrical test procedures as described under *Inspection* in this chapter.

8

11. Lightly lubricate both ends of the armature shaft before installation.

12. If the drive gear assembly is removed, perform the following:

    a. Slide the front cover onto the armature shaft.

    b. Install the drive assembly, spring and sleeve.

    c. Compress the spring and install a new snap ring into the groove in the armature shaft.

    d. Compress the spring and make sure the snap ring is fully seated in its groove.

13. Install the positive brush spring (A, **Figure 29**) and brush (B).

14. Install the brush holder assembly. Apply Loctite 242 to the threads of the 2 brush holder mounting screws. Install the screws and tighten securely.

CAUTION
If the parts are not installed in the correct order as indicated in Step 15, the positive terminal will be grounded and the starter will be damaged.

15. Install the following parts on the positive terminal, in the following order: O-ring, small insulator, washer, spring washer, large insulator and nut. Tighten the nut securely.

16. Install the housing onto the armature assembly.

17. Make sure the O-ring is installed on both ends of the front cover.

18. Install the washers onto the armature shaft next to the commutator.

19. Make sure the O-ring is installed in the end plate.

20. Align the notch on the front end cover with the tab in the housing. Push the brushes against the springs to allow armature installation and install the end plate over the armature.

21. Rotate the end plate and housing to align the match marks made during disassembly (Step 1).

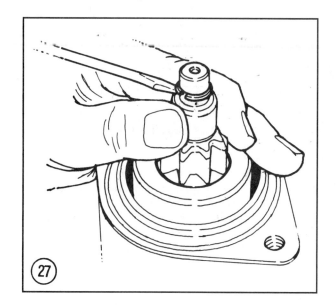

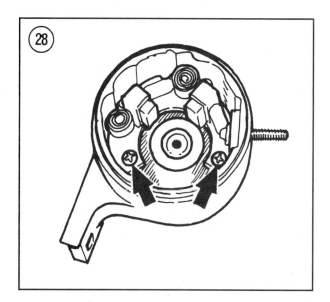

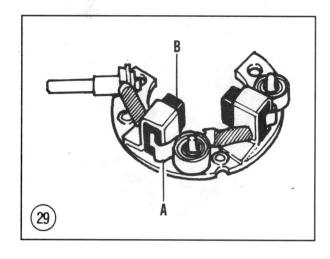

22. Install an O-ring on each long through-bolt, then install the through-bolts and tighten securely.

Starter Motor Disassembly/Reassembly (All 650 and 750 cc Models)

Refer to **Figure 30** while performing this procedure.

1. Place match marks on the cover, housing and rear cover for alignment reference during reassembly. See **Figure 31**.

2. Loosen the 2 through-bolts (**Figure 32**). Then, remove the bolts and washers.

3. Remove the front cover (**Figure 33**).

4. Remove the rear cover (**Figure 34**).

5. Slide the armature out of the housing.

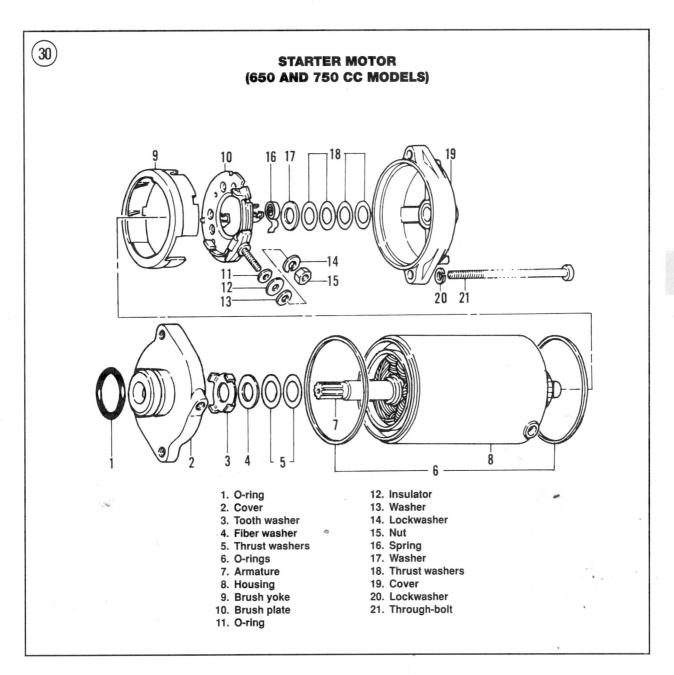

STARTER MOTOR (650 AND 750 CC MODELS)

1. O-ring
2. Cover
3. Tooth washer
4. Fiber washer
5. Thrust washers
6. O-rings
7. Armature
8. Housing
9. Brush yoke
10. Brush plate
11. O-ring
12. Insulator
13. Washer
14. Lockwasher
15. Nut
16. Spring
17. Washer
18. Thrust washers
19. Cover
20. Lockwasher
21. Through-bolt

8

NOTE
Note and record the number of shims used on both ends of the armature. Be sure to reinstall the same number during starter reassembly.

6. Remove the shims from each end of the armature.

7. Remove the toothed washer from the front cover (**Figure 35**).

8. Pull the springs back and remove the brushes from their mounting position in the brush holder (**Figure 36**).

9. To remove the brush plate and brush yoke, proceed as follows:

   a. Lift the brush plate off the center housing.

   b. Remove the nut and washer assembly (11-15, **Figure 30**) and remove the yoke and brush assembly (**Figure 30**).

10. Inspect the starter assembly and perform the test procedures as described under *Inspection* in this chapter.

11. Reinstall the brush plate and yoke assemblies as follows (if removed):

   a. Install the brush plate and yoke assembly (**Figure 30**) into the center housing. Then, install the washer and nut assembly in the order shown in **Figure 30**.

   b. Align the brush plate with the center housing and install it (**Figure 37**).

12. Insert the brushes into their holders and secure the brushes with the springs. Then, place

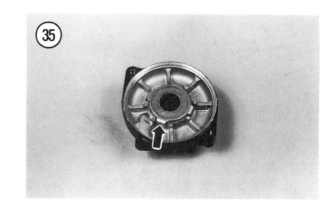

a piece of folded paper between each brush and spring assembly as shown in **Figure 38**. This reduces spring tension on the brush face to allow easier armature installation.

13. Insert the armature into the center housing. Carefully work the commutator past the brushes until it bottoms (**Figure 39**). Remove the 4 pieces of folded paper. Make sure each brush snaps against the commutator (**Figure 40**).

14. Install the correct number of shims on the armature shaft next to the commutator (**Figure 41**).

15. Install the correct number of shims on the drive end of the armature shaft (**Figure 30**).

16. Place the toothed washer into the front cover (**Figure 35**). The washer will only install one way. Make sure the washer seats flush in the end cover.

17. Install both end covers, making sure to align the match marks made during disassembly (**Figure 31**).

18. Install the 2 through-bolts and tighten securely.

**Starter Motor Inspection
(All Models)**

Refer to **Figure 24** (JS440SX and JS550SX) and **Figure 30** (650 and 750 cc models) when performing this procedure.

8

1. Thoroughly clean the armature, housing and end covers.

CAUTION
Do not immerse the brushes or wire windings in solvent as the insulation may be damaged. Clean the electrical components using a suitable aerosol cleaner designed for electrical components. Dry with compressed air.

2. Check the seal in the front cover for tearing or excessive wear. Also check the needle bearing mounted behind the seal. If the seal or bearing is damaged, the front cover must be replaced.

3. Check the bushing (**Figure 42**) is the rear cover. Replace the rear cover if the bushing is excessively worn.

4. Check all O-rings for cracks, hardness, cuts, deterioration or other damage. The O-rings should be replaced upon reassembly.

5. Check the fiber washer(s). Replace the washer(s) if excessively worn, cracked or damaged in any way.

6. Check the metal shims for damage. Replace if necessary.

7. Measure the length of each brush (**Figure 43**). If the length is worn to the wear limit specified in **Table 1**, replace the brushes as a set.

8. Inspect the commutator (**Figure 44**). The mica in a good commutator is below the surface of the copper segments. On a worn commutator the mica and copper segments may be worn to the same level. See **Figure 45**. Smooth the commutator surface using fine emery cloth (if necessary) and clean out the grooves between the segments. If necessary, have the commutator serviced by an electrical repair shop equipped to resurface armature commutators.

9. Inspect the commutator copper segments (**Figure 44**) for discoloration. If a pair of segments are discolored, grounded armature coils are indicated.

10. Measure the commutator outer diameter with a vernier caliper (**Figure 46**). Replace the

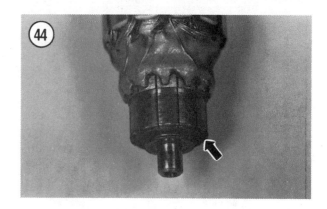

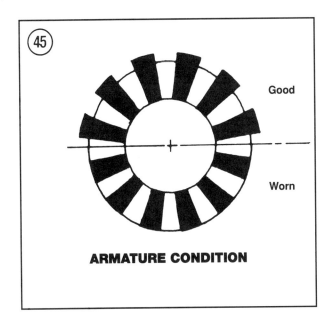

ARMATURE CONDITION

Good

Worn

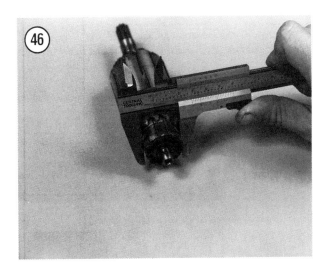

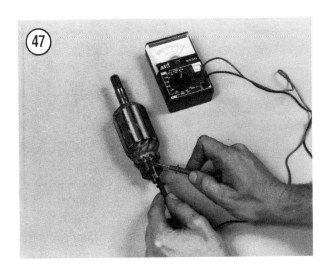

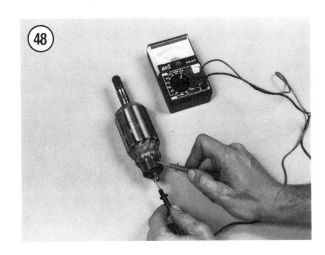

armature if the commutator is worn to less than the minimum diameter specified in **Table 1**.

NOTE
An ohmmeter is required to perform the following checks.

11. Using an ohmmeter, check for continuity between the commutator segments (**Figure 47**). Continuity should be present between the segments. Also check for continuity between *each* commutator segment and the armature shaft (**Figure 48**). No continuity should be present between any segment and the shaft. If no continuity is present between commutator segments, or if continuity is noted between any segment and the armature shaft, the armature is defective and must be replaced.

12. Set the ohmmeter on the R × 1 scale. Then, check the resistance between the insulated brushes as shown in **Figure 49**. The reading should be nearly zero ohm. If high resistance or infinity is noted, one brush lead is open. Replace the brushes as a set.

13. Next, check the resistance between the grounded brushes and brush plate. Low resistance should be noted. If high resistance or infinity is noted, the brush plate has an open circuit and must be replaced.

14. Set the ohmmeter on its highest scale. Measure the resistance between the brush plate and

8

brush holder. No continuity should be noted. If the reading is not infinity, replace the brush plate.

CAPACITOR DISCHARGE IGNITION (CDI)

All models are equipped with a capacitor discharge ignition system.

> *NOTE*
> *Refer to Chapter Two for troubleshooting and test procedures.*

Flywheel Removal/Installation

The flywheel must be removed to service the stator coils. Flywheel replacement is usually necessary only if the magnets are damaged.

JS440SX and JS550SX

> *NOTE*
> *This procedure is shown with the engine removed from the hull for clarity. Engine removal is not necessary for flywheel removal.*

1. Remove the fuel tank as described in Chapter Seven.
2. Remove the 2 bolts from the front of the starter motor (**Figure 50**).

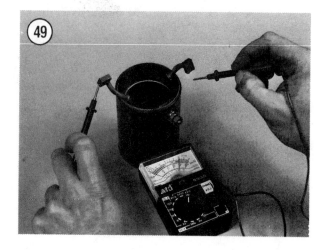

3. Remove the bolts holding the flywheel cover to the engine (**Figure 51**). Remove the cover.

4. Fold down the tabs on the flywheel nut locking tab washer (**Figure 52**).

5. Hold the flywheel with a universal flywheel holding tool or the Kawasaki flywheel holder part No. 57001-276 (JS440SX) or 57001-1313 (JS550SX). Loosen the flywheel nut (**Figure 53**). Unthread the nut until it is flush with the end of the crankshaft.

CAUTION
Do not use heat to remove the flywheel. Do not hammer on the flywheel. Striking the flywheel with a hammer can damage the flywheel or flywheel magnets. Heat will destroy the electrical components under the flywheel and could cause the flywheel to seize to the crankshaft.

6. Install the Kawasaki flywheel puller part No. 57001-259 and puller bolt part No. 57001-1099 onto the face of the flywheel (**Figure 54**). Tighten the puller bolt to dislodge the flywheel from the crankshaft (**Figure 55**). If necessary, tap the end of the puller bolt to break the flywheel free.

7. Remove the puller, flywheel nut, flywheel and flywheel key (**Figure 56**).

8

NOTE
Prior to installing the flywheel, check the flywheel magnets for metallic particles or other debris. The clearance between the magnets and the charging or pulser coils on the stator plate is close. Any debris on the magnets could result in damage to the electrical components and the flywheel.

8. Make sure the crankshaft and flywheel tapers are absolutely clean. Then, spray the tapered area of the flywheel and crankshaft with Bel-Ray 6 in 1 or WD-40.

9. Place the flywheel key into its slot in the crankshaft (**Figure 56**). Position the flywheel over the crankshaft with the key slot in the flywheel hub aligned with the key.

10. Install a new locking tab washer. Make sure its tongue is positioned in the hole in the flywheel (**Figure 57**). Install the flywheel nut.

11. Hold the flywheel using the flywheel holding tool. Tighten the nut to the specification in **Table 3**.

12. Bend the tabs of the locking tab washer up against the flywheel nut (**Figure 58**).

13. Make sure the flywheel cover O-ring is in good condition. Apply a light coat of water-resistant grease to the O-ring prior to installation.

14. Reverse Steps 1-3 to complete installation.

JF650X-2 and JS650SX

NOTE
This procedure is shown with the engine removed from the hull for clarity. Engine removal is not necessary for flywheel removal.

1. Remove the engine cover.

2. Remove the battery as described in this chapter.

3. Remove the oil tank as described in Chapter Nine.

4. Remove the fuel tank as described in Chapter Seven.

5. Remove the oil pump as described in Chapter Nine.

NOTE
Do not lose the small spring, bushing and washer when the flywheel cover is removed.

6. Remove the bolts holding the flywheel cover to the engine. Remove the cover (**Figure 59**) and O-ring seal.

7. Hold the flywheel using a universal flywheel holding tool or Kawasaki flywheel holder part No. 57001-1313 (JS650SX) or part No. 57001-306 (JF650X-2). Loosen the flywheel bolt (**Figure 60**), then remove the holding tool and bolt (**Figure 61**).

CAUTION
Do not use heat to remove the flywheel. Do not hammer on the flywheel. Striking the flywheel with a hammer can damage the flywheel or flywheel magnets. Heat will destroy the electrical components under the flywheel and could cause the flywheel to seize to the crankshaft.

8. Install the Kawasaki flywheel puller (part No. 57001-259) onto the face of the flywheel (**Figure 62**). Tighten the puller center bolt to dislodge the flywheel from the crankshaft. If necessary, strike the end of the puller bolt to break the flywheel free.

9. Remove the puller, flywheel bolt, flywheel and flywheel key (**Figure 63**).

NOTE
Prior to installing the flywheel, check the flywheel magnets for metallic particles or other debris. The clearance between the magnets and the charging and pulser coils on the stator plate is close. Any debris on the magnets could result in damage to the electrical components and the flywheel.

10. Using clean solvent, thoroughly clean the tapered area of the crankshaft and flywheel. The

8

tapers must be absolutely clean. Then, spray the tapered areas with Bel-Ray 6 in 1 or WD-40.

11. Note the slot (A, **Figure 64**) in the head of the flywheel bolt. The oil injection pump engages with the slot and is driven by the flywheel bolt. Carefully inspect the bolt and replace it if the slot is worn or damaged in any way.

12. Place the flywheel key in its slot in the crankshaft (**Figure 63**). Position the flywheel over the crankshaft, align the flywheel key slot with the key and slide the flywheel on the crankshaft.

13. Lightly lubricate the mating surface (B, **Figure 64**) of the flywheel bolt with engine oil.

14. Install the flywheel bolt. While securely holding the flywheel using the holding tool, tighten the flywheel bolt to the specification listed in **Table 3**.

NOTE
*Make sure the washer, spring and bushing (**Figure 65**) are correctly installed.*

15. Make sure the flywheel cover O-ring seal (**Figure 66**) is in acceptable condition. Apply a light coat of water-resistant grease to the O-ring prior to installation. Also make sure the cover dowel pins are properly installed. Apply Loctite 242 to the threads of the flywheel cover mounting bolts. Tighten the bolts to the specification in **Table 3**.

16. Reverse Steps 1-6 to complete installation. Bleed the oil injection system as described in Chapter Nine.

JL650SC and JF650TS

1. Remove the engine as described in Chapter Five.

2. Remove the oil injection pump (Chapter Nine).

3. Remove the bolts holding the flywheel cover to the engine. Remove the cover (**Figure 59**).

4. Hold the flywheel using a universal flywheel holding tool or Kawasaki flywheel holder part

No. 57001-1313. While securely holding the flywheel, loosen and remove the flywheel bolt (**Figure 61**). Remove the holding tool.

CAUTION
Do not use heat to remove the flywheel. Do not hammer on the flywheel. Striking the flywheel with a hammer can damage

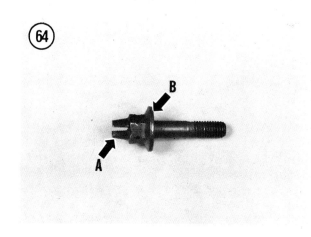

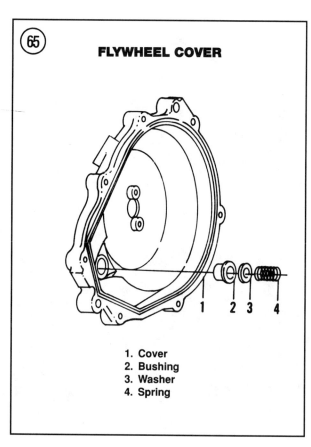

1. Cover
2. Bushing
3. Washer
4. Spring

the flywheel or flywheel magnets. Heat will destroy the electrical components under the flywheel and could cause the flywheel to seize to the crankshaft taper.

5. Install Kawasaki flywheel puller part No. 57001-259 onto the face of the flywheel (**Figure 62**). Tighten the puller bolt to dislodge the flywheel from the crankshaft. If necessary, strike the puller bolt sharply to break the flywheel free.

6. Remove the flywheel puller, flywheel and flywheel key (**Figure 63**) from the crankshaft.

NOTE
Prior to installing the flywheel, check the flywheel magnets for metallic particles or other debris. The clearance between the magnets and the charging and pulser coils on the stator plate is close. Any debris on the magnets could result in damage to the electrical components and the flywheel.

7. Thoroughly clean the tapered areas of the crankshaft and flywheel using solvent and a clean towel. The tapers must be absolutely clean. Then spray the tapers with Bel-Ray 6 in 1 or WD-40.

8. Note the slot (A, **Figure 64**) in the head of the flywheel bolt. The oil injection pump engages with the slot and is driven by the flywheel bolt. Carefully inspect the bolt and replace it if the slot is worn or damaged in any way.

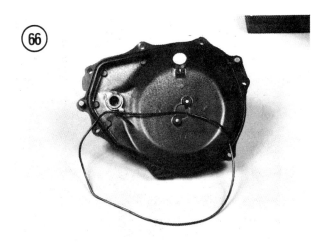

66

9. Place the flywheel key in its slot in the crankshaft (**Figure 63**). Position the flywheel over the crankshaft, align the flywheel key slot with the key and slide the flywheel on the crankshaft.

10. Lightly lubricate the mating surface (B, **Figure 64**) of the flywheel bolt with engine oil.

11. Install the flywheel bolt. While securely holding the flywheel using the holding tool, tighten the flywheel bolt to the specification listed in **Table 3**.

NOTE
*Make sure the washer, spring and bushing (**Figure 65**) are correctly installed.*

12. Make sure the flywheel cover O-ring seal (**Figure 66**) is in acceptable condition. Apply a light coat of water-resistant grease to the O-ring prior to installation. Also make sure the cover dowel pins are properly installed. Apply Loctite 242 to the threads of the flywheel cover mounting bolts. Tighten the bolts to the specification in **Table 3**.

13. Reverse Steps 1-6 to complete installation. Bleed the oil injection system as described in Chapter Nine.

8

JB650 Jet Mate

NOTE
This procedure is shown with the engine removed from the hull for clarity. Engine removal is not necessary for flywheel removal.

1. Remove the engine cover.

2. Remove the oil tank and tank mounting bracket. See Chapter Nine.

3. Remove the oil pump as described in Chapter Nine.

4. Remove the water box muffler as described in Chapter Seven.

5. Remove the bolts holding the flywheel cover to the engine. Remove the cover and O-ring seal (**Figure 59**).

6. Hold the flywheel with a universal flywheel holding tool or Kawasaki flywheel holder part No. 57001-1156. While securely holding the flywheel, loosen the flywheel bolt (**Figure 61**). Remove the flywheel holding tool and bolt.

7. An adaptor bolt must be threaded into the end of the crankshaft in place of the original flywheel bolt removed in Step 6. The adaptor bolt is necessary for the flywheel puller to push against during flywheel removal.

8. Install a bolt (10 mm diameter, 20 mm long) into the end of the crankshaft.

9. Install Kawasaki flywheel puller assembly part No. 57001-259 and 57001-1099 onto the face of the flywheel (**Figure 62**). Tighten the puller bolt to dislodge the flywheel from the crankshaft. If necessary, strike the puller bolt with a hammer to break the flywheel free.

10. Remove the flywheel puller, flywheel and flywheel key.

11. Remove the adaptor bolt installed in Step 8.

12. Thoroughly clean the tapered areas of the flywheel and crankshaft with solvent and a clean towel. The tapers must be absolutely clean. Then, spray a light coat of Bel-Ray 6 in 1 or WD-40 on the tapers.

13. Note the slot (A, **Figure 64**) in the head of the flywheel bolt. The oil injection pump engages with the slot and is driven by the flywheel bolt. Carefully inspect the bolt and replace it if the slot is worn or damaged in any way.

14. Place the flywheel key into its slot in the crankshaft. Position the flywheel over the crankshaft, align the key slot in the flywheel with the key and slide the flywheel on the crankshaft.

15. Lightly lubricate the mating surface (B, **Figure 64**) of the flywheel bolt with engine oil.

16. Install the flywheel bolt. While securely holding the flywheel using the holding tool,

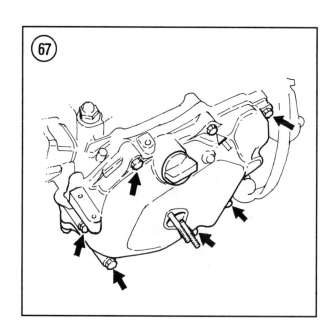

tighten the bolt to the specification listed in **Table 3**.

17. Make sure the flywheel cover O-ring (**Figure 66**) is in acceptable condition. Lubricate the O-ring with water-resistant grease prior to installation. Also make sure the cover dowel pins are properly installed.

18. Apply Loctite 242 to the threads of the flywheel cover mounting screws. Reverse Steps 1-5 to complete installation.

JS750SX and JT750ST

NOTE
On JS750SX models, the flywheel can be removed with removing the fuel tank if Kawasaki flywheel puller part No. 57001-1258 is used to separate the flywheel from the crankshaft.

1. Remove the engine hood/seat assembly

2. *JS750SX*—Remove the fuel tank as described in Chapter Seven.

3. Remove the oil injection pump as described in Chapter Nine.

4. Remove the bolts holding the flywheel cover to the engine (**Figure 67**). Remove the flywheel cover and O-ring seal. Do not lose the spring, washer and bushing (**Figure 65**) located behind the cover.

5. Hold the flywheel with a universal flywheel holding tool or Kawasaki flywheel holder part No. 57001-1313 (JS750SX) or part No. 57001-1368 (JT750ST). While securely holding the flywheel, loosen and remove the flywheel bolt (**Figure 61**). Because of limited clearance between the engine and hull, it may be necessary to use a universal-type socket to remove the flywheel bolt on JT750ST models.

CAUTION
Do not use heat to remove the flywheel and do not hammer on the flywheel. Striking the flywheel with a hammer can damage the flywheel or flywheel magnets. Heat will destroy the electrical

components under the flywheel and could cause the flywheel to seize to the crankshaft.

6. Install Kawasaki flywheel puller part No. 57001-1216 onto the face of the flywheel. If using flywheel puller part No. 57001-1258, thread the puller into the flywheel. Tighten the puller bolt to dislodge the flywheel from the crankshaft. If necessary, strike the puller bolt with a hammer to break the flywheel free.

7. Remove the flywheel puller, flywheel and flywheel key.

NOTE
Prior to installing the flywheel, check the flywheel magnets for metallic particles or other debris. The clearance between the magnets and the stator coils is close. Any debris on the magnets could result in damage to the electrical components and the flywheel.

8. Thoroughly clean the tapered areas of the flywheel and crankshaft with solvent and a clean towel. The tapers must be absolutely clean. Then, lightly spray the tapers with Bel-Ray 6 in 1 or WD-40.

9. Note the slot (A, **Figure 64**) in the head of the flywheel bolt. The oil injection pump engages with the slot and is driven by the flywheel bolt. Carefully inspect the bolt and replace it if the slot is worn or damaged in any way.

10. Place the flywheel key into its slot in the crankshaft. Position the flywheel over the crankshaft, align the key slot in the flywheel with the key and slide the flywheel on the crankshaft.

11. Lightly lubricate the mating surface (B, **Figure 64**) of the flywheel bolt with engine oil.

12. Install the flywheel bolt. While securely holding the flywheel using the flywheel holding tool, tighten the bolt to the specification listed in **Table 3**.

13. Make sure the flywheel cover O-ring seal (**Figure 66**) is in acceptable condition. Lubricate the O-ring with water-resistant grease prior to

8

installation. Also make sure the cover dowel pins are properly installed.

14. Make sure the spring, washer and bushing (**Figure 65**) are correctly installed.

15. Apply Loctite 242 to the threads of the flywheel cover bolts. Install the cover and bolts. Tighten the bolts to specification (**Table 3**).

16. Reverse Steps 1-3 to complete installation. Bleed the oil injection system as outlined in Chapter Nine.

JH750SS, JH750 Super Sport Xi and JH750XiR

NOTE
This procedure is shown with the engine removed for clarity. Engine removal is not necessary for flywheel removal.

1. Remove the engine hood/seat assembly.

2. *JH750 Super Sport Xi and JH750XiR*—Remove the carburetors as described in Chapter Seven.

3. Remove the throttle and choke cable bracket from the engine. Place the bracket and cables aside.

4. *Except JH750XiR*—Remove the oil injection pump as described in Chapter Nine. Remove the oil line clamp from the front of the engine.

5. Remove the bolts securing the flywheel cover to the engine. Remove the cover (**Figure 68**) and O-ring seal. Do not lose the spring, washer or bushing (**Figure 65**) when the cover is removed.

6. Hold the flywheel using a universal flywheel holding tool or Kawasaki flywheel holder part No. 57001-1368. While securely holding the flywheel, loosen and remove the flywheel bolt (**Figure 61**).

CAUTION
Do not use heat to remove the flywheel and do not hammer on the flywheel. Striking the flywheel with a hammer can damage the flywheel and flywheel magnets. Heat will destroy the electrical components under the flywheel and
could cause the flywheel to seize to the crankshaft.

7. Thread flywheel puller part No. 57001-1258 into the flywheel. While holding the flywheel using the holding tool, turn the puller bolt to force the flywheel off the crankshaft. Remove the flywheel bolt, flywheel and flywheel key.

NOTE
Prior to installing the flywheel, check the flywheel magnets for metallic particles or other debris. The clearance between the magnets and the stator coils is close. Any debris on the magnets could result in damage to the electrical components and the flywheel.

8. Thoroughly clean the tapered areas of the flywheel and crankshaft with solvent and a clean towel. The tapers must be absolutely clean. Then, lightly spray the tapers with Bel-Ray 6 in 1 or WD-40.

9. Note the slot (A, **Figure 64**) in the head of the flywheel bolt. The oil injection pump (except JH750XiR) engages with the slot and is driven by the flywheel bolt. Carefully inspect the bolt and replace it if the slot is worn or damaged in any way.

10. Place the flywheel key into its slot in the crankshaft. Position the flywheel over the crankshaft, align the key slot in the flywheel with the key and slide the flywheel on the crankshaft.

11. Lightly lubricate the mating surface (B, **Figure 64**) of the flywheel bolt with engine oil.

12. Install the flywheel bolt. While securely holding the flywheel using the flywheel holding tool, tighten the bolt to the specification listed in **Table 3**.

13. Make sure the flywheel cover O-ring seal (**Figure 66**) is in acceptable condition. Lubricate the O-ring with water-resistant grease prior to installation. Also make sure the cover dowel pins are properly installed.

14. Make sure the spring, washer and bushing (**Figure 65**) are correctly installed.

15. Apply Loctite 242 to the threads of the flywheel cover bolts. Install the cover and bolts. Tighten the bolts to specification (**Table 3**).

16. Reverse Steps 1-4 to complete installation. Bleed the oil injection system as outlined in Chapter Nine.

Stator Plate Removal/Installation (JS440SX and JS550SX)

The stator plate contains the exciter and trigger coils for the ignition system and the charging coil for the battery charging system.

NOTE
Refer to Chapter Two for troubleshooting procedures.

1. Remove the flywheel as described in this chapter.

2. Remove the screws securing the stator plate (**Figure 69**) to the crankcase. Remove the stator plate.

3. Spray a light coat of WD-40 or Bel-Ray 6 in 1 on the connectors and wires at both ends of the stator cable. Loosen the connector caps.

NOTE
Label the wires and connector cap before disconnecting the wires in Step 4.

4. Use a small pair of needlenose pliers to compress the spring retainer in each pin in the 5-pin connector (**Figure 70**). Pull each pin out of the connector, one at a time.

5. Spray the grommet and wires with WD-40 or Bel-Ray 6 in 1. Then, gently pull the grommet off the wires.

6. Remove the outer tube from the wire cable.

7. Pull the wires out of the crankcase and remove the stator assembly.

8. Install the stator assembly by reversing Steps 1-7, plus the following.

9. The tube covering the wires between the grommets must cover the ends of the grommets by 10 mm (3/8 in.).

10. Align the 5-pin connector halves and insert the pins into the connector so each wire will match the electric box connector wire. Make sure

8

each pin's locking tang is seated inside the connector.

11. Check and adjust the ignition timing as described in Chapter Three.

Charge, trigger and exciter coil replacement

When replacing a defective coil, be sure to properly identify the wires to be removed and unsoldered.

The trigger coil is mounted on top of the exciter coil (**Figure 71**). The remaining coil is the charge coil (**Figure 71**).

1. Remove the flywheel as described in this chapter.

2. Remove the screws securing the stator plate to the crankcase and remove it.

3. Replace the charge coil as follows:

    a. Remove the wire clamp at the front of the stator plate.

    b. Slide the insulator away from the 2 light green wires.

    c. Remove the screws holding the charge coil to the stator plate.

    d. Unsolder the light green wires at the coil.

    f. Solder each coil wire to its light green wire.

    g. Reinstall the coil screws.

    h. Wrap the new coil connections with electrical tape.

4. Replace the trigger and exciter coils as follows:

    a. Unsolder the red and gray wires at the coils.

    b. Remove the coils.

    c. Solder the wires to the coil terminals. Then insulate the new connections with electrical tape.

    d. Reinstall the coil screws.

Stator Plate Removal/Installation (650 cc Models)

The stator plate contains the exciter coil for the ignition system and the charging coil for the battery charging system. Individual stator components, however, are not available for service replacement. Should a coil fail, replace the stator plate assembly.

> *NOTE*
> *Refer to Chapter Two for troubleshooting and testing procedures. Also refer to the appropriate wiring diagrams at the end of the manual.*

1. Remove the flywheel as described in this chapter.

2. Remove the electric box cover as described in this chapter.

3. Remove the 2 screws and grommet retaining plate from the electric box. Label the stator wires for reference during installation, then, disconnect the wires at their bullet connectors, remove

the grommet from the electric box and pull the stator wires out of the electric box.

4. Place match marks (if not already marked) on the stator plate and crankcase for reference during installation. Remove the screws securing the stator plate (**Figure 72**) to the crankcase.

5. Remove the screws securing the grommet plate to the lower crankcase (**Figure 73**). Pull the wires out of the crankcase (**Figure 74**) and re-move the stator plate.

6. Install the stator plate by reversing Steps 1-5, plus the following:

a. Apply a light coat of water-resistant grease to the grommets at the lower crankcase and electric box.

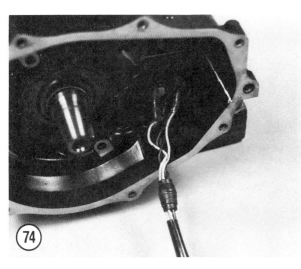

b. Align the match marks when mounting the stator plate on the crankcase.

c. Apply Loctite 242 to the threads of all fasteners and tighten securely.

d. Check and adjust the ignition timing as described in Chapter Three.

Stator/Charge Coil Removal/Installation (750 cc Models)

The stator and pickup coil (pulser) are mounted to the crankcase, under the flywheel. See **Figure 75**. The battery charging coil and exciter coil are contained in a 1-piece stator assembly. The stator and pickup coil are not available separately—if either fails the stator/pickup coil must be replaced as a unit assembly.

NOTE
Refer to Chapter Two for troubleshooting and testing procedures. Also refer to the appropriate wiring diagrams at the end of the manual.

1. Remove the flywheel as described in this chapter.

2. Remove the cap from the electric box, exposing the stator connectors (**Figure 76**, typical). Disconnect the 3- and 4-pin connectors.

3. Using a small pair of needlenose pliers or a small screwdriver, compress the spring retainer in each wire pin (**Figure 77**) in each connector, one at a time.

4. Unscrew both wire caps (5, **Figure 78**) from the electric box cap (2).

5. Spray a light coat of Bel-Ray 6 in 1 or WD-40 (or equivalent) on the grommet and gently pull each wire, one at a time out of the grommet and wire cap.

6. Remove the fasteners securing the stator and pickup coil to the crankcase. Remove any clamps securing the stator wiring harness. Carefully note how the harness is routed for reference during installation.

8

7. Remove the 2 screws (**Figure 73**) securing the grommet plate to the crankcase.

8. Pull the stator/pickup coil wires through the crankcase (**Figure 74**) and remove the stator/pickup coil assembly.

9. Install the stator/pickup coil assembly by reversing Steps 1-8, plus the following:

    a. Coat the grommets with water-resistant grease.

    b. Make sure all wires are correctly routed and clamped to prevent contact with the flywheel.

    c. Insert the stator and pickup coil wires into their respective connectors as shown in **Figure 79**.

    d. When mounting the pickup coil to the crankcase, push the coil outward, away from the stator, then tighten the mounting screws.

    e. Tighten all fasteners securely.

RPM LIMITER (JS550SX)

JS550SX models are equipped with an RPM limiter system that limits engine speed to ap-

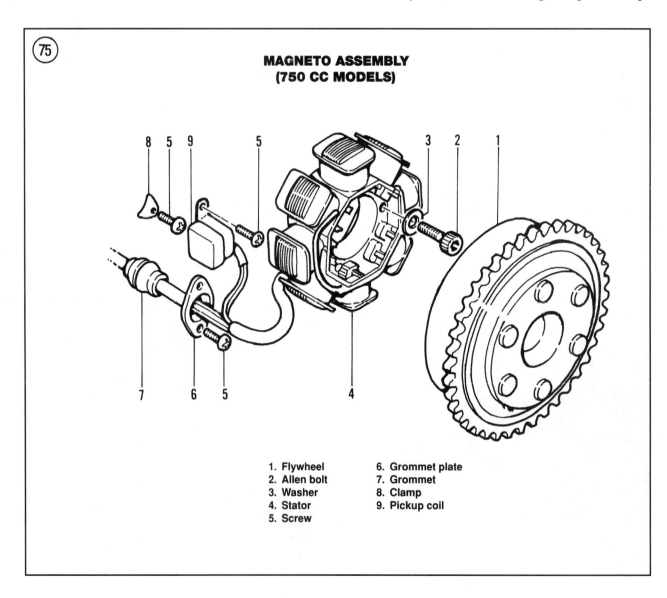

⑦⑤

**MAGNETO ASSEMBLY
(750 CC MODELS)**

1. Flywheel
2. Allen bolt
3. Washer
4. Stator
5. Screw
6. Grommet plate
7. Grommet
8. Clamp
9. Pickup coil

proximately 7750-8250 rpm. The RPM limiter system consists of the magneto (exciter and pickup coil), controller and igniter module. The controller contains crankshaft position and ignition pulse control circuits.

During operation, the crankshaft position circuit monitors engine speed. Then, if the engine speed reaches a predetermined rpm, the pulsing control circuit grounds the pickup coil output, interrupting ignition until engine speed drops below approximately 7750 rpm.

An ohmmeter is necessary to test the controller assembly.

1. Set the ohmmeter on the R × 1000 ohm range.
2. Open the electric box and remove the controller as described in this chapter.

3. Referring to the chart in **Figure 80**, connect the ohmmeter to the controller leads as shown. Replace the controller if the test results are not as indicated in the chart.

ELECTRIC BOX
(JS440SX and JS550SX)

The electric box on JS440SX models contains the following electrical components (**Figure 81**):

a. Ignition coil/igniter assembly.
b. Stop button relay.
c. Voltage regulator/rectifier assembly.
d. Starter solenoid.

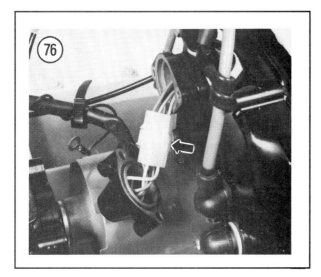

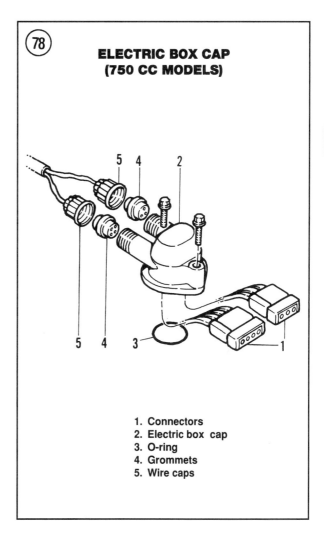

(78)

**ELECTRIC BOX CAP
(750 CC MODELS)**

1. Connectors
2. Electric box cap
3. O-ring
4. Grommets
5. Wire caps

8

On JS550SX models, the electric box contains the following components (**Figure 82**):

    a. Ignition coil/igniter assembly.

    b. Stop switch relay.

    c. Voltage regulator/rectifier assembly.

    d. Starter solenoid.

    e. RPM limiter controller

Removal/Installation

The electric box is mounted on the bulkhead.

1. Remove the engine cover.

NOTE
Label all wire connectors for reference during installation.

2. Remove the battery as described in this chapter. Disconnect the electric box ground wire from the engine.

3. Disconnect the spark plug leads from the spark plugs.

4. Remove the exhaust pipe as described in Chapter Seven.

5. Disconnect the cable from the starter motor (**Figure 83**).

6. Remove the choke cable clamp (A, **Figure 84**) from the electric box.

7. Remove the 2 bolts and washers securing the magneto wiring connector cap (B, **Figure 84**). The electric box ground wire is attached to one of the bolts.

8. Remove the cap and separate the connector from the electric box (**Figure 85**).

9. Spray the start and stop switch grommet caps with Bel-Ray 6 in 1 or WD-40 (or equivalent) to lubricate the rubber. Unscrew the caps (C, **Figure 84**).

10. Pull the switch leads out of the electric box carefully, one at a time, until their connectors are exposed (**Figure 86**). Separate the connectors.

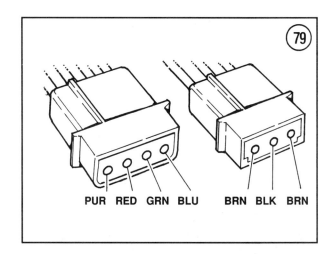

PUR RED GRN BLU   BRN BLK BRN

RPM LIMITER TEST
(JS550SX)

Unit: kΩ

	Wire color	Ohmmeter positive (+) lead connection				
		Black	Blue	Red	Gray	Brown
Ohmmeter negative (–) lead connection	Black		12 ~ 18 k	12 ~ 18 k	∞	0
	Blue	∞		0	∞	∞
	Red	∞	0		∞	∞
	Gray	∞	∞	∞		∞
	Brown	0	12 ~ 18 k	12 ~ 18 k	∞	

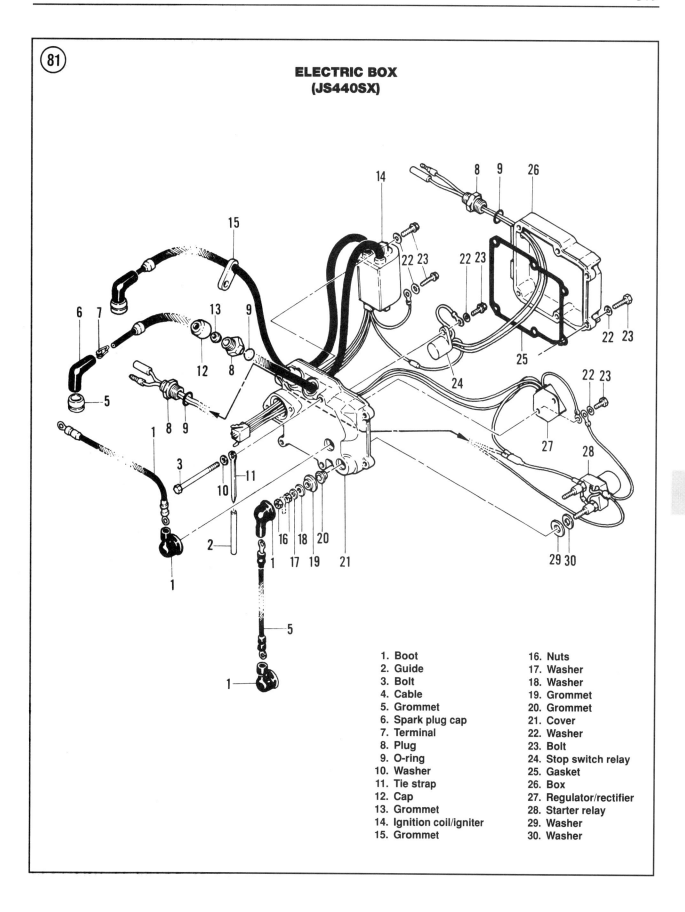

**ELECTRIC BOX
(JS440SX)**

1. Boot
2. Guide
3. Bolt
4. Cable
5. Grommet
6. Spark plug cap
7. Terminal
8. Plug
9. O-ring
10. Washer
11. Tie strap
12. Cap
13. Grommet
14. Ignition coil/igniter
15. Grommet
16. Nuts
17. Washer
18. Washer
19. Grommet
20. Grommet
21. Cover
22. Washer
23. Bolt
24. Stop switch relay
25. Gasket
26. Box
27. Regulator/rectifier
28. Starter relay
29. Washer
30. Washer

8

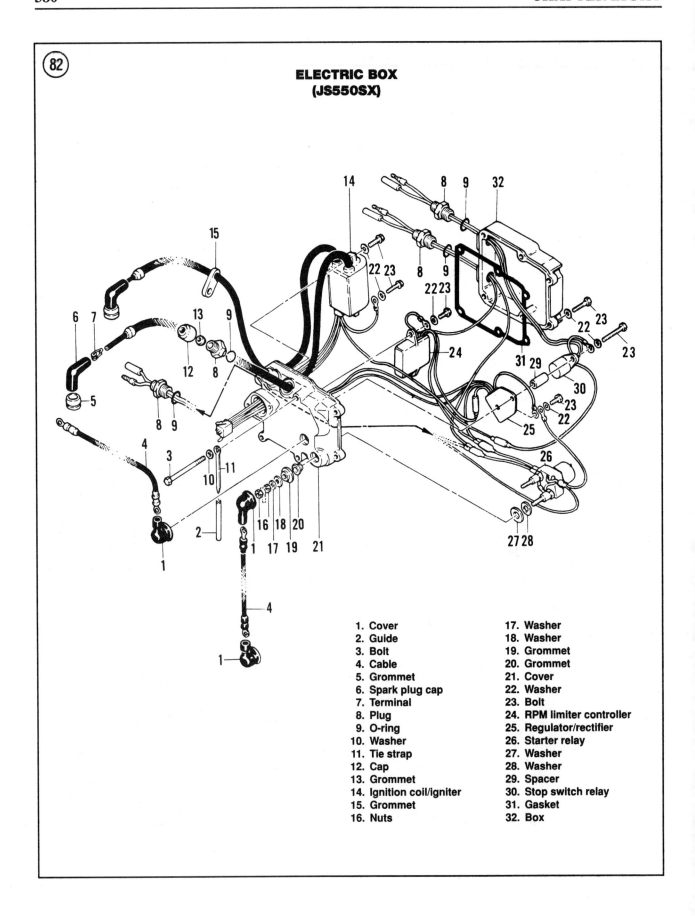

82

**ELECTRIC BOX
(JS550SX)**

1. Cover
2. Guide
3. Bolt
4. Cable
5. Grommet
6. Spark plug cap
7. Terminal
8. Plug
9. O-ring
10. Washer
11. Tie strap
12. Cap
13. Grommet
14. Ignition coil/igniter
15. Grommet
16. Nuts
17. Washer
18. Washer
19. Grommet
20. Grommet
21. Cover
22. Washer
23. Bolt
24. RPM limiter controller
25. Regulator/rectifier
26. Starter relay
27. Washer
28. Washer
29. Spacer
30. Stop switch relay
31. Gasket
32. Box

11. *JS550SX*—Repeat Step 9 and Step 10 to remove the rpm limiter cap and wires. See **Figure 82**.

12. Remove the 4 bolts and washers that attach the electric box to the control panel (**Figure 87**). Remove the electric box from the hull.

13. Install the electric box by reversing Steps 1-12, plus the following:

   a. Make sure the start and stop switch leads and the rpm limiter leads (JS550SX) are extending out of the box openings. If they are inside the box, separate the halves and thread the leads out of the box openings.

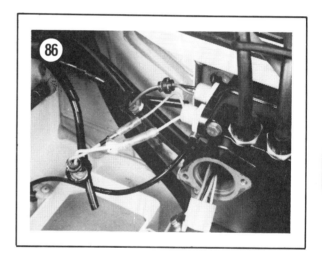

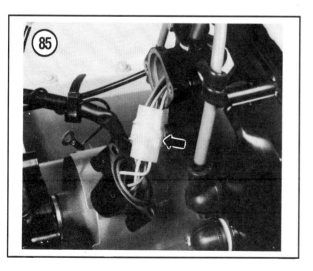

Connect the color-coded wires to wires of the same color code.

b. Apply a light coat of the water-resistant grease to the rubber switch connector grommets before tightening the caps.

Disassembly/Reassembly

Refer to **Figure 81** or **Figure 82** while performing this procedure.

1. Remove the electric box as described in this chapter.

2. Remove the bolts holding the box halves together (**Figure 88**). Open the front of the electric box (**Figure 89**).

3. Remove the defective component(s) from the box as required.

4. When reassembling the electric box, note the following:

a. Make sure all wire connectors are clean and tight.

b. Install a new gasket between the electric box halves. Coat both sides of the gasket with silicone sealant.

c. Coat the outside of all grommets with water-resistant grease.

d. Be certain that no wires are pinched between the electric box halves.

e. Apply Loctite 242 to the threads of all electric box mounting fasteners. Tighten all fasteners securely.

ELECTRIC BOX (JS650SX)

On JS650SX models, the electric box contains the following components (**Figure 90**):

a. Ignition coil/igniter assembly (mounted outside the electric box).

b. Starter relay.

c. Voltage regulator/rectifier assembly.

Removal/Installation

The electric box is mounted at the back of the engine compartment.

1. Remove the engine cover.

> *NOTE*
> *Label all wire connectors for reference during installation.*

2. Disconnect the negative battery cable from the battery.

3. Disconnect the positive battery cable from the electric box.

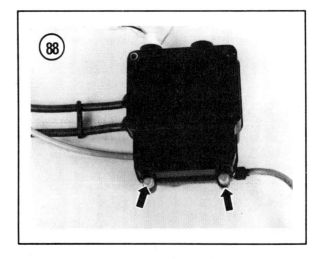

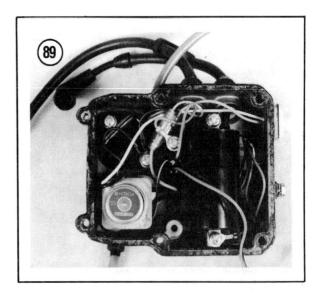

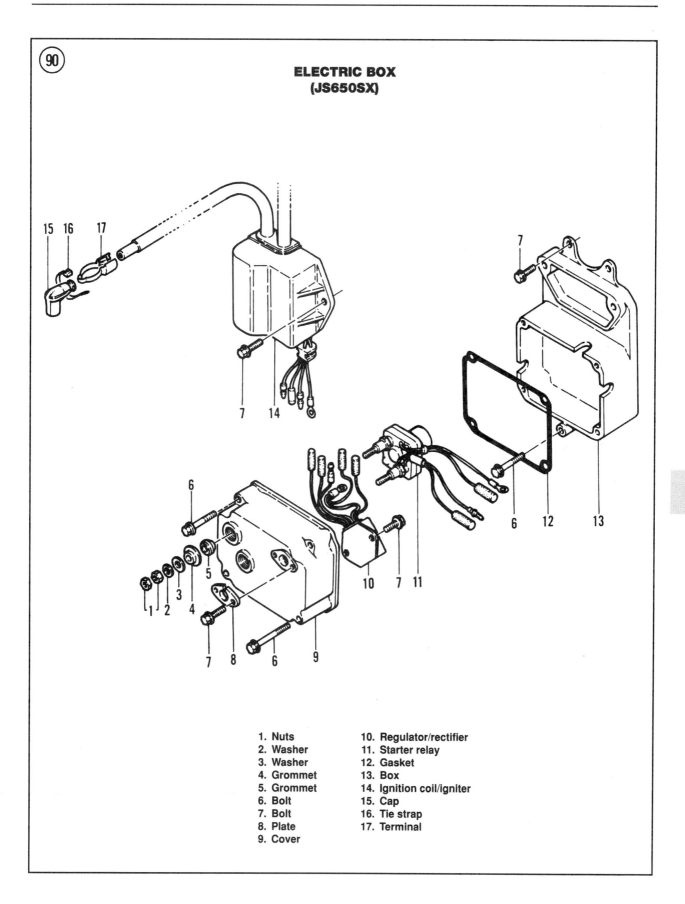

**ELECTRIC BOX
(JS650SX)**

90

8

1. Nuts
2. Washer
3. Washer
4. Grommet
5. Grommet
6. Bolt
7. Bolt
8. Plate
9. Cover
10. Regulator/rectifier
11. Starter relay
12. Gasket
13. Box
14. Ignition coil/igniter
15. Cap
16. Tie strap
17. Terminal

4. Disconnect the starter motor cable from the electric box.

5. Disconnect the spark plug leads from the spark plugs.

6. Remove the flame arrestor as described in Chapter Seven.

7. The ignition coil/igniter assembly is mounted on the outside of the electric box (**Figure 90**). Remove the mounting fasteners and remove the ignition coil/igniter assembly.

8. Remove the bolts holding the electric box to the hull. Remove the electric box (**Figure 91**).

9. Remove the grommet cap bolts at the front of the electric box. Pull the stator wires out of the box, one at a time, then disconnect the wires.

10. When reassembling the electric box, note the following:

   a. Make sure all wire connections are clean and tight.

   b. Install a new electric box gasket. Coat both sides of the gasket with silicone sealant.

   c. Coat the outside of all grommets with water-resistant grease.

   d. Be certain that none of the wires are pinched between the electric box halves.

   e. Apply Loctite 242 to the threads of all electric box fasteners. Tighten all fasteners securely.

Disassembly/Reassembly

Refer to **Figure 90** while performing this procedure.

1. Remove the electric box as described in this chapter.

2. Remove the bolts holding the box halves together. Open the front of the box.

3. Remove the defective component(s) from the electric box as required.

4. Refer to the following points when reassembling the electric box:

   a. Make sure all wire connections are clean and tight.

   b. Install a new electric box gasket. Coat both sides of the gasket with silicone sealant.

   c. Coat the outside of all grommets with water-resistant grease.

   d. Be certain none of the wires are pinched between the electric box halves.

   e. Apply Loctite 242 to the threads of all electric box fasteners. Tighten all fasteners securely.

ELECTRIC BOX (JF650X-2)

The electric box used on JF650X-2 models contains the following components (**Figure 92**):

   a. Ignition coil/igniter assembly (mounted outside the electric box).

   b. Voltage regulator/rectifier assembly.

   c. Starter relay.

   d. 5 amp fuse.

Removal/Installation

The electric box is mounted at the back of the engine compartment.

1. Remove the engine cover.

NOTE
Label all wire connectors for reference during installation.

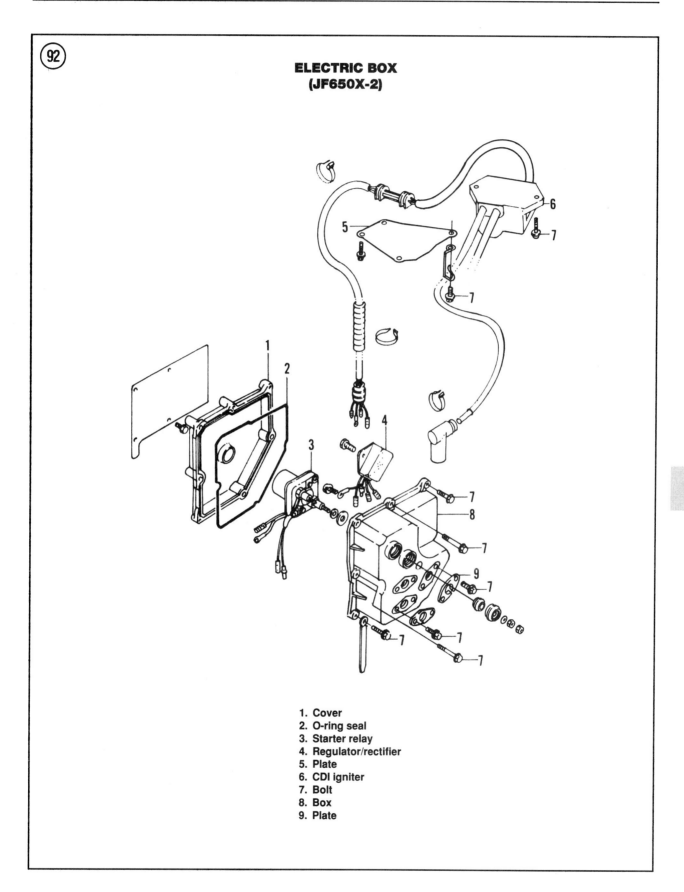

**ELECTRIC BOX
(JF650X-2)**

1. Cover
2. O-ring seal
3. Starter relay
4. Regulator/rectifier
5. Plate
6. CDI igniter
7. Bolt
8. Box
9. Plate

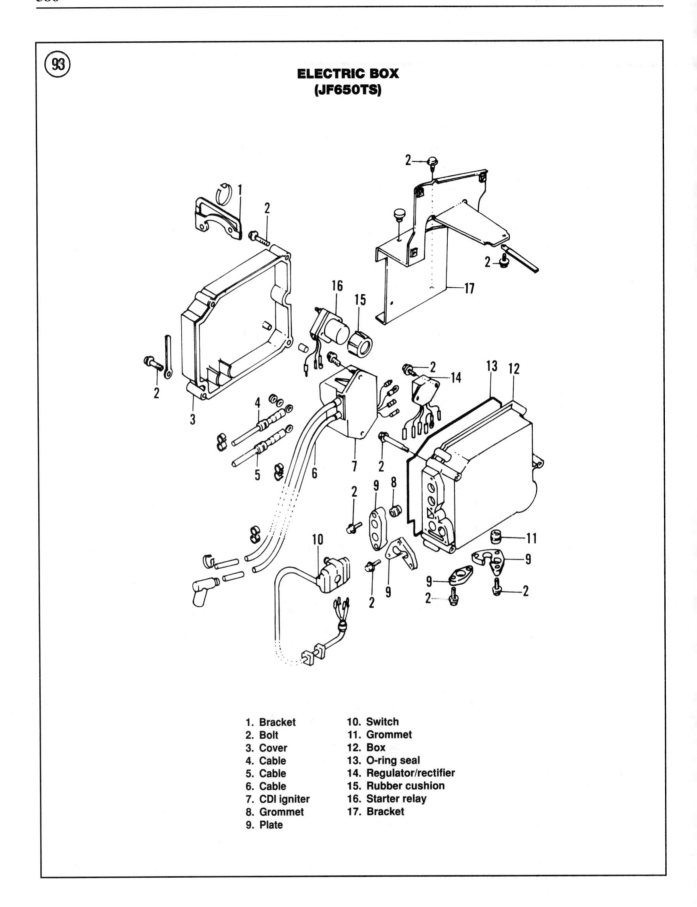

**ELECTRIC BOX
(JF650TS)**

1. Bracket
2. Bolt
3. Cover
4. Cable
5. Cable
6. Cable
7. CDI igniter
8. Grommet
9. Plate
10. Switch
11. Grommet
12. Box
13. O-ring seal
14. Regulator/rectifier
15. Rubber cushion
16. Starter relay
17. Bracket

2. Disconnect the negative battery (ground) cable from the battery.

3. Disconnect the positive battery cable from the electric box.

4. Disconnect the starter motor cable from the electric box.

5. Disconnect the spark plug leads from the spark plugs.

6. Remove the bolts holding the electric box to the hull. Remove the electric box.

7. Unscrew the grommet caps from the front of the electric box. Pull the stator wires out of the box, one at a time and disconnect them.

8. Note the following when reassembling the electric box:

    a. Make sure all wire connections are clean and tight.

    b. Install a new electric box O-ring seal. Lightly coat the O-ring seal with water-resistant grease.

    c. Be certain that none of the wires are pinched between the electric box halves.

    d. Coat the outside of all grommets with water-resistant grease.

    e. Apply Loctite 242 to the threads of all electric box fasteners. Tighten all fasteners securely.

Disassembly/Reassembly

Refer to **Figure 92** while performing this procedure.

1. Remove the electric box as described in this chapter.

2. Remove the bolts holding the electric box halves together. Open the front of the box.

3. Remove the defective component(s) as necessary.

4. Note the following points when reassembling the electric box:

    a. Make sure all wire connections are clean and tight.

    b. Install a new electric box O-ring seal. Lightly coat the seal with water-resistant grease prior to installation.

    c. Coat the outside of all grommets with water-resistant grease.

    d. Make sure none of the wires are pinched between the electric box halves.

    e. Apply Loctite 242 to the threads of the electric box fasteners. Tighten all fasteners securely.

ELECTRIC BOX (JF650TS AND JB650 JET MATE)

The electric box used on JF650TS (**Figure 93**) and JB650 Jet mate (**Figure 94**) models contains the following components:

    a. Ignition coil/igniter assembly.

    b. Starter relay.

    c. Voltage regulator/rectifier assembly.

Removal/Installation

The electric box is mounted in the engine compartment.

1A. *JF650TS*—Remove the seat/engine cover assembly.

1B. *JB650 Jet Mate*—Remove the rear seat assembly.

NOTE
Label all wire connectors for reference during installation.

2. Disconnect the negative (ground) battery cable from the battery.

3. Disconnect the positive battery cable from the electric box.

4. Disconnect the starter motor cable from the electric box.

5. Disconnect the spark plug leads from the spark plugs.

6A. *JF650TS*—Remove the bolts holding the electric box to the hull. Remove the electric box.

8

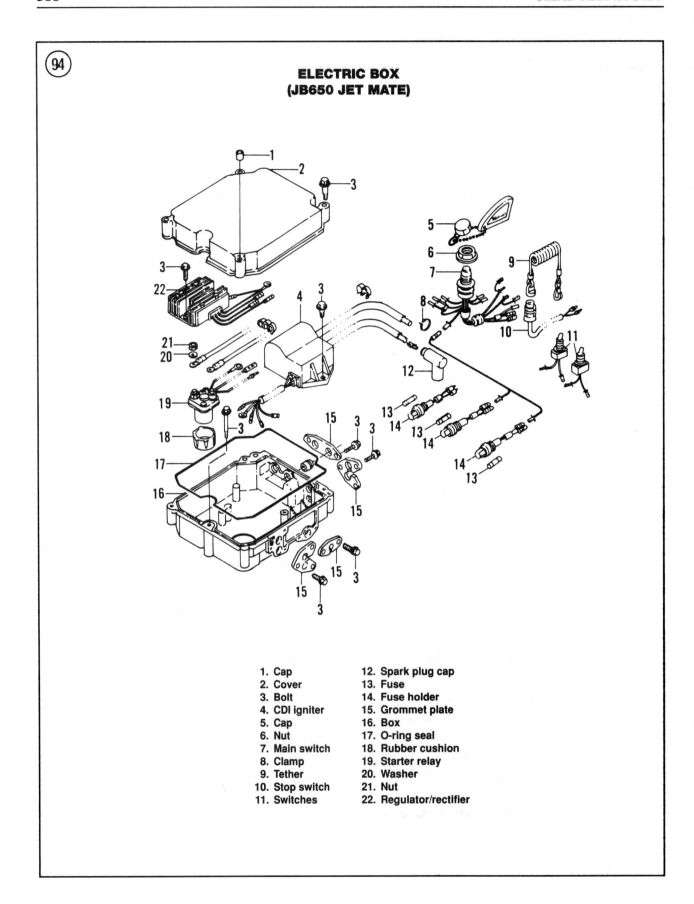

**ELECTRIC BOX
(JB650 JET MATE)**

1. Cap
2. Cover
3. Bolt
4. CDI igniter
5. Cap
6. Nut
7. Main switch
8. Clamp
9. Tether
10. Stop switch
11. Switches
12. Spark plug cap
13. Fuse
14. Fuse holder
15. Grommet plate
16. Box
17. O-ring seal
18. Rubber cushion
19. Starter relay
20. Washer
21. Nut
22. Regulator/rectifier

Then, remove the grommet plate bolts at the front of the electric box. Pull the stator wires out of the box and disconnect them.

6B. *JB650 Jet Mate*—Perform the following:

a. Remove the bolts holding the box halves together and open the front of the box.

b. Remove the bolts holding the electric box to the hull. Remove the electric box.

7. Note the following points when reinstalling the electric box:

a. Make sure all wire connections are clean and tight.

b. Install a new electric box gasket. Coat both sides of the gasket with silicone sealant prior to installation.

c. Coat the outside of all grommets with water-resistant grease.

d. Be certain that none of the wires are pinched between the electric box halves.

e. Apply Loctite 242 to the threads of all electric box fasteners. Tighten all fasteners securely.

Disassembly/Reassembly

Refer to **Figure 93** (JF650TS) or **Figure 94** (JB650 Jet Mate) while performing this procedure.

1. Remove the electric box as described in this chapter.

2. *JF650TS*—Remove the bolts holding the box halves together and open the front of the box.

3. Remove the defective component(s) as necessary.

4. Note the following points when reassembling the electric box:

a. Make sure all wire connections are clean and tight.

b. Install a new electric box gasket. Coat both sides of the gasket with silicone sealant prior to installation.

c. Coat the outside of all grommets with water-resistant grease.

d. Be certain that none of the wires are pinched between the electric box halves.

e. Apply Loctite 242 to the threads of all electric box fasteners. Tighten all fasteners securely.

ELECTRIC BOX (JL650SC)

On JL650SC models, the electric box contains the following components (**Figure 95**):

a. Ignition coil/igniter assembly.

b. Starter relay.

c. Voltage regulator/rectifier assembly.

d. Fuse

Removal/Installation

The electric box is mounted inside the engine compartment.

1. Unlock the seat.

2. Remove the screws securing both seat base brackets and remove the seat.

3. Remove the rubber plugs covering the engine hood attaching screws. Remove engine hood attaching screws and remove the engine hood.

NOTE
Label all wiring connectors for reference during installation.

4. Disconnect the negative (ground) battery cable from the battery.

5. Remove the bolts holding the electric box halves together. Open the top of the box.

6. Disconnect the spark plug leads from the spark plugs.

7. Remove the grommet plate bolts from the side of the electric box. Pull the stator wires out of the box, one at a time and disconnect them.

8. Remove the bolts holding the electric box to the hull. Remove the electric box.

9. Reinstall the electric box by reversing Steps 1-8, plus the following:

8

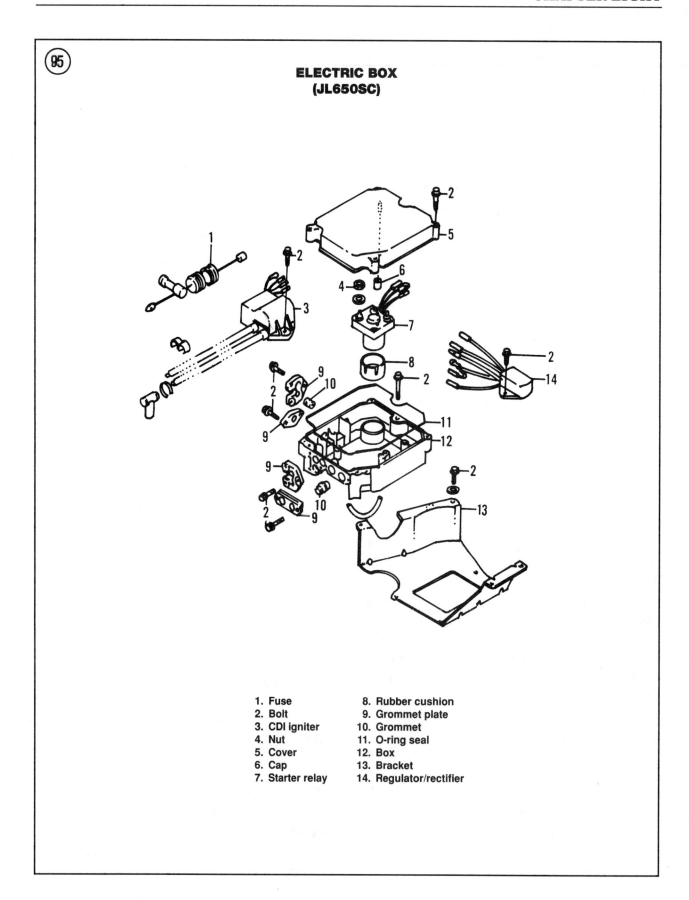

95

**ELECTRIC BOX
(JL650SC)**

1. Fuse
2. Bolt
3. CDI igniter
4. Nut
5. Cover
6. Cap
7. Starter relay
8. Rubber cushion
9. Grommet plate
10. Grommet
11. O-ring seal
12. Box
13. Bracket
14. Regulator/rectifier

a. Make sure all wire connections are clean and tight.

b. Install a new electric box O-ring seal. Lightly coat the O-ring seal with water-resistant grease prior to installation.

c. Coat all grommets with water-resistant grease.

d. Be certain that none of the wires are pinched between the electric box halves.

e. Apply Loctite 242 to the threads of the electric box fasteners. Tighten all fasteners securely.

Disassembly/Reassembly

Refer to **Figure 95** while performing this procedure.

1. Remove the electric box as described in this chapter.

2. Remove the defective component(s) from the electric box as necessary.

3. Note the following points when reassembling the electric box:

a. Make sure all wire connections are clean and tight.

b. Install a new electric box O-ring seal. Lightly coat the O-ring seal with water-resistant grease prior to installation.

c. Coat all grommets with water-resistant grease.

d. Be certain that none of the wires are pinched between the electric box halves.

e. Apply Loctite 242 to the threads of the electric box fasteners. Tighten all fasteners securely.

ELECTRIC BOX (JS750SX)

The electric box (**Figure 96**) on JS750SX models contains the following components:

a. Ignition coil.

b. Igniter.

c. Starter relay.

d. Voltage regulator/rectifier.

e. Water sensor switch.

f. Fuse.

g. Spare fuse.

Removal/Installation

The electric box is mounted at the rear of the engine compartment.

1. Disconnect the negative battery cable from the battery.

2. Disconnect the spark plug leads from the spark plugs.

3. Disconnect the 2 bilge hoses (A, **Figure 97**) from the bilge breather.

4. Disconnect the bypass hoses (B, **Figure 97**).

5. Disconnect the starter motor cable (C, **Figure 97**) and the positive battery cable (D) from the electric box.

6. Remove the 2 bolts securing the connector cover and expose the 3- and 4-pin connectors (**Figure 98**). Separate the 3- and 4-pin connectors.

7. Remove the electric box mounting bolts and remove the box from the hull.

8. Install the electric box by reversing Steps 1-7, plus the following:

a. Apply Loctite 242 to the threads of the electric box mounting bolts and tighten them to 7.8 N•m (69 in.-lb.).

b. Make sure the connector cover O-ring seal is in good condition. Lightly coat the O-ring seal with water-resistant grease prior to installation.

c. Make sure all wire connections are clean and tight.

Disassembly/Reassembly

Refer to **Figure 96** during this procedure.

1. Remove the electric box from the hull as described in this chapter.

8

**ELECTRIC BOX
(JS750SX)**

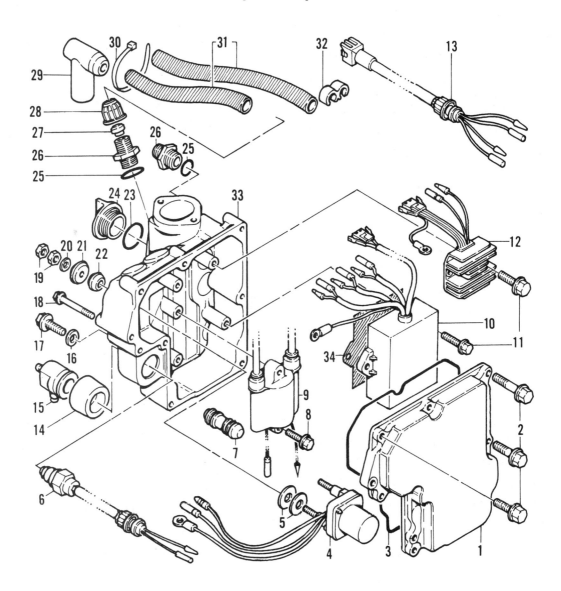

1. Electric box cover	13. Wire harness	24. Oil filler cap
2. Bolt	14. Grommet	25. O-ring
3. O-ring seal	15. Temperature sensor holder	26. Joint
4. Starter relay	16. Washer	27. Grommet
5. Washer	17. Bolt	28. Cap
6. Temperature sensor switch	18. Bolt	29. Spark plug cap
7. Fuse assembly	19. Nuts	30. Tie strap
8. Bolt	20. Washer	31. Tube
9. Ignition coil	21. Spacer	32. Clamp
10. Igniter	22. Grommet	33. Electric box
11. Bolt	23. O-ring	34. Plate
12. Voltage regulator/rectifier		

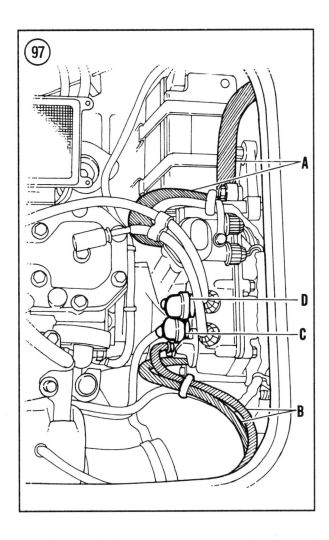

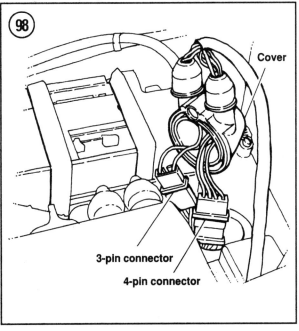

Cover

3-pin connector

4-pin connector

2. Remove the 8 bolts securing the electric box halves together. Separate the electric box halves.

3. Remove and replace the defective component(s) as necessary.

4. Reassemble the electric box by reversing Steps 1-3, plus the following:

    a. Make sure all wire connections are clean and tight.

    b. Install a new electric box O-ring seal. Lightly coat the O-ring seal with water-resistant grease prior to installation.

    c. Coat all grommets with water-resistant grease.

    d. Be certain that none of the wires are pinched between the electric box halves.

    e. Apply Loctite 242 to the threads of all electric box fasteners. Tighten the bolts that secure the electric box halves together to 7.8 N·m (69 in.-lb.).

ELECTRIC BOX (JH750SS, JT750ST, JH750 SUPER SPORT Xi AND JH750XiR)

The electric box on these models contains the following components (**Figure 99**):

    a. Igniter.

    b. Starter relay.

    c. Ignition coil.

    d. Voltage regulator/rectifier assembly.

    e. Water sensor switch.

    f. Fuse (and spare fuse).

Removal/Installation

The electric box is mounted at the rear of the engine compartment.

1. Remove the engine cover/seat assembly.

2. Disconnect the negative battery cable from the battery.

3. Disconnect the spark plug leads from the spark plugs.

8

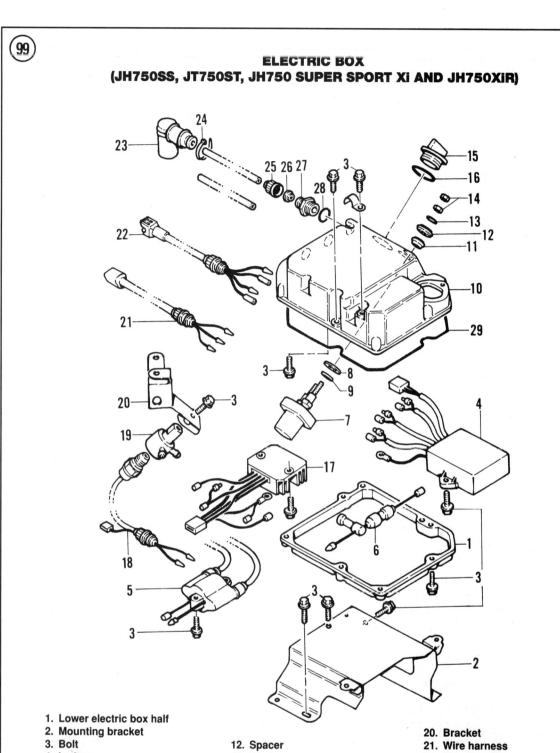

ELECTRIC BOX
(JH750SS, JT750ST, JH750 SUPER SPORT Xi AND JH750XiR)

1. Lower electric box half
2. Mounting bracket
3. Bolt
4. Igniter
5. Ignition coil
6. Fuse
7. Starter relay
8. Washer
9. Washer
10. Upper electric box half
11. Grommet

12. Spacer
13. Washer
14. Nut
15. Oil fill cap
16. O-ring
17. Voltage regulator/
    rectifier assembly
18. Temperatue sensor switch
19. Temperature sensor holder

20. Bracket
21. Wire harness
22. Wire harness
23. Spark plug cap
24. Tie strap
25. Cap
26. Grommet
27. Joint
28. O-ring
29. O-ring seal

4. Disconnect the positive battery cable (A, **Figure 100**) from the electric box.

5. Disconnect the starter motor cable (B, **Figure 100**) from the electric box.

6. Remove the 2 bolts securing the electric box connector cover (C, **Figure 100**). Remove the cover to expose the 2 connectors. Disconnect the 3- and 4-pin connectors (**Figure 98**).

7. Disconnect the temperature sensor wires at their bullet connectors.

8. Disconnect the start/stop switch and L.E.D. unit from the electric box.

9. Remove the electric box mounting bolts and remove the electric box from the hull.

10. Install the electric box by reversing Steps 1-9, plus the following:

a. Apply Loctite 242 to the threads of the electric box mounting bolts and tighten them to 7.8 N•m (69 in.-lb.).

b. Make sure the connector cover O-ring seal is in good condition. Lightly coat the O-ring seal with water-resistant grease prior to installation.

c. Make sure all wire connections are clean and tight.

Disassembly/Reassembly

Refer to **Figure 99** during this procedure.

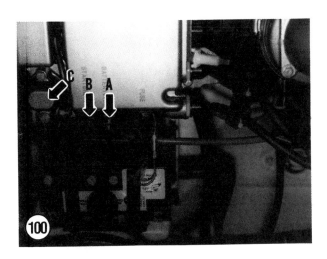

1. Remove the electric box as described in this chapter.

2. Remove the 5 bolts holding the electric box halves together.

3. Separate the electric box halves.

4. Replace the defective component(s).

5. Reassemble the electric box by reversing Steps 1-3, plus the following:

a. Make sure all wire connections are clean and tight.

b. Install a new electric box O-ring seal. Lightly coat the O-ring seal with water-resistant grease prior to installation.

c. Coat all grommets with water-resistant grease.

d. Be certain that none of the wires are pinched between the electric box halves.

e. Apply Loctite 242 to the threads of all electric box fasteners. Tighten the bolts that secure the electric box halves together to 7.8 N•m (69 in.-lb.).

**BILGE PUMP TEST
(JB650 JET MATE)**

If the bilge pump does not function properly, and the impeller area is free of obstructions, perform the following test:

1. Remove the engine hood and rear seat assembly.

2. Under the rear seat area, disconnect the pump electrical wires.

3. Using jumper leads connected to a fully charged 12-volt battery, connect the positive (+) jumper lead to the brown pump wire and the negative (–) lead to the black pump wire.

4. The pump should now run.

5. Disconnect the jumper leads.

6. If the pump does not run in Step 4, and the impeller area is free of obstructions, the pump has failed and must be replaced as described in Chapter Ten.

8

BILGE BLOWER (JB650 JET MATE)

If the bilge blower does not function properly, remove the blower assembly from the hull for testing.

1. Loosen the clamp securing the duct to the blower assembly.

2. Disconnect the blower wires.

3. Remove the blower mounting bolts and remove the blower from the hull.

4. Using suitable jumper leads and a fully charged 12-volt battery, connect the blue blower wire to the positive (+) battery terminal and the black blower wire to the negative (−) battery terminal. The blower should now turn freely.

5. If the blower does not turn in Step 4, the blower motor has failed and must be replaced. If the blower operates normally, first check the blower 5 amp fuse, then check the blower switch and wiring as necessary. Refer to the appropriate wiring diagram at the end of the manual.

TEMPERATURE SENSOR SWITCH

JB650 Jet Mate and all 750 cc models are equipped with a temperature sensor switch. The sensor is designed activate the overheat warning system should the engine temperature exceed 202° F (94° C). On 750 cc models, the overheat warning system also interrupts ignition, limiting engine speed to approximately 3500 rpm. On all models, stop the engine as soon as possible if the warning system is activated.

On JB650 Jet Mate models, the temperature sensor is screwed into a holder assembly which is connected to the bypass cooling hose near the water box muffler. On all other models, the temperature sensor is screwed into a holder assembly and is either mounted on a bracket attached to the electric box or mounted in a recess in the electric box. The bypass hose is connected to fittings on the holder assembly.

Removal/Installation

1. Disconnect the negative battery cable from the battery.

2. Open the electrical box and disconnect the temperature switch wires. Refer to the appropriate wiring diagram at the end of the manual. Unscrew the grommet cap and pull the temperature sensor wires from the electric box.

3. Disconnect the bypass hose from the fittings on the temperature switch holder.

4. Remove the temperature switch and holder from its mounting bracket or from the electric box.

5. Unscrew the sensor from the holder assembly.

6. Install the temperature sensor by reversing Steps 1-5.

Testing

1. Remove the temperature sensor switch as described in this chapter.

2. Connect an ohmmeter between the temperature sensor wires.

3. Suspend the temperature sensor and a suitable thermometer in a container of water.

4. Slowly heat the water while noting the thermometer and ohmmeter.

   a. With the water temperature under 203° F (95° C), the ohmmeter should indicate infinity (switch open).

   b. When the water temperature reaches approximately 203° F (95° C), the ohmmeter should indicate less than 0.5 ohm (switch closed).

5. Next, allow the water to cool while noting the thermometer and ohmmeter. When the water temperature falls to approximately 190° F (88° C), the ohmmeter should again indicate infinity (switch open).

6. Replace the temperature switch if it does not perform as specified.

STOP AND START SWITCHES

Removal/Installation
(JB650 Jet Mate)

Refer to the appropriate wiring diagram at the end of the manual.

1. Disconnect the negative battery cable from the battery.

2. Remove the bolts holding the electric box halves together. Open the electric box and disconnect the start/stop switch wires.

3. Remove the 2 screws securing the grommet cap to the electric box and pull the wires and grommet out of the box.

4. Remove the control stick as described in Chapter Eleven. Disassemble the control stick grip section and remove the defective switch.

5. Install the switches by reversing the removal steps. Note that the stop switch has while and black wires.

Removal/Installation
(JL650SC)

Refer to the appropriate wiring diagram at the end of the manual.

1. Unlock the seat.

2. Remove the screws securing both seat base brackets and remove the seat.

3. Remove the rubber plugs covering the engine hood attaching screws. Remove engine hood attaching screws and remove the engine hood.

4. Disconnect the negative (ground) battery cable from the battery.

5. Remove the bolts holding the electric box halves together. Open the top of the box.

6. Disconnect the start/stop switch wires.

7. Remove the 2 bolts securing the grommet plate to the electric box. Remove the plate and pull the switch wires and grommet from the electric box.

8. Remove the steering column and steering frame covers. See Chapter Eleven.

9. Disconnect the throttle cable from the carburetor. Disconnect the throttle cable joint and the start/stop switch wire connector in the steering column. See Chapter Eleven.

10. Remove the steering wheel assembly as described in Chapter Eleven. Separate the steering wheel cover from the wheel and remove the switches.

11. Install the switches by reversing Steps 1-10, plus the following:

   a. Apply Loctite 242 to the threads of all steering system and electric box fasteners.

   b. Make sure all wiring is correctly routed. Refer to the appropriate wiring diagram and reconnect the start/stop switch.

   c. Adjust the throttle cable as described in Chapter Three.

Removal/Installation
(JS440SX, JS550SX, JF650X-2, JS650SX, JF650TS and All 750 cc Models)

The start/stop switches are contained in one case mounted on the handlebar assembly. Refer to the appropriate wiring diagram at the end of the manual.

1. Disconnect the start/stop switch 4-pin connector.

2. Remove the handlebar pad or steering cover.

3. Carefully pull the switch wires up through the steering holder.

4. Unscrew the switch case mounting screws and remove the switch case from the handlebar assembly.

5. Install the switches by reversing the removal procedure, plus the following:

   a. When installing the switch case, be sure to align the case peg with the hole in the handlebar and secure the switch leads with a cable tie.

   b. Make sure to route the switch wiring exactly as it was prior to removal. Make sure

8

the wiring does not interfere with the throttle or steering cables when turning.

Start/Stop Switch Testing

Refer to the appropriate wiring diagram at the end of the manual during this procedure.

1. Disconnect the start switch wires. With an ohmmeter set on the R × 1 scale, connect the meter between the start switch wires.

2. Push the starter interlock (A, **Figure 101**) or safety switch to the right.

3. Depress the start button (B, **Figure 101**), note the ohmmeter reading then release the button.

    a. With the button pushed, the meter should indicate very low resistance (zero ohm).

    b. When the button released, the meter should indicate infinity.

4. Test the starter interlock switch (A, **Figure 101**) as follows:

    a. Push the starter interlock switch (A, **Figure 101**) to the left.

    b. Depress the starter button, note the ohmmeter reading then release the button.

    c. The ohmmeter should indicate infinity with the button pushed or released.

5. Reconnect the start switch connector(s).

6. Disconnect the stop switch connector(s).

7. Connect the ohmmeter between the stop switch wires.

8. Push the starter interlock (A, **Figure 101**) to the right.

9. While noting the ohmmeter, push, then release the stop button.

    a. The ohmmeter should indicate 0 ohm when the button is pushed.

    b. The ohmmeter should read infinity when the button is released.

10. Remove the ohmmeter and reconnect all circuits.

11. Replace the start/stop switch assembly if it does not perform as specified.

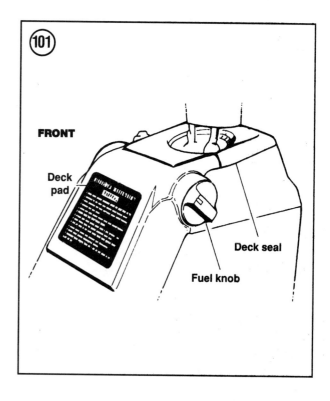

Table 1 ELECTRICAL SPECIFICATIONS

Recommended battery	
JB650 Jet Mate	12-volt 50 amp hour
JS440SX	12-volt 16 amp hour
All other models	12-volt 19 amp hour
Starter motor	
Standard brush length	12 mm (15/32 in.)
JS440SX	17 mm (0.67 in.)
JS550SX	13 mm (0.51 in.)
All other models	12.5 mm (0.49 in.)
Wear limit	
JS440SX	13 mm (0.51 in.)
JS550SX	9 mm (0.35 in.)
All other models	6.5 mm (0.26 in.)
Standard commutator diameter	
JS440SX	N/A
JS550SX	30 mm (1.18 in.)
All other models	28 mm (1.10 in.)
Wear limit	
JS440SX	N/A
JS550SX	29 mm (1.14 in.)
All other models	27 mm (1.06 in.)

Table 2 BATTERY STATE OF CHARGE

Specific gravity	State of charge
1.110-1.130	Discharged
1.140-1.160	Nearly discharged
1.170-1.190	1/4 charged
1.200-1.220	1/2 charged
1.230-1.250	3/4 charged
1.260-1.280	Fully charged

8

Table 3 FLYWHEEL NUT OR BOLT TIGHTENING TORQUE

	N·m	ft.-lb.
JS440SX	170	125
JS550SX	165	122
650 cc models	98	72
750 cc models	125	92

Chapter Nine

Oil Injection System

A mechanical oil injection system using a crankshaft driven injection pump and external oil tank is used on all 650 and 750 cc models (except JH750XiR). The pump draws oil from the oil tank and supplies it under pressure to a nozzle mounted in the intake manifold. On JH750 Super Sport Xi models (twin carburetors), the injection pump delivers oil to 2 nozzles mounted in the intake manifold. The oil is then sprayed into the incoming air/fuel mixture.

The different oil injection systems can be identified as follow:

a. **Figure 1**: JF650X-2.
b. **Figure 2**: JS650SX.
c. **Figure 3**: JF650TS.
d. **Figure 4**: JL650SC.
e. **Figure 5**: JB650 Jet Mate.
f. **Figure 6**: JS750SX.

g. **Figure 7**: JH750SS, JH750 Super Sport Xi and JT750ST.

This chapter covers complete oil injection system service.

OIL PUMP SERVICE

Oil Pump Bleeding

All air must be purged (bled) from the oil injection system if an oil line is disconnected, a leak develops or air enters the system for any reason.

> *NOTE*
> *A temporary cooling system must be used when performing this procedure. Refer to* **On Shore Cooling** *in Chapter Three.*

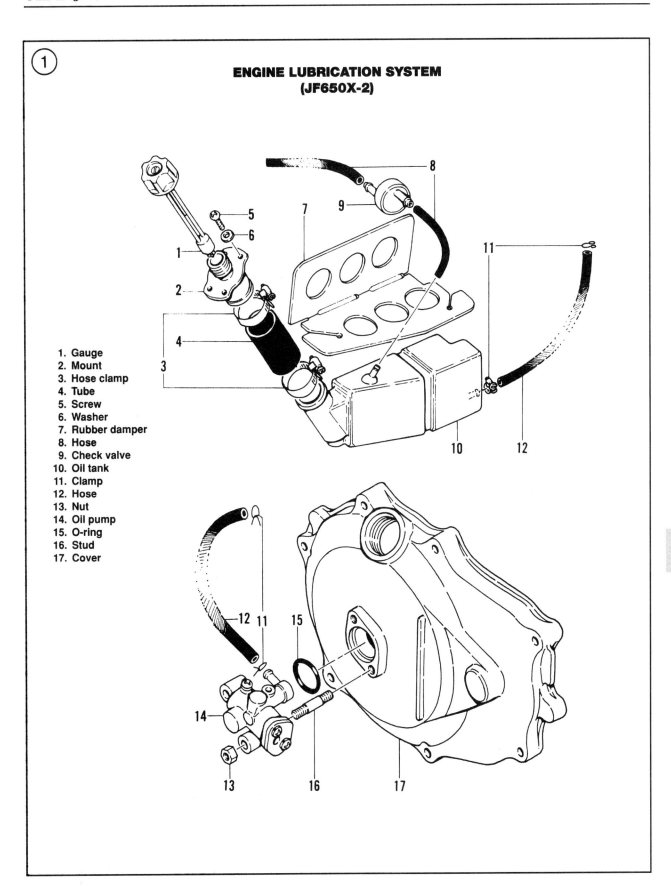

1
ENGINE LUBRICATION SYSTEM
(JF650X-2)

1. Gauge
2. Mount
3. Hose clamp
4. Tube
5. Screw
6. Washer
7. Rubber damper
8. Hose
9. Check valve
10. Oil tank
11. Clamp
12. Hose
13. Nut
14. Oil pump
15. O-ring
16. Stud
17. Cover

9

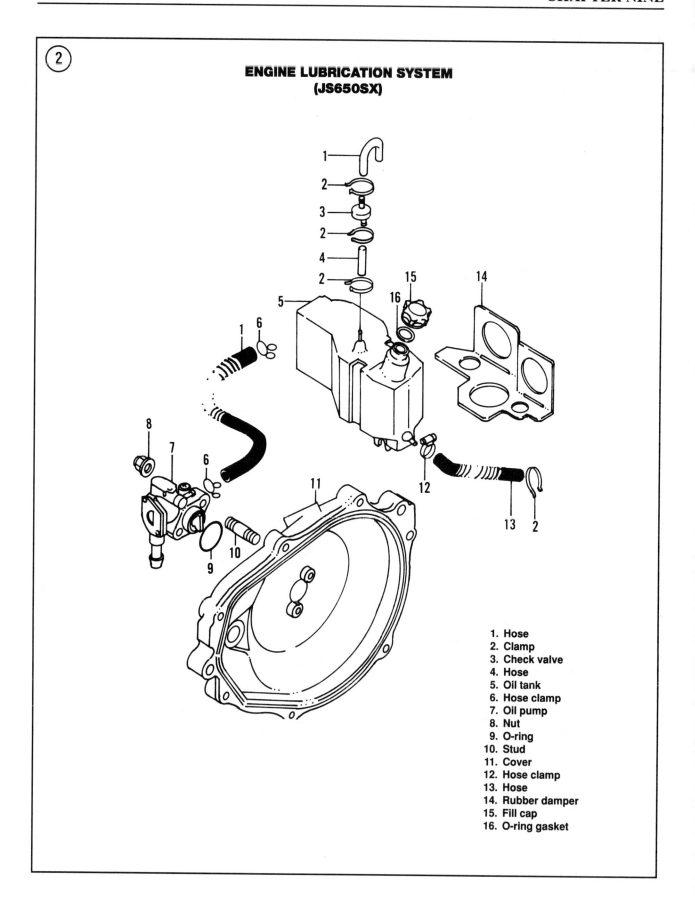

② **ENGINE LUBRICATION SYSTEM
(JS650SX)**

1. Hose
2. Clamp
3. Check valve
4. Hose
5. Oil tank
6. Hose clamp
7. Oil pump
8. Nut
9. O-ring
10. Stud
11. Cover
12. Hose clamp
13. Hose
14. Rubber damper
15. Fill cap
16. O-ring gasket

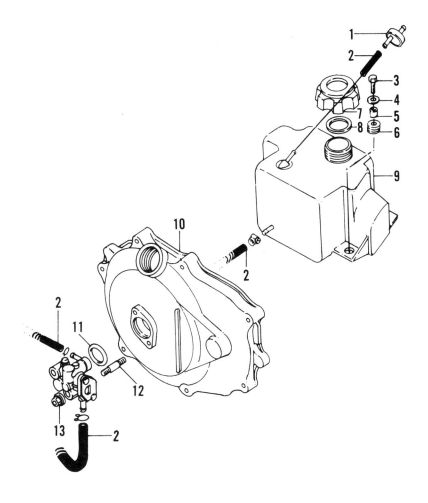

③ **ENGINE LUBRICATION SYSTEM
(JF650TS)**

1. Check valve
2. Hose
3. Bolt
4. Washer
5. Collar
6. Rubber grommet
7. Fill cap
8. O-ring
9. Oil tank
10. Cover
11. O-ring
12. Stud
13. Oil pump and mounting nut

9

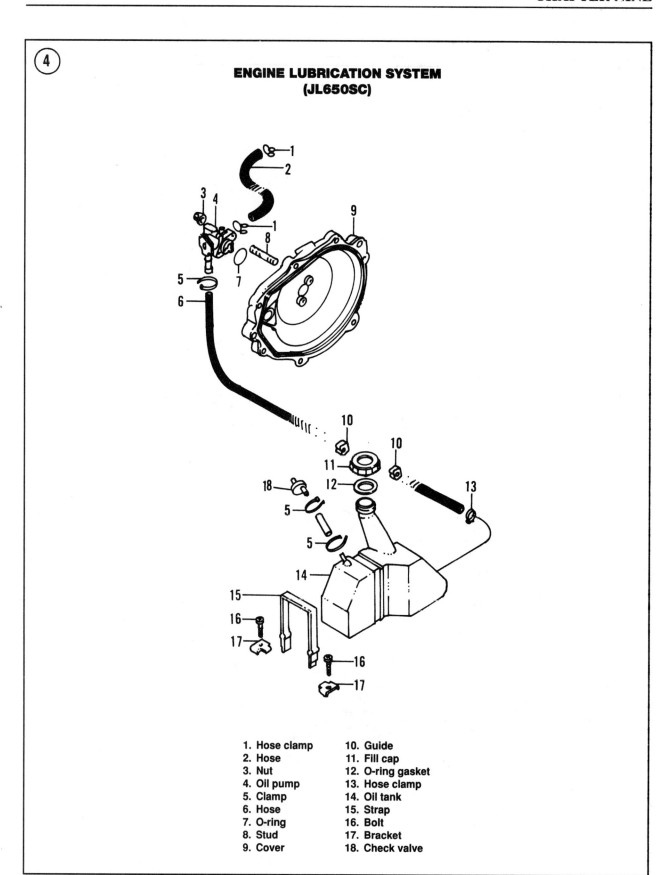

ENGINE LUBRICATION SYSTEM
(JL650SC)

1. Hose clamp
2. Hose
3. Nut
4. Oil pump
5. Clamp
6. Hose
7. O-ring
8. Stud
9. Cover
10. Guide
11. Fill cap
12. O-ring gasket
13. Hose clamp
14. Oil tank
15. Strap
16. Bolt
17. Bracket
18. Check valve

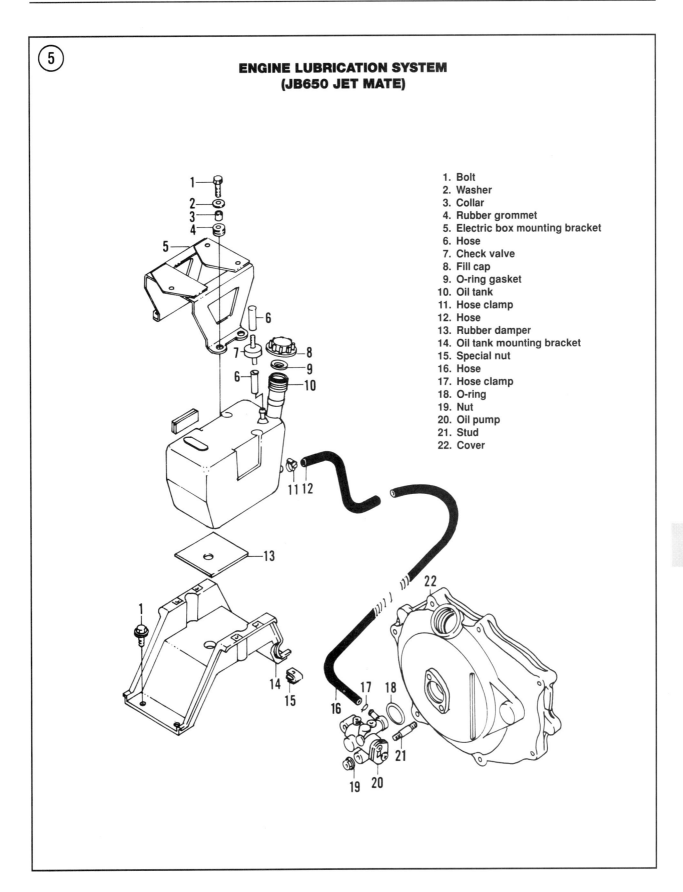

⑤

**ENGINE LUBRICATION SYSTEM
(JB650 JET MATE)**

1. Bolt
2. Washer
3. Collar
4. Rubber grommet
5. Electric box mounting bracket
6. Hose
7. Check valve
8. Fill cap
9. O-ring gasket
10. Oil tank
11. Hose clamp
12. Hose
13. Rubber damper
14. Oil tank mounting bracket
15. Special nut
16. Hose
17. Hose clamp
18. O-ring
19. Nut
20. Oil pump
21. Stud
22. Cover

9

⑥

ENGINE LUBRICATION SYSTEM
(JS750SX)

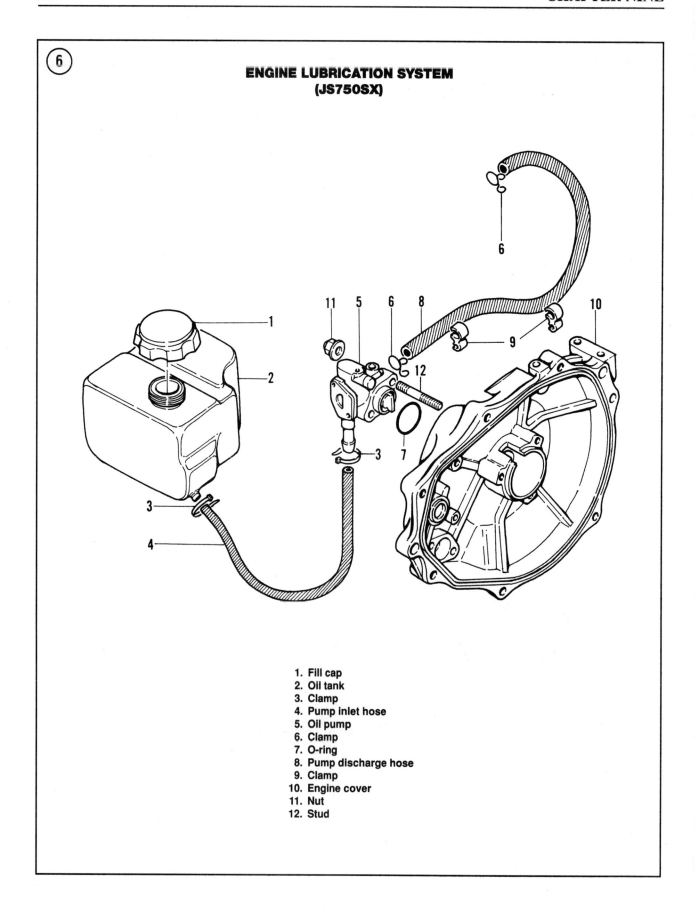

1. Fill cap
2. Oil tank
3. Clamp
4. Pump inlet hose
5. Oil pump
6. Clamp
7. O-ring
8. Pump discharge hose
9. Clamp
10. Engine cover
11. Nut
12. Stud

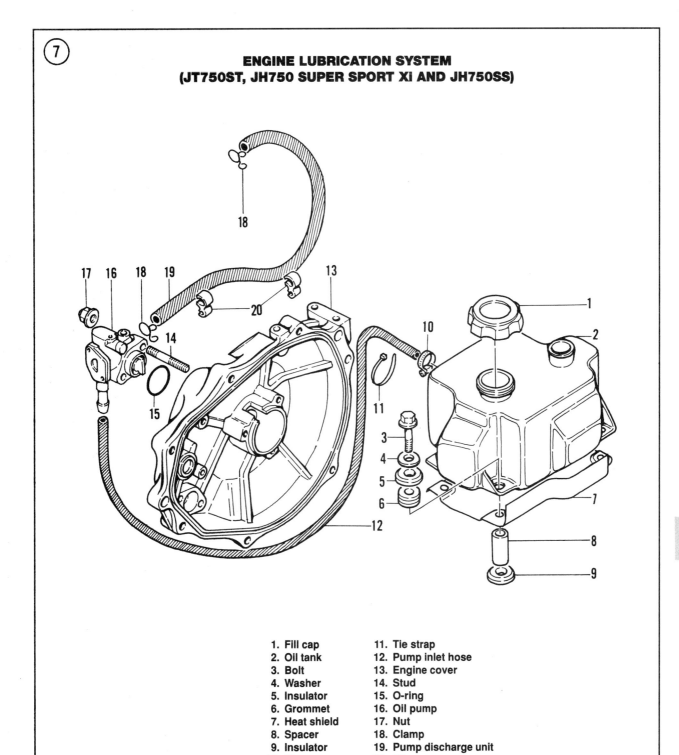

**ENGINE LUBRICATION SYSTEM
(JT750ST, JH750 SUPER SPORT Xi AND JH750SS)**

1. Fill cap	11. Tie strap
2. Oil tank	12. Pump inlet hose
3. Bolt	13. Engine cover
4. Washer	14. Stud
5. Insulator	15. O-ring
6. Grommet	16. Oil pump
7. Heat shield	17. Nut
8. Spacer	18. Clamp
9. Insulator	19. Pump discharge unit
10. Clamp	20. Clamp

9

CAUTION
Add a 50:1 fuel oil mixture to the fuel tank for engine operation during the bleeding procedure. Refer to Chapter Three.

1. Make sure the oil tank contains a sufficient quantity of a recommended oil. See Chapter Three.

2. Place a shop towel or small pan under the oil pump to catch spilled oil.

3. Open the oil pump bleed screw 3-5 turns (counterclockwise). See A, **Figure 8**). When air-free flows from the bleed screw, tighten the bleed screw securely.

4. Start the engine, then turn on the auxiliary water supply and allow the engine to idle. Observe the transparent oil pump discharge hose (B, **Figure 8**) for air bubbles. Continue to idle the engine until no more bubbles are noted.

5. After all air bubbles have disappeared, turn off the water supply, then stop the engine.

6. Drain or siphon the 50:1 fuel-oil mixture from the fuel tank and add straight gasoline.

Oil Pump Delivery Rate Test

NOTE
*A temporary cooling system must be used when performing this procedure. Refer to **On Shore Cooling** in Chapter Three.*

CAUTION
Add a 50:1 fuel-oil mixture to the fuel tank for engine operation during the bleeding procedure. Refer to Chapter Three.

1. Make sure the oil tank contains a sufficient quantity of a recommended oil. See Chapter Three.

2. Place a towel or small pan under the oil pump to catch spilled oil.

3. Install a tachometer according to its manufacturer's instructions.

4. Disconnect the oil pump discharge hose (B, **Figure 8**) from the pump. Place the hose into a suitable measuring container.

5. Start the engine and run at 3000 rpm for exactly 2 minutes, then stop the engine.

6. The oil pump should discharge 5.9-7.2 mL ((0.20-0.24 fl. oz.) in 2 minutes at 3000 rpm.

7. If the discharge rate is not as specified, first check the injection system for plugging, restrictions, leakage or contamination. If the tank and oil hoses are in acceptable condition, replace the pump assembly.

8. Bleed the injection system as described in this chapter.

OIL TANK

Removal/Installation (JF650X-2)

Refer to **Figure 1** during this procedure.

1. Remove the oil level gauge and O-ring from the oil tank.

2. Disconnect the vent hose from the oil tank.

3. Disconnect the oil pump inlet hose and drain the tank.

4. Loosen the oil tank filler tube clamp.

5. Disconnect the oil tank rubber strap and remove the tank.

6. Install the tank by reversing Steps 1-5. Bleed the injection system as described in this chapter.

Removal/Installation (JS650SX)

Refer to **Figure 2** during this procedure.

1. Disconnect the vent hose from the oil tank.

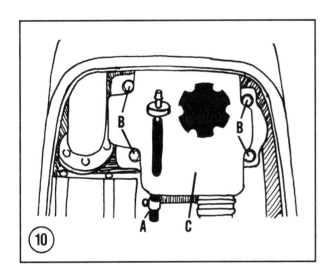

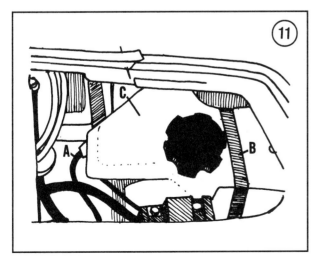

2. Disconnect the oil pump inlet hose (**Figure 9**) from the tank. Allow the oil tank to drain into a suitable container.

3. Disconnect the oil tank rubber strap and remove the tank.

4. Install the tank by reversing Steps 1-3. Bleed the injection system as described in this chapter.

Removal/Installation (JF650TS)

Refer to **Figure 3** during this procedure.

1. Disconnect the vent hose from the oil tank.

2. Disconnect the oil pump inlet hose (A, **Figure 10**) from the oil tank. Allow the oil in the tank to drain into a suitable container.

3. Remove the bolts (B, **Figure 10**) securing the tank to the hull.

4. Remove the oil tank (C, **Figure 10**) from the hull.

5. Install the tank by reversing Steps 1-4. Bleed the injection system as described in this chapter.

Removal/Installation (JL650SC)

Refer to **Figure 4** during this procedure.

1. Unlock the seat.

2. Remove the screws securing both seat base brackets and remove the seat.

3. Remove the rubber plugs covering the engine cover screws. Then, remove the screws and engine cover.

4. Disconnect the vent hose from the oil tank.

5. Disconnect the oil pump inlet hose (A, **Figure 11**) from the tank. Allow the tank to drain into a suitable container.

6. Disconnect the oil tank rubber strap (B, **Figure 11**) and remove the tank (C).

7. Install the tank by reversing Steps 1-6. Bleed the injection system as described in this chapter.

9

Removal/Installation
(JB650 Jet Mate)

Refer to **Figure 5** for this procedure.

1. Remove the rear seat assembly.

2. Disconnect the vent hose from the oil tank.

3. Disconnect the oil pump inlet hose (A, **Figure 12**) from the tank. Allow the tank to drain into a suitable container.

4. Remove the bolts (B, **Figure 12**) holding the electric box to the hull.

5. Without disconnecting any wires, move the electric box and mounting bracket (C, **Figure 12**) out of the way.

6. Remove the oil tank (D, **Figure 12**).

7. Install the tank by reversing Steps 1-6. Bleed the injection system as described in this chapter.

Removal/Installation
(JS750SX)

Refer to **Figure 6** during this procedure.

1. Disconnect the oil pump inlet hose from the oil tank and allow the tank to drain into a suitable container.

2. Remove the rubber strap securing the tank to the hull. Remove the tank.

3. Install the tank by reversing the removal procedure. Make sure the tank rubber damper is in position. Bleed the injection system as described in this chapter.

Removal/Installation
(JT750ST, JH750 Super Sport Xi and JH750SS)

Refer to **Figure 7** during this procedure.

1. Loosen the clamp and remove the oil level sensor from the oil tank (**Figure 13**).

2. Disconnect the pump inlet hose (A, **Figure 14**) from the oil tank. Allow the tank to drain into a suitable container.

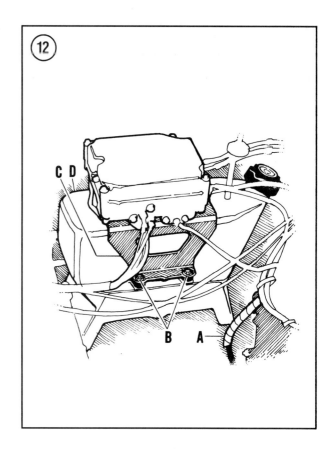

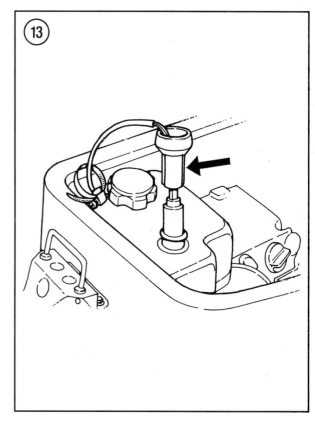

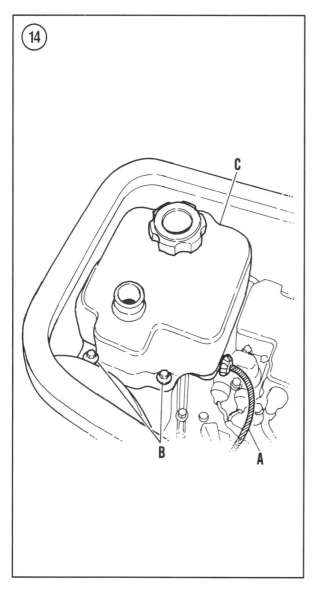

3. Remove the bolts (B, **Figure 14**) holding the tank in the hull. Remove the tank (C, **Figure 14**) from the hull.

4. Install the oil tank by reversing Steps 1-3. Make sure the heat shield (7, **Figure 7**) is in position on the water box muffler. Bleed the oil injection system as described in this chapter.

OIL LEVEL SENSOR

On models equipped with an oil level gauge, test the oil level sensor as follows:

1. Remove the clamp and remove the level sensor from the oil tank (**Figure 13**).

2. Disconnect the level sensor 2-pin connector.

3. Set an ohmmeter on the R × 1 scale.

4. Connect the ohmmeter between the level sensor wires.

   a. With the sensor held upright, the ohmmeter should indicate 0 ohm.

   b. With the sensor inverted, the ohmmeter should indicate infinity.

5. Replace the oil level sensor if it does not perform as specified.

9

OIL TANK CHECK VALVE

A check valve is connected to the oil tank vent hose (**Figure 15**, typical). The 1-way check valve prevents oil from spilling out the vent hose during rough maneuvers or if the watercraft becomes capsized.

The arrow on the check valve must always face toward the oil tank.

Test the check valve by blowing through it from both ends. Air should pass through the valve in one direction only. If air passes through the valve in both directions, or not at all, replace the check valve.

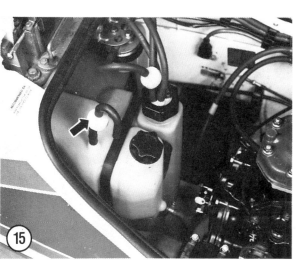

OIL PUMP

Removal/Installation

Refer to **Figures 1-7** as necessary for this procedure.

1. Disconnect the inlet and discharge hoses from the oil pump. Plug the hoses to prevent leakage or contamination.

2. Remove the nuts (A, **Figure 16**) securing the oil pump to the flywheel cover. Remove the oil pump (B, **Figure 16**).

3. Check the O-ring on the back of the oil pump. Replace it if worn or damaged in any way.

4. Install the pump by reversing the removal steps, plus the following:

a. Align the oil pump shaft (**Figure 17**) with the slot in the flywheel bolt (**Figure 18**).

b. Tighten the oil pump mounting nuts securely.

c. Make sure the oil pump fittings are clean. Wipe them off with a clean towel prior to reconnecting the oil hoses.

d. Bleed the injection system as described in this chapter.

NOTE
*The notch on the flywheel bolt (**Figure 19**) engages the oil pump shaft. If the notch appears worn or damaged in any way, replace the bolt. Refer to Chapter Eight and remove the flywheel bolt as described under **Flywheel Removal/Installation**.*

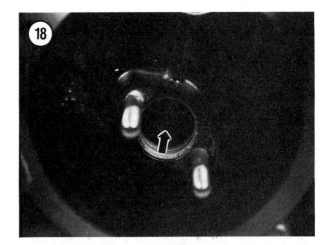

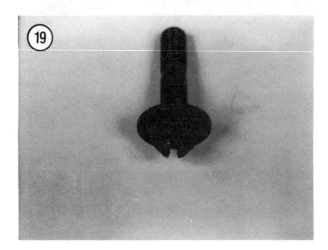

Chapter Ten

Bilge System

Despite the fact that the Jet Ski is designed to prevent water from entering the engine compartment, some will always manage to get in. The purpose of the bilge system is to remove this unwanted water.

VACUUM-TYPE BILGE SYSTEM

The vacuum-type bilge systems for the various models are identified as follows:

   a. **Figure 1**: JS440SX.

   b. **Figure 2**: JS550SX.

   c. **Figure 3**: JF650X-2.

   d. **Figure 4**: JS650SX.

   e. **Figure 5**: JF650TS.

   f. **Figure 6**: JL650SC.

   g. **Figure 7**: 750 cc models.

The vacuum-type bilge system has no moving parts. It consists of a rubber hose connected to the jet pump outlet, a metal tube through the hull, a rubber hose to a plastic breather fitting (**Figure 8**, typical) and another rubber hose running to the bilge pickup filter (**Figure 9**, typical) in the engine compartment.

When the jet pump is operating, water is forced out of the pump outlet at high speed, creating a low pressure area at the pump outlet. Mounted just in front of the steering nozzle is the bilge suction fitting, which draws water out of

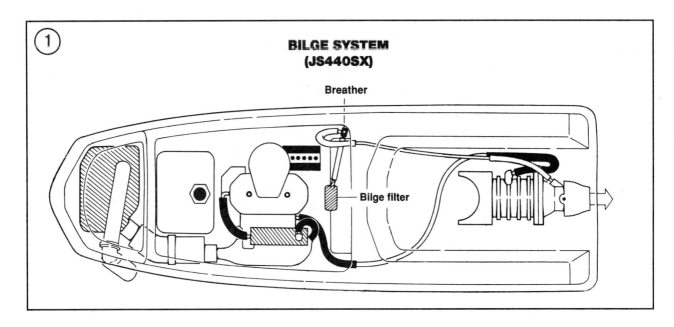

① **BILGE SYSTEM (JS440SX)**

Breather

Bilge filter

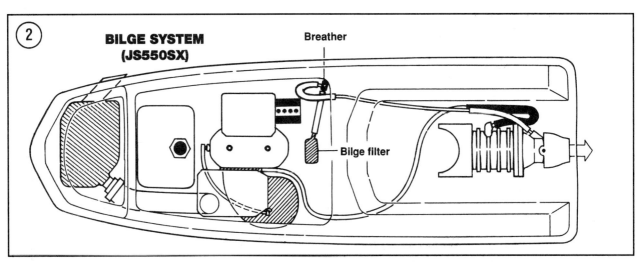

② **BILGE SYSTEM (JS550SX)**

Breather

Bilge filter

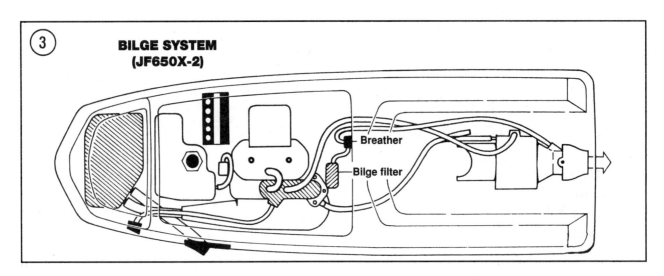

③ **BILGE SYSTEM (JF650X-2)**

Breather

Bilge filter

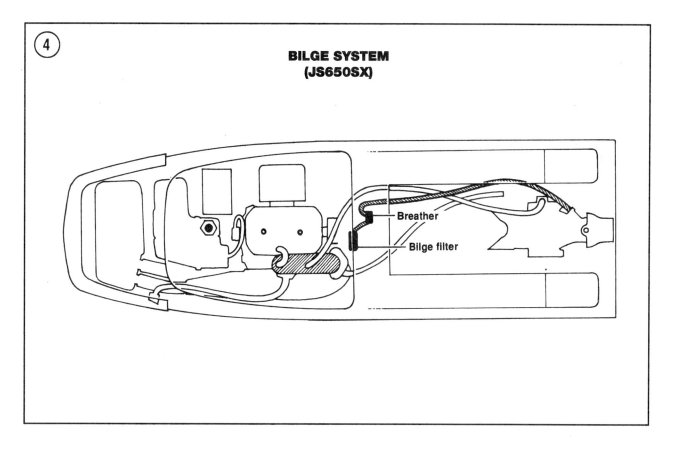

**BILGE SYSTEM
(JS650SX)**

Breather

Bilge filter

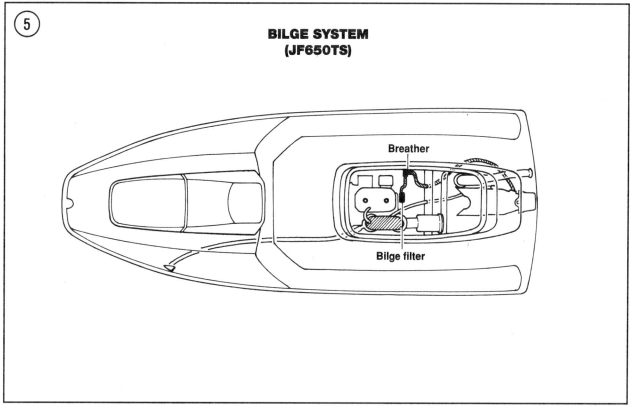

**BILGE SYSTEM
(JF650TS)**

Breather

Bilge filter

10

the engine compartment through the bilge filter, through the breather fitting and out the jet pump.

Since the bilge system depends on a fast flow of water through the jet pump to cause suction, the bilge system does not work when the engine is running at idle speed. Water is emptied from the engine compartment when the Jet Ski is operated at a speed sufficient to create a suitable vacuum. The purpose of the plastic breather fitting is to prevent water from siphoning back into the boat when the engine is not running. In the top of the fitting is a small vent hole that allows air to enter the bilge hoses to break any possible siphoning effect. However, the hole is not large enough to interfere with the normal operation of the bilge system. The vent hole must be kept clear, but it must not be enlarged or the bilge system will not function properly.

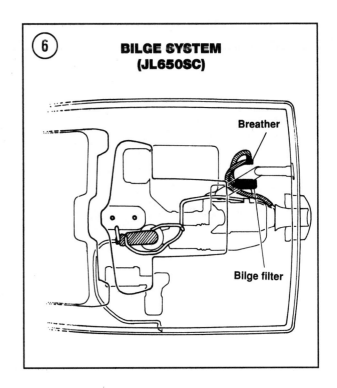

⑥ **BILGE SYSTEM (JL650SC)**

Breather

Bilge filter

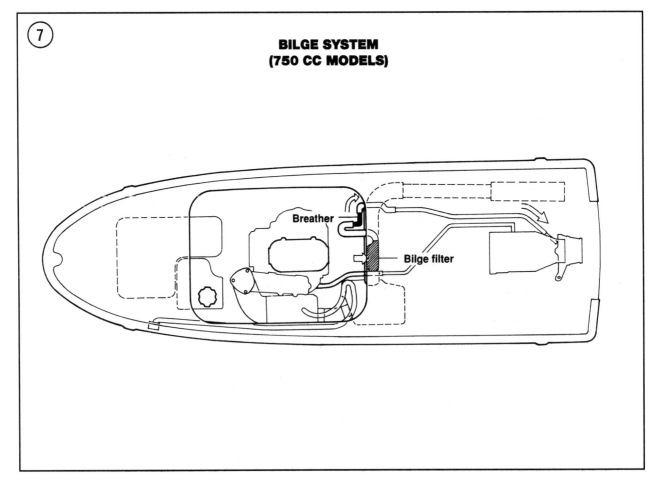

⑦ **BILGE SYSTEM (750 CC MODELS)**

Breather

Bilge filter

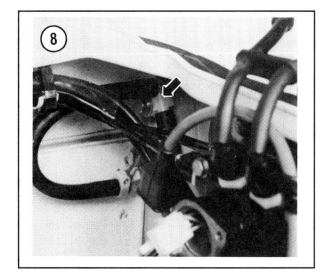

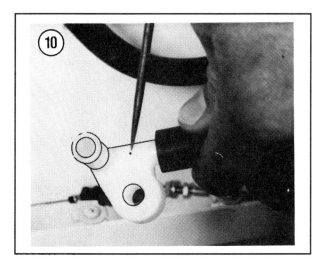

Hose

Clamp

Bilge pickup filter

Breather
Removal/Inspection/Installation

Locate the breather in the engine compartment (**Figures 1-7**). Disconnect the hoses from the breather and remove it. Make sure the small vent hole on top of the breather is clean (**Figure 10**, typical). Install the breather by reversing the removal procedure.

Bilge Filter
Removal/Installation

Locate the bilge filter in the engine compartment (**Figures 1-7**). Disconnect the hose from the filter and remove it. Install the filter by reversing the removal procedure.

Bilge System Cleaning

The bilge system can become plugged during normal operation. The system should be flushed every 25 hours of operation or whenever a restriction is suspected. A garden hose and a 3/8 in. hose adapter (**Figure 11**) is necessary to flush the bilge system.

10

1. Locate the breather (**Figures 1-7**) in the engine compartment. Disconnect the 2 bilge hoses from the breather.

2. Connect the garden hose and adapter to the bilge hose leading to the pump outlet.

CAUTION
Water will flow into the engine compartment during this procedure. Do not allow a large amount of water to accumulate in the engine compartment. If necessary, roll the watercraft onto its exhaust side to drain the water. Refer to Chapter Three. Do not roll the watercraft toward the side opposite the exhaust system or water from the exhaust can enter the engine.

3. Turn on the water and allow it to run for about 1 minute. Turn the water off and clean the engine compartment.

4. Next, connect the hose adapter to the bilge hose leading to the filter and repeat Step 3.

5. Disconnect the garden hose and reconnect the bilge hoses to the breather.

ELECTRIC BILGE SYSTEM (JB650 JET MATE)

An electric bilge system (**Figure 12**) is used on Jet Mate models. This system used an electric motor/pump assembly to remove the water from the engine compartment. The bilge pump is controlled by a switch on the control panel. The system consists of an electric motor/pump assembly and a length of rubber hose connected from the motor/pump discharge fitting to the fitting on the hull. Water is pumped from the engine compartment and exits through an opening in the hull.

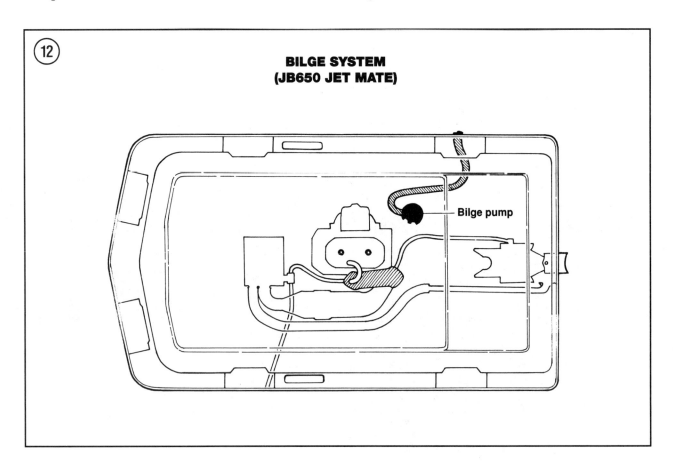

(12)

BILGE SYSTEM (JB650 JET MATE)

Bilge pump

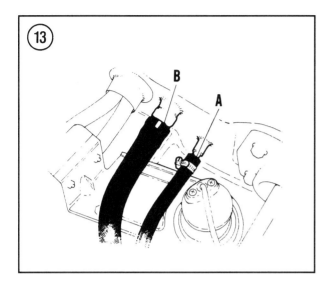

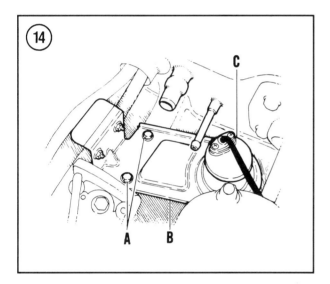

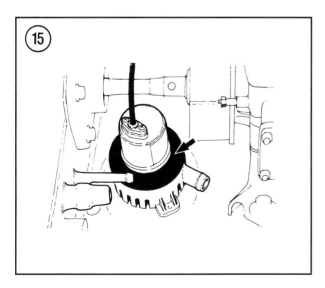

Bilge Pump
Removal/Installation

1. Remove the engine hood and rear seat assembly.

2. Disconnect the inlet cooling hose (A, **Figure 13**) and the bilge hose (B) from the fittings on the hull. Move the hoses out of the way.

3. Under the rear seat area, disconnect the pump electrical wires. Carefully pull the wires through the interconnecting pipe located between the two compartments.

4. Remove the bolts (A, **Figure 14**) securing the bilge pump bracket in the hull. Move the bracket (B, **Figure 14**) and attached fuel pump (C) out of the way.

5. Remove the bilge pump and rubber damper from the hull.

6. Install the bilge pump assembly by reversing Steps 1-5, plus the following:

    a. Be sure to install the rubber damper (**Figure 15**) on top of the bilge pump prior to installing the bracket.

    b. Install the bilge hose with the paint markings facing up.

Bilge System Cleaning

The bilge system can become plugged during operation and should be flushed every 25 hours of operation, or whenever a restriction is suspected. A garden hose with a 3/4 in. inside diameter is necessary to flush the system.

1. Disconnect the bilge hose from the fitting on the hull and from the bilge pump.

2. Run freshwater through the hose and thoroughly clear out any obstructions.

3. Connect the 3/4 in. hose to the bilge hose fitting on the hull.

4. Turn on the water and flush the bilge line within the hull for several minutes.

5. Turn off the water and disconnect the garden hose.

10

6. Inspect the bilge hose for cracks or other damage. Replace the hose as necessary.

7. If the bilge pump is suspected of not operating properly, test it as follows:

    a. Remove the bilge pump as described in this chapter.

    b. Remove the screws (A, **Figure 16**) securing the pump cover. Remove the cover (B, **Figure 16**).

    c. Visually inspect the pump impeller blades for wear or damage. Make sure the impeller rotates freely. If the impeller is damaged or does not turn, replace the pump assembly.

    d. Install the pump cover and screws. Tighten the screws evenly and securely, but do not overtighten.

    e. Install the pump and connect the bilge hose with the paint markings facing up.

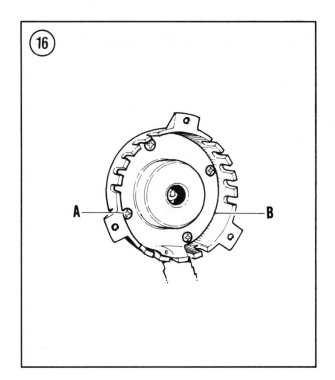

Chapter Eleven

Steering and Hull Repair

STEERING ASSEMBLY
(JS440SX, JS550SX AND JS650SX)

Refer to **Figures 1-2** when performing procedures in this section. **Tables 1-8** are located at the end of this chapter.

Handle Pole Removal

1. Disconnect the negative battery cable from the battery.

2. Steering, throttle and electric cable removal is easier if the water box muffler is removed. Refer to Chapter Seven for exhaust system service.

3. Lock the handle pole in the upright position (**Figure 3**).

4. Pull the fuel tank vent hose up through the cable boot or pull it down out of the handle pole and out of the rubber boot. The grommet in the handle pole is secured with sealant and will probably come out with the hose.

5. Slide the steering cable connector's spring loaded sleeve down and pull the connector free of the ball (**Figure 4**).

6. Remove the 2 bolts holding the steering cable bracket and remove the bracket and throttle cable holder (**Figure 5**).

7. Pull the steering cable down out of the handle pole and through the rubber boot.

8. Disconnect the throttle cable from the carburetor, or at the throttle lever, and pull it out of the handle pole.

9. Spray the start and stop switch grommet caps (and RPM limiter cap on JS550SX) at the elec-

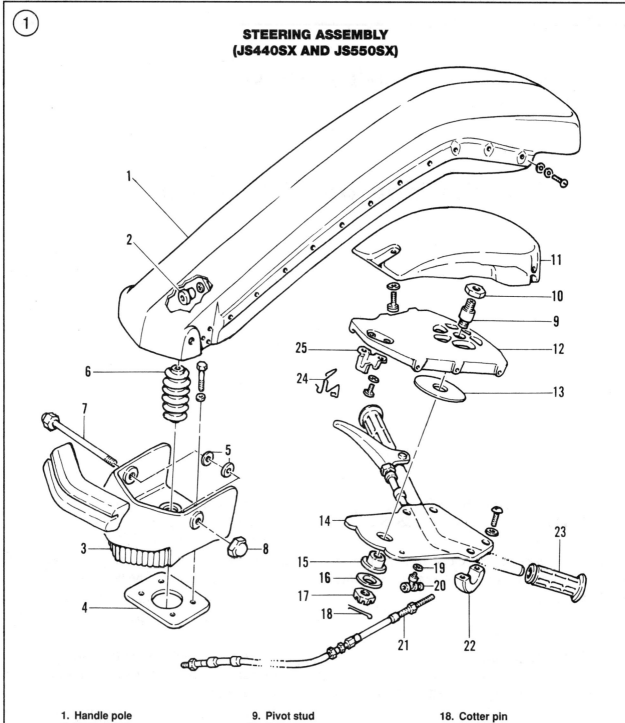

**STEERING ASSEMBLY
(JS440SX AND JS550SX)**

1. Handle pole
2. Fuel vent line
   grommet
3. Handle pole bracket
4. Bracket anchor plate
5. Plastic washers
6. Boot
7. Bolt
8. Nut

9. Pivot stud
10. Nut
11. Float
12. Steering support plate
13. Plastic disc
14. Steering plate
15. Bushing
16. Washer
17. Castellated nut

18. Cotter pin
19. Lockwasher
20. Ball joint
21. Steering cable
22. Handlebar clamp
23. handlebar grip
24. Throttle cable holder
25. Steering cable bracket

② STEERING
(JS650SX)

1. Handle pole pad
2. Rivet
3. Bracket
4. Handle pole
5. Bolt
6. Screw
7. Washer
8. Bracket
9. Screw
10. Rivet
11. Float
12. Boot
13. Nut
14. Washer
15. Pole stopper damper
16. Pivot shaft bracket
17. Pivot shaft
18. Rubber
19. Brace
20. Float
21. Screw
22. Washer
23. Pivot stud
24. Bushing
25. Screw
26. Cover
27. Handlebar plate
28. Screw
29. Ball joint
30. Bushing
31. Washer
32. Nut
33. Circlip
34. Clamp
35. Clamp washer
36. Washer
37. Screw
38. Handlebar
39. Grip
40. Cover
41. Screw
42. Clamp

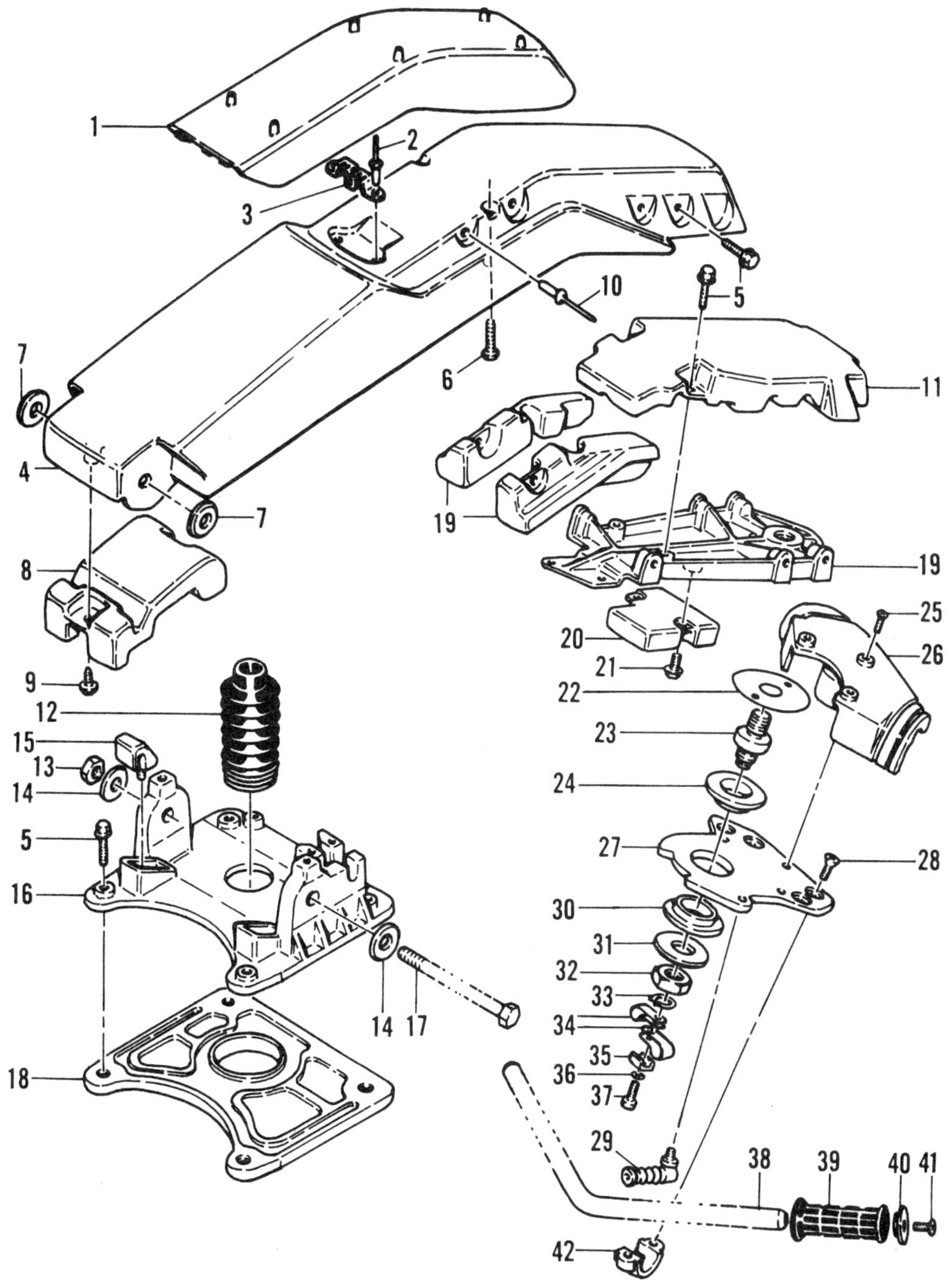

11

tric box with BelRay 6 in 1 or WD-40 (or equivalent) to lubricate the rubber, then unscrew the caps. Pull the switch leads out of the electric box carefully, one at a time until their connectors are exposed (**Figure 6**), then disconnect them.

> *NOTE*
> *If the connectors separate inside the electric box, the box must be disassembled to reconnect them. Refer to Chapter Eight.*

10. Remove the cable ties securing the wiring loom to the Jet Ski (**Figure 7**, typical).

11. Detach the rubber boot from the handle pole and carefully pull the start and stop switch wiring up and out of the boot (**Figure 8**).

12. Unscrew the acorn nut from the right side of the handle pole pivot bolt (**Figure 9**). Remove the bolt and washers.

13. Pull the handle pole up and back out of its bracket.

> *NOTE*
> *Mark the handle pole bracket with an arrow to indicate alignment.*

14. To remove the handle pole bracket, remove the 4 bolts (**Figure 10**). The bracket anchor plate will fall inside the hull when the last bracket bolt

is removed. Cut the sealant around the bracket and remove the bracket.

Handle Pole Installation

1. Install the handle pole bracket (if removed) as follows:
   a. Apply silicone sealant to the bottom of the bracket and install it.
   b. Install the bracket into position. From inside the hull, position the bracket anchor

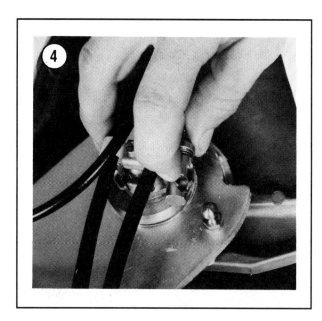

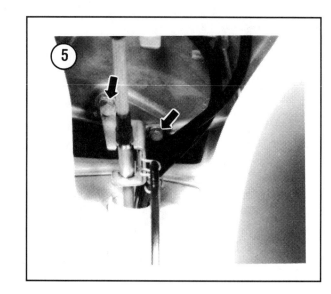

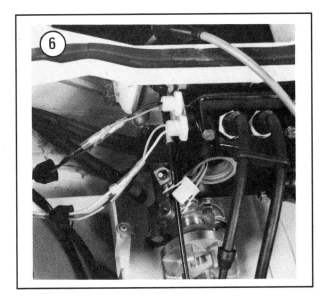

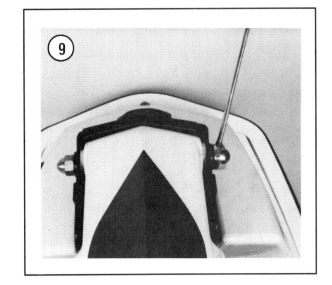

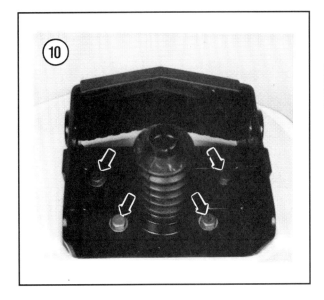

plate under the bracket and install the mounting bolts. Apply Loctite 242 to the threads of the 4 bolts (**Figure 10**). Tighten the bolts to specification (**Table 1-2**).

2. Slip the handle pole into position in the bracket. Lubricate the handle pole pivot bolt and nylon washers with water-resistant grease. Then, place one nylon washer between each side of the handle pole and its bracket (**Figure 11**).

3. Insert the pivot bolt from the left side and screw it into the bracket. Tighten the pivot bolt to the specification in **Tables 1-2**. No side play

should be present at the pivot, but it must not be so tight it binds.

4. Install the acorn nut on the pivot bolt. Hold the pivot bolt tight and tighten the nut to specification (**Tables 1-2**). Make sure the handle pole still moves up and down smoothly. If it does not, loosen the acorn nut and readjust the pivot bolt.

5. If the electrical cables were removed, spray them with BelRay 6 in 1 or WD-40 (or equivalent) to permit easy installation. Thread the cables down through the handle pole and the rubber boot (**Figure 8**).

6. Place the rubber boot in position and thread the throttle cable and steering cables up through the boot and handle pole (**Figure 12**).

7. Push the vent line through the boot and insert it into the grommet in the bottom of the handle pole. The grommet should be secured to the pole with silicone sealant. Be sure the vent line reaches at least 100 mm (4 in.) into the handle pole.

8. Assemble the steering cable bracket onto the cable and mount the bracket on the handle pole (**Figure 13**). Tighten the 2 bolts securely.

9. Attach the steering cable to the ball joint on the handlebar steering plate.

10. Make sure the steering cable is routed through its rubber guides (**Figure 14**, typical).

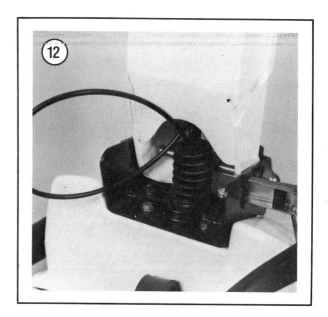

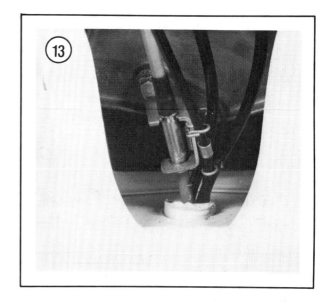

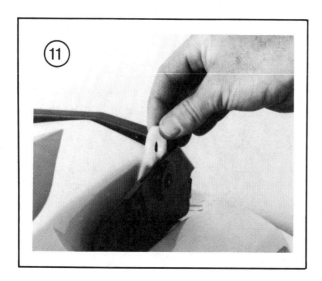

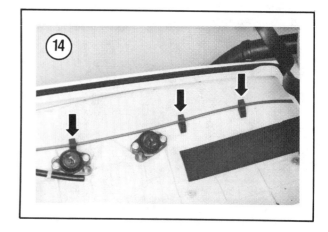

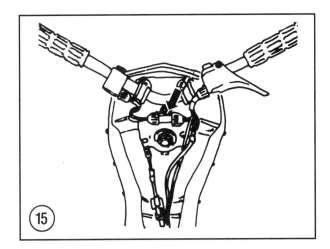

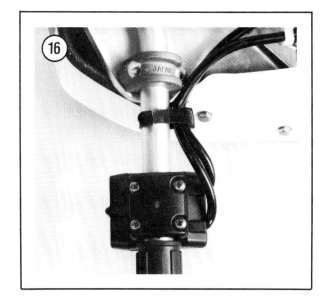

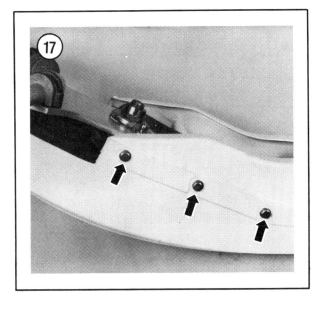

11. Attach the throttle cable holder to the steering cable bracket and install the throttle cable (**Figure 13**).

12. Route the stop and start switch leads along the right side of the Jet Ski and secure the straps (**Figure 7**).

13. Reconnect the stop and start switch wires at the electric box.

14. Apply a light coat of water-resistant grease to the connector cap threads and grommets and screw the caps on.

15. Adjust the steering as described in Chapter Three.

16. Adjust the throttle cable as described in Chapter Three.

Steering Disassembly

Refer to **Figure 1** or **Figure 2** as necessary while performing the following procedure.

1. Remove the wiring clamp screw and clamps from the pivot (**Figure 15**).

2. Remove the cable tie and remove the start/stop switch assembly (**Figure 16**).

3. Remove the 6 bolts that secure the steering support brackets to the handle pole (**Figure 17**). Remove the steering assembly.

> *CAUTION*
> *The float (**Figure 18**) mounted on the top of the handle pole should not be removed unless necessary. Removal of the float screws may damage the screw holes in the handle pole.*

4. If the handle pole float must be removed, remove the 3 screws and remove the float (**Figure 18**).

5. Remove the cotter pin from the pivot nut and remove the nut, washer and bushing (**Figure 19**).

6. Remove the steering plate from the support and remove the nylon bushing disc (**Figure 20**).

7. To remove the handlebar from the steering plate, remove the 4 handlebar clamp screws with an impact driver.

11

8. If necessary to remove the handlebar grips, cut the grips with a knife and pull them off the handlebar. Remove the grip holder (**Figure 21**) from the end of the handlebar, if so equipped. Remove all traces of tape from the handlebar with acetone, naphtha or equivalent solvent.

> *WARNING*
> *Acetone and naphtha are very flammable and poisonous. Avoid prolonged contact with skin and keep away from open flame. Use only in a well-ventilated area.*

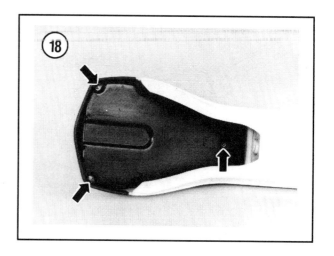

Steering Reassembly

Refer to **Figure 1** or **Figure 2** during this procedure.

1. Install the handlebar on the steering plate with its 4 screws and clamps. Apply Loctite 242 to the threads of the handlebar mounting screws.

2. Install the throttle lever assembly. Position the throttle lever about 45 mm (1-3/4 in.) from the right grip.

> *WARNING*
> *Acetone is very flammable and poisonous. Avoid prolonged contact with skin. Keep away from open flame and only use in a well-ventilated area.*

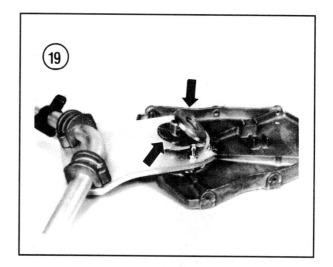

3. To install new hand grips, use a piece of sandpaper to rough up the ends of the handlebar, then clean them with solvent. Wrap the handlebar ends with double-sided tape such as 3M Scotch No. 400 or No. 410. Do not overlap layers of this tape. Treat the inside of the handle grip with a small amount of acetone and push the grip onto the handlebar. If a grip holder is used, install the holder and screw (**Figure 21**). Apply Loctite 242 to the threads of the screw.

4. Apply water-resistant grease to the nylon pivot bushings. Assemble the steering support, plate, bushings and washer.

5. Install the castellated nut and tighten it just enough so the handlebar rotates smoothly without excessive drag and a minimum of vertical

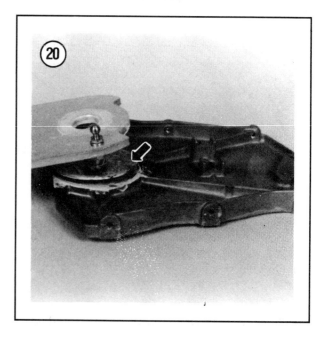

play. Install a new cotter pin and spread the ends (**Figure 22**).

6. If the float in the handle pole was removed, install it with its 3 screws (**Figure 18**).

7. Install the steering support in the handle pole. Install the 6 mounting bolts and tighten securely.

8. Install the stop/start switch assembly. A pin cast into the switch housing fits into a hole in the handlebar.

STEERING ASSEMBLY (JF650X-2)

Refer to **Figure 23** while performing this procedure.

1. Remove the handlebar pad from the handlebar.

2. Remove the bolts securing the throttle housing to the handlebar and remove it.

3. Remove the screws securing the switch housing to the handlebar and remove it.

4. Remove the handlebar holder bolts and washers and remove the handlebar.

5. If necessary to remove the handlebar grips, cut them with a knife and remove them. Remove the grip holder (**Figure 21**) from the end of the handlebar. Remove all traces of the tape with acetone, naphtha or equivalent solvent.

> *WARNING*
> *Acetone is very flammable and poisonous. Avoid prolonged contact with skin. Keep away from open flame and only use in a well-ventilated area.*

6. Installation is the reverse of Steps 1-5. Note the following.

7. To install new handlebar grips, use a piece of sandpaper to rough up the ends of the handlebar, then clean them with solvent. Wrap the handlebar ends with double-sided tape such as 3M Scotch No. 400 or No. 410. Do not overlap layers of this tape. Treat the inside of the handle grip with a small amount of acetone and push the grip onto the handlebar. If a grip holder is used, install the holder and screw (**Figure 21**). Apply Loctite 242 to the threads of the screw.

8. Tighten the handlebar holder bolts to the specified torque (**Table 3**).

Steering
Disassembly/Inspection/Reassembly

Refer to **Figure 23** while performing this procedure.

1. Remove the handlebar as described in this chapter.

2. Remove the pivot shaft cotter pin. Then, remove the pivot shaft nut and withdraw the pivot shaft.

11

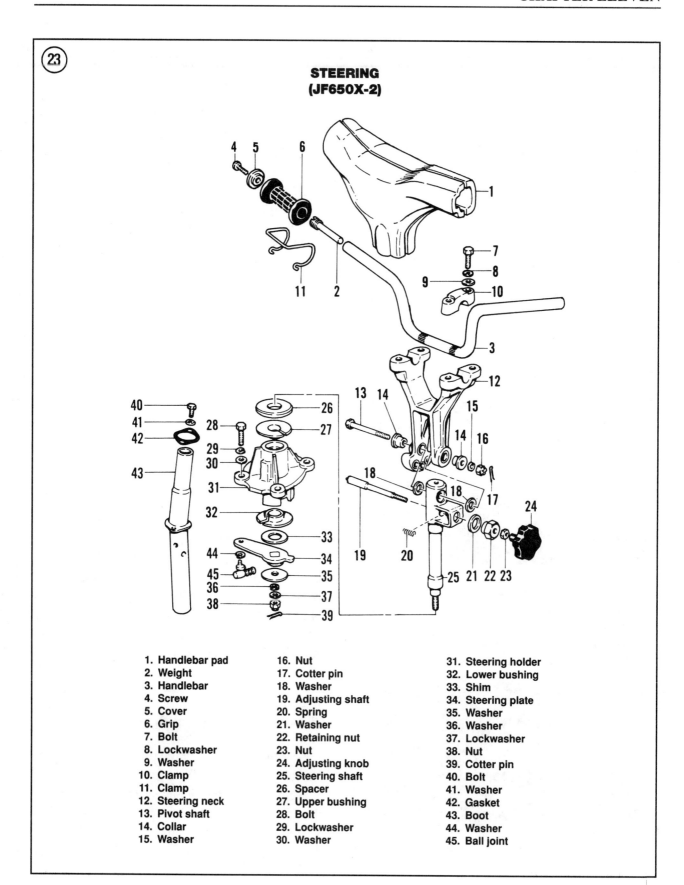

㉓

**STEERING
(JF650X-2)**

1. Handlebar pad	16. Nut	31. Steering holder
2. Weight	17. Cotter pin	32. Lower bushing
3. Handlebar	18. Washer	33. Shim
4. Screw	19. Adjusting shaft	34. Steering plate
5. Cover	20. Spring	35. Washer
6. Grip	21. Washer	36. Washer
7. Bolt	22. Retaining nut	37. Lockwasher
8. Lockwasher	23. Nut	38. Nut
9. Washer	24. Adjusting knob	39. Cotter pin
10. Clamp	25. Steering shaft	40. Bolt
11. Clamp	26. Spacer	41. Washer
12. Steering neck	27. Upper bushing	42. Gasket
13. Pivot shaft	28. Bolt	43. Boot
14. Collar	29. Lockwasher	44. Washer
15. Washer	30. Washer	45. Ball joint

3. Remove the left and right pivot collar from the steering neck.

4. Hold the steering neck and pull the handlebar adjustment knob out and remove the steering neck. See **Figure 24**.

5. Loosen the handlebar adjustment knob locknut. Then, unscrew the knob and remove it.

6. Remove the retaining nut from the steering shaft. Then, remove the adjusting shaft and spring.

7. Disconnect the ball joint at the steering cam lever.

8. Loosen the cotter pin at the bottom of the steering shaft. Then, remove the following from the steering shaft:

    a. Nut.

    b. Washer.

    c. Lockwasher.

    d. Spacer.

    e. Steering cam lever.

    f. Shim.

    g. Bushing.

9. From the top of the steering holder, remove the steering shaft, spacer and bushing.

10. Remove the bolts and washers securing the steering holer. Then cut the sealant from the around the base of the holder and remove the holder.

11. Thoroughly clean all components. Remove all sealant from the steering holder and its mounting position.

12. With all parts disassembled and clean, visually inspect for excessive wear, cracks, breakage or other damage. Replace any part in questionable condition.

13. Reassembly is the reverse of Steps 1-10. Note the following points during reassembly.

14. Apply silicone sealant to the base of the steering holder and install it. Apply Loctite 242 to the threads of the steering holder mounting bolts and tighten the bolts to the specification in **Table 3**.

15. Apply water-resistant grease to the bushings, steering shaft, adjusting shaft and steering neck pivot shaft.

16. Check steering shaft operation after tightening the steering shaft nut to specification (**Table 3**). The shaft should move smoothly from side-to-side without noticeable play or roughness. If necessary, replace the shim (33, **Figure 23**). Steering shims are available from Jet Ski dealers in 0.3, 0.5 and 1.0 mm thicknesses.

17. After installing the steering neck, tighten the steering neck pivot shaft nut to the specification in **Table 3**.

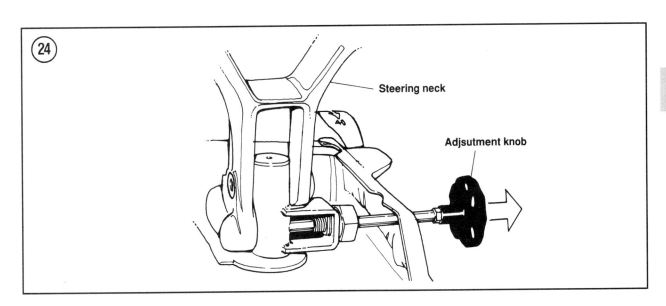

Steering neck

Adjsutment knob

11

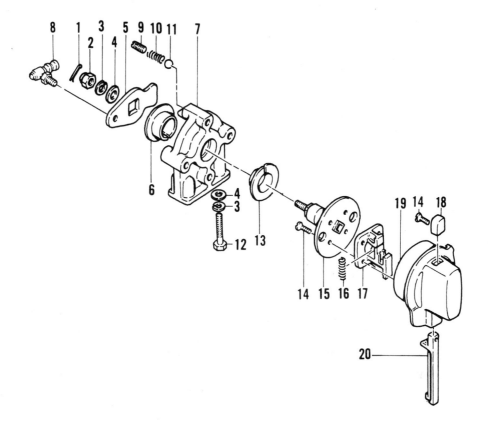

**TRIM ADJUSTER
(JF650X-2)**

1. Cotter pin
2. Nut
3. Lockwasher
4. Washer
5. Trim cam lever
6. Bushing
7. Bracket
8. Ball joint
9. Spring retainer
10. Spring
11. Ball
12. Bolt
13. Bushing
14. Bolt
15. Shaft
16. Spring
17. Bracket
18. Cap
19. Knob
20. Rod

Trim Adjuster
Removal/Installation

Refer to **Figure 25** during this procedure.

1. Remove the deck seal and deck pad.

2. Disconnect the ball joint at the trim cam lever.

3. Remove the cotter pin at the rear of the trim adjuster shaft.

NOTE
When the trim adjuster shaft is pulled away from the bracket, 4 detent balls and springs will fall out of the bracket.

4. Loosen the nut on the end of the trim adjuster shaft. Then, remove the nut, lockwasher, flat washer, trim cam lever, shim and bushing from the bracket. Then remove the knob and trim adjuster shaft assembly.

5. Remove the small left-side deck piece.

6. Remove the bolts securing the igniter to the deck and position it out of the way.

7. Remove the bolts holding the bracket to the hull. Remove the bracket.

8. Remove the spring retainer and remove the retainer, spring and ball from the bracket. Repeat for each retainer set.

9. If necessary to disassemble the knob assembly, remove the screws from the back of the trim adjuster shaft and separate the shaft and knob assembly.

10. Thoroughly clean all components. Remove all sealant from the steering holder and its mounting position.

11. Visually inspect all components for excessive wear, cracks, breakage or other damage. Replace any component in questionable condition.

12. Reassemble the trim adjuster assembly by reversing Steps 1-9, while noting the following points.

12. Apply Loctite 242 to the threads of the trim adjuster shaft and knob screws. Tighten the screws securely.

13. Apply Loctite 242 to the spring retainers.

14. Apply water-resistant grease to the trim adjuster shaft before reassembly.

15. Tighten the trim adjuster shaft nut securely and secure the nut with a new cotter pin.

STEERING ASSEMBLY (JF650TS)

Handlebar
Removal/Installation

Refer to **Figure 26** during this procedure.

1. Remove the handlebar pad from the handlebar.

2. Remove the bolts securing the throttle housing to the handlebar and remove it.

3. Remove the screws securing the start/stop switch housing to the handlebar and remove it.

4. Remove the handlebar holder bolts and remove the handlebar.

5. If necessary to remove the handlebar grips, cut them with a knife and remove them. Remove the grip holder (**Figure 21**) from the end of the handlebar. Remove all traces of the tape with acetone, naphtha or equivalent solvent.

WARNING
Acetone and naphtha are very flammable and poisonous. Avoid prolonged contact with skin. Keep away from open flame and only use in a well-ventilated area.

6. Installation is the reverse of Steps 1-5. Note the following points.

7. To install new handlebar grips, use a piece of sandpaper to rough up the ends of the handlebar, then clean them with solvent. Wrap the handlebar ends with double-sided tape such as 3M Scotch No. 400 or No. 410. Do not overlap layers of this tape. Treat the inside of the handle grip with a small amount of acetone and push the grip onto the handlebar. If a grip holder is used, install the holder and screw (**Figure 21**). Apply Loctite 242 to the threads of the screw.

11

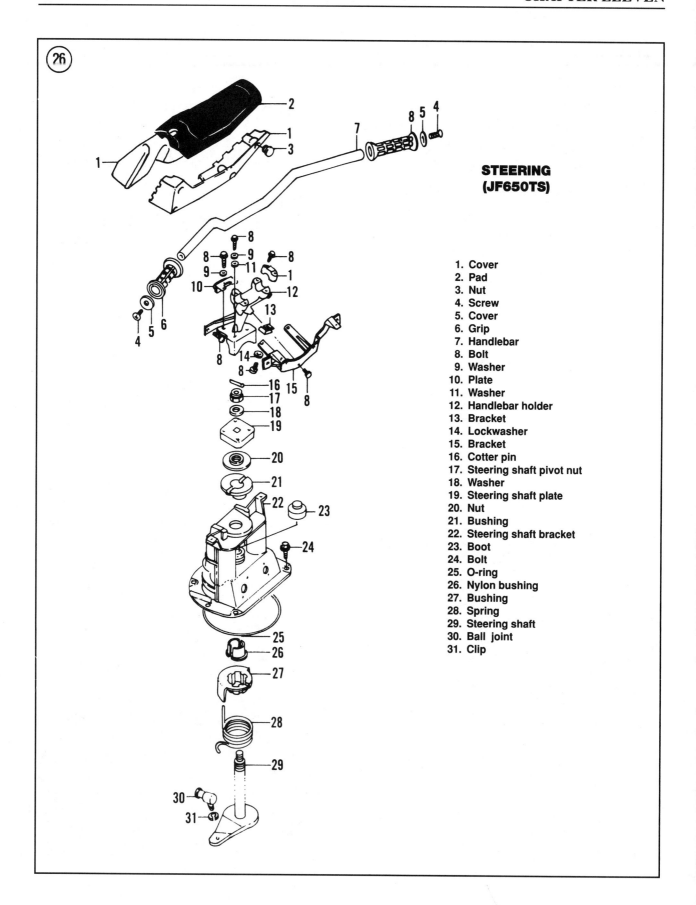

STEERING (JF650TS)

1. Cover
2. Pad
3. Nut
4. Screw
5. Cover
6. Grip
7. Handlebar
8. Bolt
9. Washer
10. Plate
11. Washer
12. Handlebar holder
13. Bracket
14. Lockwasher
15. Bracket
16. Cotter pin
17. Steering shaft pivot nut
18. Washer
19. Steering shaft plate
20. Nut
21. Bushing
22. Steering shaft bracket
23. Boot
24. Bolt
25. O-ring
26. Nylon bushing
27. Bushing
28. Spring
29. Steering shaft
30. Ball joint
31. Clip

8. Apply Loctite 242 to the threads of the handlebar holder bolts. Tighten the bolts to specification (**Table 4**).

Steering
Disassembly/Inspection/Reassembly

Refer to **Figure 26** during this procedure.

1. Remove the handlebar as described in this chapter.

2. Remove the screws securing the steering cover and remove the cover.

3. Remove the screws securing the choke and throttle knob panel cover and remove the panel cover.

4. Open the storage compartment door.

5. Remove the screws securing the storage compartment case.

6. Remove the storage compartment case and door as an assembly.

7. Remove the main fuel valve as described in Chapter Seven.

8. Remove the choke knob shaft assembly.

9. Disconnect the steering cable ball joint from the steering shaft arm.

10. Remove the bolts securing the cable grommet and plate. Remove the plate and partially pull the grommet, cables and hose from the grommet. It is not necessary to remove the cables and hose from the grommet and steering shaft bracket.

11. Remove the pivot shaft cotter pin. Then remove the pivot shaft nut and washer.

12. Remove the steering shaft plate, steering stem nut and bushing from the top of the steering shaft bracket.

13. Remove the bolts securing the steering shaft bracket to the hull.

14. Partially pull the steering shaft bracket up and off the hull, then pull the steering stem out of the steering shaft bracket.

15. If steering shaft bracket removal is necessary, perform the following:

a. Disconnect the start/stop switch connectors in the electric box.

b. Disassemble the throttle housing and disconnect the throttle cable from the housing.

c. Carefully pull the start/stop switch wires and throttle cable through the rubber grommet and the opening in the steering shaft bracket.

d. Remove the steering shaft bracket.

16. Thoroughly clean all components.

17. Visually inspect all components for excessive wear, cracks, breakage or other damage. Replace any component in questionable condition.

18. Reassemble the steering by reversing Steps 1-15, while noting the following points.

19. Apply water-resistant grease to the bushings and steering shaft.

20. Make sure the large O-ring seal is in place on the base of the steering shaft bracket.

21. Apply Loctite 242 to the threads of the steering shaft bracket bolts. Tighten the bolts to specification (**Table 4**).

22. Check steering shaft operation after tightening the bolts in Step 21. The shaft should move smoothly without any noticeable play or roughness.

STEERING ASSEMBLY (JL650SC)

Steering Wheel
Removal/Installation

Refer to **Figure 27** during this procedure.

1. Remove the screws and nylon washers securing the column lower cover (A, **Figure 28**).

2. Remove the screws and nylon washers securing the column cover (B, **Figure 28**). Remove the cover.

3. Remove the self-tapping screws and bolts securing the steering frame lower cover (C, **Figure 28**). Remove the lower cover.

4. Open the front hatch cover to expose the bolts in Step 5.

11

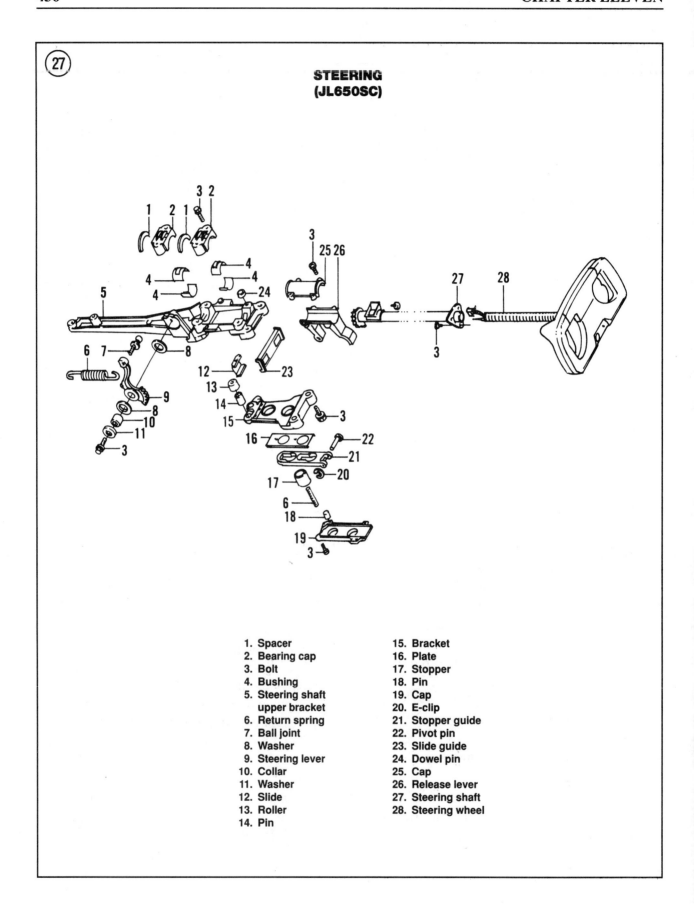

(27)

**STEERING
(JL650SC)**

1. Spacer
2. Bearing cap
3. Bolt
4. Bushing
5. Steering shaft
   upper bracket
6. Return spring
7. Ball joint
8. Washer
9. Steering lever
10. Collar
11. Washer
12. Slide
13. Roller
14. Pin
15. Bracket
16. Plate
17. Stopper
18. Pin
19. Cap
20. E-clip
21. Stopper guide
22. Pivot pin
23. Slide guide
24. Dowel pin
25. Cap
26. Release lever
27. Steering shaft
28. Steering wheel

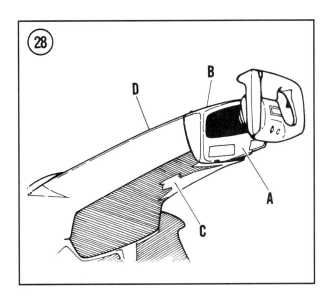

5. Remove the bolts and washers securing the steering frame upper cover (D, **Figure 28**) and remove the upper cover. Do not lose the collar located in the rubber grommet at each mounting hole in the upper cover.

6. Close the front hatch.

7. Disconnect the return spring (A, **Figure 29**) from the steering lever.

8. Remove the tie straps (B, **Figure 29**) from the steering shaft securing the throttle cable.

9. Disconnect the throttle cable lower end from the carburetor.

10. Disconnect the throttle cable joint (A, **Figure 30**).

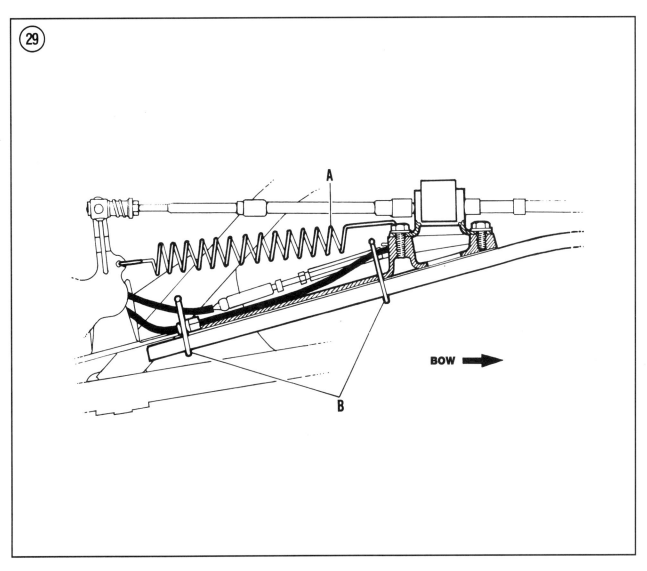

11

11. Disconnect the start/stop switch electrical connector (B, **Figure 30**).

12. Remove the bolts securing the steering wheel to the steering shaft.

13. Slowly pull the steering wheel and guide the electrical connector into the open end of the steering shaft. Continue to pull and remove the steering wheel, throttle cable and electrical harness out of the steering shaft.

14. Install the steering wheel by reversing Steps 1-13. Note the following points during installation.

15. Apply Loctite 242 to the threads of the steering wheel mounting bolts. Tighten the bolts securely.

16. Be sure to connect the return spring onto the steering lever as shown in **Figure 31**.

17. When installing the steering frame upper cover, be sure the collar and rubber grommet are installed in each mounting hole. This collar serves as a stop for the mounting bolts during tightening. If the collars are not installed, the upper cover may crack or fracture in the mounting bolt hole area.

18. Adjust the throttle cable as described in Chapter Three.

Steering Shaft and Arm Removal/Inspection

Refer to **Figure 27** while performing this procedure.

1. Remove the steering wheel as described in this chapter.

2. Disconnect the steering cable ball joint from the steering lever.

3. Remove the screws clamping the release lever cap and remove it. Place the release lever pivot down and out of the way.

4. Remove the bearing cap bolts and remove both bearing caps. Do not lose the locating dowels in each cap or the spacer on each side the front bearing cap.

5. Remove the steering shaft assembly.

6. To remove the steering arm from the steering shaft upper bracket, remove the bolt and washers and remove the steering arm. Do not lose the washer on each side of the steering arm or the collar in the pivot hole in the steering arm.

7. Thoroughly clean all components. Then, visually inspect all components for excessive wear, cracks, breakage or other damage. Replace any part in questionable condition.

8. Inspect the steering shaft bushings for excessive wear or damage. Replace the bushings as follows:

   a. Apply water-resistant grease to the inside of each bearing cap, then install the bushing onto it. Apply another coat of grease to the exposed surface of each bushing.

   b. Install the bushings in the receptacles in the steering shaft upper bracket, then apply water-resistant grease to the exposed surface of each bushing.

   c. Apply water-resistant grease to both sides of each spacer and install them onto each side of the front bearing cap.

9. If removed, install the steering arm onto the steering shaft upper bracket as follow:

   a. Apply water-resistant grease to the pivot hole, collar and washers.

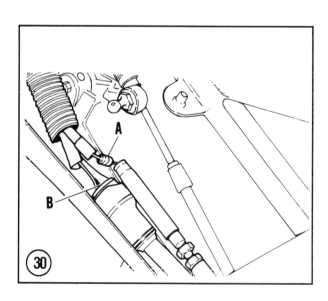

b. Install the collar in the pivot hole in the steering arm.

c. Place a washer on each side of the steering arm.

d. Position the steering arm on the steering shaft upper bracket with the sector gear facing toward the steering wheel.

e. Apply Loctite 242 to the threads of the steering arm mounting bolt. Install the bolt and an additional washer and tighten to specification (**Table 5**).

Steering Shaft and Arm Installation

Refer to **Figure 27** during this procedure.

1. Apply water-resistant grease to the sector gears on both the steering shaft and the steering gear.

2. Install the steering shaft assembly into the steering shaft upper holder. Align the steering shaft sector gear index mark with the index mark on the steering lever. This alignment is necessary for proper steering operation.

3. Next, install the front bearing cap with a spacer on each side and then the rear bearing cap.

Make sure the locating dowels are in place in the caps.

4. Install the bearing cap bolts and tighten in a crossing pattern to the specification in **Table 5**.

5. Move the release lever up into position and install the cap. Install the screws and tighten securely.

6. Connect the steering cable ball joint to the steering lever.

7. Install the steering wheel as described in this chapter.

8. Pull the release lever and move the steering wheel into the three positions: right, center and left. Make sure the steering moves freely and locks securely into each position.

9. Turn the wheel in both directions and operate the throttle. Make sure the steering wheel and throttle operate smoothly without binding.

Steering Latching Mechanism Removal/Inspection

Refer to **Figure 27** during this procedure.

1. Remove the steering shaft assembly as described in this chapter.

2. Remove the E-clip , then withdraw the pivot pin and remove the release lever.

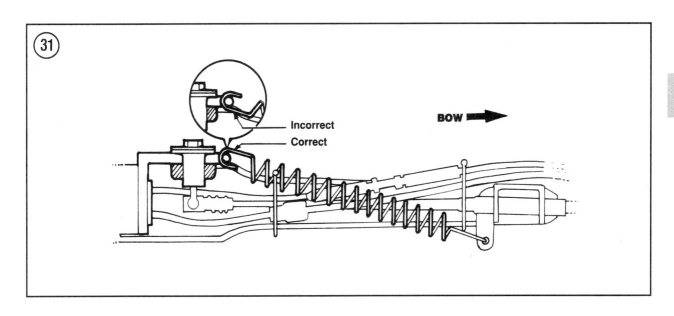

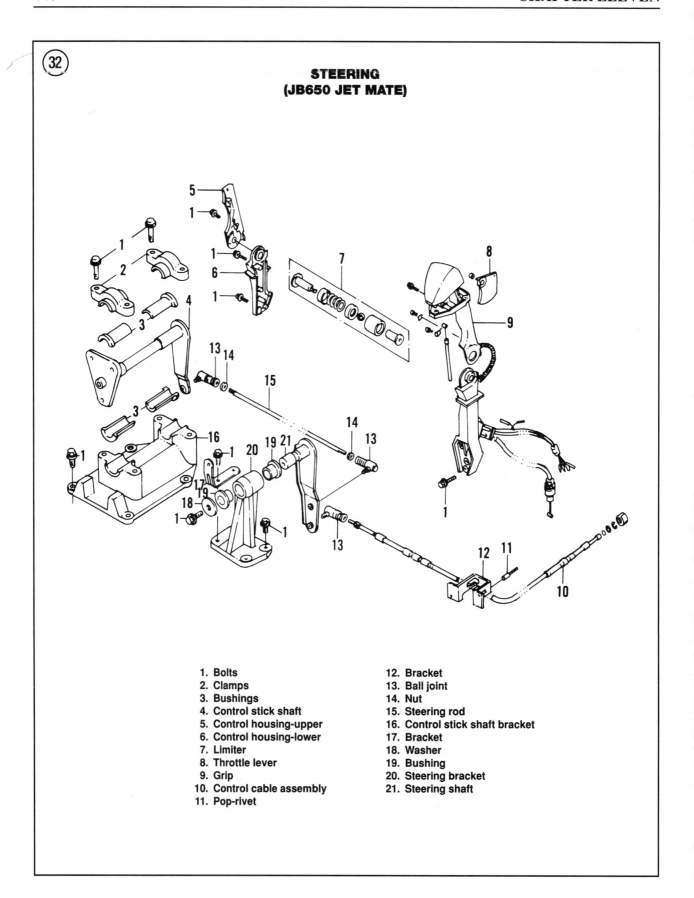

**STEERING
(JB650 JET MATE)**

1. Bolts
2. Clamps
3. Bushings
4. Control stick shaft
5. Control housing-upper
6. Control housing-lower
7. Limiter
8. Throttle lever
9. Grip
10. Control cable assembly
11. Pop-rivet
12. Bracket
13. Ball joint
14. Nut
15. Steering rod
16. Control stick shaft bracket
17. Bracket
18. Washer
19. Bushing
20. Steering bracket
21. Steering shaft

3. Remove the steering cable holder and move the cable out of the way.

4. Remove the latching bracket mounting bolts and separate the bracket from the steering shaft upper bracket.

5. Carefully lift the steering shaft upper bracket off the steering frame and remove the slide guides. Note that the longer guide is toward the steering wheel.

6. If necessary, disassemble the latching bracket as follows:

    a. Turn the latching bracket upside down and remove the bolts securing the cap to the bracket.

    b. Remove the cap then remove all internal components.

7. Inspect all components for excessive wear, cracks, breakage or other damage. Replace any component in questionable condition.

Installation

Refer to **Figure 27** during this procedure.

1. If the latching bracket was disassembled, perform the following:

    a. Apply water-resistant grease to the sliding surfaces of the stopper guide, stoppers and the springs.

    b. Place the bracket upside down and make sure the locating dowels are in place.

    c. Align the stopper ears with the grooves in the stopper guide and install the stoppers into the stopper guide.

    d. Install this assembly into the bracket and install the spring into each stopper.

    e. Install the cap, compress the springs and install the bolts. Tighten the bolts securely.

CAUTION
Never apply any type of grease to the black painted surface of the steering frame.

2. The black-coated portion of the steering frame must be free of dirt or sand.

3. Install the slide guides onto the steering frame. The front guide is the smaller of the 2 and has indexing dowels. Install this guide correctly. Install the longer guide on the rear surface of the steering frame.

4. Install the latching bracket onto the slide guides and onto the steering frame.

5. Align the bolt holes with the steering shaft upper bracket. Apply Loctite 242 to the threads of the latching bracket mounting bolts. Install the bolts and tighten securely.

6. Move the steering cable holder and cable back into place.

7. Install the release lever and install the pivot pin and E-clip. Make sure the E-clip is secure in its groove.

8. Install the steering shaft assembly as described in this chapter.

STEERING ASSEMBLY (JB650 JET MATE)

Control Stick
Removal/Installation

Refer to **Figure 32** while performing this procedure.

1. Remove the engine hood.

2. Remove the steering case as follows:

    a. Remove the screws securing the steering case.

    b. Remove the screws securing the choke knob shaft.

    c. Remove the steering case.

3. Remove the rear seat assembly.

4. Remove the top from the electric box. Disconnect the start/stop switch red/purple, green/white, white and black wires. Carefully remove the wires from the electric box.

5. Disconnect the throttle cable from the carburetor.

6. Remove the bolts securing the control stick to the control stick shaft on the bracket.

11

7. Install the control stick by reversing Steps 1-6. After installation, adjust the steering, throttle and choke cables. Refer to Chapter Three.

Steering Bracket
Removal/Installation

Refer to **Figure 32** during this procedure.

1. Remove the engine hood.

2. Disconnect the steering cable and steering rod ball joints (A, **Figure 33**). Remove the steering rod (B, **Figure 33**) and move the steering cable (C) out of the way.

3. Remove the bolts securing the steering bracket and remove the bracket.

4. Remove the control stick and steering case as described in this chapter.

5. Remove the clamp bolts and remove both clamps (A, **Figure 34**).

6. Remove the control stick shaft (B, **Figure 34**) and all 4 bushings.

7. Remove the bolts securing the control stick shaft bracket (C, **Figure 34**) and remove the bracket.

8. If necessary, remove the bolt and remove the steering shaft from the steering bracket. Remove the bushings from the steering bracket and inspect them.

9. Inspect all components for excessive wear, cracks, breakage or other damage. Replace any component in questionable condition.

10. Replace all 4 steering shaft bushings as a set. Also, if necessary, replace the steering shaft bushings as a pair.

11. Install the steering bracket by reversing Steps 1-8, while noting the following:

   a. Tighten the bolts to the specification in **Table 6**.

   b. After installation, adjust the steering, throttle and choke cables as described in Chapter Three.

STEERING ASSEMBLY (JS750SX)

Handle Pole
Removal

Refer to **Figure 35** while performing this procedure.

1. Remove the fuel tank as described in Chapter Seven.

2. Disconnect the throttle cable from the carburetor.

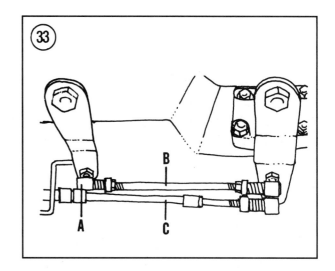

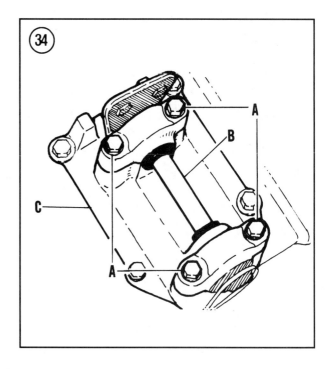

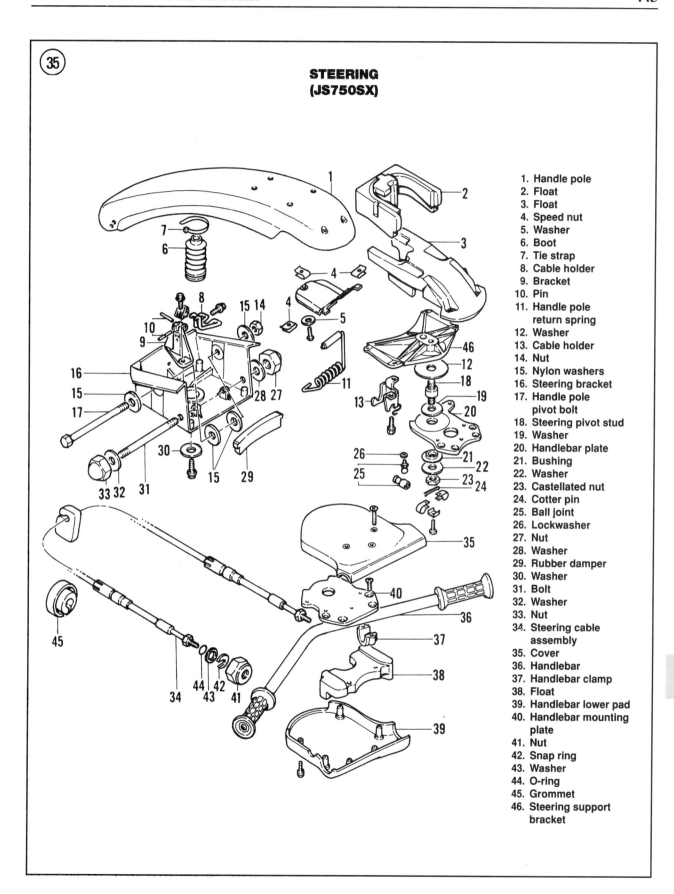

**STEERING
(JS750SX)**

1. Handle pole
2. Float
3. Float
4. Speed nut
5. Washer
6. Boot
7. Tie strap
8. Cable holder
9. Bracket
10. Pin
11. Handle pole
    return spring
12. Washer
13. Cable holder
14. Nut
15. Nylon washers
16. Steering bracket
17. Handle pole
    pivot bolt
18. Steering pivot stud
19. Washer
20. Handlebar plate
21. Bushing
22. Washer
23. Castellated nut
24. Cotter pin
25. Ball joint
26. Lockwasher
27. Nut
28. Washer
29. Rubber damper
30. Washer
31. Bolt
32. Washer
33. Nut
34. Steering cable
    assembly
35. Cover
36. Handlebar
37. Handlebar clamp
38. Float
39. Handlebar lower pad
40. Handlebar mounting
    plate
41. Nut
42. Snap ring
43. Washer
44. O-ring
45. Grommet
46. Steering support
    bracket

11

3. Remove the handlebar start/stop switch case and wiring. Refer to Chapter Eight.

4. Disconnect the steering cable from the steering support bracket. Slide the outer sleeve on the cable end away from the ball, then, pull the cable off the ball joint.

5. Remove the steering support plate from the bottom of the handle pole.

6. Remove the cushion pad from the handle pole.

7. Remove the bolts securing the steering bracket to the hull. Remove the handle pole with the steering bracket from the hull.

8. To remove the handle pole from the steering bracket, remove the nut securing the handle pole pivot bolt.

9. Push the pivot bolt from the handle pole and bracket. Be sure the retrieve the nylon washers as the pivot bolt is removed.

10. Remove the handle pole return spring, then separate the handle pole from the steering bracket.

11. Closely inspect all components for excessive wear, cracks, breakage or other damage. Replace any component in questionable condition.

Handle Pole
Installation

Refer to **Figure 35** during this procedure.

1. Install the handle pole into position in the steering bracket. Lubricate the nylon washers and pivot bolt with water-resistant grease. Install the handle pole return spring and pivot bolt, making sure all 4 nylon washers are in position.

2. Tighten the handle pole pivot bolt nut to specification (**Table 7**). Make sure the handle pole pivots freely in the steering bracket, with no noticeable side-to-side play. If necessary, tighten or loosen the pivot bolt as necessary.

3. Make sure the steering bracket and hull mating surfaces are clean. Install the handle pole and steering bracket assembly into the hull, install

the bracket fasteners and tighten to specification (**Table 7**).

4. Make sure all wires and cables are correctly routed through the rubber boot (**Figure 36**).

5. Install the steering support bracket. Attach the steering cable to the ball joint on the support bracket.

6. Make sure the steering cable is routed through its rubber guides (**Figure 37**, typical).

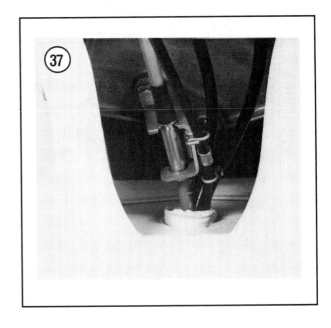

7. Complete the remaining installation by reversing the removal steps. Make sure all wires and cables are routed correctly. Adjust the steering, throttle and choke cables as described in Chapter Three.

Handlebar and Steering Pivot Removal/Installation

Refer to **Figure 35** for this procedure.

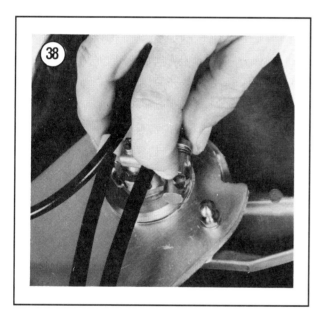

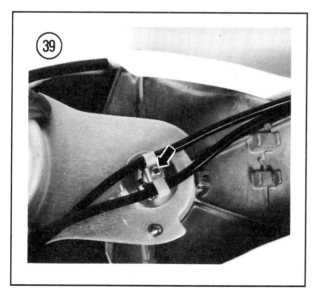

If the steering pivot binds, feels tight or becomes loose, it should be disassembled for inspection.

1. If necessary to remove the handlebar grips, cut them with a sharp knife and remove them from the handlebar. Remove all traces of the old tape with acetone, naphtha or equivalent solvent.

> *WARNING*
> *Acetone and naphtha are very flammable and poisonous. Avoid prolonged contact with skin. Keep away from open flame and use only in a well ventilated area.*

2. Remove the handle pole cover. Remove the 6 handlebar pad mounting screws (bottom side of handle pole). Remove the handlebar pad (39, **Figure 35**).

3. Remove the 2 screws holding the throttle lever case halves together. Separate the throttle case from the handlebar.

4. Remove the 4 screws holding the start/stop switch case halves together. Separate the start/stop switch case from the handlebar.

5. Disconnect the steering cable from the ball joint on the steering support plate. Slide the outer sleeve on the cable end away from the ball and lift the cable off the ball joint (**Figure 38**, typical).

4. Remove the screw securing the wiring/cable clamp to the steering pivot stud (**Figure 39**, typical).

5. Remove the cotter pin and castellated nut (**Figure 40**) from the steering pivot stud.

6. Remove the handlebar and handlebar plate from the handle pole.

7. Remove the upper pad. If necessary, remove the 4 handlebar clamp (Allen) screws and separate the handlebar from the handlebar plate.

8. Remove the 4 bolts (A, **Figure 41**) securing the steering support plate to the handle pole. Remove the support plate.

9. Carefully inspect the pivot stud (B, **Figure 41**) for excessive wear, cracks, corrosion or other

11

damage. Replace the stud if any defects are noted.

NOTE
The steering pivot stud is secured at the factory with thread locking compound. If necessary, heat the stud to ease removal.

10. Inspect all components for excessive wear, cracks, breakage or other damage. Replace any component in questionable condition.

11. If removed, thoroughly clean the pivot stud threads in the steering support plate. Apply Loctite 242 to the threads of the steering pivot stud. Install the stud into the support plate and tighten to specification (**Table 7**).

12. Apply Loctite 242 to the threads of the handlebar clamp screws. Mount the handlebar on the handlebar plate, then install and tighten the clamp bolts to specification (**Table 7**).

13. Install the steering support plate on the handle pole. Apply Loctite 242 to the threads of the plate mounting screws (A, **Figure 41**). Tighten the bolts securely.

14. Make sure all bushings and nylon washers are in place. Lubricate the handlebar pivot stud and nylon washers with water-resistant grease. Make sure the nylon washers are in position and install the handlebar and plate assembly on pivot stud. Install the washer and castellated nut. Tighten the nut so the handlebar pivots freely without noticeable play. Install a new cotter pin (**Figure 40**).

15. To install new handlebar grips, use a piece of sandpaper to rough up the ends of the handlebar, then clean them with solvent. Wrap the handlebar ends with double-sided tape such as 3M Scotch No. 400 or No. 410. Do not overlap layers of the tape. Treat the inside of the grips with a small amount of acetone and push the grips onto the handlebar.

16. Complete the remaining reassembly by reversing the disassembly steps. Apply Loctite 242 to the threads of all remaining fasteners. Adjust the steering, throttle and choke cables as necessary. Refer to Chapter Three.

Steering Cable Replacement

1. Remove the handlebar pad.

2. Remove the handle pole cover.

3. Disconnect the steering cable from the steering plate and from the steering nozzle. Slide the

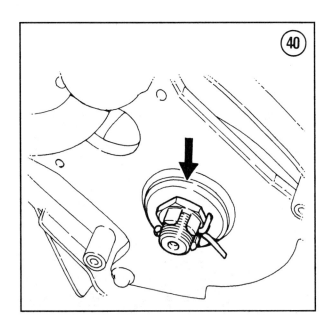

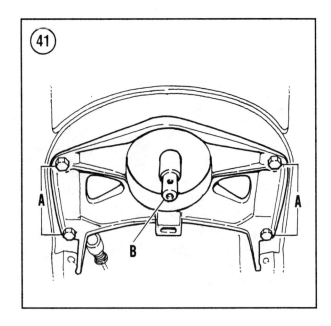

outer sleeve of the cable end away from the ball joint and pull the cable off the ball.

4. Loosen the locknut and remove the connector and locknut from each end of the cable.

5. Roll the watercraft onto its left side. Protect the hull with a heavy blanket.

6. Remove the intake grate and jet pump cover. Refer to Chapter Six.

7. While securely holding the hull fitting (A, **Figure 42**) with an open-end wrench, loosen and remove the cable nut (E). Pull the cable through the hull fitting and remove the O-ring (B, **Figure 42**), Washer (C) and snap ring (D) from the cable.

8. Remove the fuel tank and water box muffler as described in Chapter Seven.

9. Remove the steering cable by pulling the front section up through the handle pole.

10. Install the cable by reversing Steps 1-9, while noting the following.

11. The protective sheath and tap around the new steering cable should be positioned to the front of the watercraft. Lubricate the outside of the cable with Belray 6 in 1 or WD-40 (or equivalent) to ease cable installation.

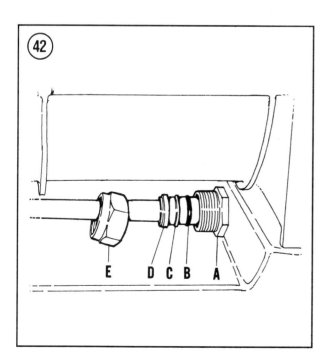

12. After installation, make sure the cable moves freely in both directions. Then, connect the cable to the steering plate and steering nozzle ball joints. Adjust the steering cable as described in Chapter Three.

STEERING ASSEMBLY (JT750ST, JH750SS, JH750 SUPER SPORT Xi AND JH750XiR)

Handlebar
Removal/Installation

Refer to **Figure 43** during this procedure.
1. Remove the handlebar cover.
2. Remove the bolts securing the throttle housing to the handlebar. Remove throttle housing.
3. Remove the screws securing the start/stop switch housing to handlebar. Remove the switch housing.
4. Remove the 4 handlebar clamp bolts. Remove the handlebar.
5. Install the handlebar by reversing Steps 1-4, while noting the following.
6. Apply Loctite 242 to the threads of the handlebar clamp bolts.
7. Align the punch mark on the left side of the handlebar with the center of the gap between the handlebar clamp and handlebar holder (**Figure 44**).
8. Tighten the front, then the rear handlebar clamp bolts to the specification in **Table 8**.
9. If necessary to remove the handlebar grips, cut them with a sharp knife and remove them from the handlebar. Remove all traces of the old tape with acetone, naphtha or equivalent solvent.

> *WARNING*
> *Acetone and naphtha are very flammable and poisonous. Avoid prolonged contact with skin. Keep away from open flame and use only in a well ventilated area.*

10. To install new handlebar grips, use a piece of sandpaper to rough up the ends of the handle-

11

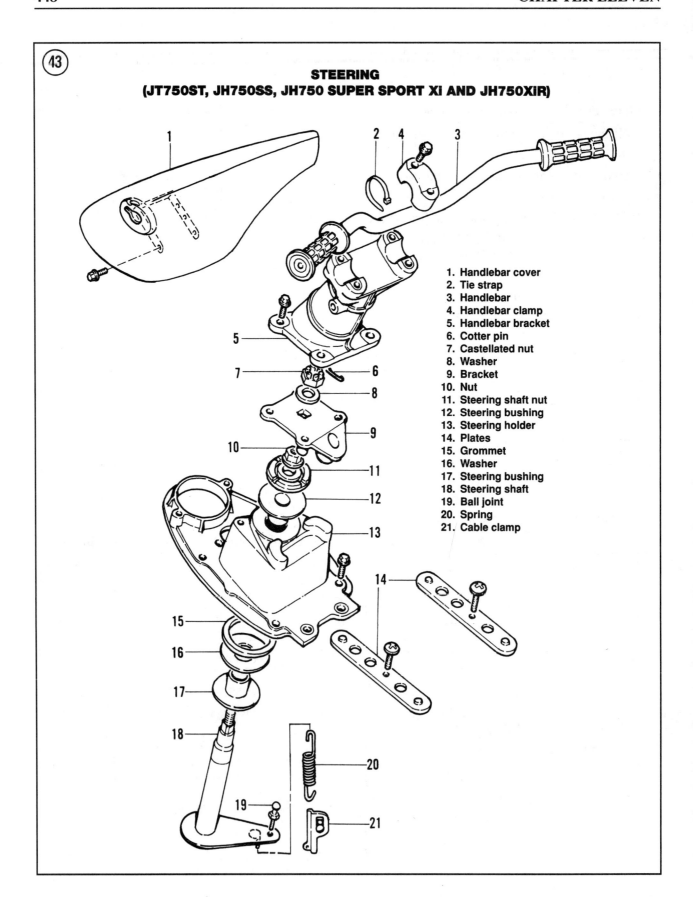

㊸

**STEERING
(JT750ST, JH750SS, JH750 SUPER SPORT Xi AND JH750XiR)**

1. Handlebar cover
2. Tie strap
3. Handlebar
4. Handlebar clamp
5. Handlebar bracket
6. Cotter pin
7. Castellated nut
8. Washer
9. Bracket
10. Nut
11. Steering shaft nut
12. Steering bushing
13. Steering holder
14. Plates
15. Grommet
16. Washer
17. Steering bushing
18. Steering shaft
19. Ball joint
20. Spring
21. Cable clamp

bar, then clean them with solvent. Wrap the handlebar ends with double-sided tape such as 3M Scotch No. 400 or No. 410. Do not overlap layers of the tape. Treat the inside of the grips with a small amount of acetone and push the grips onto the handlebar.

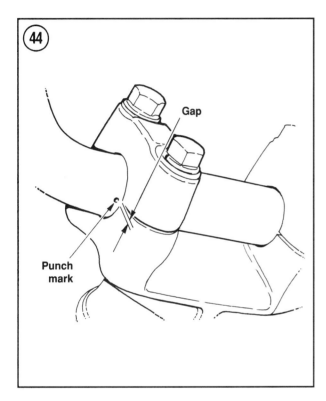

**Steering
Disassembly/Inspection/Reassembly**

Refer to **Figure 43** during this procedure.

1. Remove the seat/engine cover assembly. Remove the handlebar as described in this chapter.

2. Remove the bolts securing the steering cover. Slide the cover toward the front of the watercraft, then remove the 3 bolts securing the LED unit to the cover. Remove the LED unit from the cover, then remove the cover from the watercraft.

3. Unscrew the handlebar bracket (5, **Figure 43**) mounting bolts Remove the bracket assembly.

4. Remove the cotter pin and nut (A, **Figure 45**). Then lift the steering bracket (B, **Figure 45**) off the steering shaft.

5. Next, hold the steering shaft nut using Kawasaki steering shaft nut wrench part No. 57001-1100 (or equivalent spanner wrench) and remove the steering shaft locknut. See **Figure 46**.

6. Remove the air duct, grommet, vent hose, throttle cable, start/stop switch wires and LED unit wires from the steering holder.

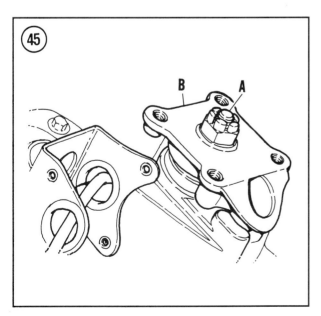

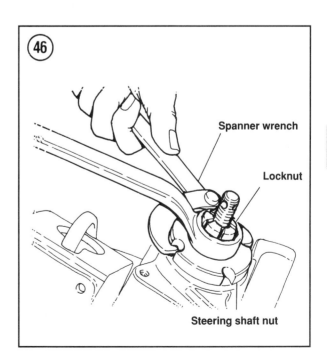

11

(47)

STEERING HOLDER AND SHAFT ASSEMBLY
(JT750ST, JH750SS, JH750 SUPER SPORT Xi AND JH750XiR)

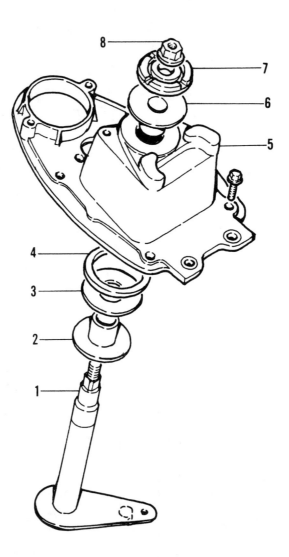

1. Steering shaft
2. Lower bushing
3. Washer
4. Grommet
5. Steering holder
6. Upper bushing
7. Steering shaft nut
8. Steering shaft locknut

7. Reaching inside the hull, disconnect the steering cable and return spring from the steering shaft. Next, remove the bolts securing the steering holder to the hull. Lift the steering holder assembly from the hull. Remove the steering shaft nut (**Figure 46**) using the spanner wrench. Then, remove the steering shaft, along with the grommet, washer and bushing from the steering holder.

8. Remove the bushings and washers from the steering holder and shaft.

9. Closely inspect all components for excessive wear, cracks, breakage, corrosion or other damage. Replace any component in questionable condition.

10. To reassemble the steering assembly, first place the washer and grommet on the lower steering shaft bushing. One side of the grommet (4, **Figure 47**) has a larger inside diameter. Make sure the larger diameter is facing the bushing. Lubricate the bushing, washer and grommet with water-resistant grease, then place them on the steering shaft. See **Figure 47**.

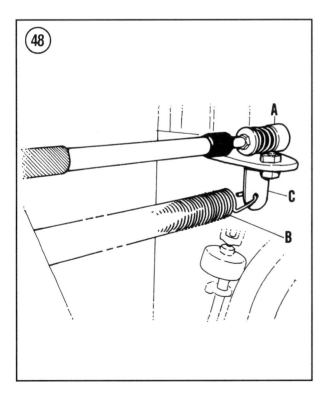

11. Install the steering shaft, with the washer, bushing and grommet into the steering holder. Install the upper bushing and steering shaft nut on the shaft. Tighten the steering shaft nut by hand.

12. Make sure the mating surfaces of the steering holder and hull are completely clean. Then coat the holder mating surface with silicone sealant. Install the holder assembly into the hull.

13. Apply Loctite to the threads of the steering holder mounting bolts. Install the bolts and tighten to specification (**Table 8**).

14. Reach inside the hull and connect the steering cable (A, **Figure 48**) and return spring (B) to the steering shaft (C).

15. Next, adjust the steering shaft nut (7, **Figure 47**) so the return spring is able to turn the steering shaft (steering cable connected), but without any noticeable up and down play in the shaft.

16. After properly adjusting the steering shaft nut, hold the nut with Kawasaki steering shaft nut wrench (or equivalent spanner wrench) as shown in **Figure 46**. While holding the steering shaft nut from turning, tighten the steering shaft lock nut (8, **Figure 47**) to specification (**Table 8**).

17. Place the LED unit wires, start/stop switch wires, throttle cable and vent hose into their grommet. Apply silicone sealant around the outside of the grommet, then install the grommet into the steering holder.

17. Complete the remaining installation by reversing the removal steps. Adjust the steering, throttle and choke cables as described in Chapter Three.

Steering Cable Replacement

1. Disconnect the steering cable at each end.

2. Loosen the locknut and remove the ball joint connector and nut from each end of the cable.

3. Disconnect the steering cable from the steering holder. Disconnect the steering shaft return

11

spring. Then, remove the bolts (A, **Figure 49**) and remove the steering cable holder (B).

4. Separate the steering cable from the holder.

5. Roll the watercraft onto its side, toward the engine exhaust. Do not roll the watercraft toward the side opposite the exhaust, or water from the exhaust system can enter the engine, resulting in severe engine damage. Be sure the use a heavy blanket to protect the hull when rolling the craft.

6. Remove the intake grate and jet pump cover. Refer to **Figure 6**.

> *NOTE*
> *On JH750 Super Sport Xi, it is necessary to disconnect the trim cable to gain access to the steering cable hull fitting nut in Step 7.*

7. While securely holding the hull fitting (A, **Figure 42**) with an open-end wrench, loosen and remove the cable nut (E). Pull the cable through the hull fitting and remove the O-ring (B, **Figure 42**), Washer (C) and snap ring (D) from the cable.

8. Pull the steering cable out of the hull toward the front.

9. Install the steering cable by revering the removal steps. Lubricate the outside of the cable using BelRay 6 in 1 or WD-40 (or equivalent) to

ease cable installation. Adjust the steering cable as described in Chapter Three.

TRIM ADJUSTER
(1993 JH750 SUPER SPORT Xi)

Removal/Installation

Refer to **Figure 50** during this procedure.

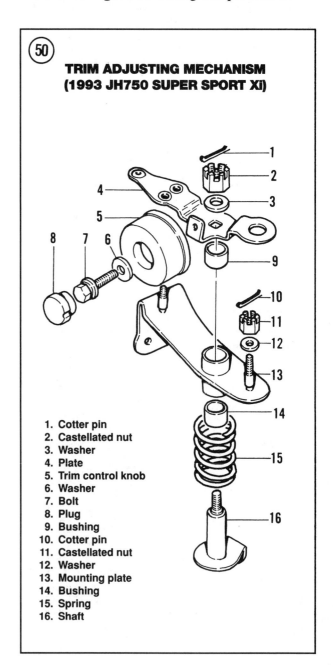

TRIM ADJUSTING MECHANISM (1993 JH750 SUPER SPORT Xi)

1. Cotter pin
2. Castellated nut
3. Washer
4. Plate
5. Trim control knob
6. Washer
7. Bolt
8. Plug
9. Bushing
10. Cotter pin
11. Castellated nut
12. Washer
13. Mounting plate
14. Bushing
15. Spring
16. Shaft

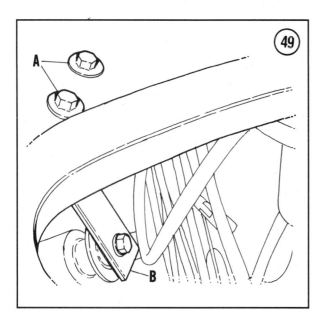

1. Remove the seat/engine cover assembly.

2. Remove the plastic plug from the center of the trim control knob. Then, remove the bolt from the center of the knob and remove the knob from the left side of the watercraft.

3. Remove the steering assembly cover.

4. Disconnect the trim cable from the ball joint on the trim control lever (inside the hull).

5. Remove the cotter pins and shaft nut (A, **Figure 51**) and plate mounting nuts (B). Then remove the plate (C, **Figure 51**).

6. Pull the shaft and spring down and out of the hull.

7. Remove the mounting plate from inside the hull. The plate may be stuck to the hull with sealant. If necessary, remove the bolt and clamp and separate the mounting plate from the trim cable.

8. Clean all sealant from the mounting plate. Inspect all components for excessive wear or other damage.

9. Reinstall the trim mechanism by reversing the removal steps, plus the following:

   a. Lubricate the shaft bushings with water-resistant grease. Install the bushings into the

mounting plate with their beveled side facing inward.

   b. Apply silicone sealant to the mating surface of the mounting plate.

Trim Cable Replacement

Trim cable replacement is essentially the same as the steering cable replacement. Disconnect the cable at both ends, remove the locknuts and connectors. Remove the trim cable clamp at the trim mechanism mounting plate, then remove and install the cable as described under *Steering Cable Replacement*.

HULL REPAIR

On all models, the hull is made of a sheet-molded compound (SMC) material. SMC is a machined-pressed and cured chopped fiberglass sheet. Hull repairs covered in this manual are limited to hairline cracks up to 8 inches long and small punctures. Larger cracks and punctures require professional repair or replacement of the damaged parts. If any structural damage to the handle pole occurs, it must be replaced.

Repair Materials

Many commonly available fiberglass repair kits will not work well on the Jet Ski hull. Kawasaki provides a hull SMC Repair Kit (part No. W61080-001). The paint supplies by Kawasaki is not the same as the original white epoxy paint; it is for cosmetic touch-up only. The original paint used on the Jet Ski is a 50/50 mixture of DuPont Imron paints No. 555U and 817U, available from marine suppliers. This is an epoxy paint and requires a catalyst to cure. A solvent such as acetone must be used to clean and prepare surfaces for bonding.

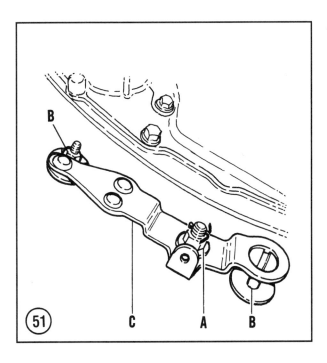

11

WARNING
Acetone is very flammable and poison-
ous. Avoid prolonged contact with skin.
Keep away from open flame and use only
in a well-ventilated area.

NOTE
When mixing the epoxy hull repair filler,
use a smooth nonporous surface. Do not
use cardboard for mixing filler.

Scratches

Use this procedure when the hull is scratched or lightly damaged.

1. Clean the damaged area with acetone. Push on the area around and, if possible, under the damage to determine the extent of the damage.
2. Use an electric drill with a burr bit or a hand file to make a V-shaped groove along the whole length of the scratch or gouge (**Figure 52**). Taper the sides of the groove at a 45° angle, but be careful not to cut the groove any deeper than the existing damage.
3. Use No. 80 emery cloth or sandpaper to remove the flaky edges and to sand away the paint up to 1-2 inches away from the damaged area.
4. Clean the area with a clean cloth moistened with acetone.
5. Refer to the repair kit instructions and mix enough filler to fill in the area. Use a plastic squeegee to apply and spread the filler, making sure to remove all air bubbles. The filler should extend a little above the original surface (**Figure 53**). Allow the filler to cure according to the kit instructions.
6. Use a sanding block to sand the area smooth. Start with No. 80 grit and finish with No. 400.
7. Use the Paint Kit to repaint the area, following the kit instructions.

Structural Damage

Use this procedure when the hull is cracked anywhere except at the engine cover rail.

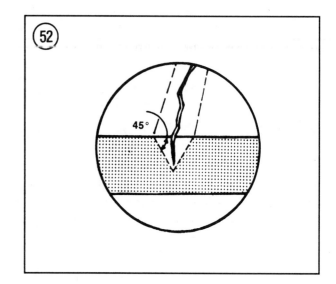

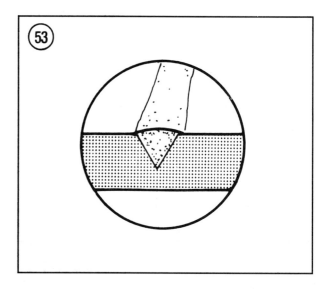

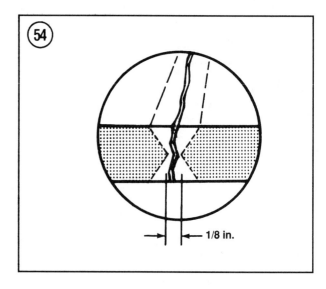

1. Clean the damaged area with acetone. Push on the area around and, if possible, under the damage to determine the extent of the damage.

2. Use an electric drill with a burr bit or a hand file to make a V-shaped groove along with the whole length of the crack or gouge. Open a 1/8 in. gap along the crack (**Figure 54**). On the hull bottom and the front deck (where the handle pole attaches), open the gap to 1/4 in. (**Figure 55**). Taper the sides of the groove to a 45° angle. If both sides of the hull are accessible, groove both sides.

3. Using No. 80 emery cloth or sandpaper to remove the flaky edges and to sand away the paint about 4 in. from the damage.

4. Clean the area with a clean cloth and acetone.

5. Refer to the repair kit instructions and mix enough filler to fill in the area. Use a plastic squeegee to apply and spread the filler, making

sure to remove air bubbles. The filler should extend a little above the original surface (**Figure 53**).

6. Before the filler sets up, lay 4 oz. fiberglass cloth over the crack, inside and outside, so that the cloth extends about 2 in. beyond the crack on each side.

7. Tap the cloth into the filler until filler comes through the cloth. Spread a light coat of filler over the cloth, inside and outside, and allow the filler to cure according to the kit instructions.

8. Use a sanding block to sand the area smooth. Start with No. 80 grit and finish with No. 400.

9. Use the Paint Kit to repaint the area, following the kit instructions.

Crack at Engine Cover Rail

See **Figure 56**. A crack in this area must be reinforced with wood for strength.

1. Clean the damaged area with acetone. Push on the area around, and if possible, under the damage to determine the extent of the damage.

2. Use an electric drill with a burr bit or a hand file to make a V-shaped groove along with the whole length of the crack or gouge. Open a 1/4 in. gap along the crack. Taper the sides of the groove to a 45° angle (**Figure 55**).

3. Use No. 80 emery cloth or sandpaper to remove the flaky edge and to sand away the paint about 4 in. from the damage.

4. Clean the area with clean cloth and acetone.

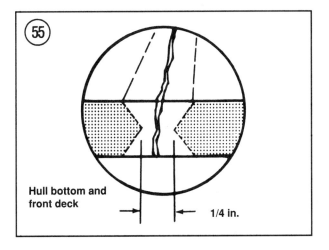

55

Hull bottom and front deck

1/4 in.

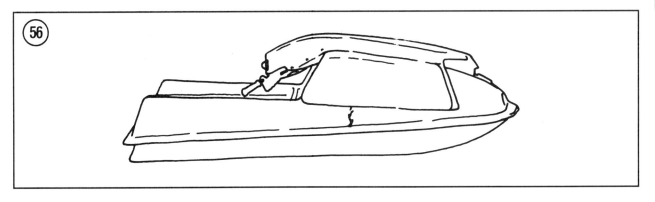

56

11

5. To align the rail and add rigidity, cut a piece of marine plywood 3/8 in. thick, 3/4 in. wide by 3 in. long. Center the wood under the crack inside the deck and clamp it at each end.

6. Refer to the repair kit instructions and mix enough filler to fill in the area. To bond the wood to the deck on both sides of the crack, apply filler to the center of the wood and the inside wall of the deck. Use a plastic squeegee to apply and spread the filler, working it into all the cracks and voids making sure to remove all air bubbles.

7. Before the filler sets up, lay 4 oz. fiberglass cloth over the crack, inside and outside, so that the cloth extends about 2 in. beyond the crack on each side. Make sure the cloth completely covers the wood on the inside.

8. Tap the cloth into the filler until filler comes through the cloth. Spread a light coat of filler over the cloth, inside and outside, and allow the filler to cure according to the kit instructions.

9. Use a sanding block to sand the area smooth. Start with No. 80 grit and finish with No. 400.

10. Use the Paint Kit to repaint the area, following the kit instructions.

Hull Extensions

The hull extension tips (**Figure 57**) are available as replacement parts. They should be bonded to the hull with the same hull repair epoxy used for repair of cracks.

Rubber Parts

1. To replace the rider's mat, thoroughly clean the deck surface and use waterproof contact cement such as Goodyear Plio-bond to glue the mat down. Refer to the adhesive container for instructions.

2. The engine cover gasket (A, **Figure 58**, typical) and the fuel tank and water muffler dampers (B), should be attached with a waterproof contact cement such as Goodyear Plio-bond.

3. The bumper strip on the front of the Jet Ski, the handle pole bracket cover and the steering cable guides should be secured with a cyanoacrylate cement such as Loctite Super Bonder. Refer to the adhesive container for instructions. Goodyear Plio-Grip adhesive can also be used.

DECK FRAME (JF650X-2)

Refer to **Figure 59** for this procedure.

1. Remove the engine from the hull as described in Chapter Five.

2. Loosen the deck frame adjuster locknuts by turning them clockwise.

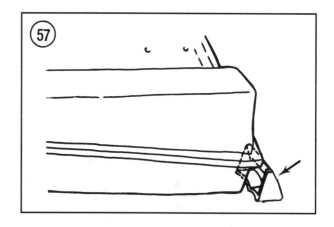

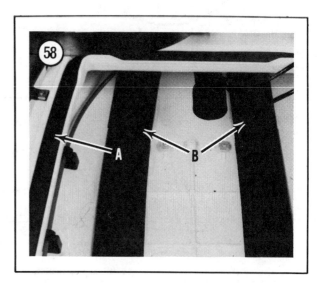

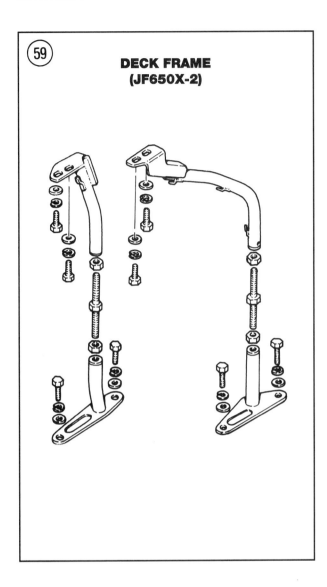

(59)

**DECK FRAME
(JF650X-2)**

3. Remove the deck frame mounting bolts. Then turn the adjuster locknuts clockwise to shorten the deck frame assembly. Repeat for each side.

4. Remove the deck frames from the engine compartment.

5. If necessary, disassemble the deck frame assembly. Store each deck frame assembly in separate boxes to prevent confusion during reassembly.

6. Check the deck frames for cracks or other damage.

7. Check the bolts, nuts and washers for damage; replace fasteners as required.

8. Installation is the reverse of these steps, plus the following:

    a. Referring to **Figure 59**, assemble the deck frame assembly.

    b. Turn the deck frame adjuster all the way clockwise. Repeat for both sides.

    c. Position the deck frames into the engine compartment.

    d. turn the adjusters so that the deck frames tough against the deck.

    e. Tighten the deck frame mounting bolts to 13 N.m (113 in.-lb.).

    f. Tighten the locknuts to 13 N.m (113 in.-lb.).

    g. Install the engine as described in Chapter Five.

Table 1 STEERING SYSTEM TIGHTENING TORQUES (JS440SX AND JS550SX)

Fastener/Item	N.m	ft.-lb.
Handlebar clamp screws	18	13
Handle pole pivot bolt	14	10
Handle pole pivot nut	35	26
Handle pole bracket anchor bolts	22	16
Steering pivot stud and nut	40	29

Table 2 STEERING SYSTEM TIGHTENING TORQUES (JS650SX)

Fastener/Item	N.m	in.-lb.	ft.-lb.
Handlebar clamp bolts	25		18
Handle pole bracket anchor bolts	19		14
Steering pivot nut	6	53	

(continued)

11

Table 2 STEERING SYSTEM TIGHTENING TORQUES (JS650SX) [continued]

Fastener/Item	N·m	in.-lb.	ft.-lb.
Steering pivot shaft nut	33		25
Steering pivot stud	39		29
Steering pivot shaft	13	113	

Table 3 STEERING SYSTEM TIGHTENING TORQUES (JF650X-2)

Fastener/Item	N·m	in.-lb.	ft.-lb.
Ball joints	7.8	69	
Handlebar holder bolts	13	113	
Handlebar weights	18		13
Retaining bolts	13	113	
Steering arm holder bolts	18		13
Steering cable nuts	18		13
Steering holder mounting bolts	23		17
Steering neck pivot shaft nut	23		17
Steering shaft nut	23		17
Trim adjuster knob nut	23		17
Trim cable nuts	18		13

Table 4 STEERING SYSTEM TIGHTENING TORQUES (JF650TS)

Fastener/Item	N·m	ft.-lb.
Handlebar holder bolts	16	11.5
Steering shaft bracket bolt	16	11.5
Steering shaft pivot nut	78	58

Table 5 STEERING SYSTEM TIGHTENING TORQUES (JS650SC)

Fastener/Item	N·m	in.-lb.	ft.-lb.
Bearing cap bolt	7.8	69	
Steering arm mounting bolt	16		11.5

Table 6 STEERING SYSTEM TIGHTENING TORQUES (JB650 JET MATE)

Fastener/Item	N·m	in.-lb.	ft.-lb.
Clamp bolt	22		16
Control stick shaft bracket bolt	22		16
Steering bracket bolt	9.8	87	
Steering shaft bolt	22		16

Table 7 STEERING SYSTEM TIGHTENING TORQUES (JS750SX)

Fastener/Item	N·m	in.-lb.	ft.-lb.
Handlebar clamp bolts	18		13
Handle pole bracket bolts	19		13.5
Handle pole pivot shaft nut	33		24
Handle pole pivot shaft	13	115	9.6
Steering pivot stud	38		28

Table 8 STEERING SYSTEM TIGHTENING TORQUES (JT750ST, JH750SS, JH750 SUPER SPORT XI AND JH750XIR)

Fastener/Item	N·m	ft.-lb.
Handlebar clamp bolts	16	12
Shift lever mounting nut		
JT750ST	18	13
Shift cable nut	18	13
Steering cable nuts	18	13
Steering holder mounting bolts	16	12
Steering neck mounting bolts	16	12
Steering shaft nut	78-88	57-65
Steering shaft lock nut	29	21
Trim adjuster shaft nut		
JH750 Super Sport Xi	18	13

11

Index

12

JS440SX

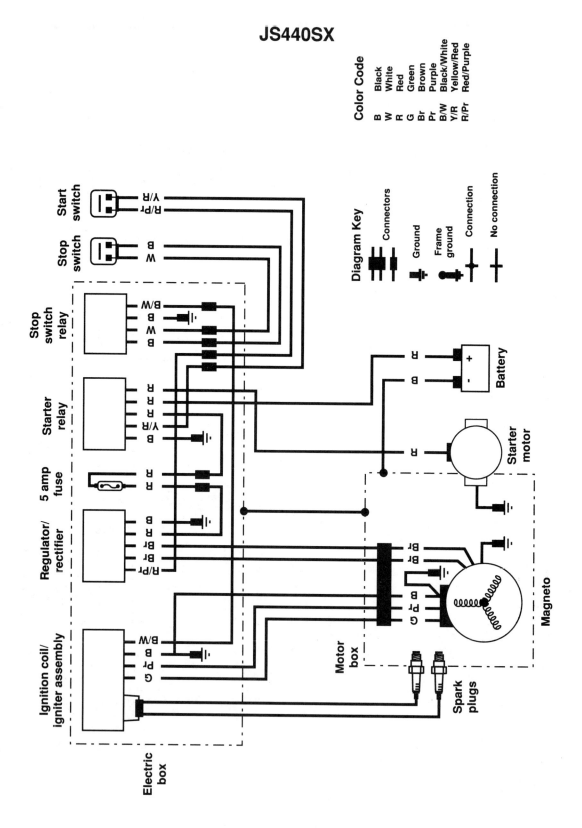

JS550SX

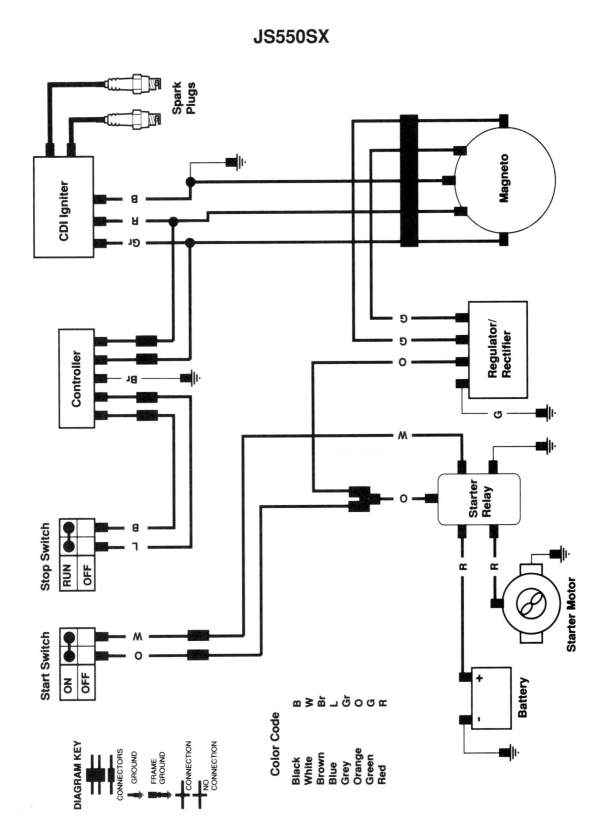

DIAGRAM KEY

CONNECTORS

GROUND

FRAME
GROUND

CONNECTION

NO
CONNECTION

Color Code

Black	B
White	W
Brown	Br
Blue	L
Grey	Gr
Orange	O
Green	G
Red	R

13

JF650X-2

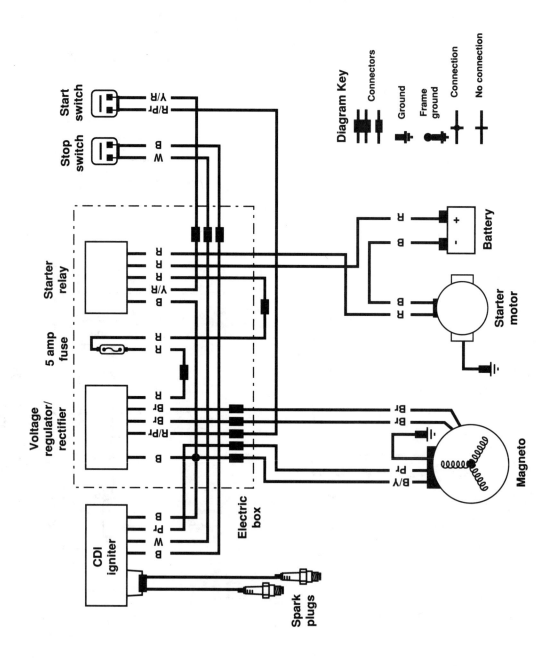

JS650SX

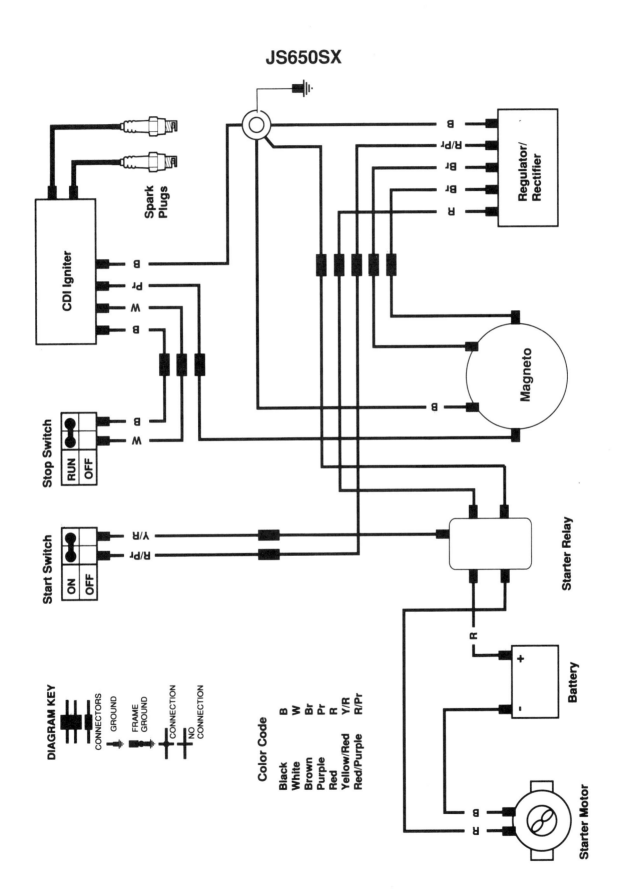

JF650TS

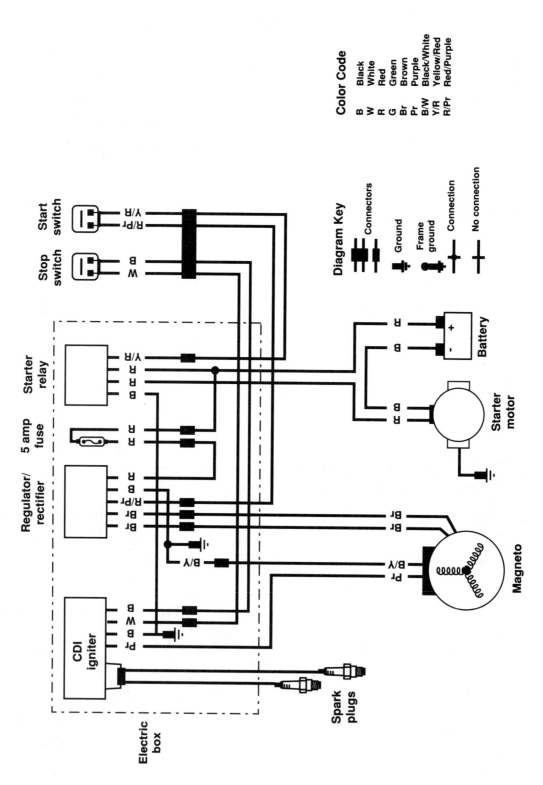

JL650SC

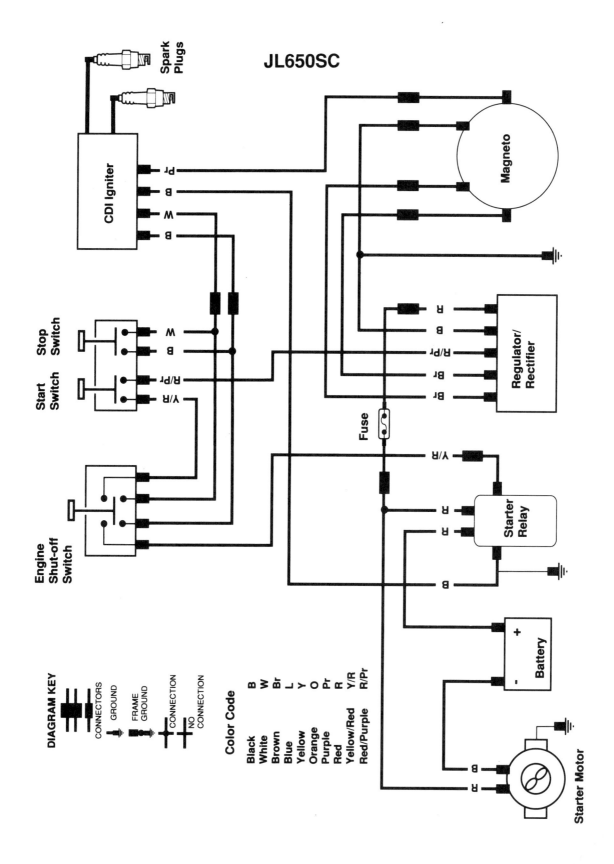

13

JB650 Jet Mate

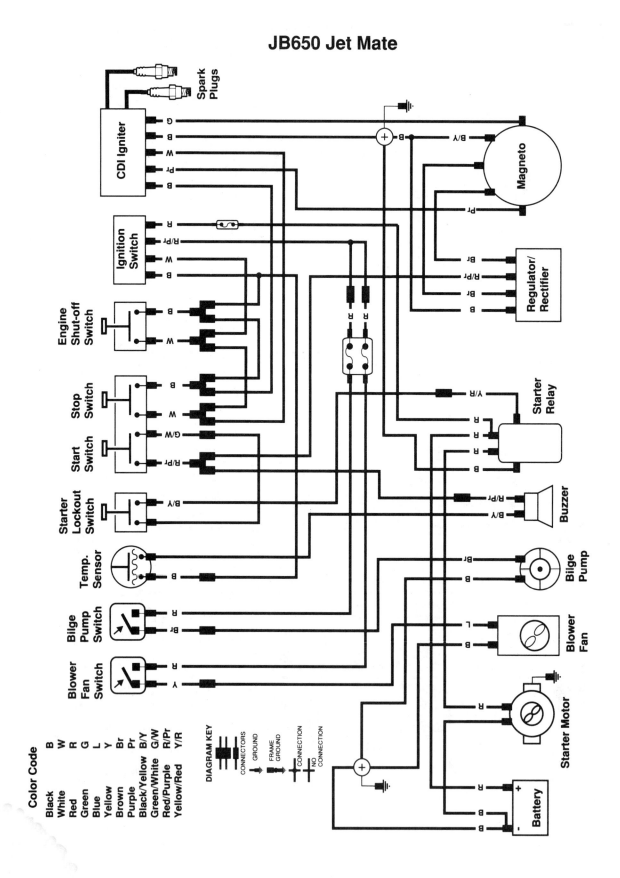

JH750SS (1992-1993) and JH750Xi (1993)

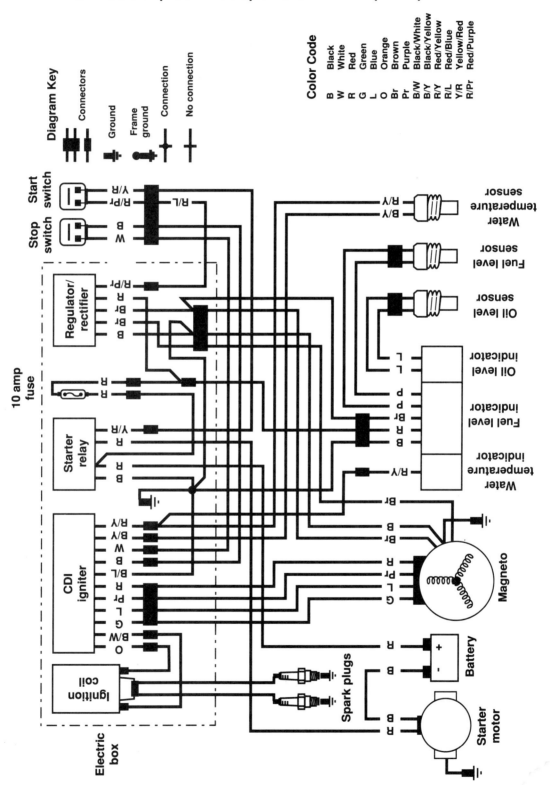

JH750SS (1994) AND JH750 Super Sport Xi (1994)

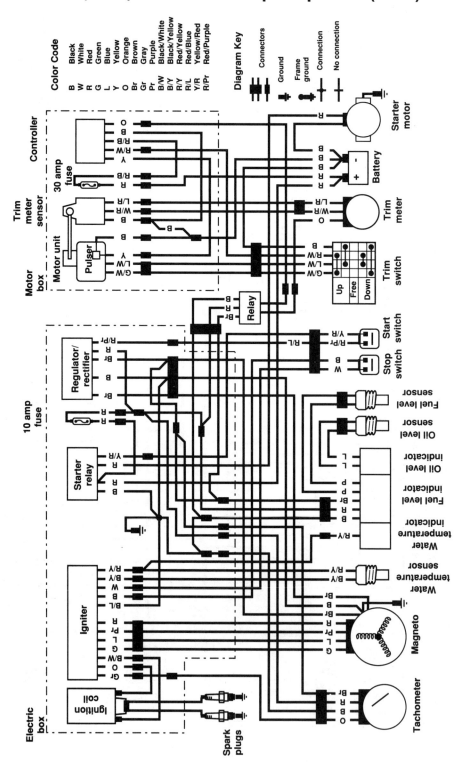

JS750SX

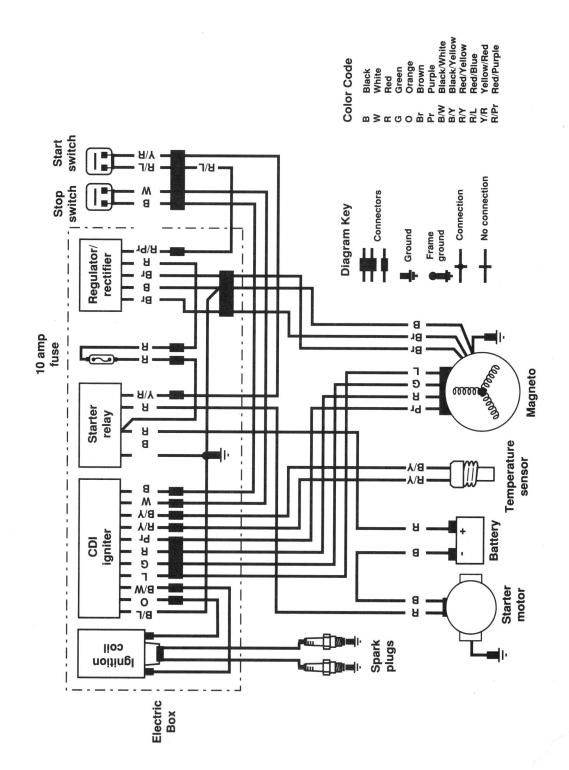

JT750ST

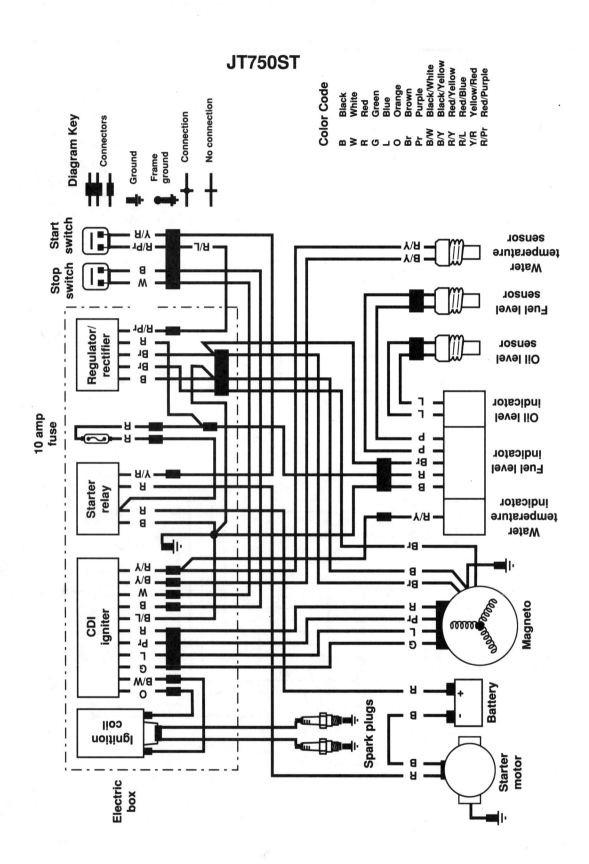

JH750XiR

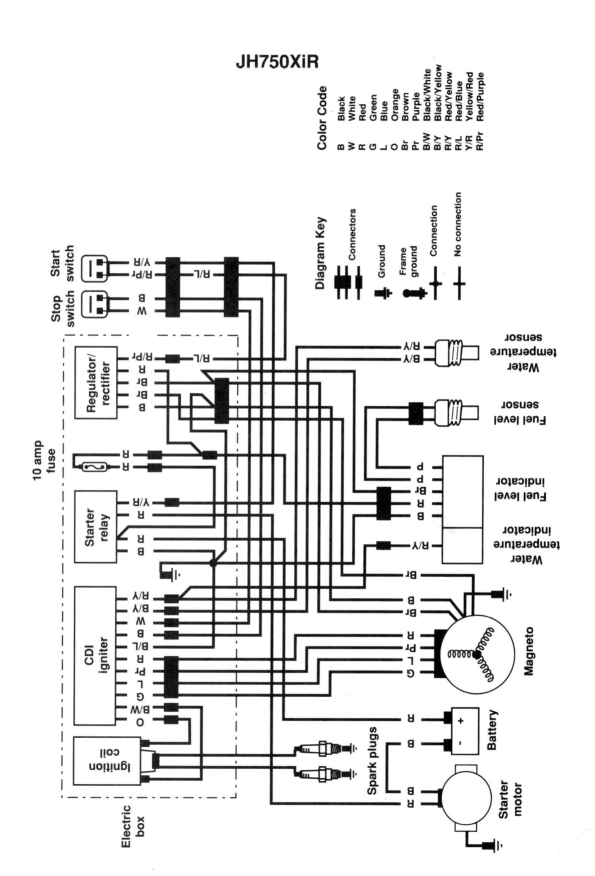

Color Code

B	Black
W	White
R	Red
G	Green
L	Blue
O	Orange
Br	Brown
Pr	Purple
B/W	Black/White
B/Y	Black/Yellow
R/Y	Red/Yellow
R/L	Red/Blue
Y/R	Yellow/Red
R/Pr	Red/Purple

Diagram Key

Connectors

Ground

Frame ground

Connection

No connection

13

MAINTENANCE LOG

Service Performed	Mileage Reading				
Oil change (example)	2,836	5,782	8,601		